HENRY JAMES
THE MASTER
1901–1916

By Leon Edel

THE LIFE OF HENRY JAMES
The Untried Years, 1843–1870
The Conquest of London, 1870–1883
The Middle Years, 1883–1894
The Treacherous Years, 1895–1900
The Master, 1901–1916

The Psychological Novel
Literary Biography
James Joyce: The Last Journey
Henry D. Thoreau
Willa Cather: A Critical Biography (with E. K. Brown)
A Bibliography of Henry James (with Dan H. Laurence)

Editor of *The Complete Plays, The Selected Letters* and
The Supernatural Stories of Henry James, *The American
Scene, The Henry James Reader,* and *The Diary of
Alice James*

HENRY JAMES 1905
Concord, Mass.

HENRY JAMES

The Master

1901–1916

★ ★ ★ ★ ★

by Leon Edel

RUPERT HART-DAVIS
LONDON
1972

Granada Publishing Limited
First published in Great Britain 1972 by Rupert Hart-Davis Ltd
3 Upper James Street London W1R 4BP

Copyright © 1972 by Leon Edel

ISBN 0 246 10532 1
Printed in Great Britain by
Richard Clay (The Chaucer Press), Ltd.,
Bungay, Suffolk

Art *makes* life, makes interest, makes importance.

CONTENTS

CONTENTS

ILLUSTRATIONS

INTRODUCTION

THIS is the last volume of my *Life of Henry James* begun in 1950 and completed—to be exact—on 12 January 1971. It consists of five volumes or "parts" after the serialized manner of certain Victorian works. In my introduction to the first part, "The Untried Years" of 1953, I projected the biography as a study of James's childhood and youth; my second volume described the development and pursuit of his career; this ultimately became two parts as did my final volume which I promised would trace "the evolution of the legendary 'Master'—for so his peers came to call him—the architect of the modern novel." I added "his was a large life and it requires a large canvas."

This biography has become a five-part portrait, or let us think of it as consisting of five panels showing the countenance of the artist during the five phases of his life. It is not a statue; nor is it a mausoleum. Moreover, it is not as long as some have made it seem. If one counted words rather than volumes this would be discovered to be one of the shorter literary lives of our time. Volumes almost as long have been accorded to artists who died by thirty; Henry James died in his seventy-third year. I claim for this work a specific form and a high selectivity, particularly when one remembers that the book covers half a century of writing and represents a synthesis of many thousands of letters, as well as diaries and other historical documents and the testimony of many of the novelist's contemporaries. It will suggest how drastic has been my selection when I mention that I had, for "The Master," as much material as for the four preceding parts. Had I used this material in its vast extent my work would be as disproportioned as Percy Lubbock's edition of James's letters which devote some 400 pages to the first fifty-seven years of his life and more than 500 to the last sixteen years covered by the present volume.

"Did nothing happen to Henry James except the writing of an

extremely long shelf of books?" I asked at the outset of this work. "And," I added, "could a man produce so much having, as it is claimed, lived so little?" Readers of this life now have the answer to these questions. My interest in my task has not been exclusively in my subject. He represented a challenge to the art of biography and I have attempted experiments in biographical narration and the use of the retrospective method; I have been "scenic" where my material permitted; I have violated the usual adherence to chronology and been scolded by other biographers for regarding the works of the imagination as possible "life" material—as if imagination could belong to a disembodied mind.

I mention these matters because I believe biography to be the most taken for granted—the least discussed—of all the branches of literature. Biographies are widely read and widely discussed; but they are treated as if they came ready-made. Our explicating critics seem to find little in them to explicate; and many indeed read the lives of poets and then hide them, as if they were ashamed of them, insisting on the sanctity of the work of art. Small wonder that Stephen Spender has asked criticism to restore the poet to his poem. Critics tell us every Monday or Friday that the novel is dying or dead, thereby showing a genuine concern for that form of literature. But biographies are accepted as they come and relished for their revelations. Biographers themselves have not on the whole been helpful. When they speak of their work, they describe either their quest in libraries and archives which is often as amusing as a detective story, or their struggle with their intractable materials, which they find always difficult. Questions of form, composition, structure are seldom raised; and the public has been taught that a heavy compendium of documents, a big inflated volume of selected excerpts from archives, is a work of art. I hold with Lytton Strachey that we have "relegated to the journeymen of letters" what he described as "the most delicate and humane of all the branches of writing." He complained, in a memorable passage, of "their lamentable lack of selection, of detachment, of design." I would claim, as I have said, selection and design for *The Life of Henry James*. As for detachment, let me say only that I have kept before me always Coleridge's dictum "how mean a mere fact is, except in the light of some comprehensive truth."

"How long, Leon, how long?" asked a friendly and witty reviewer in *The Times Literary Supplement* when my fourth part appeared in 1969. The answer is as long as was necessary—keeping in mind that a biographer has his own life to lead as well as the lives of his subjects. *The Life of Henry James* has had an organic growth; it acquired in the process the form proper to itself and the proportions suited to its materials. But one time-question of quite another sort did concern me; indeed all the resources of craft were invoked for it. This was the complex and essential question of making the reader *feel* the passage of the years in the life of my subject. It dictated many of the narrative strategies I had to adopt; it was—given the limitations imposed by my materials—the single most difficult part of the entire work. I found my personal reward in the imagination of form and structure—after all the only imagination a biographer can be allowed. I hope that I have made it rewarding for the reader as well.

LEON EDEL

Book One

Notes on Novelists
1899–1901

★

VIE DE PROVINCE

I

ON afternoons in the late autumn and early winter, when the roads were sufficiently dry, the clean-shaven master of Lamb House would descend from his hilltop into the High Street. He wrapped himself in a heavy coat. He walked massively, carrying one of his many sticks. Sometimes he wore a small peaked cap; sometimes a felt hat. There was invariably a touch of colour—in his knotted thick cravat, or, if he unbuttoned his coat, in a show of orange or blue waistcoat. Behind him, waddling slowly as if he possessed some of his master's authority, was one of James's dogs, say Maximilian, his dachshund, successor to the long-lived Tosca, of the De Vere Gardens time. When James walked alone, he walked solemnly, unsmiling and grave, greeting old and young alike with deliberate courtesy. Even when he paused and pondered he seemed remote and absent-minded; yet his searching eyes looked everywhere. Sometimes his typist walked with him —there would be three of them in all and two would keep diaries. Sometimes he was accompanied by his current guest. He also discovered walking companions among his fellow-residents in the ancient port. At the turn of the century he had for company a former Indian colonial servant, "whose face I suit and whose reminiscences I invite." Later there would be A. C. Bradley, Sydney Waterlow, Fanny Prothero, a Mr Tayleure, and others. On occasion James walked to Playden, where he had lived briefly in 1896 and had written *The Spoils of Poynton*; or along the sea by Camber, past the golf course and the grazing sheep; or he would take the road to picturesque and desolate Winchelsea. He walked across the marshes and looked on melancholy relics of the past. "Rye dares to be cheerful," he once remarked, "Winchelsea has the courage of its desolation." He still bicycled; and on some days he would sweep off to more distant towns, dressed in knickerbockers and an "exiguous jacket" of black and white stripes (as David Garnett would remember out of a boyhood glimpse), with the peaked cap which made him seem broader than he was. The walker in the Alps, the rider on horseback in the Campagna, was now a cyclist on the salt flats of the Cinque Ports.

Passers by going to Rye's church and the Ypres tower on the hilltop, near Lamb House, could hear on any morning after 10 a.m. through the bow windows of the garden room the slow voice speaking to the answering typewriter. James, looking out to the church, saw the burghers on holy days "go in to their righteousness and come out to their dinners." As owner of Lamb House he had "an immemorial pew" in the church "which I have never been in but once." Still, it made him feel all the more a part of the little town. From the first he spoke of himself as if he were a character in one of Balzac's *scènes de la vie de province*. "I am learning the lesson," he wrote to Grace Norton, "that in a small country town where local society is *nil*, fate seems to make the matter as broad as it's long by arranging compensations on strictly domestic lines. In other words, whereas in London the people you know are everywhere, in the country they are all in your own house! This is very ingenious of fate: it is good for everything except reading, writing, arithmetic and the higher branches of solitude."

He listed some of his acquaintances: John Symonds Vidler and his wife Caroline, of Mountsfield, who would remain friendly during all of James's days in Rye; old little Mrs Davies, "straight out of *Cranford*," whom he found one Christmas day stranded on the road, her conveyance having lost, "under Christmas influence, *both* its back wheels." He brought her back to town "in the frosty moonlight and under her little archaically-sculptured wooden door-canopy of the last century, to the embrace of a rosy maid-servant almost as fluttered as herself and quite as much out of *Cranford*." Or he dined with the Brookfields of Leasam, Colonel Brookfield being Member of Parliament for East Sussex and elder of the two sons of Thackeray's Mrs Brookfield. As it happened the newer Mrs Brookfield was an American, "all that there is most of from Buffalo, N.Y."

These were rural social beginnings. Presently the neighbourhood, if we take a radius of twenty-five or even fifty miles, filled
itself in for James: and he found in it men of his own craft.
Farthest away, involving a trip via London (until the motor car
shortened the way), was Kipling, at Rottingdean, soon to move
to Burwash in Sussex. Just over the county line, in Kent, near
Ashford, Joseph Conrad and his family established themselves
during the autumn of 1898, the year James moved into Lamb
House; nearby too, H. G. Wells, prophet of "the shape of things
to come," had settled at Sandgate on the Kentish Coast. The tall
young Ford Madox Hueffer, whom James had met earliest of
all—in 1896—moved into a bungalow at Winchelsea. Briefly,
too, in the picturesque and ghostly fourteenth-century Brede
Place, eight miles from Rye, there dwelt for a moment, Stephen
Crane and his Cora. To recite these names is to suggest that there
was a veritable nest of novelists in south-east Sussex and Kent.
But the word "nest" suggests community as well as propinquity,
and these novelists, each haunted by his own reveries and engaged
in his own pursuit of the fancies of his writing desk, saw less of
each other than literary history perhaps would like to believe; and
saw each other through the windows of "temperament," which
means that each one's vision of the other was perhaps even more
limited and subjectively coloured than usual. When the Conrads
visited the Hueffers at Winchelsea, James remarked to H. G.
Wells, "Conrad haunts Winchelsea, and Winchelsea (in discretion), haunts Rye." The "in discretion" suggests that James's
neighbours did not in reality visit as frequently as the memoirs
claim and that "the higher branches" of solitude were not too
often disturbed. As fellow-workers each novelist respected the
sacrosanct hours of the other; and above all those of James. He
was older and looked upon with awe; and he kept them at a distance, save when he was ready to receive them.

II

Within his first year and a half—that is from mid-1898 to 1900—
James lived himself into the provincial life of Rye. He quickly
became a local "fixture." The shopkeepers knew him; the local

gentry dined him; but with the characteristic English respect for privacy, he was registered by many of the townsfolk and his neighbours simply as an odd literary gentleman of great courtliness, who walked the roads or bicycled, and who often met his guests at the Rye station himself, accompanied by his gardener wheeling a barrow or cart for the luggage. His was a well-organized establishment; with the Smiths, his husband-and-wife cook and butler, a housemaid, and a houseboy, and George Gammon, the gardener, he was perhaps less servanted than most gentlefolk of the time living in the town's principal houses. The town was more interested in golf than in literature; and James's friends and the literary personalities who came to see him were generally unknown. Neither James nor his guests aroused curiosity; and there was little gossip about them in the town where there was understandable local pride at having a celebrity in Lamb House. There is only one recorded invasion of James's privacy early in his stay at Rye, and this was done with decorum and tact. In June 1900 Lord and Lady Wolseley came over from their nearby country home at Glynde to visit their novelist-friend. Lady Wolseley, a connoisseur of antiques, had helped James buy various pieces of furniture for his house. The word got round quickly that the great soldier was in Rye; moreover his afternoon's visit coincided with the news of the occupation of Pretoria. A wave of patriotic emotion, a sudden urge to do honour to this pillar of the British military, seized the town, and an informal delegation of officials and leading citizens knocked at the canopied door and asked permission to pay respects to the victor of the Ashantee, who, earlier in the century, had gone to the relief of General Gordon. "Rye rather lacked history," Henry wrote to Lady Wolseley afterwards, "now she *has* it. You didn't leave me where you found me. I am inches and inches higher. I believe I could really do anything with the place."

This is the only recorded moment when national grandeur touched modest Lamb House. Otherwise the establishment and its tenant blended into the town. Had James been a British citizen he might have been asked to be Rye's mayor, as E.F. Benson was in later days, for Lamb House had been the home of mayors for more than a century, mainly members of the Lamb family. But James preferred in any event to be passively civic. He was, however, on good terms with the local organizations and generous in his contributions to local charities. And when the local clergy asked him for favours, he was only too willing to help—for he was on excellent terms in particular with "a dear little all but Catholic Irish curate." During the summer of 1900 he billeted a young curate when the Bishop of Chichester came to Rye for certain ordinations. To Lady Wolseley again James wrote that the priest fasted "on fish, eggs, vegetables, tarts, claret, cigarette, coffee and liqeurs," which the generous Lamb House larder and cellar provided. James was happy to be hospitable. But the problem of finding himself "face to face with him, at meals," was more trying. Remembering his visit to the Wolseleys in Ireland five years earlier, he remarked he would on the whole have been happier to billet a soldier.

These small moments of provincial life were, however, limited in the even march of James's days in the country. "The days depart and pass, laden somehow like processional camels—across the desert of one's solitude." He felt severed from his old life— and he was sincere in describing his longing for "the blessed Kensington fields." He had originally planned to live in Rye half the year, and the other half in London; but he had sublet his De Vere Gardens flat and would have to use clubs and hotels in the city. A mild winter had led him to remain in Lamb House all through 1898–9, but during his second winter in the country, he was homesick for London. He found himself pining for its lamp-light, and the sound of its buses. There came to him in twilight vision the colours of the green and red and yellow jars in the chemists' windows and the chiaroscuro of the late London afternoons. He had been, in all the years of his maturity, a walker in cities: Paris, London, Florence, Rome; or in his American time Boston and New York. To mitigate his isolation, he constantly urged his friends to come to him; and sometimes they did. "The youth of the lyrist never was so lonely as the old age of the proser," he wrote to W. Morton Fullerton. "I am so alone here at present . . . and so nose to nose with the dark, wet country winter, and other still gloomier and embracing conditions, that the presence of a valued friend would be a luxury almost past belief." And to Howard Sturgis, "I am lonely and lean and comfortless." To Edmund Gosse he spoke of going up to London late in 1900 for a real go at town life—"I shall have been confined to this hamlet for two and a half years on end—save for three or four months abroad. You *must*, all, take me to Madame Tussaud's." To Mrs W. K. Clifford, one of his oldest and most cherished London friends, he wrote, in May of 1900, "But can't you, couldn't you, dearest Lucy Clifford, come down and see me some day next month, some pretty, summery, *possible* day as you did two years ago, and tell me everything that's going and let me drive you to Winchelsea, after feeding and tea-ing and blessing you? Think of it—do, *do*. I will make everything of a comfortable for you! Think of it, plot for it—and let me hear of it. It seems to me as if otherwise I mightn't see you for many a month." And again, writing of his domestic comforts, he tells her, "it would be so infinitely nicer to be sitting by your fire and tasting your charity—and your Benedictine."

He had made his peace with solitude long ago. But there was an important difference between solitude and loneliness. He had always known how to be alone; he had sought and invited solitude. But he also had always known how to avoid—urban dweller that he was—a feeling of loneliness. The cities, and London in particular, provided people, theatres, tea-talk, the pleasant privacy or gregariousness of his clubs, as he wished. Now in Rye he suffered "for want of social, domestic, intellectual air." And yet he was tied to Lamb House even in the winter, because he was tied to his work: his typewriter was not easily movable—the day of the "portable" was yet to come—and his way of work had changed from his old roving ease when he could set up shop anywhere. A trip to London meant divorce from his daily writing; and his writing was as necessary to him as the social, domestic, intellectual air of which he spoke; indeed it was more than necessary, for he was trying to work off his book-contracts and pay for his house. He had agreed to write three novels, a biography, certain essays, and every now and again he felt moved to write a tale. Thus occurred the conflicts of his new "exile," an intermittent debate between the life of Rye and the life of London that he would maintain, and never resolve, during the next decade. Even after he had created a work place for himself in the metropolis, as he did within the coming months, he would spend lonely weeks in inclement weather in the sea-town. To an outsider it might have seemed that Rye had been for so urban a man a grave mistake; its simplified life could not meet the needs of so complex a being. On the other hand, the world owes to the long periods of his encaged state, some of his finest writings. Work was his principal refuge and no writer—even the driven Balzac, the prodigiously diligent Walter Scott—applied himself more seriously and assiduously to his craft. The dictation in the morning; the recuperative walk in the afternoon when possible; the re-reading and revision of what had been dictated; the preparation for the next morning's work; the planning of new stories; the writing of scenarios; the long evenings of thought and toil before he was ready to meet his typist once more for renewed endeavour. Out of the hours of Rye's solitude, there took shape and were written within four years, the three last novels, the summit of his creation. It was as if his years of ceaseless wandering and dwelling in cities had prepared him for this final communion with himself, a reforging out of memory and loneliness of his visions of the civilization absorbed and studied during forty years of cosmopolitan life. In the process he would ask himself what he had really known of life. How much had he *lived*? He had not "lived" in the common meaning of that word: he had known neither the obsessive passion of a Byron nor the romantic dedication of a Flaubert; he had sought no distant exotic lands, nor indiscriminate sex, the practices of his French confrères. He had always been quiet, withdrawn, pensive, observant, contemplative: he had fled the society of passionate women. As he put it of Lambert Strether, his hero in *The Ambassadors*, who in so many ways resembled him: "It was nothing new to him . . . that a man might have—at all events such a man as *he* was—an amount of experience out of any proportion to his adventures." There was adventure and adventure. He had put this in another way in his essay on the art of fiction long before, when he had challenged Walter Besant's assertion that young women could not write about soldiers and military life. "The young lady living in a village has only to be a damsel upon whom nothing is lost to make it quite unfair (as it seems to me) to declare to her that she shall have nothing to say about the military. Greater miracles have been seen than that, imagination assisting, she should speak of the truth about some of these gentlemen." So now, living like his young lady, in what was little more than a village, Henry James could allow his imagination to bring together the essences of the world that he had known. And in some strange way his writing of his late novels, was a reliving of his earlier life; as if in middle age he had to re-examine, to try again old artistic experiences, and test them in his maturity. In setting his "ambassador" in Paris he was rewriting his old story of *The American*, who had gone to Paris and sought the high world, the feudal magnificence of Europe. But Newman was a good-hearted *parvenu*: Strether was a middle-aged romantic. And his story of a young woman doomed to die seemed to be a reliving of his old *Portrait of a Lady* which one might say had been about a young American girl doomed to live. In other words he was continuing the reliving of his life, which he had begun with his series of fictions about children from *What Maisie Knew* to *The Awkward Age*. He was done with childhood experience; now he was dealing with the years of his coming abroad, the great drama of his two worlds— all recollected in a Wordsworthian tranquillity in his little harbour, in the quiet cobbled existence of Rye.

In the end, after long trial and much work, Rye would cease to be possible as a continual abode. He would say to a friend, "Little Rye—poor little Rye—I find life there intolerable—yes, Rye has had to be deserted—no, not *permanently* deserted— heaven forbid!—but I have had to make a nest—a perch for myself in London, which involves the desertion of Rye for the winter—only temporarily, *hibernetically* speaking."

III

This was spoken at the end of the Edwardian decade when James had again established an apartment in London. But at the threshold of the decade he found himself a metropolitan perch which served him well and gave him a place for temporary work. On the leasing of Lamb House, he had taken the precaution of putting his name down for a room at the Reform Club. In the autumn of 1900 the longed-for vacancy occurred. It meant that he had "a town-cradle" for his declining years. He refurbished the room, installed his own bed, new blinds, new curtains. He kept enough things in town so that he could come up from Rye with minimal luggage. The room was located high up over Carlton House Terrace: it looked over embassies and lordly houses. He had visited in many of these during his earlier London years. "Nothing could be more *chic*," he proclaimed. It made him feel less of an outsider when he returned to the city. Nevertheless movement between Rye and London consumed time; and once in London he was divorced from the continuity of his work, even though at the Reform he also installed a typewriter and was able to dictate on certain mornings according to habit. He tended, however, to loiter and ramble and seek mild sociabilities in the metropolis. The general effect of going up to town at first was to make him want his work desk in Rye; and the effect of Rye was to make him pine for London. Circumstance had made him suburban and he rebelled. The city was no longer wholly possible. But neither was the country.

In the better season of the year he forgot the gloom and rustication, and early in his life at Lamb House he set about improving his garden. He had never been a gardener; he would not become one now, any more than he could learn to use his typewriter or ever dreamed of owning, let alone driving, one of the new cars that would soon be depositing visitors at his door. He had, however, committed himself in his lease to the upkeep of the Lamb House garden; with his purchase of the house he felt even more strongly that he wanted as much vernal beauty as possible in the private acre outside the french doors of his front parlour and his dining-room. For twenty-two shillings a week he obtained the services of his gardener. It was up to James, however, to provide the ideas, and as he looked at the available space he felt himself "densely ignorant." He barely knew a dahlia from a mignonette. To Miss Muir Mackenzie, whom he had met once at Winchelsea, he turned for expert advice; and his letters to her tell of his horticultural progress. In his "poor little tuppenny Rye," his garden looked sad and shiftless. He began by explaining that his temptation was to "go in for a lawn, which requires mere brute force— no intellect." Miss Mackenzie was a woman of knowledge and tact; presently she was suggesting that certain kinds of tobacco leaves might be decorative; and then some crocuses at strategic spots in the lawn, for a touch of purple at the right season. James found himself ordering bulbs and roses, and George Gammon industriously was executing his and Miss Mackenzie's designs. James fell promptly into the spirit of the endeavour: his missives went forth addressed to Miss Mackenzie as the "Hereditary Grand Governess of the Garden" with apologies for offering "so shabby a government." He feared that he might become too fascinated. Would the garden become a trap for his hours (which were full) and for his purse (which was empty)? As fuchsias and geraniums were planted, he exclaimed, "Your touch is magical, your influence infinite," and "what a bliss, what a daily excitement, all summer, to see it grow by leaps and bounds"—these were the tobacco leaves [nicotiana]. "We are painfully preparing to become bulbous and particoloured." Into the lawn went one hundred crocuses, while "Our Lady of Tobacco" was addressed in letters filled with images of fertility and the novelist sported his growing knowledge in a kittenish way. "Dear Grand Governess, dear Friend Florist," he saluted her, and she saluted him back "Dear Distinguished Author." In reply he signed himself Henry James D.A. The time would come when his flowers would win prizes in the local flower show. And under Gammon's care the fig tree kept him in figs, although his grapes left something to be desired, while a small kitchen garden provided for his table. The domestic side of Rye had its endearing side.

A LETTER TO RHODA

"THIS dreadful gruesome New Year, so monstrously num-
bered," Henry James wrote on 1 January 1900 to Rhoda
Broughton, his fellow-novelist whom he had known for almost a
quarter of a century. His ailing brother William, his sister-in-
law, his young niece Peggy, were staying at this moment in Lamb
House, yet he felt alone—and the last year of the old century had
dawned. Miss Broughton was sixty; Henry was fifty-seven.
They had met long ago, during the years of James's conquest of
London, at Lord Houghton's, at dinner parties, in the literary and
social world, where Miss Broughton's sharp tongue and Mr
James's wit were prized. Miss Broughton's tongue was sharper
than ever, her legend longer. She had found fame as a writer of
fiction deemed "bold" by the Victorians, always about the
palpitating young woman who discovers love and defies con-
vention. Her three-deckers were staples of the lending libraries.
Her quip, that she had begun by being compared with Zola and
was ending her career as Charlotte Yonge, has often been repeated. But in truth she was neither a Zola, nor a Miss Yonge, but
simply Rhoda Broughton, a solid British integrity who had known
life in Oxford in the days of Pater and Mark Pattison (and had put
the much-novelized Pattison and his young wife into a novel).
She had written a widely-read series of fictions with picturesque
titles—*Cometh Up as a Flower*, or *Red as a Rose is She*. James
had attacked one of her novels in the *Nation* before he met her.
"A strongly-seasoned literary article," he had described *Joan* in
1876. It contained "puerility and nastiness, inanity and vulgarity." He hadn't hesitated to say that Miss Broughton's "in-
sidiousness is like the gambols of an elephant. . . . What
immaturity and crudity of art, what coarseness of sentiment and
vacuity of thought." Then a year later he met her—and he never
reviewed her again. Having encountered the original, he ap-

parently had no need for her projection in print. Something in
her upturned nose, her unconcealed asperity, her verbal vitality
appealed to James: she was a reincarnated Mrs Procter, a younger
version of old Mrs Duncan Stewart, the gruff maternal figures of
his prime whose talk he had liked and whose occasional cruel
sayings he seemed to prefer to anything more gentle and feminine.
Miss Broughton was "an old friend . . . before whom I even now
scarce cease to tremble," he could write in 1897. "We are excellent friends, but I really don't know whether I like her books or
not; it is so long since I read one. She is not in the least a person
to whom you have to pay that tribute."

He knew enough about her love-entangled histories in which
adolescent anguish seemed as eternally fresh as the adolescent
anger seemed fresh in Miss Rhoda. She was, moreover, a slight
yet somehow cherished link with Miss Woolson. One evening
during his long stay on Bellosguardo in 1887, when he and Miss
Woolson had occupied apartments in the same villa, Rhoda had
climbed the steep hill to dine with him and meet Fenimore. She
alone of all James's London friends had known his long-dead
companion. In 1897 James wrote to Francis Boott that Miss
Broughton was "too big a subject for the passing phrase, as to
which I see, by the way, that you have an inkling in speaking of
your 'escape' from that Bellosguardo dinner that Miss Woolson
commemorated to you."

"That very mature child of nature, my old friend Rhoda
Broughton," James said of her at the end of the century. "Poor
dear heroic Rhoda," he was saying as late as 1912, and even later
—in the last year of his life—he spoke of her as delivering "her
appreciations and discriminations as straight from the shoulder as
ever." In the years when she had lived at Richmond, he would
take the Thames journey to walk with her in the park; or he
summoned her to London to a play. She would come, refusing to
be his guest and belligerently paying for her stall. Above all she
seemed to be a figure to whom he could turn, now that other and
older ladies were gone, to pour out his epistolary melancholy and
his gallantries at decisive moments, as on this occasion when
the date on the calendar was changing, and James felt himself

moving into an unfamiliar time, the dawn of an unpredictable age.

His letter to Rhoda contained his usual apologies. He had been long silent; yet on this date he found himself turning back "to the warm and coloured past and away from the big black avenue that gapes in front of us. So turning, I find myself, not wholly without trepidation, yet also with a generous confidence, face to face with your distinguished figure—which please don't consider me, rude rustic and benighted alien as I've become, unworthy to greet. The country has swallowed me up, for the time, as you foretold me that it would, but I haven't quite burnt my ships behind me, and I'm counting the months till I can resume possession, for at least half the year in future, of my London habitation." Then his pen suddenly ceased its ritualized gestures, and gave way to "I'm so homesick for the blessed Kensington fields that I gloat over the prospect of treading them, finally afresh." More candour of feeling followed: "Meanwhile, I've felt remote and unfriended and have lacked courage to write to you almost only (as it might look) to say: 'See—from the way I keep it up—how I get on without you!' I get on without you very badly—and worse and worse the *more* I keep it up."

James wanted her to know "how poor a business I find it to be so deprived of your society." He gave her his "fervent wishes for the dim twelvemonth to come." With the Boer War raging, the year looked to him "full of goblins, to be deprecated by prayer and sacrifice—and my incense rises for your immunity, of every kind, not less than for my own. . . . Think of me, please, meanwhile, as yours, dear Rhoda Broughton, always and always Henry James."

In the coming years this kind of letter to Rhoda would be repeated again and again. He saluted the hearty and rough woman, almost as if she were some deity to be appeased, some Muse, who stood by his writing table and whose wholesome anger and affection, in moments of despair and loneliness, made his life bearable. "Our dear Rhoda—our gallant and intrepid Rhoda" she would remain to the end.

AN INNOCENT ABROAD

IN March of 1900, after almost two years of continual residence in Lamb House—broken only by his Italian trip of 1899—James had descended on London for a brief holiday. He wrote amusingly of experiencing "an extraordinary sense of dissipation." His visit was "a small carnival" and he was surprised to be greeted by friends and acquaintances "almost as if I had returned from African or Asian exile." He liked to feel the pavement under foot again; he window-shopped; he wandered into back streets; he browsed in the book shops; he dined out every night, as of old. He lunched with Henry White, first secretary of the American embassy, who was entertaining Brooks Adams. Henry Adams's brother was "refreshingly fundamental and universal—most cosmic and interesting." He went to see Sargent's large new painting of the Wyndham sisters. The sisters were seated on a sofa, with Watts's portrait of their mother in the background. It was "vast and dazzling"; there was something about it that reminded James of the feeling he had had in a music-hall or at a fair when a woman was shot out of the mouth of a cannon—its force made him feel "weak and foolish." With Sargent he went to call in Tite Street on Edwin Austin Abbey, working on one of his large Shakespearian paintings, "diabolically clever and effective, with success perched on every banner. I came away biting my thumb, of course, and with my ears burning with the sense of how it's not the age of my dim trade."

His trade was at the moment almost at a standstill. Publishers shook their heads sadly and thinned their lists; the effects of the war were being felt everywhere and London was filled with mourners. Behind the show of patriotism, James sensed the depression. One day he accompanied an army surgeon to watch him check the physical fitness of a batch of recruits. On another day his thirteen-year-old niece Peggy, with three of her playmates, came to the city from Harrow, and James gave them lunch and took a box at the "Biograph" to show them the primitive movies of the war. Peggy, true to her father's anti-Imperialism, was pro-Boer. She seemed surprised that her uncle wasn't. His identification with England had been long; he was, however, sufficiently American to decry "the fetish-worship of the Queen." It had "reached an abasement that makes one wonder if one dreams." But then Victoria was almost as old as her century.

The novelty of London wore off quickly. Even before James left, he looked forward to "little restful, red-roofed uncomplicated Rye." At the end of seventeen days he was back in Lamb House with Jonathan Sturges once more as his guest. However, Rye struck him as "slightly grim and nude." So it would be, between London and Rye, during all the Edwardian years.

I

Having broken his spell of absence, James made a second descent on London in mid-May, leaving a Rye in which there had been a dazzling outbreak of spring, after the bleak winter. Tulips and hyacinths, primroses and daffodils, were in bloom; his lawn was "daisied like a Botticelli picture." In the interval between his visits he had removed his beard. Writing about his changed appearance he remarked to a correspondent "still, it will be always I." Nevertheless it seemed a new "I" that descended from the train at Charing Cross and now brought his clean-shaven countenance into the familiar drawing-rooms of Mayfair. On a late afternoon James encountered before one of London's tea-hour fires, the grizzled, white-maned Samuel Langhorne Clemens, most famous of America's "innocents" abroad — rosy as a babe, clear-eyed, clad as always in white and full of rage at the "damned human race."

James had gone to call on a friend of his youth, Helena De Kay. The De Kays had been Newport neighbours. Helena was the wife of Richard Watson Gilder, editor of the *Century*, and a sister of James's old Venetian friend Mrs Bronson. She had a special claim on James's affections: she had been a close friend of Minny Temple. James thus found himself in a familiar American circle.

B

Mark Twain, moreover, was not new to James; their paths had crossed before.

They faced each other now as changed men. James was bland and cosmopolitan before the brilliant aggressivity of Clemens. Both were in late middle life, both had passed through long periods of despair. Both had battled with private demons. The nineties had been as hard on the world-seeking prosperous Mark Twain as on the privacy-seeking Henry James. James's clean-shaven face was symbolic of his recovery and awareness of the approaching century. Mark Twain was announcing that "the twentieth century is a stranger to me."

The two writers had known each other for years in the way of celebrities who meet at public dinners or in great houses. They had shared the devotion and loyalty of their friend, William Dean Howells—Mark Twain, much more than James, because he was more in America. Twenty years before, in 1879, during the days of Henry's constant dining out, he had seen Mark Twain a number of times in various London mansions, "a most excellent pleasant fellow," he had written to Howells, "what they call here very 'quaint.' Quaint he is! And his two ladies charming." James had made a great hit with Mrs Clemens. On one of these occasions, Whistler was also present and the thought of Mark Twain and James at a single board with Whistler teases the imagination. But no Boswell was there: and one knows only the simple facts. James and Clemens had been then at the height of their first fame: the one had been writing *A Tramp Abroad*; the other, a great social success of two seasons in London, honoured author of "Daisy Miller," was writing *Washington Square*.

They had met again—in 1897—when James was teaching himself to dictate directly to the typewriter. Mark Twain wrote to Howells at the time, "I was amused when I was in London last fall, to have James tell me that he had taken to dictating all his fiction, because he had heard that I always dictated. He makes it go, but if there could be anything worse for me than a typewriter, it would be a human typewriter." Mark loved the human race or he would not have had so much fault to find with it; and Henry could not talk to a machine that did not have a human being beside it. A few months before their 1897 meeting Mark Twain, in his preoccupation with the story of Joan of Arc (which had led to his writing a book about her) had told a friend that "if a master —say Henry James—should translate it [a certain French book about Joan] I think it would live for ever." To Mark Twain, to Howells, to a newcomer in letters like Conrad, James was now indeed "master"; he had the largeness of the formidable craftsman who speaks also as an oracle. A whole new generation of writers would take the title for granted.

II

Mark Twain and Henry James were not by nature destined ever to be intimate; there was a newspaperish side to the humorist, the "lion" side, and the roar of publicity and a love of broad effects, from which James shrank. "Temperament" divided them, as it would James and his fellow-novelists in England. Mark Twain was out-going, expansive, capable of great exuberance. James was inward-turned, ruminative, secretive. No two American geniuses were more dissimilar, save in their sense of humour; this in James was highly condensed, epigrammatic, and also private, whereas in Mark Twain it was broad, visceral, and public. Both were lovers of the truth; both critical of their fellow-Americans. Mark Twain had gratified his countrymen by criticizing Europe in *Innocents Abroad*. James had shocked them by making himself a critical analyst of American innocence. Mark Twain had decried the feudal ages, the Roman barbarians, the cant of romance, the violence and brutality of the European centuries. James had discerned the eerie brutality and violence behind the façade of civilization. Nevertheless he had the nineteenth century's belief in "progress"; he could accept the forms and rituals, the myths and usages men had created in order to be less barbaric. The two writers had great respect for each other, even though Mark Twain had once said he would rather "be damned to John Bunyan's heaven" than read *The Bostonians*. James, reading Mark Twain's *Life on the Mississippi* had found in it the presence of "sublimity."

Of the particular encounter in London in early 1900 during

James's call on Helena Gilder, we know little more than about the other encounters. It was a casual meeting of two great American writers. Mark Twain had been living abroad — Switzerland, France, Austria, Sweden, England, with brief trips to the United States. At this moment he was in a flat in Knightsbridge. He was full of dreams and of rage; he sympathized with the British in the Boer War "but my heart and such rags of morals as I have are with the Boer." To Henry James he seems to have talked largely of his symptoms, probably coming to them through Henry's telling him that his brother William had returned to Nauheim for another "cure." Mark Twain, who had invested in quack medicines and elixirs as he invested in printing and machinery, was at this phase all for osteopathy. He had recently been to Henrick Kellgren's health establishment in Sweden. Kellgren could cure anything, Mark said. He told Henry he had been in correspondence with William and had offered him medical advice. He also discoursed on "albumen." He said he would put William James on to it. The talk was rather confused. When Mark Twain spoke of Kellgren, Henry thought he was referring to Lord Kelvin. "Why Sweden?" he asked of William's wife, not having apparently related the osteopath to that country. As James put it to Alice, he had met Mark who had given him "a muddled and confused glimpse of Lord Kelvin, Albumen, Sweden and half a dozen other things on which I was prevented from afterwards bringing him to book." William James knew Mark Twain more intimately than his brother; the philosopher had met the creator of Huck Finn in Florence, during the winter of 1892. "A fine, soft-fibred little fellow with the perversest twang and drawl, but very human and good," William had said. He called him also "a dear little genius."

Mark Twain was eight years older than Henry; and his finest work was done. Henry's greatest work was about to be written. In the future they would come to be archetypal figures — the one the historian and embodiment of a kind of American innocence which the other had devoted his lifetime to studying. Indeed James was now embarked on a novel that would confront America and Europe, provincialism and cosmopolitanism, innocence and evil. Lambert Strether would hardly be a Mark Twain; he would be much closer to Mark's and Henry's friend, Howells, and even to Henry himself—the Henry who listened confusedly to Mark's hypochondriacal babble. But a little touch of this babble would be imported into *The Ambassadors* in the character of the dyspeptic Waymarsh. This hypothesis gains some credence when we discover, in James's original plan for the novel, that the character was first named Way*mark*. The "sacred rage" of Waymarsh-Waymark would have in it perhaps a touch of the sacred rage of Mark Twain.

A NATURAL PECULIARITY

FORD MADOX HUEFFER, a descendant of peripheral pre-Raphaelites, whose father was a German musicologist enamoured of Wagner and Schopenhauer, had called on Henry James during the summer of 1896 when the novelist first discovered Rye. James had just moved into the Vicarage from Point Hill, on Playden, and Hueffer—who would later be known as Ford Madox Ford—came to lunch one September day with an introduction from Henry's friend, Mrs W. K. Clifford. James received the tall, lean, blonde, young man, then twenty-three, with his customary civility. He chatted with him about his relatives—his grandfather on the English side was Ford Madox Brown, a pre-Raphaelite painter—and interrogated him about his literary ambitions. By Hueffer's testimony, Smith, the red-nosed butler, served an efficient meal while markedly tipsy. James sent the young man away with perhaps less than his usual avuncular tenderness for aspirants to literature. Certainly the friendliness is absent in the extant records; there were no encouraging letters subsequently, save one, several years later, offering cautious praise of some of Hueffer's poems. And there were no immediate invitations to return.

Hueffer himself only vaguely remembered the Old Vicarage. In his vast recollections a quarter of a century later he recorded a first meeting with the clean-shaven James in Rye, where he had gone with Conrad—but that was in the era of the motor-car. Later he recalled the bearded James of 1896 and the red-nosed alcoholic Smith. His memories of this and other meetings are scrambled. They show proof of that "copious carelessness of reminiscence" which H. G. Wells attributed to him. Hueffer readily confessed to "a large carelessness," insisting, however, that he was not reporting literal fact. He was, he explained, "an impressionist." His impressions, however, were "absolute." By

38

this formula, late in life, he composed elaborate portraits which were a strange amalgam of half-truths, vague recollections, anecdotes garnered from reading, and other persons' memories. He could build an entire essay on his having offered Turgenev a chair in his grandfather's studio when he was eight years old. He had fugitive memories of Lamb House: he remembered its colour as grey, and said it was built of stone, forgetting that its characteristic russet was derived from weathered brick. Documents which have survived confirm that he was a literary Munchausen. The famous Baron told tall tales, robust and Rabelaisian. Hueffer contented himself with literary chit-chat, the manufacture of small pastiches out of a blurred imagination. He claimed, for instance, to have been the "original" of Merton Densher in *The Wings of the Dove*, and this was the slightest of the many identities he constantly borrowed to place himself in a favourable relation to great men. H. G. Wells, who like others saw the humour and the nonsense of Hueffer, called this "his great system of assumed *personas* and dramatized selves." Hueffer's tendency to change his own name was symptomatic of a lifelong quest for an identity. He seems not to have been certain at first whether he should make much of his severe German father or pose as his mother's son and an English gentleman. He was actually baptized Ford Hermann Hueffer, but on becoming a Catholic at eighteen—still another change of identity—he took two more names, Joseph and Leopold. Then, as if searching for a makeweight for the German nomenclature, he adopted his mother's name of Madox. During another phase, he claimed he was Baron Hueffer von Aschendorf. The final shift to Ford Madox Ford, which wholly eliminated his father, occurred after the First World War when he had for several years worn the guise of "the good soldier" and wanted to forget his German antecedents. Perhaps a more compelling reason for the change was to avoid a legal struggle with his wife; he was by then living with Stella Bowen. Under this name, the writings of Henry James aiding, he made his long friendship with "the Master" the very centre of his myth through four volumes of anecdotal self-inflating reminiscence.

The young man James met in 1896 was not yet the formed

myth-maker of the later decades. But he was uncertain, confused, romantic and good-naturedly poetic. Whether the American novelist recognized that he had invented Hueffer long before he met him, it would be hard to say. Life had a way of being anticipated in James's art. In the early 1880's James had dined in a London house where a lively individual provided "the woven wonders of a summer holiday, the exploits of a salamander, among Mediterranean isles," and other pleasing tall tales. Recalling Daudet's story of *Nouma Roumestan*, the meridional whose stories won him favour and political recognition in Paris, James wrote an artful tale simply titled "The Liar," about a Colonel Capadose, who "lies about the time of day, about the name of his hatter." It is quite disinterested. He is not in the least a scoundrel, "there's no harm in him and no bad intention; he doesn't steal nor cheat nor gamble nor drink; he's very kind—he sticks to his wife, is fond of his children. He simply can't give you a straight answer." This description fitted Hueffer with the exception that ultimately he did not stick to his wife. He was inclined, like James's Capadose, to a mixture of the correct and the extravagant; he had good manners and yet could tell stories in bad taste. Also like Colonel Capadose, he inspired affection. His "natural peculiarity" was forgiven by many devoted friends because it testified to an overflow of life and genial spirits. Hueffer would be kind and generous to many young writers; and from James and Conrad he borrowed a high seriousness about the art of fiction.

Joseph Conrad, who would collaborate with Hueffer, may have intuitively grasped the protean essence of his friend, for in "Heart of Darkness," written early in their acquaintance, there is a strange, mysterious character, a man dressed in motley who carries—in the midst of the jungle—a book on navigation. This man, wearing a coat of many colours, a kind of patchwork European, with the wrong book to guide him, seems a premonition of the composite Ford Madox Hueffer, with "little blue eyes that were perfectly round" and an abiding loyalty to Kurtz, the figure at the "heart of darkness." "Brother sailor . . . honour . . . pleasure . . . delight . . . introduce myself . . . Russian . . . son of an archpriest . . . Government of Tambov . . . What? Tobacco!

English tobacco; the excellent English tobacco! Now that's brotherly. Smoke? Where's a sailor that does not smoke?" Hueffer, in later years, leaning on grand pianos in the drawing-rooms of England and America, talked in this way. His passages in his memoirs about Henry James have the same kind of discontinuity.

II

It would be a large and ungrateful task to unravel Hueffer's Jamesian tales.[1] A slender thread of fact informs some of them; others were culled from his reading of James's *Partial Portraits* or *Notes on Novelists*, and became a kind of free rewrite of James's own cautious reminiscence of some of the French novelists he had known. They form a part of the false "image" of Henry James at Rye, and have been adopted by so many others as authentic that some characterization of them seems inevitable. The best-known Huefferian tale is his claim that James hated Flaubert because the French writer received him one day wearing a dressing-gown. This is ludicrous in the light of James's affectionate allusions to Flaubert; perhaps those who have looked too often at the top-hatted photographs of James have concluded that he indeed tolerated no informality among those with whom he discussed the craft of fiction. James's actual report on Flaubert's dress is to be found in his late essay on the French writer and it is wholly complimentary. He tells us the French master wore "up to any hour of the afternoon that long, colloquial dressing-gown, with trousers to match, which one has always associated with literature in France—the uniform really of freedom of talk." James here was thinking of the ways in which French writers are often described *en pantoufles*. Hueffer joined to his anecdote something he had read in the Goncourt journals. This was that Flaubert had once severely admonished an American, whose initial was given as H. That the H. turned out to be not Henry but Harisse mattered very little. In the repertoire of Hueffer, James had been scolded by Flaubert, and Flaubert had had the in-

---

[1] Simon Nowell-Smith long ago brilliantly analysed their improvised character in his *Legend of the Master* (1948).

decency to welcome him in a bathrobe. Such is the small talk of Huefferian legend.

Curiously enough Hueffer read James's critical account of Maupassant and decided that the Master liked him very much. To be sure, said Hueffer, James had been upset when he arrived at Maupassant's for lunch and found a naked *femme du monde* seated at table wearing a mask. In Hueffer's myth-making, one gathers the naked lady disturbed James less than Flaubert's dressing-gown. Reading of James's constant correspondence with Mrs Humphry Ward about how novels should be written, Hueffer said James always corrected that lady's manuscripts.[1] He pictured James in Rye as practising black magic—or so he said the townsfolk believed. He described James as using foul language; and told how a murderer once confessed his crime to James. He also made James out to have been a financial supporter of the *Yellow Book*; and said *Guy Domville* was booed because the audience did not like to pay for its programmes. A glimpse of the crippled Jonathan Sturges in Lamb House yielded the following reminiscence:

I have attended at conversations between him and a queer tiny being who lay as if crumpled up on the stately sofa in James's magnificent panelled room in Lamb House—conversations that made the tall wax candles seem to me to waver in their sockets and the skin of my forehead and hands to prickle with sweat. I am in these things rather squeamish . . . I don't wish to leave the impression that these conversations were carried on for purposes of lewd stimulation or irreverent ribaldry. They occurred as part of the necessary pursuit of that knowledge that permitted James to give his reader the "sense of evil" . . . And I dare say they freed him from the almost universal proneness of Anglo-Saxon writers to indulge in their works in a continually intrusive fumbling in placket-holes as Sterne called it, or in the lugubrious occupation of composing libidinous limericks.

One of his most charming inventions was that James telegraphed Wanamaker's to have apple butter and pumpkin pie sent to the dying Stephen Crane. In this way James was given legendary form by Hueffer's shaky ego. He described James as "the most masterful man I have ever met," and this probably was

[1] Ford probably got this from Violet Hunt who noted in her diary that James complained to her that Mrs Ward occasionally sent him typescripts "for his corrections."

true. To which he added, with equal truth, that "I do not think that, till the end of his days, he regarded me as a serious writer." How this accorded with James's consulting Hueffer, as the latter claimed, "about his most intimate practical affairs," it is difficult to see. In one of his essays Hueffer, after this kind of self-depreciation, finally remarked "I think I will, after reflection, lay claim to a very considerable degree of intimacy." He did make this claim; and it remains highly at variance with the available testimony. James's secretary recorded that James once made her jump a ditch in order to avoid an encounter with Hueffer on the Winchelsea road; on another occasion he quickly pulled her behind a tree, till Hueffer had walked by. There is also the testimony of a Rye neighbour, a writer, Archibald Marshall. In his memoirs he relates "how very coldly Hueffer's name was received." There had been some question of an invitation that would "bring that young man down upon me again" and James exclaimed to Marshall, "I said to myself, No! and again No!"

III

There was something almost pathetic in Hueffer's need to stand in the good graces of the Master, and his strange swagger and boast of later years. On one occasion he speculated that James "must have liked" him and Hueffer gave as the reason that this was because he was "a strong silent man of affairs." Hueffer boasted that James described him to Conrad as *votre ami, le jeune homme modeste*. If James said this there may have been a certain characteristic irony in the remark. Modesty was not one of Hueffer's outstanding qualities. His decision that James had converted him into the passive Merton Densher was based largely on Densher's being "longish, leanish, fairish." From the few sparse letters of James to Hueffer that survive we know that the latter did write to James about *The Wings of the Dove* but it was to inquire why the novelist had left out the scene of Milly's confrontation with Merton. James carefully explained that this was the sort of scene he wanted to avoid, lest his book be turned into a sentimental romance—the kind over which women wept. In another letter James offered qualified praise for *Poems for Pictures* which

Hueffer had sent him. James thanked him for his "so curious and interesting book of verses." He found some of them "terribly natural and true and 'right,' drawn from the real wretchedness of things. The poetry of the cold and the damp and the mud and the nearness to earth—this is a chord you touch in a way that makes me wonder if there isn't still more for you to get from it." And he ended this letter, one of his less impersonal missives to Hueffer, by asking him to stop by, if he happened to pass his way.

Flowing into Hueffer's mythology of James was the admiration of Conrad, and the worship of Hueffer's wife Elsie, and of her Garnett friends, especially that of Olivia Rayne Garnett, who wrote novels and had a curious "fixation" on the American novelist. Two years before she ever set eyes on James, Olivia Garnett recorded in her diary: "I had a dream this morning: Henry James looked up at me from writing and said smiling: 'You know, life isn't ONLY reality, it's a small part of a great whole.' I believed him and awoke." Later we find her working on a story "of what it would be like to love and be loved by Henry James." Finally there are glimpses of the Master in an entry of November 1901. Olivia relates how she goes to Winchelsea to visit Hueffer and his wife, and travels on the train with James's new cook. The Great Man is at the station. "I have come to meet my doom," he remarks as he comes up with the cook. A day or so later the Hueffers and Miss Garnett walk to Rye from Winchelsea; they enter by the Ypres gate, go past the church and then "a moment for me!"— they pass Lamb House. They have tea at the Mermaid and go to the butcher's and draper's. While at the draper's "we heard James's voice as he passed with his typist." A few days later Hueffer goes to London and Mrs Hueffer and Olivia Garnett walk to Rye after tea:

It was dark when we got there, and stopping outside a lighted chemist's shop Elsie said "I have to go in there, but I am not sure, I think that is James inside. What do you say?" I looked, and saw a huge round figure in a light overcoat, and almost sure it wasn't James said "Oh no, let's go in." So in we went and in another moment I was being introduced! The figure swung round, seemed to bend an impressive searching look on me, and a voice said, "I have met you in London." I said "Yes," and seemed to heave my face upwards. The next moment there were inquiries about walking, Ford, etc. "You did not recognize me. I have scraped my chin." "No, I should not have recognized you," and we were walking up to Lamb House. He asked me if I had known Madox Brown, and what he was like, and talked of the abysmal vulgarity of the British public, coming down the street with us as far as the toy-shop. We parted abruptly. Elsie and I went home by train and lived on the recollection till the return of Ford.

Finally there came the summons to tea in Lamb House. Elsie Hueffer describes to James how Conrad and Hueffer are collaborating on *The Inheritors*. James looks at Olivia Garnett. He speaks of the dissimilar traditions of Hueffer and Conrad, and how "inconceivable" such collaboration was. "To me," said James, and Miss Olivia later records it, "this is like a bad dream which one relates at breakfast."

The diarist meekly added, "we all munched bread and butter and no more was said on the subject."

A MASTER MARINER

FORD MADOX HUEFFER moved to Winchelsea early in 1901, and during the next two years Joseph Conrad visited him frequently, for they were collaborating on *Romance*. It was during this period that Conrad "haunted" Winchelsea and, as James said, Winchelsea "in discretion" haunted Rye. The novelist continued to marvel at this collaboration; he had a vague sense of the unsounded depths of Conrad; he could not reconcile them with the shallows of Hueffer. On occasion, Conrad alone, sometimes with Hueffer, knocked at the canopied portal of Lamb House for a tea-time talk or an afternoon's walk with the Master. James's nephew Billy, the second son of William, recalled these visits—and particularly the way in which James would take Conrad's arm and start off with him along the road, leaving Hueffer and Billy to bring up the rear. "Hueffer babbled," the frustrated nephew said, "and I didn't listen. I wanted to hear what the great men were saying up ahead, but there I was stuck with Hueffer. Occasionally a word or two would drift back and what I always heard was—French!" The two novelists, the American and the Pole, discussed the form and future of the English novel in the language of art and diplomacy—and with appropriate gestures. So it would always be between them—a mask of politeness, a kind of guarded "distance," a mixture of friendliness and anxiety.

Conrad induced a state of malaise in James. It was not his "foreignness," nor the harsh slavonic accent in his speech. James had known and liked many émigré Russians and Poles since the days of his friendship with Turgenev in Paris. Nor were there any difficulties about the professional side: indeed on this level there was great esteem between them. Conrad "put himself in relation with me years ago, when he had written but his first book or two," James told Edith Wharton in 1912, adding that his feelings about him were mixed up "with personal impressions since received." While he did not specify these, the implication was that they were not entirely favourable. Hueffer insisted that James actively disliked Conrad; but it would be more accurate to say that he was simply troubled by him—by his nervousness, his "temperament" and the signals James picked up of a deep morbidity. The Pole and the American exchanged compliments and books. James extravagantly praised Conrad's early works. The middle period—*Nostromo, The Secret Agent, Under Western Eyes*—he described to Mrs Wharton as "impossibilities" and "wastes of desolation that succeeded the two or three final good things of his earlier time." *Chance* he found "rather yieldingly difficult and charming." On his side, Conrad always saluted James as *cher maître* and in the end as "very dear Master." James responded by disclosing to him a few of the secrets of his writing desk, something he seldom did. Indeed when Wells learned that James had shown Conrad a scenario for *The Wings of the Dove* he did not conceal his jealousy. He had never been given such a privilege. In a word James honoured Conrad the craftsman; yet he was uneasy about the man. He spoke of him as "curious" and "interesting," or as "the interesting and remarkable Conrad." This juxtaposition of the weak and the emphatic adjective denoted on the part of James a degree of bewilderment. On a later occasion he spoke of Conrad as "that poor queer man." This was not condescension. One way of translating these remarks might be "that poor troubled man—who somehow gives me a queer feeling." The key to these remarks may be seen in his confiding to Mrs Wharton that he had a "realising sense" of Conrad but it was of "a rum sort." James was saying—he who prided himself on his insights—that he couldn't quite fathom the gifted Pole.

I

They met when Conrad was thirty-nine and James fifty-three. Both were occupied at that moment with a world that seemed to them "illusion." James had been in the depths of despair after his failure in the theatre; Conrad was trying to understand his two decades of seafaring and to find an outlet in the writing of fiction for his inner nightmares of violence. The sea might be the "destructive element" but he could be sustained by it; it was much more difficult to cope with life on land. James too had spoken of the sea, many times: but for him, as a landlubber, it was "far shallower than the spirit of man," shallower than man's "abyss of illusion." To Conrad all was illusion. Man when born, he said, fell "into a dream like a man falls into the sea." Conrad had left Poland in 1874—when he was Jozef Teodor Konrad Nalecz Korzeniowski—"as a man gets into a dream." He had been living that dream ever since, attempting to understand and describe, as he would later say to James, "the poignant reality of illusion." James in his subjectivity had also come to wonder about the phantasmagoria of being, but it led him always back to immediate realities—the "real, the tideless deep" of man.

The first gesture had been made by Conrad as early as 1896. He debated whether to send James his second book *An Outcast of the Islands*. He feared at first he might be thought "impudent." But so strong was the impulse that he finally dispatched the volume, writing on the flyleaf the equivalent of a letter. "I address you across vast space," he wrote to James, and he told him that he had read his novels while sailing many seas. James's characters were "Exquisite Shades, with live hearts and clothed in the wonderful garment of your prose." They had stood "consoling by my side under many skies. They have lived with me, faithful and serene— with the bright serenity of Immortals. And to you thanks are due for such glorious companionship." The inscription was flowery; yet it seemed deeply felt. James liked it. Moreover he liked the book. He waited for a few weeks, and when *The Spoils of Poynton* was published he dispatched one of the first copies to Conrad in February 1897 inscribing it "Joseph Conrad, in dreadfully delayed but very grateful acknowledgment of an offering singularly generous and beautiful." Conrad had not expected such spontaneous acceptance. "The delicacy and tenuity" of the *Spoils*, he said, was like "a great sheet of plate glass—you don't know it's there till you run against it." The image was apt. There would always be a plate glass between James and Conrad. He discerned in advance the quality of "distance" James possessed.

The American did not let the matter rest with this exchange of books. He was curious about the mariner-novelist and he sent a lively note suggesting that Conrad come to lunch. Conrad's report on it to Edward Garnett was: "He is quite playful about it. Says we shall be alone—no one to separate us if we quarrel. It's the most delicate flattery I've ever been victim to." No more delicate, it might be remarked, or flattering than Conrad's inscription of his book to James.

They lunched on 25 February 1897 in De Vere Gardens. The master mariner got a sense of the established power of James's literary life. And what Conrad could not know was that he met a James who was at odds with himself. In the midst of his fame, and with his command of the world's respect, the American was going through a bad phase. What James couldn't know—though he seems to have sensed it—was that he was faced with a powerful and deeply disturbed genius, possessed of "paranoid trends" (as one psychiatrist surmises) whose strength resided in his perception of the buried violence within himself. Conrad reached out to James with a predatory emotion—the "cannibalism" of which psychoanalysts have written—that made him want on occasion, as he himself avowed, "to howl and foam at the mouth." And he couldn't reach James. The wall of plate glass was there between them. What they talked about we do not know; but James that very morning had written to Whistler "with the artist, the artist communicates." They stood on their common ground of art. We can imagine the two face to face. Both were short men. James was all repose and assurance. Conrad, with his head tucked between his shoulders, his strong Polish accent, looked at James with eyes which seemed to live in wild dream and which somehow, for all their penetration, sought the very "heart of darkness." The man who would write a tale of such a search faced the man who would write "The Beast in the Jungle." The two stories speak for the two temperaments. Conrad, making the descent into the irrational jungle of himself, James fearing the irrationality, walking anxiously and warily through the dense growth of the human consciousness, on guard against the beasts that might leap—yet knowing that the beasts were those of his own mind. With his slow-moving eyes and settled aristocratic manner he would have listened to Conrad and answered his questions. He had always loved seamen's tales. James may have described on this occasion how he was learning to dictate directly to the typewriter: he had just begun. Conrad would allude to this in an article he wrote some years later. They may have discussed the British Navy for at some point the first volume of Pepys's diary was pulled from the shelf—James owned the stout brown-covered Braybrooke-Bright edition of 1875. In turning its pages Conrad came upon the passage describing the boarding of the *Naseby* to bring Charles II back from his exile across the water. "My lord, in his discourse discovered a great deal of love in this ship." Conrad copied the sentence. He affixed it as epigraph to the book he had completed that week, *The Nigger of the Narcissus*.

If we do not know the precise nature of their talk we know that James would speak of the "independent nobleness" in Conrad's work and the "moral radiance" that he apparently did not find in the man. He got from Conrad a vivid sense of long lonely vigils on ships in distant waters, of land looming up in the dark, of adventures such as he, in his landed cosmopolitanism, had learned only in books or from men of action. "I read you," James would later write to Conrad, "as I listen to rare music—with the deepest depths of surrender." This would not always be so. Conrad on his side liked the nobility of James's world and the way in which he created characters with "fine consciences." He would argue this with John Galsworthy, when the latter called James "cold." James's finished, chiselled, carved work might be so called, Conrad admitted, but the perfection of craft did not prevent James from imparting to his readers a full sense of "flesh and blood." Above all Conrad felt that James's people rode always to moral victory: they lost battles, yet never left the battlefield. They renounced, but it was "an energetic act"—"energetic not violent." James's books ended as episodes in life ended; one retained a feeling of life still going on. "His mankind is delightful," Conrad would write. "It is delightful in its tenacity; it refuses to own itself beaten." And in a supreme passage in his essay on James, Conrad wrote words that would inspire a novelist of a later date (William Faulkner) to proclaim the victories of life over death, of art over chaos:

When the last aqueduct shall have crumbled to pieces, the last airship fallen to the ground, the last blade of grass have died upon a dying earth, man, indomitable by his training in resistance to misery and pain shall set this undiminished light of his eyes against the feeble glow of the sun.

Conrad inscribed *The Nigger of the Narcissus* to James in French —a long inscription in which occurred the phrase *on ne communique pas la réalité poignante des illusions.* Perhaps it was difficult to communicate the poignancy of certain dreams, perhaps this poignancy could never wholly penetrate the soul of the listener—so Conrad mused in his eloquent *dédicace*: and perhaps this was because behind his deep reserve this listener seemed remote, inscrutable, sovereign. But James was not always aloof and Conrad's admiration was not lost on him. In writing to the Royal Literary Fund in 1902 in support of a grant to Conrad he said that "*The Nigger of the Narcissus* is in my opinion the very finest and strongest picture of the sea and sea-life that our language possesses—the masterpiece in a whole great class; and *Lord Jim* runs it very close." His liking for *Lord Jim* was conveyed in a letter which Conrad characterized as "a draught from the Fountain of Eternal Youth. Wouldn't you think a boy had written it? Such enthusiasm! Wonderful old man, with his record of wonderful work!"

To the Royal Literary Fund James wrote:

When I think that such completeness, such intensity of expression has been arrived at by a man not born to our speech, but who took it up, with singular courage, from necessity and sympathy, and has laboured at it heroically and devotedly, I am equally impressed with the fine persistence and the intrinsic success. Born a Pole and cast upon the waters, he has worked out an English style that is more than correct, that has *quality* and ingenuity. The case seems to me unique and peculiarly worthy of recognition. Unhappily, to be very serious and subtle isn't one of the paths to fortune. Therefore I greatly hope the Royal Literary Fund may be able to do something for him.

The Fund in due course bestowed the sum Conrad needed, £300.

We have a further record of an exchange between the two writers. In 1906 Conrad dispatched *The Mirror of the Sea* to James, and once more filled the end-paper with an epistolary inscription again in French. This time he described it as "a little preface written for you alone." In it he tried to explain why he had been self-indulgent, why he had written a book of reminiscences for his own pleasure—"a dangerous fantasy" for any writer. He was confessing this to James because he was "very sure of the friendship with which you have honoured me." And he added: "Your friendly eye will know how to distinguish in these pages that piety of memory which has guided the groping phrase and the ever-rebel pen."

James responded by telling Conrad that whatever he might say of his difficult medium and his "rebel pen," he knocked about "in the wide waters of expression like the raciest and boldest of privateers." And he told Conrad, "you have made the whole place your own *en même temps que les droits les plus acquis vous y avez les plus rares bonheurs*. Nothing you have done has more in it. . . . You stir me to amazement and you touch me to tears, and I thank the powers who so mysteriously let you loose with such sensibilities, into such an undiscovered country—*for* sensibility . . . I want to see you again." He concluded with "I pat you, my dear Conrad, very affectionately and complacently on the back, and am yours very constantly Henry James." *Complacently* we must assume, for being so admirable a disciple, so admirably a fellow-artist.

III

Concerning this discipleship perhaps not enough has been said: for dissimilar as the two writers were, and distinctive as Conrad's genius was, James played a much greater role in Conrad's craftsmanship than has perhaps been allowed. No one has noticed that "The Turn of the Screw" and "Heart of Darkness" appeared within a year of each other; and that both tales begin in the same way—the quiet circle, the atmosphere of mystery and gloom, the hint of terrible evil, the reflective narrator, the retrospective method, the recall of crucial episodes. And perhaps from the

"Mr Quint is dead" of the ghostly tale there sounds in Conrad a powerful echo, "Mistah Kurtz—he dead." The stories are as different as their authors, but they suggest that Conrad went to school at times in the works of Henry James—and notably learned James's devices for obtaining distance from his materials. In James this was inevitable, given his own shrinking from the violence of passion. In Conrad it proved a much-needed method; it helped him cope with a great flow of emotion, and "contained" his "cosmic" feeling. Of "The Turn of the Screw" Conrad said James showed how to extract an "intellectual thrill" from his materials leaving "a kind of phosphorescent trail in one's mind." There would come a time, a decade later, when James would criticize Conrad's excesses in indirect narration; perhaps the Master felt that his lesson had been too well learned. Conrad resented the rebuke; and on James's part it was ill-considered. It occurred in a two-part article 19 March and 1 April 1914 in *The Times Literary Supplement* called "The Younger Generation," James's final critical fling at the writers who followed on his heels and whose youth and talent he sometimes resented with all the vitality of his old age. He was kinder to Conrad than to any of the other writers, save Hugh Walpole and Mrs Wharton, to whom however he offered superficial accolades. He paid Conrad the compliment of taking him seriously; and for Conrad alone, in this array of writers, he reserved the title of "genius." But when it came to matters of technique, he had some fine-spun observations. Conrad was alone, as regards method, "absolutely alone as the votary of the way to do a thing that shall make it undergo most doing." James complained, nevertheless, about the "prolonged hovering flight of the subjective over the outstretched ground of the case exposed. We make out this ground, only through the shadow cast by the flight" and he took his image out of the recently developed machines of flight, for he had seen, one day at Rye, Blériot's plane over the Channel. Conrad's narration within narration (an extension of James's devices) he likened to a series of aeroplane shadows which create an eclipse upon "the intrinsic colour and form and whatever, upon the passive expanse."

The story of the impact of James's article upon the novelist he dealt with belongs to a later stage. In his complex and subtle analysis of Conrad's modes of narration in *Chance*, in forgetting that Conrad (by then fifty-one) was hardly of the "younger" generation (as he had been when James met him), and in failing to speak of other works which had pleased him more than *Chance*, James understandably hurt Conrad. The latter felt, as he said, "rather airily condemned." He added, "I may say with scrupulous truth that this was the *only time* a criticism affected me painfully." It must have been extremely painful for it came from a revered source which had hitherto given him the finest praise. In later years Conrad remembered not the rebuke but James's singular kindness. His response to James's gift of the first batch of volumes of the New York Edition shows his depth of feeling:

"*Très cher maître*," he began, "they have arrived—the six of them: I have felt them all in turn and all at one time as it were." He had taken the morning off to browse in them and read the preface to *The American*. "Afterwards I could not resist the temptation of reading the beautiful and touching last ten pages of the story. There is in them perfection of tone which calmed me, and I sat for a long while with the closed volume in my hand going over the preface in my mind and thinking—that is how it began, that's how it was done!"

The Pole thanked James for "the opportunity to breathe in the assurance of your good-will, the fortifying atmosphere of your serene achievement."

Long afterwards, when James was dead, Conrad one day found himself describing to John Quinn, the Irish-American patron of the arts, how he had felt about the American novelist. He could not bring himself to say positively that James had liked him; perhaps the memory of his hurt over *Chance* made him cautious. He spoke as if he had to infer James's feelings, in spite of the letters James had written to him. And he was right. James's feeling had been mixed. On his own side he could be affirmative. "I had a profound affection for him," he told Quinn, adding that

James "accepted it as if it were something worth having. At any rate that is the impression I have." Then, almost as if he were ruminating aloud, he said James "wasn't a man who would pretend" to like some one. What need had he? —even if he had been capable of the pretence?

A GHOSTLY RENTAL

HENRY JAMES met H. G. Wells and Stephen Crane during 1898 and within months both became his neighbours— Wells at Sandgate on the Kentish coast, across Romney Marsh from Rye, and Crane at Brede, in Sussex, an eight-mile bicycle run from Lamb House. Legend has it that Crane and James met at a bohemian party in London, at which a woman named Madame Zipango poured champagne into James's top hat. James protested this affront to the symbol of his dignity. Crane is said to have spirited the offender away from the party and addressed himself tactfully to salvaging the hat and soothing the ruffled spirit of the Master. They had been discussing literary style. Crane may have been alluding to this incident a few days later when he spoke of seeing James "make a holy show of himself in a situation that—on my honour—would have been simple to an ordinary man." He added, "it seems impossible to dislike him. He is so kind to everybody."

Crane's friend Harold Frederic, a fellow-American, and London correspondent of the New York *Times*, took a less generous view of the rituals of the Master. A down-to-earth, rough-and-ready newspaperman who had written a best-selling novel, *The Damnation of Theron Ware* (about a Methodist clergyman, the flesh and the devil) he characterized James as "an effeminate old donkey who lives with a herd of other donkeys around him and insists on being treated as if he were the Pope." And he spoke of James's "usual lack of a sense of generosity." Both Crane and Frederic lived "hard" and died young—Frederic of a stroke that very year. He had maintained two households and left illegitimate as well as legitimate children and he would have been astonished to learn that the man he described as lacking generosity was among the first to sign an appeal for money for the illegitimate children. James wrote to Cora Crane, Stephen's common-law wife, "deeper than I can say is my commiseration of these beautiful children." The sentimental and practical Cora wept when she received £50 from James. Historians of the Cranes and the Frederics have described James as disturbed and even shocked by the bohemianism of this group of American journalist-novelists. Cora had been the "madame" of a "house of joy" in Jacksonville, Florida, but there was no failure of courtesy on James's part when she became his neighbour. He had known bohemianism in all its forms from the days of his studio hauntings in Rome, Paris, London. He had chronicled the lives of dissolute artists in his novels and tales. If he passed judgment on them it was not that they led bohemian lives but that they made their bohemianism an excuse for poor art. When Cora Crane sent Frederic's posthumous work, *The Market Place*, to the Master, he read it "with a lively sense of what Harold Frederic might have done if he had lived—and above all lived (and therefore worked) differently."

I

James's meeting with Wells had in it less of the bohemian and more of the dignity of letters. The younger man had been enjoying increasing prosperity as a writer of tales about man in time and space, and as a contributor to the journals. Early in the summer of 1898, he had gone on a bicycle trip along the Kentish coast, accompanied by his wife. He found himself, however, increasingly unwell and collapsed at New Romney with a high fever. An old kidney ailment had declared itself, and he spent a number of weeks under medical care. In August there appeared at his cottage two important-looking middle-aged gentlemen, wheeling their bicycles. Wells recognized Henry James. He had seen him on the night of *Guy Domville*. The other visitor was Edmund Gosse. They had cycled over from Lamb House to inquire about his health. Wells was then thirty-two; James fifty-five. The younger writer was touched—and flattered—to have two outstanding members of the literary establishment show such a kindly interest in his welfare. They sat around a table, drank tea, talked sociably for an hour and then the visitors left as un-

ceremoniously as they had arrived. Some years later Wells put
two and two together and realized that the visit was not as
innocent as it had seemed: James and Gosse had been quietly
ascertaining, on behalf of the Royal Literary Fund, whether the
younger writer was in financial need.

From the time of this meeting, and through the Edwardian
years, Wells and James were excellent friends. James sent Wells
"The Turn of the Screw" which was published that year, and
Wells sent James *The Time Machine*, and from then on bestowed
all his books on the Master. This may have been unwise, for
James felt he would insult the younger man if he acknowledged
them in a perfunctory way. He invariably offered him a full-dress
critique. He liked the utopias for their abundance of ideas and
originality, and candidly complained to Wells that he was not
sufficiently thinking through his fiction—not concerned sufficiently with art. Wells, in an anonymous review, before he had
met James, had criticized the American's "frosted genius." He
spoke of his "ground-glass style," but admitted that James's
characters were "living men and women." James's main criticism
of Wells was that he failed to create such men and women. "I
rewrite you much, as I read—which is the highest tribute my
damned impertinence can pay an author," James said.

In the summer of their meeting, Wells decided to stay on in
Kent. He occupied Beach Cottage at Sandgate, and later built
himself a solid brick house, Spade House, symbol of his growing
prosperity. Both Wells and James, during the early months of
their friendship, would be the spectators of the passage at nearby
Brede House of Stephen Crane and his honey-haired Cora. Wells
indeed would leave some of the most vivid pictures we have of
the ill-fated young American writer.

II

James had known about Crane some time before he met him. He
knew that Howells had praised *Maggie: A Girl of the Streets* and
he had read *The Red Badge of Courage*, seeing in it qualities he
associated with Zola. Crane's subject, we may surmise, touched
James closely—the Civil War had been an anguished memory of

his youth, and then Crane—who knew it only from history—
had created a young man who was heroic in spite of himself.
This was a type of hero James had treated in his story of the young
pacifist ("Owen Wingrave") who proves a good soldier in spite
of his pacifism. James quickly appreciated Crane's intensity, his
industry, his dedication. He belonged to a new generation; and
while James speaks of him nowhere, and no letters to him have
survived, we do know how he characterized the new breed of
literary journalists. He regarded Richard Harding Davis, Crane's
journalistic contemporary, as belonging to "the possible fatal
extravagance of our growing world-hunger"—that "alert,
familiar journalism, the world-hunger made easy, made for the
time irresistible." Crane had ministered to this hunger by going
to scenes of war and violence: he was a spiritual ancestor of
Hemingway. When James met him he had returned from the
Graeco-Turkish War, and was on his way to the Spanish–
American War. It was after his brief and violent experiences in
the Cuban war, and the Puerto Rico Campaign—heedless where
his personal safety was concerned—that he returned to England.

Crane and Cora Taylor (as she was then known) had been
living together ever since the Graeco-Turkish War. They had
met at her high-class bawdy house, "Hotel de Dream," in
Jacksonville. With her pretensions to literature, her pleasure-
loving ways, her managerial abilities, she had attached herself to
Crane and followed him to Greece, taking the *nom de plume* of
Imogene Carter. She had been one of the earliest of her tribe—a
lady war correspondent. Crane edited some of her dispatches and
they were published. Cora Howorth had been married twice
before; first to a man named Murphy in New York, whom she
had divorced; then she had laid siege to London and married the
son of a baronet. They had parted early but Captain Donald
Stewart would not give her a divorce. Unable to marry Crane,
she did not relish trying to live with him as his common-law wife
in the United States where his activities were always publicized
and where she could have no status as the "wife" of a celebrity.
In England all was different. The English asked no questions and
they were more "accepting." Crane's writings had made him a

large English reputation ahead of his recognition in America. And then Cora had large social aspirations. She was an egotist, a woman slightly overblown, proud of her blonde hair and fleshly charm, and energetic in her pursuit of pleasure and "society." James had invented her long ago (as Mrs Headway in "The Siege of London"), indeed everything she did seemed to be part of his early "international" tales. Even before Stephen Crane returned from Cuba, she had arranged to rent Brede House from Moreton Frewen (young Winston Churchill's uncle through his marriage to one of the Jerome sisters). Frewen had been to America and made and lost a fortune in cattle. He was happy to let the old family house of Brede to the talented Crane, and asked £40 a year. Brede was a massive manor house, begun in the fourteenth century, to which there had been subsequent elaborate additions. It had a large hall, a chapel, great fireplaces; but it was in disrepair, and filled with cold and damp. Its sanitary conveniences were old-fashioned and minimal. Nevertheless it ministered to Cora's grandiose dreams of social glory; she would give great parties, she would play *grande dame* in baronial halls. She showed Brede House to Stephen Crane in January of 1899; in February they moved in and she wrote promptly to Henry James to announce their arrival. But James was on the verge of leaving for Italy. By the time he returned, the Cranes were well established. They had no money; they lived from hand to mouth on the charity of their friends and the credit of the neighbourhood. The unbuttoned and bohemian Crane fell in with Cora's pretensions; he began to dress for dinner. He lived the life of a gentleman and left practical affairs to Cora. The house was a centre of hospitality. People came and went; journalists turned up to interview Crane; relatives appeared from America. The place was meagrely furnished but they strewed rushes on the floors and kept mastiffs in the Elizabethan style. Whole trees were burned in the capacious fireplaces. They were aided by Frewen's servants—a butler named Heather, a brandy-loving cook, a maid. In the grounds romped "the young barbarians," as James called them, Frederic's illegitimate orphans. Crane had a wagonette and also rode on horseback, wearing riding breeches and a flannel shirt most of the day. Hueffer said this costume shocked James—but then Hueffer was always depicting James as shocked by other people's attire. Shortly after James returned from Italy, in July 1899, he cycled to Brede and left his card on which he scrawled in pencil, "Mr and Mrs Crane: Very sorry to miss you—had a dark foreboding it was you I passed a quarter of an hour ago in a populous wagonette. Will try you soon again."

The biographers of the Cranes have created an impression that from this time on there was much fraternizing between Brede House and Lamb House. So far as we know the Cranes came to Lamb House for tea on two, perhaps three occasions during the rest of that summer; and James in turn visited them at Brede perhaps the same number of times. In a word, the deep and "intimate" friendship between the Cranes and James of which so much has been made never existed: and this in part because James had little opportunity that year to be neighbourly. He was pre-occupied with his new friendship with Hendrik Andersen, the young American sculptor he had met in Rome, and who visited him that August. Then his brother William came abroad after his heart attack. Finally Lamb House at this moment was put up for sale and James bought it, in great nervousness—for he did not have much ready cash. He had promptly set to work to earn the sum needed for the initial payment.

At Brede, Crane daily sat in his study, in the tower, trying to write tales in order to provide money for the improvident Cora. In Lamb House, James was producing throughout that autumn an article or a tale a week, in a fever of writing, in order to provide himself with a home for his old age. He was fascinated—and pained—by the spectacle of the Cranes. They were living out his tales—about old English houses in need of repair let to Americans, about ambitious American women with a "past," about talented writers struggling to do the successful thing in order to dress their wives and pay for food and rent. He had satirized in his ironic tales the mixture of pretension to English manners and flamboyance and ignorance of Americans. The situation at Brede had also a touch of the eerie and the occult of James's ghostly tales. There was a legend that Brede had had an ogre, a consumer of children; he had ultimately been done to death with a wooden saw. Other legends said there were underground passages which served generations of smugglers. But more than its ghosts, its draughts, its creaking boards, its tree-consuming fireplaces, Brede was clearly the last place in the world for a malariaridden consumptive to spend cold damp English winters. Wells remembered Crane as "profoundly weary and ill." He described him as "essentially the helpless artist; he wasn't the master of his party, he wasn't the master of his home; his life was altogether out of control; he was being carried along. What he was still clinging to, but with a dwindling zest, was artistry." And what Cora was clinging to was her love of pleasure. Cora did not notice—what everyone else saw—that Crane was destined to be very soon one of the ghostliest of Brede's ghosts.

III

There are many anecdotes about the Cranes at Lamb House, and these made it seem as if the Cranes were visiting James every other day. One journalist has Mrs Humphry Ward pouring tea during one of Crane's visits; but Mrs Ward did not come to Lamb House during this period. She was busy writing *Eleanor* and Henry James was offering lengthy criticism by mail. Another journalist describes Crane as giving James Knut Hamsun's *Hunger*, and their talking about the annual mud-boat regatta, which James refereed in Rye wearing knickerbockers, ghillie-shoes, and a homburg. It is possible that much of the gossip came from the talkative and inventive Cora. There was certainly talk of the Boer War—a subject of great common interest both to James and Crane. James gave Crane a copy of *In the Cage* and also inscribed *The Awkward Age* to him. He was quoted as saying "We love Stephen Crane for what he is; and admire him for what he is going to be." At Brede, James was reputed to have turned up on one occasion with a party of "stuffed shirts" and Cora was forced to improvise lunch for the group—but this was not in character; James never organized spontaneous visits of this sort: it sounds as much an invention as a tale circulated by Hueffer that James sent over a bundle of manuscripts to Crane asking for his opinion and

for editorial help. Nothing could have been less likely—that
James with his sense of craft should at fifty-six seek counsel from
a twenty-seven-year-old. Evidence shows that James that autumn
allowed no manuscripts to linger on his desk; he sent them with
great rapidity to his agent in London, sometimes in instalments.
Many of them were rapidly placed. Indeed James's earnings
during these weeks were substantial. Crane, sickly and straining
at his desk, could not earn enough.

Late in August James attended a party at the Brede Rectory
organized by Cora. Of this occasion two significant snapshots
survive: one of James in his trimmed spade-like beard standing
beside Cora and another with his mouth wide open—he was
caught in the act of eating a doughnut. Cora had baked a large
supply. When he received "the strange images" James wrote
to Cora that they formed "a precious memento of a romantic
hour. But no surely, it can't be any doughnut of yours that is
making me make such a gruesome grimace. I look as if I had
swallowed a wasp or a penny toy, and I tried to look so beautiful.
I tried too hard, doubtless. But don't show it to anyone as H.J.
trying." He concluded by hoping Frederic's "young barbarians"
were at play "far from Crane's laboratory."

His letters to Cora, all scribbled social notes, are cordial and
friendly. She wanted information about a ladies' club at the
Mermaid Inn and James gave it to her, telling her how she could
join. At the end of September there is a telegram accepting an
invitation to tea. After that there are no communications, for a
full six months. During this period William James was in
England after his cure at Bad Nauheim. We are abundantly documented on the activities of the Cranes during this time—for
Conrads, Hueffers, Wells and his wife, Garnetts, journalists and
literary hangers-on continued to come. For Cora it was a perpetual lark; for Crane it was a continual sad grind. H. G. Wells
has told the story of the great Christmas-week party Cora
organized to welcome the year 1900. The guests were asked to
bring their own bedding. There were few furnished bedrooms in
Brede House and Cora created a dormitory for the ladies and
another for the men. They stayed late before roaring fires. Great

candles burned in sockets fixed for the occasion by the local black-
smith; guests showed marks of candlewax on their clothes. There
was an acute shortage of toilets. Troubled-looking male guests
wandered about the grounds in the early mornings. Crane tried
to organize American-style poker games which his English guests
did not take seriously. Wells called the whole house party a
"lark" but it sounds as if it wasn't much fun for some of the
visitors. On Christmas Eve a play was given in the local school
house written in part by Crane, who asked James, Conrad, Wells,
Gissing, A. E. W. Mason, Marriott Watson, and others to add a
few words to the script, making it the most "authored" play of
the century. It was about the Brede ghost—the child-eating ogre
who was sawed in half. James's contribution to the script was
part of the name of one character—who was called Peter Quint
Prodmore Moreau—Peter Quint from "The Turn of the Screw"
and Prodmore from "Covering End" (he is the sharp businessman who holds all the mortgages). The Moreau belonged to
H. G. Wells. The party had a painful finale at just about the hour
when Henry James, in nearby Lamb House, was invoking the
"gruesome" date of 1900 in his letter to Rhoda Broughton. He
had seen the new year in quietly with William and his young niece
Peggy. Eight miles away Cora was waking up Wells; Crane had
just had a lung haemorrhage. Wells's final memory of the party
was his riding into the drizzle at dawn on a bicycle in search of a
doctor.

During the first months of the new year, when Crane was ill
most of the time, Henry James wrote *The Sacred Fount*. It may
have derived some of its poignancy from the vision the novelist
had of the way in which Crane was visibly dying while Cora
thrived, seemingly unaware of the tragedy being lived out under
her roof. It was a very old theme with James—the way in which
men and women prey on one another. Late in May, Cora finally
recognized the truth. She had stayed with Crane in the damp old
house all winter, but now with the warmth of approaching
summer she rushed him off to the Continent, borrowing money
on all sides, arranging for a special train, taking the Rye doctor,
Ernest Skinner, along to give Crane constant medical attention.

HENRY JAMES 1900
Sketch for a portrait by Ellen (Bay) Emmet

LAMB HOUSE.
RYE.
SUSSEX.

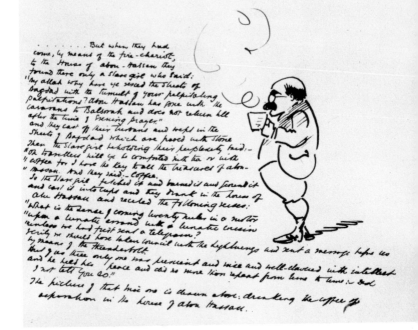

.... But when they had come, by means of the fire-chariot, to the House of Abou-Hassan they found there only a slave girl who said: "By Allah why have ye vexed the streets of Bagdad with the tumult of your palpitating palpitations? Abou Hassan has gone with the caravans to Balsorah and does not return till after the time of Evening prayer." And they cast off their turbans and wept in the streets of Bagdad which are paved with stone. Then the slave girl beholding their perplexity said:— "Oh travellers will ye be comforted with tea or with coffee for I have the key to all the treasures of Abou-Hassan. And they said:— Coffee. So the slave girl fetched it and brewed it and served it and cast it into cups and they drank in the house of Abou Hassan and recited the following verses: "What is the sense of coming twenty miles in a motor upon a lunatic errand with a lunatic cousin unless we had first sent a telegram? Verily we should have taken council with the lightnings and sent a message before us that of us three only one was prescient and wise and well-clawed with intellect and he held his peace and did no more than repeat from time to time: I not tell you so." The picture of that wise one is drawn above: drinking the coffee of desperation in the house of Abou Hassan.

A KIPLING TALE FOR THE MASTER
Philip Burne-Jones's sketch and Kipling's anecdote, on James's stationery

They paused at Dover and James and Wells planned to drive over to see Crane off. James was detained at the last minute by an urgent batch of proofs, and Wells went alone. Later Wells told of his last glimpse of the American lying wrapped in blankets before an open window at the Dover hotel "thin and gaunt and wasted, too weak for more than a remembered jest and a greeting and good wishes." Wells noted "a face of a type very typically American, long and spare, with very straight hair and straight features and long, quiet hands and hollow eyes, moving slowly, smiling and speaking slowly."

Cora got Crane to the Black Forest, and there he died. James received the news of Crane's impending end from the Moreton Frewens who had returned to Brede House; not only had Frewen never been paid his rent, but he had actually sent money to his desperate tenants. In early June 1900 James wrote his longest letter to Cora. He had heard how ill Crane was; he was sorry not to have seen him at Dover; he enclosed a cheque for £50. "I won't pretend to utter hopes about Crane which may be in vain . . . but I constantly think of him and as it were pray for him. I feel that I am not taking too much for granted in believing that you may be in the midst of worries on the money-score which will perhaps make the cheque for Fifty Pounds, that I enclose, a convenience to you. Please view it as such and dedicate it to whatever service it may best render my stricken young friend. It meagrely represents my tender benediction to him." He told Cora he had bicycled over to Brede with a couple of friends to show them the façade of the house after the Cranes had left and had found "the melancholy of it quite heartbreaking."

He had barely posted this letter when he read of Crane's death in the newspapers. Two days later he wrote to Cora, "What a brutal, needless extinction—what an unmitigated unredeemed catastrophe! I think of him with such a sense of possibilities and powers! Not that one would have drawn out longer these last cruel weeks—!" A few days later he wrote to H. G. Wells: "You will have felt, as I have done, the miserable sadness of poor Crane's so precipitated and, somehow, so unnecessary extinction. I was at Brede Place this afternoon—and it looked conscious and

c

cruel." The phrase was not accidental: the word "cruel" was used with design.

That autumn James wrote to the Royal Literary Fund at Cora's request, but he doubted whether this British fund could allocate money to Americans. She wrote to James and asked for more money—but he had already sent her the equivalent of what he was paid for one of his stories. He told his agent of this in the hope that he would explain to Cora that "I can do very little more." He added, "my heart, I fear, is generally hard to her." J. B. Pinker told James that Cora would return again to the charge and James replied that he considered her "an unprofitable person, and I judge her whole course and career, so far as it appeared in this neighbourhood, very sternly and unforgivingly." James was particularly incensed that Cora had made no effort to pay Dr Skinner who had been with Crane to the end. Nevertheless when Cora sent James Crane's posthumous *Wounds in the Rain*, he answered her that "if Crane could have lived—success and he would evidently have been constantly, no strangers. The greater the tragedy!" And then he told Cora he did not know when he would be in London, perhaps after Christmas. He concluded speaking of Rye, "it's very much in the minor key here."

The allusion to Crane's possible success, the reference to "the minor key" suggests that James's mind may have been turning on a story written some years before, in which he had described an author who writes himself to death. One of the novels the fictitious author writes in that tale is called *The Major Key*. In the end the writer gives up. He awakens one morning "in the country of the blue." The pen drops from his hand. "The voice of the market had suddenly grown faint and far . . . he had floated away into a grand indifference, into a reckless consciousness of art." Stephen Crane had done just that. He had simply come to a stop. The world had asked too much of him.

Cora, at a later time, when she had remarried, tried to call on James. He abruptly dismissed her and announced himself unavailable. His heart remained "hard" to her. This had nothing to do with her "past," as some biographers have implied. James had been too close a spectator of the tragi-comedy played out in the old manor house: Crane had been a Jamesian hero—a Ralph Limbert, or the young aspirant who tries to learn "the lesson of the master." The lesson had been that a writer must choose between art and worldliness. Crane had not even made the choice. He had simply been caught between the two and the consequences had been fatal. "His short, so troubled, yet also so peaceful passage" at Brede, James wrote, was "a strange, pathetic, memorable chapter."

DURING the last summer of the old century when Henry James was writing *The Ambassadors*—an uncommonly hot summer for England—he sat for his portrait to the gifted member of the "Emmetry," his cousin Ellen Emmet, familiarly known as "Bay." She had been studying in Paris; now she planned to live and work in America. James, to encourage her, and with characteristic generosity, insisted that he pay her for a full-length painting although she did just his head and shoulders. He wanted, in all probability, to put on canvas his newly shaven countenance. Bay Emmet was talented and skilful. James described her as "a *pure* painter, a real one, a good one," but added, in a letter to his brother, that she was "without imagination, a grain." The finished portrait is a close-up. James looks directly out of the frame: his eyes are half-veiled; half the face is in deep shadow. The wear and tear of the years is erased, and she has given the face an effect of greater length than it possessed. James wore for the sittings a beige waistcoat, a dark suit, and a prominent heavy-knotted white-speckled cravat. In his strong writing fist he has a tight grip on his spectacles. The portrait—its conception—is precocious for Bay was in her mid-twenties; it is also rather "arty," in the manner of Sargent.

Many years later, when it was being cleaned and repaired, the restorer found beneath it, on a separate canvas, a sketch made by Bay Emmet which was obviously abandoned before it was finished. She had posed James differently, at an angle, and was looking downward at him. She had applied a great deal of red to the face but had not yet finished painting the flesh; the effect, especially of the nose, resembled the colour of James's alcoholic butler rather than that of the abstemious novelist. The suggestion, in this uncompleted work, is of great ruddiness, a figure as of a country squire, a haunter of pubs. James's shortness is emphasized; his shoulders are out of proportion, the cravat is unfinished. One can see that both painter and sitter were dissatisfied with what was emerging. Nevertheless there is a great deal of life in the face, and the eyes are large, clear, alert, much more than in the "set" and on the whole rather inanimate finished portrait.

The novelist varnished the painting himself, found an old frame for it, placed it above his sideboard in his dining-room. There it hung for the remainder of his life. Visitors, seeing it, little dreamed that hidden behind the solemn and unsmiling face of the Master there existed a sketch of a more "bouncy" human being, the relaxed parochial resident of Rye. James never considered the finished portrait a good likeness. He poked fun at it in his letters, describing it to Bay as "the smooth and anxious clerical gentleman in the spotted necktie." "Do you remember," he wrote to her a couple of years later, "when you were (more or less vaguely) painting me?" If the gentleman on the wall didn't look like him, he said, he looked immensely "like *you*, dear Bay, and he reminds me of our so genial, roasting romantic summer-before-last here together, when we took grassy walks at eventide, and in the sunset, after each afternoon's repainting."

I

The Ambassadors was written as "the picture of a certain momentous and interesting period, of some six months or so, in the history of a man no longer in the prime of life." He himself had had such six months from the time in 1899 when he had met Hendrik Andersen, purchased Lamb House, written *The Sacred Fount* and suddenly found himself—after removing his beard—wanting to write things of "the altogether human order." The novel he wrote about his middle-aged hero had a single primary message, for himself as for his readers: that one must live in full awareness and "with sufficient intensity," be a source of "what may be called excitement" to oneself. At fifty-seven he seemed to be starting his career all over again: and this was suggested by his return, after almost two decades, to the "international" subject by which he had first established his fame. He came back to it with unconcealed pleasure; came back to a story of an American in Paris, as if he were once more thirty-three and writing *The American*. His new novel was about the rigidities of New England and the relaxed cosmopolitanism of "Europe." In his long-ago romantic novel he had told of Christopher Newman seeking entry into the Faubourg St Germain like a Balzacian young man from the provinces. *The Ambassadors* was to be the story of an elderly hero who, in the French capital, breaks out of the shell of his New England conscience—and discovers how much he has looked at the world with innocent eyes, in spite of his advanced years. James felt, as he dictated his work in the Garden Room, as if all his data were "installed on my premises like a monotony of fine weather." He finished the book in about eight months. Its twelve parts, one for each month of a year of serialization, were shaped in pictures and scenes, using the techniques he had perfected since his play-writing. "Nothing resisted, nothing betrayed," said James, who would speak of this book as "quite the best, 'all round' of my productions." And it is true that the novel possesses a singular harmony of theme and presentation, a felicitous symmetry of form and content.

Its story was simple, almost conventional; it told of a young man from New England who lingers too long in Paris; and of a middle-aged "ambassador" sent out by the young man's mother to bring him home. James named the principal envoy Lewis Lambert Strether after Balzac's hero in the novel *Louis Lambert*. In his opening pages he went out of his way to draw attention to this fact: few authors indeed have ever signalled a "source" more clearly. When Miss Gostrey, looking at Strether's card, says, "It's the name of a novel of Balzac's," Strether replies, "Oh, I know that!" She rejoins, "But the novel's an awfully bad one." Strether's reply is prompt. "I know that too."

Balzac's *roman philosophique* is the inflated story of the education of a young man, his inhibited compulsive constricted Latin "formation"—as constricted as a "New England conscience." Louis Lambert is a cerebral prodigy, a near-genius; he writes a portentous *Treatise on the Will* and dies young, after a painful love affair. If there is any connection between *The Ambassadors* and the Balzacian novel it may be in Lambert Strether's struggle to discover the difference between what he sees and what he imagines—between what is "real" and what is illusion. James's novel tells us that life is willed for us, that each man must make the best of his own fate. He must have felt that he too was writing a "philosophical" novel—a novel of a certain kind of "education," in which Strether, strapped tight by his New England "conditioning," unwinds in the Parisian circle of Chad Newsome's friends, discovering that the flexible cosmopolites "live" by being open to experience, while the New Englanders keep themselves closed. The book contains a certain cautious hedonism; and its moral is that high civilization derives from a life—as Balzac might have said—of "expectant attention." One learns to see into things; one recognizes that the best freedom man has is the freedom of his imagination—the freedom of his illusions. Lambert Strether refuses to accept the preconceptions of Woollett, Mass. The Newsomes, mother and daughter, have made up their minds that Chad, the son and heir, remains abroad because some woman, some Cleopatra-enchantress, has taken hold of him, as if he were a Caesar or a Mark Antony. Chad is hardly made of such heroic stuff. Strether knew him as a rough, spoiled small-town boy. Now he finds a smooth egotistical young man obviously improved and polished by his life abroad. He lives in a pleasant apartment in the Boulevard Malesherbes; he has certain pleasant cosmopolite friends—among them a young artist named John Little Bilham, who resembles Jonathan Sturges (the writer who had brought James the original idea for this novel) and other friends like Miss Barrace, in whom James drew an accurate portrait of his old friend Henrietta Reubell, the American-Parisian expatriate. Above all there is the presence in Chad's entourage of Madame de Vionnet, an aristocratic French lady who has a grown daughter. She is a *grande dame*, half English and half French, separated from her husband. She embodies French elegance, tradition, discretion; and she has also a certain Anglo-Saxon high-mindedness. Strether finds her appealing and assumes that she has been the benign influence on Chad; it is she, he believes, who has given the young man his high continental polish. He believes also at first that she is trying to marry her daughter to him.

Mrs Newsome's ambassador is in no hurry about his mission. It is, in the first place, an embarrassing one. Chad is old enough not to be accountable to his mother; and Strether has no relish in making inquiries about his Parisian way of life. He gives himself over to enjoying the city, with the aid of the sophisticated American lady he met in England, at a hotel in Chester. She is Maria Gostrey; very quickly she becomes his confidante. He has told her the details of his mission; she gives him a great deal of useful advice and helps constantly to correct his active, romantic imagination. For he is inclined to live a little in his fancies. The Woollett envoy also has as companion an American friend, Waymarsh, a distinguished Washington lawyer, who is dyspeptic, ill at ease, and always growling against Europe very much in the manner of William James. Abroad, William was always belligerently American; in America he longed for Europe. Waymarsh seems to possess the gloom of Henry Adams, William's dislike of Europe, and the hypochondriacal problems of Mark Twain. He acts as Strether's foil, and like many an American tourist, cools his "sacred rage" by frequent incursions into shops. Strether finally musters the courage to ask Little Bilham about Chad and Madame de Vionnet. Little Bilham, being a gentleman, answers that theirs is a "virtuous attachment." No Jamesian gentleman, as one remembers from "The Siege of London" is supposed to "tell" on a woman. Strether through the first half of the book has sent detailed dispatches to the "home office," to Mrs Newsome. He has reached the conclusion that Chad should stay abroad. He feels Madame de Vionnet is good for him. He encounters the grand lady one day in Notre Dame and they have a charming lunch on the quays. Over their *omelette aux tomates* and their straw-coloured Chablis, while Madame de Vionnet's "grey eyes moved in and out of their talk," he feels that he must gallantly help her. She is fond of the young man—and besides the attachment is "virtuous." The result is that in the exact middle of the book, Strether is relieved of his high office. New ambassadors are dispatched—Chad's sister Sarah and her husband, a Woollett mediocrity named Jim Pocock. On arrival Sarah proclaims to Strether that Madame de Vionnet is "not even an apology for a decent woman." Pocock goes off to the Folies.

II

The novel has two brilliant climactic scenes, set with classical symmetry in the fifth and eleventh parts of the book. The first is the scene in Gloriani's garden, which had been the original "germ" for the story. Long ago, at Torquay, James had heard how his friend William Dean Howells had murmured to Jonathan Sturges in Whistler's garden in Paris that, really, one should "live all one can." This had caused James to make a long entry in his notebook. He liked the idea of Howells saying this—he who had "never known *at all* any woman BUT his wife." James knew Whistler's garden—he knew it very well; he had visited Whistler there and had seen it years before, during 1875–6 when he visited on occasion the house overlooking the garden, and talked with old Madame Mohl, Fanny Kemble's friend, the Anglo-French hostess who had been a friend of Madame Récamier and Chateaubriand. James had stood at her window and observed the adjoining convent for the training of missionary priests. In *The Ambassadors* he endows Strether with his memories:

> Strether had presently the sense of a great convent, a convent of missions, famous for he scarce knew what, a nursery of young priests, of scattered shade, of straight alleys and chapel-bells, that spread its mass in one quarter; he had the sense of names in the air, of ghosts at the windows, of signs and tokens, a whole range of expression, all about him, too thick for prompt discrimination.

Charming indeed, an author who allows his principal character to see the ghost of himself at a window. There may be a touch of Whistler in James's image of the artist Gloriani—Gloriani, resuscitated from *Roderick Hudson*, James's Roman novel of 1875. In *Roderick*, Gloriani still had his career to make; he possessed "the mere base maximum of cleverness." This was a reproach James had addressed to Whistler in his earlier period in London. Now the fictional character, like Whistler, has matured. Gloriani has acquired greatness. It has come to him by his having the courage to live the passion of his art. Strether is "held by the sculptor's eyes ... the deep human expertness in Gloriani's charming smile—oh the terrible life behind it!"

In this garden with his sense of the beauty and terror of life, Strether delivers himself of one of the most poignant soliloquies in all of James's fiction. He begins his quiet speech to the artist-expatriate, Little Bilham, by wondering whether it is too late for someone like himself to "live." He images himself as having failed to catch the train that waited for him; now he can only hear its distant whistle. "Live all you can; it's a mistake not to. It doesn't so much matter what you do in particular," he tells Bilham, "so long as you have your life." He adds "If you haven't had that what *have* you had?" Later, Little Bilham will change the speech slightly. He will remind Strether that he had said "*see* all you can." Strether does not contradict him. *Seeing* is accordingly equated with living. After this Strether speaks the words that give the novel its "deterministic" post-Darwinian philosophy. We are all moulds, "either fluted and embossed, with ornamental excrescences, or else smooth and dreadfully plain, into which a helpless jelly, one's consciousness is poured." One takes his form and his shape. You are what you are, James seems to be saying and you must make the most of it. After this prophecy of "conditioning" Strether observes, "still, one has the illusion of freedom; therefore don't be, like me, without the memory of that illusion."

The second scene which haunts readers of *The Ambassadors* is that of Lambert Strether's relaxed day in the country. This is the crucial moment in which he discovers the affair between Chad and Madame de Vionnet. The Strether of the early part of the novel is always looking at his watch, always patting his pocket to make sure his wallet is in its place. The later Strether sets off casually in search of a certain metallic green in the French landscape that he had encountered once in a painting by Lambinet. To find this he takes a train to a station indiscriminately chosen—the exact terminus isn't needed. What is needed is a general direction. In this chapter James makes us feel the way in which Strether enters the countryside as if he were moving through the very frame of the Lambinet seen long years before in an art shop in Tremont Street in Boston. He gives us first the image of the painting; then it is as if a camera were moving towards the picture, it picks up a stream, the greens of the landscape, the church spire. Descending from the train, Strether walks into the painting "the oblong gilt frame disposed its enclosing lines; the poplars and willows, the reeds and river—a river of which he didn't know, and didn't want to know, the name—fell into composition, full of felicity, within them; the sky was silver and turquoise and varnish; the village on the left was white and the church on the right was grey; it was all there, in short—it was what he wanted; it was Tremont Street, it was France, it was Lambinet. Moreover he was freely walking about in it."

Strether has discovered a kind of freedom which can escape rigidities, omniscience and life conducted like a railway time-table. He can avoid the set journey, the designated place, even the names of places—"a river of which he didn't know, and didn't want to know, the name." We are reminded of the mysterious article—never named—manufactured by the Newsomes in Woollett, the source of their fortune. The reader is again being told that in this world we can never know everything. The name of the village is of little importance—although James was fond of esoteric names. What counts is the silver and turquoise, the poplars, the willows, the impressionistic play of light over the enchanted scene. Strether escapes Woollett during these carefree hours, he cultivates his illusion of freedom. He waits for his dinner at the inn, on the bank of the river. He sees a boat, as in one of Manet's paintings. In one of those coincidences Balzac loved, and James emulated, the boat contains Chad and Madame de Vionnet. In the rustic twilight, Strether suddenly experiences the anguish of his disillusion. Woollett has been right after all. Or had it? At any rate, he feels "sold." The grand lady is indeed Chad's mistress: their informality, their casual clothes reveal to Strether they must be staying at a nearby inn.

III

No bald sketch of *The Ambassadors* can convey the brilliance and the wit of its comedy, the ironic delicacy of its scenes and conversation, the ways in which James, with the ease and skill of his maturity, dissects America and Europe and re-imagines his international myth. He tells himself that America has always been provincial, that he has been wise to live in the high places of civilization. America is Mrs Newsome, an implacable, immobile force, intransigent and exigent: she is there, in Woollett, or a hundred cities where values are unambiguous, and where everyone pays a price—the price of muffled feeling, the conventional, the prescribed. One doesn't "live all you can." Mrs Newsome clings to her children, demands that they remain at home, refuses to allow them to grow up and lead their own lives. She "hangs together with a perfection of her own." The only solution—the one James had sought—is casually mentioned in the book, "you've got morally and intellectually to get rid of her." The ex-ambassador learns how to ease his moral and intellectual bondage. He will return to Woollett which "isn't sure it ought to enjoy life," with a recognition that if Europe is amoral (by Woollett standards) it offers him beautiful illusions of freedom. He can live by his illusions—if he remains open to experience and doesn't require life to measure up to the Woollett yardstick.

The Ambassadors was told by James in a complex indirect style he had never attempted before and it revealed that he had at last reconciled himself to diminished omniscience. One could never know everything. And he was determined to make his readers feel this, rather than accept the old tradition of the novel which told all. James paid his price for running against the very thing that had made novels the most popular art form of modern times. Instead of allowing his novel to gratify curiosity, James turned it into an instrument of mystification. He allowed his readers to know only as much as one learns in life. And he developed for the first time shifting angles of vision. In terms of old-fashioned story-telling this resulted in a novel without action. The excitement was intellectual, the pleasure resided in the unfolding of little details. Characters are glimpsed from different angles. Early in the novel we are given a feeling that we have access to a series of cameras—and James is writing long before the modern cinema. We first see Miss Gostrey through Strether's eyes, "a lady . . . whose features—not freshly young, not markedly fine, but on happy terms with each other." We first see Strether through her eyes, and in deliberate shifts of vision, "what his hostess saw, what she might have taken in with a vision kindly adjusted, was the lean, the slightly loose figure of a man of the middle height and something more perhaps than the middle age—a man of five and fifty, whose most immediate signs were a marked bloodless brownness of face, a thick dark moustache, of characteristically American cut, growing strong and falling low, a head of hair still abundant . . ." Then we look at the two together "each so finely brown and so sharply spare, each confessing so to dents of surface and aids to sight, to a disproportionate nose and a head delicately or grossly grizzled, they might have been brother and sister." It has often been said that in *The Ambassadors* the story remains wholly in the "point of view" of Strether. But we discover soon enough that James brings in clouds of witnesses, first person intruders, spectators, individuals with "adjusted" vision; he keeps his camera moving; he asks us to use our imagination and to enjoy the personal relations he is showing us at the very heart of his story.

Seen in the light of its inventions, its original style, its psychology, the novel can be recognized in literary history as a Stendhalian mirror in the roadway, past which Marcel Proust, James Joyce, Virginia Woolf, William Faulkner and so many others have since travelled. It might be called the first authentic masterpiece of the "modern movement." Its pattern-structure prefigured *Ulysses*; its long river-like sentences anticipated the reflective novel of Proust. Its quest for "auras" of feeling foreshadowed the experiments of Virginia Woolf.

IV

Beyond "technique" and its resourceful experiments in narration, beyond its neat symmetrical design, the care with which it is "composed"—its indirections, its deliberate withholding of information—that is its refusal to "specify" as in "The Turn of the Screw"—beyond all this, the novel spoke for the central myth of Henry James's life. James had long before made up his mind that his choice of Europe was wise, that Woollett and Mrs Newsome —that is the U.S.A.—could not offer him the sense of freedom he had won for himself abroad. Europe was art, manners, landscapes in old paintings, interesting women like Madame de Vionnet, in whose apartments one found the historical past of the French Empire; or it was relaxed Maupassant afternoons on the banks of the Seine—or the Thames—and wayside inns where civilization composed itself into pictures. Woollett was filled with the parochialisms and narrowness of the Newsomes; it was not a place for freedom of spirit. It was all constraint—it was rigid.

On the level of this myth and the working out of his emotions arising from the tangled early relations of his life, James seems to be struggling still with visions of a powerful, controlling yet beneficent mother—authority figures of his childhood and youth. There is first America itself, the mother sitting, waiting, in Woollett (or Cambridge), asking the son to perform in the great world into which he has ventured—but at the end of a silver cord. He struggles to free himself, to pursue his own life abroad and not be in a perpetual state of ambassadorship. In Europe he acquires other mothers. Miss Gostrey represents the mother—or even the brother—of intelligence; Madame de Vionnet is "Europe" and passion. Her being Anglo-French gives her the two streams of culture that met in James. She is also the temptress-mother, mysterious and a source of anxiety. We might pause over the names James gave to Miss Gostrey and Madame de Vionnet. James's mother's name was Mary. Miss Gostrey is Maria and Madame de Vionnet is Marie. In the mythic symbolism of the book the two motherlands of James's life take primary place —beneficent Europe, exigent America. Moreover he had had to choose. He had had to accept the idea of exile.

On psychological ground thus we can see the prolonged struggle in James to cut the silver cord that had bound him to Quincy Street and to Boston and New York. He could, at the end of his novel, send Strether back to Woollett—for he was quite prepared to go back himself. From the time of this novel, aided by the sight of his nephews, nieces, cousins, he begins to speak of the need to give a sense of rootedness to American children. Circumstances had provided him with trans-Atlantic roots, but he is no longer sure that native rootedness would not have been better. In effect he is saying also that had he stayed at home life would have been, for him, less ambivalent. Yet this ambivalence had made possible his life of art and involved him in a constant balancing of the good and the bad of America and Europe. It had enabled him to be Henry James, the Master—and to write *The Ambassadors*.

Book Two

The Beast in the Jungle
1901–1902

★

A POOR ANCIENT LADY

WILLIAM JAMES and his wife Alice had been abroad ever since William became ill with heart trouble in 1899. Now as the nineteenth century waned he was in Rome, still trying to find health and repose. His daughter Peggy, thirteen when they arrived, had been living with an English family, the Joseph Thatcher Clarkes, friends of William, at Harrow and attending an English school. Uprooted from the familiar American environment at the threshold of her adolescence, confined to English rural life, homesick, and lonely, Peggy vigorously protested to her parents, and to her uncle at Lamb House. He on his side had large sympathies for her; he remembered out of his early years what it meant to be cast adrift as a child in Europe. Peggy might have been any one of his sentient little girls, in those stories of childhood he had lately written. He had from the first—with his long-nourished theories of juvenile education—urged William to send Peggy to a school in England; and now he pleaded with her mother to worry a little less about inculcating "moral and spiritual" ideas in the child. This had always been the trouble with the James family; he said his own father had had that too-exclusive preoccupation. What Peggy could use, he told his brother and sister-in-law, was something more worldly. "With her so definite Puritan heritage, Peggy could afford to be raised on almost solely *cultivated* 'social' and aesthetic lines. The Devil (of the moral and spiritual) can—given her 'atmosphere'—be trusted to look out for himself."

Casting about, Henry James decided that Peggy could be best educated if she were entrusted to the well-known Marie Souvestre, who "has had for many years a very highly esteemed school for girls at high, breezy Wimbledon, near London (an admirable situation)—where she has formed the daughters of many of the very good English *advanced* Liberal political and professional connection during these latter times. She is a very fine, interesting person, her school holds a very particular place (all Joe Chamberlain's daughters were there and they adore her), and I must tell you more of her." Henry's only objection to Mlle Souvestre's establishment was that it was definitely "middle-class"—but then, he added, "*all* schools here are that."

The William Jameses were opposed to such a school for their only daughter. They wanted her to continue to live in a family environment which was one of the reasons they chose the Clarkes. In retrospect one wonders whether the uncle's perception of Peggy's needs, given the temporary expatriation of the William Jameses, was not more acute than that of her own parents. At Mlle Souvestre's she would have been involved in the active life of a school run with French realism and imagination; she would have found among the students such young women as the future Eleanor Roosevelt, enrolled there at that time; she would have met among English families, the Stracheys, for Lytton Strachey's sisters were close to Mlle Souvestre, and Lytton himself was deeply indebted to her for his French background. The environment would have been benign, and even a challenge to a young American girl who had lived in a family composed entirely of brothers and a celebrated father somewhat aloof from his children. Things were not much better at the Joseph Thatcher Clarkes, where the exuberant Clarke boys seem to have visited various petty indignities on Peggy. The Clarke family was good-natured, prosaic, middle class. Peggy wrote homesick letters to her parents on the Continent and received from her uncle gentle kindly letters of encouragement. He also arranged to have Peggy and some of her playmates regularly brought to London and escorted them to the primitive movies being shown then, or to some theatrical show he judged fitting for their tender ages. Apparently this was not always the case, for we find him writing to Peggy early in 1900, "I hope, too, that your journey home a week ago was comfortable and easy and that some of the rather horrid figures and sounds that passed before us at the theatre didn't haunt your dreams. There were too many *ugly* ones. The next time I shall take you to something prettier." And again, "your poor old lonely uncle misses you very much and takes the greatest interest in your new form of life and feeling greatly." This had a depth of truth in it far beyond what little Peggy could have known; for little Harry James in his early years had led a lonely life on the Continent, mixing with foreign children and profoundly resenting his uprooting from familiar New York and later Newport.

The lonely uncle asked his lonely niece to come and stay with him at Lamb House that Christmas of 1900. It was a bleak time. England was in mourning for its dead and dying in Africa; the war had cast a blight over everything. The old Queen was unwell, her life running to its end. And Henry was uncomfortable—a troublesome eczema had bothered him ever since the middle of the year and would continue throughout the writing of *The Ambassadors*. In the midst of the general depression, and his own discomfort James acted with his customary formalities and with his quick empathy for the female young. He gave Peggy the unrestrained affection of which he was capable, plied her with sweets and good food, and planted her in his oak-parlour with the novels of Sir Walter Scott. A serious, solemn, slightly depressed girl, Peggy was a good reader and she made her way, during the wet and windy days at Lamb House, through *Redgauntlet*, *Old Mortality*, *The Pirate*, *The Antiquary*, and since she could read French, Rostand's *L'Aiglon*. When weather permitted novelist and niece went forth for walks with their little wire-haired fox terrier Nick, one of the Master's most beloved dogs. As with his Emmet cousins, James corrected Peggy's American speech, and later he would express confidence in her "heroism" not to lose what she had learned in resuming life in Cambridge.

It was a little like Mr Longdon and Nanda, although Peggy, now turned fourteen, was a few years younger than James's grave intelligent girl of *The Awkward Age*. "We make together a very quiet and cosy couple," he wrote to Clare, the niece of Miss Woolson. And on Christmas Day he wrote to another friend, Jessie Allen: "I have just come up to a small upstairs study that I rejoice in here—after a *tête-à-tête* with my niece over a colossal turkey on which we made no perceptible impression whatever;

and I have left her alone, by the fire and the lamp in the little oak-parlour—if a young thing may be said to be alone who is deep down in Sir Walter. The sea-wind howls in my old chimneys and round my old angles; but the clock ticks loud and the fire crackles fast within."

And so the uncle and Peggy spent their Christmas. The clock was ticking out the dying hours of the old century but James did not allow himself to remain in Rye to the very end. He retreated to London on 31 December taking his niece with him to restore her to Harrow. Before leaving he wrote quick notes to various friends, wishing them "a solid slice of the new era." There was even a little note to Cora Crane, that betrayed no sign that his heart was hard against her. He could imagine "how little of anything but heaviness" this Christmas had for her, "in the dark and dreary town and with little but ghosts at your fireside." She had missed nothing in Sussex he said save "deluges of wet, a howling gale . . . The midwinter here is at best gruesome."

I

The old Queen was dying; with her unusual physical strength she had survived into a new time that was not her own. England at war, and in mourning, prepared itself for deeper mourning still.

Profoundly American though Henry James was, he experienced to the full the public emotion. Victoria was too much a part of his own life, too much a kind of presiding mother, for him not to feel strangely stirred; the public's silver cord and the private were intertwined. He spoke of England feeling "quite motherless" adding "and I to some extent have my part in the feeling." He wrote of her empathically as "a poor and ancient lady," a tired creature of pomp who had patiently lasted and laboured. Victoria had been on the throne, an immovable presence, when he had reached London in 1855, a boy of Peggy's age. He had seen her riding in her carriage from the time when the Prince Consort still lived; then in her widowhood, and at the last in her final dropsical old age "throwing her good fat weight into the scales of general decency." Ensconced in the Reform Club, and with his other club, the Athenaeum just around the corner—his two

London "homes"—James watched the very heart of England give itself over to a changing of monarchs with the changed century.

The tiny figure on the canopied bed in Osborne House, wasted by illness, took its last breath on the evening of 22 January 1901, surrounded by children and grandchildren in prayer. "Darling Grandmama," wrote Princess May [Mary], wife of the future George V, who would herself a decade later be Queen, "looked so lovely and peaceful dressed all in white with lace, and the bed covered with flowers." So ended the life and era of Victoria, a moment in time yet almost a century. It had embraced the greater part of Henry James's life.

The novelist, coming out of the Reform Club on his way to dine with his tenants in the De Vere Gardens flat, the younger Stopford Brookes, saw the big bulletin, "Death of the Queen." The streets of London seemed to him "strange and indescribable," the people dazed and hushed as if helpless—almost, he wrote, as if scared. It was "a very curious and unforgettable impression." He had not thought that he himself would experience grief, for it had been "a simple running down of the old used up watch." "One knew then that one had ended by taking her for a kind of nursing mother of the land and of the empire, and by attaching to her duration an extraordinary idea of beneficence. This idea was just," he told Bourget, "and her duration is over. It's a new era—and we don't know what it is." However there were other feelings too and he wrote to Miss Woolson's sister and her niece, who were in Austria:

> The Prince of Wales is an arch-vulgarian . . . the wretched little Yorks are less than nothing; the Queen's magnificent duration had held things magnificently—beneficently—together and prevented all sorts of accidents. Her death, in short, will let loose incalculable forces for possible ill. I am very pessimistic.

Edward was an "ugly" omen "for the dignity of things," he felt, and his accession would make for "vulgarity and frivolity." Was he not called "Edward the Caresser?" There would probably be a year's mourning; and he told the Woolson relatives they ought to wear mourning at least for a month, as a gesture—Victoria had been "always nice" to the U.S.A. When he found himself at the Reform Club writing letters on the club's black-bordered stationery, James continued to experience strange emotions of grief. They were only partly for Victoria; the old figure was an embodiment of his lifetime experience of strong, guardian women. "It has really been, the Event, most moving, interesting and picturesque. I have felt *more* moved, than I should have expected (such is the *community* of sentiment,) and one has realized all sorts of things about the brave old woman's beneficent duration and holding-together virtue." Dining amid various Privy Councillors and the leaders of England at the Reform, Henry James kept abreast of all the ceremonials and rituals. He caught the traditional wave of sympathy which always flows towards the new monarch as he heard John Morley say that Edward "made a good impression" at his first Council. But, James added in a letter to William, "*speriamo*."

II

From a window in the home of old James family friends who had once lived in New England, Peggy James watched the procession built around the tiny coffin—it seemed almost a child's coffin— in which the great dead Victoria was borne through the streets of the capital she had graced so long, to Paddington Station, to last obsequies at Windsor. Peggy's uncle had fully briefed her; and he had insisted she wear a little black mourning hat which he purchased for her as befitted the occasion. It was a day of great pageantry: Europe's princes and kings, not least the Emperor of the Germans, rode and marched; bells tolled; the streets were black with people, and they were dressed in black. The solemn slow procession was lit by a break in the cloud-canopy; and within the black-bordered frame of funeral the empire at war asserted its pride and glory in a multiplicity of uniforms, handsome bedecked horses, great lines of soldiers. Victoria's reach had been long—it went back almost to the edge of a remoter century. Henry James had met his niece the previous afternoon and arranged for her to spend the night at their friend's home. This left him free on the day itself to see the procession from other windows, those of still another friend, at Buckingham Gate. It was a good window; the view was splendid; but the visual-minded novelist was not altogether happy. His hostess had invited too many guests. The ladies wore high plumes and bows and as a "lone and modest man," (he explained to his niece) "I had the back seat, as it were, of all. However I saw a good deal and our windows were close to the show." The formidably large gun carriage on which the coffin was placed "just grazed the ridiculous" (James confided to Miss Robins) yet he found it all "impressive and really picturesque." He came away from his vantage point with Alice Stopford Green, widow of the historian, who had a lively tongue and quick mind and also wrote history. A loyal Irishwoman she had strong views on colonialism and the Boer War; she had bravely gone to St Helena a few months before to inspect the prisoner-of-war camps set up there by the British. James found her "troubled about many things—too troubled perhaps and about too many. But on some of them I much feel with her." He had said he "loathed" the war; he felt "that if this dear stupid old Country doesn't stop trying to bite off more than she can chew . . . she will sink."

"I mourn the safe and motherly old middle-class queen, who held the nation warm under the fold of her big, hideous Scotch-plaid shawl and whose duration had been so extraordinarily convenient and beneficent," he wrote a few days later to Wendell Holmes. She had been for him "a sustaining symbol."

Shortly afterwards he found himself mourning another sustaining symbol of his life. Mrs Bronson, who had presided queen-like over the Grand Canal in her charming Ca'Alvisi also died with the new century. Her death made James feel "older and sadder," he wrote to her daughter, the Contessa Rucellai. "It is the end of so many things—so many delightful memories, histories, associations—some of the happiest elements of one's past. It breaks into my tenderness even for the dear old Italy and seems to alter and overshadow *that* cherished relation. From years ever so far back she was delightfully kind to me and I had for her the most sincere affection. Those long Venetian years will be for all her friends—

had indeed already become so—a sort of legend and boast."
James would write a memorial tribute to Mrs Bronson, hostess of
Browning and himself, and of so many others; and later that year
he would begin his novel whose greatest scenes would be set in
the city of Mrs Bronson's adoption.

MISS WELD

I

JAMES had lost the habit of London, but he came back to the metropolis during the winter of 1901 with all his old energies, and this in spite of the fact that his skin irritation continued to trouble him. He felt a great burning in his face and described it to his brother as "visible *gout*"—in spite of "extreme sobriety and abstinence: small, very small, too small, eating and no drinking. The smallest drop of wine or spirits sets my face on fire." Nevertheless, for a while, he dined out strenuously, as of old; and he worked strenuously too. This was the first occasion on which he occupied his newly furnished room at the Reform Club and he was delighted with it. He was able to have MacAlpine in from midmornings until almost two o'clock to receive dictation of *The Ambassadors*. He worked with a certain desperation, for he had decided some weeks before to part with the Scottish typist "not in anger or as a catastrophe," but simply because "he's too damned *expensive*, and always has been—and too place-taking in my life and economy. I can get a highly competent little woman for half, or a less full-blown young man at a great abatement. He has taken long, in every way, too much for granted—but we part on excellent terms." MacAlpine had worked for James on and off for more than four years; he was an expert shorthand reporter, but James had no use of this skill since he dictated directly to the typewriter. Early in the new year he found a new position for MacAlpine, which the latter would assume after Easter. In the interval he sought to get as much of his novel as possible completed before reorganizing "this branch of my establishment."

His mornings were consistently given over to work; after a late lunch he was ready for the sociable occasions of his renewed town life. The occasions were muted, because of the universal mourning, but they still had a large interest for the novelist. He noticed, in some of the great houses, how much more the diamonds gleamed against the mourning black of the ladies' dresses; and the lower classes, in ubiquitous black, looked "as if they were of more exalted stations." He relished the pageantry which went with the public grief, for a new king was to be crowned. He had come back to the capital, he wrote to his old friend Wendell Holmes, after two suburban winters only to fall on "pomps and pageants . . . We are going to have a pompous king." Edward would provide circuses, if not bread. "We grovel before fat Edward," he wrote. To his friend Morton Fullerton he repeated that "the old Queen's death was a real emotion—quite big and fine, but we have dropped again to Edwardism quite unvarnished and Chamberlainism quite unblushing." He saw many old friends; he dined with the Humphry Wards, and with certain of his intimates— Jonathan Sturges, A. C. Benson, Gosse. He drank tea with the writer Violet Hunt at her club. However, he did not lose sight of his niece. Regular letters were dispatched to her, and when he could not go out to Harrow on a Sunday to visit her, he made arrangements for her to come into town, sometimes with some of the Clarke children. Years later she still remembered his courtliness and gentleness on these occasions. He took her to a performance of *Twelfth Night*; he marched her through museums; and in gentle letters to her guardian he spoke of his search for "some innocent place of entertainment—say the Hippodrome or the Alhambra."

In the cold days of March, after little more than eight weeks of London life, he felt "a yearning for cabless days and dinnerless nights." The William Jameses were coming north again after their winter in Rome and would arrive at Lamb House after Easter. William had been preparing a series of lectures on "the varieties of religious experience"—the Gifford Lectures—to be delivered that spring at Edinburgh. His brother and sister-in-law had been abroad for two years and his niece was nearing her fifteenth birthday. Recognizing that there would be interruptions of his work he addressed himself to a secretarial bureau. He wanted a young woman, he explained, willing to live out in Rye, capable of learning to take dictation directly to the machine. He

could promise few distractions for a young person save those of
rural charm and the bicycle.

II

Henry James's literary situation at the moment of his change of
secretaries was as follows: he had published the previous autumn
his volume of tales *The Soft Side*, containing a dozen stories
written by him, most of them during the weeks when he was
attempting to "finance" the purchase of Lamb House. At Easter
1901 he had almost completed *The Ambassadors* for which he had
not yet signed a contract. He had already begun another novel,
not yet committed to any publisher, and there loomed before him
still the biography of William Wetmore Story promised to
Blackwood in Edinburgh. In addition he was to do an introduction to a new edition of *Madame Bovary* and one to a volume
of Balzac—these promised to Edmund Gosse, who was editing a
series entitled *A Century of French Romance*. Also the *North
American Review* had asked James to do a series of literary essays.

The William Jameses arrived at Lamb House at the end of the
first week in April, Peggy coming with them. Just after their re-
installation, Miss Mary Weld, young, clear-eyed, round-faced,
fresh from a holiday in Berlin, came to Rye to discuss working for
Mr James. He interviewed her in the Garden Room where she
would do her typing. She had first-class references. Her father
had been a classical scholar at Trinity in Dublin and had published
English translations of certain of the Greek tragedies. She had
attended a college for young ladies; and then, in the emancipatory
spirit of the times, she had gone to secretarial school. She seemed
modest, willing, and delighted at the prospect of Rye and the
bicycle. James was nervous during the interview (she later recalled) and she herself felt anxious. They discussed what she
would do during the long pauses that sometimes occurred during
dictation. MacAlpine had smoked; it was settled that she would
crochet. James escorted her into Lamb House proper for lunch,
where she met the William Jameses. There was a long discussion
at table as to what an amanuensis should wear for such duties.
Mrs William agreed that a "suit"—that is a coat and skirt—

would be appropriate. That same afternoon Miss Weld went hunting for a room in Rye and she agreed to start work the following week. Her diary records that there was snow in the town on 15 April, when she arrived; and the next morning she began her duties. As it turned out, her first task was not for Henry James. What she found herself typing were William James's lectures on religion. Miss Weld would say later that typing for Henry James was like accompanying a singer on the piano. In a letter to a friend she wrote that James's dictation was "remarkably fluent. The hesitation and searching for the right word people talk about, was simply nervousness and vanished once he knew you well . . . when working I was just part of the machinery, but out of school, so to speak, he was extraordinarily kind, courteous, and considerate." Sometimes in the afternoon he bicycled with her. Sometimes she accompanied him on his walks. It was she who recalled how James hid to avoid encountering Hueffer during one of their walks towards Winchelsea. She also recalled that a certain woman in Rye came to Lamb House to make sure that everything was "respectable"—since so young a lady was working for an elderly bachelor. In little more than a month Henry James was writing that "Miss Weld proves decidedly a *bijou*," and to the Duchess of Sutherland in June of that year, who inquired about her compatriot MacAlpine, James replied the latter had found "more exalted employment," adding "he had too much Personality—and I have secured in his place a young lady who has, to the best of my belief, less, or who disguises it more." Miss Weld did have her own more modest kind of personality. At times it may have seemed mouse-like to the Master, but she was always at ease with him and always helpful and tactful. MacAlpine's "lady successor is an improvement on him! and an economy!" James wrote. And again: "Miss Weld continues dressy and refined and devoted." So he reported to the William Jameses. In later letters he Italianized her name, as he had often done with others in his letters to Lizzie Boott. His typist became "the little Weldina"—and he was delighted when she took up bookbinding with the help of a friend. "Little Weldina," he wrote, "is still in the foreground—but she has now a background of bookbinding that greatly helps." He saw that this employment would relieve the monotony of Rye for so young a person. He made available to her the adjacent studio in Watchbell Street, which he had offered repeatedly to Hendrik Andersen. "The Diversion," he wrote of the bookbinding, "seems to have been quite successfully operated." He allowed Miss Weld to bind certain of his French books and told her "poor binding is an abject thing, good a divine. Go in for the latter."

It fell to Miss Weld to have dictated to her the latter part of *The Ambassadors* and the two large works that followed it, *The Wings of the Dove* and *The Golden Bowl*. Her typewriter also took down great masses of correspondence, the biography of W. W. Story, some of James's finest late essays, and some of his most remarkable tales, those contained in *The Better Sort*, not least the tale of "The Beast in the Jungle." Her punctuality, efficiency, and good nature contributed markedly to the environment he needed for this sustained period of his labours, during the last writing of his long career.

A FAMILY SUMMER

WILLIAM JAMES, looking at his brother after a winter's absence, wrote to Dr Baldwin "he works steadily, and seems less well than he did—possibly the result of a London winter." The London winter had, as a matter of fact, done Henry much good; and what William saw, but could not recognize, was Henry's usual worried state whenever his brother was on the scene. In a letter to Miss Robins, the novelist spoke of "anxiety-breeding relations in my house." Part of the anxiety was a concern for William's health. The psychologist-philosopher was better, but he had not fully recovered from his severe heart attacks of the previous year and he planned a further cure at Bad Nauheim before sailing that summer for home. The family party was joined by Harry, his elder son, now grown to young manhood, who came out from America to attend his father's Edinburgh lectures. With four more mouths to feed in Lamb House, Henry found himself once again in constant consultation with his cook.

The novelist wanted to get on with *The Ambassadors* which was almost finished, but the distractions were numerous. He found himself finally free in May, when his relatives left for the Continent. On 9 May 1901 he dispatched the first nine parts of his novel to his agent in the form destined for its serialization. The remaining parts were transmitted shortly afterwards, James warning that in the book form he would restore three and a half chapters omitted in the serial. In the restoration a chapter was misplaced in the American edition, but the English edition was accurate. There is no record that James noted the error.

He enjoyed the early days of summer at Lamb House. Miss Weld brightened his house and garden room by arranging flowers in strategic places. "She does so charmingly—has a real gift," he

THE ANGEL OF DEVASTATION
Edith Wharton in 1905

95 IRVING STREET

Henry James in William's garden in Cambridge, with Peggy James
(left) and William and his wife

THE BROTHERS 1905

told his niece. The novelist would later speak of this summer as "a family summer," for Peggy stayed with him while the William Jameses were on the Continent. James's correspondence shows however that Lamb House was filled with many other guests as well. On a day in June, H. G. Wells brought over George Gissing to meet James and the two spent the night at Lamb House. James was fascinated by Gissing, disapproved of his "amazing" relations with women—"why will he do these things?"—but at the same time approved of *New Grub Street*. However, he deplored its style. He found it colourless and surfaced as with some mechanical gloss. Gissing's best quality, James held, was that he really described the life of the lower middle class; other novelists seemed to prefer the extremes of "low life or lords." Gissing had led a life among prostitutes and his face was disfigured by a purple syphilitic scar. He had left his second wife and children to live with a mistress in France. He spoke French, James noted, "with a precise affectation that made it almost too well." From then on James followed his career through Wells, and was touched by Gissing's sufferings and Wells's loyalty: the latter went to France and was with Gissing during his rapid decline and death.

On another day James received the Kent contingent, "Joseph Conrad, wife, baby and trap and pony" who came to tea and stayed all afternoon. The previous day he had had the Winchelsea contingent, the Hueffers, Ford, his wife and guest "for hours." Various Bostonians turned up, including Wendell Holmes; and English intimates such as Edmund Gosse, and the old dilettante, Hamilton Aïdé whom James characterized as "the Diane de Poitiers of our time." As between Holmes, Aïdé, and Peggy, he was happiest with his niece. Holmes's views "on the course of Empire and other matters," he disliked, so they confined themselves to a few chosen topics; with Aïdé "the superficial is imposed by the very nature of his mind." Peggy imposed no strain; she showed off her continental frocks to her uncle and he approved of her speech and manners. Her two years in England had done much for her—not least her long periods of exposure to James. "She is a most soothing and satisfactory maid, attached

D

and attaching to her (poor old) Uncle," James wrote to Morton
Fullerton. "We are spending the summer days, (amazing for unbroken beauty, but too rainless,) here together in idyllic intimacy
and tranquillity . . . We take longish late afternoon walks, and
this afternoon off—two miles by the Golfists little steam-train—
to the beautiful sands of the shore, vast and firm and shining, with
the dear old Romney Marsh on one side, and the blue, blue sea of
August on the other—where we wandered far and far and missed
you awfully and awfully. Ah, you must come." Fullerton wrote
back beautiful and affectionate letters, but remained embedded in
his Paris.

II

By the middle of July, Henry James was at work on his new novel.
He announced its title, *The Wings of the Dove* and said it would be
a love story. He had actually had the story in his notebooks since
1894 and had made a start on the book in 1900 but had dropped it
to write *The Ambassadors*. Before returning to it, he wrote the
last of his theatrical articles—he had written a sufficient number
during all his years to fill a stout volume. This one dealt with the
French neo-romantic, Edmond Rostand. He had seen Sarah
Bernhardt in *L'Aiglon* and *La Princesse Lointaine*, and Coquelin
in *Cyrano de Bergerac*. He considered Rostand a journalistic
Victor Hugo; he liked his theatricality, his swagger, his combination of whimsicality and nationalism, the sentimental with the
sublime. As always, something beside his admiration made James
write such fugitive essays. What fascinated him in Rostand was
his success; he equated this with the success of Kipling, finding in
both writers "the patriotic note, the note of the militant and
triumphant race." As always he pondered the phenomenon—
the way in which these men, with one or two works, suddenly
captured the public, suddenly became personalities and, above all,
suddenly became wealthy. Rostand's themes were close to his
own—Cyrano's love and renunciation; the frustration of the
faraway princess and the pilgrim; the play about Napoleon II,
"who lives over the vast paternal legend, the glories, the victories,
the successive battlefields, the anecdotes, the manners, the personal

habits, the aspect and trick of the very clothes." The Napoleonic story as always had a magical appeal for James—it was also a story of success—and then of fall, in the old tragic sense. Above all it spoke for great power and for *gloire*. *L'Aiglon* was about an "eaglet" who is unable to soar—and James was writing a novel about a dove, who also could not soar. The poetry, the melancholy, the gloom in Rostand touched James; although we gather not as deeply as that which he found at this time in the plays of Maurice Maeterlinck, about whom he did not write an article but whose works he saw. He very quickly grasped their crepuscular symbolism, their veiled allegory. There are explicit references to Maeterlinck in *The Wings of the Dove* and careful evocation of the mood of certain of his scenes.

The William Jameses sailed at the end of August. Henry gave them a sad send-off at Euston station. With all the anxieties William induced in him, Henry had a deep love for his brother. And his attachment to the young "Peggotina" was now profound. She had enlivened many hours for him. Like his Mr Longdon, he would have been delighted to have her always in Lamb House. "I feel very lonely and bereft," he wrote to his brother, "more than ever eager to borrow a child from you, if you only had the right one." He returned to Rye having caught a cold, and feeling seedy. "The beautiful vanished days . . . they have continued here, the beautiful days, of an exquisite quality." Lamb House remained, as he ruefully testified, "an hotel." Gosse returned from Venice and reported on his adventures. The annals of the house record that for the first time young Percy Lubbock "of long limbs and candid countenance" visited Henry James that summer; and most important of all, Hendrik Andersen gave signs of wanting to come. He was due in Paris and promised to dash over for a few days. James was expecting Lily Norton, various other Boston ladies, and a writer friend, T. Bailey Saunders and he warned Andersen they would have very little time alone; he added, however, "I shall at the station, take very personal possession of you." Andersen's visit, so long and so eagerly awaited, with all its overtones of affection and love, occurred in the midst of a series of unscheduled events. "A below-stairs crisis that has been maturing fast for some time, reaches visibly its acute stage," James wrote to a friend on 19 September 1901. Three words in Miss Weld's diary, the next day, "the Smith tragedy," tell us that the crisis had—after many years—been reached.

A DOMESTIC UPHEAVAL

I

FOR some sixteen years—ever since he had originally settled in De Vere Gardens (in 1886)—James had had as servants an English couple, the Smiths, husband and wife. They had kept house for him with great efficiency, the husband as butler, the wife as cook. The two, with the addition of a parlour maid, and his house-boy Burgess, constituted his total staff in the country. There had been long intervals in the old days when James travelled on the Continent—periods of idleness for his servants—during which the Smiths became increasingly alcoholic. James had been, from all evidence, a generous employer. He paid them well. They did not work hard. They had more work, however, at Lamb House than in London, especially with so many visitors, during the summers. And they had never wholly accommodated themselves to their absence from the metropolis. Rural life encouraged their alcoholism. One of Hueffer's memories had been his first luncheon with James served by the red-nosed Smith with great skill and elaborate control of his tipsiness. Only ten days before Andersen's arrival, James had written to his brother, "I am living from hand to mouth with the Smiths, who remain exactly the same queer mixture of alcohol and perfection." Sooner or later the "perfection" had to give way.

On their side, the Smiths seem to have been content with their distinguished master. In 1892, when James was mourning the death of his sister, he had allowed Mrs Smith to bring into De Vere Gardens her ailing sister during one of his absences. He had returned to discover that the woman was seriously ill. She had cancer and he permitted her to come back to De Vere Gardens after her operation. He brought nurses in, and for a time turned his flat into a hospital. Finally he had her removed to a nursing home, and paid most of the medical bills. The gratitude of the

Smiths had been shown through the years. However, James could also be demanding and irritable and a hard taskmaster.

The collapse of the Smiths was sudden although fully expected. On 19 September, a Thursday, Lily Norton came to spend the night at Lamb House. The next day she and James were joined at lunch by Ida Agassiz Higginson, an old Boston friend, wife of the financier and patron of the arts, Henry Lee Higginson, who journeyed from London to be with them for the day. In the afternoon T. Bailey Saunders, arrived from Eastbourne to spend the week-end. Smith seems to have managed the lunch; but he was out cold shortly thereafter. James got the ladies off to London without their suspecting that a domestic crisis was under way around them. "Smith," Henry wrote in a letter to Mrs William James (who was by now back in Cambridge) "was *accumulatedly* so drunk that I got him out of the house—i.e. all Friday and Saturday and Sunday." Andersen arrived on Saturday. James got the local doctor, Skinner, to treat the man, but his employer "could not really communicate with him to the extent of a word." In the meantime Mrs Smith anaesthetized herself. James summoned Mrs Smith's sister, whom he knew to be in service at the home of England's poet laureate, Alfred Austin, at nearby Ashford. She arrived, helped to pack their belongings (they still too drunk to help themselves) and on the Monday they left— dismissed at last, and leaving James's house unstaffed, save for "the gnome" Burgess, as James playfully called his loyal local boy, and the housemaid, Fanny.

"They were, at the end, simply two saturated and demoralized victims, with not a word to say for themselves and going in silence to their doom; but great is the miracle of their having been, all the while, the admirable servants they were and whom I shall ever unutterably mourn and miss." James said he had always paid them well and they had had to spend very little; Smith usually inherited James's clothes, and it was clear at the end that most of their wages had gone into liquor. James thought it an extraordinarily lucky thing he had been able to find their relatives "otherwise my case would have indeed been queer." He gave the Smiths "an almost foolishly liberal" severance pay of two months' wages each, "till they can turn round." He added, to Alice James, "They will never turn round; they are lost utterly; but I would have promised *anything* in my desire to get them out of the house before some still more hideous helplessness made it impossible. A new place is impossible to either; they wouldn't keep it three days; and their deplorable incriminating aspect alone damns them beyond appeal. What they looked like going to the Station!"

James paid their liquor bill in the town and settled down to makeshift living, taking some of his meals at the Mermaid Inn, while he sent out appeals to his London lady friends for help.

II

In retrospect James wrote good-humouredly to Andersen of the débâcle. He spoke of "my little squalid botheration." In the midst of the crisis, and with Bailey Saunders present, the long-awaited reunion of the old Master and the young sculptor lost some of its intimacy. James was too upset, too anxious. "Saunders and dear young Andersen remained with me through it and were really a comfort," the novelist reported to Mrs William, who had met the sculptor in Rome. Andersen, however, prolonged his stay into the middle of the week and the two re-captured at the end a few hours of privacy. Once again James found Andersen enormously appealing: once again he offered him all the tenderness and affection of which he was capable. He had described Andersen to the William Jameses, when he had arranged for the sculptor to meet them, as "a sincere and intel-ligent being, though handicapped by a strange 'self-made' illiteracy and ignorance of many things." The sculptor had had a difficult time in America. He had been commissioned, however, to do a statue of Lincoln; he had also done a nude on com-mission, but the statue had been turned down because of the nudity. James was consoling. "What a dismal doom for a sculptor to work for a great vulgar stupid community that revels in every hideous vulgarity and only quakes at the clean and blessed nude—the last refuge of Honour!" He urged Andersen to come away from Rome and live and work in the Watchbell Street studio, which he again offered him. "What I should like is that you should come and stay with me till you are wholly rested and consoled and cheered—no matter how long it takes: the longer the better." The longest time the sculptor gave him was this brief, and as it happened, interrupted visit.

Their personal relationship was one thing; the matter of art was another—and when it came to the statue of Lincoln, of which Andersen sent James a photograph, the novelist was direct and uncompromising in his criticism. He reminded Andersen that in his youth he had been "drenched with feeling" about the President. He found a seated Lincoln, as Andersen had done him, unthinkable; he said it shocked him. "He was for us all, then, standing up very tall." He began by saying he liked the head but thought it "rather too smooth, ironed-out, simplified as to ruggedness, ugliness, mouth, etc." His principal complaint, however, was that Andersen had not conveyed the sense of a *physical* Lincoln. "I don't feel the length of limb, leg, shanks, loose-jointedness, etc.—nor the thickness of the large body in the clothes—especially the presence of shoulders, big arms and big hands." He told Andersen that he had made "a *softer*, smaller giant than we used to see." The face lacked light and shade," and what was needed was "more breaking-up, under his accursed clothing, more bone, more mass." Also he was too "placid." The image of history and memory was "benevolent, but deeply troubled, and altogether tragic: that's how one thinks of him."

The young sculptor took these criticisms with good grace. They were gently given "for the love of your glory and your gain." Moreover, Andersen's ego was impervious to subtleties. When they were together it was Andersen's stature, his shoulders, his arms and hands, the solid physical presence that counted. James escorted him as far as the junction point of Ashford and wrote to him promptly, "I miss you—keep on doing so—out of all proportion to the too few hours you were here—and even go so far as to ask myself whether visits so damnably short haven't more in them to groan, than to thank for." He said also "the memory *is* a kind of beggarly stopgap till we can meet again." When he got word of the sculptor's safe return to his studio in Rome he imaged him as a young priest returned to his altar—but a pagan priest, for he saw him with "your idols, bless their brave limbs and blank eyes, ranged roundabout."

"I wish you, my dear Boy, such a high tide of inspiration and execution as will float you over every worry and land you in peace and renown."

With Andersen gone James addressed himself with Napoleonic precision to restoring his household. "Peace now reigns—I am happy to say—though peace a little sharply distinguished from Plenty," he wrote to his other recent guest, Bailey Saunders. A charwoman was recruited as emergency cook. With the aid of the "knife-boy" Burgess and maid, some semblance of normal life was restored. To Peggy, with whom he now began a fairly regular correspondence, he described his staff and household as reduced to "picnicking lines." "Mrs Bourne, who sleeps here, roasts chickens, fries soles, makes custard puddings, etc. Fanny and the gnome Burgess affect me as a delightful simplification. I have no desire for the present to alter it." He was glad the catastrophe had been stayed until after the William Jameses had left. Their handsome tips on departure had all been invested in liquor. "I see now," he told Peggy, "how heavily for years, the accumulated (the thousands of gallons of) whisky of the Smiths has weighed on my spirits, how odiously uneasy I had chronically been."

AUNT LUCY

OF the London ladies to whom Henry James appealed for help there was one who entered most into his domestic crisis. This was Mrs W. K. Clifford. He had known her since the 1880's and their friendship had deepened every year. Lucy Clifford, the former Lucy Lane, had been in her youth a golden-haired, red-cheeked art student, who sketched the antique statues in the British Museum. She had married in due course one of the greatest mathematicians of the Victorian era, W. K. Clifford, who died at thirty-four. Finding herself a widow—she was then twenty-four —with two young daughters to support, Lucy bravely turned to writing—journalism, fiction, and later, plays. Her courage, her steadfastness, her alertness, and her abilities won her wide admiration. She was still wearing mourning when James met her. He liked her from the first. When they met in 1880 he was of the same age as her husband, but she had treated him as if he were one of her young literary protégés who came regularly to her Sunday salon. In the 1890's, when he had been discouraged by the failure of his plays, she had induced the editor of the *Illustrated London News* to publish a Henry James serial—one of the strangest mediums in which the novelist ever appeared. This was *The Other House*. By that time she had become a hearty, mothering, energetic, enveloping woman, direct in her conversation and formidable in her ability to get things done. It was she who helped to launch Rudyard Kipling in literary London after reading some of his work published in India. James was an habitué of her home and he liked nothing better than to sip a liqueur by her fireside after an evening at the theatre; or to take tea with her and listen to London literary gossip. Her novel *Mrs Keith's Crime* proved a great success; and also *Aunt Anne*, which still has its place on the shelf of minor Victorian fiction. Because of the latter, James often addressed her in his letters as "Dearest Aunt

Lucy." She responded by calling him her "nevvy." On other occasions she was his "Beloved girl." She was brisk, original, loyal, self-assertive, and full of warm feelings. Even the young Hueffer, whom she sent to James in the first instance, found her friendly.

Unlike the ladies James had cultivated in his younger years, Lucy Clifford did not possess a sharpness of tongue, or an underlying cruelty that he had accepted and even found attractive in them. Lucy Clifford was genial; she spoke well, and to the point; and she was eminently expressive and generous. One would not have called her a pretty woman. Her irregular features had much charm and, then, one always knew where one stood with her. She had loyal friends among London's most distinguished men—Huxley, Tyndall, among her husband's scientific friends; Browning, John Morley, Lowell, during his ambassadorial time, and Henry James. Frequenters of her salon encountered Bernard Shaw, when he was still the red-bearded music critic of his nonage. In the twentieth century she was still befriending the literary young, Hugh Walpole, among others, and after him Charles Morgan. Late in life James would speak of "that admirable Lucy Clifford—as a character, a nature, a soul of generosity and devotion." She was, in these ways, he said "one of the finest bravest creatures possible." Mrs Clifford was one of three London friends who would be remembered in Henry James's will.

II

She had just returned from Vienna when James wrote her of his domestic débâcle, using the language of cataclysm. His letters record the event as a tidal wave, a whirlwind, a shooting "into space" of the drunken Smiths. He told Lucy he had had a "domestic cyclone." One feels in reading his letters to her that she was ready to swoop down on Rye and keep house for him. "How noble and generous your instant impulse of succour in respect to my disabled house and how deeply I am touched by it! I thank you with all my heart." She immediately got into touch with a housemaid and she canvassed others for interviews. James reassured her. He was not "in extreme discomfort; therefore don't pity me or think of me too much." It was really a relief not to have whiskyfied servants around; it was "a blissful cessation of nightmare." He would be in town early in the new year and probably could make do until then. And he told Mrs Clifford that other friends had recommended a certain lady named Paddington, with a record of having held only two posts, nineteen years in one and ten in another. "Bear with the lonely celibate," he wrote to loyal Lucy, "who has, as it were to boil his own pot . . . It's horrible not immediately to see you—and to know that you must all the while be letting off steam by which I shan't—or don't— profit. Do bottle a little up for me, and I will come and uncork the wine on the earliest possible day." Lucy, however, continued to send telegrams; she had a standby housemaid readied in case of emergency; and James came to confer with her when he arrived in town for his interview with the matronly Mrs Paddington.

The matron had impeccable references. She seemed to like the idea of a bachelor establishment. She was ready to come for £3 a month. Such was the wage-scale of the time for a good housekeeper-cook. She would not, however, be free until mid-November. James was prepared to go on with his improvised household until then. He was working peacefully at *The Wings of the Dove* and the autumn at Rye that year was exquisite—"the tree forms grow in beauty as they simplify in dress; the grey sky is streaked with vague pink; peculiar delicacies and poetries abound; and the stillness is like the long gulp or catching of breath that precedes . . . a long sob, or other vocal outbreak." He added, "May this fine image not fit too closely my own hushed personal condition." He was writing then to his garden-lady Miss Muir Mackenzie. "I go down at last, only tomorrow (to the station) to meet the lady of the Gorringe's costume, on whose convenience I have been waiting all this time. She is my Fate! may she not be my Doom. May a 'long sob' not have cause to ensue upon this period of quite resigned suspense."

It will be recalled that Olivia Garnett, she who had dreams of Henry James saying profound things to her, stepped off the train at Rye station on her way to visit the Hueffers the next morning and beheld Henry James approaching a matronly lady and heard

him say, "I have come to meet my doom." Thus began the long
régime of Mrs Paddington in Lamb House, a woman who was
severe and autocratic with her fellow-servants, but who knew her
business thoroughly. Three weeks after her arrival, James was
writing of the "peace" she promised his household—"a *real*,
trained, all-round, excellent cook, up to the wildest want, or
flight . . . a *supreme* economist, manager, mistress of thrift, fore-
sight (my tradesmen's books going steadily down and down;)
and an equally excellent, genial, sensible, good-tempered, friendly
woman—safe with her fellow-servants altogether . . . *The* blessing in Mrs P. is that she clearly likes my service, as much as I
cling to *her*."

THE WINGS OF THE DOVE

HENRY JAMES had begun dictating *The Wings of the Dove* to Miss Weld on 9 July 1901; he had worked on the book intermittently during August when Peggy had been with him; and he continued through the upheaval of his domestic life in October and on into the new year. The only interruption was a three weeks' absence that included some days with E. L. Godkin, his old *Nation* editor who had come out to England to spend his last days. He died at Torquay shortly after James had his last glimpse of him.

Jonathan Sturges paid one of his longish visits to Lamb House through Christmas and the year's end, with the consequence that James stayed on until the end of January before going up to London where he planned to remain during the worst part of the winter. Great gales made Rye as mournful and as lonely as a lighthouse. So confident was James of completing his novel at an early date that he sent off five hundred pages of the manuscript to Constable and was reading proof of his book even while writing its final two sections—the pages devoted to the rage of the elements in Venice as Milly, his heiress, dies in her rented palazzo. In the Venetian chapter James was reliving old memories, not only the long-ago death of Minny Temple, but the long wasting illness of his sister, and then the violent end—in Venice—of Miss Woolson. He reached London on 27 January—the anniversary week of Miss Woolson's death—and had no sooner settled in the Reform Club when he became "painfully" ill. He described it as an "inflammation of the bowels." He continued to have stomach upsets and gout; in mid-February, in a moment of remission of his symptoms, he dashed back to Rye. Lamb House, even in the depths of winter, was better than the single room at the Reform Club; at home he had a household to take care of him.

During the ensuing weeks he had "botherations, aberrations,

damnations of the mind and body." The subject or central dilemma of his novel, the death in Venice, was a heavy charge on his emotions. Within the year his memories of Miss Woolson's suicide had been stirred in particular by a visit to Rye of Grace Carter, Fenimore's cousin, whom he liked. She had seen Miss Woolson in death, had made the funeral arrangements in Rome; and from that troubled time they had been friends. He had not met her for some years, but now he wrote her a series of letters, cherishing "our common memory of, and common affection for, dear C.F.W." Then in recent weeks he had learned that Miss Woolson's dog, Otello, had died. "This end of his career," James wrote to the Benedicts, "takes me back in memory to that other end—the melancholy days in Venice." Otello had come to them for refuge and he stood, James reminded them, "for a particular terrible passage" in their lives. The passage had been terrible in his life as well; and he was in a sense reliving it for he had decided to have his heroine die, as Miss Woolson had done, in an old Venetian palazzo. He had direct news of the palace he had in mind—from Edmund Gosse, who visited James's friends the Curtises in "the divine Barbaro, noblest of human habitations." To Mrs Curtis he wrote that "Venice . . . seems such a museum of distressed *ends*." They were discussing the disappearance from the scene of many familiar figures. By a coincidence, the news of the death of Miss Woolson's dog had been followed a few weeks later by the sudden death of his own beloved little wire terrier. Everything seemed to contribute to the encroachment on mind and memory of the crowded past of his recent years—not least the publication of Graham Balfour's biography of Robert Louis Stevenson who had died less than a year after Miss Woolson. James's illness caused postponement of the novel; the final pages were written late in May. In June he had a return, in attenuated form, of his winter's illness, but he recovered rapidly, and after that Lamb House began to receive its summer quotas of visitors. His novel, delayed by his illness, was published on 21 August 1902 in England and seven days later in New York.

I

The idea for the novel had been with him ever since the early death of Minny Temple in 1870. In mourning his beloved cousin he had foreshadowed the situation of his future work, and in personal terms. He had seemed almost to welcome her death because he could take total possession of her in his mind and memory; he had told his mother Minny would be an inspiration to him in years to come. This she had been. The young woman had died of "galloping" consumption. James, thinking at the time of his own ill-health during the Civil War, had spoken of himself as "slowly crawling from weakness and inaction and suffering into strength and health and hope; she sinking out of brightness and youth into decline and death." He had made it sound as if she had laid down her life that he might live. The death of one or the other partner in love: this had been his theme in tales such as the early "De Grey: a Romance," or "Longstaff's Marriage." In later years, re-worked, it had become the unpleasant story of "Maud-Evelyn" in which a young man falls in love with a dead girl he has never known, and finally convinces himself she has been his wife. When James's heroes do not actively renounce marriage, they can passively displace love from the living to the dead.

He had published a story, as late as 1884, called "Georgina's Reasons," in which the recurrent theme expressed itself in still another form. In it two women bear names that would be used in The Wings of the Dove, Kate and Mildred Theory. Mildred Theory would become Milly Theale. Both Mildreds are doomed by illness, Mildred Theory by consumption, Milly Theale by an unnamed disease. Mildred Theory is "as beautiful as a saint, and as delicate and refined as an angel;" in short, she too is a "dove," like Milly. Kate must adjust her life to her sister's needs. "So long as Mildred should live, her own life was suspended." She cannot allow herself to feel love for the handsome naval officer, who comes to see her and her sister in their temporary home at Posilippo. He is Raymond Benyon, secretly married to a woman in New York named Georgina, as Merton Densher will ultimately be secretly engaged to Kate in *The Wings of the Dove*. In the earlier tale we find a recognition scene in front of a portrait, a foreshadowing of the dramatic moment in which Milly Theale will face a Bronzino portrait of a lady. Minny Temple—Mildred Theory—Milly Theale—the three belonged to a single line of fantasy—life into art: in its essence it was that of the Henry James who could not bring himself to love and marry. He could worship a younger woman in a utopia of the mind. In life he required the friendship of protective and sheltering females, to whom he could be kind and attentive, but who gave him everything and seemed satisfied that he be "kind" in return. The ending of the story of the Theory sisters is pure melodrama. Benyon discovers that the woman to whom he is secretly married —she has borne his child and abandoned it in Italy—has remarried. He is free to marry his Kate, when her sister dies; but he is held back by his unwillingness to duplicate the bigamy of his wife. He sails away on his ship for another long voyage. Kate Theory will wait. Once again James had arranged his story so as to leave his uncomfortable hero unmarried and his heroine suspended as in a void.

The notes for *The Wings of the Dove* were written in the autumn of 1894 in James's notebooks, in the year of the death Constance Fenimore Woolson, in Venice. She had been the most important of his "protective" ladies in all the years he had known her; only after her death had it occurred to him that she might have loved him more than he had been ready to admit. He had always been attentive, dutiful, kind to her because, as he thought, she was so devoted to him. What we can read in these repeated patterns of fantasy which spoke for inner passional life, is a reflection of an old situation in the James family, present to him from earliest childhood. There had been two sisters in the Walsh family, in Washington Square. Henry James's father married the older one, Mary. The younger, Catherine, had been quite as spell-bound by the fervour and eloquence of Henry Sr, and she had come to live with the Jameses. A strong assertive woman, Aunt Kate had tried to break away late in life; she had married but she left her husband shortly after to return to her familiar place at the James family hearth. The real-life Mary and Kate, the omnipresent older female figures of Henry James's childhood, may be regarded as the figures behind his cousin Minny Temple and the Milly and Kate of fiction, the idealized mother and the down-to-earth Aunt—Kate Theory and Mildred, Kate Croy and Milly—the strong and the weak, the good and bad heroines of the various stories, the representatives of spirit and flesh. They were an outgrowth in the novelist's mind of elements in his buried life, the everlasting vision of a mother who seemed compliant and sacrificial and an aunt, assertive and manipulative. In such complex equations resided the personalized form of Henry James's myth of women. The myth had been translated early in life into the apotheosis of Minny Temple as the "heroine of the scene." Later, with the entry of Miss Woolson into his life, the old triangle of his father's life, and of his own, was redrawn. Minnie Temple remained a "luminary of the mind." Fenimore was a fellow-writer, a woman with womanly demands. The myth of the ethereal and the fleshly, of spirit and body, continued to have reality. Otherwise stated, in James's equations, they were formulated as art and passion—and in his existence they could not be reconciled. The solution: renunciation. One renounced love, or was deprived of it. Accepted, it could prove ruinous.

In returning to these themes now, James was making a supreme attempt to understand and resolve a life-dilemma in which he had feared the love of woman and learned to keep himself emotionally distant from all human relations lest he commit himself to unforeseen disasters. In all his tales of authorship this is the semi-humorous, but at bottom deeply serious "lesson," given by literary masters to their acolytes. Marriage destroyed art; passion could destroy life.

II

To understand James's return to his myth of the "sacred woman," a kind of personal virgin-worship that he disliked when he saw it in the Church, we must recognize that he had begun a kind of re-writing of his past. *The Ambassadors* had been in effect a return to *The American* in which the writer at fifty-seven redreamed into his maturity what he had written at thirty-four. So now he began a retelling of *The Portrait of a Lady* which had been his attempt to construct a story for Minny Temple as if she had gone on living. He had shown that she would have been frustrated by life, that the dancing flame would in any event have been quenched. In the fullness of time he was reverting to the idea of death. He created an "heiress of the ages" who is to be deprived of her patrimony—of life itself. "Live all you can" had been the theme of *The Ambassadors*; but the question now was, "What if life is denied?" The answer would be, in part at least, "One can still love—and love can endure from beyond the grave." He was still governed by the idea of renunciation and sacrifice. But now it was coupled with thoughts of fleshly love. In opening himself to feeling in recent months, in allowing himself to experience the touch, the presence, the embrace, of the young sculptor, James had learned the meaning of physical love. Life was at last proving more attractive than fiction. His novel had, he told Howells, "a prettyish tale . . . It's moreover, probably, of a prettyish inspiration—a 'love-story' of a romantic tinge." He had never written such a novel. All his earlier tales had been stories of artists seeking glory and power, and finding passion incompatible with their art; of businessmen seeking to conquer a wife as they had conquered their fortunes; of young American heiresses marrying "sensibly" because they fear marriage as a form of bondage and an invasion of their sovereignty. In no novel had James pictured a pair of lovers or made love the very heart of his action. In his sixtieth year he found himself writing about a love affair—and on a grand scale. There would be scheming and treachery, as in *The Portrait of a Lady*. Kate Croy, discovering that Milly the heiress is doomed, will tell a civilized lie, a "constructive" lie: she will deny to the heiress that she loves Merton Densher. The heiress will be left free to love him; and Kate will instruct Merton to be "kind" to the dying girl. Her hope is that the heiress, dying, will "endow" Merton—and so endow their marriage. Milly will have her love in the moments of her fear and trembling over her impending separation from the world. What would have been a meaningless death could become, through Kate's lie, a beautiful journey to an illuminated Paradise. This was Kate's reasoning.

As with *The Ambassadors*, Henry James brought all the resources of his art to bear on this melodramatic tale. He had begun by seeing it as "ugly and vulgar." He would gild the ugliness and the vulgarity with his prose and his style. To do so he summoned the full orchestra of his symbolic imagination. He had never paid attention in his critical writings to the symbolist movement in France, he who had otherwise watched closely the art of the novel in the Third Republic. There is no mention of Verlaine in his essays nor of Mallarmé. And his essay of the 1870's on Baudelaire shows how limited was his vision of that artist whom he condemned with the eyes of a "realist" for his unpleasant concern with "flowers of evil." His early reading of Hawthorne to be sure had shown him the uses of allegorical symbolism; but he had enrolled himself instead under the banner of Balzac. James came late to the symbolist movement, even as he had been tardy in accepting impressionism in painting. He discovered it in the theatre, in Ibsen, and even then it had had to be called to his attention by William Archer. Once James had grasped the uses of the symbol he possessed the power and the poetry to assimilate it promptly into his art: to discard the literal realism of Balzac for the evocative realism of Ibsen. We have but to call the roll of Henry James's novels to see the change—the label titles give way first to the ironic-symbolic, and then wholly to the symbolic—*Washington Square*, *The Bostonians*, *The Princess Casamassima*, change to allusive titles such as *The Spoils of Poynton*, or collections of tales called *Terminations* or *Embarrassments*. And now for the first time he finds a new kind of title—*The Wings of the Dove*—as he will find *The Golden Bowl*.

> Oh that I had wings like a dove! for then would I fly
> away, and be at rest.

The 55th Psalm also speaks of "deceit and guile," and its lines record treachery and despair. We must, however, take note of lines in the 67th Psalm as well, "yet shall ye be as the wings of a dove covered with silver, and her feathers with yellow gold."

Milly the dove who wants ultimately to fly away and be at rest has gold-covered wings; with her fragility she possesses the gilded power of an heiress. And beyond this suggestive title, James fills this novel with the beating of wings, the sense of the abyss, as if we were in the opening pages of Balzac's *Seraphita*, the novel of the androgynous nature of love (which would fascinate Yeats) with its Swedenborgianism and its use of the fjords of Norway and great effects of sky and clouds and mist to suggest the empyrean. Like *Louis Lambert*, the story of *Seraphita* was one of Balzac's *études philosophiques*. Was it a coincidence that in Balzac's novel there should be a Minna—as there had been a Minny? And that we should meet Milly perched on a crag in the Alps in Switzerland with the world "all before her." (James will repeat the final words from *Paradise Lost* thrice in the novel.) In *Seraphita* James found echoes of the Swedenborgianism of his father. Moreover, during the year of the writing of the *Wings*, Lamb House was filled with talk of William's *Varieties of Religious Experience*, his lectures which sprang out of the depths of James family history—deeply related to the religious passion and mystical revelations experienced by the elder Henry James. *The Wings of the Dove* borrows the symbolism of Christianity to clothe the sordid drama it has to tell, to convert the gold-weighted Milly into a seraph and a dove and the predatory Kate into a creature motivated by her poverty to seek a better life for herself. In the novel's imagery, Kate is a panther and she is named Croy— the crow, a blackbird, of which the name in French is *merle* (and Madame Merle in *The Portrait of a Lady* had played a similar role). The bird imagery is sustained in the name Theale—the silver-and-gold dove is also thus a little duck. The realist of the novel, turned poet, seemed to be trying to reconcile the divine and the earthly. Memories of Milton and Blake: his father had edited a volume of Blake's poems—the marriage of heaven and hell. And then Henry James had seen, after Ibsen—with his *Wild Duck* and his *Doll's House* and his *Peer Gynt*—the evocative plays of Maeterlinck, vague, mystical, crepuscular. There are two allusions to Maeterlinck in *The Wings of the Dove*: the Boston lady, Susan Shepherd Stringham, the shepherdess of

Milly, has read her Maeterlinck along with her Pater; and in the heart of the novel we are invited to look at Milly as if she were a princess, in her plumes and jewels, with Kate as her handmaiden, circling about in the twilight "in the likeness of some dim scene in a Maeterlinck play."

In *The Portrait of a Lady* there had been a physician who was given a brief walk-on part; James had named him Sir Matthew Hope. In the *Wings* he is at the centre of the action and his name is that of the healer, Luke—Sir Luke Strett. There is also Lord Mark, who journeys to the city of St Mark as the *deus ex machina* of Milly's drama. The very introduction of Mark and St Mark brings a new pair of wings into the novel, not those of the dove, but of the winged lion, emblem of Mark, and emblem of Venice. *The Wings of the Dove* seems a riot of symbols, not least that of the ascending dove of the title, whose wings shelter those left behind. Since they are wings of gold, the gold weighs down Merton Densher at the end. As in the early story of the naval officer who sails away and leaves his Kate, Densher turns from Kate Croy. Their cruel gambit has succeeded only too well; but they can no longer be as they were. The solution of *The Wings of the Dove* still finds James rewriting an old equation. The dead interfere with the living; the worship of woman as goddess acts as prohibition to human love.

III

This is the deepest flaw within the inventive poetry and form of *The Wings of the Dove*. For all his disguises as active and even coercive lover, Merton Densher, is in reality the classical passive, renunciatory Jamesian hero. He drifts in his passivity into a solution comfortable to himself. He sits back and allows women to be kind, devoted, sacrificial. Kate serves him, and plots for him; Milly is a fine rare creature who loves him; he "takes the comfort of it." James has tried to suggest a certain opaque quality within his passivity, as if to provide some reason for it: and his name is interpreted for us when we are told that Kate is "almost tired of his density." But there is nothing "dense" about Merton Densher. In drifting, and accepting, he becomes irritated by his "so extremely manipulated state." The result is one of the coolest–hottest scenes in all of James's fiction. He threatens to spoil Kate's plans — as if she were doing everything for herself and not also for him; and exacts as his price for continued passivity that the woman he loves come to his rooms, and sleep with him. It is in this sudden show of active (but also aggressive) male force, that Densher finally differs from all his predecessors. Kate yields; Densher feels himself "master in the conflict." Yet there has been no conflict. There has been only the demands of an irritated lover, asking Kate not only to continue to do everything for him, but to surrender to him. She is willing, for she loves Densher.

The effect of this change in the old Jamesian equation, however, is simply to offer a new justification for old conclusions. Densher's physical love of Kate frees him for his spiritual love of Milly. What he has not counted on, and does not recognize, is his guilt. The hand reaching from beyond the grave and offering him continued sustenance fills him with remorse: fills him with a need to rush to the altar in the Brompton Oratory. In the final scene Densher has withdrawn into a greater passivity than ever. Kate now believes that Densher is in love with Milly's memory. Yet it has been clear throughout that Densher did not love the sick girl. If Milly's wings cover him from beyond life, his freedom has been diminished; he chooses to live with a ghost rather than with the strong and living woman, like the young man in "Maud-Evelyn." The renunciation is as complex as all of James's renunciations; nevertheless it is touched by the exquisite delicacy with which James describes the final meeting of the lovers. And for the first time in all his fiction James writes believably of the sexual passion of his hero. Kate and Merton are aware of one another as physical beings. Moreover he writes with an awareness of love's vulnerability. He muses at one point on the impatience of love, "how ill a man, and even a woman could feel from such a cause." He complains that men have been unimaginative in their vocabulary of love. Nowhere in his novels is there a stronger sense of the physical than in the account of Densher left alone in his rooms after Kate's visit. The entire place is changed. Eros has touched everything. Densher can lay on Kate "strong hands almost in anger" and she closes her eyes "as with the sense that he might strike her but she could gratefully take it." James had come face to face at last with "the great relation." But he had not been able to banish his other ghost—the ghost of doubt, of guilt, the double-love of the heroine of the spirit and the heroine of the flesh; they were still the "good" and the "bad" heroines of all his stories. The resolution would have to be attempted once again: and James did, the following year, and for a last time.

IV

James would speak later of his quest for a "compositional key" to the structure of *The Wings of the Dove.* This was made necessary by his subject. "The way grew straight," he wrote, "from the moment one recognized that the poet essentially can't be concerned with the act of dying. Let him deal with the sickest of the sick, it is still by the act of living that they appeal to him, and appeal the more as the conditions plot against them and prescribe the battle." The novelist recognized that to depict the stages of Milly Theale's illness, as in the doleful last act of some opera, was merely to create a novel of the "graveyard" school or what we might call in the language of today a "soap opera." Death resulting from the accidents of life is sad, but it is not tragic. James had a subject likely to cause an unmotivated flow of tears rather than provide the catharsis of tragedy. His solution was to omit the tearful scenes, the very scenes which the sentimental novelists put in so as to wring every possible emotion out of the audience. Venice in the *Wings* remains the Venice of Othello or of Volpone. But the reader is kept out of certain rooms; he may not be present at certain encounters. We remain with the living—their greed, their guilt, their ultimate anguish. The expected moments do not materialize. We are allowed to see Milly in thought and action so long as she is still physically strong: or as James put it in his preface, he had been reduced, out of the "tenderness of his imagination" to watching her "through the successive windows of other people's interest in her." We see her in her passionate scene before the Bronzino, proclaiming that the woman in the picture is "dead, dead, dead," and as she looks she holds in her hand a cup of iced coffee, a chill reminder of her mortality. We see Densher in the autumn downpour in Venice when the winter winds lash the lagoon as if we were with Lear—all the elements enter into the climax of the drama. We are present at the splendid confrontation—one of James's greatest moments of drama—in the National Gallery when Milly comes upon Kate and Densher together. We accompany Densher in the gondola, as he goes for his "last interview" with Milly. We expect to see her on her couch, to hear her words, to listen to Densher's explanations. He is received at the palace. And the doors close in our face. When we turn the page we are no longer in Venice. We will never know what passed between the hero and the heroine, although Densher will later have brief moments of memory. It was to this that Ford Madox Hueffer alluded when he inquired why the Master had deprived him of the "last interview." James's answer had been that the book had had to be "composed in a certain way, in order to come into being at all, and the lines of composition, so to speak, determined and controlled its parts and account for what is and isn't there; what isn't e.g. like the 'last interview' of Densher and Milly." In a parenthesis he had inserted "Hall Caine would have made it large as life and magnificent, wouldn't he?"

This is a part of the strange organization of *The Wings of the Dove*. The Master plays with fire but he does not burn his fingers. He creates a novel in which all the "great scenes"—all the *expected* ones—are left out. He substitutes other scenes which belong to Kate and Densher—"the subject," he told Hueffer, "was Densher's history with Kate Croy—hers with him, and Milly's history was but a thing involved and embroiled in that. I fear I even then let my system betray me, and at any rate I feel I have welded my structure of rather too large and too heavy historic bricks." By this he meant that he had developed each section of his structure with great solidarity until the novel was four-fifths finished; and had then had to foreshorten and truncate in the fifth. He spoke of the *Wings* as suffering from a "misplaced pivot," or he humorously described its structural flaw, in a letter to Mrs Cadwalader Jones, as having too big a head for its body. He said the book was "too inordinately drawn out and too inordinately rubbed in. The centre, moreover, isn't in the middle, or the middle, rather, isn't in the centre, but ever so much too near the end, so that what was to come after it is truncated." To Lucy Clifford he wrote that *The Ambassadors*, which still remained unpublished—and would not appear until more than a year after the publication of the *Wings*—was "much better and less long."

Whatever its defects, the latter novel has the strong interest of its subject and the scenic structure by which the subject is rendered. A new generation of dramatizers and opera writers would be attracted by the book, and would put into it the very scenes James had purposely left out. In other words, they made it into the "tear-jerker" it was not supposed to be. In his text, James made direct allusion to his intention. Densher, returning to London, talks with Kate and "she sat there before the scene . . . very much as a stout citizen's wife might have sat during a play that made people cry." Seeking popularity, James nevertheless worked very hard to fashion his book in the way of art; he did not intend it, apparently, for stout citizens' wives. If James resorted to omission and indirection, thereby further disposing of the omniscient author, as he had done in *The Ambassadors*, he gives full play to those scenes in which we are allowed to see Milly resisting her fate. The novel is never more in command of itself, nor of its existential materials, than in the quiet give-and-take of Sir Luke Strett, the physician, and his doomed patient. There are many things in Sir Luke which suggest the authority and the bedside manner of Dr W. W. Baldwin who had been doctor of Henry, William, Alice, and in Florence of Miss Woolson. Moreover, in naming the Italian doctor who substitutes for Sir Luke in Venice Taccini, James was using the actual name of Baldwin's Falstaffian friend, an Italian-teacher, with whom the novelist and the American doctor had gone on a walking tour in Tuscany in 1890. Once again James is careful not to specify. The only medical word he uses in these scenes is "auscultation." There is never a hint of the nature of Milly's illness. We are present rather at a comparatively modern therapeutic session, as if James were predicting, two years after Freud's book on dreams, the future of the psychoanalytical relation. Sir Luke is "supportive;" he emphasizes the immediate, the real. Milly has had only premonitory symptoms; she is still in possession of her faculties and her strength; the physician is determined not to allow her to be sorry for herself, nor to convert self-pity into pity for him. She speaks of her isolation. He is not convinced. Who had accompanied Milly on her first visit? A devoted friend—well then, "doesn't that make another friend for you?" And he amusedly reminds her that her being American makes her a member of a large national gregarious family, "it puts you with plenty of others—that isn't pure solitude." We are also made party to Milly's day-dreams. She dreams of offering her doctor a gift; she suggests that she is kind to him by being so easy to treat "since you've already done me so much good." He refuses to play her game. "Oh no, you're extremely difficult to treat. I've need with you, I assure you, of all my wit." He dismisses the past—her past of dead parents, dead relatives, her being alone in the world. "Don't try to bear more things than you need . . . Hard things have come to you in youth, but you mustn't think life will be for you all hard things. You've a right to be happy. You must make up your mind to it. You must attempt any form in which happiness must come."

Milly feels as if she has been to confession and been absolved. She faces the world with renewed hope. She rents a palace in Venice and invites her friends to join her there. And in Venice life and art are deeply mingled for James. He embodies in these beautiful chapters memories of his various sojourns at the Palazzo Barbaro. The palace itself is described, with its *piano nobile* and the shuttered light playing across its floors. He had stayed there with the Curtises (he was in active correspondence with them during the writing of this novel), and he had been there during Mrs Gardner's rental of the palazzo early in the '90's. There is a recall of Mrs Gardner and her famous string of pearls, in the scene in which Kate studies Milly's pearls, and recognizes that the weak dove has the strength of her wealth.

. . . the long priceless chain, wound twice round the neck, hung, heavy and pure, down the front of the wearer's breast—so far down that Milly's trick, evidently unconscious, of holding and vaguely fingering and entwining a part of it, conduced presumably to convenience. "She's a dove" Kate went on, "and one somehow doesn't think of doves as bejewelled. Yet they suit her down to the ground."

Densher, listening, knows that Kate is "exceptionally under the impression of that element of wealth in her which was a power, a great power, and which was dove-like only so far as one remembered that doves have wings and wondrous flights, have them as well as tender tints and soft sounds."

The centre of emotion in this novel is fixed in Merton Densher, a figure not unlike James's Parisian friend W. Morton Fullerton, who was a journalist and a man of sentiment. Fullerton spent his days writing cables for the London *Times* and lived a life similar to James's hero. He was curious about this character, for he wrote James inquiring whether Densher was modelled on a man named T. A. Cook. "*Ah, que non!*" James responded, "he was *not* my poor distinguished Densher. I never dreamed of him." He did not say, however, of whom he had dreamed. Certainly it was not Ford Madox Hueffer. The personality of Morton Fullerton and the use of the name Merton, permits us to speculate that the Parisianized journalist had ground for his inquiries. We must recognize nevertheless that there is much of James's own moral feeling in Densher, his own reticences, his problems in relating to women. Reading the parallel columns of James's life and James's art we seem to recognize that in memory he was much in Venice during the closing months of the century's first year. In writing this novel he touched the whole mystery of Fenimore and the painful weeks of questioning and mourning when he had lived in Fenimore's Venetian apartment—above all the great riddle of death. This is suggested in the closing pages of *The Wings of the Dove* and may explain James's uneasiness and uncertainties—and troubled health—during these months. If he could not find an answer to the riddle he could try to answer the riddle of life—and this may to some extent explain why he could not stop writing, even though he had published three volumes between 1900 and 1902 and had written still another that awaited publication.

BILLY

WHEN Billy James, William's second son, had been told in his boyhood that his uncle was a famous writer, he remarked a trifle enviously, "I suppose there's nothing that Uncle Henry can't spell." Now eighteen, an enthusiastic oarsman and a fine tennis player, he was being sent abroad to spend a year on the Continent. His turn in the family hierarchy had come for exposure to his uncle. Henry James had last seen him when he was eight. He was now a tall slender youth, well turned out by his tailor, and wearing a small military moustache. He had an elegant upright carriage and manner, and a certain hesitancy of speech; he possessed a well-modulated voice and an intensity and sincerity that endeared him promptly to James. Billy was distinctly unlike his elder brother Harry, who had visited Lamb House four years before and spent his time writing a diary wondering what his uncle thought of him. The younger nephew was interested in what went on around him; he began by wanting to draw things—he seemed to have his father's early addiction to sketching although he was at the moment not destined for art—and the novelist reported to Cambridge, "we have had the happy inspiration of his taking lessons in water colours from a modest but skilful little artist who is living here—so that he may simply learn how to use colour." Perhaps this "inspiration" contributed to Billy's decision later to abandon medical studies and go to Julien's in Paris to study painting.

Billy was unlike his elder brother in many respects. Harry was deeply serious, unsmiling, thoughtful; he had the cognitive and intellectual qualities of his father, but not his easy spontaneity. Harry also had none of the liveliness of the Jameses, and little of their "Irishness." The novelist was fond of him and in later years greatly valued his help in practical matters, particularly relating to his financial affairs. But it would be Billy and Peggy who would have the largest share of their uncle's affection. William's youngest son, Alex, arrived much later on the scene.

Billy came early in October 1902. He was on his way to Geneva and planned to spend a fortnight in Lamb House and then a few days in Paris visiting the Louvre. "I congratulate you all on him," Henry James wrote to Billy's elder brother, "so beautiful he is, and so attaching; so formed to charm and interest and, as it were, repay. I *knew* well enough that I should take satisfaction in him, but I take . . . still more than I expected." Billy little dreamed that the voice he heard in the mornings in the Garden Room, during his brief stay, was dictating what were to be two celebrated tales, "The Birthplace" and "The Beast in the Jungle." His vision was of a short, rotund man, with a quick sensibility and a boundless capacity for affection. The lesson he carried away from his elderly uncle was the memory of hearing him say "three things in human life, are important. The first is to be kind. The second is to be kind. And the third is to be kind." He always remembered the days of his first stay at Lamb House, spent on the bicycle, with long walks in between, and with the central drama revolving around the arrival of his Emmet cousins, Bay and Leslie, whom he found "devastatingly" beautiful and who made a great fuss over their handsome cousin. He remembered, too, how the age of the motor-car came to Lamb House — the Rudyard Kiplings driving up in their new £2000 machine, an object of curiosity and wonder. There had been a lively lunch in which Rudyard was talkative, anecdotal, poetic. Kipling greatly liked Billy, as his subsequent letters to Henry James showed. Then, when they got into the car to return to Burwash, twenty miles away, where the Kiplings had just bought a fine house, the vehicle "in the manner of its kind" wouldn't start. Rudyard grew increasingly angry over its behaviour. He had baptized it Amelia. It behaved as he believed all women behaved. The Kiplings ended up going home by train. There followed a long letter from the author of *The Jungle Book* describing the struggle of the successive "engineers" to get Amelia started. "It's not as easy as it looks, a sick motor," Kipling wrote to James. The factory finally sent another "engineer" from Birmingham who "vowed that the accident which had befallen her was unique in all mechanics and motoring." Kipling ended by inviting the novelist and his nephew to lunch, urging them to take the train which "tho' slow is safe" and promising Amelia would take them home.

Billy left for the Continent, but he was not a letter-writer, and his uncle became worried. He had visions of the innocent nephew "swindled or bamboozled in Paris," or even "robbed and murdered in your night train in Geneva." His violent fantasies caused him to send an uneasy wire to Geneva. All was well though the doting uncle wondered "when you *did* mean to write!" And he expressed pleasure that his nephew was "under a human roof, and at a nourishing board and in a coherent curriculum." Remembering his own days in Geneva, Henry James added he had found the city attractive "all except the Slavonic females, who I should think *would* be a great thorn in the flesh." Pleasant people turned up at Swiss pensions, he added, and "so long as you don't meet your 'fate' in yours, I hope you may be beguiled." Henry was being quite maternal. To William James the novelist wrote that he had "rejoiced" in Billy, and found him "an ornament to my life." Their harmony had been "without a cloud." At a later stage he expressed the belief that Billy's "personal charm" smoothed his path through life; it invited "general good-will."

Billy stayed briefly at Geneva and then spent the winter at Marburg, where he attended classes at the university. In emulation of his father he returned to study medicine in Cambridge, after another stay at Lamb House. Ultimately he would be back in Europe studying art. In the coming years uncle and favourite nephew would see each other on many occasions; and Henry would watch and encourage his work. As he had advised Bay Emmet to "beware of finding yourself not able to feel your subjects at your ease and with true inwardness," so he one day gave Billy advice that remained fixed in the young man's memory for the rest of his life. What he recalled was his uncle standing behind him as he was struggling with a canvas. After a long period of silent watching, the voice slowly and with characteristic deliberation said: "Bill, remember that no captain ever makes port with all the cargo with which he set sail." A long pause. "And Bill—remember—there is always another voyage."

IN THE WORKSHOP

THERE were eight writing tables or secretary-desks in Lamb House. Henry James could write comfortably in almost every room, although he worked largely in his upstairs Green Room during the winters and in the detached Garden House as soon as the warm weather permitted. Visitors used to hear him dictating from 10 a.m. until 1.45. What they did not know were the hours spent in revising what had been dictated, the close attention he gave to proofs, the number of notes he made, the amount of reading he did, and the time he devoted to letters, which he preferred writing in longhand since he deemed many of them too personal to share with his typist. Also he did not want to waste time on correspondence during Miss Weld's working hours. As he grew older and wrote less—in the years to come— he began to dictate the long letters of his late years as if he were writing epistolary fiction.

Life in Lamb House had a certain military regularity. At eight every morning Burgess mounted the stairs to the Master's bedroom, and brought him his hot water for shaving. There followed the hot bath, the meditated choice of what to wear and finally the descent of the sartorially neat and often bright-cravated novelist, with an equally colourful waistcoat, into the dining-room. The typical breakfast consisted of cereal with cream, followed by three shirred eggs. It was always served at 9 a.m. and while James slowly ate this repast he issued his instructions and complimented the housekeeper on her wise economies. At 10 a.m. Miss Weld arrived and work began. Visitors knew they could never see the Master before lunch. The voice dictated rhythmically—with long pauses—in the workshop. They could hear James pacing forward and backward, he paced constantly with the quality of a restless animal, and, it seemed, in rhythm with the familiar response of the typewriter. When various friends suggested that dictation affected his style—which to a degree it did—he was vehement in his denial. "Don't undermine me by general remarks," he replied to one friend who asked whether the oral method had not determined the form of *The Wings of the Dove.* "The value of that process for me is in its help to do over and over, for which it is extremely adapted, and which is the only way I can do at all. It soon enough becomes *intellectually*, absolutely identical with the act of writing—or has become so, after five years now, with me; so that the difference is only material and illusory—only the difference, that is, that I walk up and down; which is so much to the good."

This was precisely the difference. In the old days he had been unable to "do over and over." His novels of the middle period had all been written with little revision and dispatched in longhand to the magazines. There had been revision in proof, and from magazine to book. Now he revised constantly; and while revising, new metaphors, large elaborate similes, found themselves inserted into the text. Miss Weld repeatedly retyped the manuscript—James could as it were read proof on his work continually, from day to day. The late style is a "revised" style, a building of the prose page by a process of accretion. In this process certain mannerisms crept in—attempts to get away from old familiar forms of expression: displacement and splitting of verbs, the emergence of unexpected adverbs, the removal of the given phrase from that part of the sentence where the reader expected to find it, into another part. And then James's prose was now spoken prose. Writing had become a matter of controlled speech, of constant qualification and emendation.

Dictation also enabled James, as never before, to work at several things at once. He had tended, when he wrote in longhand, to push ahead with a given piece of work. The brief but illuminating record kept by Miss Weld of her work-days shows us how James would start a story one day, drop it for other work the next, go on with still another story, return to the first, start still another: there were always now several hares running at once. The physical effort of penmanship would have slowed James down as he grew older; the method of dictation enabled him to be as productive as ever—indeed more productive—with the aid of his active, fertile crowded imagination. An illustration of simultaneity of work on various stories occurs immediately after the completion of *The Wings of the Dove* during the summer of 1902. While James is reading the final proofs he is already assembling a collection of tales published in the magazines at the turn of the century to make up a book called *The Better Sort*. He discovers the volume will not be of proper length. Two or three more stories are needed. On 1 July 1902 he begins a story titled provisionally "John Marcher," the tale destined to be known as "The Beast in the Jungle." The start apparently was made on that day; there is then no further reference to it for three months, to be exact not until 12 October. In the interval James has been working on three other stories. They consisted of a story first called "Maud Blandy" later the very long tale of "The Papers;" the story called "The Birthplace," and a tale known in Miss Weld's record only as "The Beautiful Child" never completed. This may have been a development of a fragment among James's papers written in longhand, a tale based on an anecdote of Bourget's, of two parents who ask a painter to paint a portrait of their nonexistent child. The following will suggest how James moved between one tale and another, between his various tasks and the usual interruptions of his gregarious social life:

Beast	Papers	Birthplace	Child
1 July	24 July	14 August	11 July
12 October	1 August	30 September	22 July
16 October	11 August	10 October	
	11 October		
	16 October		
	5 November		
	13 November		

Miss Weld's entries say very clearly when each tale was completed —"The Birthplace" on 10 October, "The Beast in the Jungle" 16 October, "The Papers" 13 November. This would suggest that the tale of John Marcher, a remarkably unified tonal picture and perhaps James's finest story, was written in three sessions, due allowance made for manual revisions. There were days when

Miss Weld was allowed to idle: an entry of 8 August 1902 tells us "no work, Mr James revising." There were other days when the typist was pressed into overtime: thus in 1903 the record shows that to meet a deadline for an article, Miss Weld worked "nine hours with Mr James on D'Annunzio to finish."

During the summer of 1902 James finally disposed of the lease of his flat at De Vere Gardens. It had been his home for more than ten years, from 1886 until 1898. The flat had been let for the past three and a half years; it still had in it many fine pieces of furniture and many of James's books. The novelist turned over some of the furniture to the William Jameses and it was shipped to America; other pieces found their place in Lamb House, and some time was consumed in finding a place for the hundreds of books that arrived. Three entries made by Miss Weld give the elements of the story:

> Saturday, July 19—Furniture arrives. Assist in stowage and lunch at Lamb House.
> Sunday, July 20—Books!
> Monday, July 21—Hanging of pictures. Lunch and tea at Lamb House.
> Tuesday, July 22—Work again, continue "The Beautiful Child."

In between work on these tales, Henry James was sorting out the papers of William Wetmore Story and Miss Weld typed such letters as he would use in the long-postponed memoir. This was the next large piece of work he intended to do, and an entry of 22 September records that she had finished copying the letters "so really begin W.W. Story."

Within his workshop Henry James found himself studying closely the working methods, the large creative designs, of his predecessors. During the opening years of the new century the Master began his revaluation of the writers who had meant most to him, those who, as he put it, have "done something for us, become part of the answer to our curiosity." Circumstances aiding, he was led to write the series of papers on George Sand, and large explanatory essays on Balzac, Flaubert, Zola. He had dealt with them in the past, often in piece-meal fashion, either by reviewing them or discussing various editions of their works. But now he found himself looking at their total achievement. Criticism had always been, for Henry James, an extension of his creative act: one always felt, in what he wrote of other novelists—and he rarely discussed poets—that he was asking himself "What are they trying to do? What has been their intention?" and this was a surfacing of a buried question, "Is there anything I can find out, for the work I have to do?" His essay of 1902 on Balzac begins with his asking himself what he had learned from the French master: and the answer would be given in his later lecture "The Lesson of Balzac." He had read him in his youth. Now, re-reading him on the threshold of his old age, he recognized that Balzac had passed long ago into the very texture of his life. "Endless are the uses of great persons and great things," he told himself, and what he discerned, in each of these large "cases" was the manner in which the ultimate literary monument had been erected.

At sixty James could well ask himself—looking back at all the books he had written, and in the very midst of this period of extraordinary fertility—where he stood in the history of the novel? He had asked himself this question at the beginning of his play-writing. He had sought always to win success, and had always remained an ambiguous figure in the market-place. What future did he have? What would be the fate of his "reputation?" Thus he embraced the new opportunities given him by Edmund Gosse to preface a Balzac novel and a new edition of *Madame Bovary*. He had watched the growth of this classic from the day when, as a boy in Paris in 1856, he had read the first instalments in the *Revue de Paris*. He had also watched, since the death of Balzac in 1850, the slow growth of a formidable reputation, the way in which the *Comédie Humaine* had established itself in the mind of Europe—and the world. And he remembered Zola, just beginning his fame, and their talks during Flaubert's Sunday afternoons in 1876.

In his essay on Balzac we find James writing of that novelist's "mass and weight," his "scheme and scope." From this he is led to "the question of what makes the artist on a great scale." This was what interested Henry James above everything: what had made James an artist—perhaps on the grand scale? Balzac's imagination had encompassed all his experience. He had created with enormous fertility. He had in his "active intention" tried to read "the universe, as hard and as loud as he could, *into* France of his time." He had been "a beast with a hundred claws," hugging his material close to him with enormous energy. "He is the only member of his order really monumental, the sturdiest seated mass that rises in our path," wrote Henry James and he added "we are never so curious about successes as about interesting failures . . . the scale on which, in its own quarter of his genius, success worked itself out for him." James might have been trying to work this out for himself. So in his essay on Flaubert, also of 1902, he discusses, in a final survey, the uneven work of that master to the end of discovering how he "built himself into literature." Flaubert was the opposite of Balzac. He did not have abundance in him. He was not on the "monumental" scale. But then one could hardly have wanted, James implied, more books of the type of *Madame Bovary* or *Salammbo*. "When the production of a great artist who has lived a length of years has been small," wrote James, ". . . the case is doubtless predetermined by the particular kind of great artist the writer happens to be." George Sand, James wrote, had had great abundance, but she had produced much less *literature* than Flaubert. "She had undoubtedly herself the benefit of her facility, but are we not left wondering to what extent *we* have it?" The omniscient Balzac had created a world. Flaubert had created a single classic. Zola, in his particular and grosser way, had established a "massive identity." And George Sand, in her fluency, her liquid qualities, had been "a supreme case of the successful practice of life itself."

Thus in the midst of his great fertile years, when he summoned to his work the greatest powers of his maturity, James interrogated the literary reputations of the great novelists of France, in the interest of his own literary reputation. He was like a Napoleon of literature surveying conquered territories. His exploration would lead him to shore up, against the ravages of posterity, a great part of his *œuvre*—in the New York Edition, the "definitive edition" he had planned for years. The time was now almost ripe for the creation of this monument.

In his exploration of what made the artist "on the grand scale" the Master was led to the question of biography. What distinctions were to be made between the man and the artist? He was about to write a biographical memoir, the only one he had ever undertaken; and in his stories there had for a long time been an increasing interrogation of the question of the private life of art and the public life of the work issuing from that art. At this moment, however, on the evidence of his stories, a more fundamental question seemed to trouble James. He had never been a great success on the scale of Kipling—or of Rostand. He had a small general reputation even if a formidable authority among other novelists. He knew too well how artists create during all their lives only to go down, in death, into oblivion. He had, very early in his career, written in "The Madonna of the Future" the record of the impotent artist, who wishes for fame and can only struggle helplessly in front of his canvas. He had had his own show of fame; he had certainly never been impotent. But what if he had lived all his life for his great moment, for that *gloire* in which he believed—and what if the moment in the decades of the future, in the annals of literary history and of the novel, would never come? Out of this troubled emotion, the "ferocious ambition" to which he had early testified, he now fashioned two tales, one tragic and mysterious, the other comic and ironic. Both were parables of the artist-life. "The Beast in the Jungle" was about a man who thinks himself destined for a role "rare and strange," and who ends up being someone to whom nothing happens—save his having had a negative life. "The Birthplace," satirizing the rituals of Stratford-on-Avon, has in it the corollary to this: it is the story of "the human character the most magnificently endowed, in all time, with the sense of the life of man, and with the apparatus for recording it." The man is almost invisible; yet he is luminous in his work. In this way, after a lifetime devoted to novelists of his time, James came to the question of the supreme poet and dramatist; he came to William Shakespeare.

THE IMPENETRABLE SPHINX

"THE Beast in the Jungle" as we have seen was begun in July of 1902 but seems to have been written largely in two sessions that autumn, during the first days of Billy James's stay in Lamb House. Miss Weld's diary tells us, "October 12, return to John Marcher or The Beast in the Jungle." The next day she notes that Kipling lunched at Lamb House. This was the day that Amelia broke down. Three days later "Finish the Beast in the Jungle. Back to The Papers."

Presence of the author of *The Jungle Book* in Lamb House at the moment of the writing of "The Beast in the Jungle" was a coincidence. However, James had mentioned Kipling when he was writing, earlier, about Rostand; he had evoked him as a figure who, like the French dramatist, had had a phenomenal public success. Henry James himself had had, in the English-speaking world, what might be termed a private success, a *succès d'estime*. In "The Beast in the Jungle" we can discover a remarkable coalescence of this theme with themes which the novelist had been unable to resolve in the just-completed *Wings of the Dove*—the question of men who in this world believe themselves reserved for a special destiny only to discover that their name is writ in water. Or the one who believes—like Keats—that he is condemned to oblivion—yet in his posthumous life becomes a hero of culture and civilization. Corollary to this, James used the theme of egotism: the man so absorbed in his ultimate destiny, that he fails to live the life given him; worse still, he fails to discover the meaning of love. The eerie passion of "The Beast in the Jungle" resides in a consummate threading of these themes into a parable in which James finally casts the woman in the story in the role of the eternal keeper of man's riddles—casts her and visions her, as a Sphinx.

It was as if, in his own life, after wandering about the world seeking the answer to the mysteries of his life—as the frantic narrator had done in *The Sacred Fount* or the little critic in "The Figure in the Carpet"—he at last had decided to confront, in her awesome majesty, the mythic figure, Theban or Egyptian, she who was half lion, half woman, guardian of the needed answers. In all his work there is no tale written with greater investment of personal emotion. The unlived life of so many of his heroes here is embodied in John Marcher, the great Anonymous Man, who in thinking of his fate blinds himself to his anonymity.

There may be a link between this majestic tale and a little story of Maupassant's called "Promenade," which James marked when he read it in the 1880's. It is a tale of a drudge-clerk in Paris who on a spring evening goes out to dinner and pleasantly content, strolls into the *Bois* only to be overcome suddenly by the emptiness of his life. "He thought of the life he had led, so different from the lives of others, this life so sombre, so dull, so flat, so empty. Some people simply have no luck. And suddenly as if a thick veil was being rent, he saw the infinite misery, the monotonous misery of his existence: past misery, present misery, future misery; recent days, no different from earlier days, nothing lying ahead, nothing behind, nothing around him, nothing in his heart, nothing anywhere." The story ends with the police finding the man's body. He has hanged himself.

I

"The Beast in the Jungle," sustained in its mood and in its evocative poetry, is a tale of melancholy and loneliness. The passage of an entire lifetime is told in six neatly balanced sections. Thirty pages encompass years of futility. John Marcher feels "lost in the crowd" at the start of the tale; and he finds this anonymity unbearable. In a house called Weatherend, filled with art objects out of the centuries, he meets a woman named May Bartram. They have met before—ten years earlier, at Naples; and one day at Sorrento (she reminds Marcher), on a sudden impulse, he had confided to her his secret: he believed himself reserved for an unusual experience. What it is to be, or its strangeness, he does not know. The prophesied occurrence is imaged as a beast tracking him in the jungle, waiting for its moment to spring. He is not sure whether the climax will be beautiful or horrible. He is certain that it will come.

Marcher and May are thirty-five and thirty when they renew their acquaintance at Weatherend. May says she believes in Marcher's haunted vision and is ready to participate in his life's vigil. He has the thought that "a man of feeling didn't cause himself to be accompanied by a lady on a tiger hunt;" he therefore will not marry her, but he nevertheless allows her to share in his fantasy—in which he is not at all sure whether he is hunter or hunted. Their encounter occurs on an October afternoon, when the sky is sombre and flushed with red; and in the next two sections of the story Marcher and May keep company—and the years pass. He goes with her to art galleries; he takes her to the opera. He is devoted to her as Henry James had been to Miss Woolson, in the first days of their friendship when they had been tourists in Florence during a certain April and May in the early 1880's and had sought each other out almost daily. The first of the two crucial episodes in the story is set in April. Half a lifetime has passed; Marcher now is aware that May is ill; and for the first time he begins to recognize that they have both grown old waiting for the beast to spring. In this climactic section we are told of the "long fresh light of waning April days which affects us often with sadness sharper than the greyest hours of autumn." May stands before a fireless hearth. She wears a green scarf, but like her life it is faded. As in the story "The Aspern Papers," in which Juliana sheds her green eyeshade, and the narrator sees for the first time the bright intensity of her eyes, so here Marcher looks once more into May's eyes and finds them "as beautiful as they had been in youth, only beautiful with a strange cold light—a light that somehow was a part of the effect, if it wasn't rather a part of the cause, of the pale hard sweetness of the season and the hour." At this moment before the cold hearth and the Dresden china on the mantelpiece, and with a sense of "the odd irregular rhythm of their intensities and avoidances," John Marcher images her as "a serene and exquisite but impenetrable sphinx, whose head, or indeed all whose person, might have been powdered with silver."

We are at last face to face with the supreme keeper of the Riddle, the possessor of "the figure in the carpet."

May Bartram keeps the riddle of John Marcher's life. She tells him that the beast has sprung, that his fate—or doom—has already occurred. "You were to suffer your fate," she says. "That was not necessarily to know." It is an agony for Marcher. He has been deprived of the one anchor to which he has clung all his life. Suddenly his jungle is empty and "poor Marcher waded through his beaten grass, where no life stirred, where no breath sounded, where no evil eye seemed to gleam from a possible lair, very much as if vaguely looking for the Beast, and still more as if acutely missing it."

At this moment, Marcher joins another image to that of the Sphinx. He sees May, in her whiteness of age, as a lily under a bell of glass, the green of her scarf forming the leaves. Thus John Marcher's dream of woman mingles with the eternal dream of Henry James; she is sphinx, matron, virgin, beast, all in one—artificial and safely preserved under glass, like an artefact. The novelist had long ago imaged the virginal Minny Temple, when he mourned her death, as shut within the "crystal walls of the past."

"You've had your experience," Marcher desolately says to May—"you leave me to my fate." May can do nothing else. They have a final interview, almost as if James, avoiding the last confrontation between Milly and Densher in his just-completed novel, still had to get the scene out of his system. We are given the last confrontation between Marcher and May, and May's last words come to him as "the true voice of the law; so on her lips would the law itself sound." The Sphinx has spoken. He never sees her again. She has left him with the unsolved riddle. He must live with it for the rest of his life, as James lived with the unsolved riddle of Fenimore's death. As the grave closes over her he stands looking at the gravestone, "beating his forehead against the fact of the secret" kept by the name and date, "drawing his breath, while he waited, as if some sense would, in pity of him, rise from the stones. He kneeled on the stones, however in vain; they kept what they concealed; and if the face of the tomb did become a face for him it was because her two names became a pair of eyes that didn't know him."

II

In "The Figure in the Carpet" everyone who knew the secret died and the secret remained untold; in "The Friends of the Friends" the woman who could tell about the ghost remains silent in death; death turns the key on something the jealous narrator is concerned to know. The time had come when James could no longer stand such eternal frustration; and his imagination gives John Marcher a final scene, one of the most intense and dramatic he ever wrote in any of his tales. It occurs at the cemetery. In the interval between his visits to this cemetery Marcher has travelled to the East, to Asia, India, to Egypt—to the lands of the Sphinx. But the riddles of history offer him nothing that doesn't seem "common" compared with the dream he has nourished of being one of the elect of this world. Turning from the great temples and sepulchres he comes back to his private sepulchre, now both an altar and a grave. In a sense James here revisits the tale he wrote immediately after Miss Woolson's death, which he called "The Altar of the Dead." In that tale a woman had deprived a man of his altar—and of the secret of his life. Now, face to face with May Bartram's tomb, Marcher happens to notice a mourner at another grave. For one moment he suddenly allows himself to see not his own grief, but the grief of another, an "image of scarred passion." Insight has come at last. He witnesses the grief of love. Now he realizes what the Sphinx had wanted him to see on that April day beside her cold hearth, when he had turned her into an artificial flower and put her under glass. "No passion had ever touched him, for this was what passion meant . . . He had seen *outside* of his life, not learned it within." The message is there for him to read in his memories of the chill room, with its atmosphere of death. The expected climax in Marcher's life is an anti-climax. The event is a non-event. He had been singled out—such might be his consolation—as someone to whom "nothing on earth was to have happened." He had not allowed himself to "live" or to love. He had circled perpetually in his little private jungle—a hunter hunted—and haunted—stalked by the beast of his own blindness. He had not recognized love when it had been offered to him. The final passage in James's story rises to great heights of passion, of tenderness, of guilt, of self-accusation. It is as if Marcher's revelation were his own.

The escape would have been to love her; then, *then* he would have lived. *She* had lived—who could say now with what passion?—since she had loved him for himself; whereas he had never thought of her (ah, how it hugely glared at him!) but in the chill of his egotism and the light of her use. Her spoken words came back to him—the chain stretched and stretched. The Beast had lurked indeed, and the Beast, at its hour, had sprung; it had sprung in that twilight of the cold April, when pale, ill, wasted, but all beautiful, and perhaps even then recoverable, she had risen from her chair to stand before him and let him imaginably guess. It had sprung as he didn't guess; it had sprung as she hopelessly turned from him, and the mark, by the time he left her, had fallen where it *was* to fall. He had justified his fear and achieved his fate; he had failed, with the last exactitude, of all he was to fail of; and a moan now rose to his lips as he remembered she had prayed he mightn't know.

In the final sentences the passionate words James was setting down seemed to carry with them the deepest message of his own egotism, the blindness he had ironically written into "The Aspern Papers" which he now saw with eyes unsealed, as if it were some vast hallucination, like his father's "vastation" long ago at Windsor, when the elder Henry James had suddenly felt a figure of evil squatting invisible in the room beside him:

This horror of waking—*this* was knowledge, knowledge under the breath of which the very tears in his eyes seemed to freeze. Through them, none the less, he tried to fix it and hold it; he kept it there before him so that he might feel the pain. That at least, belated and bitter, had something of the taste of life. But the bitterness suddenly sickened him, and it was as if, horribly, he saw, in the truth, in the cruelty of his image, what had been appointed and done. He saw the Jungle of his life and saw the lurking Beast; then, while he looked, perceived it, as by a stir of the air, rise, huge and hideous, for the leap that was to settle him. His eyes darkened—it was close; and instinctively turning, in his hallucination, to avoid it, he flung himself, face down, on the tomb.

These were the last words of the tale. In this moment of perception Henry James was, it would seem, revisiting the grave in the Protestant cemetery in Rome, near the grave of Keats, where Constance Fenimore Woolson's name and her dates were simply carved on the stone embedded in violets. Long ago James had imaged the frosty Winterbourne, a predecessor of John Marcher, standing on this spot unable to answer the riddle of Daisy Miller: the continuity of his imagination may be seen in Winterbourne and Marcher—two frosty names. Marcher at last had had his vision. He had learned the meaning of egotism. What he had lost would have made him mortal, and to be mortal—that is to live one's life—was the real escape from anonymity.

And so, into this strange and haunted story, James translated universal symbols of the riddle of man's life, his struggle against annihilation and anonymity, his belief that love alone makes existence possible and preserves man from the dark abyss. In its use of myth, its mood of desolation, its portrait of alienated man, it is perhaps James's most "modern" tale.

THE REAL RIGHT THING

"THE Beast in the Jungle" had provided a catharsis for Henry James: it was a moment of vision and of insight such as his brother, William, described in his book on *The Varieties of Religious Experience*. The novelist, we know, was reading this book when he wrote the tale. He was recognizing anew—and more intensely than ever—the ways in which people "use" one another, and this may have helped lighten some of his old feelings of guilt which had coloured the ending of *The Wings of the Dove*. Miss Woolson had killed herself in Venice for reasons of her own. Her death had been *her* decision and no one else's. It had been *her* fate and *her* mystery; and it would remain a mystery. In "The Beast in the Jungle" James seems to have reached a moment when he could say to himself that his solution was to occupy himself with his own mysteries, to light up the gloom in his own soul. He had behaved with Miss Woolson like one of his vampire-people in *The Sacred Fount*—and like John Marcher with May Bartram. His recognition that he was capable of love and was vulnerable, enabled him to revisit his past and ease his soul.

His perceptive friend in Paris, Morton Fullerton, reading the story of "the Beast" with some attention questioned James's underlining of the emotion in the final section of the story. The novelist admitted he had been over-insistent, "as of the school-slate and the column of figures." And yet "I did it, consciously, anxiously, for the help of the unutterable reader at large, who would have been incapable, down to his boots, of your discrimination." But James rarely made concessions to the reader. He had been over-insistent because it was his need; he was finding out the riddle of the "impenetrable Sphinx." Long ago he had reminded his friend Grace Norton that each life was a special problem "which is not yours but another's," and he had urged her to content herself with "the terrible algebra" of her own. He was well on the way to working out some of his own terrible algebra. *The Wings of the Dove* and the tale of John Marcher had provided insights; the "deep well of unconscious cerebration" had sent up a series of signs and symbols. The answers seemed simple enough —yet he had had to wait until he was ready to understand them. Strether's "live all you can" had been answered by Milly's fate; one really hadn't lived until one had learned to love. The story of Marcher and May implied that one could love only when one ceased to love oneself. James had treated Miss Woolson as if she had been his Aunt Kate. And he had expended his love for years on ethereal heroines of the mind. Now, on the edge of sixty, he had had a profound moment of revelation. It freed him for the things he had to do. First among these was the great sustaining question of his life's work. Scattered in the magazines, arrayed on the bookshelves, were the works he had written in his early chamber in Cambridge, in dim lodgings in Bolton Street, in a hundred hotels on the Continent, amid the affluence of De Vere Gardens—some with so much passion of art and intensity of intellectual effort—his whole life, all the adventures of his soul, were in these works. Was he to leave these to the vulgarizing multitude, to the newspaper critics who were interested in chatter not in art, to the biographers who might exploit him not for what he had written but for the irrelevant "facts" of his daily life? He had said this in his little tale of "Sir Dominick Ferrand," about a bundle of letters found in an old desk and the newspaper that wanted to publish them; in "The Aspern Papers" and its curious history of the "publishing scoundrel;" in "John Delavoy," in which the artist was "the most unadvertised, unreported, uninterviewed, unphotographed, uncriticized of all originals. Was he not the man of the time about whose private life we delightfully knew least?" The artist was what he did—he was nothing else. And there was the great question "what makes the artist on the great scale?" He had written these words lately in discussing Balzac. He felt that he had been such an artist—on the grand scale, astride two continents, writing out personal histories, exploring in the Balzacian sense, the underside of the human tapestry. The time had come for him to take stock: it was time to pay attention to his own legend. A writer on the grand scale had to shore up all that was worth preserving out of his years of endeavour. No one else could do it for him. He thought, as the French did, of his personal *gloire*—had he not always really thought of it, in those early days when he had confessed to his mother that he had a "ferocious ambition?" The great men of the earth lived by the legend they left behind them; their tangible works were their monument. Time had spilled itself out for Henry James: the spinning years had brought him to the moment when he could reflect on the lessons of literature—the example of Balzac, the mystery of Shakespeare—and make the decisions that would lengthen his shadow beyond the grave. He had always said that an artist should not leave his personal papers to accident. In the coming time he would act on this. He burned his manuscripts and hundreds, thousands, of letters received from the great men he had known and the multitude of persons who had come into his orbit. What he could not destroy were the letters he had written to others; and it does not seem to have occurred to him that his letters—so full were they of style, individuality, eccentricity—had been saved by everyone.

Two years before his death he would take another step. He issued explicit instructions to his literary executor, his nephew Harry, William's oldest son who had inquired about his papers:

My sole wish is to frustrate as utterly as possible the post mortem exploiter—which, I know, is but so imperfectly possible. Still one can do something, and I have long thought of launching, by a provision in my will, a curse no less explicit than Shakespeare's own on any such as try to move my bones. Your question determines me definitely to advert to the matter in my will—that is to declare my utter and absolute abhorrence of any attempted biography or the giving to the world by "the family", or by any person for whom my disapproval has any sanctity, of any part or parts of my private correspondence. One can discredit and dishonour such enterprises even if one can't prevent them, and as you are my sole and exclusive literary heir and executor you will doubtless be able to serve in some degree as a check and a frustrator.

I

The Shakespearian curse, recalled in this letter to his nephew, written as late as 7 April 1914, eight days before James's seventy-first birthday, was implicit in the Shakespearian story "The Birthplace" James wrote while he was writing "The Beast in the Jungle," and also in the brilliant if long-drawn-out prophecy of modern "public relations," a story called "The Papers" also written during the autumn of 1902. The novelist at that moment was embarking on the one biography he ever wrote, the life of William Wetmore Story. His actions could have been predicted from his tales of letter-burning or the story "The Real Right Thing" published in December 1899. It deals with a young biographer who works in his subject's study. Ghostly hands move the papers away from him; they turn the pages of certain books; they seem to warn him to leave privacy alone. In the end the biographer tells the widow—who simply wants to do "the real right thing"—that the right thing is to leave the dead alone. As if to drive the lesson home, the biographer (to whom James gave the symbolic name of Withermore) one day finds the ghost of his subject standing on the threshold of the chamber. Shakespeare's curse had been stated explicitly enough in James's tales.

His discussion of biography is nowhere more brilliantly sustained than in an 1899 essay on George Sand: indeed that essay and "The Real Right Thing" both seem to have been products of his agreeing that year to write the life of Story. It was as if James, about to join the ranks of biographers, wondered whether this was the real right thing for a novelist to be doing. George Sand offered the "special case" enabling him to weigh the problems of an artist's public and private life. She had always lived in public. She had made of her work "the affirmation of an unprecedented intensity of life." Long after she died the revelations had come: her violent "love-life" with Musset, her affair in Venice with Pagello, the endless train of lovers she had taken in bold assertion that a woman had as much right to them as men had to mistresses. If all this seemed to make George Sand a "rueful denuded figure" on the broad highway of life, it raised the deeper question of what was to be done when the figure was encountered. Modesty caused one to avert one's eyes, James supposed, but after all "we have *seen* . . . and mystery has fled with a shriek." This disappearance of mystery was like turning down the incandescent light of genius and substituting the light of common day. The heroic figure of the artist shrank, was diminished, ceased to be the transcendent figure of the imagination; the unearthly voice of great poetry and divine inspiration became the ordinary human voice—the voice of another marcher in the multitude. Reading at this time the life of Robert Louis Stevenson by Graham Balfour, James had had a new glimpse of his beloved Louis, who had vanished into the South Seas like some mysterious bird after its brilliant passage in the western world. His beloved friend had become merely a picturesque figure in literary history. James had high praise for Balfour; but he wrote him with affectionate candour that Stevenson's books were now "jealous and a certain supremacy and mystery (above all) has, as it were, gone from them. The achieved legend and history that has *him* for subject, has made so to speak, light of *their* subjects, of their claim to represent him." The biographer had made Stevenson too "*personally* celebrated." Of course Stevenson himself had been picturesque—and to that extent he was "in some degree the victim of himself." James reminded Balfour he was saying all this "from the literary vision, the vision for which the rarest works pop out of the dusk of the inscrutable, the untracked."

In writing of George Sand, James suggested that perhaps the artist, the subject, should organize the game of biography on his own terms, rather than leave it to the terms of the biographer. "There are secrets for privacy and silence, let them only be cultivated on the part of the hunted creature with even half the method with which the love of sport—or call it the historic sense —is cultivated on the part of the investigator. They have been left too much to the natural, the instinctive man." The thing was indeed to burn papers, keep the secrets, challenge the biographer to dig harder for his facts, demand of him a genuine effort of inquiry and research. It was all too easy to leave him a massive archive which he could draw upon at will. "Then," wrote James, "the cunning of the inquirer, envenomed with resistance, will exceed in subtlety and ferocity anything we today conceive, and the pale forewarned victim, with every track covered, every paper burnt and every letter unanswered, will, in the tower of art, the invulnerable granite, stand, without a sally, the siege of all the years."

II

Shakespeare had withstood the siege of the years; he had survived as invulnerable granite: even generations of actors, raving and ranting, could not spoil him. There had been, to be sure, some of the subtlety and ferocity of which James spoke; critics and biographers had had their say; they continued to build a great library around the First Folio and the Quartos. Yet Shakespeare seemed immune in his great "tower of art"—immune as no other artist in literary history. In "The Birthplace" Henry James wrote still another of his parables—he had written so many—about the life of art. He had always mocked the legends of Stratford-on-Avon. He had spoken of "the lout from Stratford" and had been dressed down by his acerbic friend Rhoda Broughton—"A lout—me divine William a lout! I won't have yer call me divine William, a lout. Me beloved Jamie calling Shakespeare a lout!" But James had not intended condescension or depreciation. He argued that the facts of Stratford did not "square" with the plays of the genius. The facts spoke for a commonplace man; the plays for the greatest genius the world had ever known. This was "the most attaching of literary mysteries." And James wrote to a friend, "take my word for it, as a dabbler in fable and fiction, that the plays and the sonnets were never written but by a Personal Poet, a Poet, and Nothing Else, a Poet, who being Nothing Else, could never be a Bacon." James refused to accept the Baconian theory, or the parochial *bêtise*, as he called it, of the Ciphers. The Baconians would overlook this and claim him as their own.

To Violet Hunt, James reiterated that he was "haunted by the conviction that the divine William is the biggest and most successful fraud ever practised on a patient world . . . I can only express my general sense by saying that I find it *almost* as impossible to conceive that Bacon wrote the plays as to conceive that the man from Stratford, as we know the man from Stratford, did." Miss Hunt compared the genius of a writer like Shakespeare to a passenger on a liner who has a cabin and great reserves of luggage in the hold. The analogy did not satisfy James. The point about genius he replied was that "it gets at its *own* luggage, in the hold perfectly (while common mortality is reduced to a box under the berth) but it doesn't get at the Captain's and the First Mate's, in *their* mysterious retreats." In a word the artist knows only his own consciousness. When James was twenty-two, and writing an early book review, he had formulated this very clearly: "To project yourself into a consciousness of a person essentially your opposite requires the audacity of great genius; and even men of genius are cautious in approaching the problem." In his answer to Miss Hunt, James remarked that "William of Stratford (it seems to me) had no luggage, could have had none, in any part of the ship, corresponding to much of the wardrobe sported in the plays."

All of Henry James's work shows that he had been saturated with Shakespeare from his earliest days. He had known him as a boy in Lamb's retelling of the plays; he had seen Shakespeare acted in many forms — not only the Shakespeare of old New York theatres, but the Shakespeare of Dickensian London, and the Shakespeare of the Lyceum, the heavily costumed creatures of Henry Irving. He had written about these productions, often quite sharply and he had made his pilgrimage long ago — in the days when he had been a "passionate pilgrim" — to Warwickshire, to the Shakespeare country. As early as 1872 he had remarked on "the excess of nutritive suggestion" in the land — it savoured of the larder and the manger — and it helped "enliven my own vague conception of Shakespeare's temperament, with which I find it no great shock to be obliged to associate ideas of mutton and beef." The Warwickshire pastures were ovine and bovine — that is in the service of human needs — as was "the underlying morality of the poet."

He had revisited and written again of Warwickshire and Stratford five years later, in 1877, on the eve of "Daisy Miller." The densely grassed meadows and parks were perhaps not as prettily trimmed in Shakespeare's day; yet this had been the Bard's "green picture of the world." Even then, at Stratford, he found a "torment" in Shakespeare's "unguessed riddle." If it was "the richest corner of England," it was also the most mysterious.

James expanded his view of "the lout," or as he put it with greater gentleness in writing, "the transmuted young rustic," on only two occasions. The first was in the form of "The Birthplace," published in *The Better Sort* of 1903; the second was in a preface to *The Tempest* of 1907 written for an edition of Shakespeare edited by the Bard's biographer, Sir Sidney Lee. James had met Lee during visits to Sir George Otto Trevelyan, the historian, at Welcombe, near Stratford, where we find him writing "it's lovely here—and awfully Shakespearian—every step seems somehow, on William's grave and every word a quotation." He knew the grave well; he admired the spire and chancel of the church in which the Bard was buried; and he knew by heart the cryptic doggerel he invoked bespeaking the curse on anyone who would disturb Shakespeare's bones. Long ago, when he had spent a Christmas with Fanny Kemble, at Stratford, they had gone to the service in this church—Fanny Kemble, whom James in his boyhood had heard in her readings of Shakespeare and whose talk was so saturated with the language of the plays that she made the Bard "the air she lived in." Hawthorne had visited the Birthplace and described it in a touching essay. He had felt, he said, "not the slightest emotion while viewing it, nor any quickening of the imagination." For "the Shakespeare whom I met there took various guises, but had not his laurel on." And one suspects that Henry James, knowing this essay, must have very early accepted Hawthorne's view, so close was it to his own—that "it is for the high interests of the world not to insist upon finding out that its greatest men are . . . very much the same kind of men as the rest of us, and often a little worse." Hawthorne also said that "when Shakespeare invoked a curse on the man who should stir his bones, he perhaps meant the larger share of it for him or them who should pry into his perishing earthliness, the defects or even the merits of the character that he wore in Stratford, when he had left mankind so much to muse upon that which was imperishable and divine." In Henry James this view was filled with the ambivalence he always showed when faced with the "facts" of biography. The artist in him was curious about the life of art: if an artist was careless enough to leave his papers and they were not destroyed the world could hardly ignore them. Moreover, one supposes, James believed that it was proper for artists to write about artists. It was the public, and the penny-catching journalists, who never understood.

III

James's little-known preface to *The Tempest* tells us, in many subtle ways, and with all the *finesse* of his late prose, that he could under no circumstances swallow the legend that Shakespeare wrote *The Tempest* and then gave up writing. This was not the way of a genius with so much abundance in him. *How*, James asked, "did the faculty so radiant here contrive, in such perfection, the arrest of its divine flight? By what inscrutable process was the extinguisher applied and, when once applied, kept in its place to the end? What became of the checked torrent, as a latent, bewildered presence *and* energy, in the life across which the dam was constructed?" Recorded circumstances were of course dim and sparse. They indicated at any rate, James wryly remarked, "that our hero may have died—since he did so soon—of his unnatural effort." Shakespeare, the man, did not exist. What existed was simply the Artist—"the monster and magician of a thousand masks . . . so generalized, so consummate and typical, so frankly amused with himself, that is with his art, with his power, with his theme, that it is as if he came to meet us more than his usual half-way," gave us the illusion of "meeting and touching the man." But the man was "locked up and imprisoned in the artist." In an exquisite passage of summary James elaborated what he had meant in his private letter about the Personal Poet:

The subjects of the Comedies are, without exception, old wives' tales— which we are not too insufferably aware of only because the iridescent veil so perverts their proportions. The subjects of the Histories are no subjects at all; each is but a row of pegs for the hanging of the cloth or gold that is to muffle them. Such a thing as *The Merchant of Venice* declines for very shame, to be reduced to its elements of witless "story;" such things as the two Parts of *Henry the Fourth* form no more than a straight convenient channel for the procession of evoked images that is to pour through it like a torrent. Each of these productions is none the less of incomparable splendour; by which splendour we are bewildered till we see how it comes. Then we see that every inch of it is personal tone, or in other words brooding expression raised to the highest energy.

If energy were pushed far enough—"far enough if you can!"—then, said Henry James, what you had was Character.

Tone, energy, character—the chemistry of Shakespeare which Henry James described, as he described that of Balzac—showed his belief that artists live not in the data of their lives but in the ways in which they express themselves. They were not—Shakespeare was not—a sensitive harp set once for all in a window to catch the air: he had descended into the street in quest of every possible experience and adventure. And he was to be grasped as a questing spirit, not as a static harp—"the genius is part of the mind, the mind a part of behaviour, so that, for the attitude of inquiry, without which appreciation means nothing, where does one of these provinces end and the other begin? We may take the genius first or the behaviour first, but we inevitably proceed from the one to the other. James was prepared to accept the art of biography only if it became "a quest of imaginative experience." In such circumstances it could be "one of the greatest observed adventures of mankind."

IV

This was Henry James's prophecy of the criticism of the future, and of the future of biography. His tale of "The Birthplace" is of a piece with all the stories he had written in which he scoffed at newspaper-made fame, and placed himself wholly on the side of the imagination. The tale does not mention Shakespeare; nor does it mention Stratford. But the birthplace of which it speaks is "the Mecca of the English-speaking race." The story follows closely the original idea given James in May 1901 during one of his visits to Welcombe. Lady Trevelyan had told him of a man and his wife who had been placed in charge of the Shakespeare house. They were "rather strenuous and superior people" from Newcastle. They embraced the job eagerly, only to find at the end of six months that they could not stand the "humbug" imposed upon them by the tourists. Morris Gedge, in the story, the newly appointed keeper, realizes soon enough that the birthplace is a lot of humbug. He would have liked to stick to hard facts, but the visitors impose upon him their desire for homely detail. He finds, in a visiting American couple, kindred spirits. And to them he confides "there *is* no author . . . There are all the immortal people—*in* the work; but there's nobody else." And then, when he realizes that he may lose his job, he is able to yield to his own reconstructing imagination. He starts to embroider the legend; he becomes a creator himself. His wife now fears he will be discharged for weaving too much romance. Apparently the visitors cannot have too much. When the appreciative American couple return, he gives them an example of his delicate improvisations as he stands in the Birth-room: "Across that threshold He habitually passed; through these low windows in childhood, He peered out into the world that He was to make so much happier by the gift to it of His Genius; over the boards of this floor—that is over *some* of them, for we mustn't be carried away!—his little feet often pattered, and the beams of this ceiling (we must really in some places take care of *our* heads!) he endeavoured, in boyish strife, to jump up and touch." In this vein Gedge creates a fanciful fabric. He is now a success. The directors vote to double his pay. The creative imagination triumphs over the mundane. In the tale James gives us the levels of art-appreciation—that of the flat-footed public, which merely wants to know how like itself greatness is; the sensitive appreciators, like the American couple, who represent higher criticism, and finally the keeper of the shrine, who pays his tribute to art by being imaginative.

Book Three

The Better Sort

1903–1904

★

GOODY TWO SHOES

THE crowded years had fled; but the new years, the approach of old age, had their own crowdedness, and the traveller to the Continent—the tourist in France, the voyager in Italy—now had his beaten path from Rye to London. Henry James might pose amusedly as a rural aristocrat, a member of the landed gentry; he had his eye nevertheless on the metropolis that had sheltered him during most of his expatriation. It was his little joke that he lived a dutiful life among his "peasantry;" he performed local social obligations with punctuality and friendliness as antidote to winters of lonely writing—"the solitudinous and silent nature of Lamb House." These only sharpened his appetite for London. "You have no idea," he wrote to the distant Grace Norton, "what a small personal world I live in, in having come to live so much as I do in the country." He had thought he knew how to live alone; he was learning better each month. But was this kind of life good for him? He asked the question of Miss Norton and answered it promptly—yes, it was beautiful—for three quarters of the year! For the remaining quarter he needed the amplifications of the capital. The *impersonal* life, he explained, "is provided for among my Sussex yokels." Various neighbours were dutifully dined at the Yule-time—the parochial, golf-playing, walking, gardening, tea-drinking retired generation with whom he was "gorged to such repletion that I am heavy even as with their heaviness." And if his friends would ask, "Why have them?" his answer would have to be "What will you have? The Squire——! One's 'people.'" He had such a sense of being "looked to" from humble quarters, "that one feels with one's brass knocker and one's garden-patch, quite like a country gentleman, with his 'people' and his church-monuments." *Noblesse oblige.*

I

Two of his paths in London led him to certain ladies. When he was younger the ladies he had cultivated were older, they had memories reaching back to the eighteenth century. Now they were closer to his own years. One path always led to Lucy Clifford's—that was the road to the literary salon, a hearth where one talked of old friends and met the children of the New Novel and the New Poetry over whom Aunt Lucy fussed hen-like and devoted. The other path led to Eaton Terrace, to Jessie Allen's, and the echoes of the grand world offered by his newer friend, two years younger than himself, whom he had met in Venice in 1899. He had begun by going to her small corner house at No. 74 by invitation, but increasingly was allowed to turn up at the tea-hour, uninvited; although he sometimes risked the absence of his hostess. Thus he could write to her on one such occasion in 1903 "on Saturday *week* last the 14th—or was it Friday 13th—when being in town for three days and near Eaton Terrace, a gentleman of distinguished though faded, appearance, with the remains of once remarkable beauty distinguishable under the flickering street lamps, might have been seen to hurry, all intent to No. 74 (about five o'clock) and then, at the sight of its darkened windows and closed shutters, stop short, smite his still noble brow, glare wildly about him, murmur a deep imprecation and stride gloomily away." The artisan of the "modern" wasn't above mocking the clichés of Victorian fiction.

James found Elizabeth Jessie Jane Allen lively and amusing from the first days of their Venetian acquaintance. They had met under the noble and hospitable roof of the Curtises in the Palazzo Barbaro (renamed Palazzo Leporelli in *The Wings of the Dove*) and thereafter Miss Allen, who was very *écrivassière*, as James put it, sent him her thirty-page letters filled with news of castles and country houses. She couldn't, for her life, as James said to Mrs Curtis, write a simple note. Her letters were full-length and filled with "the bright pageant of her pen." She came of the Allens of Cresselly. Her great-grandfather had been the Earl of Jersey, and in the way of distinguished British families, various relatives in various generations married Wedgwoods and Darwins. Raised by devoted aunts and trained in the hope, it was said, that she might become a lady-in-waiting at Court, she had, however, lacked the requisite lineage. But she moved through the world as if she were a noble attendant bent on the highest service. She was always on the move, to Wales, to the castles of the Scottish border, to great English homes. In Eaton Square, with her two loyal maids, her cat, her delicate Victorian water-colours, her choice miniatures and fine antiques, she served tea or dinner to Henry James usually in her upstairs drawing-room. And they talked. She might have been in earlier years a Madame Merle, though less calculating. Now she was more like Maria Gostrey. Indeed James compared her to that lady of *The Ambassadors* in a letter in which they gossiped, as they invariably did, of the Curtises of Venice who "see all the greatness of the earth and bestrew their path with anecdotes and witticisms." The Curtises, James told Jessie, had a kind of "dim theory that we, you and I, sort of daily conspire together—if only, as it were, towards an indiscreet alliance, in which we communicate over *their* heads!" And he went on to tell her (he was actually reading proof of his novel) that he had been writing "some stuff in which a woman who has in certain circumstances"—and his pen slipped at this moment and in wanting to write the word "rather" James wrote "Strether" instead. He corrected this, and went on, "who has in certain circumstances rather launched a man, has occasion to say to him an afterwards: 'Ah, I did it all, but now you can toddle alone!'" The Curtises had made him acquainted with Miss Allen. Now the two toddled alone "in a manner that their sponsors have possibly a vague, uneasy, uncanny conception of."

They toddled magnificently for the last seventeen years of James's life; and the more than two hundred letters he wrote and Miss Allen saved, are filled with ardent anecdote, now ancient, of the Curtises and others of the cosmopolite-English world. Miss Allen used to write her letters in a low chair with a small table at her side. Her penmanship was beautiful and as each letter was ready for the post she dropped it on the floor to be mailed by one of her maids. She affected a cape and bonnet when she went to

the theatre with Henry. She attached great importance to her
little glass of port at lunch. Her voice was deep and low. She was
above all an old-fashioned Lady Bountiful. James had begun by
saying to her that her letters brought him "something of the
rattle and the fragrance—as of a thousand expensive essences—
of the great world" and exclaiming "how much good you must
do and how many people you make happy!" But soon his letters
were filled with warnings and with dismay at the way in which she
spent herself doing her good deeds for vampires. He spoke of her
"hungry genius for relieving humanity," of "the sad and dreary
things—things of woe and wretchedness—that you seem always
condemned to be doing."

Very early Henry James found himself included in Miss Allen's
largesse. On the first Christmas of their friendship, in 1899, Jessie
sent her new friend a Venetian *cinquecento* taper. James gracefully
thanked her with full euphemism: it would be the joy of his eye—
"the flower of my collection, and the pride of my house." The
following Christmas, Miss Jessie's gift consisted of two fine brass
Venetian candlesticks. James told her he bowed his head very low
in gratitude. All Venice—the Salute, San Giorgio, the Dogana
—was in her gift; but he also had an uneasy feeling he said that
"the positive frenzy of your altruism" required close watching.
The Christmas after that, still keeping up the Venetian memory,
it was a fine casket, doubtless like one of Portia's. In the fourth
Christmas, and perhaps because it was a winter of blizzard at Rye,
Jessie departed from the Venetian mood. What descended on
Lamb House, in the midst of the deep snow, were two large bearskin rugs.

II

Henry James had addressed her as "Dearest and unspeakable Miss
Allen" for her earlier gifts. Now he wrote to "Dearest and worst
Miss Allen." He told her he would have to bring the bearskin
rugs back to Eaton Place. They were "impossible, unspeakable,
unforgivable." He refused to regard them as his. "I really, dear
lady, can *not* again receive *any* object of value from your hands,
of value or even of *no* value." What was more, he said, he

wouldn't even "growl" his "thank you" for the bearskins. To such ungraciousness was he reduced by her perversity. He wanted a solemn promise she wouldn't do it again. "And even thus the bearskins will be deposited at no distant date either on the top of your house or at its foundations, or thrust into one of its windows or down one of its chimneys; for I thought I had made all this plain last year. There!—And do you see what a Pig you make of me. And a Pig that I shall *remain*, that I shall continue to be, elaborately, inexorably, always, *always!*" He added: "See, too, what you compel me to sit up nights writing about, when I might be either reducing my oil-bill or at least writing about Shakespeare, and the musical glasses, or the Kenmares and the crimes of the aristocracy."

A day or two later James went up to London. There was a confrontation in Eaton Terrace between the Great Novelist and the Altruistic Lady. Whether he carried the bearskins with him on this occasion we do not know. But he seems to have faced utter defeat. He returned to Lamb House and a letter of 15 December 1902 shows him in a mood of compromise. He agrees to keep the gift. "I promise," he wrote, "to wear the bearskins in Bed in the blizzard that I feel to be now again preparing; but all on one condition." The implacable, great condition was that from this time on he would address Miss Allen as "Goody Two Shoes." This was an allusion to the eighteenth-century moral tale attributed to Oliver Goldsmith and written for the edification of the young:

The History of Little Goody Two Shoes otherwise called Mrs Margery Two Shoes with the Means by which she acquired her Learning and Wisdom and in consequence thereof her Estate; set forth at large for the Benefit of Those
> who from a state of rags and care
> and having shoes but half a pair
> Their fortune and their fame would fix,
> and gallop in a coach and six.

Little Goody had been an orphan possessing but one shoe and when given a mate she went about the town saying "see two shoes."

Miss Allen was hardly an orphan and she had all the shoes she

F

needed. But she had Goody's addiction to good deeds and noble sacrifices. Thus it came about that the descendant of the Allens of Cresselly became, in the Jamesian mythos, for all her future "dear generous Goody" or "my dear Goody—best of goodies." Books were inscribed to her thus by James. Sometimes she was "Dear St Goody," or "my eternally martyred and murdered Goody." She was indeed too good—"wherever I look, in your existence, it strikes me as bristling with merciless monsters, with devouring dragons. I would like to St George them all into the bottomless pit."

John Singer Sargent, who was both James's friend and Miss Allen's, and also a friend of the Curtises, characterized Miss Allen's letters to James—which the novelist burned with his other papers—as "mischievous tattle about James's friends, whom she always tried to alienate from him." He said that James's letters were "sympathetic replies." Shorn of their associations, this abundant correspondence remains a monument of elegant, ironic persiflage and personal reference; many of the details have been rendered meaningless by time; but in them one finds a comedy of old-fashioned manners, that of the latter-day Goody Two Shoes and her Novelist, humblest, yet most Napoleonic of her courtiers.

A QUEER JOB

I

HENRY JAMES called his book about William Wetmore Story "a queer job." It was a mixture of biography, documents, reminiscence. The tone of reminiscence dominated the book. The two thick volumes published late in 1903 at the same time as the long-delayed *Ambassadors*—held back by Harpers who doubted the success of the book—were distinctly autobiographical. The novelist had found that he had to eke out the scant history of his subject with "my own little personal memories, inferences, evocations, and imagination." James was not in reality a biographer, and he had no intention of becoming one. Moreover, he had never liked Story. Faced with bundles of letters and certain diary notes he had neither the time nor the inclination to do the required "research" which would have provided him with a full background; nor did he have the patience of the scholar accustomed to using always "given" material. His own creative and organizing imagination played around the impersonal and inanimate documents and sought constantly to "novelize" them. He had undertaken the book in a moment of financial need and under the pressure of Story's children. He had known Story, the Bostonian-Roman, not intimately, but had seen him long ago in his forty-room apartment in the Barberini Palace; he had visited his studio, with morsels of marble shining in the yard and with expert Italian stonecutters to carry out Story's ideas. Story had lived in a kind of general grandeur in the artistic ambiance described in James's *Roderick Hudson*, which had dealt with an American sculptor in Rome—though he had by no means been the "original" for Roderick. The novel indeed had had no original; it was based on James's friendship with a whole group of painters and sculptors in the Holy City in the early 1870's. Story himself, with his consistent amateurism—he

163

sculptured, wrote verses, plays, essays, staged theatricals — James had considered a case of "prosperous pretension." He had made his reputation in Victorian England with a statue of Cleopatra. All his sculptures were narratives; and American businessmen visiting Rome and seeking "art" purchased them. The world had been more than kind to Story. Set against his time and his generation, he was almost an archetypal American subject, a Jamesian subject — the American expatriate with a penchant for the artist life. Story had originally been a lawyer and a professor of law; he had never learned the law of the artist.

This James said at several points in his book with finger-tip tact and explicitness which always enabled him to speak the truth — highly varnished with his verbal felicities. "How could he be, our friend, we sometimes find ourselves wondering, so restlessly, sincerely aesthetic, and yet, constitutionally, so little insistent." By "insistent" James meant the act of "throwing the whole weight of the mind" into what an artist is doing. With artists this was instinctive, a necessity. "They feel unsafe, uncertain, exposed, unless the spirit, such as it is, be at the point in question 'all there.' Story's rather odd case, if I may call it so, was that when he wrote, prose or verse, he was 'there' only in part." Having in this passage, as in others, clearly shown Story's amateurism, James turned to the other question that must have made him originally want to write the biography — Story's expatriation. Had Story paid in his art for having chosen to live abroad — and in a seductive country that beguiled, tempted, distracted the artist? Robert Browning, Story's friend, had lived in the same country and produced some of his finest work. "Italy, obviously, was never too much," for the author of *Men and Women*. "That weight of the whole mind which we have speculatively invoked was a pressure that he easily enough, at any point, that he in fact almost extravagantly, brought to bear. And then he was neither divided nor dispersed. He was devoted to no other art." Story had been divided and dispersed, more social than artistic, and much too worldly.

Out of such mixed elements, James produced this book; he was already thinking of *The Golden Bowl* as he wrote it, and he disposed of his "queer job" in about two months, dictating eloquent commentaries around a series of letters to Story from the Brownings, from Norton, Lowell, and others. He gave the book a careful title: *William Wetmore Story and His Friends: From Letters, Diaries and Recollections*. The key word was "re-collections." He always fell back on his own memories, and speaking always in the first person he created a series of exquisite pictures of the old Roman time. To start remembering was to run away from his material. The digressions were numerous. An instance of this was James's coming on a reference to the thick ankles of the ballerina Taglioni in one of the letters. There ensues in these pages a passage in which James reminds himself of dining in the great houses of London with Taglioni when she was old and her ankles were no longer visible on the stage of the world. So too, a reference to Mrs Procter enabled him to yield to an old desire to commemorate that caustic old lady, whom he had liked so much, when he had known her in his early London days. Small wonder certain of his critics in the United States described the life Story as the "sacrifice" of a fine subject to Henry James's egotism. The statement was true. Yet one must recognize, in the fullness of time, that the Story volumes now stand as a separate work of art, and are full of lessons for the modern biographer—hints from a powerful creative intelligence how to use the significant detail, the organizing imagination, the transfiguring touch. It also suggests what style and evocation can do when it is used to illuminate inanimate documents. The loosest kind of biography, the life of Story suggests to us how fine an historian James might have been had he not been a novelist. Houghton Mifflin editors, reading the book, promptly asked James to do a life of Lowell. His reply showed how clearly he understood the biographer's task. The interest of a biographical work, he wrote, "must depend on intrinsic richness of matter. If a man has had a quiet life, but a great mind, one may do something with him; as one may also do something with him even if he has had a small mind and great adventures. But when he has had neither adventures nor intellectual, spiritual, or whatever inward history, then one's case is hard. One becomes, at any rate very careful."

This was the lesson he had learned. In the history of biography the Story volumes should be given a particular place: not only do they show the struggle of the free imagination within the documentary prison; they illustrate how a work of art can be created about a subject the biographer dislikes. The Story life is not a "debunking" biography. James addresses himself instead to extracting such richnesses as he can: and the richness he ends up with comes from his own discipline, his own experience, his own mind. The writing had proved a "damnedly difficult job — to make an at all lively and shapely and artful little book — which should not give poor dear W.W.S. simply clean away." Or as he put it to the Duchess of Sutherland late in 1903, he had, in this biography made bricks without straw, he had chronicled "small beer with the effect of opening champagne." Story was the dearest of men, "but he wasn't massive, his artistic and literary baggage were of the slightest, and the materials for a biography *nil*. Hence (once I had succumbed to the amiable pressure of his children,) I had really to invent a book, patching the thing together and eking it out with barefaced irrelevancies — starting above all *any* hare, however small, that might lurk by the way. It is very pleasant to get from a discriminating reader the token that I have carried the trick through. But the magic is but scantly mine — it is really that of the beloved old Italy, who always *will* consent to fling a glamour for you, whenever you speak her fair." What we can say now, looking at the two artful volumes, is that they represent still another instance of the power of the artist to transfigure whatever crosses his path. Story's sculptures rest in the deepest basements of the art museums; and few pause to look at his public statues. But in the pages of Henry James he is enshrined in the grandeur of a great style — decidedly not his own.

II

Henry James's old friend Henry Adams, read the Story volumes during a stay in Paris in the autumn of 1903. The two had not met since the period of the Spanish-American war, five years earlier, when their friend John Hay had become Secretary of State. Adams was moved by the book, and with his asperity and melancholy, he read a deeper message in it. The result was a remarkable, and very personal, letter to Henry James. His New England generation, Adams told James "were in actual fact only one mind and nature; the individual was a facet of Boston." Henry James had thus chronicled, in writing Story's life, the history of a generation. "Harvard College and Unitarianism kept us all shallow," wrote Henry Adams. "We knew nothing—no! but really nothing! of the world." And Adams went on to say that one could not exaggerate "the profundity of ignorance of Story in becoming a sculptor, or Sumner in becoming a statesman, or Emerson in becoming a philosopher. Story and Sumner, Emerson and Alcott, Lowell and Longfellow, Hillard, Winthrop, Motley, Prescott and all the rest, were the same mind—and so, poor worm—was I!" Turning the lens of history on himself, Adams said he and the others had been the "*type bourgeois bostonien!*" Doubtless a type as good as another, but

What you say of Story is at bottom exactly what you would say of Lowell, Motley and Sumner, barring degrees of egotism. You cannot help smiling at them, but you smile at us all equally. God knows that we knew our want of knowledge! the self-distrust became introspection, nervous self-consciousness, irritable dislike of America, and antipathy to Boston. *Auch ich war in Arcadien geboren.*

Adams concluded by saying James had written "not Story's life, but your own and mine—pure autobiography, the more keen for what is beneath, implied, intelligible only to me and half a dozen other people still living." He ended, "You make me curl up, like a trodden-on worm. Improvised Europeans we were, and—Lord God!—how thin!"

James could have replied that *he* certainly wasn't an "improvised European" and certainly not a Bostonian. He had made himself long ago into an Americano-European. Yet in the long historical perspective Adams had touched an important truth. The Bostonians, products of a puritan tradition, Story, Sumner, Emerson, Alcott, Lowell, Holmes, Longfellow had all been intellectuals, to a degree writers of disguised sermons; they had lacked the larger imagination. One might speak of the "flowering of New England" but the flowers were tame and confined to a well-

ordered churchly garden. It had been New York that supplied
the largest imagination in American literature—in Melville's
reaching out to the South Seas, in Whitman's democratic "barbaric yawp," and in the super-civilized psychology of Henry
James who went to Europe as Melville had gone to the Pacific, in
quest of himself and of freedom.

What James thought of Adams's reaction to his book we do
not altogether know. We can only read between the lines of his
reply, which was gentle and mild and quietly reproving, for he
could not join Adams in his pessimism. There was, said Henry
James, "a kind of *inevitableness* in my having made you squirm."
But he himself had been pushed "to conclusions less grim."

The truth is that any retraced story of bourgeois lives (lives other than
great lives of "action"—*et encore!*) throws a chill upon the scene, the time,
the subject, the small mapped-out facts, and if you find "great men thin" it
isn't really so much their fault (and least of all yours) as that the art of the
biographer—devilish art!—is somehow practically *thinning*. It simplifies
even while seeking to enrich—and even the Immortals are so helpless and
passive in death.

James had wanted, he said, to invest old Boston out of which
William Wetmore Story came with a mellow and a golden glow
and he had succeeded only in making it bleak for Henry Adams.
He ended by telling Adams he had not yet heard from the Story
family. "I think they don't know whether they like it or not!
They are waiting to find out—and I am glad on the whole they
haven't access to *you*."

THE MASTER AT SIXTY

THE book on Story was at the printer's and Henry James was making a fresh adjustment to London in his annual winter flight from Lamb House. If he had in the metropolis his usual distractions—his tea ceremony at Eaton Place, his visits to the Gosses at Delamere Terrace, his quiet hours with Lucy Clifford —he at the same time maintained his ceaseless industry in his comfortable room at the Reform Club. *The Ambassadors* was being serialized at last and he was reading proof; and he had promised the *Atlantic Monthly* an article on Zola, who had died of carbon monoxide poisoning the previous autumn as a result of a blocked chimney in his home. James had written his summing up of Balzac and of Flaubert a few months earlier. It was fitting that he should now call on his memory, and his reading, to offer a final tribute to the author of *Les Rougon-Macquart* and the courageous defender of Dreyfus. The essay is of a piece with its predecessors and those he had written earlier on George Sand; in effect he was rewriting his 1878 book *French Poets and Novelists*. He had then at the threshold of his middle years recorded his appreciation and his debt to the French writers. Now he was re-visiting them, looking at them from the distance of his maturity. He had begun by being fascinated by Zola, but had disliked his subject-matter; "a combination of the cesspool and the house of prostitution" he had said of *Nana*; at least officially, in the journals of the New World, he had deprecated Zola's tendency to deal with "dirty" subjects, his pronounced physicality. But he had always shown in these criticisms that he also liked the determination and persistence, the dogged seriousness of the man—ever since he had heard him one day at Flaubert's describe how he was compiling for himself a dictionary of coarse language to write *L'Assommoir*. He had been struck "with the tone in which he made the announcement—without bravado and without apology,

as an interesting idea that had come to him and that he was working, really to arrive at character and particular truth, with all his
conscience." James remembered how the novel's audacity had
got it banned, and how now it was judged, in the fullness of time,
a masterpiece. As in his other late essays, his concern at maturity
was no longer with the power of individual works. He looked at
the total work, the figure, the legend, the making of a "classic."
In a few passages of reminiscence, in this essay, in which he
allowed his full admiration for Zola to be expressed at last, he
remembered their talk when the French novelist had come to
London: and the factitious side too, of his creation, Zola's
account of how he intended to do a series on Lourdes, Paris,
Rome. James was prepared to allow Zola the first two: but
Rome! Zola confessed to having been once in Italy, in Genoa.
"It was splendid for confidence and cheer, but it left me, I fear,
more or less gaping . . . he was an honest man—he had always
bristled with it at every pore; but no artistic reverse was inconceivable for an adventurer who, stating in one breath that his
knowledge of Italy consisted of a few days spent at Genoa, was
ready to declare in the next that he had planned, on a scale, a
picture of Rome. It flooded his career, to my sense, with light; it
showed how he had marched from subject to subject and had 'got
up' each in turn—showing also how consummately he had
reduced such getting-up to an artifice." James thought of his
own "frequentations, saturations"—a history of long years in his
adored Rome. And here was Zola already giving Rome away
"before possessing an inch of it."

So James mused, recalling also how in his talk with Zola in the
1890's, the French writer appeared to him to have lived only for
the writing of his great series of novels. He had wondered what
else he had lived for. It was almost "as if *Les Rougon-Macquart*
had written him as he stood and sat, as he looked and spoke, as the
long, concentrated, merciless effort had made and stamped and
left him." But then something fundamental had happened. Zola
had been shaken to his roots. *J'Accuse* had happened—and
Zola's defence of Dreyfus was that of a man who finally found his
commitment to life as well as to art—"a man with arrears of

personal history to make up, the act of a spirit for which life, or for which at any rate freedom, had been too much postponed, treating itself at last to a luxury of experience."

II

Henry James was sixty; but this birthday, which placed him now in the autumn of life, came and went on 15 April in a heedless London. Moreover James himself would have liked to forget it. He wrote to Grace Norton, "Any age is in itself good enough— even the latest." The devil of it was that its identity was so brief; it passed so quickly. Landmarks of time there were, on all sides, and in the faces of American and English and French friends, those who had survived out of earlier years. Grace Norton's brother, Charles Eliot Norton, loomed one day, on James's horizon, at Lamb House, but he was distinctly a figure in an ancient gallery; he belonged, James felt, to "some alien epoch of my youth;" even Norton's terminology, filled with echoes of the days of Carlyle and Ruskin, seemed quaint. He was of another age indeed, and James felt he had "travelled thousands of miles from the order and air" of Cambridge and Shady Hill. "It takes one whole life," he wrote to Miss Norton, in the vein of his hero of *The Ambassadors*, "for some persons *dont je suis*, to learn how to live at all; which is absurd if there is not to be another in which to apply the lessons."

Another Cambridge friend of the old days seemed indestructible and had just crowned his career by being named to the Supreme Court. Henry James had predicted long ago, when they were mere youths, that the younger Oliver Wendell Holmes would some day rise to eminence "in a specialty, but to a high degree." Holmes visited James in Rye during the summer of 1903, and the novelist continued to marvel at the associate justice's "faculty for uncritical enjoyment and seeing and imagining." What struck him as unusual about Holmes was that he remained himself, in all his integrity, unmodified by time. "The people of such perfect sameness are usually those who *haven't* lived." Wendell moved through life "like a full glass carried without spilling a drop." To the new associate justice Henry wrote "you were *born* historic."

Holmes, he said, would remain "solidly seated . . . a beautiful great portrait, as it were, hung up in the chamber of my life."

Norton, and Holmes—and then, there was Howells, "the dear man." He too belonged to James's old Cambridge. Miss Norton told Henry James that Howells, in an intimate moment, had confided to her his feeling that he had lived his life under the dominion of fear. James, commenting on this, said he had always felt the depression in Howells. He hadn't felt this in his verses—but then he hadn't much cared for these. Real as Howells's depression was, however, James believed he was able to disconnect it from his "*operative* self." It had never been, said James "the least paralysing, or interfering, or practically depressing." On the contrary, Howells had arrived at compensations "very stimulating to endeavour." The melancholy wasn't to be found in his prose at all "and he has in short been so inordinately and cheeringly and cheerfully 'successful.'" Still James had always known that Howells had a strange, sad, "kind of crepuscular *alter ego*, a sort of 'down cellar' (where they keep the apples of discord) a gloom and apprehension." He could quite believe that Howells had tried to explain the merits of James's later work to Miss Norton. Henry James said he would enjoy Howells's "zeal and deplore your darkness even more had I not reached a state of final beatitude in which one cares not a fraction of a straw what any one in the world *thinks* of one. How they *feel* for one, yes—or even against one; that as much (almost!) as ever. But how they *judge*— never again, never! And it is a peace worth having lived long and wearily to have attained."

In James's letters of his sixtieth year we obtain new glimpses of old faces. Thus late in the year he sums up Edmund Gosse "our immortal Gosse, who has been here for a couple of days and whom, also, last winter in town (I was there from January to May) I occasionally communed with. All news of him, however, you can construct for yourself, in exact correspondence with the genuine article—the grand features of his career and character reproduce themselves from month to month in the most punctual and genial way. He is only rather *more* a child of the World and a presider at the Table than hitherto, and his World and his Table

and his relations to the same and his pursuit of society and conversation, and of the Great—and of the Small—and of everything and everyone, remain the same bewildering and baffling
enigma as ever to me (in respect to their compatibility with the
cultivation of Letters, and with the interests of the Board of
Trade.)" Gosse was still librarian at the latter institution; and
James's quick sketch of him, written for W. E. Norris, did not
alter the fact that they remained excellent friends; for if Gosse was
a busybody of letters, he was also a fount of gossip; and then the
two were connected by so many old threads of friendship and
memories winding through so many years.

Time had brought also distancings and estrangements. In the
matter of distance Jules Jusserand, the diplomat, James's walking
companion of London in the 1880's, had long been away, in other
scenes, serving at other embassies. James felt "the little able and
ambitious, contracted and concentrated (*in* ambition) demon that
he is" would return to his orbit. Jusserand was now France's
Ambassador to Washington; and there he had become one of the
intimates of President Theodore Roosevelt. The novelist believed he might again catch up with Jusserand in Washington, for
his thoughts had been running on a journey to America.

Perhaps because he had written of Zola and Dreyfus, James's
mind turned in one of his letters to Paul Bourget whose deep-
seated conservatism and anti-semitism had revealed itself during
the Dreyfus affair. Bourget's "views and convictions, obsessions
and fanaticisms," these were, in the French novelist's brilliant
talk, "perverse," but animated, characteristic. "It is his form,
manner and general laxity and monotony in the novel, that I
regard as a greater menace to his prosperity, and that make his
future doubtful and darksome to me . . . However, with an intelligence so great, a literary sense so great, and a humanity, after
all, by no means exhausted, a man, at his age, ought still to have a
large margin. *Patientons!*" But Bourget would never use that
margin. Presently he and James ceased altogether to correspond.

At sixty, scattered in his letters of the times, we thus see James
glancing at the ageing countenances of some of his contem-

poraries. But his own face remained the brooding unsmiling countenance that Max Beerbohm described; and if James's life was peopled alike with ghosts of the long-dead, and the presence of the ageing like himself, it had wide room in it for the newer generation. Late in 1903 we catch him, as it were, on the threshold of the nascent Bloomsbury—in the presence of Virginia and Vanessa Stephen, now fully grown, daughters of his old friend, Sir Leslie Stephen. He had known Sir Leslie longer than most of the other Londoners; in the days of his *Cornhill* editorship, Stephen had published *Washington Square*; and he had befriended James as far back as the novelist's first adult journey to England in 1869. Now old, weak, Sir Leslie was slowly dying. Henry visited him and talked with him, although their communication had always been more in silence than in speech: James had told of the long walks he had taken with Stephen—walks of many hours —in which Stephen spoke not a word. Stephen's first wife had been Thackeray's daughter; and to her sister, Anne Thackeray Ritchie, another friend out of the late Victorian London, James wrote of one of his last visits to Leslie in the house at Hyde Park Gate. He had found him brighter and firmer than he had hoped. "He is as infinitely touching and backward-reaching as you say, and particularly beautiful in his humorous kindly patience with his long ordeal." James had visited him in Cornwall in the scenes his daughter Virginia would enshrine in *To the Lighthouse*. His dying seemed to James "very handsome, noble, gentle and, full of all the achievements behind it and surrounded with such beauty in present and past—beautiful ghosts, beautiful living images (how beautiful Vanessa!) beautiful inspired and communicated benevolence and consideration on the part of everyone." James found Stephen lying on his couch reading; and told him of some new French books that might interest him.

III

He lived now on a new plane; after the long desolation of the 1890's he had greeted the new century with an outburst of writing. Since 1900 he had published three novels, two volumes of tales, a series of articles; the life of Story was on the press. He might complain during the winter stretches in Rye of solitude, but no writer of his age was more productive, and no American author had ever, so late in life, written with such power and such serene command of craft. James could look back to the Victorian creators—in France, Flaubert and the *cénacle*, and his beloved old friend Turgenev; in England, the wide circle of the late Victorians. Now the young Edwardians were emerging. Among them he stood, still a presence in the bookshops and the magazines, and a great authoritative voice that spoke of old and new, past and present, a voice awesome, uncompromising, on the subject of art. This presence was a living force—still providing new works, and works strange in style and "difficult," works emanating from a writer remote from press and publicity, a figure mysterious to the literary world beside the ubiquitous Gosse, or those who wrote for the newspapers. Distinctly a figure of the élite, his private life unknown, his rare public appearances always portentous and unsmiling, he could be pointed to in the clubs and be sought after by hostesses, and still remain aloof and oracular. His speech had grown slower and more elaborate. His short frame had become heavy. When he spoke he delivered himself with a kind of dramatic wit, in sedate, austere phrases, phrases that amplified, described, touched, retouched. There was something Johnsonian about him—a Johnson who spoke not with the voice of the oracle or of dogma, but with inner laughter, the essence of wit. He was always clothed elegantly but sometimes—as the Bay Emmet portrait shows—with a certain extravagance of colour. Henry Dwight Sedgwick glimpsing him in 1901 in the New Forest, where James was visiting the Godkins, saw him as a figure of vaudeville—tight check trousers, waistcoat of a violent pattern, coat with short tails like a cock sparrow—and none matching; and this topped by a cravat in a large, a magnificently flowery bow.

Gosse, remembering him at this moment, was reminded of a canon he had seen preaching in the Cathedral of Toulouse—in the unction, gravity, yet vehemence of his speech. James had about him the suggestion of an actor; there was a theatrical look in the extravagant costume. Whatever the costume, or the tone of speech, the effect was, as Gosse also said, of a "radically power-ful and unique outer appearance. The beautiful modelling of the brows, waxing and waning under the stress of excitement," dwelt in his memory. An American publishing lady, Elizabeth Jordan, on first meeting him at a dinner saw someone who might have been a successful lawyer or banker; and it was not until the dinner was half over that James suddenly turned and looked at her very closely. Then she realized "the strange power of Henry James's eyes. They made me feel in those instants as if he had read me to the soul and I rather think he had." An English journalistic lady, Ella Hepworth Dixon, described his eyes as "not only age-old and world-weary, as are those of cultured Jews, but they had vision—and one did not like to think of what they saw." Lady Ottoline Morrell in her memoirs said "they were unlike any other eyes I have ever seen." Conrad's were "tragic and worn and suffering," James's, she wrote, was a "clairvoyant exhausting vision" and his eyes "were of a fluid quality." They seemed to absorb and distil what they apprehended. Hueffer quoted his servants as saying, "It always gives me a turn to open the door for Mr James. His eyes seem to look you through to the very back-bone." Thomas Hardy was distinctly in the minority in speaking of James's "nebulous gaze"—but then this may have been the Master's way of looking at the author of *Tess*.

As we turn the pages of volumes of Victorian and Edwardian reminiscence, James is there, in this drawing-room or that, and the images invoked for him are usually images of power—he recalls Caesar or Napoleon, or he reminds one of a Rothschild, or the Catholic "Lacordaire in the intolerable scrutiny of the eyes." His sentences have become intricate and labyrinthine; sometimes he seemed to carry over his literary dictation into the salon. And he could be "as ceremonial as an Oriental." "The greatest com-pliment that can be paid to that subtle, complex mind of his is that notwithstanding his mannerisms and hesitations that would be so tediously unbearable in the case of most of us, Henry James never came even near to being a bore," wrote the dramatist Alfred Sutro. "One had to wait a long time for the thought to be expressed; one watched the process of its germination and development; but when it came one felt that it had been tremendously worth waiting for, and that it was a thought peculiarly his own and expressed as no other man could have expressed it." It depended on the listener. There was in this behaviour, without doubt, a form of aggression—this coercing of the listener—that what would be uttered was important; the end of the sentence was unpredictable, the search for the right word, the piling up of metaphors, was necessary even to the small change of daily talk. "He talked as if every sentence had been carefully rehearsed; every semi-colon, every comma, was in exactly the right place, and his rounded periods dropped to the floor and bounced about like tiny rubber balls." Thus Gertrude Atherton. Edith Wharton described the elaborate hesitations as like a cobweb bridge flung from James's mind to the listener "an invisible passage over which one knew that silver-footed ironies, veiled jokes, tiptoe malices, were stealing to explode a huge laugh at one's feet." It was, she said, a "unique experience."

Anyone who rummages through the memoirs—they are endless—is led to the conclusion that James was a bore to the bores; but when he found his intellectual peers he could relax; the "front" of the Master dropped, the sentences became shorter, the give and take easier. The image of James at sixty, the common denominator of these multiple pictures, is that of a man who, if he seemed at moments idiosyncratic, eccentric, even comical, exuded great and aggressive strength. He was a presence, assertive and uncompromising, a formed figure, shaped by two continents and many journeys, a tireless observer with an ability to see behind the frail and doubting, the conflicted and ambiguous façade of humanity. Gloriani's eyes in *The Ambassadors* are James's—and we remember how Strether is "held" by them. He thinks of them as "the source of the deepest intellectual sounding to which he had ever been exposed." "Was it the most special flare, unequalled, supreme of the aesthetic torch, lighting that wondrous world for ever, or was it above all the long straight shaft sunk by a personal acuteness that life had seasoned to steel?" One wonders whether in the case of Henry James this power of vision was not both—the aesthetic torch, the "long straight shaft." The torch lit up the surface and found external loveliness, the other sought the inner world—its beauty and its terror. For one remembers "the terrible life" to be found in Gloriani's smile.

IV

In the midst of his work in London James had to rush back to Rye for "a tiresome little episode, one of the sorrows of a proprietor." He found himself having to purchase a large piece of garden, next to his own, which had been acquired by an individual named J. H. Gasson, a "blatant tradesman and scourge of Rye." Gasson could have built on the lot and ruined James's view. The property had been for sale, but James had not heard of this; Gasson had purchased it and now offered it to James at what was then a high price—£200. "The danger poisoned my rest, and would have ruined my one view and all my little place, practically —so that there was nothing to do but to buy—and save the situation," he wrote to William James. "I have done so, and the (*this*) property is proportionately improved and defended, for ever." But he now had to have a wall built around the lot before letting it to a neighbour.

Then a little while later another townsman named Whiteman threatened to tear down two "little old-world whitey-grey cottages" at the end of his garden wall, in the direction of the church. James's gardener lived in one of them. Both had their old gables, and a silvery surface, and were often sketched and painted by artists. The would-be destroyer proposed to put up two modern "raw, cheap, sordid" cottages which he would rent. New negotiations ensued. James consulted his architect and the destruction was averted, at what cost we do not know.

As always in such matters, James moved very quickly to rectify the depletion of his bank account. He received from Blackwood £250, the balance of his advance on the Story biography; but he also signed a contract for a new book—over and above two contracts he had signed to produce two novels during the ensuing year. Macmillan had for some time wanted James to write a book about London. It was to be one of a series for which F. Marion Crawford had just done a book on Rome and would be illustrated by Joseph Pennell. James told Macmillan he would need space to turn around in, at least 150,000 words. He agreed to a royalty of 20 per cent and an advance of £1000 to be paid on publication. "I must do, as I reflect with pleasure, a good deal of fertilizing reading, besides other prowling and prying; but once these things get themselves adequately done, I think I shall be able to *write* the book in some eight months." The book would never be written, but the traces of what it would have been can be found in a series of pencilled scrawls in a small red pocket notebook, as he visited old corners of London; and in his annotated volumes on London in his library. Too many other things intervened, not least his journey to America. But with the Blackwood money, and assurance of the Macmillan advance, James had a renewed sense of margin; his newly-acquired property, and the defence of the picturesqueness of Rye, was thoroughly financed—with a possible surplus.

He returned to Rye in the early summer of 1903, happy with all that had happened, and with his productions of the past two years on the press. He returned also with the most famous of his dogs, Max, the ruby-red dachshund. The acquisition was announced to Miss Weld, early in May, when James had run his cycle of London. "I am very homesick at last for house and garden and even for High Street and the Military Band, so I am counting the days. Likewise I have bought a very precious red Dachshund pup—hideously expensive but eight months old— and undomesticated; but with a pedigree as long as a Remington ribbon. So I have work cut out."

A few days later he was enjoying his garden, his flowers, the late spring "the last whistle of the blackbirds sounding in the trees and a wonderful red hawthorn . . . quite glowing and flaming in the sunset." The typewriter ticked again in the Garden Room. James had begun a new novel. It was called *The Golden Bowl*.

THE REVERBERATOR

FIFTEEN years earlier James had written a brilliant little comedy of manners he had called *The Reverberator* (it was the name of a newspaper), about a young American girl whose romance in France is almost ruined by a snooping gossip writer named George Flack. James long ago had foreseen—as he measured the future of America—how freedom of the press in his homeland would lead to licence; how responsibility would cease—and so would privacy. As Mr Flack, who is a more extreme version of Henrietta Stackpole of *The Portrait of a Lady*, or Matthias Pardon of *The Bostonians*, put it with reportorial vehemence; "The society news of every quarter of the globe, furnished by the prominent members themselves (oh, *they* can be fixed—you'll see!) from day to day and from hour to hour and served up at every breakfast-table in the United States—that's what the American people want and that's what the American people are going to have." There came a moment, in the wake of his novel *The Wings of the Dove*, when James himself, lover of privacy, student of private lives, was served up on the American breakfast-table as a "lover" (at sixty) of a young scandal-creating beauty, mistress of a tycoon, who barged into British society like one of James's early American girls. Once again—he might ruefully tell himself—his fiction had a way of coming true.

I

That spring of 1903 in London, at a tea party or some social occasion, a young woman, dressed in white, fresh and radiant, had detached herself from those present and confronted the author of *The Wings of the Dove*. She was small, plump, alert, and had beautiful red hair. Her smile revealed a row of even teeth. She fluttered up to James, a vision of white skin and Titian hair. "Oh, Mr James, everyone says I look like Milly Theale. Do *you* think I look like Milly Theale?" The anecdotes do not record Henry James's reply. But if he was hesitant and qualifying, he was also pleased that she seemed to have read his novel. The fictional Miss Theale and the real-life Miss Grigsby had one thing in common; they possessed red hair and a great deal of wealth. It little mattered to Miss Grigsby that she was meeting James almost a year after publication of the novel. With a fine disregard for chronology, she would always give herself out as the "original" of James's heroine. She had probably not read the book. She may have taken her cue from a charming article Howells had devoted to *The Wings of the Dove* in January of that year in the *North American Review*. In this he had spoken of Milly Theale's "lovely impalpability."

There was nothing impalpable about Miss Emilie Busbey Grigsby. Her vague earlier history records that she was the daughter of a Confederate officer and a certain Sue Grigsby of Kentucky; a writer of a later generation would speak of the mother as a kind of "super Scarlett O'Hara." Emilie was convent-bred; but all her history is a tissue of rumour and publicity. Her wealth came from her "protector," the Chicago traction magnate Charles T. Yerkes who was perhaps "an elderly platonic infatuate" as one commentator put it, or her lover. He had installed her in a five-storey mansion at 660 Park Avenue in New York, which the press called "The House of Mystery." She was twenty-three when James met her. At seventeen she had described herself as having "a tingling sense of a young pulsating life. I loved my hands because they were so fine of touch and tint and my long firm untried limbs, which could dance all night and hardly know it; in fine, I loved the body of me with a hearty animal relish and yet I was not sensuous." Sensuous she was, as these words suggest; and she was worldly, and socially ambitious. Her "natural history" was known to James; had he not been the historian of the American girl? Miss Grigsby's siege of London was conducted from the Savoy; later she would acquire a house and still later a flat in Mayfair, where Sir Rupert Hart-Davis recalled seeing walls covered with military mementoes, chiefly of Sir John French and some of Lord Kitchener. James knew of her from his friends the Henry Harlands, and from Meredith's daughter. Miss Grigsby would claim in due course that Meredith, seeing her, had said he had at last met the heroine of *The Ordeal of Richard Feverel*. She seems to have had a self-image of herself as heroine in many novels; and in her pursuit of literature as well as "society" she resembled an earlier adventuress, Blanche Roosevelt, who had made friends in America with Longfellow and in France with Victor Hugo and Maupassant, whose mistress she was for a while; in England she had sought, but had not conquered Henry James. Emilie Grigsby, later annals would record, dined Yeats; and one legend said that Rupert Brooke "spent his last night in England at Old Meadows" where Miss Grigsby lived. Indeed it was said that the lines he wrote in the visitors' book were afterwards engraved in bronze over Miss Grigsby's door. But then she also turned up in Westminster Abbey for the coronation of George V, and claimed an acquaintance with Princess Mary, later Queen. The press established that her acquaintance was with someone backstairs in Buckingham Palace.

She was the sort of woman, it may be judged, who created her own legend. When she was old, and lived in a fine house in New York, she spoke of Henry James as an intimate friend, who had admired her when she was young and had put her into his novel. By James's account he saw her only four or five times. She invited him to various parties. He declined. Then feeling that he at least should be civil, he paid a formal call on her at the Savoy, and spent ten minutes chatting with her. This was all that Miss Grigsby needed: the Master had actually called on her. The only allusion to the ambitious Emilie in his correspondence of this year is to be found in a letter of 5 May 1903 to Goody Allen. "Grigsbina is, thank the Lord, in her natural dressmaking Paris—but I *have* seen her too. But of her and every thing anon." This would suggest that James studied Emilie as he had studied other such females from the farther shore of the Atlantic. Miss Grigsby is not reported to have sent James such gifts as Goody Allen's bearskins; there was, however, a story that she dispatched to the Master at Christmas a fine ham, cooked in champagne.

II

She would always pass as "a mysterious and beautiful" figure who, like so many young Americans, had been a part of the Mayfair of the Edwardian years. Her meeting with Henry James would be a matter for scant attention had not her subsequent history proved so lurid. Two years after that London springtime, Miss Grigsby's patron, Charles T. Yerkes, the very prototype of an American tycoon, died at the Waldorf and Miss Grigsby was with him at the time. This projected the indomitable Emilie from the society pages into the front pages of all the scandal sheets of America. She carried with her among many names the name of Henry James—and the name of Milly Theale. In the fullness of time she would get herself into a novel, indeed a series of novels. Yerkes became Theodore Dreiser's "financier" in his trilogy; and Emilie Grigsby figures in *The Titan* of that series as Berenice Fleming.

Logan Pearsall Smith, an inveterate polisher and amplifier of Jamesian anecdote, long after used to say that the ham cooked in champagne was at the heart of the story. His version was that Henry James one day, in 1905 or 1906, after Yerkes's death, entered the Reform Club and joined a group of men who were gossiping idly. One among them at a given moment suddenly remarked, "Whatever became of that Grigsby woman?" In the ensuing silence, Pearsall Smith used to recall, James began to issue denials, like a Foreign Office. He denied he had ever known her, save to meet her on a few impersonal social occasions; he denied that she was the original of Milly Theale; he volunteered, and then denied, saying that it was simply a *canard*, that she had sent him a ham cooked in champagne.

This was Pearsall Smith's way of building up from slender threads his elaborate stories about the Master. There are two documents, however, which testify to the extent of the legend. For the story finally reached the Hearst press. "Heroine in Master's Novel; Grigsby in Language of Love." The *New York Evening Journal*, which published it on 4 January 1906, carried a caricature of a long-faced, lecherous-looking bald-headed Henry

James seated at his writing desk looking at a bust on a pedestal and at a portrait on his wall of Miss Emilie Grigsby. The caption read "Henry James and his Shrine: This is the celebrated author, reported to be in love with Emilie Grigsby, who is Mildred Theale, heroine of his novel *The Wings of the Dove*, whom he describes in terms of adoration, has placed on a pedestal as an object of adoration, an image of Miss Grigsby." The paper affirmed that the heroine of James's novel "in reality is Emilie Grigsby" and a sub-heading pushed harder. "Famous Author, some say, has Romantic Attachment for Girl he idealized as Mildred Theale."

This is the only time in recorded history that the Jamesian prose and the Jamesian style figured in the Hearst press. The story began, with the usual qualifications of journalism: "Out of the pages of fiction from the pen of one of the greatest master geniuses that America has given the world in modern years— Henry James—comes a wonderful, a close and detailed psychic and physical portrait of Emilie Grigsby, the girl whose wondrous beauty and strange, startling personality, fascinated Charles T. Yerkes, a foremost financier of the world, fascinated foremost society men and women in England, and in turn, it is also declared, absolutely entranced men of such amplitude of genius and almost uncanny intuitive gifts as George Meredith and her portrayer, Henry James.

"It may or may not be true that Henry James was, as report has stated of him, at one time deeply in love with Emilie Grigsby— that at sixty-five he sneered at conventionalities and in full knowledge of her past laid his great fame at her young feet and asked her to marry him. Men who came to him warning him that there was in the girl's career and antecedents that which would turn his romance over to the sneers of the world, are said to have been sent away from him with crackling words of anger and scorn. It is further said that when she left England and travelled to the Isle of Wight he followed her, and his recent return after years and years of absence to America was solely because of her return also to America."

The reporter went on:

"Friends of Miss Grigsby, while not denying that Henry James honoured her with his admiration, declare as fiction itself the tale of his love for her and his proposal of marriage to her. James himself is simply silent on the subject." There followed lengthy passages from the *Wings*, those in which James had described Milly Theale. These were prefaced as follows:

"There can be little doubt that the remarkable girl who had the devotion of Yerkes, the millionaire, was also the inspiration for the great writer's character-drawing of the strange, intense, fascinating girl, Mildred Theale . . . So much of Emilie Grigsby's life is like that of Mildred Theale, her voyage in Europe in the hope of securing the communion with cultured people that was denied her by her peculiar position in New York, her half successes, her trials in London life, and, so much in his actual description of the heroine's appearance and temperament coincide, that reading the splendid novel one feels of a certainty that Mildred Theale in real life was none other than Emilie Grigsby."

The Hearst version of James's novel was that "the tale takes the fabulously wealthy girl with her vague antecedents along the outskirts of English society not without heartache and wounds and it finally brings her in love with a young English journalist whose betrothed is so greatly the girl's friend that she is willing to abdicate in favour of the wonderful Milly. Milly has become afflicted with an illness affecting her heart, and it is in the belief that the marriage she wanted might bring her new life that the other girl offers such a big self-sacrifice."

The second document in the case is Henry James's letter to his brother William, dated 6 May 1904. William had inquired whether it was true that he had proposed marriage to Miss Grigsby.

Dearest William. Your "Grigsby" letter, which has just come in, would be worthy of the world-laughter of the Homeric Gods, if it didn't rather much depress me with the sense of the mere inane silliness of this so vulgarly chattering and so cheaply-fabricating age—the bricks of whose mendacity are made without even as many wisps of straw as would go into the mad Ophelia's hair. My engagement to *any one* is—as a "rumour"—exactly as fantastic and gratuitous a folly as would be the "ringing" report that Peggy, say, is engaged to Booker Washington, *ouf*! or that Aleck is engaged to Grace Norton. There *is* a Miss Grigsby whom I barely know to speak of, who has been in London two or three June or Julys.

He had seen Miss Grigsby, he said, half a dozen times in all. "She is, I believe, a Catholic, a millionaire and a Kentuckyian, and gives out that she is the original of the 'Milly' of my fiction *The Wings of the Dove*, published before I had ever heard of her apparently extremely silly existence. I have never written her so much as three words save two or three times, at most, to tell her I wouldn't come up from Rye to lunch or dine with her (I've never done it!) and I hadn't till your letter . . . so much as (entailing these so burdensome denegations—for a busy pen and a minding-one's-own-business-spirit) so much as been conscious of the breath of her name for practically a year—since about last June, that is, when I met her once at dinner in London (being there for a few days,) and *never* afterwards beheld her or communicated with her in any fashion whatever. *She* must have put about the 'rumour' which, though I thought her silly, I didn't suppose her silly *enough* for. But who—of her sex and species—isn't silly enough for *anything*, in this nightmare-world of insane *bavardage*. It's appalling that such winds may be started to blow, about one, by not so much as the ghost of an exhalation of one's own, and it terrifies me and sickens me for the prospect of my visit to your strange great continent of puerile *cancans*. Who and what, then, is safe? When you 'deny,' deny not simply by my authority please, but with my explicit derision and disgust." He signed himself as "always your hopelessly celibate even though sexagenarian Henry."

AN EXQUISITE RELATION

DURING the spring of 1903, when the sexagenarian bachelor was still in London, he received a letter from the famous Mrs Sitwell, who had been the "muse" of Robert Louis Stevenson's early days. She told Henry James that she and Sidney Colvin would marry that summer, and invited him to the wedding. Theirs had been a romance of forty years' standing. Colvin, keeper of prints and drawings at the British Museum, was fifty-eight—almost a sexagenarian; and the bride was six years older. Henry James had known the two ever since the early days of his friendship with Stevenson, that is the middle 1880's, when he saw Louis regularly at Skerryvore, near Bournemouth. Mrs Sitwell was then separated from her clergyman husband, who was now dead. Colvin long had had to support an aged mother. Now they were free to marry. Mrs Sitwell was a plump white-haired lady with a large nose and soft eyes; she wore large hats and feather boas. She had always maintained a literary salon, especially for young writers; Stevenson had been her great celebrity. She had been hostess for Colvin when he entertained in his British Museum residence, and all Victorian London knew that they had been in love for decades. "How charming and interesting your note, and how deeply touched I feel at having your news from you in this delightful way," James replied to Mrs Sitwell. "Besides being good, your intention is beautiful, which good intentions always aren't. It has a noble poetic justice." She had talked, he wrote, "of the crown of your romance coming late, but what do you say to the total absence (at the same lateness) of all crowns whatever, whether of romance or of anything else?— which is the chill grey solitary portion of your faithful old friend Henry James." Just before the wedding James sent his old friends a small silver salver "big enough to hold a glass of wine or a vase of flowers." He little dreamed that the wedding, a quiet, almost a secret one in view of the ages of the bride and groom, would prove an extraordinary occasion in his own life. He had given away the bride at Kipling's marriage; he had long ago gone to "a very cold church, to see my friend Mrs Carter, married: a rather dreary occasion, with a weeping bride, a sepulchral clergy-man who buried rather than married her, and a total destitution of relatives or accomplices of her own, so that she had to be given away by her late husband's brother." The bachelor of Bolton Street and De Vere Gardens had participated in many such intimate moments. And he came up for this marriage from Rye on 7 July 1903 with genuine pleasure.

Only four guests were invited to the Marylebone Church, where Browning, whom they had all known, had romantically married Elizabeth Barrett so many years before. James went in the com-pany of Lucy Clifford. They met at the side door of the church and entered to find beautiful floral decorations. "Are these for Mr Colvin's wedding?" James asked the verger. He received an almost indignant reply—"No, they are for a fashionable wedding at half past two." The Sitwell–Colvin party consisted in fact of the Bishop who married the couple, a cousin of Robert Louis Stevenson named Mrs Babington and his one-time friend Basil Champneys. Stevenson was thus an invisible presence. His memory linked everyone on this occasion. The ceremony was soon over and the party went on foot to the Great Central Hotel a quarter of a mile away for luncheon. Victorian reticence continued to prevail; they walked on different sides of the street, so as not to attract atten-tion. At least this was what Lucy Clifford reported later on, though she added "no one would have suspected six sedate middle-agers in everyday clothes, of anything unusual. We sauntered casually into the hotel, where a quiet little luncheon party had been arranged." It was very quiet indeed. The Colvins were obviously full of happy embarrassment and the guests were afraid to laugh and spoke only in low tones lest the waiter should suspect it was a marriage feast. "We did not even drink their health," said Mrs Clifford, "till someone, Basil Champneys I think, suggested that it ought to be done; then a bottle of still white wine was brought, our glasses were filled, and when the waiter was out of sight and hearing we drank to the bride and bridegroom with little nods and whispers."

The party was joined at the hotel by a young friend of Mrs Sitwell's, a handsome, elegant man, who seemed a dandy, and who looked younger than his years. Amid the group of elderly guests he seemed very young indeed: but he was actually thirty. His name was Dudley Jocelyn Persse. He was a Persse of Galway, a nephew of James's friend, Lady Gregory. Jocelyn carried himself with ease; he was gentle, poised, self-assured, yet with a touch of shyness. He was lively and good-natured; he laughed a great deal. James found him attractive from the first. He would speak later to Mrs Sitwell of Jocelyn's "constituted *aura* of fine gold and rose-colour." Persse on his side was drawn to the square and stocky elderly man, who looked at him in so friendly a way with his piercing eyes, and spoke with so much humour and had such an avuncular manner. We are left with the impression that the Master's eyes were always on Jocelyn. They found each other irresistible. The party proceeded afterwards in high spirits to Paddington. The newlyweds were waved on in their wedding journey. And a week later Henry James wrote to Mrs Colvin of the presence in Lamb House "of your delightful young Irish friend Jocelyn Persse. I feel as if I ought to thank you for him."

I

It seemed indeed a case of love at first sight. Two days after the wedding Jocelyn had called on the Master at the Reform Club. That same week-end he journeyed to Rye, where the two spent three days together, apparently not unlike the long week-end four years earlier when Henry James had discovered how much he loved the young sculptor, Hendrik Andersen. He loved Persse one judges quite as much—if not more. The first letter from James to Persse, written nine days after their meeting is addressed from the Athenaeum Club with an absence of formality to "my dear, dear, Jocelyn." James was snatching a minute, he said, to scribble a few friendly words. "You were as happily inspired to write me so humanely as when you had that other inspiration— days ago—of coming to see me at the Reform." The "days ago"

suggests the extent to which James felt himself Jocelyn's friend—
for exactly a week had elapsed. "Cultivate always, in the future,
inspirations as happy and as generous." He was, he said, lunching, tea-ing and dining out, "but finding it all less good, by a long
shot, for soul and sense, than the least moment of that golden
westward walk and talk of ours on Monday afternoon. A blessing
rested on that, still rests, will ever rest." James added that it
would "rest better still if you will remember that you promised to
send a photograph to yours always and ever" and he signed his
name with his customary grand flourish. He added an exhorta-
tion: "Let me find the photograph at Lamb House when I go
back."

When four days later James returned, Jocelyn's photograph
"welcomed me home to my empty halls and made them seem for
the moment less lonely." The novelist evicted another picture
from a frame to make room for his new friend, wishing Jocelyn
had autographed it—"for you are one of those of whom the
beholder asks who you are." James added, possessively, "You
are not for the staring crowd." He told Jocelyn of a visit he had
paid to Surrey, and a drive he had taken in that rural countryside
"which is so absurdly near the dire South London. But these will
seem pale adventures to *you*, luxurious youth, whom I seem to see
launched on the huge (and agitating) wave of the King's visit,
and into endless Irish junketing. May these things not float you
too direfully far—far, I mean, from the virtuous *grind* of life and
the sober realities that a homely friend can hope to share with
you!" He ended by enjoining Jocelyn to remember—"and never
doubt of it"—that "no small sign of your remembrance will ever
fail even of its most meagre message to yours, my dear Jocelyn,
always Henry James."

Thus was struck the note, the consistent tender note, of a
friendship that would grow in warmth and feeling and remain
devoted and loyal to the end—into the time when James grew old
and ill and Jocelyn's golden hair turned white. The refrain was
that of the young man-about-town, who moves in the great wide
world and brings tidings of it to the elderly writer, in his Rye
hermitage—the great wide world of country houses, visits to

Ireland and Scotland, and the Riviera, dinners and parties, which had been James's life during the period of his conquest of London. Even more than Andersen, Jocelyn Persse became a kind of image in a mirror of James's own younger days. Jocelyn was half James's age; and he made James feel as if he were still thirty. Andersen had helped break the plate-glass front of James's life, and Persse and the novelist were able to approach one another with an ease and friendliness James had not allowed himself in his earlier and more reserved years.

II

The more than seventy letters Persse kept—there probably were others—had been hastily thrown into drawers of old desks; their pages are mixed up; some are partly torn; some sheets are missing; some have cigarette or cigar holes burned in them. Their condition suggests that Persse lived much in the moment; that his friendship with James depended on their direct meetings rather than on the written word. Through these letters, in their tattered state, shines the constancy of James's affection and the evidence of Jocelyn's loyal response. The letters have none of the desperation, or anguish, or ache of passion that occurs periodically in the letters to Andersen (these by contrast preserved meticulously, perhaps with a sense of their future value as autographs). There was for James "something admirable and absolute" between him and Jocelyn. This was true. He would speak also of "this exquisite relation of ours." Jocelyn wasn't the least bit "literary." He was a finely-turned-out specimen of the Anglo-Irish gentry— addicted to good manners, the enjoyment of food and drink, fine cigars, fine brandy, hunting, flirtation, romance, the "fun" of living. Very early in their friendship James wrote to Jocelyn: "I seem to see you roll, triumphant, from one scene of amiable hospitality and promiscuous social exercise to another; and, sitting here, on my side, as tight as I can, with a complete avoidance of personal rolling, I quite rejoice in the bright brave vision of you, who are willing to do these things (that I can't do) for my mind, and to take me with you, so to speak in thought—so that, even while I crouch in my corner, I get through you, more or less, the vibration of adventure and the side-wind of the unfolding panorama. May you to the end of the feast, retain a stout young stomach! which is a manner of saying—may you suffer yourself to be pelted with as many of the flowers of experience as you can (we won't talk just now of the thorns;) so that when we next meet you shall have at least some of the withered leaves to show me and let me sniff." And James told him that "the record of your eternal Bacchanalia (do you know what Bacchanalia are?) continues to excite my vague envy, or at least my lively admiration, of your social genius, social good health, the mysterious genial power that guides and sustains you through the multitude of your contacts and the mazes of your dance. What I do envy is the magnificent *ease* with which you circulate and revolve—spinning round like a brightly-painted top that emits, as it goes, only the most musical hum. You don't *creak*." Or again: "I rejoice greatly in your breezy, heathery, grousy—and housey, I suppose—adventures, and envy you, as always, your exquisite possession of the Art of Life which beats any Art of mine hollow."

Others—Hugh Walpole for instance—who watched James's friendship with Persse wondered what the two talked about, how this young man whose spelling wasn't up to scratch and whose talk was wholly social and gossipy, could hold the formidable Master. But then Hugh stood in awe of James; Jocelyn didn't. Hugh mentioned this once to James (for he was jealous of Jocelyn) and asked what "subjects in common" they found to talk about. He got a clear answer. "One gets on with him in a way without them, and says to one's self, I think, that if *he* doesn't mind, well, why should one either? At any rate I am glad you were gentle with him. I am infinitely and gladly so." Hugh Walpole was often intensely bored by Jocelyn, who had none of Hugh's ambition or his literary and social pretensions. But Walpole did write in his diary that he found Jocelyn "nice, eager to be liked, easily pleased" and again "very agreeable—a good creature," "the kindest and nicest of creatures." One entry as late as 17 March 1914: "Spent evening with Jocelyn who was perfectly delightful with his simplicity and charm."

His simplicity, his charm, his good looks, *these* mattered for

"Just as one tumbles back into the street in appalled reaction to them."

"But there would be too much to say just here were this incurable eccentric to let himself go."

THREE CARICATURES 1905
by F. Opper

"Some such close and sweet and whole national consciousness as that of the Switzer and the Scot."

TWO CARICATURES 1905

by F. Opper and another

James much more than any high intellectual talk. Jocelyn, faced with a literary question, usually ducked it. "Well, I think there are things to be said *for*—and *against*—don't you?" So Walpole remembered. James had had enough of that sort of thing in the *grand monde* of literature. Early in their friendship Jocelyn was off to Greece and James wrote him: "God grant that I be here when you turn up with the rich glow of travel on your manly cheek and the oaths of all the Mediterranean peoples on your moustachioed lips (as I hope, at least, I should like to hear you rip them out.) But I yearn, dear Jocelyn, for all your sensations and notations, and think with joy of your coming to me for a couple of days, near at hand a little later on, shaking the dews of Parnassus from your hair. When I think you are living with Phidias and the Hermes, with the divine race, in short, I am ashamed of writing you a prosy Pall Mall note. *Je t'embrasse bien tendrement.*"

James was "peculiarly *touched* by every letter of yours that reaches me." What existed between him and Jocelyn was one of those friendships in which neither friend makes large demands on the other; Jocelyn wandered in "society," visited, travelled—and eventually came to Lamb House. James went to America and was away for many months. When they met they did so with a fullness of appreciation of one another and a great joy in their companionship. When Jocelyn was in London, in his flat at Park Place, James periodically issued one of his elaborate invitations to the younger man to join him for dinner and a theatre in town. "Can you miraculously dine with me either tonight or tomorrow *here*—at 8.15—and perhaps 'go' somewhere; or at any rate *talk?*—when I will tell you many things—most of all how indeed I remember last year." James was writing on the first anniversary of their first week-end together at Lamb House. He had been to the British Museum "where, between Colvin and Colvina, our meeting of last summer always comes romantically back." When Jocelyn considerately wondered whether he wasn't keeping James from work and from doing important things instead of simply gossiping with him, James replied, "Don't, my dear boy, afflict me again by talking of my 'sacrifices.' There is, for me, something admirable and absolute between us which waves away all

G

that. But these things are beyond words—words almost vulgarize them. Yet the last ones of your note infinitely move me." They went to see the new Shaw plays at the Court Theatre. They saw Gerald du Maurier, son of James's old friend, in *Raffles*. They went to plays given by the Stage Society—Persse remembered one such occasion when they saw Gertie Millar and James was "bored to distraction." "The humour of a country circus" he exclaimed and they walked out at the end of the first act. Then for lighter entertainment there were always the music-halls. James had always been a devotee and so was Jocelyn. The younger man remembered taking James "to the low" Middlesex, which Walter Sickert painted, and where "the primitive audience appealed to him." And some years later, when James had a play produced in Edinburgh, Jocelyn journeyed non-stop all the way from Algiers to be present at the opening night as James's guest. James sent Persse *The Ambassadors* when it was published—"if you are able successfully to struggle with it try to like the poor old hero, in whom you will perhaps find a vague resemblance (though not facial!) to yours always Henry James." He knew that Jocelyn probably wouldn't read him. Jocelyn wasn't bookish. But this mattered not at all to James. What mattered was the air of charm and enchantment they seemed to weave for one another. "Why he liked me so much I cannot say," Persse would write many years later. And he said also James was "the dearest human being I have ever known."

III

Thus James found himself, in his sixty-first year, with two attachments to ease the loneliness and melancholy of ageing. He continued to write passionate letters to Andersen—although letters increasingly critical of him—even while he enjoyed his periodical meetings with Jocelyn. The letters to Jocelyn do not contain the quantity of verbal embracings and laying on of hands that we find in those addressed to Andersen. Perhaps the intimacy with the young Irishman was close; it did not need so much verbalizing— "words almost vulgarize them," James had said of his feelings. But for Andersen words were available. We may speculate, in trying to read between the lines, that James's involvement with Andersen had in it a part of his passion as artist. Andersen was trying to become a great sculptor. He had a strong touch of megalomania that James, with his own Napoleonic drive, would recognize: and on that "wave-length" their feelings were deeply enmeshed, or at least James's seemed to be, so that when Andersen did not measure up to James's high standards and codes of art, there was strong and poignant disillusion; this younger version of himself was proving a failure—which he himself, in his youth, had not been. With Jocelyn no such tensions seem to have existed. Percy Lubbock, whose involvement with James as ultimate editor of his letters, would be posthumous rather than actual, would write a novel called *The Region Cloud* about a great artist and his disciples, picturing the artist as a powerful vampire, who needed young admirers to feed his incredible egotism. Whether he was thinking of himself and James we do not know: but in the very style of the novel, with its Jamesian imitations, and hinged and dramatized sentences, Lubbock created a portrait-caricature of James of considerable power and a certain amount of truth. The artist in the novel is both vampire and cannibal: he is so creative that he "makes his own life, every hour of it—he is the author of it all; and when he has made an hour of it his life is not what it was before, it is changed by the value of that hour; and so it's a new man, a new author, who passes on to the next hour and the next, and each of his days is a creation as fresh as the first." In a very Jamesian passage, Lubbock describes his character's charm —"he dazzled the intruders with his mirth, or he flattered them with his grandeur, or he caressed them with his irony—always according to his mood, giving them what he was pleased to give; for they mightn't choose, they had to take what he offered them, the greatest with the least. Sometimes he bullied and trounced them without mercy, and on this mood, too, they thrived as well as ever . . . he overruled the intruders, one and all, with that lordly possession of himself."

This is the extreme of discipleship. It has in it some of the flavour of James's letters to Andersen, to Persse and later to Hugh Walpole. Lubbock's fictional recreation suggests a ruthlessness and a lack of a sense of reality. But if James could be ruthless with others he was no less ruthless with himself. And he never lost sight, even in his moments of love and loftiness of the realities in his personal relations.

Years later Hugh Walpole spoke of James's "inevitable loneliness" and of the conflict in James's temperament, between his "reticent Puritanism" and his "intellectual curiosity." He believed the loneliness in James came from his remaining an exile in Europe, while never at peace with America. In America "he longed for the age, the quiet, the sophistications of Europe." And his young friends, the young men who clustered around him, whether disciples in letters or caught up in the magnetism and egotism of the artist, fed his powerful feelings. "His passion for his friends—Lucy Clifford, Edith Wharton, Jocelyn Persse, Mrs Prothero, among others—was the intense longing of a lonely man. It was most unselfish and noble." Walpole was partly right; it was noble in its grandiosity, but not always unselfish; there was in it some of the egotism James himself described in "The Beast in the Jungle;" but it had in it also the nobility of his art.

In referring to James's Puritanism Walpole may have sought to varnish the eroticism of the novelist's letters to his acolytes. It is difficult to say. The exact nature of James's friendship with Jocelyn, as that with Andersen, we cannot at this late date describe. Sir Rupert Hart-Davis recalls meeting Persse while walking down Piccadilly with Walpole and Hugh saying, after they left him, "Believe it or not, Henry James was madly in love with him." The evidence is tenuous: we have so little beyond the affectionate language of James's letters. We must remind ourselves that if on the one hand there was a buried life of sexual adventure among some Victorian men, as evidenced by the revelations of the Wilde case and the more recent evidence in the papers of John Addington Symonds, there were also many friendships which were romantic rather than physical. The Victorian world was a man's world: men met in clubs; there were very few women in offices or in business. The women had their world of the home and of society. Whether the homo-erotic feeling between Persse and James was "acted out" is perhaps less important than the fact that a great state of affection existed between them. We must remind ourselves that James was old, stout, Johnsonian. He probably loved Persse in some ways as Johnson had loved his Boswell. Boswell had been a candid young man about town with stories of his escapades and his adventures. But Boswell was a "publishing" individual who consumed his life in his diaries—and planned to write the life of Johnson. Persse simply lived his life; and years afterwards his memories of James remained un-recorded; they were absorbed into one great memory—that of an abiding affection. He was not a keeper of diaries; and James's date-books, and the letters, tell us all we know of their meetings. We are left with the impression that James's love meant more to Persse than James's greatness. They both pos-sessed a large fund of hedonism. It was the love of an ageing man for his own lost youth, and the evocation of it in a figure of masculine beauty, as with Hendrik Andersen. He found in his relationship with Persse what he did not find with Andersen, the serenity that enabled him to make *The Golden Bowl*, which he was now writing, a work unique among all his novels: it is James's only novel in which things come out right for his characters—the marriage survives, there is progeny, and the hero has a strength and masculinity not to be found in James's other works. James's feelings of the moment were always incorporated into what he was writing. Prince Amerigo may have in him some touches of Jocelyn—but he has much more the strength and self-assertion of James himself. In his relation with Persse, James finally freed himself from the prolonged innocence of his earlier years. Persse helped complete the process begun four years earlier when James had met Andersen in Rome. And while James tried to write more novels after *The Golden Bowl*, he no longer needed to do so: he had finally resolved the questions, curious and passionate, that had kept him at his desk in his inquiry into the process of living. He could now go back to America and make his peace with it; and he could now build the altar of himself, collect and unify the work of a lifetime.

LESSONS OF THE MASTER

HE had become a presence, an oracle, a legend. Not only the increasingly conferred title of "Master," but the adulation of the young men, the awe he seemed to inspire in the drawing-rooms, the way in which he was publicly quoted, the fact that he was now imitated, parodied, caricatured—all this spoke for the imprint of a style and a personality. The very headlines in the New York newspapers—or their reverberations—had in them the overtones of reputation. If there was laughter at James's odd-ness, or complaint that he was "difficult," this suggested he was read and discussed. People took sides. Where was there admira-tion that didn't inspire envy, irritation, hostility? Articles were appearing, "The Queerness of Henry James," or "In Darkest James." Frank Moore Colby, taking his readers on a tour of the jungle of James would speak of chapters in *The Wings of the Dove* that were "like wonderful games of solitaire, broken by no human sound" except for the author's "own chuckle when he takes some mysterious trick or makes a move that he says is 'beautiful.'" But Colby also admitted that James produced "very strange and powerful effects" even when he was "wearisomely prolix." People had cared for Browning not because he had a "message," but because of his presence in his poems; "part of the obscurity of Henry James," Colby said, "springs from the same pleasing and honorable egotism."

Young writers began to write like him. Henry James received a sample of this in late 1902 from his friend Morton Fullerton, who had long before been accused by his editors at *The Times* of writing in Jamesese. Fullerton's sister Katherine, who would later be a successful magazine writer, (Katherine Fullerton Gerould), had written a tale which Henry read with strange feel-ings of embarrassment and pleasure. "Am I so much that *as* that?" he queried Morton, "it *is*, but too sensitively, too insanely *me* ... She may see a little where she's going, but I see where she's *coming*—and oh, the dangers scare me." He himself, he said, would much sooner have written like Anthony Hope or F. Marion Crawford, naming the best-selling authors of the hour, "and I think she ought accordingly to ask herself if the real tribute shouldn't be to do what the accident of myself only has prevented me from doing. Let her apply my inclination, my yearning, as I can't apply it."

I

He had a particular and even painful instance of the effect of his personality and his literary power in the autumn of 1903 when Howard Overing Sturgis brought him the galleys of a long-planned novel. Sturgis was a very particular friend whose name sometimes got him confused with James's other friend, the crippled "little demon," Jonathan Sturges. Howard visited Lamb House rarely, but James stayed quite often in Howard's comfortable oversize Georgian villa, Queen's Acre—called by everyone "Qu'Acre"—on the edge of Windsor Park. Here at various times during the coming years James would be at the centre of Sturgis's entourage, Benson, Lubbock, the young American historian Lapsley who taught at Trinity College, Cambridge, Rhoda Broughton, and a bit later Edith Wharton who had known Sturgis at Newport. Howard was the youngest son of the American banker Russell Sturgis, whom James had known and visited in the 1870's in his fine residence in Carlton House Terrace. James had remembered the youthful Howard Sturgis, but he had not really got to know him until the young man completed his education at Eton and Cambridge. He inherited considerable wealth and settled promptly into Victorian domesticity. As George Santayana later put it, Howard Sturgis believed that there was nothing women did that men could not do better; and Howard's most characteristic eccentricity was his addiction to embroidery and knitting. He would sit with his thick golden hair—which later became silvered—beautifully brushed, his small feet daintily crossed, in the middle of a square carpet on the lawn, or by his fireside, with his basket and his dogs about him, working on some large golden-threaded design. He lived with a friend, a younger man, William Haynes Smith, known to the Qu'Acre circle as "The Babe." He might have been the child Howard might have borne if he had been of the opposite sex; or the younger brother he never had, for he himself had been the youngest. His mother's boudoir had been Howard's nursery and playroom; she had clung to him in her widowhood. Santayana said Howard was "her last and permanent baby." The philosopher added that Howard became in due course "a perfect young lady of the Victorian type." There are more friendly characterizations, for in spite of his eccentricities, "Howdie"—even his nickname carried with it a flavour of childhood—had had a very successful career at school; he had embodied his Eton experience in a sentimental novel called *Tim*, long before he met James. He was witty, poetic, sociable, gentle, and not at all intellectual. We can see him through the eyes of one of the younger Etonians admitted to his circle, Percy Lubbock. "He sat at home," wrote Lubbock, "wound his wool and stitched at his work; he took a turn on the road with his infirmary of dogs; with head inclined in sympathy and suavity he poured out tea for the local dowager who called on him." His villa had a quiet domestic air, with its white-panelled walls hung with water-colours, its furniture of faded slippery chintz, its French windows opening on an old-fashioned large American-style verandah. Edith Wharton remembered the view from the windows—a weedy lawn, uneven shrubbery, a neglected rose garden, a dancing faun poised above an "arty" blue-tiled pool. Small wonder that Qu'Acre, and its homey atmosphere provided such a warm hearth for those of Howdie's intimates who weren't bothered by his feminine traits—as Santayana seems to have been. Howard attracted endless visitors, dandies, distinguished dames, the *literati*. And over his salon he presided, a passive nature lodged in the sturdy frame of a moustachioed and vigorous male. The atmosphere was a mixture of the maternal, paternal and even matriarchal. Perhaps this was why James once told Howard he could find it possible to live with him—an unusually affectionate declaration from a novelist who cherished his privacy, and lived so proudly alone. It would have been for James a little

like living with his mother—and the American females he had
described in his early Civil War tales seated by the fire endlessly
knitting. James spoke of "Howard in his infinite Howardism"—
finding no other way of defining his friend except in his own
terms. His other image for him recalled childhood goodies.
Howdie was like a richly-sugared cake, said James, always available on the table. "We sit round him in a circle and help ourselves. Now and then we fling a slice over our shoulders to some-
body outside." Sometimes they even allowed a newcomer to join
the closed circle. Henry James, during his Qu'Acre visits, would
pad about the room in his comfortable bulk, or stand hugely by
the fireside, "listening, muttering, groaning disapproval or
chuckling assent to the paradoxes of the other tea drinkers." And
he would talk when tea was over—about Paris, or his earlier
London, or some novel he had read, or play he had seen, or about
Balzac, Tolstoy, or Meredith. This was one of the stranger and
more home-like salons of the many he had frequented; and its
frequenters were all amusing and brilliant, and all of "the better
sort."

II

Howard Sturgis had long before this time told James of the novel
he was writing, and had received strong encouragement. After
Tim he had published a short fiction with a Trollopeian title, *All
That Was Possible*, written in the old-fashioned epistolary style.
Now he had completed his long work, *Belchamber*. It was about
a young English marquis, of an extremely passive nature, who
marries a rather pushing young woman more out of chivalry than
affection, flattered that she should be interested in him. She has
wanted his title and his wealth, but she despises him and the
marriage is never consummated. She takes lovers and he continues his bachelor existence. In due course she presents him with
an heir. The young nobleman remains passive. Howard thus
provided himself in his novel with a babe, without having to
sleep with any woman. The best part of the novel is the affection
Sainty—Howdie's hero—bestows on the infant.

"Bring your book and read it aloud!" James told Sturgis, in-

viting him to Lamb House early in October 1903. Jocelyn
wanted to come at this time but James postponed his visit. Then
Howard postponed his, and his stay overlapped with a visit long
planned by Hendrik Andersen, who, being in Paris, came over to
Rye for four or five days. Howard seems not to have read his
novel aloud to James, but he left behind a batch of galleys. In a
matter of days he received the first report. The novel was going
"very solidly and smoothly," James wrote. Having delivered a
series of compliments, James settled down to the essentials. He
was, he warned Sturgis, a bad person to read other people's novels.
After all he was "a battered producer and 'technician'" himself,
and could read only critically, constructively and "*re*constructively." James was up to his old tricks; this was the way he always
dealt with Mrs Humphry Ward, or H. G. Wells; he would do the
same to the young Hugh Walpole. Critical though he was, he
said he was ready to "pass" Howard's book. The one detail over
which he paused was Howdie's choosing as his main character a
member of the English nobility and of such high rank, a Marquis.
"When a man is an English Marquis, even a lame one, there are
whole masses of Marquisate things and items, a multitude of inherent detail in his existence, which it isn't open to the painter *de
gaieté de cœur* not to make some picture of." James was sure
however other readers wouldn't notice this. "No one notices or
understands *any*thing and no one will make a single intelligent or
intelligible observation about your work. They will make plenty
of others." And James applauded the way in which Howdie had
stayed with the inner world of Sainty.

These observations were mild enough, but Howard Sturgis
was understandably sensitive about his work; he was worried by
James's implying that an American, like himself, however much
identified with England, could hardly know the inner world of the
nobility. What James perhaps overlooked was that Howdie had
recorded, with great accuracy, the natural history of a passive
male. James, however, came to the question of the passivity in
his second letter, after he had read a further batch of galleys. It
wasn't only Sainty's aristocratic "point of view," said James, it
was that he was "*all* passive and nullity." Where was the *positive*

side? James suddenly expressed the wish that he might have talked with Sturgis while "the book was a-writing" in the interest of producing a Sainty "with a constituted and intense imaginative life of his own." He did not question the existence of so virtuous and innocent a young man, who came through to the reader in so negative a way: this was however because Sturgis gave Sainty "*no state of his own* as the field and stage of the vision and the drama." The novel didn't seem to happen to Sainty, but *around* him. When Sturgis replied that after Sainty's marriage "nothing happens to him" James replied as from Olympus: "Why, my dear Howard, it is the part in which *most* happens! His marriage itself, his wife *herself*, happen to him at every hour of the 24—and he is the only person to whom anything does . . . If he had only felt everything else as he feels his wife's baby . . . the subject would have been fully expressed. But it is the baby, as a baby, that he actually feels—for a pleasure—most."

James pointed out to Howard that to have Sainty living with his wife day after day as if he were a bachelor who had no thoughts or feelings on the subject was to have nothing "happen" in the novel—"to whom *is* it happening?" To have married this young woman in the belief that she cared for him and to find her then wholly avoiding him "would be really for him an experience of some kind of Intensity. There was something in him (at the worst!) to which this was to be *shown as happening*—horribly, tormentedly, strangely—in some way or *other* happening." James's unveiling of the work's central weakness overwhelmed Howard. We do not have his letter, but we know that he announced to the Master he was withdrawing his novel from publication. James wrote in haste, clearly upset, of "your too lamentable letter, in which you speak of 'withdrawing' your novel—too miserably, horribly, impossibly, for me to listen to you for a moment. If you *think* of anything so insane you will break my heart and bring my grey hairs, the few left me, in sorrow and shame to the grave. Why should you have an inspiration so perverse and so criminal? If it springs from anything I have said to you I must have expressed myself with strange and deplorable clumsiness."

Thus James realized that lessons of a Master, however truthful and right, however close to the sanctity and integrity of art, could overwhelm. He reassured Howdie: "Your book will be the joy of thousands of people, who will very justly find it interesting and vivid, and pronounce it 'disagreeable,' etc., vivid, and lively, curious and witty and *real*." James said his own "esoteric" reflections would occur to no one else "at all, and the whole thing will excite marked attention." If Howdie loved him, said James, "let your adventure take care of itself to the end."

There exists an independent report of the Master's essentially uncompromising attitude towards the novel, in the diary of Arthur Christopher Benson. The latter, in April 1904, was cross-examining James at the Athenaeum, on how his ideas came to him for a book. James replied "It's all *about*, it's about—it's in the air —it, so to speak, follows me and dogs me." At this point Thomas Hardy came and sat on the other side of Benson, so that he felt "like Alice between the two Queens." The conversation flowed to Cardinal Newman, and then to Flaubert about whom James was oracular. "Then Hardy went away wearily and kindly. Then H.J. and I talked of Howard's *Belchamber*," just published —for Howdie had been mollified. James said it was a good idea, a good situation. He had read it and "Good Heavens, I said to myself, he has made nothing of it! . . . Good God, why this chronicle, if it is a mere passage, a mere ante-chamber, and leads to nothing." He had tried he said "with a thousand subterfuges and doublings such as one uses with the work of a friend" to indicate the fault.

This was more harsh than anything James had written to Sturgis. But even with the "subterfuges and doublings" James's criticisms came through to his friend with distinct clarity, and Howdie felt the disapproval all the more profoundly because he loved the Master. Edith Wharton, contending that James was never to be trusted about the value of any fiction "not built according to his own rigid plan," said that Sturgis—his "native indolence and genuine humility aiding"—accepted James's verdict and "relapsed into knitting and embroidery." But in the privacy of his study Sturgis wrote out his painful feelings in an unpublished tale called "The China Pot"—about a great writer who demolishes the work of a younger man. The younger man takes this so to heart that he commits suicide; and in a scene at the cemetery, the Great Author and another friend discuss why the young man has taken his life. He had had everything to live for, youth, good looks, freedom from care, intelligence. The Great Author says he finds his death "amazing, mysterious and inexplicable." But the other man "could see that he knew as well as I did, and that he knew that I knew." This was an ending worthy of James himself, and one that would have given the deepest pain to the Master, which is perhaps why Howdie never published the story. James had had a signal, however, of how powerful his effect on others could be.

The signals were there; the incidents occurred—and yet James never learned. So massive was he in his authority and doctrine that one had but to thrust a novel under his nose and the great machinery went to work. The habits of a lifetime were hard to outlive. A few months after the *Belchamber* incident, James received a novel by the young Forrest Reid—*The Kingdom of Twilight*. It was an offering of homage from a young admirer. James promptly read the book "with interest and attention." The attention was weighty. "Up to the middle at least, you see your subject where it *is*—in the character and situation of your young man." But—the invariable *but*—"I confess however, that, *after* the middle you strike me as *losing* your subject—or, at any rate, I, as your reader, did so. After the meeting with the woman by the sea—certainly after the parting from her—I felt the reality of the thing deviate, felt the subject lose its conditions, so to speak, its *observed* character and its logic." And then the final flourish and the accolade—"it's not of your young (as I take it) your airy and enviably young inexpertnesses that I wished to speak—for many of these you will obviously leave behind you. There are elements of beauty and sincerity in your volume that remain with me." Thus the doctrinaire lessons of the Master: much kindness, much truth, great integrity—yet often the weighty foot stepping on tender toes.

AN AGREEABLE WOMAN

FOR some years the Master had been quietly pursued by another American writer, an elegant lady, more professional in her work than Howard Sturgis, more determined, more ambitious. Her name was Edith Wharton. She came out of James's "old New York" although born two decades later. His locale had been essentially Washington Square (before the city had moved uptown), with its prosperous upper middle-class merchants and doctors. Mrs Wharton's was the higher reach of the then residential Fifth Avenue, and the aristocracy of wealth and tradition that had developed from the days of the "patroons" during the Dutch régime. She had Joneses, Schermerhorns, Rhinelanders, Pendletons, Gallatins, and Ledyards for ancestors. Her maternal ancestor, General Ebenezer Stevens, had served under Lafayette in the defeat of Cornwallis. She had a large inheritance and had grown up to "a life of leisure and amiable hospitality," as she put it. Edith Newbold Jones came to maturity in a small and wealthy Manhattan society that was now threatened by the new industrialism, the *arrivistes* James had only tentatively sketched in his fiction. She herself would describe her group as having "a blind dread of innovation, an instinctive shrinking from responsibility." Edith Jones met her responsibilities. She knew to the core this tight little world, with its old decencies, its stratified codes, its tradition of elegance, and the daily life within its brownstone mansions already fenced in by tall buildings.

She had been reared in a masculine family circle. Her two brothers were grown men when she was still a child, and she was deeply attached to her father. In her memoirs she sketches an intimate portrait of him but adopts towards her mother a tone of condescension, an aloof tolerance for her love of fashionable clothes and the life of "society." Edith herself would insist later in life, not successfully, that her name be dropped from the

"Social Register." The male circle which framed her childhood would lead Edith Jones to have more men friends than women and they were always men high in the life of the country. It was said of her that she brought a man's strength to the sympathy and solicitude of a woman, and a man's organizing power to a woman's interest in dress and the decoration of houses. James would put it in another way, comparing her with the volatile and "liquid" George Sand and the intellectually powerful George Eliot. In her novels he found "the masculine conclusion" tended "so to crown the feminine observation." She was, in James's life, one of the "queenly" women he had studied closely in earlier years. Mrs Gardner's assertiveness had attracted him to her—but Mrs Wharton did not have to assert her queenliness in the eccentric ways of Mrs Jack. It was instinctive, inborn, inbred—and what endeared her to James was that she possessed also a civilized mind and an artist's style. Indeed her "set" never forgave her for her devotion to her art. And it took her many years, as her novels show, to free herself from the fetters of her class.

I

She would later recall that she had crossed Henry James's path twice in the 1880's and the early 1890's: but she was then too shy and in awe of the Master to speak to him, and he paid no attention to her. The first occasion had been at the home of the Edward Boits in Paris, where Mrs Wharton had sported a specimen of the *haute couture* in the hope that she might catch the attention of the pensive bearded novelist. She failed. She tried again one day in Venice in the Curtis entourage, where she made a point of wearing a particularly fetching hat. To this display of finery he seems to have been impervious: or perhaps to Edith's assertion of personality through dress. She had not, then, published anything and was living with her socially prominent husband, Edward Robbins Wharton, largely at Newport, and paying extended visits to Europe. In the closing years of the century, the Bourgets began to speak to James of their valued American friend, Madame Whar-*ton*. He heard of her also from Mary Cadwalader Jones, the divorced wife of Edith's older brother, whom he had known

for some years and liked. Through the Bourgets, Mrs Wharton
sent James a message of good-will at the moment of *Guy Domville*. And in 1899 she sent him her first book of tales, *The Greater
Inclination*. James reported this to Bourget saying he had received
"a fruit of literary toil" from Mrs Wharton and a note that she
expected to be at Claridge's—"the sojourn of kings." As the
remark implied, James had no intention of calling on her in such
a royal place. Towards the end of that year he wrote Bourget he
had read Mrs Wharton's stories. What was best in them was "her
amiable self." What was "not best was quite another person."
He had recognized himself, his style, "I should like a quiet hour
with that almost too susceptible *élève*. In which of the hemispheres
does she happen for the moment to be?"

If the Master was willing to give the susceptible pupil one of
his famous lessons, he seems to have made no particular effort to
do so. Almost a year elapsed before he acknowledged the tales.
What prompted him finally to write was a story in *Lippincott's*,
called "The Line of Least Resistance." He found Mrs Wharton's
tale "brilliant." It possessed "an admirable sharpness and neat-
ness and infinite wit and point." And in his most charming law-
giving vein he continued, in his first letter to her, dated 26
October 1900:

> I applaud, I mean I value, I egg you on in your study of the American life
> that surrounds you. Let yourself go in it and *at* it—it's an untouched field,
> really: the folk who try, over there, don't come within miles of any civilized,
> any "evolved" life. And use to the full your remarkable ironic and valeric
> gifts; they form a most valuable, (I hold) and beneficent engine.

Still her irony and her "valeric" quality needed moderating. The
Lippincott tale was "a little hard, a little purely derisive." He
hastened to tone this down by his usual invocation to Youth—
"you're so young, and with it, so clever. Youth is hard—and
your needle-point later on will muffle itself in a little blur of silk.
It *is* needle-point!" The allusion to her youth was generous: she
was by now almost forty. He ended by urging Edith Wharton to
send him what she wrote. "I'll do the same by you!" he promised.
He asked her also to come to see him some day.

She had finally made a distinct impression. But she was then writing a long novel and creating one of the finest of her houses in America (her first book had been a collaboration with an architect, *The Decoration of Houses*.) The house was The Mount, at Lenox, Massachusetts, where she would receive the Master some years later. They had not yet met when in 1902 she sent him her two-volume historical fiction, *The Valley of Decision* which she dedicated to Bourget; and Mrs Cadwalader Jones followed this up, sending Mrs Wharton's new collection of tales, *Crucial Instances* and her short novel *The Touchstone*. James acknowledged the historical novel and told Mrs Wharton he had read it with sympathy, "high criticism, high consideration" and "generally most intimate participation." He did not tell her that he disliked this kind of novel; instead he returned to the charge of his earlier letter. He wanted "crudely" but "earnestly, tenderly, intelligently to admonish you, while you are young, free, expert, exposed (to illumination)—by which I mean while you're in full command of the situation—admonish you, I say, in favour of the *American Subject*. There it is round you. Don't pass it by—the immediate, the real, the ours, the yours, the novelists' that it waits for. Take hold of it and keep hold, and let it pull you where it will." He drove home the lesson. "Profit, be warned, by my awful example of exile and ignorance. You will say that *j'en parle à mon aise*, but I shall have paid for my ease, and I don't want you to pay (as much) for yours." Pausing to apologize for his "impertinent importunities" he still returned to the charge with "All the same DO NEW YORK! The first-hand account is precious."

The Master thus saw, with great clarity, where Mrs Wharton's talent and subject lay. He meant what he said for a few days later he sent to Mrs Cadwalader Jones his famous statement that Edith "must be tethered in native pastures, even if it reduce her to a backyard in New York." He further told the authoress's sister-in-law, that he was "very taken with Mrs Wharton—her diabolical little cleverness, the quantity of intention and intelligence in her style, and her sharp eye for an interesting *kind* of subject."

II

They actually did not meet until December 1903, when James had passed his sixtieth birthday and Mrs Wharton her fortieth. In the interval she had installed herself in The Mount. She came abroad that year, and when she arrived in London, James called on her, one day just before Christmas. He seems then also to have met her husband. James saw a woman of about his own height, dressed with taste and distinction, who spoke in the civilized manner of her tales. Her husband was genial and wholly non-intellectual. Mrs Wharton was all the blue-stocking, with a range of literary knowledge and quotation, a saturation in German— part of her childhood had been passed in Germany—and a thorough knowledge of things French. She was cosmopolitan like himself. She had lived much in her imagination during her European childhood. Yet she was grounded in New York; and she was concrete and observant. On her side, she saw a different James from the bearded "Penseroso" of Mrs Boit's Parisian drawing-room, or the light-jacketed James of Venice. For the first time she looked upon his shaven countenance, "the noble Roman mask" of his face and "the big dramatic mouth," and she noticed well-tailored clothes which now loosely enveloped the considerable embonpoint. James was massive and masterly. Her report of her meeting, to her editor at Scribner's, spoke of his looking, without his beard, like a blend of Coquelin and Lord Rosebery. Thus she caught the histrionic aspect of James as well as the aristocratic. He seemed to her "in good spirits" and she said he talked "more lucidly than he writes," for she did not like his later manner. The once-shy younger woman had herself changed to matronly middle age. She no longer stood in awe of the Master. But he remained, and would remain, a figure of mag-netic charm and force—her greatest literary friend. His first impression of her was, as he put it to Henrietta Reubell, that she was *sèche*, although agreeable and intelligent. The word "dry" continued to characterize her in his letters for some time. He would grow to admire her, with careful qualifications, but she would never occupy in his existence the role that Goody Allen then occupied, or Lucy Clifford, or his friend in Rye, Fanny Prothero. He and Mrs Wharton had their common American background, their friends abroad, their "international" feeling. Their sense of irony and humour was tuned to the same key and on this ground Mrs Wharton said that "Henry James was perhaps the most intimate friend I ever had though in many ways we were so different." James would not have used the word "intimate." Mrs Wharton was always for him the *grande dame*; but he admired her intellectual and literary qualities and her style. His affection was genuine; his reservations were strong. One writer has attempted to inject a feeling of romance saying they should be portrayed "almost as though they were a married couple or acknowledged lovers." But this was hardly the case; nor can their friendship be considered "one of the unique attachments of literary history." Mrs Wharton was inclined to be "possessive," and James kept his friendly distance. She was right, however, in remembering that "suddenly it was as if we had always been friends." The friends of the friends—the Bourgets, Mary Cadwalader Jones, the Edward Boits, Howard Sturgis, a wide circle of common acquaintance—had prepared the ground. "I mustn't omit to tell you, though you probably by this time know it," James wrote to Mrs Cadwalader Jones, "that Mrs Wharton has gone and come—gone, alas, more particularly, fleeing before the dark discipline of the London winter afternoon. I was in town for a day or two during her passage, and I lunched with her, with very great pleasure, and had the opportunity of some talk. This gave me much desire for more—finding her, as I did, *really* conversible (rare characteristic, *par le temps qui court!*) and sympathetic in every way." To Mrs John LaFarge, formerly Margaret Perry and an old Newport friend, he wrote a few days later that he found in Mrs Wharton "a slightly cold but quite individual grace."

III

The following spring, at Whitsuntide, Edith Wharton and her husband, familiarly called Teddy, hired a motor—they did not then own one—and were chauffeured to Rye where they spent twenty-four hours with the Master. By that time Henry James had no doubt of Mrs Wharton's role in her marriage. He treated her as if she were Teddy's husband. "The Edith Whartons," he told Howells, had been with him "in force." In her late reminiscences, written long after James was dead, she would describe Lamb House with careful and observed detail and with the eye of one accustomed to living in much larger and more palatial establishments. The Garden House with its Palladian windows pleased her; the general air of amiability and the constantly bubbling wit and acerbity of the Master delighted her. He would always be candid with her and even aggressive in his criticism. And it is clear from her account of the ways in which he spoke to her that he assumed his best "courtier" style, the style he had used with Mrs Jack, even though Edith's aristocratic tone was genuine and Mrs Jack's assumed. What James reacted against was the wealth of both these ladies—that is he felt that a condition of chronic luxury tended to insulate and to produce a certain blindness in them. He had long before expressed his suspicion of "the great ones" of the earth; he had complained that they lacked imagination. This was true sometimes of Mrs Wharton. It can be discerned in the things she noticed in Lamb House and her description of Jamesian hospitality. She alone of all his guests would speak of his "anxious frugality," would comment on the "dreary pudding or pie of which a quarter or a half had been consumed at dinner" and its reappearing on the table the next day "with its ravages unrepaired." She who had gardens and gardeners—and woe to them if a protruding twig or two were discovered on the trimmed hedge—remarked on the "unkempt" flower borders of James's small Lamb House plot. From her point of view James—whose servants called him a martinet and "an old toff"—did not know how to give them orders. She also would speak of him as being helpless in choosing items of dress or making travel arrangements. These comments were strange. James had travelled alone since the last days of the stage-coach in the middle nineteenth century; and he had always been smartly turned out by his tailors. What is clear is that when James visited Edith Wharton she took command; and before a commanding woman—as with his older brother—James withered and passively surrendered. He took on a helpless air. She made him feel powerless—he who otherwise exuded power. Mrs Wharton's remark that James "lived in terror of being thought rich, worldly or luxurious" must be understood as stemming from his continued ironies about his inability to live up to *her* style. She tells us he was for ever "contrasting his visitors' supposed opulence and self indulgence with his own hermit-like asceticism and apologizing for his poor food while he trembled lest it should be thought too good." There is a singular failure in this on the part of Mrs Wharton to understand what James was doing. James's visitors usually testified to the solid bourgeois comfort of his house and the quality of his table; his claret had been praised and the efficiencies of his small household staff. What Mrs Wharton did not grasp—she could be very literal in such matters—was that James amusedly posed as a country squire and treated her with great flourishes as a visiting lady of high estate. He could be the most humble of her servants; nothing he could do would be good enough. In the same way, he would refer later to his penny royalties and compare them with Mrs Wharton's large success in the literary market-place. James was in fact, especially during these years when his maturing annuities increased his income, decently well off; he had about £2000 a year as against Mrs Wharton's £10,000. Moreover, James liked to mock forceful ladies. To his friends he spoke of her "devouring, burning and destroying energy." That was why she was sometimes "the Firebird" and sometimes the "Angel of Devastation." Mrs Wharton's failure to understand James's candid if ironic declarations that he simply could not offer her customary luxuries is exemplified in her saying years later that James "denied himself (I believe quite needlessly) the pleasure and relaxation which a car of his own might have given him, but took advantage, to the last drop of petrol, of the travelling capacity of any visitor's car." This was perhaps ungenerous. The last thing James wanted, or could afford in the early days of motoring, was a car. He had poked fun at Kipling's large motor-monster, and had mused on the large royalties that made such a machine possible; and while he greatly enjoyed motoring with Mrs Wharton, his complaints are numerous. A little motoring with her went a long way. Yet there was no stopping her when she arrived on his horizon for what James called "the eagle pounce and eagle flight."

James was writing of Mrs Wharton's world in the novel he was finishing when she and Teddy came for their first visit to Lamb House. The Whartons were on their way back to the United States and he promised Edith he would visit her at Lenox later that year—for by this time it was settled that the native would return after his twenty-year absence. To Mrs La Farge he described how Mrs Wharton had been at Lamb House and had been presented by Miss Weld with one of James's books, beautifully bound in her little bindery. It had been an act of homage "to no less a *raffinée* than Mrs Wharton." He had seen "more of them— of her—than ever before, and greatly liked her, though finding her a little dry." He added these significant words "she is too pampered and provided and facilitated for one to be able really to judge of the woman herself, or for *her* even, I think, to be able to get really *at* things." The judgment would be muted in later years. Her energy would enable her to get at some things; but when James wrote of the Prince in *The Golden Bowl* that "below a certain social plane, he never *saw*" he was describing in effect Edith Wharton's failures in perception. These misunderstandings between Mrs Wharton and Henry James would reach an ultimate climax. But this would occur at a later time, after James had become also her counsellor and comforter in her marital difficulties and her complicated affairs of the heart.

THE GOLDEN BOWL

DURING the Christmas season of 1902, in that busy year in which he had published *The Wings of the Dove* and written the life of Story, Henry James had had an opportunity to view an *objet d'art* which belonged to the descendants of the Lambs, the family that had built the house he now owned. It was a golden bowl, presented by George I after his ship had put in to the Sussex coast during a storm. The King had slept in Lamb House; and during his stay he attended the christening of a recently born baby in the Lamb family. The bowl was the King's gift to the child. James saw the vessel at a local bank, where it was kept in the vault. He studied it as if he were visiting a museum. To one of the Lamb descendants, he wrote he had been "delighted to rest my eyes on this admirable and venerable object." It had "a beautiful colour—the tone of old gold—as well as a grand style and capacity." He added that he was eager for "every ascertainable fact" about Lamb House and felt "personally indebted to your peculiarly civilized ancestor who kindly conceived and put together for my benefit, so long ago, exactly the charming, graceful, sturdy little habitation (full of *sense*, discretion, taste) that suits alike my fancy and necessity, and in which I hope in time (D.V.) to end my days."

King George's Bowl, viewed by James in the waning days of 1902, was more than an "ascertainable fact" about Lamb House. It became a symbol for the theme of the novel which he began early in 1903—the last novel he would complete during his final years.

I

He had written *The Ambassadors* and *The Wings of the Dove* each in less than a year: but he spent more than a twelvemonth over *The Golden Bowl*, rewriting almost every page, as he had done long ago with *The Portrait of a Lady*. When he sailed in August

215

1904 for America the manuscript had been delivered to Scribner's for autumn publication. It would appear during James's visit in the United States. In England it was scheduled for the following spring.

The idea for *The Golden Bowl* had been in his notebooks for more than ten years: that of a father and daughter who both become engaged, the daughter to an Englishman and the father, a widower, still youngish, to an American girl of the same age as his daughter. "Say he has done it to console himself in his abandonment—to make up for the loss of the daughter, to whom he has been devoted." Then and there (it was on 28 November 1892) he sketched his plot for what he thought would be a short story. The marriages would take place "with this characteristic consequence" that father and daughter would continue to see one another and in fact maintain their old interest, while the husband of the one and the young wife of the other would in turn be thrown together—with the father's second wife becoming "much more attractive to the young husband of the girl than the girl herself has remained." The subject for James resided in "the pathetic simplicity and good faith of the father and daughter in their abandonment. They feel abandoned, yet they feel consoled with *each other*, and they don't see in the business in the least what every one else sees in it." James described the situation as "a vicious circle"; it was a kind of crisis of mutual abandonment and consolation. A necessary basis "must have been an intense and exceptional degree of attachment between the father and daughter—he peculiarly paternal, she passionately *filial*!" James originally thought he would make the daughter's young husband a Frenchman; and the father and daughter he would make "intensely American." He returned to the idea in 1895 just after *Guy Domville* and now thought of it as subject for a novel. At the end of that year, he reminded himself of "the Father and Daughter, with the husband of the one and the wife of the other entangled in a mutual passion, an intrigue." It was the kind of story that would be attractive for Harpers, except for its "adulterine element," but he also told himself, "may it not be simply a question of *handling* that?" At that time the other element in the plot, the "in-

cestuous" element of father and daughter, did not constitute a
difficulty. The Victorian daughter was expected to be devoted to
the father; she was expected to sacrifice her own interests. From
the days of *Washington Square*, James had written stories of
"dutiful" daughters in various stages of revolt. Or of daughters
so "fixated" on their fathers that they ruin the paternal chances of
remarrying, as in "The Marriages" in which a daughter tells the
fiancée a lie, while persuading herself that she is being faithful to
the memory of her dead mother. James's sister Alice had been a
dutiful and invalid daughter, who had remained at home, and kept
house briefly for her father after their mother's death. Even more,
there remained with him the image of Lizzie Boott who had
grown up in Italy under the care and education of her father, the
amateur composer Francis Boott. The New England Boott had
been widowed young and in his grief had fled America for Italy.
He had been in the Italy of William Wetmore Story and James
had alluded to him in his recent life of Story. Old Boott was
dying at the very moment that James was completing *The Golden
Bowl*; and when he died in the spring of 1904 he remembered
Henry in his will, for the novelist had been an old and loyal
friend. What had struck James long before, and he had incorporated this in *The Portrait of a Lady*, had been the way in which
Lizzie and her father, in their beautiful apartment in the Villa
Castellani, on Bellosguardo, had led a self-sufficient life: this
image gave him Pansy and Osmond. Then had come the
moment when Lizzie had fallen in love with her art teacher Frank
Duveneck, the bohemian painter in Munich, and had married him
in the late 1880's. Nevertheless life with her father had gone on as
before and Duveneck had seemed to James very much of a third
party. At the time of this marriage the novelist saw Boott as
suddenly bereft of the single interest of his life. "Take care," he
warned, "lest between two easels you fall to the ground, you can
so easily trip over the legs."

It is doubtful whether James himself could know how much of
his life was in this book, the richest of all his creations. *The
Golden Bowl* seemed indeed a final attempt to resolve the problems
he had approached from so many different angles in his earlier

works. The adulterous couple forced to make marriages of "convenience" rather than of love: Charlotte and the Prince in this novel had been foreshadowed by Madame Merle and Osmond, by Kate Croy and Densher or even by Christina who had married Prince Casamassima and later taken lovers. Maggie Verver had appeared earlier as Pansy Osmond; and Adam Verver as a whole generation of fathers. But in the close-knit family constellation he created in *The Golden Bowl* James was dealing with the deepest webs of his own inner world—his father's having had in the house not only his wife Mary Walsh, Henry's mother, but her sister Catherine, the loyal Aunt Kate. There had always been triangles in James's life. In the little tale of "Georgina's Reasons" which had anticipated some of the themes of *The Wings of the Dove*, there had been the young man and the two sisters, one dying of consumption. But there was also in that story another triangle, the strange situation resulting from the young man's marriage in New York to Georgina, who had kept the marriage secret, and had given their secretly born child away for adoption. She had blandly committed bigamy, thus creating another triangle. Moreover she had urged her husband to feel free to marry again—that is to commit bigamy too. Strange fantasies, these of triangular human relations, and they culminated, in this ultimate work of James's, in two joined triangles: father, daughter, and daughter's husband; and the husband's mistress, who then marries the father and so becomes the stepmother of the heroine, and mother-in-law of her lover. The implication of emotional "incest" is not as relevant in this work as the fact that in the situation everyone begins by having his cake and eating it. The daughter marries but remains close to her father. The father acquires a bride, but still possesses his daughter. The Prince acquires his Princess, but doesn't have to give up his mistress. The mistress makes the marriage she had waited for, a marriage of wealth and position, but keeps her lover. In an Elizabethan tragedy such situations could lead to a sanguinary ending. In *The Golden Bowl* the energies of the characters, and of the work, have as their goal an extraordinary attempt to maintain balance—without rocking the boat.

II

There is little doubt that, in addition to the memory of King George's offering to the Lambs, James had in mind Ecclesiastes 12:6-7—"Or ever the silver cord be loosed, or the golden bowl be broken, or the pitcher be broken at the fountain, or the wheel broken at the cistern, Then shall the dust return to the earth as it was: and the spirit shall return unto God who gave it." He may also have remembered Blake's lines, "Can wisdom be kept in a silver rod, Or love in a golden bowl?" The golden bowl is seen originally by Charlotte and the Prince in a London curiosity shop; she wants to offer it as a marriage gift, but the Prince, whom James names Amerigo, is deeply superstitious; he discerns from the first a flaw in the bowl: it is not made of gold, but is gilded crystal; and it contains a crack, like the porcelain cup handled by Osmond one day during a crisis with Madame Merle in *The Portrait of a Lady*. The symbol was an old one in Henry James—but in this novel the flawed artefact is emblematic not only of the marriage of the Prince and Maggie (he too is a discoverer of America) but of the entire civilization in which this marriage has been consummated. The Prince, Maggie, and her father belong to the world exemplified for James by Edith Wharton. The Prince's aristocratic lineage, and the American aristocrats of wealth were insulated—and therefore blinded—from certain truths of life within their charmed circle. This world is also imaged for us in the large metaphor of the pagoda with which the second half of the novel begins, an "outlandish" artefact, "a structure plated with hard, bright porcelain, coloured and figured and adorned, at the overhanging eaves, with silver bells that tinkled, ever so charmingly, when stirred by chance airs." The great surface remains "impenetrable and inscrutable" to Maggie. It might have been a Mahometan mosque, "with which no base heretic could take a liberty." She has never really sought admission. She has remained outside, living in proximity to this artificial hard-surfaced, beautiful but lifeless, object. And it will be the plebeians who will break the artificial world: the dealer in antiques will reveal inadvertently the liaison between the Prince

and Charlotte to Maggie; she will come into possession of the
flawed golden bowl; and it will be another plebeian, Fanny
Assingham, who will perform the single act of violence in the
novel; she will deliberately drop the Bowl on the polished floor
and it will split neatly into three pieces.

James was writing, in this strange and heavily loaded symbolic
drama, a story of the education of a princess, an American
princess. Nothing in Maggie's life has prepared her for her crisis
—her discovery that the person closest to her, the aristocratic
husband she has acquired as if he were still another artefact, is
treacherous and unfaithful; and that he is being unfaithful with
her friend, Charlotte, whom she had induced her father to marry,
in order to "console" him for the loss of herself. Maggie's insulated life had provided her with no means to deal with such a
situation; the loss of innocence is violent, a complete collapse of
her pagoda-life. What she possesses is the knowledge of her
power: and the innate strategy of her insulation. She has learned
long ago that one does not upset boats; there is a risk of everyone
drowning; and where in a hundred novels such a heroine would
have torn her passion to tatters, raged, threatened, exposed, made
grand scenes, James remains true to Maggie's delicate upbringing
and also her state of ignorance. He is writing the story of her
growing-up. In the process of her education, and by her recognition of the elements of power in her predicament, she is able to
get rid of the disequilibrium in her life. She comes to recognize
that the Prince, having married wealth, will hardly wish to renounce it; that Charlotte in turn has gained the position of
comfort and ease she has wanted. With the coolness of an heiress
of all the ages, she brings about a "palace" revolution that gives
her full command. By degrees she recognizes that a daughter is
supposed to grow up; that she has involuntarily—through force
of habit and the conditions of her life—thought that she could be
both a wife and a daughter. She now sees that if she is to remain
a wife she must indeed cease to be a daughter. She accepts the
idea that she cannot continue to have her cake and eat it. She dispatches her father to America to lead his own life. Charlotte, the
adulteress, is thereby banished from Europe. And the Prince, who

has wanted a wife instead of an immature father-attached girl, finds that he now has one. They have a child, a boy, and for the first and only time in all of James's fiction this novel ends with a family in which the offspring is allowed to live. Many lies have had to be told to save the marriage, but they have been, as in *The Wings of the Dove* and *The Ambassadors*, "constructive" lies— the lies by which civilization can be held together. The whole truth, James suggests, could destroy civilization, for everything, as the Prince is made to say, is "terrible in the heart of man." All the more reason, this novel seems to imply, that the terrors of the heart should not be translated into life. They would be unbearable. As James had felt, in his early days in Rome, that the dead past must be kept buried, that the primitive uncovered, becomes too dangerous to continuation of life, so in the last of his "philosophical novels" he places himself on the side of the "illusions" by which man lives. Like Marlow, in Conrad's "Heart of Darkness," James's characters tell lies because the truth can serve no useful purpose. Certain lies can be extremely useful.

A few critics, reading this novel, have tried to make Maggie out to be evil and destructive; in their sympathy for the cool and admirable Charlotte, who is one of James's most remarkable "bad heroines," they have blinded themselves to the fact that at the end of the novel the latter is better off than she was at the beginning. At the beginning she had lost the Prince; he has preferred to marry a rich heiress rather than continue a love affair that reduces him to poverty. Charlotte ends with the wealth and power and freedom of her marriage to an American tycoon; and if Adam takes her back to America this does not mean that she is necessarily being taken to prison. We know she will ultimately be free, like James's other American wives, to travel, to build houses, to acquire art treasures, or other lovers. She can become Mrs Touchett or resemble the real-life Mrs Gardner. And Maggie, far from being a "witch," has simply learned that a revolution cannot restore the *status quo ante*. It was exactly this status that had ruined her marriage. By thinking she could live in a fool's paradise of perpetual daughterhood—that is a perpetual child—she had lost her husband. By acquiring her maturity, she recovers him. She shows herself capable of facing realities in the great scene of the novel, when she paces the terrace and watches the game of bridge played by her father and Mrs Assingham with the two lovers.

. . . meanwhile the facts of the situation were upright for her round the green cloth and the silver flambeaux; the fact of her father's wife's lover facing his mistress; the fact of her father sitting, all unsounded and unblinking, between them; the fact of Charlotte keeping it up, keeping up everything, across the table, with her husband beside her; the fact of Fanny Assingham, wonderful creature, placed opposite to the three and knowing more about each, probably, when one came to think, than either of them knew of either. Erect above all for her was the sharp-edged fact of the relation of the whole group, individually and collectively, to herself—herself so speciously eliminated for the hour, but presumably more present to the attention of each than the next card to be played.

It is one of Henry James's great scenes, in its fine-toned "awareness," in the revealed sensibility of Maggie Verver, and in its open theatricality. But its greatness perhaps resides in that James had finally been able in a novel to bring into the open the deeply buried scenes of his childhood—that of a curious little boy who has to contend with triangular enigmas of father, mother, aunt—and having to make choices, not always knowing to whom exactly he belonged—like his Maggie, who belongs to her father and to her husband, and yet must surrender one, if she is to have the other. In some dim and difficult way James, having tried the Vionnet–Strether–Chad combination in *The Ambassadors*, and the Kate–Densher–Milly combination in *The Wings of the Dove*, had finally found the combination that could unlock the closed secrets of his life. The Prince–Adam–Charlotte combination seemed to work. Everything in this novel is at last—and for the only time in Henry James—resolved; and above all the marriage —which had seemed impossible in all his other fiction—is consummated. He had written nineteen novels and in many of them he had affirmed that no marriage was possible between the Old World and the New—that America and Europe were irreconcilable. Now at last in his twentieth he brought the marriage off. Prince Amerigo, descendant of explorers, could as it were "marry" the continent of their journeyings; and Maggie—and America—could with the proper will respond not in ignorance but in awareness.

In terms of another of his favourite symbols—that of the cage—Henry James in this novel is able at last to set free the young female adolescent imprisoned within his spirit and his imagination. She had grown from childhood with his growth; she had been Daisy and Maisie, and the governess, and Nanda, she had tried to deduce the outer world studying the telegrams passed to her in the branch post office; or she had revolved in the glass cage of *The Sacred Fount*. Now she emerges from the pagoda-cage. She has ceased to observe actively while remaining physically passive; she refuses to "renounce." She can act—with strength, with resolution, even when necessary with hardness and cruelty. The fable is at last complete.

III

The symbolic statement of *The Golden Bowl* is most personal, most biographical, if we search for the meaning not of the artefact but of the crack in the artefact. In the earlier work of the novelist society was accepted as a *status quo* and James was interested in personal relations within that society. In this philosophical novel, he finds answers to the questioning of society which had begun with *The Awkward Age* in 1898 and had continued into the final three novels. Having put together the strange pagoda of Maggie Verver's life—for such is the central image in the novel next to the golden bowl itself—the novelist is able to face the truth reflected by the image. The golden bowl contains a crack, moreover it is only a *gilded* bowl. One can live a life of artifice; but it will always have a crack in its seemingly smooth and metallic surface. The pagoda's bells tinkle when brushed by "chance airs"; but they give off a remote sound. The flaws must be discovered, the correct values re-established. In his questioning James re-expresses what he had once asserted as an epigram: that life could get by sufficiently without art; but that "art without life is a poor affair." The Ververs are patrons of the arts, collectors of discrimination and taste; they possess sufficient wealth to endow large museums; even Prince Amerigo, a work of art of the ages, can be acquired as husband and son-in-law. One can possess a pagoda, and it can be exquisite, yet in the end it is no substitute for life, for living; it remains an ornament of life. The golden bowl may have great beauty of form, but in reality it is a fake. The crack in the bowl stood thus for the cracks in James's life: as in the life of the Ververs. He had for too long cast his life too exclusively with art; he had not allowed himself to experience the force of life itself. In *The Golden Bowl* Prince Amerigo thus becomes the strongest and most assertive of James's heroes: he possesses a long and corrupt family history; and he faces life without illusions. He wants the genuine, not the fake. In adumbrating a hero who no longer rationalizes away the claims of love, of physical love, James reflected the presence in his life, at the moment that he began to write this book, of the fun-loving Jocelyn Persse, whom James adored. "Live all you can," had been central to *The Ambassadors*: man had to learn to live with the illusion of his freedom. Life without love wasn't life—this was the further conclusion of *The Wings of the Dove*; and having found love James had come to see at last that art could not be art, and not life, without love. He had become his own Sphinx; he was answering his own riddles. Step by step he had discerned the crack in the beautifully contrived British society originally admired but finally attacked in *The Awkward Age*; he had discerned the crack in the purely artistic object, the artefacts of the centuries, the museum world that fascinated *within* the museum but had no place in the daily drawing-rooms of life. And he had worked through the crack in his relationship with Fenimore which revealed itself in the writing of "The Beast in the Jungle." In the larger experience, he saw the crack in civilization, which has to contend with human force and human frailty and the grandeurs and terrors of the human heart. The "sinful" relations of Chad and Madame de Vionnet, Densher and Kate, the Prince and Charlotte were no longer the essence of the matter; each had had to make the most of the process of living and the vulnerability of love—and of life itself. Civilization might be a subtle deceit, a façade, a series of myths created by man—yet it was one

THE YOUNG JAMES AND THE MASTER
from an unpublished Max Beerbohm cartoon

a memory of Henry James and
Joseph Conrad conversing at an afternoon party—
circa 1909.

max
1926

A MEMORY OF HENRY JAMES AND JOSEPH CONRAD

Max Beerbohm's recollection of the novelists "conversing at a
party circa 1904"

of man's greatest creations. Behind the smile, the experience, the ravage in the countenance of the artist Gloriani there had been the sense of the lived life. To be sure, one could not always have the best of all worlds. Maggie had to lose her father to keep her husband; the Prince had to lose his mistress to keep his wife. Henry James had had to give up America in order to have Europe. But in all such decisions, civilization alone assured equilibrium and a rule of law and a code of decency by which man sought to stay primordial violence. A few decent lies or "sins" mattered very little, if ultimate truths were to survive. Such would seem to be the conclusions of Henry James in the three pragmatic novels with which he ended his career as novelist. *The Golden Bowl* is the summit of that career.

IV

As he wrote his novel, Henry James believed (so he told his agent and his publisher) that he was "producing the best book I have ever done." He had worked on it, day after day, for thirteen months and written 200,000 words "with the rarest perfection." To Scribner's he wrote, as he was reading proof, "it is distinctly, in my view, the most *done* of my productions—the most composed and constructed and completed, and it proved, during long months, while it got itself step by step, endowed with logical life, only too deep and abysmal an artistic trap." He added, "by which I don't mean an abyss without a bottom, but a shaft sunk to the real basis of the subject—a real feat of engineering." He concluded by saying he would shamelessly repeat, and his publisher could quote him, that "I hold the thing the solidest, as yet, of all my fictions."

Some of his readers would say that it was too solid, too compact, too filled with suggestions and associations, too crowded and imaged. Reviewers would call it "detached," "cold," "cruel," and "a psychological dime-novel." They would find it over-intellectual, and over-loaded. But few denied its greatness in 1904. Read with the kind of leisure that went into its writing, *The Golden Bowl* on every page shows clarity of intention and consummation. The prose is dense, yet fluid, and the surfeit of

H

architectural and museum-world imagery, the gathering of social and artistic materials to suggest the fabric of civilization, combined the art of realism James had learned long ago from Balzac, with the old art of the fable. The novel, in its "story-line," is a fable, a moral tale built out of symmetries and patterns, and a tissuing together of organic materials—emotional sensibility, taste, "spiritual" quality, into a charged and subjective narrative. James divided the book into two parts: the first half belongs to the Prince, the second to the Princess. These are the two "points of view." The Prince's story begins with his arrival in London to arrange his marriage and his feeling—this descendant of an old *Imperium*—how much the centre of the Empire had shifted to the British capital. James makes us see him and the civilization that has produced him in large architectural terms, the spaciousness of old palaces and formal gardens, the thousands of years and human endeavour that moulded him into a certain kind of heir of the ages. Image becomes character; metaphor and simile become vision. The prevailing imagery is the imagery of voyage and of exploration; the descendant of Amerigo Vespucci is created out of allusions to ships and quests, harbours and searches for the North-West Passage or Golden Isles, or even the narrative of Arthur Gordon Pym and his macabre polar journey. He is seen also in architectural terms—his dark blue eyes "resembled nothing so much as the high windows of a Roman palace, of an historic front by one of the great old designers, thrown open on a feast-day to the golden air." Grandeur and history, old and new, lead the novelist to the ironic marriage that unites this descendant of one kind of Imperium to the daughter of the still newer Empire that has been created out of exploration and voyage, and even bears the name that originally belonged to the family of the Prince. The symbolic statement of exploration, wealth, conquest, hard masculine adventures are compounded into the sense the Prince has of achieving at last the life he wanted, a life of ease and affluence: and then his gradual isolation and his turning for companionship to the woman he had known before meeting the innocent Maggie, the American Charlotte, who is imaged for us, in turn, in many ways, not least in the form of James's familiar evocation of Diana the huntress. The imagery changes when we come to the second half of the novel, in which Maggie must face the crack in her life and her phantoms—"the horror of finding evil seated, all at its ease, where she had only dreamed of good; the horror of the thing hideously *behind*, behind so much trusted, so much pretended nobleness, cleverness, tenderness." For the first time the insulated American innocent learns that life has its treacheries and that the pagoda, with its pleasant bright surfaces and the gentle sound of its tinkling bells can conceal the ominous and sinister, as in a nightmare—"it had met her like some bad-faced stranger surprised in one of the thick-carpeted corridors of a house of quiet on a Sunday afternoon." The terror behind the bland surface of common day—this had always been James's most powerful evocative instrument: the latent horror that had made "The Turn of the Screw" one of his most deeply felt creations. Animal imagery, the prowl of predatory creatures, is felt in the gradual unveiling of Maggie's inner world; she must live through her jealousy, her sense of the collapse of her world, her re-education, and do it with the calm duplicity she prescribes for herself; she remains ironically close to the tinkling bells and the pagoda-existence. James makes us feel the power of her subdued passion —the power of the "really agitated lamb." Lions are as nothing compared to them, "for lions are sophisticated, are blasés, are brought up from the first to prowling and mauling," as the cynical Fanny Assingham remarks to her husband.

Within the houses of London—Portland Place of the Prince and Princess, Eaton Square of the Ververs, and the lowlier Cadogan Place of the Assinghams—moves Adam Verver, the enigmatic, poker-faced, check-suited American tycoon: and James treats him as a mystery figure, a kind of "Uncle Sam" whose thoughts are never known, but who represents American indulgence where his daughter is concerned, and American shrewdness in the gathering in of Europe's creations. If he is Adam, the first man, he seems often in this novel to be still living in the Garden, "in a state of childlike innocence," as the Prince observes. He is that great anomaly, the American who has inherited the ages without having had to suffer; things have fallen into his lap; the other nations suffered; he has reaped the rewards of suffering. However he has his insights, and his perceptions. When Maggie tells her father she doesn't believe he is selfish, he rejoins "But we're selfish together—we move as a selfish mass. You see we always want the same thing and that holds us, that binds us, together. We want each other, only wanting it, each time, *for* each other. That's what I call the happy spell; but it's also, a little, possibly, the immorality." And when she questions "the immorality" he acknowledges "we're tremendously moral for ourselves—that is for each other." Yet he finds too "there's something haunting—as if it were a bit uncanny—in such a consciousness of our general comfort and privilege." Father and daughter throughout the book "protect" one another, and also understand one another. In silence, and with calm, they work out their problem with the calculations of a game of chess. The imagery in the book of the Princess is filled with the sense of her pagoda-claustrophobia; it gives way to the confrontation with Charlotte and the mounting tension in which the Prince discovers he is no longer married to a passive little girl, clinging to her father, but to a determined woman, a woman of character, who exercises her power without "making a scene." In the final meeting of the two women, the "bad heroine" and the "good," James cannot resist piling up his mythic allusions and artefact-images. Maggie waiting and wondering whether she and Charlotte will meet, feels herself to be like Io, in the old legend, goaded by the gadfly, or Ariadne, who having helped Theseus find his way out of the labyrinth, is left "roaming the lone sea-strand." She is "some far-off harassed heroine." The final artefact is the work of a printer, a book, a three-decker novel, of which Charlotte has in error picked up the second volume instead of the first. As they meet, Maggie can say "You've got the wrong volume, and I've brought you out the right." Order, sequence, chronology are restored. Maggie has her husband, Charlotte hers. Each has the right volume. Charlotte too cannot have her cake and eat it.

In the last of his novels, as in the earliest, James is concerned with the dynamic of power. What is new here, as in *The Wings of the Dove*, is a quality of eroticism, an awareness of love, absent in the earlier works. We witness only one passionate encounter between Charlotte and the Prince. It suffices. Once we have seen, we know. The lovers have been saying to one another that they must protect the happiness of father and daughter—and by this see themselves protected in their adultery.

> And so for a minute they stood together, as strongly held and as closely confronted as any hour of their easier past even had seen them. They were silent at first, only facing and faced, only grasping and grasped, only meeting and met. "It's sacred," he said at last.
> "It's sacred," she breathed back at him. They vowed it, gave it out and took it in, drawn by their intensity, more closely together. Then of a sudden, through this tightened circle, as at the issue of a narrow strait into the sea beyond, everything broke up, broke down, gave way, melted and mingled. Their lips sought their lips, their pressure their response and their response their pressure; with a violence that had sighed itself the next moment to the longest and deepest of stillnesses they passionately sealed their pledge.

This is perhaps not characteristic James: and at this distance from its time there is something cloying in the prose. However, read with a backward view it tells us how far the author of this passage had come in his treatment of the relation between man and woman. One has only to recall the kiss—the only kiss—in *The Portrait of a Lady*.

Of such passages Stephen Spender has said—discerning the latent biographical meaning as no other critic has done—that they were written by "a person who, profoundly with his whole being, after overcoming great inhibition, has accepted the *idea* of people loving . . . after a lifetime of deep human understanding, has arrived at a stage where in suffering and pity he could accept the physical fact of love."

A PASSION OF NOSTALGIA

ONE day in November of 1903 while in London, James went to the Tilbury dock to see Mrs John La Farge and her daughter off to America. He seems to have told the story of this little adventure to Ford Madox Hueffer who recorded James as returning to Rye "singularly excited, bringing out a great many unusually uncompleted sentences." Hueffer quoted him as saying "And once aboard the lugger . . . And if . . . Say a toothbrush . . . and circular notes . . . and so something for the night . . ." We have, however, James's own account of the minor episode. James had been in London for a few days; he went out to the dreary dock, because his friends were "rather helpless and alone." He did indeed go aboard the ship, the *Minnehaha*. He seems to have visited the cabin, because he spoke of going "almost into their very bunks in the electric-lighted dark of the day." And he reported that he had said to himself: "Now or never is my chance; stay and sail—borrow clothes, borrow a toothbrush, borrow a bunk, borrow $100; you will never be so near to it again. The worst is over—the arranging: it's all arranged *for* you, with two kind ladies thrown in." So strong was this feeling, he said, that if he had only had a thicker overcoat and the ladies had had an extra bunk, "I would have turned in *with* them and taken my chance." As it was, he experienced a moment of aching desire, a sudden acute wish to be in America again, resisted it, shoving his way "out of the encumbered tubular passages." He stopped his ears against the "squeak" of the voices of his compatriots. He "turned and fled, bounding along Tilbury docks in the grimy fog and never stopping till I clutched at something that was going back to London."

I

Behind the flourishes and exaggerations of this little episode lay a profound emotion. He had become aware of it during the writing of *The Ambassadors*; it had primed him to urge Edith Wharton to make the most of her American subject; he had suddenly found himself, in letters to friends, remembering the leaves he had kicked in the autumn along the lower reaches of Fifth Avenue, "as I can to this hour feel myself, hear myself, positively *smell* myself doing." But perhaps there were "no leaves and no trees now in Fifth Avenue—nothing but patriotic arches, Astor Hotels and Vanderbilt Palaces." He had in all his younger years known only the eastern seaboard and had made a single foray into the midwest, as far as Wisconsin, on a business trip. Now the land of his birth extended to California. It had become quite as "romantic" as Europe had seemed to him in his younger dreams. Visits from Justice Holmes, the La Farges, the Edith Whartons, his recent exchange of letters with Henry Adams—all spoke of an America no longer known to him. It was time to go back. And then it seemed to him that in dealing with his work of a lifetime, in bringing together his scattered novels and tales—for he now talked of a collective, a "definitive" edition—he needed to take stock of his reputation in the United States, his business connections with American publishers. When he had turned sixty, in April of 1903, he had begun to feel as never before the memories of childhood and youth. "I must go before I'm too old, and, above all, before I mind being older," he wrote to William James. To Howells he gave further proof of the longing for youth and the older time, "I *want* to come, quite pathetically and tragically—it is a passion of nostalgia." On the eve of his birthday he wrote a long letter to his brother that revealed his inner debate between his desire for the journey and the practical obstacles that seemed to loom—the letting of his house, the unaccustomed voyage, the proper itinerary, the financing of the trip. "The desire to go 'home' for six months (not less,) daily grows in me," he wrote, "before senile decay sets in." His dilemma was largely economic. He felt he should look after his long-neglected literary interests and examine what opportunities there might be in order to "quicken and improve them, after so endless an absence." But the process would be so "damnedly expensive." There would be six months of American hotels. He couldn't "stay" with friends; moreover, he wanted to move about. He could finance the trip in part by writing a book of "impressions"—it would have to be "for much money." He wanted to *see* the country at large, yet "I don't see myself prowling alone in Western cities and hotels, or finding my way about by myself and it is all darksome and tangled."

William's answer was characteristic. Henry remained to him— in his elder brotherly mind—"powerless." He said he could imagine "the sort of physical loathing with which many features of our national life will inspire you." William listed the things in America that displeased him and he thought would displease Henry—the sight of Americans having boiled eggs for breakfast with butter on them and the *vocalization* "of our countrymen." Couldn't Henry have his copyrights and literary matters taken care of by an agent? In effect he seemed to urge him not to come. Of course Henry might lecture at the Lowell Institute. On the other hand, there was the American out-of-doors. If Henry would avoid the *banalité* of the eastern cities and travel to the South, to Colorado, across Canada, possibly to Hawaii, he might find the journey rewarding, but he would have to pay the price. William advised him to come in spring and to leave in October. He invited Henry to spend the hot months with him and his family at Chocorua, their summer home. He would even go with Henry to certain places if he wished. But he was busy, and he urged Henry not to do this before the spring of 1904. The letter was on the whole friendly and helpful, but it had a certain diffidence in it and the younger brother had his usual emotional response. There was no possibility, he said, of a trip before August of 1904. William had been very "dissuasive—even more than I expected." It was all very well for him to speak, said Henry: he had moved around America at his ease, but Henry had always travelled very little; there was only the well-beaten path to Italy, that had been all. He had never been to Spain, or Greece, or Sicily; he had had no glimpse of the East. He could not see himself writing little travel articles in these countries as he had done in his younger years. If he couldn't bring off his American trip he would have to settle down to oscillation between Rye and London, London and Rye, with nothing to speak of left for him "in the way of (the poetry of) motion." He regarded this as "a thin, starved, lonely, defeated, *beaten* prospect: in comparison with which your own circumgyrations have been as the adventures of Marco Polo or H. M. Stanley." Thus spoke the younger brother, in his perpetual sense of "deprivation." The trip to America would represent "the poetry of motion, the one big taste of travel not supremely missed." It would furnish new literary material. An American agent wouldn't begin to do for him what he could do for himself. As to the boiled eggs and the "vocalization" and "the Shocks in general" all this was really irrelevant. The ways in which Americans ate their eggs was just the sort of thing that interested him as a novelist. "I want to see them, I want to see everything. I want to see the Country, scarcely a bit New York and Boston, but intensely the Middle and Far West and California and the South." He was talking a little like Christopher Newman. He did not want to spend the summer in America; arriving in August, he would have the American autumn, which he had always loved, and he could go to the warmer areas in the winter months.

This was what he would do, and it is clear that the entire plan for his journey was complete in his mind. There remained only the practical matters and time would take care of these. Goody Allen was already on the alert for tenants for Lamb House. He had already discussed with his agent, Pinker, the idea for the collective edition to be negotiated in America, probably with Scribner.

What astonished him was that his friends and relatives seemed to have a picture of him as likely to get lost in America and to hate everything he would see. They were right in certain ways; but they did not reckon with Henry's eagerness for experience. Grace Norton had written him that she talked with Mrs William James of Henry's "dislike" of his native land. He severely admonished her in his reply: "Never, never, my dear Grace: you must have misunderstood Alice—or she herself—as to the fabled growth of my still more fabled 'dislike.'" On the contrary, "I have never been more curious of it, nor more interested in it, nor more sensible of loss by absence from it (in certain ways,) than in the light of so much talk with her and William . . . The idea of *seeing* American life again and tasting the American air, that is a vision, a possibility, an impossibility, positively romantic." The possibility, he explained, was in effect his wish to return and revisit. The impossibility was that it would be "a very expensive and bewildering luxury and amusement, and a very difficult and complicated one to organize. But if I *could*!—if I *can*!" How take care of his servants? his typist? the unfinished books? This correspondence occurred when he had been writing *The Wings of the Dove*; he then still had the life of Story to write. And by 1903 he had promised two more novels to his publishers.

Miss Norton spoke, he later said, in Cassandra tones and with Cassandra warnings. His answer was that "the thought of breathing my native air again for a few months (at the latest decent date before I may begin to cease to breathe at all) strikes me as a singularly normal and natural impulse, round which no cloud of complications or other bedevilments should be *allowed* to settle." To another friend he wrote, "I think with a great appetite in advance, of the chance, once more, *to lie on the ground*, on an American hillside, on the edge of the woods, in the manner of my youth." He wasn't sure he could lecture—he was about as capable of that, he said, as of doing a trapeze act. "If I do achieve a few months in the country at large," he told Miss Norton, "the thing will have been the most private and personal act of my very private and personal life."

He was wrong and he should have known better as author of *The Reverberator* and other stories about the lack of privacy in America. When Louisa Loring wrote to him in the same vein about his not liking America his answer was "I really have the advantage of not caring whether I like it or not (and, better still, of *its* not caring;) so much must it be for me, a matter of *seeing*, quite apart from loving or loathing." By the autumn of 1903, the whole thing had become a challenge. It would be "ignobly weak" of him not to find solutions to his problems. Presently all his friends seemed involved in his travel plans. The peripatetic Benedicts, Miss Woolson's relatives, wrote as if crossing the ocean were as routine as a bus trip in London. James had crossed the sea in the old days when voyages were still dangerous and the potential rage of the ocean was a constant anxiety. The Benedicts described the luxury of the new "liners;" with their regular travel habits, they were quite ready to book James's passage for him. He could cross with them, when they returned in August 1904 from their annual jaunt to Italy, to Bayreuth, to Vienna.

In January of 1904, with the end of *The Golden Bowl* in sight, he paid his deposit on an upper promenade deck cabin on the *Kaiser Wilhelm II*, sailing from Southampton in August. He was at last ready for the return. In spite of the long inner debate there had never been any real doubt from the first. "I should greatly like before I chuck up the game," he wrote Howells, "to write (another!!) American novel or two—putting the thing *in* the country; which would take, God knows—I mean would require —some impressions."

He was ready to have his impressions.

II

He had said he would not lecture in America. But the question kept coming up. His sister-in-law asked him whether he wouldn't be interested in doing the Lowell lectures in Boston, and he replied, "I am sixty years old, and have never written a lecture in my life." It would take too much time. Would it pay sufficiently? "You impute to me, alas, a facility that I'm far from possessing." Nevertheless he kept an open mind. The proposal had been, apparently, that he deliver no less than eight lectures on "The English Novelists." Overtures began to be made the moment the word got around that he was going. *McClure's* asked him to write for them; Colonel George Harvey, head of Harper and Brothers, agreed to serialize James's American impressions in the *North American Review* and make a book of it afterwards. Both Harvey and Howells, who was literary adviser to Harper, were in London that spring, and James had direct aid in making his plans. Also abroad was an energetic young woman journalist named Elizabeth Jordan, one of the Harper editors. She was asked to canvass lecture possibilities. James became interested from the moment he learned that he could command substantial fees. Colonel Harvey spoke of $500 a lecture; Howells more modestly mentioned $150 or $200. "He ought to lecture very, very few times," Howells wrote to Miss Jordan, "and *not* on any terms of public vastness. He should read as I have done, in drawing-rooms, country-club rooms, and the like, and the public should be more or less invited, and made to feel itself privileged." James had intimated that he was prepared to deliver a lecture on Balzac, and on the novel generally, but not "if the personal exposure is out of proportion to the tip."

To Miss Jordan he wrote a few weeks before sailing concerning "the Conceivable Appetite of the Ladies for Words of Wisdom from H.J." He said he was content with the formula that the field "will not deny a very modest harvest to the artful, the *very* artful, gleaner."

Joseph Pennell wrote to James offering to illustrate his American impressions. Always jealous of his prose and disinclined to give any place to illustration the Master replied, "I can imagine a (pictorial) New York, and a ditto Chicago, and, in a manner, a ditto South; but a pictorial Boston eludes, defies, almost infuriates me—and I'm afraid I shan't rise, or fall to *that*." More pressing than the American arrangements was the problem of Lamb House and the servants. The irrepressible Goody had come up with some possible tenants, the Miss Horstmanns, one of whom was in England to marry John Boit of Boston. Lamb House would be a "honeymoon" house. James asked for a flat rental of £5 a week that would include "the servants, the forks and spoons, and house linen and books, and in short everything that is in the house except my scant supply of clothing." Also the care of the dachshund, Maximilian. In reality the rent would just cover the wages of his servants. He hoped that "the Young Things" would be "bribeable by frantic cheapness." A bare four weeks before sailing, he was able to telegraph Goody Allen,

"Little Friends accept for six months hooray and glory to immortal Goody."

His letter to his prospective tenants outlined all his domestic arrangements. There were five servants including the gardener, and Burgess, the house-boy. The gardener always took the hand-cart to the station to carry the luggage of visitors. Mrs Paddington, the cook-housekeeper, was "an absolutely brilliant economist" and a very orderly person. She was happiest if allowed to "take you into the confidence, a little, of her triumphs of thrift and her master-strokes of management." The parlour-maid, Alice Skinner, had been with James for six years, "a thoroughly respectable, well-disposed and duly competent young woman." The housemaid was "very pretty and gentle—and not a very, *very* bad one. The house-boy, Burgess Noakes, isn't very pretty, but is on the other hand very gentle, punctual, and desirous to please." He cleaned shoes, knives, doorsteps, windows, and took letters to post and so forth. Burgess was then nineteen.

"Lastly," James wrote, "I take the liberty of confiding to your charity and humanity the precious little person of my Dachshund Max, who is the best and gentlest and most reasonable and well-mannered as well as most beautiful, small animal of his kind to be easily come across—so that I think you will speedily find yourselves loving him for his own sweet sake." The servants would take care of his welfare and he wasn't to be fed between meals. But he would appreciate being taken for walks. If indulged in this way "all the latent beauty of his nature will come out."

James bought a new steamer trunk. He visited his London tailor, and made last-minute calls. From America invitations poured in—Mrs Gardner expected to see him; also the Secretary of State, John Hay in Washington and his friend Henry Adams; so did the Emmets at their farm in Connecticut; and then Peggy wrote, and the William Jameses. It was settled he should go first to Chocorua. His nephew Harry would meet the liner at Hoboken. The Paul Bourgets were briefly in London and he lunched with Bourget alone, Minny being ill. Edith Wharton sent him her volume of tales, *The Descent of Man* and he praised her "wise and witty art." He would presently be seeing her at Lenox. On 19 August he said good-bye to his servants, buried his nose in Max's little gold-coloured back, "wetting it with my tears." Rudyard Kipling sent him warm wishes and to Howells James wrote, "I feel my going not only as a lively desire but as a supreme necessity."

Miss Weld, not involved in James's domestic arrangements, and employed on an hourly basis, sought other employment during James's absence. But before his return from America she had become engaged and married and had left his employ.

As he made his way to the boat-train at Waterloo Station he was conscious of "a pandemonium of uncertainties and mysteries." He sailed 24 August 1904, having said his farewell to Jocelyn a few days before, and written also a long letter to Hendrik Andersen, the first of a series in which he began to express misgivings about Andersen's statues, of which he had received photographs. "They terrify me so with their evidence as of a *madness* (almost) in the scale on which you are working." Andersen was planning an enormous fountain—it was magnificent, heroic, sublime, said James, but where would it have any practical use? "I yearn for the *smaller* masterpiece; the condensed, consummate, caressed, intensely filled-out thing." He patted Hendrik "lovingly, tenderly, tenderly" and sailed with the sense of further "dreary and deadly postponements" of their meetings.

Henry James's lifetime had been spent in adapting his Puritan heritage to the more flexible—and more realistic—standards of Europe. He had been unable to make his peace with his native land; and in his choice of exile had, like Lambert Strether, to accommodate himself to "Europe." At the end of *The Golden Bowl* he resolved the situation by sending Charlotte and Adam back to the United States. It is a cruel fate for the interesting Charlotte, the Europeanized American. Once the novel was written, and this resolution found, James had been able to book his own passage home. He was quite as free, indeed freer, than his Charlotte. His was a voluntary voyage, where hers had in it elements of coercion. James, pacing the deck of the *Kaiser*

Wilhelm II as it left Southampton, may have felt himself acting out some significant part of his destiny. He had been abroad too long; he needed to recover a sense of his homeland. He had lived a great part of the past two decades not so much between two worlds as in a cosmopolitan world of his own making. He had said that he felt the romance and curiosity of his journey—the return to the landscapes of his childhood and youth—as if it were a new voyage of discovery. The vision was expressed by Mrs Assingham in the passage he had written towards the end of *The Golden Bowl*. "I see the long miles of ocean and the dreadful great country, State after State—which have never seemed to me so big or so terrible." Henry James was returning to the "dreadful great country."

Just before leaving, he instructed his agent to inform Charles Scribner that he thought the time had come for a definitive edition of his works. "Mr James's idea is to write for each volume a preface of a rather intimate character, and there is no doubt that such a preface would add greatly to the interest of the books." What would contribute to the intimacy of the prefaces would be the seeing again of scenes and places in which his great adventure —in art, in life—had begun. The "passionate pilgrim" was returning home at last, to the New York of his boyhood, the Cambridge of his youth, the new America of which he had had so many hints and glimpses for twenty years.

Book Four

The American Scene

1904–1905

★

THE JERSEY SHORE

A REPORTER covering the waterfront in Hoboken found Henry James guarding his luggage on the pier in the big shed, waiting for a customs inspector. Some three thousand persons were milling about, passengers who had crossed on the North German Lloyd liner *Kaiser Wilhelm II*, many of them German-American Jews. The reporter noted James's "regular and sharp" features; he described him as an "immensely robust figure" with a firm elastic step. His nephew Harry had met him, and a representative from the firm of Harper and Brothers. James seemed unruffled and relaxed amid the confusion attending a late summer steamship docking. For a celebrity, he appeared to the reporter "remote," inconspicuous. But then the author of *The Reverberator* seldom talked to reporters. And his coming had not been heralded. After the baggage was cleared, James personally supervised its removal to a carriage; but he was in no hurry to get started. As he came out into the sunshine he turned and surveyed the New York skyline. Detaching himself from the little group he paused, and said the reporter, "almost gasped for breath." He walked to a railing; he looked for a long time, "deaf to the questions of his friends." He might have been Rip Van Winkle awakening out of a deep twenty-year sleep. He had last seen New York in 1883. It was now 30 August 1904.

Henry James had indeed skipped two decades of his country's life. And yet certain things were unchanged. Crossing to Lower Manhattan he saw New York from the ferry as held in the embrace of its two good-natured rivers; he likened the city to an overblown beauty held in the arms of a not-too-fastidious gallant. The new buildings, called skyscrapers, seemed stuck in here, there and everywhere like extravagant pins in an extravagant pincushion. There were recognizable smells. As the ferry approached the terminal he saw that the waterfront was true to a "barbarism it had not outlived." The same old sordid facts, all the ugly old items—loose cobbles, unregulated traffic, big drays pulled by struggling long-necked sharp-ribbed horses. Corpulent constables stood in high detachment with helmets askew. There were huddled houses from the older time; red-faced in their glazed paint, and off balance, amid an assortment of newer buildings and saloons.

The light of the end-of-August day was clear; the sun of New York rested with a laziness all its own on the crimson buildings. James rode up-town, discovering familiar things among the unfamiliar. At Washington Square he noted the truncated arch, an arch wholly without suggestion of grandeur or "glory." He saw some of the buildings of his childhood; and pausing at a turn of a staircase in a house near by, James suddenly found himself recalling old empty New York afternoons in waning summers. He continued to Gramercy Park where apparently he paused for rest in the home of a friend. Here certain decisions were made. James had planned to leave that evening for Boston with Harry, to join William James at Chocorua in New Hampshire. However, Colonel Harvey, president of Harper, had sent a pressing invitation—almost a summons. James was expected at his country place on the Jersey shore. Having agreed, when they met earlier that year in London, to publish James's American impressions, Harvey was also taking James under his wing, generally, during this visit, although the novelist tended increasingly to give his books to Scribner's. As James explained in a letter to his agent in London, he had found "an amiable representative of the House of Harper awaiting me on the dock, with urgent instructions to take possession of me and carry me down to the New Jersey coast to pay such a visit as I would to Col. Harvey and his wife—which in view of the general lavish kindness, was the course for me appreciatively to take." He felt that he was falling into some kind of a social "trap;" nevertheless he yielded. His nephew took most of his baggage and went on to New England; James, in Gramercy Park, piled into another four-wheeler and returned to the docks. There were a great many suburban "young men of business" aboard the ferry, returning to the Jersey shore at the end of their day's work in downtown Manhattan. James listened to their talk and looked at the breezy bay, "the great unlocked and tumbled-out city on the one hand and the low, accessible mystery of the opposite State on the other." What struck him most about the young men was their "unconscious affluence."

Presently he was being driven along a straight road, following a blue band of sea, between the sandy shore and a chain of big villas. They looked like a bunch of white boxes. Each villa presided over a small bit of bright green lawn; these looked like a skirt sharply pulled down over the knees. They passed through Long Branch. There were still big brown wooden barracks of hotels. Someone pointed out the cottage where Grant had lived; and the cottage where Garfield had died. The little dwellings were outclassed, however, by a general expensiveness surrounding them.

Colonel Harvey's cottage was spacious and substantial. It stood near the sea, at Deal Beach, N.J. The tall sociable host and the plump Mrs Harvey greeted the distinguished visitor, who discovered that there was a fellow-guest awaiting him—the grizzled, white-suited, cigar-smoking "natural" Samuel Langhorne Clemens, archetypal innocent abroad and quintessential American. Colonel Harvey had gathered in his two literary lions. "Poor dear old Mark Twain beguiles the session on the deep piazza," Henry James scrawled in pencil to William James, informing him of the delay in his arrival at Chocorua.

II

Colonel George Harvey was a symbol of the new America, as Mark Twain represented the old. A native of Vermont, he was the epitome of the advertising, newspaperism and public relations that James detested; but the novelist knew he could take the smooth, efficient colonel in his stride. Harvey had been a "boy-wonder," one of Joseph Pulitzer's clever lieutenants. He was on good terms with everyone especially in Washington. Forced by his health to leave the *World*, he had, with the aid of William Whitney and J. P. Morgan, amassed a fortune in Wall Street and purchased the *North American Review*. When at the century's

turn Harper and Brothers went into receivership, Morgan had
him appointed administrator of the firm. Howells remained its
principal literary adviser, Mark Twain its principal author, and
Henry James its principal ornament. It was probably because of
these various connections that James had decided to pay this
visit, although he shrank from the clear signals that the colonel
would make the most of his presence. Harvey was already talking
of the big public dinner he planned to give in honour of James.
The novelist swept the idea aside. He was off to New England;
like the travellers in his "An International Episode" who fled
Manhattan because of the heat, James had no intention of staying
in the city's end-of-summer dust and grime. He would come back
after he had seen the leaves turn to russet and gold.

James's "poor dear old Mark Twain" sounded condescending,
but it was in reality sympathetic. Clemens had lost his wife a few
months earlier, during a stay in Florence; James had heard about
this in some detail, not only from his friend Dr Baldwin, who was
Mrs Clemens's physician, but from Howells when he saw him in
London in June. The author of *Huckleberry Finn* was now at
loose ends; he was living for the moment in a hotel in lower
Fifth Avenue, and behind his volubility and wit he was more
depressed than ever. Four years had elapsed since the two had
met in London, when Mark Twain had talked to James about
Swedish health cures. With his halo of white hair, his brilliant
aggressive loquacity, he continued to charm, as he had always
done. The repatriated novelist enjoyed his brief interlude in New
Jersey although he stayed only the next day. The weather was
good and he found the air, and the play of light over the coast
"delicious." But he had no illusions about the nature of his visit.
He had gone in common courtesy. "The basis of privacy was
somehow wanting," he would write in the opening pages of *The
American Scene* quite secure in the feeling that the extrovert
Colonel Harvey would miss his allusions. He was describing the
Jersey shore and the white boxes. The white boxes seemed to
say, "We are only instalments, symbols, stop gaps; expensive as
we are, we have nothing to do with continuity, responsibility,
transmission, and don't in the least care what becomes of us after

we have served our present purpose." James was driven to various places during this day and on the roads saw "the chariots, the buggies, the motors, the pedestrians—which last number, indeed, was remarkably small." The entire thirty-six hours at Harvey's appeared to be summed up in his allusion to "the air of unmitigated publicity, publicity as a condition, as a doom, from which there could be no appeal." On his arrival in New Hampshire his thank-you note to Harvey spoke of having "a bushel of Impressions already gathered." The note of affluence and advertising, of impermanence, of a civilization created wholly for commerce, had already been struck for him.

A NEW ENGLAND AUTUMN

HE had a strange feeling the evening he stepped out of the South Station in Boston, a sense of "confused and surprised recognition." The town seemed vacant. He rode through the warm September night to Cambridge without so much as seeing a single policeman between the depot and Harvard Square. The immediate Cambridge impression was its "earth smell." In the darkness it "fairly poetized the suburbs, and with the queer, far, wild throb of shrilling insects." Cambridge was still faithful to its type—but the rustle of the trees had a larger tone and there was more lamplight. There were also ampler walls and the University seemed in more confident possession. New and strange architecture loomed through the dark. Harvard stretched acquisitive arms in many directions.

James drove to 95 Irving Street, the large shingled house William James had built ten years before, which he had never seen. Here he spent the night. The next day he took the train into the White Mountains, to Chocorua where he found—so he wrote Edith Wharton—"the Domestic circle blooming for the poor celibate exile."

I

William James's summer home at Chocorua was a low rambling two-storey bungalow on the edge of a forest-fringed slope. From the high ground on which it stood, Henry James looked at a great sweep of country, a chain of small lakes, and off to the right the grey head of Chocorua mountain. It was all "quite Fenimore Cooper but without the danger of being scalped." He had a warm reunion with his brother and sister-in-law, his nephews, his niece. The family installed him in a suite of rooms at one end of the L-shaped house. He liked the spacious verandahs and the smell of the woods. He had a sense of total privacy. Later he spoke of the

"Arcadian elegance and amiability" of this part of New England. It reminded him of an old legend, an old love story, one of those written by Mademoiselle de Scudéry in fifteen volumes—an allusion to the way in which she had travestied her time by disguising her personages as Greeks and Romans. The place was Arcadian because it was poetic, romantic, and unburdened with too much history. Such history as it had he saw soon enough— the "old, hard New England effort, defeated by the soil and the climate and reclaimed by nature and time." He had seen the great ruins of the centuries in old European cities; but here he looked on crumbled chimney-stacks, overgrown thresholds, dried-up wells, vague cart-tracks of another time. There was the immediate richness of the leaves turning to crimson. He liked the hush of the landscape; he found an elegance in common objects, the silver-grey rock showing through thinly grassed acres, the boulders in the woods, "the scattered wild apples . . . like figures in the carpet." He found everything "funny and lovely." The loveliness resided in nature. The "funny" element was represented by the people, their incongruities and manners—and absence of form. In *The American Scene* there are beautiful verbal landscapes; James obviously went on long rambles in the woods, and he had always been a student of nature in a pictorial way. There is also a great deal of social criticism in his recollections. He was troubled from the first by what he saw—the "sallow, saturnine" people driving teams, carts and conveyances, their slovenliness of dress and careless articulation; there was a kind of general "human neglect" surrounding farmhouses and towns. With his old interest in comparing Old World life and American, he felt the difference "in a land of long winters" made by the suppression of the two great factors of the familiar English landscape, the squire and the parson. The shrill New England meeting house was no substitute for "the seated solidity of religion," which in England provided so much social furnishing. James would write of the villages, their lack of civic pride, their absence of standards. He wondered at the high wages paid unskilled "hired" men and servants, not because he grudged them their earnings but because there was no matching of skill with remuneration. He disliked the attitude of the employed. They seemed to feel that everything was "owed *to* them, not to be rendered, but to be received."

Henry James thought too many roads were being built in New England. He wasn't happy when he was driven about in buggies or wagons behind ostrich-necked horses at breakneck speed. However, he enjoyed the domestic life in William James's house; he had an enormous appetite for the country butter, cream, eggs, chickens, and the delectable home-baked loaf, such as he had not eaten in years. Shortly before leaving England he had decided to try the new fad of "Fletcherism." An American, Horace Fletcher, was teaching the virtues of slow and lengthy chewing of food. James's deliberate mastication seemed to go hand in hand with his slow ruminative conversation.

He had boasted of his escape from interviewers in New York, but one intrepid young woman, armed with a letter from Scribner's, made her way to Chocorua. James, who had never given an interview, felt it would be unkind not to see her. He stipulated, however, that she must send him no clippings. She described a man of middle height, slightly bald, his black hair turned to iron grey at the sides, wearing a plain rough sack suit of dark grey, and not as "different from other people as his fiction is different from other fiction." His face was "long and strong, broad of cheek-bone and jaw, narrower in the high doming forehead." James's blue-grey eyes had "seen, rather than seemed to see"—perhaps testimony of his lack of interest, for he described his interviewer as "a pathetic bore." Today her account has a certain documentary value. "His nose is massive and fine, his mouth large and tender," she wrote and found a "delicate, young expression of the chin." Superficially, she said, one would not count the whole as striking, but the distinction lay in the play of expression—strength, mellowness, shyness, kindness. His manner was more American "than it might have been considering his long residence in England." They talked in a low-ceilinged room "where the dreamy space of grass surmounted by a rim of trees" provided a natural panorama. James throughout was simple and relaxed.

"One's craft, one's art, is his expression," he told his interviewer, "not one's person, as that of some great actress or singer is hers." He said that "after you have heard a Patti sing why should you care to hear the small private voice of the woman. One rather discounts mere talk. In such a matter, too, the artist is practically helpless, practically at the mercy of the hearer. The author in his work has meant something perhaps, but if he had to express this meaning in a different way it would never have been written."

The young woman asked the Master about the "moral purpose" in his way of ending his stories leaving everything up in the air. "Ah, is not that the trick that life plays?" James rejoined. "Life itself leaves you with a question—it asks you questions."

Perhaps the most interesting part of the interview, which was heavily interlarded with appreciative references to certain of his novels, was James's description of the reading public. He called it "dissolute;" he said it was omnivorous, gulping, either ignorant or weary, reading to soothe or indulge. He felt that people in America did not like to think. In older civilizations there were more defined differences of public desire, "conditions that have had time to accumulate and so to be observed." James said that the French writers he had known wrote out of a strong tradition "and I wish to say that an author for whom I entertain a great esteem is Balzac." James would have a great deal to say about Balzac during his journeying in America.

II

The novelist seems to have been restless at Chocorua. He had always been active; he liked to move about; and he made three trips within a matter of days after his arrival. The first involved Balzac. He went to Jackson, New Hampshire, to spend a day with the seventy-four-year-old Katherine Prescott Wormeley, who had devoted her life to translating and writing about Balzac. She was a sister of Ariana Curtis, his hostess in Venice at the Palazzo Barbero. He had spoken of Miss Wormeley in his 1902 essay on Balzac as an "interpreter, translator and worshipper," an example of "the passionate piety" that the novelist could inspire. He arrived at nightfall, high in the White Mountains, and was

reminded of a Swiss village; he stayed at the inn next to the Wild-
cat River and climbed to Miss Wormeley's house the next morning where he found five verandahs for the view, and "images of
furnished peace, within, as could but illustrate a rare personal
history."

His second journey was to join Howard Sturgis, who was
spending a few weeks in America, on Cape Cod. James had
visited the Cape twenty years before, and had described it in *The
Bostonians*. This time he went, by the slow jogging train from
Boston, to West Barnstaple and thence to Cotuit by horse and
buggy, driven by "a little boy in tight knickerbockers." The
horse "was barely an animal at all . . . a mere ambling spirit in
shafts on the scale of a hairpin." The drive was long and James
enjoyed "the little white houses, the feathery elms, the band of
ocean blue, the strip of sandy yellow, the tufted pines in angular
silhouette, the cranberry swamps, stringed across, for the picking,
like the ruled pages of ledgers." The place looked for him like a
pictured Japanese screen; and the communities were locked up
tight, as if painted on Japanese silk. He had three pleasant days
with Sturgis; otherwise he found little human company. He
carried away a glimpse of a young man, waist high, prodding the
sea bottom for oysters. He saw a mute citizen or two packing
oysters in boxes for shipment to Boston; he listened to "the un-
abashed discourse of three or four school-children at leisure,
visibly 'prominent' and apparently in charge of the life of the
place." As during his visit twenty years before, he was convinced
that America in its permissiveness was surrendering itself and its
culture to the uncultivated young.

His third trip was farther away, a sally into Connecticut to visit
his Emmet cousins, whom he hadn't seen since 1900 when Bay
Emmet had painted his portrait. They were now living on a farm
near Salisbury—the mother, Mrs Hunter and Rosina, Leslie, and
Bay. Going there James suddenly realized that every trip in
America involved distance, compared with the easy little journeys
in and out of London he had been making for years. He found
Connecticut "a ravishing land," and he was pleased particularly
by the fine houses, the elms, the general aspect of Farmington.

Here he found "the note of the aristocratic in an air that so often affects us as drained precisely and well-nigh to our gasping, of any exception to the common." In one house he was shown an array of impressionist paintings, "wondrous examples of Manet, of Degas, of Claude Monet, of Whistler." It made him realize, he said, that he had been starved of such things in his early weeks in America. Everywhere he had discovered a desire among people for "sameness" rather than difference. When he asked about the conditions of life, even at Farmington, the answer he got was "The conditions of life? Why, the same conditions as every-where else." James bowed his head to this kind of "monotony of acquiescence."

III

He explored, that autumn, as the colours of the trees continued to change and the leaves began to fall, the no-longer familiar con-tours of Cambridge, the mysteries of the expanded Boston. He revisited Newport, scene of his younger self, as well as Concord and Salem. The personal America of his earlier years seemed shrunken; the new America, and the new racial mixtures, con-fronted him everywhere. In William James's spacious house in Irving Street he had his anchor; here there were memories of his father and mother, including the striking paternal portrait by Duveneck, and objects of furniture, such as his father's old large work-table which William now used. These referred him back to a remote past. William's house was spacious with a smallish verandah, a square garden at the side, and a long and wide study-sitting-room, behind the front parlour, in which the family could gather round the fire in the evenings. The novelist had his isolated quarters in the upper reaches of this house and worked in the mornings as usual, but without a typist. Accustomed always to talking and observing, he strolled in the afternoons, he read, he took notes. Just across the way from William's home lived the ageing Grace Norton, his confidante of many years; long ago she had come to represent a substitute for his mother to whom, from abroad, he had continued to chronicle his doings, as he had done in his youth to Quincy Street. Now he found her much less the personage he had made of her; he still felt an old affection for her, in her spinsterish aloofness; but she was "intellectually inaccessible" and this fact destroyed his old desire to write to her, once he was abroad again. But in her possession were some of the finest letters he had written, many more than he remembered.

In October he paid a long visit to Mrs Wharton in the Berkshires. He visited also that other *grande dame*, the indomitable "Mrs Jack" Gardner at Green Hill in Brookline, and saw the all-but-completed and already inaugurated Venetian *palazzo* she had built in the Fenway, admiring her gift in shoring up the fragments of her far-flung purchases abroad. He had once spoken of "the age of Mrs Jack"; that age had now composed itself into a set form, a museum-mould, as he had imagined in his creation of Adam Verver and his dream of an art centre in American City. He wrote to Paul Bourget that Mrs Gardner's *palais-musée* "is a really great creation. Her acquisitions during the last ten years have been magnificent; her arrangement and administration of them are admirable, and her spirit soars higher still. Her spirit is immense, and proof against time and fate. It has greatly 'improved' her in every way to have done a thing of so much interest and importance—and to have had to do it with such almost unaided courage, intelligence and energy! She has become really a great little personage."

IV

James's inspection of Cambridge began, as might be expected, with Harvard, where he found himself musing anew at the shape of the Harvard Yard and the fact that it was still not sufficiently enclosed. In the old days it had been wide open, and the stray horse or cow could amble through the campus as if the animal too had a claim on American education. With his novelist's need for shape and form, the unenclosed gave an effect for him of extemporization and thinness. And he remembered the high grills and palings at Oxford, and the sense of mystery these created for him. His nephew Harry, so lately a graduate of these halls, guided him one day to the various buildings; and the novelist, thinking back on the small Harvard of his own youth, and the few brief months he had spent at the old law school in Dane Hall, looked at each item of the new "pampered state" of the students—"multiplied resources, faculties, museums, undergraduate and postgraduate habitations . . . pompous little club-houses." He went into the Law Library and saw in the distance, the dean, John Gray, whom he had known in his youth when they had both admired his cousin Minny Temple—but "to go to him I should have had to cross the bridge that spans the gulf of time;" he was nervous whether the bridge would hold him.

He stepped into the student union, admiring the Sargent portrait of the donor, Major Henry Lee Higginson; he paused before the tablets carrying the names of members of the university who had died in the Civil War. He felt in all this "the too scant presence of the massive and the mature." Walking about the yard he scanned the faces of the young men. Many of them already seemed to have for James a "businessman" face; he was speaking of facial cast and expression alone, leaving out of account questions of "voice, tone, utterance, and attitude." The American women seemed to be "of markedly finer texture" than the men; and this led James to wonder how American men could satisfy American women, or as he put it "this apparent privation, for the man, of his right kind of woman, and this apparent privation, for the woman, of her right kind of man." On this subject he had already written much, his general vision having been that American men were absentee husbands, and absent not only from home but from culture; American men intervened in the life of the American women "by occult, by barely divinable" courses. Inspecting the young man at Harvard, James continued to ask himself what would happen, "in what proportion would he wear the stamp of the unredeemed commercialism that should betray his paternity?" and to what extent would he have absorbed the different social values which his mother might have interposed. Such were the inquiries of "the restless analyst." They were social, psychological, historical, based not on any scientific method or any dialectic but rather the intuitions, the feelings, the soundings, of an artist who had the deepest trust in his own senses and faculties, not least the supremacy of his intellect.

Meanwhile, however, his concern was most often with the relation of the past—his personal past—to what he saw in the America of 1904 and 1905. One of his first pilgrimages in Boston was to Ashburton Place, in quest of the house in which he had lived during the two far-away years of his youth, the last two years of the Civil War—the house of his early "initiations." He found it, although it stood isolated behind the State House in an area already much cleared-out; some of the little old crooked streets had disappeared. He looked on with profound emotion remembering his old public and private "vibrations." Here had come the news of the death of Lincoln, the end of the war, and word of the death of the presiding genius of the American novel, Hawthorne. Here he had counted the first dollars earned by his book reviews and early tales. He seemed now to hear ghostly footsteps, "the sound as of taps on the window-pane heard in the dim dawn," the place seemed to hold old secrets and old stories, "a saturation of life as closed together and preserved in it as the scent lingering in a folded pocket handkerchief." Yet when he returned a month later, for another look, the old house was gone —every brick of it—"the brutal effacement, at a stroke, of every related object, of the whole precious past." He got thus a vivid impression of the impermanence of American life, the discontinuity of objects and places. "I had been present, by the oddest hazard, at the very last moments of the victim in whom I was most interested; the act of obliteration had been breathlessly swift, and if I had often seen how fast history could be made I had doubtless never so felt that it could be unmade still faster."

Beacon Hill was full of memories. There was Mount Vernon Street where his father had died and where he had stayed, in the house of death, through the spring of 1883 with his sister Alice. This is probably the meaning of his allusion to "intenser ghostly presences" in the passage he devotes in his book to this street. And here he can speak with intensity of habitations built of brick as against those of wood he found in so many of the New England towns. "Oh, the wide benignity of brick, the goodly, friendly, ruddy fronts, the felicity of scale, the solid *seat* of everything . . . to walk down Mount Vernon Street to Charles was to have a brush with that truth . . . the preservation of character and the continuity of tradition." But what he saw in great measure was "the lapse into shabbiness and into bad company." Descending to Charles Street he passed the house which had been the centre of culture in his day—the home of J. T. Fields and his beautiful wife, where Dickens and Thackeray and all the Brahmins had been entertained, even himself as a young aspirant to letters— where he had met Mrs Stowe and listened to Julia Ward Howe read the *Battle Hymn of the Republic*. Behind the effaced anonymous door he could remember the long drawing-room looking over the water towards the sunset, like the finished background of a Dürer print. He felt a deep anguish in speaking of this "temple to memory" and he added, "Ah, if it hadn't been for *that* small patch of common ground, with its kept echo of the very accent of the past, the revisiting spirit, at the bottom of the hill, could but have muffled his head, or but have stifled his heart, and turned away for ever." James neither muffled his head, nor stifled his heart; he wasn't capable of such acts. In the same locality he passed the spot where Dr Oliver Wendell Holmes had lived and remembered the feeling of August emptiness in the street, the closed houses, the absent families, and how he had in his youth come to ask for news of Wendell Holmes "then on his first flushed and charming visit to England and saw his mother in the cool dim matted drawingroom of that house and got the news, of all his London, his general English success and felicity, and *vibrated* so with the wonder and romance and curiosity and dim weak tender (oh, tender!) envy of it." He had remounted Mount Vernon Street to the Athenaeum on that occasion filled with longing for London "humming with it, and the emotion, exquisite of its kind." He never seems to have forgotten that hour, for he dwelt on it in his notebooks as "a sovereign contribution to the germ of that inward romantic principle which was to determine so much later (ten years!) my own vision-haunted migration."

In Back Bay he revisited Marlborough Street, comparing it to Wimpole Street and Harley Street. He remembered the winter winds and snows and the eternal dust; he studied the individual

I

house-fronts, finding too many bow windows and suddenly recalled a phrase from Tennyson, "long, unlovely street." Yet
Marlborough Street, unlike the English street, did not have a
monotony of leasehold brick and there was evidence of architectural experiment. Nevertheless Harley Street had character and
depth: Marlborough Street was thin and had the tone of a precocious child.

He looked closely at the Florentine palace that was the new
public library in Copley Square; he had watched Abbey paint
some of its murals. He inspected those of Puvis de Chavannes
and noted the comings and goings of readers, and yet found—it
was his common complaint—that the majesty of such a place was
diminished by the absence of "penetralia." One failed to get the
feeling in these American buildings that there was an innermost
shrine, some sacred centre. His feeling of this was increased by
the ubiquity of the American child, "*most* irrepressible little
democrats of the democracy." Even works of art in the city, like
Saint-Gaudens' noble monument to Robert Gould Shaw and the
Fifty-fourth Massachusetts Regiment in which James's brother
Wilky had served, seemed placed with a casualness that was a dis-
respect to both art and memory. There was an absence of
majesty. America could scatter emblems of things far and wide;
it seemed to pay no attention to their symbolic meaning.

Much of James's progress through America, during these in-
tensely-felt weeks is recorded, with swelling phrase and large
metaphor, in his book. In Newport he experienced the bitter-
sweet of finding little corners full of old recall and the work of the
real estate operators and American wealth and pretension, that
had superseded old views and old values. There is a beautiful
tenderness in which James describes the topographical contours
of Newport—"a little bare, white, open hand, with slightly-
parted fingers" and remembers the days of his youth on its lonely
beaches. He visits the villas and palaces "into which the cottages
have all turned" as if he were living in a fairy-tale—or some
ancient story of King Midas. The place seemed heaped with gold
"to an amount so oddly out of proportion to the scale of nature
and of space." He would locate here the opening scene of the

American novel he started to write seven years later, *The Ivory Tower*.

At Concord he remembered Emerson in his orchards; he had attended Emerson's funeral during his visit twenty years before. He found less change here; and he saw anew the Old Manse, and looked closely at the scene of Concord's single historic event, where the minute men had made their stand. He hung over the Concord River and remembered how Thoreau, Hawthorne, and Emerson had expressed "the sense of this full, slow, sleepy, meadowy flood;" he imaged it as setting its pace and taking its twists "like some large obese benevolent person." His youngest brother, Robertson James, who had fought in the Civil War, was living in Concord with his family. Bob had aged much; he talked however as brilliantly as ever. Henry had seen him at various times abroad. The three years that separated them in age, and the war experience, had made great differences between them; and then Bob had had great spiritual struggles, and had never found a focus in his life. Henry James could remember when Robertson, and their long-dead brother Wilky, had gone to school in Concord. Personal memories ranged deeply under the elms and in the sleepy streets; and yet what prevailed above all was the sense of the two geniuses of the place, Hawthorne and Emerson. James went in quest of Hawthorne also, to Salem; he found the birthplace, set in an area now taken over by industry; he looked at what was said to be the house of the seven gables. He did not venture into it—he had a horror of "reconstituted antiquity." And for the same reason he paused before the Salem Witch House with a kind of "sacred terror" and a "sacred tenderness;" he was somehow put off by the flimsiness of all the wooden houses. "They look brief and provisional at the best—look, above all, incorrigibly and witlessly innocent." His entire visit left him wondering how this place had nurtured Hawthorne, and how "merely 'subjective' in us are our discoveries about genius. Endless are its ways of besetting and eluding, of meeting and mocking us . . . we recognize ruefully that we are for ever condemned to know it only after the fact."

THE LADY OF LENOX

I

AS might be expected of a woman who had written a book on the decoration of houses, Edith Wharton had built her new home at Lenox, Massachusetts, in the Berkshires, with a sense of style and comfort. The Mount stood on a slope; it was spacious; it was dignified. It overlooked the dark waters and wooded shores of Laurel Lake. In the French style, its drawing-room, dining-room and library opened through large glass doors on a terrace beyond which was a stretch of formal garden. Henry James sank into the house as into a luxurious bed. He had come to the United States, he explained to Goody Allen to whom at intervals he reported on his American progress, "with a neat little project of paying no visits" and he was carrying this project out "still more neatly, by having spent but two nights at an hotel, and done nothing but proceed from one irresistible hospitable house to another." The Mount was "an exquisite and marvellous place," he wrote to Howard Sturgis "a delicate French Chateau mirrored in a Massachusetts pond" and a monument to "the almost too impeccable taste of its so accomplished mistress." Every comfort prevailed, "and you needn't bring supplementary apples or candies in your dressing-bag. The Whartons are kindness and hospitality incarnate, the weather is glorious-golden, the scenery of a high class."

"Everyone is oppressively rich and *cossu* and 'a million a year' (£200,000) seems to be the usual income," he explained to Miss Allen. He was having, he said, "a most agreeable and absorbing adventure and this golden glorious American autumn (such weather, as of tinkling crystal, and *such* colours, as of molten topaz and ruby and amber!) a prolonged fairy-tale." The country was "too terrifically big—and yet all this New England is but the corner of a corner of a corner." Mrs Wharton motored constantly, with her handsome heavily moustached husband, a poodle, and the increasingly absorbed and fascinated distinguished visitor. Henry James proclaimed himself won over to this form of travel in spite of bad roads, and "the mountain-and-valley, lake-and-river beauty extends so far, and goes so on and on, that even the longest spins do not take one out of it." They visited every accessible part of this corner of Massachusetts and crossed into New York to large Hudson vistas. James in the horse-and-buggy days of his earlier years had known but limited areas of the eastern seaboard and to find himself in the heart of New England and of New York State was to make him feel as if a great deal of freshness was breaking through old staleness, "when the staleness, so agreeably flavoured with hospitality, and indeed with new ingredients, was a felt element at all." They drove through the great Lebanon bowl and the Shaker settlement—skirting on the wide hard floor of the valley rows of gaunt windows that resembled parallelograms of black paint, criss-crossed with white lines, as in Nuremberg dolls'-houses. The place wore "the strangest air of active, operative death . . . the final hush of passions, desires, dangers." Mrs Wharton must have provided an active commentary also on the New England villages through which they passed, for James would write of "those of the sagacious who had occasionally put it before me that the village street, the arched umbrageous vista, half so candid and half so cool, is too frequently, in respect to 'morals,' but a whited sepulchre." It had been put to him, he said, that "the great facts of life are in high fermentation on the other side of the ground glass that never for a moment flushes, to the casual eye, with the hint of a lurid light." This caused the novelist, who had seen sex in the open in Europe, who had written of Maupassant, D'Annunzio, and Serao, and French morality, to wonder profoundly whether American "realism" had really had the necessary "veracity and courage." The village street and the lonely farm, as he looked at them from the moving motor, "became positively richer objects under the smutch of imputation." He had heard not only of desire but of incest under the elms, for he wrote that "twitched with a grim effect, the thinness of their mantle, shook out of its folds such crudity and levity as they might, and borrowed, for dignity, a shade of the darkness of Cenci drama, of monstrous legend, of old Greek tragedy, and thus helped themselves out for the story-seeker more patient almost of anything than of flatness." Edith Wharton would write of these subjects in *Ethan Frome* and her short novel, *Summer*.

They found themselves one day foraging for dinner in a town by the Hudson, with the dim Catskills in the distance. The car had broken down, and they walked the long straight street to the hotel where they were barred from the dining-room because of Mrs Wharton's poodle. They found a quiet cook-shop instead, where the dog and its human companions could enter and where there was little denial, as James remarked, of "the superstition of cookery." What remained was the memory of that long straight street. The Hudson stretched back "with fumbling friendly hand, to the earliest outlook of my consciousness." The river had been a central fact in the lives of the Jameses between their parental Albany and their own New York—"small echoes and tones and sleeping lights, small sights and sounds and smells that made one, for an hour, *as* small,—carried one up the rest of the river, the very river of life, indeed, as a thrilled, roundabouted pilgrim, by primitive steamboat, to a mellow, medieval Albany."

II

The days at the Mount, both that autumn, and the following summer, when James revisited it, had a great calm, a luxurious ease. Hostess and guest spent their mornings writing; Teddy Wharton smoked his cigars and came and went. Lunch was late; they motored afternoons and spent evenings by the fire, in talk, in jest; and when Howard Sturgis was there they might as well have been at Qu'Acre or Lamb House. Edith Wharton had considerable "style," and grace; she appreciated a good story and could tell her own stories very well; and she had a love of poetry even though her own published verses are indifferently stiff and solemn. Her admiration for James was profound—he was becoming one of the largest figures in her life. And her account of his various remarks to her, about her work, convey a feeling of a certain sharpness on his part that may have been mitigated by his voice, and complete acceptance, on her part, of their barbed quality. On one occasion Teddy Wharton made some remark about "Edith's new story" just published in *Scribner's*, and the Master's answer was prompt: "Oh yes, my dear Edward, I've read the little work—of course I've read it. Admirable, admirable; a masterly little achievement." And turning towards her, "Of course so accomplished a mistress of the art would not, without deliberate intention, have given the tale so curiously conventional a treatment. Though indeed, in the given case, no treatment *but* the conventional was possible; which might conceivably, my dear lady, on further consideration, have led you to reject your subject as—er—in itself a totally unsuitable one." Mrs Wharton recognized in this the characteristic tendency of James, to begin with praise and then find himself "overmastered by the need to speak the truth." He had done the same to Miss Jewett in a letter in which he suddenly cast aside "the mere twaddle of graciousness" and criticized her historical novel, *The Tory Lover*, as a falsified pastiche. So on another occasion, after praising *The Custom of the Country*, he burst forth to Mrs Wharton: "But of course you know—as how should you, with your infernal keenness of perception, *not* know?—that in doing your tale you had under your hand a magnificent subject, which ought to have been your main theme, and that you used it as mere incident and then passed it by." Mrs Wharton recorded still another instance of this kind of cushioned cruelty of criticism. She had written a tale in French for the *Revue des Deux Mondes*, and when someone spoke of this as "remarkable," James came crashing in with, "Remarkable—most remarkable! An altogether astonishing feat. I do congratulate you, my dear, on the way in which you've picked up every old worn-out literary phrase that's been lying about the streets of Paris, for the last twenty years and managed to pack them all into those few pages." He then added, thoughtfully, "a very creditable episode in her career. *But she must never do it again.*"

Small wonder Mrs Wharton found such comments "withering" at times, even though she joined in the laughter and spoke

good-naturedly of "our literary rough-and-tumble." The sharpness of James's remarks, as she recorded them—so stark when
compared with the tone of similar strictures made in letters to Mrs
Humphry Ward, or some of the young writers—suggests that
there existed between the Master and the lady novelist a direct-
ness, an openness and freedom—and truth—that gave to their
friendship a rare quality of mutual "ease." This, at any rate, is
what Mrs Wharton tries to suggest in her reminiscences. At the
same time we may imagine that James's tone of voice could have
softened the seeming harshness of his Johnsonian dicta and
blunted their aggressivity. Perhaps too, in remembering them,
Mrs Wharton was recalling the "message" in all its nakedness,
and not the surrounding euphemisms.

III

Mrs Wharton would remember James's reading poetry by her
fireplace in Lenox, remembered his taking up Emily Brontë's
poems and "with some far-away emotion" his eyes filled and in
his rich flexible voice chanting

> Cold in the earth, and the deep snow piled above thee,
> Far, far removed, cold in the dreary grave,
> Have I forgot, my only Love, to love thee,
> Severed at last by Time's all-severing wave?

His reading she felt was "an emanation of his inmost self, un-
affected by fashion or elocutionary artifice." On another evening,
they began to quote Whitman. In his young manhood James had
been sharply critical of old Walt; he had published an uncompromising review attacking his "flashy imitation of ideas."
Recently he had mentioned this article to an old friend who
threatened to dig it up: James's recantation was vigorous. The
review had been, he said, "a little atrocity." "Nothing would
induce me to reveal the whereabouts of my disgrace, which I only
recollect as deep and damning." If it were to cross his path he
would not look at it; wherever he encountered "the abominations
of my early innocence" he destroyed them. He had indeed made
his peace with Whitman in the long years since the Civil War.
Perhaps it was a result of his renewed vision of America, the

touching of old emotions; or Whitman's homo-eroticism. At any rate "his voice filled the hushed room like an organ adagio as he read from 'The Song of Myself' and 'When lilacs last in the door-yard bloomed' and 'Out of the Cradle' which he crooned rather than read. We talked long that night of *Leaves of Grass*," Mrs Wharton remembered, "tossing back and forth to each other treasure after treasure." At the end, the Master flung his hands upward, a characteristic gesture, and with eyes twinkling said: "Oh yes, a great genius; undoubtedly a very great genius! Only one cannot help deploring his too-extensive acquaintance with the foreign languages."

On another evening, when they had sat late on the terrace, there was some allusion apparently to his recent visit to his Emmet cousins, at Salisbury. A member of the party said, "Tell us about the Emmets—tell us all about them." James began, said Mrs Wharton, and suddenly he seemed to forget where he was, the place, the surrounding friends; he was lost in visions of his youth. "Ghostlike indeed at first, wavering and indistinct, they glimmered at us through a series of disconnected ejaculations, epithets, allusions, parenthetical rectifications and restatements, till not only our brains but the clear night itself seemed filled with a palpable fog; and then, suddenly, by some miracle of shifted lights and accumulated strokes, there they stood before us as they lived, drawn with a million filament-like lines." It was "a summoning to life of dead-and-gone Emmets and Temples, old lovelinesses, old follies, old failures, all long laid away and forgotten under old crumbling gravestones." The artist in Edith Wharton responded fully to the Master's sense of his personal past.

IV

At Lenox, Henry James met Walter Berry whom he would see intermittently during the ensuing years, and would like—his conversation, his logical mind, his general enjoyment of life. Berry would be a peripheral friend of the two masters of the modern subjective novel—Marcel Proust in France and Henry James in England and America; and he was already, and would continue to be, one of the closest of Edith Wharton's friends.

James corresponded with him playfully, amusedly, ironically, and the handful of letters printed when Mrs Wharton was still alive, disguised her presence in them, although allusions to "the Lady of L——" could hardly escape the notice of those who knew her. She is also "the Princesse Lointaine" and "the Angel of Devastation" in these letters; and there are allusions to the rue de Varenne where she later lived and the "sarabandistes" of that *rue*, as James came to call Mrs Wharton's attendant friends. One postscript has contributed to the legend that Walter Berry was Edith Wharton's lover, for James wrote to Berry "it adds to my joy *de vous savoir* in such bowers of bliss, abysses of interest, labyrinths of history —soft sheets generally *quoi.*" This allusion need not be read too literally. In private James found him very much a man of the world and a familiar cosmopolite figure—one of the characters he had invented. Berry came out of old New York—his full name was Walter Van Rensselaer Berry. He was in his forties when James met him. Born in Paris, educated at Harvard, admitted to the bar, he was at one time president of the American Chamber of Commerce in Paris, and practised as an international lawyer. Mrs Wharton has described how Berry filled an intellectual void in her life and he motored with her in many parts of Europe in later years. There survive joint postcards, written by them to James during their travels. Of Mrs Wharton's love for Berry we know a great deal: of Berry, the confirmed bachelor said to have been interested in Mrs Wharton's intellect, and in young dancers at the Folies (as one who knew him said) we know perhaps less. He was handsome, tall, a bit stiff, a bit dry—so some saw him—deeply committed to the cause of France against Germany. Percy Lubbock would describe Berry's effect on Mrs Wharton's art in nothing less than disastrous terms; Nicky Mariano, Bernard Berenson's companion, would remember how radiant Mrs Wharton was in Berry's presence. But all this was of a later time. In James's letters to Mrs Wharton he is "the brave Berry" and James speaks of him as having "greatly endeared himself to me" with his mixture of his "gifts and his unhappinesses," his alertness, and his melancholy. He writes on occasion "I hope you've not wanted for the sight of Walter Berry."

From Lenox, Edith Wharton wrote to Minnie Bourget in France of the visit of her distinguished guest. The self-effacing Minnie responded with words that showed how deeply the Bourgets loved Henry James. "Nobody," wrote Minnie in Gallic-tinged English, "who has not actually lived with him will ever completely appreciate this *great artist*, the wonderful companion, the charm of whom resides in that perfect simplicity and adaptation of everyday life with the ever-springing source of comprehension and keen sensitiveness. There are early Italian days in my memory when I became for ever attached to what I must call his genius, in an antique sense of that word." She was she said glad to know of this "new link between you and us." Minnie also spoke of Mrs Wharton's having discovered "the compatriot" in James—"he loves his country, perhaps even when he does not know himself to what extent." And then, in a strange self-revelation Minnie spoke of feeling in the presence of the artists around her, her husband, James, Mrs Wharton, like a boy in a painter's studio who cleans the palette and brushes and finds inspiration in the fragments of the "aerial atmosphere or divine outline" of the artist's blurred patches of colour.

"I am immensely touched," James wrote to Mrs Wharton when she sent him this letter. The image of the little studio boy was "exquisite" and "veracious" as a picture of Minnie's services to her husband. "It is all very beautiful and helpless and I am glad of your communication of it." But the Bourgets didn't *really* know him, he added. He did not comment on Minnie's observations concerning his patriotism. He was giving proof of that in his unremitting and restless study of the American scene. Lenox and the rides with Mrs Wharton were one part of this. His exploration of old Cambridge haunts and shrines was another.

THE MEDUSA FACE

HE went in search one Sunday in Cambridge of the Fresh Pond of his personal past. In his youth, when Howells was also young and learning to edit the *Atlantic*, the two used to walk beside the pond and speak of the novels they wanted to write and what a novel should be. He found the muses of the place had fled; and "the little nestling lake had ceased to nestle." Still, James remarked, in a personal sentence, that he could "at this day, on printed, on almost faded pages, give chapter and verse for the effect, audible on the Sunday afternoons" of those Fresh Pond muses. Which was to say that he and Howells had not simply talked; they had carried out their plans and certain of their early writings had issued from these promenades. A charming Country Club now stood on the ground towards Watertown, all verandahs and golf-links, "all tea and ices and self-consciousness." And there was a great deal of highway "the arms of carnivorous giants" across the rural scenery. The old haunt, "desecrated and destroyed," could no longer be a place for "shared literary secrets." Henry James spoke of "angrily missing" among the ruins the atmosphere he had gone to recover—"some echo of youth, the titles of tales, the communities of friendship, the sympathies and patiences, in fine, of dear W.D.H." With the tact and reticence of the time he reduced Howells to his initials in *The American Scene* since the latter still lived, and Henry was determined to stay with impressions and not go "smash on the rock of autobiography."

I

He reserved, however, one stroll in Cambridge for a special time. It would have to be a "favouring hour," when he was in the right mood, when he could face his long-dead personal past that lived in him alone. The moment came one evening in November, some

268

time after his return from Lenox. He set out on foot. There was a wintry pink in the west, the special shade of late fall "fading into a heartless prettiness of grey"—heartless because it silhouetted in gaunt and grim tracery the bare trees of November. James walked past Longfellow's house, admiring its ample style and its symmetry, thinking of it before it had become a tourist-haunted spot, when he used to visit the poet and talk of his travels. He walked past high, square, sad, and silent Elmwood, and lingered around it, remembering his best-loved Cambridge friend, James Russell Lowell, whom he mentions also only by initials—remarking it was difficult to put him into the past tense. The passage in *The American Scene* describing this walk is charged with autobiographical feeling even if it avoids autobiographical reminiscence. He thinks of Lowell as "the very genius of the spot." He had been a "rustic;" James had often said this, and he said it now with gentle words: Lowell had been "without provision, whether of poetry or of prose, against the picture of proportion and relations overwhelmingly readjusted." Even more than Longfellow, however, Lowell had given Cambridge its literary cachet. And James could not say whether in this new time Harvard, looking "very hard at blue horizons of possibility, across the high table-land of her future" could offer as much as Lowell had offered when James had visited his classroom. "The light of literary desire is not perceptible in her eye"—this was James's verdict on the new Harvard. He spoke of the "tragic intensity" in the faces of the ghosts of Longfellow and Lowell; they had represented "literary desire." Lowell had had a perhaps humorous thesis that "Cambridge, Mass., was, taken altogether, the most inwardly civilized, most intimately humane, among the haunts of men." With this thesis James's friends at least had committed themselves to cultivating the *genius loci*.

His lonely walk was carefully planned. Presently he was making his way among the graves in the Cambridge Cemetery, slowly and deliberately, until he came to the James family plot, on its little ridge—an "unspeakable group of graves." There were four then—those of his mother, his father and his sister Alice, and near by that of one of William's children who had died young. Long ago when he had last visited America, Henry had come here in heavy snow to see his father's newly dug grave, and had stood in the deep whiteness to read aloud, over the raw gash in the earth, William's letter of farewell which had arrived too late.

Henry James stood again on this spot. It was 1904: he had last been here in December 1882. It was as if he had returned to America precisely for this vision, and for this moment. So he said, at any rate, in the moving words he scribbled in a notebook some weeks later when he was in California—"I seemed then to know why I had done this; I seemed then to know why I had *come* —and to feel how not to have come would have been miserably, horribly, to miss it. It made everything right—it made everything priceless." The moon was rising, early, white, young and seemed reflected in the white face of the great empty stadium where a few days before he had witnessed the Harvard–Dartmouth game and "the capacity of the American public for momentary gregarious emphasis." The stadium formed the boundaries of Soldiers' Field that "stared over to me, through the clear twilight, from across the Charles." James carefully took in the scene, noting the quality of the air, the stillness, the waning light. The place "bristled with merciless memories. Turning back to look at the graves, the tears came—the recognition, stillness, the strangeness, the pity, the sanctity and the terror, the breath-catching passion, and the divine relief of tears."

Through his tears he read the words from Dante on the little marble urn of his sister's ashes, which William had had carved in Florence: *ed essa da martiro e da essilio venne a questa pace.* The line "took me so at the throat by its penetrating *rightness.*" It was as if he had sunk on his knees before the symbols of family past and family history "in a kind of anguish of gratitude before something for which one had waited with a long, deep *ache.*"

Henry James stood there a long time; he looked again across the Charles. It was the old Cambridge—and he had moved past ghosts of friendship to reach ghosts of family. This was "the cold Medusa-face of life." He thought of "all the life *lived* on every side." He remembered "the old thinner New England air and more meagre New England scheme." "But why do I write of the all unutterable and the all abysmal?" he asked himself as he sat beside the Pacific with these autumn memories. "Why does my pen not drop from my hand on approaching the infinite pity and tragedy of all the past? It does, poor helpless pen, with what it meets of the ineffable." And he exclaimed—"Oh, strange little intensities of history, of ineffaceability; oh delicate little odd links in the long chain, kept unbroken for the fingers of one's tenderest touch! Sanctities, pieties, treasures, abysses! . . . Basta, basta!"

CITY OF CONVERSATION

BETWEEN the time of his visit to Lenox and his travels at the
beginning of 1905, Henry James went through "an interminable and abysmal siege of American dentistry." This lasted
during the greater part of November and December, "a monument of technical art but a bottomless gulf of physical and
financial ruin." He slipped away from Boston to New York,
however, in November to keep his promise to Colonel Harvey;
the dinner, long-planned, was a modest one for the publicity-
loving colonel—only thirty guests and not at Delmonico's, but at
the Metropolitan Club. Mark Twain, Booth Tarkington, G. W.
Smalley, Hamlin Garland, and the journalist Arthur Brisbane,
were among the guests. The novelist sat between Mrs Harvey
and Mrs Cornelius Vanderbilt. His dental difficulties deprived
him of the full enjoyment of the food; moreover he disliked
Harvey's ostentation, mentioning in particular the floral decorations which cost $500. After Christmas, when the Boston dentist
released him, he returned to New York, first staying at Mrs
Cadwalader Jones's, at 21 East Eleventh Street, in that part of the
city crowded with most of his boyhood memories. He moved
uptown right after the new year to visit at Mrs Wharton's flat,
884 Park Avenue—"a bonbonnière of the last daintiness naturally," he told Howard Sturgis, "but we were more compressed
than at Lenox and Teddy more sandwiched between, and we gave
a little more on each other's nerves, I think, and there was less of
the Lenox looseness." Still, James added, "she was charming,
kind, and ingenious, and taste and tone and the finest discriminations, ironies, and draperies mantelled us about." After eight days
uptown he returned with relief downtown to Mrs Jones's in the
Village, just before going to Washington where he had been
invited to stay with Henry Adams and to attend a dinner in his
honour to be given by the Secretary of State, John Hay. From

this time on, in his comings and goings in Manhattan, he made Minnie Jones's place on East Eleventh Street his headquarters. She provided privacy and quiet, and her daughter Beatrix showered attention on him. He felt himself "half-killed with kindness." Mrs Jones had a pet name for James out of a French farce by Labiche—Célimare—perhaps because the central character "*le bien aimé*" inspires universal affection (he carries on love affairs with two ladies whose husbands also dote on him, and manages to keep their love when he marries a young woman half his age.) James was not capable of the comedy—Célimare's prodigalities of *amour*, but he seems to have been the centre at Mrs Jones's of an adoring circle.

En route to Washington the novelist stopped in Philadelphia to see his old friend Mrs Wister, Fanny Kemble's daughter, and to deliver the first of what would prove to be a series of lectures—or as one critic who watched him closely described them, "oral essays." He had finally decided to ask $250 as his fee for speaking to a ladies' group in Boston; the honorarium was designed to discourage them. It did; but the Contemporary Club of Philadelphia was not easily discouraged, and had the money for such occasions. James read a lecture on "The Lesson of Balzac." The "Clover Room" at the Bellevue-Stratford overflowed—more than one hundred elegantly dressed ladies and gentlemen stood during the lecture which was attended, said the press, by the most distinguished representatives of letters, art, the learned professions, and public life in Philadelphia. James read his paper without a trace of embarrassment, holding the loose sheets of his manuscript in one hand and keeping the other hand in his pocket "save," said the newspaper "where two or three times there came an involuntary gesture." There was no emphasis; the delivery was bland. Agnes Repplier, the cultural leader of Philadelphia, well known for her familiar essays, presided with style and charm. And James, who had suffered stage fright, was elated. "A dazzling success," Célimare reported to his New York admirers, "a huge concourse, five or six hundred folk, a vast hall, and perfect brazen assurance and audibility on Célimare's part. *Il s'est révélé conférencier*." The novelist was put up at the Rittenhouse Club by Sargent's friend, the eminent surgeon Dr J. William White, who supported James before the ordeal and gave him a triumphant supper afterwards. Carey Thomas, president of Bryn Mawr, had also invited James, offering him the standard $50 given to lecturers. James replied he did not have anything suitable for young girls but then, having tasted triumph, he added "to be lucid, the honorarium you offer is not sufficient." He reduced his fee, however, to $200 and agreed to double back from Washington to speak at the college before proceeding south.

I

Washington seemed bland and soft. Henry James was pleasantly surprised. He remembered it from his visit in 1882 as a gossipy but masculine town; now the women dominated the social scene while the men legislated—a town devoid of industry or trade, indeed of any distinctive economic life. But then he had known it in the days when it was still a rather nude capital, with the dome and the shaft presiding over much parochialism, and the President visiting in various houses as if he were a local—rather than a national—celebrity. James had encountered President Chester Arthur in a private home during his former visit and even put the encounter into one of his stories. This time everything was on a much grander scale. He stayed with Henry Adams in his big house on Lafayette Square, next to Adams's bosom friend, Secretary of State Hay, with whom James shared common memories of Miss Woolson. As fellow-guest, James found at Adams's his friend of his youth, John La Farge. Thus old circles, old familiarities were briefly re-established. As in 1882, Adams's house was a hotbed of Washington gossip; but James missed Adams's wife, who had committed suicide in the 1880's. She had always been a lively companion. Adams seldom spoke of her; and James hesitated to ask him about her tomb for which Augustus Saint-Gaudens had carved a much-talked-of mourning figure. In his prolonged grief and shock Adams had left to John La Farge and Saint-Gaudens most of the artistic decisions. At lunch at Adams's one day James whispered to Mrs Winthrop Chanler that the one thing in Washington he wanted to see was this statue in

Rock Creek Cemetery, but that he felt he could not make the wish known to Adams. Mrs Chanler took him there in her brougham immediately after lunch. It was a mild wintry day and the trees around the tomb had snow on their boughs. James stood uncovered for a long time before the bronze symbolic figure, with its draperies shrouding its head. "He seemed deeply moved." Marion "Clover" Hooper, whom he had known long before she married Adams, had been a "Voltaire in petticoats" to him; she belonged to a past now quite remote. Mrs Chanler remembered that on their return to Lafayette Square James talked of Clover's career as a Washington hostess, her perpetual lunches, her careful choice of guests in spite of the informality, and her command of the capital's social strategies. There had always been good talk at Clover's table—indeed James had ever after that visit spoken of Washington as a "city of conversation."

II

In 1882, although he was the author of the much-discussed *Portrait of a Lady*, Henry James had received no official recognition during his Washington visit, nor had he expected it. Washington had then hardly discovered the arts, save those of architecture and monuments to its dignitaries. In January of 1905, thanks to the Secretary of State, and the artistic entourage at Adams's, James was welcomed as a literary Master, so that even President Theodore Roosevelt—who disliked and had even denounced the novelist as "effete" and "a miserable little snob"—opened the White House to him. Henry James had quite as low an opinion of Roosevelt. He considered him "a dangerous and ominous jingo." The amenities were observed to the last letter of the alphabet, and the novelist was flattered. With his Napoleonic propensities, he was fascinated by power—particularly power in the American style.

"Theodore Rex," the gentle Célimare informed East Eleventh Street, "is a really extraordinary creature for native intensity, veracity, and *bonhomie*—he plays his part with the best will in the world and I recognize his amusing likeability." To William James he wrote that the President "did me the honour to cause me to be placed"—the precision of this statement, the monarchical "cause" could not have been lost on William—"at his table (of eight) and on the right of the lady at *his* right . . . It was very curious and interesting . . . The President is distinctly tending—or trying—to make a 'court.'" James sounded less impressed in his report to Edith Wharton.

I went to Court the other night, for the Diplomatic Reception, and he did me the honour, to put me at his table and almost beside him—whereby I got a rich impression of him, and of his being, verily, a wonderful little machine: destined to be overstrained perhaps, but not as yet, truly, betraying the least creak. It functions astonishingly, and is quite exciting to see. But it's really like something behind a great plate-glass window on Broadway.

As for Washington itself, it was "oddly ambiguous." It seemed to James to sit "for ever saying to your private ear, from every door and window, as you pass 'I am nothing, I am nothing, nothing!' and whose charm, interest, amiability, irresistibility, you are yet perpetually making calls to commemorate and insist upon." It had a kind of "spacious vacancy." Secretary Hay gave an impressive dinner for James; so did Ambassador Jusserand. He lunched with Senator Henry Cabot Lodge. And then, at the invitation of Charles McKim, he went with La Farge and Saint-Gaudens to a dinner of the American Institute of Architects at which official and artistic Washington was present in force—the President, John Hay, Elihu Root, Justice Harlan, and Jusserand. The dinner was "a big success and beautifully done—but the Eagle screamed in the speeches and I didn't know that that fowl was still (after all these years and improvements,) *permitted* to do. It was werry werry quaint and queer—but so is *everything*, *sans exception*, and the sensitive Célimare absorbs it at every pore."

President Roosevelt did not forget Henry James. Some years after the death of John Hay he spoke of the latter as "not a great secretary of state." Hay's close intimacy with Henry James and Henry Adams—"charming men but exceedingly undesirable companions for any man not of a strong nature—and the tone of satirical cynicism which they admired . . . marked that phase of his character which so impaired his usefulness as a public man."

To Henry James, Roosevelt had been "the mere monstrous embodiment of unprecedented and resounding noise."

III

James spent eight days in Washington, enjoying his role of literary lion, but was bewildered when Admiral Dewey, hero of Manila, left his card. A call from a naval personality seemed the last thing he expected; perhaps it was a case simply of one celebrity paying respects to another. If James was amused by the glitter of Roosevelt's Washington it left him with no illusions. "To *live* here," he wrote to Mrs William James, "would be death and madness——" and doubtless, he added, one would pay calls forever "in one's delirium." He found Washington's size "dreary" as of "a great sunny void furnished only with a drizzle of paste-board." He returned to his civilized friends in Philadelphia, and enjoyed his night at Bryn Mawr. He was put up at the Deanery; the audience of young women was enchanted by James's charm and delicacy. James found the occasion so felicitous that he agreed to return as Commencement speaker in the spring.

He spent several days in Philadelphia, visiting with the Whites and Mrs Wister, and seeing something of Dr J. Weir Mitchell, the medical-novelist, who was perhaps a little sensitive because James refused to take him seriously as a writer, treating him with respect but apparently with the coolness of a professional addressing an amateur. Mitchell was a friend of Mrs Wharton and was credited with having started her on her career as a writer (prescribing it as a kind of "occupational therapy.") James found Philadelphia to be, after Washington, a city of culture and refinement; but even more a city which was a "society" in the sense of having "human groups that discriminate in their own favour;" he liked the serenity, the fact that it was "settled and confirmed and content." In that sense New York was "not a society at all," and Chicago, he would later judge, was still less. Neither had been able to discriminate in its own favour—had not been able to recognize and maintain its identity. If Boston, as it was said, was "a state of mind," Philadelphia was a "state of consanguinity." And James clearly indicated what he meant when he used the word "society"—he meant "the number of organic social relations" it represented. Philadelphia in 1905, satisfied James more than other cities "of all goodly villages, the very goodliest, probably in the world; the very largest, and flattest, and smoothest, the most rounded and complete." His less official view was that Philadelphia was "kind, plentitudinous, promiscuous."

We can obtain a glimpse of James through the eyes of a Canadian, the distinguished Dr George Robert Parkin, who happened to be visiting Dr S. Weir Mitchell in Walnut Street during the week James was in Philadelphia. Parkin was in the United States helping to set up the machinery by which young Americans would receive Rhodes scholarships to Oxford. A staunch imperialist, he had been principal of Upper Canada College and was now the organizing secretary of the Rhodes Scholarships. He was taken by his host on a round of visits—to call on Benjamin Franklin's great-granddaughter, on Mrs Dana, and then to another home of a lady identified in Parkin's letter to his wife only as Mrs M. Here he found himself introduced to a "Mr James." Mr James, apparently not realizing Parkin's involvement, listened as the idea for the Rhodes scholarships was explained and promptly denounced it as "deplorable." What, the Master asked, in his most law-giving Johnsonian manner "does Oxford want of men from Nebraska and Canada?" His next logical step was to inquire "Why should we all be asked to fall down and glorify Rhodes?" Dr Parkin defended his mission, unaware that his opponent was the celebrated novelist. "He was and is an absolute surprise to me. I had always thought of him as an alert, versatile man. In looks and talk he seems much more like a heavy, opinionated, self-satisfied English businessman of exceedingly contracted views. But the whole affair was too absurd." However Parkin discovered, facing Henry James at dinner at Dr Mitchell's, that he could be "quite different from yesterday." At the dinner, James, in a mood of persiflage, began "in some absurd connection" to explain how he would elope with his hostess; the elaborateness of his plan, as he worked it out seems quite to have charmed away the Canadian's ruffled feelings. "We got on capitally," he wrote.

In the midst of these sociabilities, a series of minor difficulties suddenly developed. James's dental siege apparently wasn't over; an upper front tooth, loosened, came out, "and I look like a 'fright' but I am cynical, indifferent, desperate—I don't mind it," he told William. And then, when he would have sought local dental help, snow came, more than a foot; deep drifts were under his window at Mrs Wister's "and you may therefore imagine the temperature of the room I write in . . . The trolleys don't run, I can't get to the station; high drifts and a polar hurricane bar the way." He restlessly waited in this "fatally (and oh so 'complacently'!) uncomfortable house." Philadelphia now seemed a "fearsome ordeal." He took train for Richmond—"the southern sun, for which I fairly sicken, will re-create me." A night in the Pullman shook his faith. There was snow at Richmond and "the ugliness appals." He put up at the Jefferson Hotel, discovered that he had run out of linen and shirts, and waited for his laundry to be done before going on to visit the George Vanderbilts in North Carolina. The hotel was comfortable "but the land and place, all under snow and as cold as New York, are utterly featureless and dreary—so that I am wondering what the deuce I suppose myself to be getting out of it." While here he received word that he had been elected to the newly founded American Academy of Arts and Letters. On 3 February, his laundry done, and feeling thoroughly rested, he set out for Biltmore, the palatial Vanderbilt home. There was a new, driving snowstorm; but he was confident that he would be expensively sheltered from it.

CASTLE OF ENCHANTMENT

HE was sitting in front of a large picture window—"a hideous plate-glass window like the door of an ice-house." It had no curtains, no shutters, no blinds; north light shone cold and intense, reflected from a vastness of snow. His room was icy. He had gout in his left foot. When he rang the bell for a servant none came. He found himself hobbling and hopping down long corridors to a remote bathroom to fetch hot water. And this the consequence of his having fled south to escape winter in New York—fled in the direction of Florida. In a moment of sociability and curiosity he had accepted the invitation to stop en route in the fantastic Biltmore—"the chateau of Biltmore" he called it —built by George Vanderbilt, culture-seeking youngest son of the railroader. The place was "impractically spacious." His room was "a glacial phantasy." It looked over an ice-bound stable yard. He estimated it to be half a mile from the "mile-long library." "We measure by leagues and we sit in Cathedrals," he wrote to Mrs Cadwalader Jones.

He had arrived at the dream castle in the North Carolina mountains on 3 February 1905, from Richmond in the midst of a snowstorm. The land was buried, bleak, dreary. The first thing that happened was this sudden flare-up of his gout. He needed bran footbaths; he was taking pills. He was minus a front tooth. In an agony of pain he hopped about—alternating between anger and despair, furious at the circumstance that had brought him into deeper cold than any he had fled; "helpless snow-congested New York like a huge baffled machine roaring at a standstill *did* simply (as a place of convenience and *agrément*) appal me." Biltmore appalled him no less and his gout had brought him to a standstill. He would be a prisoner until it subsided; he was trapped in a chateau set 2500 feet in the air—the Château de Blois enlarged and glorified. "Roll three or four Rothschild houses into one, surround them with a principality of mountain, lake and forest,

200,000 acres, surround *that* with vast states of niggery desolation and make it impossible, through distance and time, to get anyone to stay with you, and you have the bloated Biltmore." The place was the *gageure* of "an imperfectly aesthetic young billionaire." Magnificent, imposing "and utterly unaddressed to any possible arrangement of life, or state of society."

After the first pain subsided, and his foot was reduced to manageable proportions, Henry James took in his surroundings with less violence of feeling, but with continuing bewilderment. He would later ironically call Biltmore "a castle of enchantment." The place would have been almost anywhere miraculous and it certainly affirmed possession of great resources. In *The American Scene* he saluted the will, purpose, patience, knowledge, involved in creating a composite castle-cathedral in a mountain wilderness; at the same time he expressed the fullest meaning for himself when he alluded to it as a "vast parenthetic Carolinian demonstration."

As he began to move about Biltmore he wrote to Mrs Wister he hoped to "escape" at the first opportunity. Yet he put in the better part of a week there; with his swollen foot and the inclement weather he was confined indoors. "There are five or six different tapestried cathedrals (of size) to sit in, and 36 empty guest rooms—wondrously appointed—besides the small, chill (with a vast glacial window) retreat in the 'bachelor wing' to which I am relegated." Moreover, "the climate stalks about in the marble halls in default of guests." His stay was lonely. There were a Mrs Hunt of Washington, and a British military personage, Sir Thomas Fraser, as fellow-guests. He had come at the wrong season. The place might have some beauty in the warmer time of the year.

In the end he saw Biltmore as "a phenomenon of brute achievement." When he was able to put a normal shoe on his gouty foot at the week-end, he made the night-long journey to Charleston, where he was met by Owen Wister. After that he went to Palm Beach where the sub-tropical landscape, such as he had never seen before, the green palms, the flaming hibiscus, the oranges and grapefruit, the general softness, restored him to a more comfortable state of mind.

THE BLIGHTED INVALID

HENRY JAMES's visit to the South was brief: the few days at Richmond, in the snow, the pleasant interlude at Charleston, with Owen Wister as his guide, a glance at Jacksonville; then a stay in Palm Beach, and three days at St Augustine where he went to see his brother Robertson's wife and their daughter Mary, later Mrs Vaux. They had preceded him to Florida. Four decades had elapsed since the Civil War: but the old muffled ache, the anguish of fratricidal struggle remained. James looked upon the South with time-wearied eyes—also with eyes that had seen the ravage of history in Europe. The hurts and wounds, the stirred feelings of defeats and victories, had shrunk now to paper mementoes, hollow-eyed statues and renovated ruins. In Charleston, visiting an old cemetery, he seems to have walked about with memories of Miss Woolson. An allusion to Venice, in the midst of his description of the place, suggests that he remembered Fenimore's "Rodman the Keeper;" and then she had talked to him of these very places—for she had lived in the post-bellum South and had been its modest fictional historian. He strolled in an old cemetery, by the lagoon, and he remembered "the golden afternoon, the low, silvery, seaward horizon, as of wide, sleepy, game-haunted inlets and reed-smothered banks, possible site of some Venice that had never mustered the luxury, in the mild air, of shrub and plant and blossom that the pale North can but distantly envy." He found in this place a certain "proud humility."

The South was a "society still shut up in a world smaller than what one might suppose its true desire, to say nothing of its true desert." He looked at Fort Sumter, and the other forts at Charleston, remembering the far-off historical moment: the forts in the twinkling blue sea seemed not like military bastions but simply vague marine flowers. Owen Wister, standing beside him, remarked, "I never at Charleston look out to the old betrayed Forts without feeling my heart harden again to steel." Wister's was perhaps not the most authoritative voice, even though he lived in the South and felt its sadness and sorrow; for he wrote about the West and had had a boyhood abroad. His grandfather, however, had been a famous slave-owner and his grandmother had been James's old friend, Fanny Kemble, who had written an anti-slavery book, describing her life on a Georgia plantation. In the Richmond Confederate museum, where James looked at framed letters, orders, autographs, tatters of paper currency, together with faded portraits, emblems of woe and glory, he found another kind of witness. He got into conversation with a young Southern farmer who had come to the city for the day and was filling in an hour by reliving the war between the States. James paid close attention to his southern accent, and followed him about as he pointed out certain relics preserved also in his family. He seemed thoroughly familiar with his father's exploits; he related a war adventure to Henry James "which comprised a desperate evasion of capture, or worse, by the lucky smashing of the skull of a Union soldier." James added: "I complimented him on his exact knowledge of these old, unhappy, far-off things," and received in return the candid remark, "Oh, I should be ready to do them all over again myself." Then with a smile, the young farmer added, "That's the kind of Southerner *I* am." James "allowed that he was a capital kind of Southerner, and we afterwards walked together to the Public Library, where, on our final parting, I could but thank him again for being so much the kind of Southerner I had wanted." He wouldn't hurt a Northern fly—*as* Northern; but his consciousness James felt "would have been poor and un-furnished without this cool platonic passion." James reflected too that though he wouldn't hurt a Northern fly, there were things— for they had talked of the blacks—that "all fair, engaging, smiling, as he stood there, he would have done to a Southern Negro."

The blacks in the South struck James as "ragged and rudi-mentary," unlike Northern Negroes he had known; and he recog-nized that there was no way to preach "sweet reasonableness" to

the South about them. The novelist had been reading W. E. B.
Du Bois' *The Souls of Black Folk* which he characterized as the
only Southern book of any distinction that he had ever read. He
wondered at the way in which the Confederate world had pinned
everything on the institution of slavery. Deprived of this, a great
vacuity remained. He saw the South as in an eternal false position
—"condemned as she was to institutions, condemned to a state
of temper, of exasperation and depression, a horrid heritage she
had never consciously invited, that bound up her life with a
hundred mistakes and make-believes, suppressions and prevarica-
tions, things that really all named themselves in the noted provincialism." At the end he imaged the South as "a figure
somehow blighted or stricken, discomfortable, impossible seated
in an invalid-chair, and yet fixing one with strange eyes that were
half a defiance and half a deprecation of one's noticing and much
more of one's referring to, any abnormal sign."

II

Part of his small "historic whiff" he got simply by looking out of
the train windows in "the Pullmans that are like rushing hotels
and the hotels that are like stationary Pullmans." In Palm Beach
he put up at the Breakers, enjoying the hotel luxuries and con-
cluding that one might live in the soft climate "as in a void
furnished at the most with velvet air." One might even live in
Florida with an idea, "if you are content that your idea shall consist of grapefruit and oranges." He enjoyed the sea and the air; he
liked the little golden fruit-ranches, but he shrank from the
human picture—"decent, gregarious, and moneyed, but overwhelmingly monotonous and on the whole pretty ugly," and
moreover, "unacquainted with the rudiments of tone or indeed
with any human utterance." In St Augustine, wearing a recently
purchased bowler too large for his head, he stayed at the hotel
Ponce de Leon, and wrote to his brother William of his pleasure
in meeting his niece Mary, "very matured and very agreeable,"
and "highly susceptible, I think, of culture." They went sight-
seeing together to look at the little Spanish fort and the old
Spanish cathedral, "these poor little scraps of Florida's antiquity

so meagre and vague." But his true impression of Florida was conveyed to the matron in whom he was now confiding most, Mrs Cadwalader Jones: "Florida is a fearful fraud—a ton of dreary jungle and swamp and misery of flat forest monotony to an ounce or two of little coast perching-place—a few feet wide between the jungle and the sea. Nine-tenths of this meagre margin are the areas of the hotels—the remaining tenth is the beauties of nature and the little walk of the bamboozled tourist. It's really *mauvaise plaisanterie*."

Ten days sufficed for this one venture into the South. He turned North again, for word of his Philadelphia performance had got round, and lecture engagements were now giving sign that he could travel farther and more widely than he had thought, and pay his way with "The Lesson of Balzac." He was due in St Louis, Chicago, South Bend, Indianapolis, San Francisco. Other places beckoned. Indianapolis, thanks to Booth Tarkington, had arranged a double-audience of two cultural organizations with the result that he was offered $400 and could have had $500. With a grand gesture he accepted the lower sum, murmuring "bloated Indianapolis!" to Elizabeth Jordan, who was making his lecture arrangements. A lecture bureau tried to entice him into its "circuit." He wrote to Edmund Gosse: "If I could come back here to abide I think I should really be able to abide in (relative) affluence: one can, on the spot, make so much more money—or at least I might." He added: "But I would rather live a beggar at Lamb House—and it's to that I shall return. Let my biographer, however, recall the solid sacrifice I shall have made."

A WESTERN JOURNEY

HENRY JAMES, having chosen to lecture to his fellow-Americans on—of all subjects—"The Lesson of Balzac," was to talk to them intimately about his own craft, as if they were novelists like himself. He did them this honour, even though America was addicted then to "molasses fiction" as critics used to say. *The Golden Bowl* consorted in the book shops with the current bestsellers—*The Little Shepherd of Kingdom Come*, *Mrs Wiggs of the Cabbage Patch*, *Rebecca of Sunnybrook Farm*. James was not concerned with what the public might want. He had always argued (even in his theatre days) that the artist must try to lead—and go his own way. James chose to speak out of the full life of his art and its skills. He had no illusions as to why men and women—and especially women—came in such numbers to hear him. He was aware that they came to see the lecturer, rather than hear the lecture. He had been a name so long in America, and now they could look upon his face and form. Everywhere people still remembered "Daisy Miller." Her spirit went marching on even though a quarter of a century had elapsed since he had captured her stylish figure in the hotel corridors at Vevey. One waggish Chicago reporter, however, with more literary sense than most, wrote his account of the novelist's arrival as if James were Lambert Strether casting a weary eye on "the bleak parks, the jumbled gray masses of tenements and the engulfing avenues of warehouses and freight sheds." He imitated James's technique of putting the reader into the character's angle-of-vision:

Mr James gave himself up to the little dreary pictures of Chicago life, which framed themselves on either hand in the square of cab door glass. It came home to him in the orthodox Jamesian manner that all he had heard of Chicago was stockyards and boards of trade and dirt and coarse fearful exploits in the getting of money.

It was perhaps flattering to be reported in his own style. But James paid little heed to the chattering press. Most of the newspapers were not quite as caressing. They spoke of James as "a novelist of the aristocracy," a condescending expatriate who talked of "the advance of civilization" in America as if he were still in the world of Fenimore Cooper. Americans did not seem to want to be described as still advancing. An Indiana editor angrily rejoined that if there was an advance it surely could not have been stimulated by reading Mr James's "inane" fictions.

I

James left Boston on 4 March 1905 and travelled for forty hours across great tracts of snow to the banks of the Mississippi—to St Louis. "Oh the dreariness of getting here." He had covered a thousand miles—"a single boundless empty platitude." The middle west was friendly but "featureless," and "the ugliness, the absence of any charm, is like a permanent plague—chronic and miserable." St Louis was "a vast grey, smoky, extraordinary *bourgeois* place" and "as languid and dreamy as the possession of coal-smoke and skyscrapers will permit." A soft gentle rain fell most of the time he was there. He read "The Lesson of Balzac" for the first time in the middle west before the Contemporary Club of St Louis on 7 March. There was first a long stifling dinner; and before that he had stood in line shaking the anonymous hands of local celebrities. He felt depleted from the start. He did not like to meet people *en masse*. He had a feeling as he read his lecture that it was "too special, too literary, too critical." But the audience was enthusiastic; and he also experienced a sense of embarrassment when, *coram publico*, the chairman handed him the cheque of payment—almost before he had said the last word. Business was distinctly business in America. However, people smothered him with hospitality. He went to lunch at the "Noonday Club" and to a reception held in his honour at the University Club of St Louis. He mentioned that the reception was to be without his making any speeches, but he found himself seated at a large table with some forty club members around him, relaxed and eager for literary gossip. The occasion resulted in one of those rare documents in which we catch the aphoristic flavour of James's talk. It was a minute of the occasion, written afterwards by a lawyer, in question and answer form. Among the questions James handled, with great delicacy and tact, were some relating to the work of Mrs Humphry Ward and whether she could be compared with George Eliot. James carefully replied "George Eliot was a great woman. I have the profoundest respect for the cleverness of Mrs Humphry Ward." Someone asked what Matthew Arnold had thought of his niece Mrs Ward's work. James said that Arnold's reply to this question used to be that if any Arnold could have written a novel "I would have done it long ago." James was asked if he had ever met Ruskin. He said he had found him "unhappy" and also "despondent and sentimental." Ruskin had surrounded himself with beautiful things and to visit his home was an experience worth having. Asked who was the most agreeable Englishman he had ever known, James suggested Sir Leslie Stephen, "a purely literary man of the very best type, an ideal literary man; and no one could know him without feeling a warm affection for him." Gladstone, James said, "qualified too much" but his speeches "sounded grandly," his voice was delightful and his manner imposing. Oscar Wilde he called "one of those Irish adventurers who had something of the Roman character— able but false." He considered Whistler "a much more interesting man" and told some Whistler–Wilde stories. He said that Wilde had returned to "the abominable life he had been leading" as soon as he got out of prison and his death was "miserable."

One other matter was discussed, a novel close to the midwesterners. This was *Ben Hur* by Indiana's Lew Wallace. James said he could not account for its success "except that there are multitudes of people who have little taste; or upon the ground that religious sentiment is more prevalent here than elsewhere."

II

He was in Chicago. First he stayed with Higginson cousins at Winnetka, and later at the University Club. From here he swung over to Notre Dame where he spoke to two Catholic groups in a single day; then he returned to Chicago, and went to Indianapolis, where he spoke before a massing of culture-groups, assembled by Booth Tarkington. He was handsomely paid. At one of his Chicago lectures, the chairman insisted that Daisy Miller had been a Chicago girl (James had actually given her Schenectady origins) and that now she must be grown up and sitting in James's audience. "Perhaps every woman here is a Daisy Miller," the novelist rejoined. But then, professorially, he explained that Daisy had not been a portrait; she was a type. His old complaint that his craft confined him "uptown"—in the American woman's world—was still true. One newspaperman making a joke of it noted that his Chicago audiences were mostly women and that at the second Chicago appearance there were only two men—one of them asleep, and the other penned in by females and unable to escape.

We get a glimpse of James in Chicago one day when he returns from a luncheon engagement on the far south side by way of a suburban train, along the wintry shore of the Lake, accompanied by Robert Herrick, the Chicago novelist. They ride through "the smudged purlieus of the untidy city into the black gloom of the Loop." James sits huddled on the dingy bench of the suburban car, draped in the loose folds of his mackintosh, his hands clasped about his "baggy" umbrella, "his face haggard under the shuttling blows of the Chicago panorama." "What monstrous ugliness!" he murmurs in a tone of pure physical anguish. (Three years later, an English diarist would record that James, recalling this trip, spoke of "ugliness, ugliness"—"he repeated it in a kind of groan!" On the other hand he said it was interesting to meet men in America "who had never thought of themselves as belonging to any class—a thing impossible in feudal Europe.")

In Chicago he visited the studio of the sculptor Lorado Taft; and he was invited to dine at Hamlin Garland's studio. Garland, novelist of the "middle border" and friend of Howells, brought together some of the local literary and artistic folk. He went to the University Club to pick up James, and noted, when the novelist came down the elevator, how "worn and haggard" he looked. "His derby was too large for him, his vest being a little

K

awry and his collar was a trifle wilted, but his face was kindly and his greeting warm. He met the people at the studio with entire friendliness but with only an abstract interest so far as most of them were concerned." Among them was Henry Blake Fuller, the Chicago novelist, whom James was happy to meet. But one gets the impression from Garland's notations that James was vague and dissociated on this occasion. "He had forgotten many of his books and spoke of them rather vaguely as though they represented another phase on various planes of his life. He has lost his enthusiasm but still has his intellectual interests. He is going on now out of sheer momentum. Chicago people have seemed very remote to him and aside from his visit to Taft's studio he met only such people and their friends." Garland added: "He unbent with us, that is certain. We were to him a reminder of Paris—the Paris of his youth when painters and writers and sculptors met informally . . . without the influence of that life our studio supper would not have taken place." What these diary notes tell us is that James was exhausted—and bored.

III

"The Lesson of Balzac" was decidedly not the lecture of a man who had lost his enthusiasm; and apparently James's delivery of it was an admirable piece of conversational reading. Edna Kenton, a magazine writer who would spend a lifetime reading James, remembered him as massive and clear-eyed on the Chicago platform, reading with a total absence of oratorical effect, in a voice filled with subtle tones. Van Wyck Brooks, who heard James that spring at Harvard, recalled his voice rolling "like an organ through a hall that could scarcely contain the aura of his presence." Brooks added that James's years of distance from America had apparently lent enchantment. One listener who heard the novelist in Brooklyn wrote that if James's sentences were long they were perfectly passable and "the average high school boy of today would have been able to grasp all that he said." This listener found a dry shrewd humour in the lecture; James's speech was "that of a sincere man with something to say, and he says it delightfully." The listener found also "scarcely a trace of English accent despite the fact that he was born in New York and has lived twenty years or more in England."

James read his lecture before the assorted audiences quietly, usually—as in Philadelphia—keeping one hand in his pocket, and removing it only to turn the pages or to make an involuntary gesture. He was always deliberate; when his witticisms were appreciated and the audience laughed, he nodded and smiled. Otherwise he was solemn. The loose sheets of his manuscript were typed on thick paper. There was never an attempt at emphasis, never a lapse into insistence. Everything was low in key and "evenly modulated," although some listeners noted a falling inflection "so often heard in pulpit delivery." One critic spoke of "the pleasant even voice" uttering "strings of images" so that the audience seemed to say to him "O still delay, thou art so fair!" and (added the commentator) "Mr James delayed."

In the content of the lecture there was no compromise with popular standards. James was his Jamesian self. He spoke of Balzac as "the master of us all"—no novelist but had learned something from him. The opening sentences suggest his strategy of formal informality:

I have found it necessary, at the eleventh hour, to sacrifice to the terrible question of time a very beautiful and majestic approach that I had prepared to the subject on which I have the honour of addressing you. I recognize it as impossible to ask you to linger with me on that pillared portico—paved with marble, I beg you to believe, and overtwined with charming flowers. I must invite you to pass straight into the house and bear with me there as if I had already succeeded in beginning to interest you. Let us assume, therefore, that we have exchanged some ideas on the question of the beneficent play of criticism, and that I have even ingeniously struck it off that criticism is the only gate of appreciation, just as appreciation is, in regard to a work of art, the only gate of enjoyment.

No audience in America, we might speculate, had ever been so ingratiatingly approached; the tone was confidential; the suave assumption was that the listeners were the speaker's peers, and that they all had deep and intimate matters to deal with. James went on to deplore the absence of a genuine criticism. Readers needed help when literary production was "uncontrolled" and "untouched by criticism, unguided, unlighted, uninstructed."

He resorted to his favourite pastoral imagery. American readers were the biggest flock straying without shepherds and "without a sound of the sheepdog's bark." Worse still, "the shepherds have diminished as the flock has increased."

From this it was a direct step to Balzac as a novelist who offers example and invites criticism. There followed an amusing passage on Jane Austen, who left readers hardly more curious about her process, James said, "or of the experience in her that fed it, than the brown thrush who tells his story from the garden bough." He went on to deplore the Jane Austen cult, "the body of publishers, editors, illustrators, producers of the pleasant twaddle of magazines; who have found their 'dear,' our dear, everybody's dear, Jane so infinitely to their material purpose."

These preliminaries led James to say that "even in this age of superlative study of the cheap and easy" Balzac stood as an extemporizer whom closeness and weight had preserved. "I speak of him," said James, "and can only speak, as a man of his own craft, an emulous fellow-worker, who has learned from him more of the lessons of the engaging mystery of fiction than from any one else, who is conscious of so large a debt to repay that it has had positively to be discharged in instalments, as if one could never have at once all the required cash in hand."

The lecture repaid that debt. Balzac was all prose, "with huge feet fairly ploughing the sand of our desert" yet he was "the very type and model of the projector and creator." With many subtle strokes James sketched Balzac's qualities but with constant reference to novelists more familiar to his audiences. Perhaps the most beautiful passage in the lecture was the following:

Why is it that the life that overflows in Dickens seems to me always to go on in the morning, or in the very earliest hours of the afternoon at most, and in a vast apartment that appears to have windows, large, uncurtained, and rather unwashed windows, on all sides at once? Why is it that in George Eliot the sun sinks for ever to the west, and the shadows are long, and the afternoon wanes, and the trees vaguely rustle, and the colour of the day is much inclined to yellow? Why is it that in Charlotte Brontë we move through an endless autumn? Why is it that in Jane Austen we sit quite resigned in an arrested spring? Why does Hawthorne give us the afternoon hour later than any one else?—oh late, late, quite uncannily late, as if it were always winter outside?

Such passages provoked charmed murmurs from certain members of his audience and brief stirrings of applause. Balzac's plan, said James, was "to handle, primarily, not a world of ideas, animated by figures representing these ideas; but the packed and constituted, the palpable, proveable world before him, by the study of which ideas would inevitably find themselves thrown up." Taking a hint from Taine, he showed how Balzac loved his men and women even when they were horrible; how he identified himself with them, all the more to make us see them as they were. Balzac's handling of Valérie de Marneffe he contrasted with the way in which Thackeray sat in judgment on Becky Sharp. Valérie is given enough rope to act herself out. "Balzac loved his Valérie then as Thackeray did not love his Becky." A great part of the lecture was devoted to a close analysis of Balzac's way of painting the conditions and environment of his characters, his possession always of all the elements of his picture, his ability to "foreshorten" and in the midst of detail stay with his "principle of composition" and convey, as few novelists have done, the lapse and duration of time. "It is the art of the brush," said James, "as opposed to the art of the slate pencil." He interpolated a long passage in which he praised Zola, but showed exactly where that disciple of Balzac had lacked his master's art of "representation." Balzac, "with all his faults of pedantry, ponderosity, pretentiousness, bad taste and charmless form" still achieved his subject "the complicated human creature or human condition." Only at the end did James artfully take notice that he was speaking "as if we all, as if you all, without exception were novelists, haunting the back shop, the laboratory, or, more nobly expressed, the inner shrine of the temple." His lecture terminated with the language of primitive religion. Balzac was in the sacred grove, the idol, "gilded thick with so much gold—plated and burnished and bright, in the manner of towering idols." And his final sentence —"it is for the lighter and looser and poorer among us to be gilded thin!"

IV

With $1350 in his pocket and complaining of "the fatigue of the good kind but too boresome people," Henry James boarded a Pullman in Chicago for the west coast. He had made a side-trip to Milwaukee for a brief visit with the wife and children of his long-dead brother Garth Wilkinson. "I am just escaping with my life," he wrote to his sister-in-law in Cambridge. "The visual ugliness of it all . . . the place a desolation of dreariness." He went straight to Los Angeles: three days and three nights, "through unspeakable alkali deserts" across Kansas, Arizona, and New Mexico. He almost broke down, he said, from tension, sickness, and weariness; he did not find the clattering of the train and the chattering "Pullman civilization" helpful. He would never again, he said, attempt a journey "of that confined and cooped up continuity." The train arrived many hours late, and the old backache of his youth had threatened to return; but a night in bed restored him. Also the soft California light and the warmth.

"This country is too *huge* simply, for any human convenience," he wrote to Jocelyn Persse, "and so unutterably empty that I defy any civilization, any mere money-grabbing democracy, to make on it any impression worthy of the name." The great green Pacific, the golden orange groves, the huge flowers, and Southern California "manners and human forms" gave promise of interest. Nevertheless he was "well-nigh *rotten* with the languishment of homesickness."

He received promptly an invitation to lecture to a ladies' "culture club" in Los Angeles and decided to give himself a holiday in the interval. He moved into the Hotel del Coronado at Coronado beach near San Diego in a room hanging over the Pacific, to work at his American travel essays. The days were of "heavenly beauty." He was reminded of Italy. He enjoyed the flowers, oranges, olives, and he lay awake nights listening "to the languid lisp of the Pacific." A series of entries in his notebooks shows him organizing the materials published in "New England: An Autumn Impression." "Everything sinks in," he wrote, "nothing is lost; everything abides and fertilizes and renews its golden promise." After the strain and tension of the winter he felt his heart "uplifted;" and he dreamed of the time when in Lamb House he would plunge "my hand, my arm *in*, deep and far, and up to the shoulder—into the heavy bag of remembrance—of suggestion—of imagination—of art—and fish out every little figure and felicity, every little fact and fancy that can be to my purpose." Sitting by the "strange Pacific" he found himself thinking of what he would say about Cambridge in his American sketches, but soon his memory wandered to his youth in Boston—the time of his "obscure hurt" during the Civil War and he wrote a vivid passage on the "*initiation première* (the divine, the unique)" when in Ashburton Place in 1865 he had experienced his first adulthood and had begun his career as writer. These memories would only be hinted at in *The American Scene*, but he would return to them in his later autobiographies.

Some eight hundred ladies came to his Los Angeles lecture; one, aged ninety-five, spoke to him familiarly of his mother and father whom she had known in New York, and of her memories of Margaret Fuller. After this James spent a few days at Monterey and journeyed on to San Francisco. He wandered up and down its primitive hills (it was before the earthquake) but enjoyed being fêted by the Bohemian Club, where he talked with Charles Warren Stoddard, author of books and sketches about Hawaii and Tahiti, and met the tenor Enrico Caruso. He had more talk of Polynesia with his old friend, Mrs Robert Louis Stevenson, in her house in Hyde Street. He warned her not to prepare a repast; a plate of oranges would suffice. They had not seen each other since the day when she and Louis had sailed on their romantic journey, in the 1880's. Mrs Stevenson remembered James's enthusiasm for the flowery hill-slopes and the green canyons. "Poor lady, poor barbarous and merely instinctive lady," he would murmur later to a cultivated San Francisco bachelor, a man of artistic taste and wide culture named Bruce Porter, whom he met during this visit. James little dreamed—and would never know—that this man was destined to become the husband of his beloved niece, Peggy. Porter was one of San Francisco's most distinguished amateurs of the arts. He had a flair for architecture, landscape gardening, verse-making. He was a charming conversationalist and with Gellet Burgess he edited a little magazine of the time, *The Lark*—coyly named because it was a "lark" to do it. He would ultimately design the Stevenson memorial in Portsmouth Square in San Francisco. He was addicted to the theory of the Shakespearian ciphers, a matter in which he received no support from Henry James. They became, however, good friends at once and James would remember that he had been "adorably kind" during the three or four days in which they prowled together in the streets of the coast city. James was critical of San Francisco; he found in it "a poverty of aspect and quality" and he left it, he said, without a pang. Nevertheless he experienced a touch of western openness when the owner of St Dunstan's, the hotel where he stayed, refused to render him a bill —it had been a privilege to have so distinguished a guest. "Brave golden California, more brave and golden for *such* possibilities surely, than any other country under the sun!" James took a train for Seattle, passing through the beflowered valleys of Oregon and spending a night in Portland. In Seattle he visited his brother Robertson's eldest son, Edward Holton James. Ned James would be one of the most eccentric of the novelist's nephews and would later be cut out of his uncle's will because he espoused attacks against George V, who he alleged had made a morganatic marriage. But this occasion was genial, and we have Ned James's account written years later for his children. "When Uncle Henry came to see us, he found the west rather crude. I sat by the hour, with wide open mouth, drinking in his wonderful exotic conversation. He was bored by the west, by the 'slobber of noises,' which we call our language, by the stream of vacant stupid faces on the streets and everywhere the 'big ogre of business.'"

James stayed at a club where he was put up by a son of his old friend John La Farge; but he was in a hurry to return to the east. His nephew got him a comfortable Pullman bedroom and arranged for a break in the journey at St Paul. At Chicago his Higginson cousin guided him to the night train to New York. The next morning, when he reached Albany, scene of so much of his childhood, he had "the absurdest sense of meeting again a ripe old civilization and travelling through a country that showed the mark of established manners." He seemed now back in history. There was "thicker detail"; and then there was the familiar Hudson which the train followed into New York. The river's face was veiled by the mists of a premature spring. James gave himself up to romantic feelings, remembering old night journeys by boat from parental New York to grandmotherly Albany. Once again in Manhattan he relapsed into the safety and comfort of Minnie Jones's house in Eleventh street, and wrote of his bliss in "having (approximately) done with Barbarism." The "approximately" suggested he expected a few more encounters with it before setting sail for England.

THE TERRIBLE TOWN

HENRY JAMES had left to the last his exploration of New York, his home-city, and during May and June, when his stay in America was nearing its end, he inspected thoroughly what he called, half-lovingly, half-seriously, "the terrible town." He had had a panoramic vision of it one day, arriving from Washington where he had lectured. He was bound for Boston and he remained in his Pullman while his car was taken by barge around the tip of Manhattan, descending the western waters and remounting to Harlem. It was a vision "of the most extravagant of cities, rejoicing, as with the voice of morning, in its might, its fortune, its unsurpassable conditions." What he studied, once he had settled again into his first-floor back rooms in Eleventh Street, was its planning, its architecture, its institutions, its ethnic groups. He had looked, from his Pullman window, at New York's "pin-cushion profile," noted the cool assurance of the Bay, the impersonal harbour which had "no item of the romantic, or even of the picturesque," and pondered the "depressingly furnished and prosaically peopled" shore. New York had made no use of the natural beauty of its surroundings, the little islands, the farther shores. There was space and light and air at the open gates of the Hudson, but the city seemed somehow to defy these with vehemence. It was crowded: it was shrill. Everything "rushed and shrieked." He felt as if he were looking at "some colossal set of clockworks, some steel-souled machine-room of brandished arms and hammering fists and opening and closing jaws."

The tall buildings were "impudently new—and still more impudently novel." They had this in common "with so many other terrible things in America"—they were "triumphant payers of dividends." He had compared them to pins stuck irregularly into a pin-cushion; but now he saw the skyline as a jagged up-ended comb, a "loose nosegay of architectural flowers." The buildings were like "American beauty" roses that possessed an "interminable stem," and were grown to be picked in time with a shears; nipped short off, by waiting fate, as soon as American science, applied to gain, "has put upon the table, from far up its sleeve, some more winning card." James's prose, as he surveyed "the thousand glassy eyes" of the giants, was sufficiently blunt:

> Crowned not only with no history, but with no credible possibility of time for history, and consecrated by no uses save the commercial at any cost, they are simply the most piercing notes in that concert of the expensively provisional into which your supreme sense of New York resolves itself. They never begin to speak to you, in the manner of the builded majesties of the world as we have heretofore known such—towers or temples or fortresses or palaces—with the authority of things of permanence or even of things of long duration. One story is good only till another is told, and sky-scrapers are the last word of economic ingenuity only till another word be written.

This would be the theme of all his poetic pictures of Manhattan as he viewed the city during the spring of 1905—the new city spreading itself into the modernity of the new century. It was a city created on a foundation of impermanence. America seemed to build only to rebuild. Remembering the beauty of Giotto's tower in Florence, James shifted his attention to the beauty of Trinity Church in downtown New York, which he had known when its simplified Gothic towered over Wall Street. Now it was submerged, surrounded, smothered, caged, dishonoured. James wrote of it as if he were endowing it with a physical hurt his own body seemed to feel. Trinity Church seemed to say to him, "Yes, the wretched figure I am making is as little as you see my fault—it is the fault of the buildings whose very first care is to deprive churches of their visibility." And New Yorkers seemed to take this for granted "with remarkable stupidity or with remarkable cynicism." The skyscrapers towering over the spire created an effect of a mountain wall; one usually expected an avalanche to drop from such a wall on village and village spire at its foot.

He looked at Castle Garden, doomed to extinction; here he had heard Patti warble like a tiny thrush when she was a child. He had, for that matter, been scarcely older. He visited Ellis Island

and felt that the aliens, flooding into New York, were taking full possession of it. James, the old New Yorker, who had known the city when it seemed a village, felt dispossessed. Would the racial mix achieve a "whole national consciousness as that of the Switzer and the Scot?"

II

He went first in search of personal memories, in the lower Fifth Avenue neighbourhood. On East Eleventh Street or West Tenth Street he felt as if he were still keeping clear "of the awful hug of the serpent;" he studied an old house on Waverly Place that had survived and the "lamentable little Arch of Triumph" built into the Square since that time—suggesting in its truncated form so little the glories it was supposed to celebrate. The author of "The Birthplace" walked over to Washington Place, to that part of the street leading from the Square to Broadway, where his father's house had stood and where he had been born sixty-two years before. The house was gone. In its place had been built a high, square, impersonal structure, proclaiming its lack of interest in the past with a crudity all its own. James felt "amputated of half my history." There was no original wall left on which a tablet might commemorate the fact that Henry James, novelist of New York, had been born here on 15 April 1843.[1] Such tablets swarmed thickly in Europe. Henry James would find a solution to this neglect. He would bestow on the collective edition of his works the name of his birth-city. The sense of personal affront was perhaps not so powerful as the thought that the city lacked self-confidence; it didn't really believe in itself. Otherwise it would not tear itself down so often. Its mission seemed to be "to gild the temporary with its gold, as many inches thick as may be, and then, with a fresh shrug, a shrug of its splendid cynicism, give up its actual work, however exorbitant, as the merest of stop gaps." James walked through streets "to which the rich taste of history is forbidden." He mused that the few landmarks, like the City Hall, illustrated exactly his feelings that multiplied floors and

---

[1] In 1966 such a tablet was unveiled on the spot where the Brown Building of New York University now stands.

windows hardly represented "any grace of building." Only in the uptown reaches did he feel that some attempt was being made to inject a human note: to build certain homes with feeling for Style.

II

The record of Henry James's energetic exploration of Manhattan is to be found in three closely written and evocative chapters in *The American Scene*. "New York and the Hudson; A Spring Impression," "New York: Social Notes," and "The Bowery and Thereabouts." These pages, filled with nostalgia and shock, surprise and resignation, reflect both James's delight in the poetry of the urban and despair at the sordid works and self-doom of the city. New York had created not a social order but an extemporized utility-life that substituted the glamour of technology for the deep-rooted foundations of existence. He cared for "the terrible town," cared for it deeply, as one born in it; and it therefore hurt him all the more that man could create so blindly and so crudely the foundations of inevitable "blight." Long before the word gained currency in the language of urban decay, Henry James had used it as he wandered in the Italian and Jewish neighbourhoods. He was struck by the alienation of the Italian immigrants when compared with those he had known during his many trips to Italy. In Italy one could address them in a give-and-take of traveller and native; here they seemed to have suffered a sea-change; they seemed remote and melancholy. On the other hand he found the Jewish ghetto, on the lower east side, animated and bewildering. His view of the Jews in the mass had always been distant; he had repeated the clichés by which their national distinctness was marked in the English novel, very much as Dickens had depicted them in *Oliver Twist*. He saw them swarming over the fire-escapes attached to the tenements and wondered what would become of them in the New World. He went to a Jewish home, in a converted tenement, for dinner.[1] The windows looked on a teeming little square. He noted the overtowering school that dominated the ghetto, harbinger of its education. He

---

[1] James's correspondence does not disclose the names of his Jewish acquaintances except for the mention of Jacob Gordin, the Yiddish playwright.

listened to the babel of children in great numbers, and the old, with marked distinctive faces, occupying doorstep and pavement, kerbstone and gutter. The "individual Jew" was for James "more of a concentrated person, savingly possessed of everything that is in him, than any other human, noted at random." He commented on "the unsurpassed strength of the race"; it had withstood the forces of history that sought to chop it into "myriads of fine fragments." An array of Jews resembled in this "diffused intensity" a "long nocturnal street where every window in every house shows a maintained light." With their reverence for intellect, he would have toasted them as "an intellectual people," but America seemed to do its work and he saw the "hard glitter of Israel." Pondering the abundance of the ghetto shops, James wondered whether the United States wasn't inventing "a new style of poverty." To be sure, he had not had a chance to see all the elements of the sordid and squalid in New York; but he saw enough to feel that "there is such a thing, in the United States, as freedom to grow up to be blighted." And he reflected that this "may be the only freedom in store for the smaller fry of future generations."

Under the wing of his Jewish friends he was taken on a round of beer houses and cafés. At the Café Royal, on the lower East side, where Jewish literati and café-philosophers mingled, James listened to the accents of Europe as they fractured the English language. Language for the novelist was sacred, and in especial the language with which he worked. He had written an address to the graduating class of Bryn Mawr on the way the young played fast and loose with English. He would describe with much pain the language he heard in these cafés, invoking the torture room of the Tower of London (where he used on occasion to take tea with the curator, Angelina Milman). In these warm-lighted cafés he felt himself in "the torture rooms of the living idiom." What would this do in America to "the Accent of the Future?" It might become of course the most beautiful in the world, James mused, but "we shall not know it for English."

He inspected Riverside Drive, bemoaning the unimaginative name given to the avenue that provided such fine Hudson vistas;

he paused at Grant's tomb, liking its situation, and its direct democratic accessibility to spectators who didn't remove their hats in the shrine. He wandered in upper Fifth Avenue and looked at the palatial houses of the rich seeing them as a "record, in the last analysis of individual loneliness." They never became seats of family; they were as discontinuous as much else of American life, reduced to "the present, pure and simple." This present squared itself "between an absent future and an absent past." He wandered in Central Park and found it filled with "eruptive and agitated effect" and afraid "to be just vague and frank and quiet." He likened the park to an actress destitute of talent, ranging in the course of a given week from roles such as the tragedy queen to the singing chambermaid. The intention of beauty in the Park was too "insistent." In the Metropolitan Museum he winced "at the expense which, like so much of the expense of New York, doesn't educate . . . There was money in the air, ever so much money—that was, grossly expressed, the sense of the whole intimation. And the money was to be all for the most exquisite things—for *all* the most exquisite except creation, which was to be off the scene altogether; for art, selection, criticism, for knowledge, poetry, taste."

Seeking to recapture fragments of the past, he went to a Bowery theatre, with the cosmopolite name of Windsor; he remembered old Bowery evenings, "the big bare ranting stupid stage, the grey void smelling of dust and tobacco-juice." The new audience was filled with alien faces, Moldavian, Galician, Hebraic. It sat munching candy—the Cult of Candy he commented seemed prodigious in the United States. The play was a farce melodrama. There was a wonderful folding bed on the stage. The villain of the piece pursued the virtuous heroine round and round the room trying to leap over the bed; and the heroine closed the bed so that the villain was engulfed in it "as in the jaws of a crocodile." After a while James left "perhaps from an excess of suspense." It all seemed to him "a queer, clumsy, wasteful social chemistry." He visited also the Yiddish theatre, guided by the reigning Jewish dramatist, Jacob Gordin. The place was convivial; the ventilation left much to be desired, and after looking at some broad passage of a Yiddish comedy of manners he walked out—"it was a scent, literally, not further to be followed." He was happier in an upper east side bowling alley and billiard room, a German beer-hall which however served no beer, but where in the shadows he remembered the faint click of the moved domino, and the quiet honest men, playing silently. This little temple of relaxation seemed a triumph amid all the "surrounding triumphs." James was relieved that the host had omitted learning "the current American." He did not fracture the English. He spoke but a dozen words—and since he talked little, James felt the stillness to be friendly. In this dingy place James found a conception "of decency and dignity." There was a real barrier against vulgarity in "a few tables and chairs, a few coffee cups and boxes of dominoes." And James concluded: "Money in quantities enough can always create tone, but it had been created here by mere unbuyable instinct. The charm of the place in short was that its note of the exclusive had been arrived at with such a beautifully fine economy."

THE BROTHERS

HENRY JAMES's incursion into the orbit of his elder
brother, after a three-decade absence, revived the long-
buried struggle for power that had existed between the two—
ever since their nursery days in Washington Square. The infant
Henry had made his original incursion by the very act of birth and
caused William to flee instinctively from the threat to his
dominion. William had been the only son of his young parents
for more than a year; and suddenly this uniqueness had ended.
The rivalry, in its childish essence, may seem altogether too
remote and too simple; but in the development of two geniuses,
malaise and avoidance, reinforced over the years, had become a
prevailing mode of existence. In their youth they had been like
Jacob and Esau. In the language of that myth Henry James now
spoke of his return as "taking up again my birthright." Mutual
guilt had made them feel as if each were encroaching upon the
other's birthright. Henry had felt most free in his young days
when William was away. William had felt free only when he
could escape—to Brazil, to Germany. Both relapsed into petty
illnesses when they had to be together for too long a time. But
between 1875 and 1905 each had carved out his own empire.
Henry James had made himself the culture bearer of America in
Europe. William had made himself the hero of American pragmatism in the world. George Santayana would see them in still
another light, as classic and romantic. Henry, as the analyst of
American manners, overcame the genteel tradition—"in the
classic way, by understanding it." William, whose student
Santayana had been, overcame it "in the romantic way, by continuing it into its opposite" by his prophetic sympathy "with the
dawning sentiments of the age, with the moods of the dumb
majority." Both brothers with their early exposure to Europe
and their father's mixture of mystical feeling and hard-headed

realism, were grandchildren of the romantic movement. Henry, however, had become a formalist in art. Composition alone was "positive beauty" he would say, and art preserved life. William, as Santayana saw, had a spontaneity and vitality which made him scatter words that "caught fire in many parts of the world." What Santayana could not foresee was that Henry's large glimpse of the American myth would capture a still later imagination in the West. The differences between the brothers was never more marked than in 1904-5 when Henry, all power and drive, came as a "restless analyst" to study William's America, and suddenly caught the public eye in a country where the philosopher's public image was large. The two brothers had renewed their ties in the autumn of 1904 in Chocorua and for a brief period there were walks and talks and the old communion of their youth. "It is a pleasure to be with anyone who takes in things through the eyes," said William. On his side Henry wrote "whenever one is with William one receives such an immense accession of suggestion and impression."

Henry did not spend much time with his brother. He was in New York; he was in Lenox; he went south; and then that spring when he arrived in the middle west and the press began to pay increasing attention to him, William quite suddenly set sail for the isles of Greece. He went on an impulse. He had never been in Athens or for that matter southern Italy. His reason for departure at this moment seems curiously flimsy: he wanted to escape the "influenza season" in Cambridge, although other such seasons had come and gone without his seeking flight. He was apparently escaping something else, and perhaps in part, his brother. Henry applauded his desire for travel; Mrs William was relieved to have him escape from some of his academic burdens. The departure of the elder brother, during the time of Henry's presence in the country was, on the surface, understandable enough. Each had his own destiny to fulfil; and then they often grated on one another. "He and I are so utterly different in all our observances and springs of action, that we can't rightly judge each other," William had written a couple of years earlier. Henry would write that autumn to William, in response to William's criticism of *The Golden Bowl*, "how far apart and to what different ends we have had to work out, (very naturally and properly!) our respective intellectual lives."

Although William always attacked Europe and pleaded with Henry to "drop your English ideas and take America and Americans as they take themselves," he was, during his trip to Greece, in a somewhat different mood. The end of middle age, his heart attacks, his years of work, seemed to make him conscious of missed opportunities; and his letters to his wife during his journey had in them strains of his brother Henry's early romantic discoveries of Italy. "I have come here too late in life," he wrote, "when the picturesque has lost its serious reality. Time was when hunger for it haunted me like a passion." Was it the sense of "too late?"—the theme his brother had written into *The Ambassadors* and "The Beast in the Jungle" that made William—in defiance of his heart condition—journey through rugged Greece and stand before the Parthenon, as so many romantics had done before, with tears in his eyes? *J'ai vu la beauté parfaite*, he wrote lapsing into the language he criticized his brother for using so often. Turning to Rome, he attended a philosophical congress, and with great spontaneity read a paper in French on "consciousness." He rejoiced to find that his ideas had sparked a whole group of European pragmatists. He was quite the hero of the meeting. And then he went on a long motor drive with his former student Bernard Berenson, and an Austrian Princess— Pisa, Genoa, Cannes. He returned in May to Cambridge, strengthened, refreshed, to find his brother Henry in Irving Street full of impressions of old New York. They saw each other briefly. Henry went off to stay with Mrs Wharton at Lenox just before sailing. William left for Chicago to deliver a series of lectures. Irving Street seemed like a railroad station with all the comings and goings. The brothers did not meet again during Henry's American trip. William sent Henry a cheerful letter of good-bye. Henry waved back one of his regular epistolary flourishes.

II

What Henry did not know—and would never know—was that William had just accomplished one of the most unusual epistolary flourishes of his life—with Henry as object if not subject. The brothers were both members of the National Institute of Arts and Letters, having been elected in 1898 when the Institute was founded. During 1905 the Institute began procedures for establishing an Academy of Arts and Letters of limited membership, like the French Academy, its members to be chosen from the ranks of the Institute. In effect the Institute became the parent body of the otherwise autonomous Academy. A group of seven academicians was elected—among them Mark Twain—and these members in turn proceeded to the election of the full complement, ultimately limited to fifty. Henry James was among those elected during the second ballot in February 1905; William was elected during the fourth ballot in May and found the notification of election awaiting him on his return that month. He seems to have brooded over the matter for a month and then, in a letter dated 17 June 1905 informed the Academy secretary, Robert Underwood Johnson, that he could not accept the honour. He began by giving as reason that he never accepted honours in academic bodies which did not have some work cut out for them, and this Academy seemed to him purely honorific. His second reason was that it would be contrary to his preachings of a lifetime "against the world and its vanities." His third reason was that with his brother also a member, the James influence in the Academy might be held excessive. He phrased this part of his letter as follows:

I am the more encouraged to this course by the fact that my younger and shallower and vainer brother is already in the Academy and that if I were there too, the other families represented might think the James influence too rank and strong.

The gesture was private, and Johnson wrote, years later in his memoirs: "I have always regretted that I did not go to Cambridge to explain to Professor James more fully the character and purpose

of the new organization to which he would have been a distinguished and appropriate addition. I mention his selection lest it
should be thought that a man of such admirable scholarship and
style had been neglected."

There were two matters in which William was not being consistent or truthful—with himself—in writing this letter. The
first was that he had not considered there was a redundancy of
Jameses when he and Henry had been elected to the Institute in
1898. He was having this afterthought only now, when Henry
was elected ahead of him to the new body. His letter rectified this
inconsistency by adding, "I think I ought to resign from the Institute (in which I have played so inactive a part) which act I here
also perform." And then he quietly overlooked the fact that he
had accepted a number of honours in spite of his claim that for "a
philosopher with my pretensions to austerity and righteousness"
the only "consistent course is to give up this particular vanity and
treat myself as unworthy of the honour, which I assuredly am."
He had not taken such a position in accepting honorary membership in the Institut de France in 1898; and he had accepted a
number of honorary degrees—from Padua, Princeton, Edinburgh, and his own Harvard before he wrote this letter, from
Durham and Oxford three years later, and Geneva as late as
1909.

A deeper and more palpable reason existed than those he gave
for his refusal to accept election to the Academy chair. He had in
effect articulated it by his characterization of his "younger
brother." The Academy had elected Henry James—"younger,
shallower, vainer"—ahead of the older brother, who considered
himself wiser, more serious-minded, and without vanity. The
letter seemed to imply once again that it was impossible for Jacob
and Esau to live under the same roof, to be in the same room—
or Academy—and occupy seats side by side. The adult William
admitted in his letter that his act was "sour" and "ungenial." In
fact he added a sentence "if you knew how greatly against the
grain these duty-inspired lines are written, you would not deem
me unfriendly or ungenial, but only a little cracked." The philosopher of pragmatism sensed he was committing—under some

strange impulse—an irrational and inconsistent act. Still, under the guise of modesty and consistency, he bowed himself out of the American Academy of Arts and Letters and its parent, the Institute.

III

In the ensuing months William James would express this hidden animus in the most consistent barrage he had ever laid down against his brother's work. He launched a measured attack on *The Golden Bowl* which he had not read earlier and when, in 1907, *The American Scene* was published he displayed his own great virtuosity by writing his sharpest words against his brother's "later manner."

Reading *The Golden Bowl* had put him "as most of your recenter long stories have put me, in a very puzzled state of mind." The method of elaboration went "agin the grain of all my own impulses in writing, and yet in spite of all," he acknowledged, "there is a brilliancy and cleanness of effect, and in this book especially a high-toned social atmosphere that are unique and extraordinary." Such stricture and praise were not new; William had done this many years before when Henry was having his first successes. The philosopher now added:

Why don't you, just to please Brother, sit down and write a new book, with no twilight or mustiness in the plot, with great vigour and decisiveness in the action, no fencing in the dialogue, or psychological commentaries, and absolute straightness in style. Publish it in my name, I will acknowledge it, and give you half the proceeds. Seriously, I wish you *would*, for you *can*; and I should think it would tempt you, to embark on a "fourth manner."

Henry James's answer was sufficiently direct, and he fell in with William's barbed aggression. He would write "some uncanny form of thing, in fiction, that will gratify you, as Brother—but let me say, dear William, that I shall greatly be humiliated if you *do* like it, and thereby lump it in your affection with things of the current age, that I have heard you express admiration for and that I would sooner descend to a dishonoured grave than have written." William wanted him, he suggested, quoting from his lecture on Balzac, to take up the art of the slate pencil instead of the art of the brush.

I'm always sorry when I hear of your reading anything of mine, and always hope you won't—you seem to me so constitutionally unable to "enjoy" it ... I see nowhere about me done or dreamed of the things that alone for me constitute the *interest* of the doing of the novel—and yet it is in a sacrifice of them on their very own ground that the thing you suggest to me evidently consists.

Always the younger brother, Henry softened his firm response by assuring William he was reading him "with rapture."

William returned to the charge in 1907. *The American Scene* seemed "supremely great." He went on to remind Henry, how opposed "your whole 'third manner' of execution is to the literary ideals which animate my crude and Orson-like breast." His were "to say a thing in one sentence as straight and explicit as it can be made, and then drop it forever; yours being to avoid naming it straight, but by dint of breathing and sighing all round and round it, to arouse in the reader who may have had a similar perception already (Heaven help him if he hasn't!) the illusion of a solid object, made (like the 'ghost' at the Polytechnic) wholly out of impalpable materials, air and the prismatic interferences of light, ingeniously focused by mirrors upon empty space. But you *do* it, that's the queerness!"

William the scientist, added: "Say it *out*, for God's sake, and have done with it." He accused Henry of having become a "curiosity of literature." "For gleams and innuendos and felicitous verbal insinuations you are unapproachable, but the *core* of literature is solid. Give it to us *once* again! The bare perfume of things will not support existence, and the effect of solidity you reach is but perfume and simulacrum." He enjoined Henry not to answer "these absurd remarks." Henry obliged. He went his own way as he had always done.

By now Henry James had outlived the hurts he used to experience at such attacks. His rejoinder to William was simply that he found the critical letter "rich and luminous." He promised he would have "a reply almost as interesting as, and far more annihilating than, your letter itself." He then said that perhaps

William needed to read the book in handsomer print than the American edition and promised to send him the English edition. The younger brother let it go at that. In the intervening weeks William had a change of heart toward the book. He read the chapter on Florida and was delighted with it. Henry's ultimate rejoinder took the form simply of an inscription in the English edition: "To William James, his incoherent, admiring, affectionate Brother, Henry James, Lamb House, August 21st 1907."

IV

In attacking his brother's style William James was adding a private fraternal voice to hostile voices raised in the press throughout Henry James's visit to the United States. Not a Sunday passed without a letter to the New York *Times* about the form or moral content of Henry's books. Jokes went into circulation in cultured circles—the lady who knew "several languages—French, New Thought, and Henry James," or the lady who boasted she could read Henry James "in the original." When James delivered "The Question of Our Speech" at the Bryn Mawr Commencement in the Spring of 1905 the press paid scant attention to the fact that James's remarks were addressed to the slipshod ways in which American girls spoke. It assumed James was attacking the American language itself, and Dr Woodrow Wilson, the president of Princeton, defended newspaper English against the "laborious" style of the novelist. One letter-writer to the *Times* said James's style would "drive a grammarian mad." Another "wished he would not put the tail of his sentences where the head belongs and the head where the body should be or the body where one naturally expects to see the tail."

James had his defenders. His "morality" seems to have offended even more than his style. *The Ambassadors* was described by one correspondent as a "notably warped situation." Did not Lambert Strether advise the nice clean American youth to cleave unto the questionable married woman in Paris? and to harden his heart to the tender claims of his mother and sister in far, humdrum, inartistic Massachusetts? "Which Henry James ending do you like best?" queried the lady who wrote this letter, "the one which turns to the left and says nothing—or the one which turns to the right and says 'So there we are.'" Obviously the woman had read much of James; she reminded him that in *Transatlantic Sketches* he had disapproved of the liaison between Rousseau and Madame de Warens; and yet in *The Ambassadors* he had written "in these places such things were."

One reader was unhappy that in *The Golden Bowl* he had allowed Charlotte to be "dragged over to exile in dreadful California." The "dreadful" proved ironic, however, for the writer added "if only Mr Henry James would migrate with Adam Verver to California and there make us one of his old-time magic books under clean blue American skies." The writer of this letter spoke of James's "politely vicious literary behaviour." There was no doubt that James was a man of genius, she said, who "sees far into hearts and minds of men and women" but the substance of his books was "like a beautiful and radiant soul" in a "deformed body." A letter-writer signing "Optimist" asked "is not the world worse for the decadence shown on the pages of Henry James?" A Brooklyn correspondent reported that in a reading club of one thousand only three out of every hundred read Henry James. The popular novelist Alice Duer Miller, who was reaching a large audience, said that James, within *The Golden Bowl*, indulged in "a situation only scandalmongers are supposed to discuss." On the other hand Claude Bragdon defended James's extended metaphors and the way in which "intellectuality overpowers the sensuous." Others found the novelist "detached," "cold," "cruel." One correspondent linked James and Edith Wharton. "Is a delicate dissector like Edith Wharton, writing *The Sanctuary*, to spoil us? Is Henry James writing about that loveliest of all women Milly Theale in order to pollute us young Americans? . . . if James, Wharton and their disciples be decadents, then may I join the choir invisible that sings where they will sing in what's beyond."

V

Things moved at an accelerated pace as the day of James's departure approached. He had never been a public figure on this scale. There were more caricatures and editorials in the press; he was recognized in the street and in the shops. One observer, Robert Cortes Holliday, then a book salesman in Scribner's, recorded later a meeting at the foot of the elevator of W. C. Brownell, Scribner's senior editor, Henry James, and Mrs Wharton. Teddy Wharton sat in the bookshop waiting and smoking a cigar. Holliday remembered James stepping out of the store, "overhauled by Mrs Wharton under full sail" and then the three moving down the avenue, James on one arm, Teddy on the other, and "in this formation, sticks flashing, skirt whipping, with a somewhat spirited mien, the august spectacle receded." Holliday watched James browse in the bookshop. "He ran his nose over the tables, and inch by inch along the walls, stood on tiptoe and pulled down volumes from high places, rummaged in dark corners." Not knowing he was recognized he explained, "I live in England myself and am curious to know this," and he asked what percentage of the novels on the fiction table was the product of English writers. He barely glanced at a high pile of *Golden Bowl*s.

Le Roy Phillips, a cousin of James's friend Morton Fullerton, wrote to inform the novelist he was compiling a bibliography of his writings. He asked for help to identify certain anonymous pieces. James's reply was Olympian. He wondered "why and how any such wretched little question can matter, at this hour, to any human being endowed with the responsibility of intelligence." But he added kindly that "your great good-will in the matter almost brings to my eyes tears of compassionate remonstrance for misapplied effort." James said he would rather with his own hand heap mountains of earth on his old writings and so bury them deeper, "beyond any sympathetic finding-out." Phillips was not discouraged; by looking up old account books he unearthed a large body of James's unsigned early writings.

At the very end James found himself involved in a series of visits. Hendrik Andersen turned up in Boston and the two went briefly to Newport. He journeyed to Kittery Point in Maine to say farewell to Howells and also saw Miss Jewett. Mrs Wharton beckoned emphatically from Lenox. James, remembering her knowledge of German, replied, "*Ich kann nicht anders*. Be indulgent and don't shoot. I am doing my best." He managed to squeeze in a few days with her. Teddy was in Canada fishing. She had a "big, commodious new motor" and they swept through the countryside. It was a fine way to rope in "a huge netful of impressions at once." They made in particular a trip to Ashfield to see their old friend Charles Eliot Norton, covering eighty miles between lunch and dinner. During the last days Pinker arrived from London and in a series of conferences with Scribner's worked out the initial plans for a "definitive edition" of James's novels and tales. Things were sociable to the last. Walter Berry, Europe-bound, booked a cabin on James's ship, the *Ivernia*; so did Elizabeth Robins, the actress, who had been revisiting her homeland. On 5 July James bade farewell to America. He had spent ten busy months. His journey had been a minor triumph. He had renewed contact with his kin-folk and he had crossed a continent. Tired, stimulated, his expenses fully covered by his lectures, he would now try to sort out his impressions. The voyage was lively. James sat on deck revising *Roderick Hudson* for the collected edition. Berry and Miss Robins played a game called "hunt the adjective"—they tried to see how many adjectives could be eradicated from whatever they were reading. James hunted superfluous commas in his own past writings. Miss Robins remembered James "sending that melancholy look of his out over the Atlantic waste" and protesting against light-minded flittering of Americans back and forth across the sea. James was eloquent on the segregation of the sexes in the United States "beyond anything existing out of the Orient"—the men always in their offices, the women "uptown" or at Newport. He had long ago described this in his tales. The *Ivernia* docked at Liverpool after a nine-day voyage. Restored to his London club, James briefly saw Jocelyn Persse. Then he was in Lamb House facing a vast accumulation of books, papers, magazines, letters—and a staff in revolt. The servants had not been happy with the tenants. His housekeeper threatened to leave. Mrs Paddington was comforted by an increase in wages and the prompt discharge of two super-fluous maids. Young Burgess was promoted from house-boy to valet, "a very improved little auxiliary." "The situation is clear-ing—Rye and my four-square little garden better and sweeter than they ever were," James reported to Mrs William in far-away Cambridge. The Master was home again.

Book Five

An Elaborate Edifice
1906–1910

★

THE SUPREME RELATION

THE BETTER CHANCE

THE HOUSE OF MIRTH

THE VELVET GLOVE

MISS BOSANQUET

THEATRICALS: SECOND SERIES

THE TONE OF TIME

THE YOUNGER GENERATION

HUGH

A PASSION ON OLYMPUS

WOMAN-ABOUT-TOWN

THE SUPREME RELATION

IN his earlier years Henry James had longed for Europe when in America, but in Europe had felt himself a claimant to kingdoms not his. In Quincy Street he had been always a second son, except when William was away; in Bolton Street he was for a long time an "observant stranger." Now, in the fullness of time, he had reclaimed his birthright. He had re-annexed lost provinces of his life. He could claim America as his own. It was "cruelly charmless" to be sure. The wreckers had destroyed the physical landscapes of his youth. Everything seemed to proceed "by cataclysms and violence and enormity—leaps and bounds from one kind of excess to another kind." James ached with this vision; he winced, he said, with the very noise of it. He wanted to crouch for ever in Lamb House. He "couldn't do it all *again* and survive." He winced; he ached; he crouched; and yet "my ten months among you renewed my curiosities and sympathies and possible understandings." In some way his visit had answered an old riddle, resolved a double-exile. He had thought of America as having rejected him: now he found that when it laughed at him it loved him. He recognized, as he said in his book of impressions, that "one's supreme relation, as one had always put it, was one's relation to one's country."

I

He talked of that "supreme relation" one evening in June 1906 with Hamlin Garland, the son of the "middle border" who had entertained him in Chicago, and who came to Rye to spend a night. James found Howells's friend simple, provincial, dull. He spoke to Garland of his being both American and cosmopolitan. He had long ago suggested that this was a highly civilized state, even if the ideal were to be a "concentrated patriot." Garland quoted James years later as saying, "The mixture of Europe and

319

America which you see in me has proved disastrous. It has made of me a man who is neither American nor European. I have lost touch with my own people and I live here alone." This has been read by many as Henry James's acknowledgment that his expatriation was a large mistake. Garland's notebook of the time shows, however, that James did not speak as positively. It has him saying "if I were to live my life again I would be American — steep myself in it — know no other." He then added that the "mixture of Europe and America is disastrous" — so Garland originally noted — but he did not use the words "which you see in me." These were inserted by Garland. James always felt that he was a consistent cosmopolitan. In a letter some years later he made this point to Edith Wharton, telling her she lacked "the homeliness and inevitability and the happy limitation and the affluent poverty of a Country of your Own." To which he added *"comme moi, par exemple."*

Two months after Garland's visit, during the night of 3–4 August 1906, Henry James found himself kept awake by an idea for a story — a story about a repatriated American who goes in search of himself in a house in New York — himself *as he might have been* had he stayed at home. He wrote the next morning to his agent, "I have an excellent little idea through not having slept a wink last night *all* for thinking of it, and must therefore at least get the advantage of striking while the iron is hot." He called the story at first "The Second House;" presently it was renamed "The Jolly Corner" and James seems to have written it during the next few days. He had a feeling that he was discounting his unfinished novel *The Sense of the Past* of half a dozen years before. The work dealt with an American who inherits a house in London, and finds himself, on entering it, within the past of his English ancestors. The reverse of this idea was the tale of Spencer Brydon, who has lived abroad for thirty years. He returns to rebuild a Manhattan house for rental purposes; but also finds himself wandering in his own private past, in his other house on a corner in lower Fifth avenue, the house of his birth and childhood — the house of Family. Brydon wanders through the rooms night after

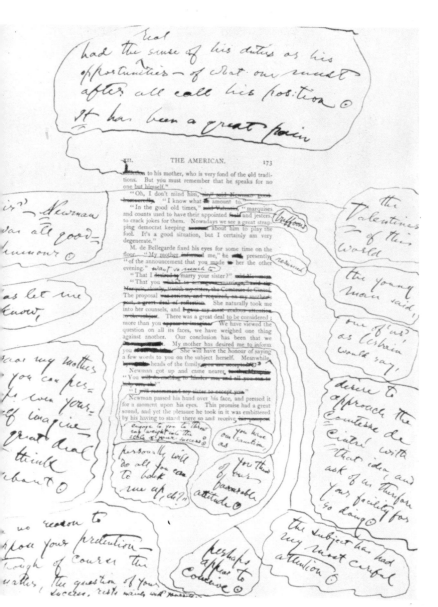

THE REVISED "AMERICAN"
A page of the 1883 version revised for the New York edition of 1906

THE MASTER 1905
Alvin Langdon Coburn's photograph, the frontispiece to the New
York Edition

night, restlessly, hauntedly, carrying a sputtering candle. He is haunted by the thought of what he might have been had he not gone to live in Europe. He has discussed this with his friend Alice Staverton, who had liked him long ago and had remained a spinster in her old house in Irving Place. It becomes an obsession with him—"how he might have led his life, and 'turned out,' if he had not so, at the outset, given it up." To Miss Staverton he says: "What would it have made of me, what would it have made of me? I keep for ever wondering, all idiotically, as if I could possibly know! I see what it has made of dozens of others, those I meet, and it positively aches within me, to the point of exasperation, that it would have made something of me as well."

This "rage of curiosity never to be satisfied" is expressed by Brydon as he looks through his monocle at Alice Staverton and drinks his tea by her fireside. He had been, at twenty-three, he ruefully says, too young to judge what kind of American life was possible to him. He doesn't admire those who had remained so much; he isn't sure what charm the country has exerted on them "beyond that of the rank money-passion;" yet he feels he had, in his early American years "some strange *alter ego* deep down somewhere within me." He had transferred this other self to a strange climate in which it didn't have a chance to grow. Alice Staverton says she feels that if Brydon had remained in America he would have had "power."

"You'd have liked me that way?" he asked.

She barely hung fire. "How should I not have liked you?"

"I see. You'd have liked me, have preferred me, a billionaire!"

"How should I not have liked you?" she simply again asked.

His nights of curiosity and meditation in "the jolly corner" become a quest, or hunt, for the *alter ego*—the self that might have been. The tale is a kind of active "Beast in the Jungle;" Brydon unlike John Marcher goes in pursuit of the "beast" instead of waiting for it to spring. The story is more than a revisiting of a personal past; it becomes a journey into the self, almost as if the house on "the jolly corner" were a mind, a brain, and Spencer Brydon were walking through its passages finding certain doors of resistance closed to truths hidden from himself. On one

L

occasion he notices with a *frisson* that a door hitherto closed is open; someone must have opened it. Descending the staircase to the vestibule he sees dark shadows taking material form. A figure rises before him rigid, conscious, spectral, yet human—a man of his own substance and stature awaits him. Brydon sees

... his planted stillness, his vivid truth, his grizzled bent head and white masking hands, his quiet actuality of evening dress, of dangling double eye-glass, of gleaming silk lappet and white linen, of pearl button and gold watch-guard and polished shoe. No portrait by a great modern master could have presented him with more intensity, thrust him out of his frame with more art.

The apparition stands there with its hands over its face, "splendid covering hands, strong and completely spread!" But two fingers are missing from the right hand, as if they had been "accidentally shot away." Then the hands move; the answer Brydon has sought is revealed to him. What he sees is a face of horror.

Then harder pressed still, sick with the force of his shock, and falling back as under the hot breath and the roused passion of a life larger than his own, a rage of personality before his own collapsed, he felt the whole vision turn to darkness and his very feet give way.

Alice Staverton arrives to rescue him from his fainting spell. She has seen the same figure in a dream; she confirms her occult experience by her knowledge of the two missing fingers. But she doesn't agree with Brydon that the figure is a "horror." "I had accepted him," she says.

It is a profoundly autobiographical tale. In it James's imagination has completed full circle from 1871, when he wrote "The Passionate Pilgrim" about an American claimant in Europe, through *The Sense of the Past* about an American heir in Europe. Like Peer Gynt, the hero has returned to his own land after endless wandering to find his Solveig has waited for him, was always there, the accepting mother in the accepting motherland. Great personal myths seem bound together in this strange tale of the occult by which James announced to himself that had he stayed at home the hand that held the pen might have been crippled, but that he might also have been a titan of finance, a remodeller of old houses, a builder of skyscrapers—even as this enterprising side of himself was about to remodel his writings in the New York Edition. Beyond Henry James's incorporation in this mythic tale of the memory of his father's amputation, associated with the New York of his childhood, we can read in "The Jolly Corner" the recognition of his own ambivalence about his Americano-European legend. He sees at last his own dual nature—the "me" and the "not-me" the self of intellect and power and the self of imagination and art; the self that for so long had tried to live in his brother's skin, but could now shed it, and the self that reflected his creativity. Spencer Brydon and Alice Staverton—James had given her his sister's and his sister-in-law's name—agree that if Brydon had remained at home he would by now be a millionaire. "The Jolly Corner" embodied James's recurrent dream of pursuing a ghost or other self—a haunting creature—and defying and conquering it. He was always more powerful in his night-dreams than in his waking thoughts. He would tell Lady Ottoline Morrell one such dream, a version of his dream of the Louvre which he also had during these late years. He walks into a house filled with antiques, cabinets, tables, chairs, a veritable *spoils of Poynton* house. He feels vaguely there is a strange presence in one of the rooms. Upstairs he finds an old man sitting in a chair and he calls out to him "you're afraid of me, you coward." The man denies this. James contradicts him. "You are, I know it. I see the sweat on your brow." Always his dreams begin with a sense of foreboding and terror; an anxiety that seeks relief. Threatened, he then turns the tables; it is *he* who suddenly frightens the *alter ego*. James would never forget this—the idea that a haunted person's fright can also frighten others. This was what he tried to put into *The Sense of the Past*. In "The Jolly Corner" Spencer Brydon is frightened by his own creation—the Self he has materialized, the thought of what his life might have been. The resolution of the story is that he had had to fulfil his destiny; that he must accept himself even as America accepted him. By the same process he was laying the ghost of his old rivalry with William. He did not have to be William; he could be himself. The myth of Past and Present, of the conquest of brothers and mythical worlds—worlds of enterprise and art—

and of "the supreme relation"—are embodied in this low-keyed tense little tale. Its elements seemed to compose themselves in some magical way out of unconscious depths where they had lain hidden for years. Small wonder it kept him awake. James called it "a miraculous masterpiece" in writing to his agent. It was a story he said of "the supernatural-thrilling." The thrill for him was that it settled the whole question of his American journey. He had always banished his own ghosts by writing about them. The next four years would be years of great fertility in spite of his advancing years; and they would be Henry James's "American years," more American even than the years of his lost youth. The decade that remained to the Master would assert his recaptured self. Out of them would emerge the edition of his novels and tales—his personal monument—designed as the "New York Edition." His late tales would be set in New York; his last unfinished novel would be on an American subject and would open in Newport. His memoirs would dwell on his New York childhood, on Newport and Boston. He was ready to complete *The American Scene*; to write papers about American manners. All that he did from now on was intimately related to his American past. And he would return once again to his homeland—for a last look, for last visits, for a final embrace.

II

The American Scene, published in 1907, was written with all the passion of a patriot and all the critical zeal of an intellectual who could not countenance national complacency and indifference. George Santayana would understand this when he defined James's stance as "classical." Civilization meant order, composition, restraint, moderation, beauty, duration. It meant creation of a way of life that ministered to man's finest qualities and potential. Using this standard of measurement, James found America terribly wanting. It was founded on violence, plunder, loot, commerce; its monuments were built neither for beauty nor for glory, but for obsolescence. It was science and technology in the service of the profit motive; and in this there resided an inherent decay of human forms and human values. Older nations had known how to rise above shopkeeping; they had not made a cult of "business" and of "success." And then James hated the continental "bigness" of America. Homogeneity, rootedness, manners —modes of life—these were his materials and everywhere James looked he found there had been an erosion of the standards and forms necessary to a novelist, necessary also to civilization. The self-indulgence and advertisement of the plunderers was carried over to the indulging of their young. Americans had interpreted freedom as a licence to plunder. This was the burden of the impressions James set down, in the days when they were still vivid, and in the light of his native, his early emotion. He wrote in a vein of poetry: buildings address him; monuments meditate; he offers us a continual monologue sometimes rhapsodic often reportorial. He looks everywhere with scrupulous attention—and with passion. He touches the America of his own past with great personal tenderness and melancholy. The book is both elegy and oration. The stages of his journey are told as they might have been painted by an impressionist painter; but the accompanying script might have been written by a documentary poet, like Zola. The book ends with a peroration on the rape of the land that makes him a prophet of the pollutions of the future. He put his words into the mouth of an Indian, looking at what the white man has done. "Beauty and charm would be for me in the solitude you have ravaged, and I should owe you my grudge for every disfigurement and every violence, for every wound with which you have caused the face of the land to bleed" in the name of "your pretended message of civilization." He made him say also "you touch the great lonely land—as one feels it still to be—only to plant upon it some ugliness about which, never dreaming of the grace of apology or contrition, you then proceed to brag with a cynicism all your own." Perhaps feeling that the passage might be jarring to American self-assurance Harpers simply left it out. It is to be found in the English edition. James apparently did not read the American proofs.

"I would take my stand," wrote James, "on my gathered impressions." Then, perhaps remembering how he had been pilloried in America for his little study of Hawthorne a quarter of a century before, he added he was prepared to "go to the stake" for what he had written. The American critics had no violent reaction; they were rather tepid. They spoke of James's "antipathy" and they complained about his style. At the same time the usual compliments were paid to his "fastidiously probing mind." H. G. Wells, who had written a book on *The Future in America* published almost at the same time wrote James—"you take the whole thing as an ineffectual civilization and judge it with so temperate and informed a decisiveness." He added, "I wish there was a Public worthy of you—and me . . . How much will they get out of what you have got in?"

III

He could not resist an opportunity offered him shortly after his book was done to amplify on the ways in which American women sacrificed the tone and the form of their inherited speech. Asked by Elizabeth Jordan to write three articles for *Harper's Bazar* he ended by doing eight, four on American speech and four on American manners. These he did not try to publish in England. They were intended for Americans; they contained intimate incidents from his American travels used to demonstrate what he felt was a collapse into "barbarism" of human forms of address and communication. Bad speech bred bad manners. He blamed American men for cultivating and fostering a state of "queenship" in the women; and he blamed the women for their failure to meet the responsibilities of sustaining and moulding the young. The essays were written in haste and with great looseness. James had spent his best efforts on *The American Scene*. These chips from the workshop are fragmentary and prolix; yet they reflect the same critical spirit, the same indignation, and possess the same energy. What James deplored was the "universal non-existence of any criticism." This led to "the unlighted chaos of our manners." The American language was undermined by "the unequalled potency of advertisement." He remembered the older time when speech in New England had been "an interesting, a really tonic form of English utterance"—touched always "with a certain Puritan rusticity, as by the echo of the ox-team driven, before the plough, over stony soil, and of the small and circumspect town-meeting." It had its "coherence, its congruity, its dignity." It offered an excellent basis for individual intelligence and virtue," the expressional effect of the few "capable of taking themselves, and of keeping themselves in hand—capable even of taking and of keeping their wives, their daughters, their sisters." What hurt James in a country with so large a heritage was "the apparently bland acceptance of the rising tide of barbarism by those who had so many reasons to 'know,' and who would have had so many rights to protest."

His papers on manners were of a piece with those on speech. He amusingly characterized the strange feminine diets "slobbering up a dab of hot and a dab of cold, a dab of sweet and a dab of sour, of mixing salads with ices, fish with flesh, hot cakes with mutton chops, pickles with pastry and maple syrup with everything" and all the while reading newspapers—"the vast open mouth, adjusted as to the chatter of Bedlam."

"We have, as a people, no sense of manners at all," said James and by manners he meant the totality of the forms of human relations. This reflected "an absence of discipline." His conclusion was that manners were above all "an economy; the sacrifice of them has always in the long run to be made up, just as the breakages and dilapidations have to be paid for at the end of the tenancy of a house carelessly occupied . . . By an excess of misuse moreover a house is fatally disfigured."

He had planned a second volume of American impressions. He wanted to write a paper on the middle west; another on "California and the Pacific Coast;" there would be one on the universities and the colleges, for he had lectured at almost a dozen from Bryn Mawr to Harvard, from Notre Dame to Berkeley, and had even visited an eccentric "School of Antiquity" of theosophical orientation at Point Loma, California. By the time he had completed *The American Scene* and the articles on speech and manners he found his impressions fading; he felt also he had sufficiently exploited his trip. Other and more important work needed to be done. The western journey was never written.

THE BETTER CHANCE

THE next four years were spent by Henry James preparing the collective edition of his novels and tales. "I should particularly like to call it the New York Edition if that may pass for a general title of sufficient dignity and distinctness," he wrote to Scribner's, adding that it "refers the whole enterprise explicitly to my native city—to which I have had no great opportunity of rendering that sort of homage." The months of unrelieved toil James expended in the preparation of the Edition (its full title was *The Novels and Tales of Henry James*, New York Edition) shows beyond question that he regarded this as his literary monument. He had written to Paul Bourget, who had collected his own works into a finely printed series some years earlier, "*heureux homme* to be building and gilding, carving and colouring, yourself, already, your marble, your mosaic sarcophagus." His Edition, however, was no sarcophagus; it became a living organism possessing an identity all its own. With a courage and zeal few writers had shown, he rewrote his early works to bring them up to the level of his maturity. He did not adhere to the chronological order of his works, but grouped them according to themes and subjects; he wrote an extraordinary series of prefaces, discussing publicly for the first time in his life the history and theory of his work, the "poetics" of his fiction. And he embarked with youthful enthusiasm on a quest to discover the right symbolic scenes to serve as frontispieces. He was ruthless in his omissions. He left out any work that did not seem to meet certain standards of perfection. As his publisher announced in a carefully worded prospectus, the New York Edition contained "all of the author's fiction that he desires perpetuated."

I

From the very beginning James had decided the set should consist of twenty-three volumes. "I quite adhere," he wrote to Scribner's, "to my original idea as to the total number of volumes and as to the number of those for my shorter productions. I regard 23 volumes as sufficient for the series and have no wish to transcend it. I shall make what I wish to 'preserve' fit into the number and only desire to sift and re-sift, in selection—so as to leave nothing but fine gold!" Although later, in a letter to Howells, James would shift ground and say the number of volumes was imposed by his publisher, the preliminary correspondence indicates that Scribner was ready to print all of James's "collected" fiction. The "complete" novels and tales would have totalled thirty-five volumes. The idea of making the edition *selective* was entirely James's, and was emphasized by him in a long memorandum to his publisher. There was a kind of Procrustean process involved; but then James was accustomed to shaping and fitting his work into magazine instalments, and while he had a tendency to overflow, he had demonstrated recently how he could fit *The Ambassadors* into twelve instalments—a year's serialization. The choice of twenty-three was thus not arbitrary. There seems to have been a special reason for it. The figure seems indeed to have had a certain magical quality for James; when he needs a date, a youthful age, a general number, he often fixes on twenty-three. One recalls in particular a scene in *The Awkward Age* when Vanderbank explores Nanda's library: "I see you go in for sets—and, my dear child, upon my word, I see *big* sets. What's this—'Vol. 23: The British Poets.' Vol. 23 is delightful—do tell me about Vol. 23." We might speculate about the significance of the combination of 2 and 3—and we might recognize that James had always been the "third person" in his relations with his mother and his brother; and then his Aunt Kate was the third person in a combination with his parents. Triangular relations are at the heart of his novels. But we need not go afield in seeking an answer to the odd number. James's first essay on Balzac in 1875 was inspired by the issue of the collected edition of that novelist and in it we find him saying "Balzac's complete works occupy 23 huge octavo volumes, in the stately but inconvenient *édition définitive* lately published." The Master, who had lectured to his countrymen on Balzac, who had written several major essays on the French novelist, who regarded Balzac as "the father of us all," paid homage not only to New York in his Edition. He bowed respectfully to—and imitated—the *Comédie Humaine*. His edition would be, in effect, the "*comédie humaine*" of Henry James.

II

James's idea of confining his Edition to twenty-three volumes offers us a key to its organization. As Balzac had grouped his scenes of provincial life, Parisian life, political and private life, we can discern that James planned the New York Edition as a series of "scenes of the international life," to which he added a group of "scenes of English life." In his correspondence with Scribner's he fell also into Balzacian designations, referring to his "stories of the literary life" and his "tales of the quasi-supernatural and 'gruesome'" each grouped in separate volumes. The effect of this limitation was that the novelist did not give himself room to turn around. Six of his novels were of such length that they required two volumes. With the addition of three single-volumed novels, he used up fifteen of his twenty-three volumes at the very start. He had then to fit his shorter novels, and a selection of his tales, into the remaining eight volumes. Thus of the one hundred and eight short stories he had written up to this time, only sixty-six found their way into the definitive edition.

This kind of selection and arrangement meant that James had to juggle with stories according to their length as well as their classification by subject or theme. Chronology, however, he had to admit was "absolutely defeated" not only by thematic arrangement but by still other "adjustments" such as making sure the title stories matched the frontispieces. In the Scribner archive are preserved loose sheets on which James listed the contents of his volumes of tales. The tales were considerably shuffled. In the end part of his scheme collapsed. He had not counted his wordage carefully: his volumes of tales proved too long. They spilled over into a twenty-fourth volume. James did not reply to Scribner for a week. Then he wrote a long letter in which we can read his deep irritation and disappointment. The magic plan was broken. "My groupings had been, of course, affinities much observed, so that each volume should offer, as to content, a certain harmonious physiognomy; and now that felicity is perforce—I abundantly recognize—disturbed." If this was true of two or three of the volumes containing tales, it nevertheless did not affect the fundamental structure of the edifice. The architectural form of the monument was preserved; it constitutes, in the totality of Henry James's work, a work of art in itself.

III

In preparing the New York Edition James seems to have had an image of himself as the "American Balzac." The language of the prospectus accords him this kind of position. "He is *par excellence* the American novelist. In the words of no other writer have American types of character and ideas appeared in such high relief and been characterized with such definite reference to *nationality*. He is the representative cosmopolitan novelist, also. And it is because of the frequent foreignness of his scene, which serves as a background, and of the society that peoples it, which affords a contrast, that his American characters and American point of view are set off with such marked effect."

The prospectus went on to say in similar Jamesian sentences that in this notable aspect James was the true successor to Fenimore Cooper and shared "with the greatest of our earlier novelists the distinction of performing a patriotic service in the world's field of letters. But for his novels America would figure far less importantly in this domain than it does. And but for his exquisite literary art, developed in a degree hardly conceived of a generation ago, America would stand far lower in the cosmopolitan scale of artistic literary production. As a matter of fact, owing to Mr James, America holds the world's primacy in fiction." The New York Edition was designed "to give Mr James's work the material form and presentment proportionate to his literary fame."

Balzac had "read the universe, as hard and as loud as he could, *into* the France of his time." Henry James set himself a comparable task—he read America and Americans into the world—the European world—read them back into the civilization from which they had seceded. His choice of his tales and their arrangement by category with the insistence on a definitive number of volumes, suggest the conscious design. The first three novels deal with three pilgrims abroad—Roderick Hudson, the artist, Christopher Newman, the man of business, Isabel Archer, the archetypal American woman. The next volumes contain James's "English novels." There follow the short novels and the long tales which are arranged thematically: and then the volumes of short stories, those of the artist life, the ghost stories, and the international scene. What James left out is abundantly clear. He omitted his "Scenes of American Life"—*The Bostonians, Washington Square, The Europeans*, and nearly all of his American short stories. They would have required too much revision; and so he seems to have set them aside to be a later extension of the original edifice, in the way that Balzac's twenty-three volumes were augmented so that the set of Balzac on the Master's shelves consisted finally of fifty-two volumes. "I treat certain portions of my work as unhappy accidents (many portions of many—of all men's works are)" he explained to one inquirer. He had tried to reread *Washington Square* but couldn't "and I fear it must go." Also set aside was the early pot-boiler *Confidence.*

Of the Edition's size James said to Howells, "Twenty-three do seem a fairly blatant array—and yet I rather surmise that there may have to be a couple of supplementary volumes for certain too marked omissions . . . I have even a dim vague view of reintroducing with a good deal of titivation and cancellation the too-diffuse but, I somehow feel, tolerably full and good *Bostonians* of nearly a quarter of a century ago; that production never having, even to my much-disciplined patience, received any sort of justice. But it will take, doubtless, a great deal of artful redoing, —and I haven't now had the courage or time for anything so formidable as touching and retouching it."

IV

In his tale "The Middle Years" Henry James described an elderly writer who dreams of a "second existence" and "a better chance" in which to do the supreme writing of his life. He is "a passionate corrector, a fingerer of style." He is, in a word, Henry James, who in creating the New York Edition got his better chance. Not only could he correct his old texts, but he could apply the varnish of his late style. James used the imagery of picture-restoration in describing his process of revision. He found "a strange charm" in going over old work. It affirmed a "creative intimacy;" moreover, "critical apprehension" became active again. James "nowhere scrupled to rewrite a sentence or a passage on judging it susceptible of a better turn." Later he would borrow an image from Alphonse Daudet: he had once heard him speak of Turgenev's luck in having a field of white snow in which to cultivate his style. Russian literature was new and fresh, whereas in France, Daudet felt, the snow had become a trampled slosh. James described his early work as "a shining expanse of snow spread over a plain" on which his exploring tread had "quite unlearned the old pace and found itself naturally falling into another." Sometimes his tracks followed old footprints; often the surface was broken in new places.

Revision for James was not a matter of choice but of "immediate and perfect necessity." Even much-revised older work found itself revised again. His first successful novel, which constituted the first volume of the Edition, *Roderick Hudson*, had been retouched in its progress from magazine to book in 1875. Preparing the English edition four years later James added a note saying the book had received "a large number of verbal alterations." Several passages had been rewritten. Now in 1905 he was rewriting portions of it again. From *Roderick* he went to *The Portrait of a Lady*, the novel which received the most detailed renovation since it occupies so large a place in his canon. His revisions strengthen his characters and eliminate ambiguities in his earlier text. The later Isabel Archer is so altered as to be almost a new personage. In this "fingering" of his text, James did not alter the substance of his story; he introduced no new scenes or new incidents. The essential structure remained. His skill in emendation consisted in the use of reinforcing imagery to overcome earlier failures in explicitness. If erotic feeling was absent in the earlier work, the Master now made amends. The best-known example is that of Caspar Goodwood's kiss in the closing paragraphs of *The Portrait of a Lady*. In the first edition James described the kiss in a single sentence. "His kiss was like a flash of lightning; when it was dark again she was free." In the New York Edition this becomes a paragraph:

His kiss was like white lightning, a flash that spread, and spread again, and stayed; and it was extraordinarily as if, while she took it, she felt each thing in his hard manhood that had least pleased her, each aggressive fact of his face, his figure, his presence, justified of its intense identity and made one with this act of possession. So had she heard of those wrecked and under water following a train of images before they sink. But when darkness returned she was free.

The earlier Isabel was incapable of this kind of feeling. Her fear of passion had been suggested; here it is made explicit—and in the language of Eros.

The American which James revised after the *Portrait* is the most rewritten of all the novels. It had originally been written in a great hurry to support the novelist during his first winter's residence in Paris; re-reading it now, twenty-eight years later, James said he was "stupefied" by his failure to create an atmosphere of feeling between his American hero and the French noblewoman, Madame de Cintré. Newman's relation to Madame de Cintré at a given moment in the story takes a great stride "but the author appears to view that but as a signal for letting it severely alone." In the first edition of 1877 Newman says to Madame de Cintré, "Your only reason is that you love me!" and James makes him murmur this "with an eloquent gesture, and for want of a better reason Madame de Cintré reconciled herself to this one." James now altered this:

"Your only reason is that you love me!" he almost groaned for deep insistence; and he laid his two hands on her with a persuasion that she rose to meet. He let her feel as he drew her close, bending his face to her, the fullest force of his imposition; and she took it from him with a silent, fragrant, flexible surrender which—since she seemed to keep back nothing—affected him as sufficiently prolonged to pledge her to everything.

In revising *The American* James made a certain number of significant substantive changes. He added five years to Christopher Newman's age—made him forty rather than thirty-five. By this stroke he altered the time-scheme of the entire novel. He wanted a more mature Newman. There probably were other reasons for this change which necessitated James's altering many of his allusions to Newman's past. He had originally given Newman too little time in which to make his fortune between the end of the Civil War and his going to Paris. The general effect of most of the revisions in the New York Edition is in the direction of verbal precision, clarification of motive and a strengthening of the fibre of the work. James took care of certain overworked words like "picturesque" and "romantic." He seems to have been less inclined to drop his much-used "dusky." In all his revisions James simplified conversation, substituted more direct language for certain pompous words and introduced much fresh colloquial utterance. Some of his revisions went in the opposite direction; new pomposities and verbal eccentricities were set down. The classical example is a change made by James which substitutes the verbal baroque for direct statement. In the first edition James described Newman—"his eye was of a clear, cold grey, and save for a rather abundant moustache, he was clean shaved." In the New York Edition this became: "His eye was of a clear cold grey, and save for the abundant droop of his moustache he spoke, as to cheek and chin, of the joy of the matutinal steel." James had been experiencing this joy ever since he had shaved off his beard. Its inclusion here, in this form, however, added a note of comedy perhaps not intended by the author.

It is possible to see at Harvard the paste-up and revisions of *The Portrait of a Lady* and from these it can be noted that James freely mixed editions. He pasted up on a larger sheet leaves from both the Boston edition of 1882 and the one-volume London edition of the same year. Sometimes even his trained eye had missed errors which were carried through most of the earlier editions to be

corrected now in the New York Edition. Thus Palazzo Roccanera is called *Piazza* Roccanera in all but the first serial version,
the London 1883 edition and the New York Edition. In six other
printings the error is uncorrected. Such technical matters aside,
the net effect of James's revisions, and particularly in the *Portrait*,
is to enhance the text and in this instance, the rewriting has been
so subtle and skilful, as to create a new novel. A striking altera-
tion was James's omission of two pages in the twenty-ninth
chapter devoted to the nature of Osmond and the egotism of
bachelorhood. Perhaps his own years as a bachelor and his concern with egotism made him feel that his reflections on this subject
at thirty-eight were superficial. At any rate, for some ninety-four
lines of early analysis of his character James substituted ten lines
in which he simply tells the reader that Isabel has discerned
Osmond's "style" and that this has a certain uniqueness. As
James elsewhere put it, Osmond suggests "the elegant complicated medal struck off for a special occasion."

James's revisions—of the *Portrait* in particular—have posed a
complicated problem for textual editors. The editions cannot be
harmonized into a single text; to do so would be to create still
another version of the novel. James created a situation in which
the early text must be regarded as having its own validity quite
distinct from that of the later text. The New York Edition becomes a separate and unique entity.

"How sickly I used to write!" James exclaimed to Brander
Matthews who wanted to reprint an old James essay in an
anthology. Max Beerbohm must have heard of this, for he one
day drew on the flyleaf of a volume containing another revised
Jamesian essay, a caricature of the obese Master, clean-shaven,
facing the slimmer bearded James of the middle years. The
cartoon could have figured in Max's famous series of "the old and
the young self." In a balloon over the heads of early and late
Henry James, Max wrote the words "How badly you——" the
Old James ending the sentence with "wrote" and the young James
with "write." Beside James's footnote, saying the essay had been
published originally in 1887, Beerbohm scribbled "and was very

obviously—or rather, deviously, and circuitously—revised in the great dark fulness of time, for republication in 1915."

V

The prefaces—eighteen in number—which Henry James wrote for the Edition enabled him to say what he had hoped all his life the critics would say for him. He defined his exploration of the novel form, discussed his belief that the novelist must create an organic whole, and explained technical innovations, particularly his addiction to "point of view." The novel in English had long been taken for granted as simple story-telling. James, arriving on the English scene late in the century, had taken the novel-machine apart in a very American way, given it a technology it had not possessed, and like the Americans of the future, had practised his craft strenuously and professionally, whereas most of his English confrères practised it in a relaxed and spontaneous way—as something designed to add to the joy of life. James's joy lay in the skill he deployed, in the pride of his inventiveness. He valued craft even beyond *gloire*. In his prefaces, to list but a few of the subjects, James discussed the extent to which the sense of place has to be created; the way in which a novelist must make his reader feel the passage of time; the need, as he felt it, for placing the novel's vision in a "central ingelligence," so that the world is seen through a Hamlet or a Lear and not through some "headlong fool" who can only see so much less of it. He discussed the use of first person narration, and the fluidity of self-revelation resulting from this kind of story-telling. He himself was willing to use the first person only in shorter tales; not one of his long novels is told by a character involved in the action. In perhaps the finest of the prefaces, affixed to *The Portrait of a Lady*, James discussed the way in which a novel must be considered an "organic" structure —quite like the human body—in which everything is related to everything else. He discussed also the secrets of the imagination, the "deep well of unconscious cerebration," recognizing like Coleridge—and Freud—that within the unconscious the deepest and richest part of man's art invisibly grows and finds its shape. He talked of form, and the way in which it is substance; he described how some of his characters began as *ficelles*, that is as puppets drawn by a string, placed as "the reader's friend" in stories from which the omniscient author withdraws and lets the narrative unwind by itself; and how a *ficelle* can take on flesh, cease to be a puppet, become a part of the action. He talked of indirection in story-telling, and how to arouse terror in the reader by artful ambiguity; he had clearly analysed, long before modern psychology, the ways in which a novelist involves his reader in the story and plays on the reader's feelings. He dealt with the plasticity of the novelist's medium and the use in alternation of "picture" and "scene;" he described his way of turning narrative into drama—and how he used to say to himself "dramatize! dramatize!" These were but a few of the subjects he dealt with on the level of craft, using vigorous imagery and highly condensed verbal statement. And then there were definitions and "terms"— a whole terminology of fiction which critics have since borrowed and made universal. To say this is not to describe the complexity of the prefaces; for woven into them was also a consideration of his own essential themes—the "Americano-European legend" he had created, the variant situations of the myth he had explored. Playing through the prefaces is the human light by which James worked—the situations he chose to develop and explore. Thus in his preface to "The Aspern Papers" there is an eloquent excursion on the uses of the past, the "visitable" past, in which the artist can still recover the human fact and the human dilemma, instead of the broken artefacts of the early centuries, whose creators are out of reach of the modern mind. A great sense of poetry is infused into these prefaces; and then they are touched by a gentle mood of reminiscence. James begins by recalling the occasion on which the first idea came to him; a dinner-table conversation, a sudden flash of inspiration while riding in a horse-car in Boston, an anecdote told by a lady in Rome (of a young girl from America whose brashness shocked the Roman "set"), or how Turgenev, talking to him long ago in Paris, made him feel that plot isn't important—that what counts is the novelist's seeing his character. Then the character itself possesses and provides its "story." In the prefaces, James recalled the places in which his stories had been written, how the chattering water-side life had floated in through his hotel window in Venice as he composed certain pages of *The Portrait of a Lady*; or how he had written parts of *The American* in elaborate rooms in Paris with medallions on the walls; or how one day on a pottering train in Italy, in the hot summer, he whiled away the time listening to an American doctor speak of his practice, and got the theme for "The Pupil." He spoke of the fog-filtered Kensington mornings, when he had worked in De Vere Gardens in that comfortable bourgeois flat with its sky windows; or his hotel bedroom during the centenary exhibition in Paris in 1889. Into this mixture of memory and theory he dropped the names of the novelists and poets who had meant most to him—and to the art of fiction— the lessons learned not only from Balzac but from Browning, Cervantes and Coleridge, Dickens, Turgenev, and George Eliot —she who had written of the "frail vessels," the young women who also became James's subject—and Flaubert and Ibsen, Maupassant and Meredith, Shakespeare and Stendhal, Stevenson and Thackeray, Trollope and Tolstoy—the Russians whose works he called "large loose baggy monsters" because they did not shape their materials, but gave the readers great chunks of life "with their queer elements of the accidental and the arbitrary." James would always argue that Tolstoy's greatness lay not in his art but in his vision of life—and that no one could learn anything about novel-writing from him.

In these crowded pages Percy Lubbock quarried the essence of his book *The Craft of Fiction*; and in studying the prefaces Richard Blackmur developed his recondite critical style. James's famous declaration to Howells that his prefaces were "in general, a sort of plea for Criticism, for Discrimination, for Appreciation on other than infantile lines—as against the so almost universal Anglo-Saxon absence of these things" has been proved true. Less than a treatise, these prefaces, in their colloquial ease, and flow, dictated at intervals between 1906 and 1908, show the embodied truths of the art of fiction as James had practised it and the distillation of a lifetime of close reading of major and minor novelists of the West. In the end there is a noble peroration which sums up

James's belief in the "religion of doing," that is the life of action in art—by which he meant "the imagination in action." The prefaces were James's supreme gift to criticism: and at the same time they elucidated what criticism in its chronic blindness had failed to perceive in his work. It took fifty years of hindsight for criticism to catch up with the lesson of Henry James.

VI

From the first, Henry James had taken it for granted that each volume of his definitive edition would have a frontispiece. The tradition was well-established. A long line of illustrators, not least Cruikshank, had added pictures to prose fiction. James himself had been illustrated by Du Maurier as early as *Washington Square*. In his tale of "The Real Thing" the narrator is an illustrator preparing a series of drawings for a "definitive edition" designed to be "the tribute of English art" to a representative of letters. James in reality wanted to be spared such a tribute. He had always resented illustration. For one thing, it delayed publication; his prose had to lie about in the magazines waiting for the illustrator to get his drawings done. On more important ground, he felt that pictures—much as he loved them—when combined with text, were an affront to the written word. The English language did not need visual aids. James was "jealous" of illustration. He looked askance at any effort "to graft or 'grow' at whatever point, a picture by another hand on my own picture." He accordingly took the precaution of telling Scribner that he would appreciate "a single good plate, in each volume." To make certain there would be no mistake about it he added "only one, but of thoroughly fine quality."

Scribner left the decision to James. The name of a well-known artist and illustrator was suggested, and James replied, "I like Albert Sterner; but are twenty Albert Sterners desirable or even thinkable ——???" Twenty or more frontispieces were needed— "some scene, object or locality, and associated with some one or other of the tales in the volume, both consummately photographed and consummately reproduced." To obtain this would be costly. Scribner underwrote the cost.

In the United States early in 1905 Henry James had been approached by a young photographer named Alvin Langdon Coburn, an artistic young man of twenty-three who photographed him for a New York magazine. Talking with Coburn, finding him sympathetic, James had the idea of trying him out on some of the scenes needed for the edition. Coburn was at this time, in spite of his youth, already considered a pioneering figure in the new art of the camera. At his one-man show in London he had been praised by an ardent amateur photographer, George Bernard Shaw, as "one of the most accomplished and sensitive artist-photographers now living." Henry James had seen his work; not only his portraits but his pictures of London, his landscapes, photographs of docks at Liverpool and arches in Rome, all attempting, in the fashion of the time, to give a painter-like texture to photographic surface. During Coburn's visit in 1906 to Rye, James gave Coburn his preliminary instructions. One of his first tasks was to obtain a suitable picture for *The American* which James had begun to revise. Out of Coburn's photographs evolved the principle that satisfied James completely. His illustrations would be "optical" symbols. They would be photographs of general scenes, material objects. They would enhance, but in no way intrude irrelevant images upon, his own literary images. Photographs could have a total "objectivity," an impersonal quality necessary for illustrating the edition. It was clear to James that Coburn would do full justice to the undertaking.

James entered into it with a zest the photographer would always remember. He dispatched Coburn to the Continent, to the cities of his fiction, and promised that he would himself guide him in London. In a series of letters he gave Coburn specific instructions—as if he were an envoy on a delicate mission. These missives add a specificity to the pictures perhaps not intended by James; they become one more autobiographical and historical note in the "story of the story." In the French capital, Coburn carried with him an envelope on which James had written "Memoranda for Paris from Henry James. For the Paris Subjects." First James wanted a portal of an aristocratic hotel in the Faubourg St Germain—a *porte-cochère* "a grand specimen of the

type." "Tell a cabman that you want to drive through every
street [in the Faubourg St Germain] not but that there are there
plenty of featureless houses too." After the drive James urged
Coburn to "go back and walk and stare at your ease." The streets
he suggested were the rue de l'Université, the rue de Lille, the rue
Bellechasse, where James had often gone to the Daudet home, and
the short rue Monsieur and possibly rue Madame. To this he
added the rue St Dominique and the rue de Varenne, where
presently Edith Wharton would live.

He asked Coburn to look out in the Place de la Concorde "for
some combination of objects that won't be hackneyed and
commonplace and panoramic; some fountain or statue or balus-
trade or vista or suggestion (of some damnable sort or other) that
will serve in connection with *The Ambassadors* perhaps. James
wanted a photograph of the Théâtre Français; also "go into the
sad Luxembourg Gardens, and, straight across from the arcade of
the Odéon, to look for my right garden-statue (composing with
other interesting objects)—against which my chair was tilted
back. Do bring me something right, in short, from the Luxembourg. These are the principal things I think of." He would
welcome one or two "big generalizing glimpses or fragments
(even of the Arc de Triomphe)." He concluded with "my blessing on your inspiration and your weather." Coburn carried out
the Parisian instructions to the letter and the Parisian scenes served
James not only for *The American* and *The Ambassadors* but for
one volume of *The Princess Casamassima*.

Early in December 1906 Coburn proceeded to Venice. For
guidance James sent the photographer to his old friend Constance
Fletcher, the American writer who, under the name of George
Fleming, had written *Kismet* and other successes. Miss Fletcher
lived with her infirm old mother and her mother's second hus-
band, Eugene Benson, a painter James had known long ago in
Rome in the *Roderick Hudson* time. They lived in the Palazzo
Capello on the Rio Marin, diagonally opposite the railway station;
it had that rare thing in Venice, a garden. This was the Palazzino
Henry James had had in mind in 1887 for "The Aspern Papers."
James began by advising Coburn to walk and "obtain guidance,

for a few coppers, from some alert Venetian street-boy (or of course you can go, romantically, in a gondola.") Reflecting on the extremely tortuous and complicated walk from the Piazza San Marco, he changed his mind and advised a *vaporetto*. Then he fell into the language of the story itself, that passage which long after would be used by T. S. Eliot in the epigraph to "Burbank with a Baedeker." "It is the old faded pink-faced battered-looking and quite homely and plain (as things go in Venice) old Palazzino on the right side of the small Canal, a little way along, as you enter it by the end of the Canal towards the Station. It has a garden behind it, and I think, though I am not sure, some bit of a garden-wall beside it; it doesn't moreover bathe its steps, if I remember right, directly in the Canal, but has a small paved Riva or footway in front of it, and *then* water-steps down from this little quay. As to that, however, the time since I have seen it may muddle me; but I am almost sure. . . . You must judge for yourself, face to face with the object, how much, on the spot, it seems to lend itself to a picture." James particularly wanted Coburn to get the "big old Sala, the large central hall of the principal floor of the house" but in the end he accepted the atmospheric courtyard that figures as "Juliana's Court." The other Venetian picture was a photograph of the Palazzo Barbaro, scene of so many of James's visits to Venice in his later years. James referred to "the beautiful range of old *upper* Gothic windows" and it was these Coburn photographed. "And do any other odd and interesting bit you can, that may serve for a sort of symbolized and generalized Venice in case everything else fails; preferring the noble and fine aspect, however, to the merely shabby and familiar . . . yet especially *not* choosing the pompous and obvious things that one everywhere sees photos of."

In London the Master was a strenuous guide. "Henry James knew his London as few men have known it, in all its quaintness, its mystery, and its charm," Coburn recalled. He had already taken a picture of the Dome of St Paul's, which James wanted for the first volume of *The Princess Casamassima*. Other London subjects were searched out together—the front of the old anti-quarian shop for *The Golden Bowl*, the front of the grocery shop for "In the Cage," a house in St John's Wood. James's memories of this part of London went back to his boyhood; and it is probable that the house and wall photographed may have been one which the novelist at one time thought of buying, during the middle 1880's. Coburn did not remember its location. What he recalled was James's high spirits. "It was a lovely afternoon, I remember, and H.J. was in his most festive mood." After the pictures were taken, they were hungry; finding no tea-shop they bought some bath buns and walked through the streets munching them. James had eaten bath buns in St John's Wood as long ago as 1856. It was now 1907.

On another occasion they went to Hampstead Heath in search of a bench needed for the volume containing "tales of the literary life." The photograph appears there labelled "Saltram's Seat"— Saltram being the Coleridge figure in James's tale "The Coxon Fund." In the story the bench is supposed to be located in Wimbledon; but this bench symbolized something more than was in the story. On such a bench, and perhaps this very one, Henry James had sat, long ago, with George du Maurier, during their rambles on the Heath, talking of Paris and French novels. For the last of the series Coburn took a memorable much-reprinted picture—that of a slightly blurred Portland Place, used in the second volume of *The Golden Bowl*—the rear view of a hansom in the broad thoroughfare, the distance fading into a haze. "The thing was to induce the vision of Portland Place to generalize itself," James wrote, "at a given moment the great featureless Philistine vista would itself perform a miracle, would become interesting for a splendid atmospheric hour, as only London knows how."

There was one other London picture which James wanted specifically. He arranged with Claude Phillips, keeper of the Wallace Collection, for Coburn to photograph "a divine little chimney piece, with all its wondrous garniture, a couple of chairs beside it, and a piece on either side, of the pale green figured damask of the wall." This was to be the frontispiece to *The Spoils of Poynton*. The novelist told Phillips that the treasures in the Wallace Collection were indeed rare, "the *Spoils* of my story, though precious, were not so good as that, but this is a fault in the right direction. They *would* be things to make possible a dire dispute even between mother and son." The Master introduced still another hidden autobiographical note when he had Coburn photograph the entrance to Lamb House to serve as frontispiece to *The Awkward Age.*

In his preface to *The Golden Bowl* the novelist paid tribute to Coburn's art. He felt that the photographs suffered somewhat by their reduced dimension; those which had been least reduced possessed the greatest beauty. "Anything that relieves responsible prose of the duty of being good enough, interesting enough, and pictorial enough does it the worst of services," James wrote. The quest for the small antiquarian shop was in reality a quest for "a shop of the mind;" for this reason James added nothing would induce him to say where they had found their picture. Coburn, years later, fell in with James's view, and refused to divulge the actual shop. He did say that by a curious coincidence they had found it to be almost exactly where James had placed it in his book. This was the meaning of James's allusion to "the marvel of an accidental rightness." They had sought always "certain inanimate characteristics of London streets." London always ended by "giving one absolutely everything one asks."

Long before he had finished his work on the New York Edition, Henry James was exhausted and even bored with it. The volumes began to be issued, in December 1907 and continued into 1909. To his nephew Harry, James wrote of "the Nightmare of the edition . . . my terror of not keeping sufficiently ahead in doing my part of it (all the revising, rewriting, retouching, Preface-making and proof-correcting) has so paralysed me—as panic fear—that I have let other decencies go to the wall. The printers and publishers tread on my heels, and I feel their hot breath behind me."

There were in reality only certain moments when this pressure was intense. James gave himself an excellent head start, and the issuing of the novels—that is the first fifteen volumes—proceeded with great regularity. When he got to the volumes containing his selected tales he found he had crowded himself too much; and the overflow into twenty-four volumes meant dismembering some of the prefaces already written to suit the new story-arrangements. While he addressed himself promptly to rectifying and rearranging, he said he would not write any more prefaces, "heaven forbid I should attempt any new ones." The rearrangement meant that he had to put the tale of "Julia Bride" into his volume of ghost stories; and certain late tales on other themes consorted with "Daisy Miller" in the "international" volume. Chagrin gave way to indifference. The rearrangements were awkward; he wasn't sure that the prefaces now alluded to the stories in the volumes they prefaced (most of them did) "but at any rate let matters stand as they are, please, in spite of any such small irregularity." Long afterwards—in the last year of his life —he would describe the Edition as "really a monument (like Ozymandias) which has never had the least intelligent critical justice done to it—or any sort of critical attention at all paid to it——" He added that "the artistic problem involved in my scheme was a deep and exquisite one, and moreover, was as I held, very effectively solved. Only it took such time—*and* such taste —in other words such aesthetic light. No more commercially thankless job of the literary order was (Prefaces and all—*they* of a thanklessness!) accordingly ever achieved."

THE HOUSE OF MIRTH

BY the spring of 1907, after almost two years of unremitting labour, Henry James began to feel restless. *The American Scene* was on the press. He had given himself a long head start on the New York Edition and was revising and reading proof of *The Princess Casamassima*, which would constitute the fifth and sixth volumes of the series. He had written "The Jolly Corner" and several fugitive pieces, and had just finished a chapter for a composite novel *The Whole Family*, a literary stunt originated by Harpers. He longed to be out of his Rye-cage. He needed some relief from the usual little run to London. For some weeks the "Angel of Devastation" had been beckoning. Mrs Wharton was on the verge of leasing an apartment in Paris at 58 rue de Varenne from George Vanderbilt, James's erstwhile host at Biltmore. Would Henry come and stay with her and Teddy? Would he go on a motor trip to the south of France? Eight years had elapsed since the novelist's last visit to the Continent, two since his return from America. The Master muttered to various friends about "pampered Princesses," and the Whartonian "eagle pounce and eagle flight." He squirmed at the pounce; he loved the flight. He characterized Mrs Wharton's energy as "devouring and desolating, ravaging, burning, and destroying." She destroyed by taking him away from his work. But he wanted to be taken away. New imagery began to creep into his letters. Now the eagle had become a "Firebird;" she rode in "a chariot of fire." When she looked at him, in her serious way, with a touch of smile at the edge of her lips—looked at him out of her round face with her hazel eyes—Henry James found it difficult to say "no." "The Rich, rushing, ravening Whartons"—this they might be, yet Henry James at sixty-four was not yet prepared to give up the social adventures of his prime. "I won't deny," he wrote to his old Gallo-American friend, Edward Lee Childe, "that for the

charm of Mrs Wharton's society I would go far." He didn't have
to go far. Early in March of 1907 he crossed the Channel, and
presently, in the rue de Varenne, he announced himself in "gilded
captivity." He came for a week or two. He had never paid long
visits anywhere. As it happened, this was to be the longest visit
he ever paid. He remained in Paris a fortnight and then they went
for the tour Mrs Wharton would celebrate in *A Motor-Flight
through France*; after that there would be a further stay at No. 58
which James spoke of as "the house of mirth"—an allusion to
Mrs Wharton's successful novel. James felt this might be his last
visit to the Continent and he consequently prolonged it. There
had been an elegiac feeling in his travels for some time. He may
not have had a "pure" holiday because Scribner proofs kept
catching up with him. But when had he not worked as he
travelled?

I

Mrs Wharton respected James's working hours; moreover she
had hers as well. Both novelists—the inventor of the American-
European legend and the dissector of "old New York"—stayed
in their rooms until lunch, sometimes into the afternoon. Mrs
Wharton scribbled amusing little messages and sent them by her
servants to divert the Master. There were no serious interruptions. James had never penetrated the life of the Faubourg
St Germain and now he found himself agreeably ensconced in it,
in one of the series of little Left Bank streets not far from the
Invalides. He had only lately asked Coburn to photograph a
porte-cochère in one of these streets as a frontispiece to *The
American*. Mrs Wharton, an American aristocrat, had little difficulty encountering the newer French aristocracy—an aristocracy
less rigid and more open than that described by Honoré de Balzac.
She moved with ease and elegance among countesses and
duchesses. James's old friend Paul Bourget, now an "inflamed
academician" had given Mrs Wharton *entrée*. "Our friend is a
great and graceful lioness," James told Howard Sturgis; keeping
up the image he said he had "come in for many odd bones and
other leavings of the Christians (if Christians they can be called)

who have been offered to her maw in this extraordinary circus."
There were charming small dinner parties in the rue de Varenne.
Mrs Winthrop Chanler remembered that "the guests were carefully chosen for their absolute compatibility." She remembered
that when the parties were over and the guests were gone, James
would draw his chair to the fire, invite his American friends to
approach and opening his eyes wide would murmur: "Now let us
say what we really think." Mrs Chanler was struck by the esteem
in which the sexagenarian novelist and the forty-five-year-old
Mrs Wharton held one another. "In a small and thoroughly
familiar circle, these two were at their most enchanting best—
their wit and their wisdom could flash back and forth in cosy confidence." The house of mirth was cosy: and James felt himself
admired.

Mrs Wharton remembered the Master's keen enjoyment of this
society which "lent a schoolboy's zest" to his Paris visit. The
lady novelist's French friends told her they had never met an
Anglo-Saxon who spoke such admirable French. He was not only
correct and fluent, but he avoided platitudes and pomposities. He
used the language as if it were his own, translated the Jamesian
style into it. The schoolboy's zest of which Mrs Wharton speaks
is to be read in his letters to his friends. He reported he had had
"an indigestion of Chères Madames"—he who had always wanted
to meet French society. The most attractive woman he met
wasn't French, but she had been absorbed into that society as a
graft in the Faubourg St Germain. Descended from Viennese
Jewish bankers, the widowed Comtesse Robert de Fitz-James—
a new form of Henry's own name—entertained and amused him.
He was susceptible to her charm, her social reach. Then there was
the Comtesse d'Humières, with her "pretty salient eyes and her
pretty salient gestures," whose husband had translated Kipling—
they both would call on James later in Lamb House; and there
were such old Faubourg names as de Béarn and D'Arenberg and
others, like Madame Waddington, once Mary King, the American
wife of a French deputy, later foreign minister. "Mrs Wharton
has been exceedingly kind—she is a dear of dears," James told
Howard Sturgis. Teddy Wharton's amiability exceeded the

novelist's fondest hopes. "It has really been lovely," he wrote on
the eve of their motor tour to the South of France.

II

They left on a bland March morning, the first day of spring, in the
Wharton's new Panhard, with the Yankee chauffeur Charles Cook
at the wheel, and various servants dispatched ahead with the luggage and to prepare hotel suites—as for a royal progress. The
car climbed the hill to Ville d'Avray and proceeded to Versailles.
Henry James, warmly wrapped in his greatcoat, experienced to
the full the amenity of this form of travel. They were "on india-
rubber wings." They visited Rambouillet, they paused in
Chartres, they looked at chateaux, they lingered in churches. It
was leisurely; it was princely. They went to Blois, to Poitiers, to
Bordeaux, and thence to the Pyrenees. There were local stops and
delightful lunches at various inns. "The motor is a magical
marvel," James wrote, and "this large, smooth old France is
wonderful." He had never seen France in such a beguiling
sequence of panorama and close-up. At Pau, Teddy Wharton
was ill for several days, and Henry and Mrs Wharton made a
series of neighbourhood excursions. Then they went to Carcas-
sonne and Toulouse; remounting the valley of the Rhône they
paused at Nîmes, Arles, and Orange. The stop at Pau enabled
James to write some letters. A long one to Goody Allen reveals
the only serious discomfort he experienced in this otherwise
cheerful journey. He had always stayed at first-class hotels but
had never cultivated the hotel de luxe: and he discovered that the
delights and comforts of this kind of travel drained his modest
purse. He was living, as he put it, "an expensive fairy-tale," proof
again of the old saying, he remarked, that it was "one's rich
friends who cost one!" He blushed, he told Goody Allen, "for
such sordid details in the face of my high entertainment." Jessie
Allen, all discretion, kept this letter, but pasted strips of paper
over the sordid details.

They stopped at Nohant in their progress southward, to visit
the home of George Sand which Mrs Wharton had seen the
previous year. James was enormously curious about it. They

wandered through the old country mansion, inspected the family graves, James reading every word on the tombstones; then after looking at the marionette theatre of George Sand's children they went into the garden. James surveyed the plain house which had harboured so much ancient passion: "And in which of those rooms, I wonder, did George herself sleep?" Edith heard him muse. He looked at her with a twinkling eye. "Though in which, indeed, in which indeed, my dear, did she *not?*" Years later James would write of "that wondrous day when we explored the very scene where they pigged so thrillingly together. What a crew, what *mœurs*, what habits, what conditions and relations every way —and what an altogether mighty and marvellous George!—not diminished by all the greasiness and smelliness in which she made herself (and so many other persons!) at home."

The Master and Mrs Wharton had a great community of interest: it was Teddy Wharton who was the "third person" in this party. And it is clear that when the Panhard turned again into the Parisian traffic, after three exciting weeks, and they found themselves once more beside the Seine, the Master and the lady novelist felt they had had a charming adventure together, a little tour of high intelligence and perception and a great deal of luxurious living for James. The Master complained, however, to the end that it had been costly: there would be seven servants including the chauffeur to tip. But "Ah, the lovely rivers and the inveterately glorious grub." And to friends at Rye, "Ah, the good food and good manners and good looks everywhere!" Followed by "Ah, the poor frowsy tea-and-toasty Lamb House."

He was in no haste to return to his tea-and-toasty abode. Waiting in the rue de Varenne were piles of Edition proof. He settled down to the galleys. The life of the Faubourg continued. "We *déjeunons* out, and we dine, and we visit countesses in between." James was writing to their friend Gaillard Lapsley. "The Teddies are divinely good—and their inflamed Academician lunches here Sunday." James continued to be shocked by the changes in Bourget's person and character. He had once admired him; now he spoke of his "almost *insane* bad manners, snobbishness, and folly," a talent spoiled by social pampering and worldliness. He found a great alienation in him, "a detachment and irrelevancy of attitude, tone, and direction." His old friend Thomas Sergeant Perry turned up in the French capital; they had gone to school together in Newport, and then Perry had married a Cabot; the years had passed; they had drifted apart and they had ceased to communicate. They met again almost as if there had been no gap; they took long walks, and went to a concert. Perry's version was, "I saw Harry James several times when he was here, tho' his hostess, Mrs Wharton kept a pretty tight clutch on him, and didn't let him stray far out of sight. To make more certain of him she carried him on a three weeks motoring tour." James spent agreeable hours with his nephew Billy, who painted at Julien's when he wasn't playing tennis or rowing. The novelist's letters to William have a little of the tone of Lambert Strether talking about Chad Newsome as he urges his brother to allow Billy to remain in Paris and keep at his painting. "He ought absolutely to stay another year and not *retomber* to the art-desert of home, before, like a camel, he has filled his stomach-pouch with water to see him through." Henry James was thinking of his own art-starved condition in Cambridge forty years earlier.

James remained in Paris for three more weeks, well into May, "steeped up to my chin in the human and social imbroglio," even though he felt himself to be "rather keyed up" by ten weeks of the *grand monde*. He had enjoyed his weeks with the Whartons. They had marked a difference "from one's promiscuous boule-vardian quarters of the past," and he continued on this theme to Jocelyn Persse: "I have had a very interesting agreeable time—one of the most agreeable I have ever had in Paris, through living in singularly well-appointed privacy in this fine old Rive Gauche quarter, away from the horrible boulevards and hotels and cos-mopolite crowd." He had "come in for a great many social im-pressions of a sort I hadn't had for a long time—some of them of a more or less intimate French sort that I had *never* had; mixed, all, with a great deal of wondrous and beautiful motoring." In most of his letters to his younger friend, it had been James who pleaded with Persse to bring him news of the great world. Now he had "plenty to tell you on some blest Sunday, after my return,

THE VENETIAN PALACE
The Curtis's Palazzo Barbaro (Coburn's photograph), frontispiece to
The Wings of the Dove in the New York Edition

PORTLAND PLACE
Frontispiece (Coburn's photograph) to *The Golden Bowl* in
the New York Edition

when you come down and stroll with me in the alentour of poor dear russet Lamb House; which appears to me from here *so* russet and so humble and so modest and so British and so pervaded by boiled mutton and turnips; and yet withal so intensely precious and so calculated to rack me with homesickness." The homesickness was a mere spasm. Italy called. He had matured plans for a little trip south—it would be the twelfth of his lifetime. Howard Sturgis was in Rome; Hendrik Andersen beckoned to him to stay at his studio. James, however, settled on the old Hotel de Russie in the Piazza del Popolo. He had lodged there so often in times past. He travelled *en route* in a sleeper to Turin, pausing to revise certain pages of the *Princess Casamassima*; it was a way of ministering to his constitutional need for a few—even if very few—days "of *recueillement* and solitude."

III

He kept speaking of this as the "last continental episode of my aged life," which it was not. A year later he would visit Mrs Wharton in Paris once more. Yet he felt quite correctly that he would never see Italy again. It was grossly changed from the time he had known it—the time when the Colosseum was still filled with earth and flowers grew out of the ruins. He spent seventeen days in Rome. Here he found Alice Mason, whom he remembered as young and beautiful in the days when they had gone riding on a Campagna that was fast disappearing. She was now "very gentle and easy and coherent"—a "silvery ghost" of the strong and passionate woman he remembered. He had some hours with Howard Sturgis whom he found rather depressed; they would meet again at the Edward Boits at Cernitoio. He spent much time with Hendrik Andersen who executed a bust of the Master making him look like a Roman senator, but with much less life in his face than is to be found in the relics of the times of the Caesars. On one day James went out by himself to the Protestant Cemetery; he had visited it long ago to look at Shelley's grave and at Keats's; and here he had described the burial of Daisy Miller. He returned this time to see once more the violet-covered grave of Miss Woolson. Thirteen years had passed since the anguish of her

M

death. James communed silently there—feeling it to be his last farewell. He had written out that experience in his imagination, in "The Beast in the Jungle," and his only reference to this personal pilgrimage was in a letter to Fenimore's niece, in which he spoke of the grave as "the most beautiful thing in Italy— almost" and "tremendously inexhaustibly touching." He added "its effect never fails to overwhelm." The old emotion remained; and the old mystery remained as well.

Rome itself had ceased to have its old grip on James. "The abatements and changes and modernisms and vulgarities, the crowd and the struggle and the frustration (of real communion with what one wanted) are quite dreadful," he wrote to Billy. "I quite revel in the thought that I shall never come to Italy *at all* again." He was glad he had come, nevertheless. He dined one evening with his old friend Henry Brewster, one of the most perfect examples of the cosmopolitan-American type James had ever met. He had been fond of him of old; this was the last time he saw him, for Brewster died shortly afterwards. The latter, in a letter, described this dinner: "I had an impression of great goodness and kindness, almost tenderness; of an immense *bienveillance* and yet of fastidious discrimination; something delicate and strong morally." He noted too James's "puffy vegetarian look, and the spring, the flash of steel has gone." He also said "all joys, sorrows, hopes, trials, and strivings find a prompt and delicate echo in him."

James seems to have enjoyed very much his renewed contact with Hendrik Andersen—they had seen so little of each other during the eight years of their friendship. One gets a feeling, however, that James's original ardour had cooled; a certain warmth and tenderness remained. James's memories were of his hours with Andersen in "the cool arched workshop" fraternizing with the sculptor's models and posing for his bust; there were mild sessions at a restaurant, visits to a foundry where some of Andersen's work was being cast, and a long last evening together on a terrace. Andersen lived with his sister Lucia and several of her snapshots have survived in which the sculptor, thin, bony, tall but no longer handsome looms beside the portly and "puffy" novelist.

James was to have the novelty of motoring in Italy with Filippo de Filippi an Italian explorer and traveller who had married an American wife. Filippi had the English manner of hospitality; he gave fine dinner parties over which he presided with his dark southern features and powerful voice—a voice that one friend said seemed to give him stature, for he had a small compact figure. A man of great temperament and violent rages he seems to have been, however, in good form as James's host. The Filippis, with the explorer himself driving, took James on two or three Roman excursions, including a crossing of the Tiber "on a medieval raft," and then a picnic on the edge of the sea; there was "a divine day" at Subiaco and then a two-day jaunt to Naples, going down by the mountains, to Monte Cassino, and returning by Gaeta, Terracina, the Pontine Marshes, and the Castelli, "quite an ineffable experience. This brought home to me," James wrote to Mrs Wharton later, "with an intimacy and a penetration unprecedented how incomparably the old *coquine* of an Italy is the most beautiful country in the world—of a beauty (and an interest and complexity of beauty) so far beyond any other that none other is worth talking about." James spoke out of the limitations of his journeyings. In his busy life he had not known Greece, or Africa, or the tropical parts of the world. Italy—had sufficed. The "dishevelled nymph" of his youth, however, was now an "old *coquine*." Of the Naples journey James told Mrs Wharton "the day we came down from Posilippo in the early June morning is a memory of splendour and style and heroic elegance I never shall lose—and never shall renew!" This journey was memorialized in a vein of beautiful nostalgia in certain pages James added to his old writings about Italy when he assembled *Italian Hours*—that book in 1910 was his way of saying farewell to the Italy of all his years. The added pages were titled "A Few Other Roman Neighbourhoods." In them we find the delight he took in the ferrying of the Filippi car over the saffron-coloured Tiber "on a boat that was little more than a big rustic raft," the visit to Ostia, to Castel Fusano with the massive Chigi tower and "the immemorial stone-pines and the afternoon sky and the desolate sweetness and concentrated rarity of the picture." These "all kept their appointment, to fond memory, with that especial form of Roman faith, the fine aesthetic conscience in things, that is never, never broken." James saw the ubiquitous bicycles of the Roman youth who had "a great taste for flashing about in more or less denuded or costumed athletic and romantic bands and guilds." He harboured special memories of Subiaco—a plunge into "splendid solitary gravities, supreme romantic solemnities and sublimities, of landscape." The Benedictine convent, clinging to vertiginous ledges and slopes of a vast gorge within that setting was for James "the very ideal of the tradition of that *extraordinary in the romantic*, handed down to us, as the most attaching and inviting spell of Italy, by all the old academic literature of travel and art of Salvator Rosas and Claudes." As always, in his pictorial travel sketches, James brought in the hints of the personal —his exploration of "sordidly papal streets" in the heterogeneous city "in the company of a sculptor friend." And he ended the pages of memory with an allusion to the last dinner with Andersen "an evening meal spread, in the warm still darkness that made no candle flicker, on the wide high space of an old loggia that overhung, in one quarter, the great obelisked Square preceding one of the Gates, and in the other the Tiber and the far Trastevere and more things than I can say—above all, as it were, the whole awkward past, the mild confused romance of the Rome one had lived and of which one was exactly taking leave under protection of the friendly lanterned and garlanded feast and the commanding, all-embracing roof-garden. It was indeed a reconciling, it was an altogether penetrating, last hour."

IV

He had in effect long ago said farewell to Florence. We have no record of this final visit. He had known so much of the old Americano–Florentine life, the days when Bellosguardo had been familiar with its drama of Frank Boott and his daughter Lizzie, and Duveneck, and the days he had spent there with Fenimore. We know only that he lingered briefly and spent four days with Howard Sturgis and "the Babe" who were in turn staying with James's old friend, the painter, Ned Boit at Cernitoio, over against

Vallombrosa "a dream of Tuscan loveliness." A photograph of James standing cigarette in hand on the long terrace of the Boits, with Sturgis in the foreground, offers us a less bloated figure than the Roman snapshots, and a more characteristic one. James had "a really adorable *séjour*" and went on to Venice to the familiar Palazzo Barbaro and the Curtises.

Venice was his old Venice, unique, exquisite, beloved of all his years. "Never has the whole place seemed to me sweeter, clearer, diviner," and this in spite of a sirocco that blew during part of the time. He found the Curtises restrictive, formal, rigid, bound up by their prejudices and with "such a terror of the vulgar" — but perhaps this was because he himself had so considerably "loosened up." They had grown older — Daniel Curtis indeed would soon die and Ariana would leave Venice for perpetual visits to friends and a lonely life chronicled in long letters to their mutual friend Goody Allen. The Curtises had made James feel "they discriminated so invidiously against anyone I might weakly wish to see, of my little other promiscuous acquaintance in Venice that I felt I could never again face the irritations and the inconvenience of it." So it was farewell to Venice too. Yet it was the most difficult farewell of all. "I don't care, frankly, if I never see the vulgarized Rome or Florence again," James wrote later that summer to Edith Wharton — "but Venice never seemed to me more loveable." And he added by way of useful information for the motoring Edith, that cars were left parked at Mestre.

Late in June he turned north again. He spent three days at Lausanne at the Hotel Gibbon visiting one of his relatives. On 4 July he was in Paris where he stayed at the Hotel du Palais d'Orsay. Edith was no longer in the rue de Varenne. A few days later he was back at Lamb House. This was one of the rare occasions when his little English home seemed to him after the glories of Rome and the delights of Venice "flat and common and humiliating. But here I am — and in my little deep-green garden, where the roses are almost as good as the Roman, and the lawn is almost as smooth beneath the feet as your floors of No. 3 — I try to forget what I've lost." Thus to Hendrik Andersen.

V

His farewell to Italy was unmistakable. His farewell to Paris was
more tentative. After a busy autumn and winter James repeated,
in the spring of 1908, his visit of the year before. This time Mrs
Wharton was in a rented apartment at 3 Place des États Unis.
James came with the understanding that his stay would be brief.
Moreover Teddy was ill in America; Mrs Wharton planned an
early sailing. They met first at Amiens to inspect the cathedral;
Morton Fullerton, James's friend, may have been with them. The
"chariot of fire" seems to have taken James and Mrs Wharton on
another literary pilgrimage: this time to Croisset, to the house of
Flaubert. In Paris, the Olympian world was quite as fascinating
as the year before, and Mrs Wharton was possessive, to judge by
T. S. Perry's again remarking that James was "in her clutch," and
that she "very unwillingly relaxed her hold." The great lady had
arranged for the Master to have his portrait painted by the
littérateur-painter Jacques-Émile Blanche, who had an enormous
facility, was a great social lion in the Faubourg, and usually
worked in his studio before an audience of society ladies—it was
always a performance. He posed James full face. When the
portrait was finished it turned out to be in profile. It is a good
likeness of the Master. Mrs Wharton always considered it the best
portrait of James ever painted. Writing to Bay Emmet, who had
painted him in 1900, James described himself as looking "very
big, and fat and uncanny and 'brainy' and awful." He characterized Blanche as a "do-you-any-way-you-like sort of painter." It
is not clear whether Mrs Wharton paid Blanche; what we do know
is that the latter had invited James to sit, having just done a
portrait of Thomas Hardy which was a great success. When
James saw the portrait exhibited in London he could not recognize
it. It was a *chic'd* thing, but had "a certain dignity of intention."
Blanche had entirely repainted the canvas with the aid of photographs.

Paris was "wonderful" in all respects, although James found
his social calendar too crowded and finally spoke of "this fatal and
prostrating vortex." "I am kept here in gilded chains, in gorgeous

bondage, in breathless attendance and luxurious *asservissement*,"
he wrote to Henry Adams who had sent him his privately printed
Education.

The visit was soon over and James rushed back to his Edition.
By this time he had had a larger vision of Mrs Wharton. She was
"the wonderful, the unique Edith Wharton" to James, and also,
in a variant on his earlier characterization "the angel of beautiful
ruin"—the devastation "of one's time and domestic economy."
He spoke of "her frame of steel" and of "the iridescent track of her
Devastation." She was "an amiable and highly imperative friend"
but also "a very great person." He imaged himself as a "poor old
croaking barnyard fowl" pitted against "a golden eagle." If we
discount the euphemisms and playful ironies, we may still accept
one designation as carrying the essence of his feeling about
her—she was, he remarked, "almost too insistently Olympian."

THE VELVET GLOVE

HENRY JAMES wrote a bit of history—literary history—after his two visits to the world of Edith Wharton. He incorporated her high life—of society, of literature, her grand style, and Princess-like existence—in a tale, incorporated it with such flourish of fine-spun allusion that few have recognized his elaborate joke and the deeper criticism it contains. Mrs Wharton saw the joke at once, it would seem, but apparently closed her eyes to the meanings that might be read in it. Years later she drew attention to the tale in her reminiscences—perhaps a way of throwing dust in readers' eyes—saying it originated one night in Paris when she had taken James on a long drive in the "chariot of fire"—so called in the tale—"high above the moonlit lamplit city and the gleaming curves of the Seine." That drive is told in the Master's high style in the last part of the story. The tale's origin was more complicated than Mrs Wharton knew. An agency in New York had written to James saying that Mrs Wharton had suggested he write an article about her. Its stationery carried a Marxian motto, "from each according to ability, unto each according to need." Apparently a socialist publication was interested in Mrs Wharton's discussion of labour–management relations in her new novel, *The Fruit of the Tree*. "She has indicated," the letter told James, "that if the leading opinion could be from your pen, it would be gratifying to her."

From the first James did not believe Mrs Wharton would, in this indirect fashion, ask for a "puff" from him. Mrs Wharton denied any knowledge of the matter. However she did say (James told his agent) "that she would be sorry to stand in the way of my writing the little article—or *a* little article—if I am moved to it." He added, "I seem to make out that the thing would give her pleasure indeed—*should* I do it." He thought it would be "amiable" of him to produce 3000 words and was tempted to use her new novel as a peg for such a tribute. He added, however, "I rather detest the man's false statement—unless he can account for it."

Perhaps behind his willingness was a feeling that there was practically no other way in which he could reciprocate Mrs Wharton's extended hospitalities. It was largely a matter of gesture; but such gestures had always been a challenge. He had long ago written an ambiguous tribute to Mrs Humphry Ward, a mixture of caution and generosity, which he could make with a clear conscience. For Mrs Wharton's art, even with its limitations, he had a much higher regard. He put the matter to her with candour. A seed had been dropped in his mind he said, "by however a crooked *geste*," and he was now conscious of "a lively and spontaneous disposition to really dedicate a few lucid remarks to the mystery of your genius." Mrs Wharton expressed proper caution to her editor at Scribner's. She asked him to send *The Fruit of the Tree* to Henry James who wants to write "a few words on the mystery of my genius," adding that this sounded "as if he meant to make mince-meat of me."

James had told Mrs Wharton he was writing "to the inquirer whose letter I sent you that if he can explain his so highly imaginative statement about your expressed wish (really, evidently, a barefaced lie, and as I judge, a common trick of the trade,) I will send him 3000 words." He did not receive a satisfactory answer; by the time he got a reply he had read *The Fruit of the Tree* and lost all desire to write about it. The novel was good; it was simply not good enough. He told Minnie Jones that it was of "a strangely infirm composition and construction;" he said as much to Mrs Wharton, praising, however, the element of good writing in it." It had "more *kinds* of interest than anyone now going can pretend to achieve." Still "I don't feel that I can 'enthuse' over you in a hole-and-corner publication." Thus the matter ended.

I

There was, however, an idea for a story in the incident. What if a great lady—of the world and the pen—did ask a great writer for a puff? How amusing the irony? to have a writer ascend to her Olympus and then have her forget her goddess-state and invite, from a mere mortal, a particular tribute? He seems to have written the tale in an open spirit of mockery, for his first title was "The Top of the Tree." In the end he decided to be more cautious. The story was given a mysterious title, "The Velvet Glove."

In the tale James resorted to the Balzacian "going on with a character." He resurrected Gloriani out of *Roderick Hudson* and *The Ambassadors*. At a great reception in Gloriani's studio in Paris a young English nobleman approaches a novelist-playwright who has written "a slightly too fat volume" called *The Heart of Gold*—a Jamesian allusion perhaps to the size and shape of *The Golden Bowl*. The author of that book is named John Berridge, perhaps an allusion to Walter Berry. The young English lord is an intermediary—like the inquirer from New York; he asks whether Berridge wouldn't take a look at a book by a friend of his. He would value his opinion. Berridge happens to find life more interesting than literature—"what was the pale page of fiction compared with the intimately personal adventure?" Berridge prefers "the grand personal adventure on the grand personal basis." He is an outsider in Society, a mortal on Olympus who is enchanted with the romances of the Olympians. The word Olympian is sprinkled with great regularity through the pages of the tale, and allusions to Endymion, Hebe, Apollo, Astarte are made together with a reference to *The Winter's Tale* and to Claude Lorrain—in a word to elements of the pastoral, great personages masquerading as shepherdesses and shepherds. The slight tale is thus weighted with mythic reference. Berridge meets a glamorous Princess and is astonished, after admiring her elegance and beauty, to discover that her disguise is that of plain Amy Evans (a name as plain as Edith Jones) a writer of novels. He has read her recent novel *The Top of the Tree* in its "tawdry red cover," an allusion to the binding of *The Fruit of the Tree* and other fictions of Mrs Wharton's.

The Princess is a figure of Romance and she floats through Gloriani's studio as a creature of magic. Berridge is delighted when she suggests to him they leave together; she will take him away for a ride in her "chariot of fire." In the cushioned vehicle Berridge feels himself to be carried on the wings of Romance. It is a soft April night; they hang over Paris "from vague conse-crated lamp-studded heights and taking in, spread below and afar, the great scroll of all its irresistible story, pricked out, across river and bridge and radiant *place*, and along quays and boulevards and avenues, and around monumental circles and squares, in syllables of fire, and sketched and summarized, farther and farther, in the dim fire-dust of endless avenues; that was all of the essence of fond and thrilled and throbbing recognition, with a thousand things understood and a flood of response conveyed, a whole familiar possessive feeling appealed to and attested."

This beauty so touching to John Berridge seems not to touch the Princess who pursues her purpose relentlessly. Her new novel "The Velvet Glove" would benefit greatly from a preface by John Berridge. That is really the point of this sudden intimacy—the preface "would do so much for the thing in America." She says this "with the clearest coolness of her general privilege. 'Why, my dear man, let your Preface show, the lovely, friendly irresist-ible log-rolling Preface, that I've been asking you if you wouldn't be an angel and write for me'"—and she also says "'of course I don't want you to perjure yourself; but——'" and the Princess "fairly brushed him again, at their close quarters, with her fresh fragrant smile"—'I do want you so to like me, and to say it all out beautifully and publicly.'"

And Berridge had thought she valued him for himself and the successful play he had written! He wonders what "could lead a creature so formed for living and breathing her Romance, and so committed up to the eyes, to the constant fact of her personal immersion in it and genius for it, the dreadful ama-teurish dance of ungrammatically scribbling it, with editions and advertisements and reviews and royalties and every other futile item." Berridge meditates on "the really great ease of really great ladies, and the perfectly perfect facility of everything once they were great enough."

In effect James seems to be saying that Princesses should not step off their pedestals; they thereby cease to be Princesses. It is deeply disillusioning for Berridge; it hurts his pride and his self-esteem. John Berridge replies to mere "Amy Evans" by breaking the barriers between himself and her exalted state—since she has broken them first. He kisses her hand; and then unceremoniously presses his lips against hers. "You are Romance," he tells her with a show of gallantry. "Don't attempt such base things. Leave those to us. Only live. Only be. We'll do the rest."

There was something deeply mocking and hostile in the tale in spite of its verbal gauze; as if James still resented the very idea of Mrs Wharton approaching him indirectly through a New York hole-and-corner publication for a puff—even though he had established her innocence. James put the icing on the story as thickly as he could. Berridge is aware of "these high existences," of "the Olympian race" and "the affairs, and above all the passions, of Olympus." The Princess strikes him as "some divine Greek mask overpainted say by Titian . . . she might have been, with her long rustle across the room, Artemis decorated, hung with pearls, for her worshippers, yet disconcerting them by having under an impulse just faintly fierce, snatched the cup of gold from Hebe." "The cup of gold" may be still another allusion to *The Golden Bowl*, and perhaps to the fact that the author of *The Fruit of the Tree* had been critical of that novel. Mrs Wharton once remarked to James, "What was your idea in suspending the four principal characters in *The Golden Bowl* in the void? What sort of life did they lead when they were not watching each other, and fencing with each other? Why have you stripped them of all the *human fringes* we necessarily trail after us through life?" James had answered in a disturbed voice "My dear—I didn't know I had!"

Within the story James extended his mockery—but it would be visible only to those who had read *The Fruit of the Tree* with some closeness. In her novel Mrs Wharton writes of a character as "with *all the ardour* of her young motherliness," or of a young man roused "with *all the boyhood* in his blood" or "*all the spirit* in him rode" or longing "with *all the warm, instincts* of youth." The embracing word was resorted to again and again by James in his references to Amy Evans's "The Top of the Tree:"

   . . . which all the Amy Evans in her, as she would doubtless have put it . . .
   . . . all the conscious conqueror in him, as Amy Evans would again have said . . .
   . . . while all the conscientious man of letters in him, as she might so supremely have phrased it . . .

He is also parodying Mrs Wharton's writing in this book in a sentence such as: "It was too much for all the passionate woman in her, and she let herself go, over the flowering land that had been, but was no longer their love, with an effect of blighting desolation that might have proceeded from one of the more physical, though not more awful convulsions of nature." He seems also to be rapping Mrs Wharton over the knuckles for some awkward sentences in the following passage from "The Top of the Tree:"

   The loveliness of the gaze, *which*[1] was that of the glorious period in *which* Pheidias reigned supreme, and *which* owed its most exquisite note to that shell-like curl of the upper lip *which* always somehow recalls for us the smile with *which* wind-blown Astarte must have risen from the salt sea to *which* she owed her birth and her terrible moods.

The allusion to Astarte may have greater meaning than meets the eye. Astarte was a deity of fecundity whose rites were celebrated by men dressed as women. It was not the first time James had looked at the element of the transvestite in popular literary circles —his tale of "The Death of the Lion" had featured men who wrote under women's names and women who wrote under men's. Amy Evans may herself be an echo of Marion Evans who had written as George Eliot or a reminder of George Sand. The allusion to Astarte may sound the fundamental theme of disguise in "The Velvet Glove" in which lords and ladies convert themselves into nymphs and shepherds and princesses became commoners by writing novels. Behind this over-elaborate joke there is a suggestion of trust betrayed, of the mighty who cease being mighty when they scribble, of hostility against that *grand monde*

---

[1] The repeated *which* has been underlined by me to emphasize the parody.

James admired and studied but also criticized. In a letter to Grace Norton, on the eve of his first visit to the rue de Varenne, he had spoken of getting news of the Nortons from Mrs Wharton adding "so far as the Pampered Princesses of this world, can when very intelligent and very literary and very gracious, *ever* arrive at real news of anything!"

James seems to have been sure that his joke would not offend — that its fun would be treated simply as fun. He had perhaps noticed a sentence in *The Fruit of the Tree* about characters "blent in that closest of unions, the discovery of a common fund of humour." When the story appeared in the *English Review* of March 1909 Mrs Wharton apparently told him it was "really good" and queried him about it. He had a ready answer. Two periodicals had declined the tale of John Berridge and the Princess "which was a good deal *comme qui dirait* like declining *you*: since *bien assurément* the whole thing *reeks* with you — and with Cook, and with our Paris (Cook's and yours and mine:) so no wonder it's 'really good.'" Asked about this tale years later, Mrs Wharton rejoined with a smile, "Oh but I would never have asked Henry to write a preface for me." And she told of "a very beautiful young English woman of great position and unappeased literary ambitions" who had once tried to beguile James "into contributing an introduction to a novel she was writing — or else into reviewing the book, I forget which."

Whatever further "sources" there may be for the story, its theme and the expression of it suggests that James's compliments to Mrs Wharton had their barbed side: that he stood his literary ground as Master and law-giver, and that he felt Edith Wharton should stand on her ground, that of a great and perceptive lady. She clearly swallowed the story as she accepted all of James's criticisms: their friendship was strong: it could withstand this kind of heavy Olympian satire. Mrs Wharton was prepared to make allowance for anything in the Master. On his side, his admiration for her grew with the passing years.

MISS BOSANQUET

WHEN Miss Theodora Bosanquet went that summer's day in 1907 to Miss Petherbridge's secretarial office and employment agency, she had no notion that this would be one of the most eventful days of her life. She felt somewhat slack and headachy. She was disinclined to brave the noise of the tube, and took a bus to Conduit Street. For some time she had been proof-reading an index to the Report of the Royal Commission on Coast Erosion. She was wearing her usual office outfit, a white blouse and green skirt, a belt and a tie, a "business-like and, I hoped, becoming costume." At about noon she learned that Mr Henry James was in the office. She had expected an interview but had not known on which day. She fidgeted nervously; she felt cold. She was a young, slim woman in her early twenties, rather boyish, with bright blue eyes and a shy manner. After a childhood on the Isle of Wight and at Lyme Regis, she had gone to Cheltenham Ladies' College and then to University College where she had taken a degree. She had, thus, much more education than Miss Weld, who had married while the novelist was in America and left his employ. He had required no typist during the revising of the New York Edition. Miss Bosanquet had no intention of parading her education, or her "literary" interests. Her precaution was confirmed later when she learned that Mr James liked his typists to be "without a mind"—and certainly not to suggest words to him, as some had done. It is doubtful whether he ever learned that Miss Bosanquet had trained herself especially to be his amanuensis. Earlier that summer she had heard chapters from *The Ambassadors* being dictated at one end of the office. She knew the novel and wondered why James's prose was being put to this service. On inquiry she had learned James needed a typist. Miss Bosanquet promptly set herself to learn typing. By the end of August she had become sufficiently proficient.

She was intelligent and observant. She had learned long ago to take mental notes. Her diary of that August day gives us a distinct picture. "He is like Coleridge—in figure—one feels that he ought to be wearing a flowered waistcoat—very expansive— 'unrestrained' in the lower part. He wore green trousers and a blue waistcoat with a yellow sort of check on it and a black coat —that was rather a shock. I'd imagined him as always very correctly dressed—in London. He is bald—except for tufts of not very grey hair at the sides. His eyes, grey I think, are exactly what I should expect—but the rest of his face is too fat. He talks slowly but continuously—I found it hard to get in any words of my own. But he is *most* kind and considerate."

James seems to have paid on this occasion little attention to Miss Bosanquet. He was interested in two or three essential things. Rye was remote; would she find it too lonely? Would she come to lunch and look for satisfactory lodgings. He would lend her books to read. And he probably also told her about walks and bicycle rides. He asked no questions. He informed her he was slow at dictating; she would have to amuse herself while he was evolving a sentence. "He was careful," Miss Bosanquet noted, "to impress on me the danger of boredom."

Miss Bosanquet observed that he did not have "the self-possession I should have expected." He seemed, however, "most kind and nice—and so absolutely unassuming." They could start in the autumn. This would give Miss Bosanquet time to make the move from London.

II

Miss Bosanquet arrived in Rye on 10 October 1907. Henry James met her at the station. His grimy gardener took her luggage. James apologized, "he ought not to have shown himself like that." He walked her to her rooms, "the talk," Miss Bosanquet noted, "being slightly constrained." He talked of the days when he used to go to see "dear old Burne-Jones" in this neighbourhood. He left his amanuensis in the care of her landlady, telling her to come around to Lamb House later and inspect the new Remington. This she did. She felt "horribly desolate." Her rooms were nice but she missed her London flat.

Miss Bosanquet rose early the next morning and took a stroll after breakfast. She was struck by the pretty view across the levels reclaimed from the sea and the masts in Rye harbour. Sharp at ten-fifteen she mounted the cobbled street to Lamb House. James let her in. He began by showing her shelves of books and telling her she could borrow anything she pleased. Then he led her to the Green Room upstairs, a little square room with two windows. There were more books, easy chairs, a table for the typewriter. Dictation began. James was working on a preface to *The Tragic Muse* "in a tone of personal reminiscence." Her diary records, "he dictates considerately—slowly and very clearly—giving all the punctuation and often the spelling. I was abominably slow and clumsy—but he was very kind—even complimentary though he admitted that he hoped I should soon go a little faster. He sat in a chair at first—then paced about, smoking—finishing soon after half past one." Miss Bosanquet then helped herself to a topical book and a volume on Meredith's poetry given to James by Meredith himself "so presumably worth reading." She ended her diary of her first day's work, "Mr James assumes complete ignorance of any literary knowledge on the part of his amanuensis. He told me that *The Newcomes* was in one word and that it was by Thackeray!"

Things were easier on the second day. She was less nervous and was able to type more rapidly. "The preface to *The Tragic Muse* continues and grows ever more interesting now that he is dealing with the interrelations of the characters. I mentioned that I had read it quite recently—and, after a moment of some murmur of 'oh—my rubbish,' said deprecatingly, he seemed, on the whole, pleased—and remarked that his former amanuensis had never at all fathomed what he wrote and made many 'exceedingly fantastic mistakes.'" Miss Bosanquet herself was worried, for once or twice she had written down the wrong word. She left on this occasion with Howells's *Heroines of Fiction* under her arm. She discovered also that the novelist worked on Sundays. The entry in Miss Bosanquet's diary for 13 October, a Sunday, reads "Mr

James was more—to use a quite inappropriate word—'sharp' this morning, at least much engrossed. He dismissed me at half past twelve, as he had by then completed the preface to *The Tragic Muse* and only wanted to look through it. I could wish he weren't extremely likely to find it crowded with my careless mistakes."

Miss Bosanquet need not have worried. In a very short time James knew that he had an accomplished amanuensis. A week after she had begun work for him he was writing William James "a new excellent amanuensis, a young boyish Miss Bosanquet, who is worth all the other (females) that I have had put together and who confirms me in the perception afresh—after eight months without such an agent—that for certain, for most, kinds of diligence and production, the intervention of the agent is, to *my* perverse constitution, an intense aid and a true economy! There is no comparison!" James did not keep his feelings from Miss Bosanquet. Nine days after her arrival "at the close of the morning, Mr James looked out of the window and said 'Ah—it's coming better today—I don't mean the dictation—though as to that I have great pleasure in saying that I'm extremely satisfied Miss Bosanquet. You seem to have picked things up so quickly and so intelligently.'" Miss Bosanquet replied in her shy way that she found the work so interesting that it was natural she would do her best. James replied, "Among the faults of my previous amanuenses—not by any means the *only* fault—was their apparent lack of comprehension of what I was driving at." So, added the amanuensis "we parted quite pleased with each other." James might have been less pleased had he read her diary on the day on which he started dictating his preface to *The Awkward Age*—"The nervous tension of the situation when he is 'agonizing' for a word is appalling—but may grow less. I hope it will . . . He goes in, more than I had noticed, for alliteration, and I didn't *quite* like 'a fine purple peach' which occurred this morning. Peaches have too *mellow* a colour to be called purple."

Miss Bosanquet would become increasingly worshipful of the Master, yet it was not blind worship. She retained a strong sense of her own identity. She was often critical of his social weaknesses; and his occasional duplicities. She sometimes protested, to herself, over his orotund sentences. Her diary of 15 October 1907 records that she was much flattered "to notice that one or two sentences I had thought rather obscure were the very ones he had picked out for revision." On another day James made her observe how he altered "a second-rate phrase" to "a first-rate one." She doesn't, however, give us the phrase. He dictates a letter to Gertrude Atherton about hotels in Paris prefacing it by saying "I abominate the woman" and, Miss Bosanquet adds, "at frequent intervals he groaned about having to write to her." On one occasion she glimpses the Master's bedroom while he is in London. She had cleaned the typewriter and put on a new ribbon. "I was allowed hot water and washed my hands in Mr James's room—*such* a nice room, panelled, all quite simple, photographic reproductions on the walls. Two *charming* little silver candlesticks by the bed. A very good old mirror against the wall."

When James was away she found other employment and stayed in her flat in London. From this time on, with certain gaps (some of her diaries were lost during the Second World War) James is mirrored almost daily in the lucid prose of his typist. Miss Bosanquet was always discreet, always tactful, always efficient. Her subsequent career would be distinguished. She wrote books—one on Paul Valéry—and an admirable little pamphlet for the Hogarth Press describing James's working methods. She was for a number of years secretary to the International Federation of University Women. One of the early feminists, she was associated with *Time and Tide* as its literary editor and for years was known to the young writers in Bloomsbury. In her work for Henry James she was submerging her own distinct personality and cultivated literary tastes. She was in every way a true hand-maiden to the Master. When he was dead she was able to enter on her own career.

Miss Bosanquet received twenty-five shillings for her first fifteen hours of work, that is just a little more than a shilling per hour. It was the regular pay at the time; and it was, she told James, the first money she had ever earned. There were certain gallantries between them. On a day when Miss Bosanquet would be indisposed, he usually turned up at her lodgings with a bouquet

of roses; if he kept her overtime and she grew hungry he would
strip the silver foil off a chocolate bar and lay it beside her typewriter. At Christmas he sometimes had her to dinner at Lamb
House and gave her a glove-box as a gift, which the boyish side of
her did not appreciate; especially when on a later Christmas James
duplicated this gift. After a while she stopped recording details of
her routine in her diary, but she made a point of setting down any
incidental remarks made by the novelist. In this respect the diary
offers us many little touches, a kind of "work-table-talk" of the
Master that could not have been otherwise preserved. What
James did not know was that Miss Bosanquet was writing as well:
she tried her hand at poetry, an occasional essay for such pub-
lications as *Hearth and Home* and even a bit of fiction. She wrote
for literary contests in the *Westminster Gazette*.

III

One day James dictated a letter to his brother William and Miss
Bosanquet wrote in her diary "I *am* in luck's way—fancy *me*
being in a sense the *medium* between Henry James and William."
Her diary records during the summer of 1908 what James meant
when he said to a friend "I am deep in family." The William
Jameses came abroad in the spring of that year. William was to
give the Hibbert Lectures at Oxford; and he accepted—quite
forgetting his reason for resigning from the American Academy
—an honorary degree of Doctor of Science. These were the
lectures which became *A Pluralistic Universe*. The typist's diary
reveals what a complex life James led during such family visits.
He was on the fifteenth volume of his Edition and writing his
preface on tales of the supernatural. He worked regularly every
morning. But thereafter he was with his brother and Alice.
Three of William's children also came to Lamb House at various
times. During the summer the figures of Kipling, H. G. Wells
and Chesterton moved through the Rye streets. Various
Americans came and went. At the summer's end Mrs Wharton
was there "fairish-bright hazel eyes, brown much-wrinkled skin
—looks tired—quite pleasant," Miss Bosanquet records. Her
own shyness bothered her. She adds "I was an awkward fool as

usual." She seemed, however, comfortable with the James family and liked William. "He *is* a charming man—there's something so simple and fresh about him somehow." In another entry—"a delightful man—small and thin—he looks about ten years older than Mr Henry James but is only one more, I believe." William walked with her down the road one day as he was going to post a letter, commenting on the picturesqueness of Rye; on another day she found him using the typewriter and enjoyed having him dictate part of a page to her. There were moments when she was less happy with him. 10 September 1908: "Saw Professor James and told him of my interest in the Society of Psychical Research report [on automatic writing]. He said I evidently had a logical mind! He found it hard to keep the threads clear! Horrid sarcasm." On another occasion seeing that Miss Bosanquet was reading a book on spiritualism he told her a "new era" was dawning in these matters. Miss Bosanquet discussed psychical research with Peggy, now a young woman of twenty-two. Seven years had elapsed since her uncle had taken her to Queen Victoria's funeral. Peggy often sought Miss Bosanquet's company and they went on walks together. "Miss James hasn't much sense of humour, which makes her just a bit heavy in hand." She described Peggy as swarthy-complexioned, pleasant and intelligent-looking with a lot of literary taste. James took his niece to a suffragette lecture in Rye and Miss Bosanquet reported the occasion was "very inspiring." She found Mrs William James "most pleasant" —"a fine strong face framed with white hair. Her daughter is just like her."

On 27 July 1908: "In the course of the morning Mr James made me go and peep through the curtain to see 'the unspeakable Chesterton' pass by—a sort of elephant with a crimson face and oily curls. He [James] thinks it very tragic that his mind should be imprisoned in such a body."

Chesterton's presence in Rye produced another incident which H. G. Wells remembered. On this occasion it was William James who climbed the gardener's ladder to peep over the wall at Chesterton. Henry apparently felt it all right to look out of his own window at Chesterton as passer by, but that it was wrong to invade privacy in William's fashion. They quarrelled about this, Wells remembered, when he arrived in a car to fetch the William Jameses and Peggy for a visit to his home at Sandgate. James appealed to Wells. "It simply wasn't done, emphatically, it wasn't permissible behaviour in England"—this was the gist of Henry's appeal. "Henry had instructed the gardener to put away that ladder and William was looking thoroughly naughty about it." To Henry's relief Wells carried off William in his car. They passed Chesterton, so the pragmatist met him after all—and Chesterton invited William to come and see him. Henry and William paid a call. William's diary records "at nine to Chesterton's where we sat till midnight drinking port with Hilaire Belloc."

Harry, William's oldest son, now twenty-nine, visited briefly at Lamb House that summer and was interested in his uncle's methods of dictation. A successful executive, he had taken the Syracuse properties of the Jameses in hand and improved their yield. When Henry James began to receive more substantial sums he tended to impart occult financial powers to his nephew. Harry had the dignity and the distinction of the Jameses and the same "heavyness" that Miss Bosanquet noted in Peggy. He would stand all his life in the shadow of a distinguished father and a celebrated uncle. But he would achieve a certain quiet eminence of his own. From William he picked up a certain condescending air towards his uncle which appears in his letters to his parents. But his uncle loved him and his financial skill, and made him his executor. During this summer William's youngest son Alex, aged seventeen, came to Lamb House also and Henry found him shy, silent, too withdrawn, but "a dear young presence and worthy of the rest of the brood."

William, in a letter to their younger brother Robertson, said he found Henry James stolid and grave, the natural result of the years; he seemed to have lost none of his early pleasure in the possession of Lamb House. Henry on his side was impressed by William's vitality. In spite of several heart attacks, William refused to obey the doctors. He took long walks, insisted on vaulting over gates and stiles and was "in general better, I think,

than I have of late years *ever* seen him." To his Emmet cousin,
Bay, the painter, Henry wrote late that autumn: "It was an infinite interest to have them here for a good many weeks—they
are such endlessly interesting people, and Alice such a heroine of
devotion."

THEATRICALS: SECOND SERIES

IN the midst of his work on the New York Edition, Henry
James received new overtures from the theatre which he had
abandoned in such pain twelve years earlier. To be sure, in 1895,
immediately after the failure of *Guy Domville*, he had written a
one-act play for Ellen Terry, but that had been for her American
tour. She had never produced it: one more proof for James that
the stage was an "abyss." Yet it was this very play which now
returned to haunt the Master. In 1897 he had remade it into a short
story called "Covering End" and published it as a companion
piece to "The Turn of the Screw." Suddenly the actor-managers
were writing to tell him the story would make a good play!
Two managers approached James in 1899; he politely turned
them down. He had had enough of the treacheries of the
theatre.

Now, in 1907, Johnston Forbes-Robertson returned to the
charge. "Covering End," he told James, would be an ideal vehicle
for himself and his American wife, Gertrude Elliott, sister of the
famous Maxine. James was more receptive now; he found himself "re-aching and re-brooding and re-itching for the theatre in a
manner very uncomfortable to other concentrations."

With Miss Bosanquet installed behind the big typewriter and
his work on the Edition going smoothly, it seemed to James he
could try once again—it was after all simply a matter of re-
converting "Covering End" to its real, its original form. Moreover, Forbes-Robertson had asked him to expand the one act into
three; the thought of enlarging rather than cutting a play appealed
to James. He had always hated the cutting. To his friend Lucy
Clifford he wrote that he had re-read "Covering End" and it
seemed to play itself, "and I assented, for the lust of a little possible gold." It was to be played "without one bloody cut (which
is bribery and balmery to me)." It would be like doing some-

376

AET. 64 THE HIGH BID

thing in three Cantos or Stanzas with "two very short curtain drops without fiddles—in which case I get three-act terms for it." To which he added, as of old, the injunction that it was a deep secret, "I breathe the weird tale into your ear alone."

The language of his dramatic years was again on his lips—he would do it for gold; it had to be kept a secret; he hated the conditions of the theatre—but he would participate in the rehearsals. His old distinction between drama-stuff and theatre-stuff was suddenly voiced again, this time to another confidante, Edith Wharton. "I loathe the Theatre, but the Drama tormentingly speaks to me." It spoke sufficiently for James to write *The High Bid* (as "Covering End" was now called) in twenty days; and then to go on to a scenario of one of his old short stories "The Chaperon," (Pinero had told him it would make a fine comedy), and then a one-act play based on his story "Owen Wingrave." After that he began revising *The Other House*, which he also had converted to fiction, and now reconverted into its original form. Miss Bosanquet found herself typing scripts and underlining the stage directions. James began attending rehearsals. He was repeating his old experiences with the Comptons and the 1890 production of *The American*. He was charmed; he was sanguine. "Whatever happens," he wrote to Lucy Clifford, "it is a very *safe* and neat and pleasing (orthodox-pleasing) little invention— which no monstrous doom can overtake." This was his way of saying that he did not fear a repetition of the débâcle of *Guy Domville*.

The try-out took place in Edinburgh in March 1908. James had joined the troupe at Manchester and they journeyed by special train, "I travelling with the animals like the lion-tamer or the serpent-charmer in person and quite enjoying the caravan-quality, the bariole Bohemian or *picaresque* note of the affair." The omens were good. The little play was "pretty and pleasing and amusing and orthodox and mercenary and *safe* (absit omen!)—cravenly, ignobly *canny*: also clearly to be very decently acted." James was so confident that he invited Lucy Clifford to the first night and when Jocelyn Persse, then travelling in Algeria, expressed an interest, he invited him also. Jocelyn made the long journey and was James's guest throughout the first-night festivities. The production was well received; but James cautiously disappeared at the time of the curtain calls. As with *The American*, he felt the play needed a London production. He liked the way in which Gertrude Elliott played Mrs Gracedew, the American widow who arrives as a tourist in an English country house and pleads with its owner, Captain Yule (played by Forbes-Robertson) for the house's preservation on grounds of tradition, history, art, a cherishing of the past. James's central irony was that the American woman should turn out to be more English than the English. It was the sort of thing that might have been expected from James before *The American Scene*, but hardly after. The play would have been fine in the 1890's; in the Edwardian period it was out of date. Audiences had had a great deal of Bernard Shaw; they were "socially-minded." To the embarrassment of Gertrude Elliott they applauded the "radical" speeches of her husband in the play rather than her own romantic–historical flights. When she delivered her emotional appeal, "Look at this sweet old human home, and feel all its gathered memories," the audience refused to share her feeling. But when Captain Yule, a liberal and socialist-tinged member of parliament answered, "I see something else in the world than the beauty of old show-houses and the glory of old show families. There are thousands of people in England who can show no houses *at all*," the audiences burst into applause. Gertrude Elliott asked James to do something about this. The Master could do nothing, short of scrapping the entire play and writing one in the vein of Shaw.

Forbes-Robertson sensed this. He felt the play was far too delicate for the theatre audiences, it had too much "literary elegance." His actor's instincts told him that a script he had received from Jerome K. Jerome titled *The Passing of the Third Floor Back*—about a stranger in a lodging house, who seemed to be a reincarnation of Christ—might have greater success. James was derisive and angry. He predicted to Lucy Clifford instant failure or at least an "imperfect success." Then remembering that strange things could happen in the theatre, he also said that it might have a "most rapturous success." To Miss Bosanquet he remarked that "Jesus Christ is the main character and of course one has to realize that He's a formidable competition." The play ran for four years; it made Forbes-Robertson's fortune. The best the actor and his wife could do, to keep their commitment to James, was to perform *The High Bid* for five matinées. This attracted the Jamesian type of audience and got him excellent notices from such ardent followers as Max Beerbohm and A. B. Walkley. Max's review began by describing Forbes-Robertson making his exit in *The Passing of the Third Floor Back* with enough of a halo of light to suggest there had been something holy about his presence in the Bloomsbury lodging house; then it seemed as if the stage had revolved and Forbes-Robertson re-entered the old English house, in his street clothes. It was "rather a long way for an actor to travel," said Max but Forbes-Robertson accomplished the journey with distinction. One moment he was the Christ-figure and the next he was a radical member of parliament saying, "What are you exactly?" to an old family butler—"I mean, to whom do you beautifully *belong*?"

"There, in those six last words," wrote Max, "is the quint-essence of Mr James; and the sound of them sent innumerable little vibrations through the heart of every good Jacobite in the audience . . . The words could not have been more perfectly uttered than they were by Mr Forbes-Robertson. He realized at once to whom *he* beautifully belongs. It is to Mr Henry James . . . In his eyes, as he surveyed the old butler, and in his smile, and in the groping hesitancy before the adverb was found, and in the sinking of the tone at the verb, there was a whole world of good feeling, good manners, and humour. It was love seeing the fun of the thing. It was irony kneeling in awe. It was an authentic part of the soul of Mr James." To which Max added, from the authority of his critical position and out of his adoration, "little though Mr James can on the stage give us of his great art, even that little has a quality which no other man can give us; an in-alienable magic."

James's renewed confidence in the theatre in spite of the limited production of *The High Bid*, sprang in part from the evolution of the English stage since the 1890's. The battle for Ibsen had been won. Arthur Pinero and Henry Arthur Jones had demonstrated, in their strong social dramas, that British audiences did not need to be fed trivialities. The new repertory theatres had followed. The plays of Bernard Shaw, aided by the directorial art of Harley Granville Barker, had taught audiences to accept a discussion of ideas if properly seasoned with a certain amount of clowning and a goodly measure of Irish wit. There were new men and new audiences in the theatre; and if they did not wholly satisfy the Master, they were the sort of people he could talk to — they were closer to art and letters than the older stage-tinkers. James had seen the Shaw plays, usually with Jocelyn Persse — *Man and Superman*, *Major Barbara*, *The Doctor's Dilemma*; he had gone to Barker's *Voysey Inheritance*. He had met Barrie and Galsworthy and joined them in their attack on the censorship of British plays, writing a letter which was read into the proceedings of a Royal Commission and is buried in an ancient blue book — a letter almost Miltonic in its phraseology. Censorship tended to deprive the theatre, James wrote, "of intellectual life, of the *importance* to which a free choice of subjects and illustrations, directly ministers, and to confine it to the trivial and the puerile." Censorship in England had the effect of relegating drama "to the position of a mean minor art, and of condemning it to ignoble dependencies, poverties, and pusillanimities."

If James stood now with the dramatists, and was received in their midst with respect and even awe, he found himself engaged in an unexpected debate with the wittiest and most didactic of the new men. The Master had converted "Owen Wingrave," his old ghost story about a young pacifist in a military family, into a one-act play *The Saloon*, in the hope that the Forbes-Robertsons would use it as curtain-raiser to *The High Bid*. Another play was used and James was induced by St John Hankin to submit it in 1909 to the Incorporated Stage Society which gave subscription

performances of non-commercial plays. The script was read by
the board members and rejected by them. The minutes of the
board of 12 January 1909, record that "Mr Bernard Shaw under-
took to write to Henry James with reference to *The Saloon*." Five
days later Shaw carried out his undertaking beginning, in anticipa-
tion of the era of broadcasting: "Shaw's writing—Bernard
Shaw."

He had read *The Saloon* he wrote and it had been "sticking in
my gizzard ever since." That play needed another act—by
James's father, an allusion by Shaw to the elder Henry's general
optimism. Shaw found the play too deterministic and pessimistic
for his taste. "What do you want to break men's spirits for?" he
queried. "Surely George Eliot did as much of that as is needed."
The dramatist then developed a Shavian version of the play. Did
James think his hero would have been seriously beaten by the
ghost? He was referring to the fact that Owen Wingrave is killed
by his military ancestor, punished for his strong pacifism. James
had tried to establish the irony that the military "conditioning"
Owen had received enabled him to fight and die for his pacifism
like a young soldier. To Shaw, arguing as a socialist, this kind of
determinism was anathema. He spoke of "that useless, dispiriting,
discouraging fatalism which broke out so horribly in the 1860's at
the word of Darwin, and persuaded people in spite of their own
teeth and claws that Man is the will-less slave and victim of his
environment." As a Marxist he knew "the enormous power of
the environment as a dead destiny," but "we can change it: we
must change it: there is absolutely no other sense in life than the
work of changing it." In effect Shaw argued that the play should
be rewritten—Owen Wingrave should kill the ghost, not the
ghost Owen. And Shaw quoted Dr Johnson's "I, sir, should have
frightened the ghost." Instinctively Shaw touched a deep part of
James's life. Had not his dream of the Louvre been just that? In
his dreams James succeeded in frightening his ghosts. It was in
his waking state that he found them overpowering. Shaw ended
his letter:

It is really a damnable sin to draw with such consummate art a houseful of
rubbish, and a dead incubus of a father waiting to be scrapped; to bring on

for us the hero with his torch and his scrapping shovel; and then, when the
audience is saturated with interest and elated with hope, waiting for the
triumph and the victory, calmly announce that the rubbish has choked the
hero, and that the incubus is the really strong master of all our souls. Why
have you done this? If it were true to nature—if it were scientific—if it
were common sense, I should say let us face it, let us say Amen. But it isn't.
Every man who really wants his latchkey gets it. No man who doesn't
believe in ghosts ever sees one. Families like these are smashed every day
and their members delivered from bondage, not by heroic young men, but
by one girl who goes out and earns her living or takes a degree somewhere.
Why do you preach cowardice to an army which has victory always and
easily within its reach?

People needed, Shaw said, "encouragement" and he repeated that
word five times and signed his name. Thus spoke Shaw, espousing
in effect the idea that art should be didactic, that it should be a
vehicle for a social idea—especially a socialist idea. James pondered the letter for a week. It must have given him some trouble:
for Shaw had the same wit and a certain native irrationality akin
to James's father's. There was indeed much in common between
the Irishness of Shaw and the elder Henry James; to answer Shaw
was a little like trying to answer the father in Quincy Street.
Which explains why Henry dictated 3000 words of reply to Miss
Bosanquet, beginning with a long explanation of "why" and
"how" he had written the play. James chose, however, not to
argue with Shaw's Marxism. On this point he simply answered
"you strike me as carrying all your eggs, of conviction, appreciation, discussion etc. . . . in one basket, where you put your hand
on them all with great ease and convenience; while I have mine
scattered all over the place—many of them still under the hens!
. . . You take the little play socialistically, it first strikes me, all too
hard." Shaw has asked him why he did such things and James's
answer was:

I do such things because I happen to be a man of imagination and taste,
extremely interested in life, and because the imagination thus, from the
moment direction and motive play upon it from all sides, absolutely enjoys
and insists on and incurably leads a life of its own, for which just this vivacity
itself is its warrant. . . . Half the beautiful things that the benefactors of the
human species have produced would surely be wiped out if you don't allow
this adventurous and speculative imagination its rights.

James went on to say the only way in which *The Saloon* could be "scientific" would be that it be done "with all the knowledge and intelligence relevant to its motive." As for people wanting not works of art but "encouragement," James could only reply that works of art were "capable of saying more things to man about himself than any other 'works' whatever are capable of doing." The Master concluded that he viewed with suspicion the "encouraging" *representational* work. It would be necessary to determine "what it is we have to be encouraged or discouraged *about*." He added he had been "touched and charmed by the generous abundance" of Shaw's letter.

Shaw answered briefly and militantly. James was trying to evade him, he said. "The question of whether the man is to get the better of the ghost or the ghost of the man is not an artistic question: you can give victory to one side just as artistically as to the other. And your interest in life is just the very reverse of a good reason for condemning your hero to death. You have given victory to death and obsolescence: I want you to give it to life and regeneration."

James's rejoinder pointed out to Shaw that he was quarrelling with the subject itself and that every artist had to be allowed his subject. Criticism had to criticize what was *done* with the subject; the subject itself belonged to the artist. One could dislike it, but that was another matter. There was no competition between man and ghost in the play. Owen Wingrave actually wins the victory, James argued, even if he pays for it with his life. What sort of play would it be if there were no danger and no resistance? It was Owen's resisting this danger and doing so with the courage of a soldier that constituted the drama. So James argued. "You look at the little piece, I hold, with a luxurious perversity; but my worst vengeance shall be to impose on you as soon as possible the knowledge of a much longer and more insistent one, which I may even put you in peril of rather liking."

Thus ended James's first debate with one of the new men: a debate which foreshadowed the entire question of didactic art in the twentieth century—art in the service of a theory or a state. In reality it was also a debate between a writer concerned with the deeper psychological truths and one whose art rested on satire and intellectual humour. "Almost all my greatest ideas have occurred to me first as jokes," Shaw said to James. Implicit also in this debate was James's taking the world as he found it, and seeking to demonstrate its realities and existential absurdities. Shaw took the world as a place in which art had to serve revolt. There is no doubt that Shaw could have written a diverting play on the same theme, but it would not have touched the conflict and ambivalence of James's hero, whose energies and courage derive both from his constituted temperament as well as his pacifistic ardour. In a word James was saying to Shaw there was the question of "human nature." Shaw was brushing this aside and saying "let's change the system."

III

In this second series of theatricals—a mere skirmish in the theatre compared with the battles of his "dramatic years"— James had in effect two failures. *The High Bid*, written ostensibly for revenue, had had its five matinées and was on the shelf; *The Saloon* had yielded only a pleasant exchange on the high plane of "the purposes of art." James was, however, not discouraged. He refurbished *The Other House*. He had sketched it in 1894 as an "Ibsen-type" play. In 1896 he published it as a novel. The novel had been all dialogue and stage-scene from beginning to end. It was easily reconverted. In June of 1909 Herbert Trench, the Anglo-Irish poet-scholar, planned a repertory at the Haymarket and paid James £100 for an option on this play. James pocketed the money. The play was not produced.

Early in the same year Charles Frohman, the American producer, began to plan a repertory season in London at the Duke of York's Theatre. The moving spirit behind the plan was J. M. Barrie who enlisted the help of Granville Barker. Allan Wade, a former actor associated with the Abbey Theatre's season in London, joined Frohman's staff; Wade believed that the theatre was suffering a great loss in not finding a place for the work of so great an artist as Henry James. Granville Barker and Barrie agreed with him; and thus it came about that James was invited to write a play especially for this repertory season. During the spring of 1909 he read *The Other House* to Harley Granville Barker one morning at the Reform Club. "But what we wanted from him was an original play, not an adapted novel," Granville Barker wrote, overlooking the origin of the play. The other dramatists were Shaw, Galsworthy, Granville Barker, Somerset Maugham, John Masefield, and Barrie. This time James found himself dealing not with a "managerial abyss" but with fellow-craftsmen. Shaw wrote *Misalliance*, Galsworthy *Justice*, Barker *The Madras House*, Barrie contributed *The Twelve-Pound Look*, and James wrote *The Outcry*. Wade later recalled his excitement in reading the manuscript "and my conviction that it would be far over the heads of our rather stupid audiences." He added: "It is true that James's dramatic sense was more in tune with the French than the English theatre of his day—but had he been given more occasion for actual and practical work in the theatre he would probably have been able to modify his tendency to excessive length and our theatre would have gained a really fine dramatist."

The Outcry was long and required cutting. Granville Barker remembered "he had to be induced to part with first one bit; then after a while another. But it was really necessary." The play was "topical." James made a comedy out of connoisseurship and the moral question involved in selling works of art abroad. In its quiet way it probably satirized Bernard Berenson and the whole question of art expertise. The young amateur art historian of the play, whose appearance, though not his personality, is almost an exact description of Hugh Walpole—he is called Hugh Crimble—recognizes in a great house a major work of art. The owner decides to sell it to Breckenridge Bender, an art dealer from America, a hard-headed and predatory Christopher Newman, not unfavourably drawn, but a man with a "really *big* Yankee cheque." The young art scholar and his fiancée, who is the daughter of the owner of the picture, decide to raise an "outcry." The picture must be kept in England. Then the Berensonian experts are called in. Was the picture a Moretto or a Mantovano? There was Pappendick, of Belgium, who says it isn't a Mantovano; and then Caselli is called in from Milan. He contradicts Pappendick.

N

James had never met Berenson and would meet him on only one occasion when he would describe him to Mrs Wharton as a "concentrated little commentator." But he had heard about the young Harvard precocity from Grace Norton as early as 1903. "I read over your letter and I come upon the Berensons, whom I don't know," he had written, "and as to *him* confess to him by others"—meaning he had heard about the young Berenson from Mrs Jack Gardner. James added that he knew him only by his association with that "writing upon art" which he had "long since come to feel as the most boring and *insupportable* identity a man can have. I am so weary, weary of pictures and of questions of pictures, that it is the most I can do to drag myself for three minutes every three years into the National Gallery. If *you* are not it is only because you live at Cambridge, Mass. You *would* be if you lived—at Rye, Sussex." Berenson would later say he didn't get along very well with James because James didn't like Jews. But the evidence seems to be that James was not interested in expertise and connoisseurs. At any rate his comedy on the subject seemed thoroughly manageable in the hands of another kind of expert, Granville Barker, who defended it from attacks on its "inhumanly literary" dialogue—Shaw's phrase. He said it was no more difficult to produce than a play of Chekhov's "and we long ago found out how to do that." The real problem with *The Outcry* was finding a cast capable of speaking James's lines. As Granville Barker put it the dialogue was "artificial—very; but that is legitimate. It might be hard to speak but I think that most of it could be made very effective once the right method had been found." Actors certainly could not blend it with "melodramatic" acting, this was probably the fault with *The Saloon*. He suggested that if *The Outcry* were placed "beside a Congreve and a Wycherley" it might "not be so good as the first but I believe you'd find more style and bite in it than in the second."

At the moment when the last volume of James's New York Edition came off the press, late in 1909, Harley Granville Barker was seeking a cast for *The Outcry*.

THE TONE OF TIME

HENRY JAMES was sixty-two when he began his work on the New York Edition and sixty-six when it was done. During these four strenuous years he had given proof of great resourcefulness and undiminished creativity—he had worked and taken holidays, written plays, and maintained his social life—to be sure at a reduced pitch, yet with a liveliness of spirit that showed him to be mentally and spiritually younger than his ageing body. He commented on this in one of his new year's letters to W. E. Norris. "I am engaged in a perpetual adventure, the most thrilling and in every way the greatest of my life, and which consists of having for more than four years entered into a state of health so altogether better than any I had ever known, that my whole consciousness is transformed by the intense alleviation of it and I lose much time in pinching myself to see if this be not, really, 'none of I.'" The value of it, he wrote, still outweighed "the formidable, the heaped-up and pressed together burden of my years."

This sense of well-being had been evident ever since the completion of *The Golden Bowl*. That novel had represented some kind of resolution of old unconscious stress; and his subsequent trip to America had smoothed the sharper edges of his years'-long quarrel with his homeland, as well as the buried sensitivities of his relation with his brother. William's heart attacks which blighted his ageing, had reduced some of the tension in Henry. The Master, however, had the normal revolt of a powerful individual who feels his powers shrinking. To a friend he spoke with philosophical resignation of having left behind the period of "the Passions." He likened this to "the quiet Atlantic liner alongside the wharf after the awful days out in the open." He continued to identify himself with the young; and he expressed this as a mixture of affection and envy. Long ago he had written in his notebooks that "youth" was the most beautiful word in the language.

He had accustomed himself to the dropping away of old friends. It was always a wrench. Henry Harland died in 1905, comparatively young, of tuberculosis. He had had an easy talent which James praised; he considered him the supreme case not of the expatriate—*that* case was himself—but of the *dis*patriate. Harland had genuinely detached himself from America. He had worshipped James, maintaining the novelist's intellect ranked with Aristotle's; and he insisted also that James was as great as Tolstoy and Balzac. This was a large order: but James glowed in his praise. Then the Master had lost Hamilton Aïdé, whom he had met in endless drawing-rooms of late Victorian London. Aïdé had been a supreme dilettante: he wrote novels, verses, plays, composed music, gave admirable parties, was the cultivated man-about-town. James went up to London for his requiem service and was deeply moved. He looked about the church for the faces of certain common friends. For a while he wondered that they had not come; and then it came to him that they weren't there "simply because they were dead." Writing to several ladies of their common generation—Anne Ritchie, the Ranee of Sarawak, Rhoda Broughton, James said Aïdé's death made him feel as if the room "of the dusky p.m. of our common existence" had become greyer and poorer. One of its pink lampshades was gone.

In 1908 he lost one of his oldest friends, Charles Eliot Norton, who had published James's first book reviews, taught him to look at early Italian art, introduced him long ago to Ruskin, Darwin, Leslie Stephen. Norton had been a votary of culture in a barren America. James pictured him as a transmuted puritan who "could still plead most for substance when proposing to plead for style, could still try to lose himself in the labyrinth of delight while keeping tight hold of the clue of duty, tangled even a little at his feet." This had been Norton's ironic New England role.

II

His country life, with all its limitations, offered much solace to the ageing Master. "I have lived *into* my little old house and garden so thoroughly that they have become a kind of domiciliary skin, that can't be peeled off without pain." The time would come when he would shed this skin; but between 1905 and 1910 he found in Rye a new circle of friends whose firesides offered him tea and conversation at the end of his long walks; he found certain ideal walking companions; his life was not too lonely. He could enjoy many of the consolations of old age, not least his garden. His flowers won prizes at the local exhibitions; there had never been so many roses and carnations. And also there were perpetual teas and motors pulling into the cobbled street with un-expected visitors. The prevalence of the motor-car began to trouble him—"the realization of what, in a country as small as England, the motor may come to mean for people in quiet in-tended hermitages." He lost his dachshund Max and buried him in the small row of dog-graves at one end of his garden. He de-cided he would have no more pets. One hot summer a chameleon turned up on his lawn as from nowhere; it blushed and flushed black and brown and blanched to pinkish grey ten times a minute. James found him to be an exquisite little pet. And one night in a rage against a too-audible feline, he killed the creature on the lawn with a blow of his stick—and promptly was sick at the stomach.

To these years belonged a series of friendships in Rye itself. He had complained earlier of the dullness of his neighbours. Now he found an excellent walking companion in Sydney Waterlow, a brilliant graduate of Cambridge and contemporary there of Strachey, Woolf, Keynes, and others who would be part of the later "Bloomsbury Group." Waterlow was in the Foreign Office and married then to Alice Pollock, daughter of the eminent jurist. James had known her since her childhood. At a cottage called The Steps, James could stop for tea with an "elfin" lady named Alice Dew-Smith, who believed in psychical phenomena and had written a book called *The Diary of a Dreamer*. She had a witty pen and wrote miniature essays in the *Pall Mall Gazette*. One of her books was called *Soul Shapes*. He liked The Steps for on clear days it offered him a view across the Channel of Cap Gris-Nez. His characterization of Mrs Dew-Smith's dog as "a positive emetic" was long remembered in Rye. Miss Bosanquet described Mrs Dew-Smith as having "a rather plaintive face and weird brown eyes." She found her "interesting . . . I can well imagine her to be gifted with psychic powers." Above all James found in Fanny Prothero, wife of George Prothero, editor of the *Quarterly Review*, a new and lively woman companion. She was "Irishly amiable." They lived in Dial Cottage. Small, bird-like, direct, veracious, Fanny Prothero had easy access to Lamb House; she gave James advice unceremoniously about simple household matters; she used to descend below stairs, put her feet up on a chair, and chat with James's servants. They liked her easy democracy, little realizing that this was her way of keeping an eye on them for the Master. There is a kind of high euphoria in James's letters to her, a mixture of formal domesticity and easy affection. Fanny Prothero—later Lady Prothero—understood Henry James very well, and especially his ability to focus intensely on persons and things in their immediacy. She had been sitting with the novelist one day when he was ill and Miss Bosanquet remarked Henry James would miss her after she went up to London. "Well, Miss Bosanquet," Fanny answered, "Henry James is very fond of people when they are here, but I don't believe he cares a bit when they aren't. Anyone else who would sit by his bedside would do just as well. I've often noticed that, friendly and charming as he is, he is really quite aloof from everyone." She added: "It's the artist in him." It was also the Henry James who preferred to be alone rather than be bored. Fanny was never boring.

Leonard Woolf remembered Waterlow as an "infant prodigy" at Cambridge; E. M. Forster recalled him as "affectionate and kind" but also apt to alternate "the dictatorial with penitence." To Waterlow, who had the precision of his diplomatic training and kept an admirable diary, we owe a vivid account of James's characteristic talk during the long walks they took in and around Rye. James talked about current affairs, his immediate reading, his literary friends, his old memories. *On politics:* "He often wondered how so complete and cumbrous a thing as the British Empire managed to go on at all; there must be some mysterious tough element in it; perhaps it was simply easier for it to go on

than to stop . . . He felt tempted to call himself a rabid Socialist."
On the suffragettes: "all the signs of the beginning of a great
movement, in spite of the ease of ridiculing them for desiring
martyrdom on such cheap terms, 'for the terms *are* cheap.'" *On
Christian Science:* "A new religion growing before our eyes, just
like Christianity or Mohammedanism, but (stroke of genius)
addressed only to the comfortably rich." *On Taste:* "James said
his taste grew more and more delicate and sensitive. I said I found
I attached less and less importance to taste. A foolish remark, but
it drew the reply: 'Attach importance: that isn't what one ever
does or did to it. Why it attaches importance to one.'" *On Ibsen*
—James had been reading Gosse's book on the dramatist: "What
a bare, poor, miserable existence he had! What absence of contacts! That horrible café life . . . when he would sit day after day
on the red plush benches, glowering at every one and drinking—
champagne of all things, and more of it than was good for him.
What a way of establishing a contact with life!" *On Meredith:*
"You give these men of genius an inch and they take an ell . . .
Vittoria was like the opening of a series of windows on history
. . . But H.J. is always beset by a sense of the immense difficulty
of being really inside things . . . Then again what are we to make
of the England which Meredith draws: an England of fabulous
'great' people, of coaching, and prizefighting and yachting,
flavoured with the Regency, yet incapable of precise location
anywhere in space or time." *On Lord Acton:* "He was an intellectual dilettante—wallowing in curious intellectual luxury. An
interesting figure from his social station and his cosmopolitan
. . . There must have been a great fund of stupidity in anyone
who could write such long letters to Mary Gladstone." *On
Jusserand:* "A demonic little man, passionately devoted to his
country, and with a corresponding hatred of all others . . .
Jusserand's enthusiasm for our literature, and indeed for *any*
literature, was entirely fictitious—ingeniously worked up as
réclame to get him advancement and reputation some day."

One day James improvised a possible dissertation that could be
written about "the vulgarity of modern French literature." He
defined the vulgarity of the French "as consisting not in the

absence, but in the badness of their moral standards . . . They are blind to all real distinction of good and evil: hence that emptiness and thinness in their work which is what we mean by vulgarity. And it is just as real, he insisted, in France as in England tho' masked in France by perfection of form. In England there is constant vulgarity of form in addition to other vulgarities." *On Flaubert:* James described him as head and shoulders above the other members of his group. "His letters to his niece, indiscreetly published, are a wonderful picture: they show him *en pantouffles*, with trousers loose—unbuttoned—sitting on his w.c.—scribbling away to her. He was a gentleman—tho' sometimes not without a touch of *cabotinage*. None of the others were gentlemen; De Goncourt was only a *gentilhomme*."

Waterlow noted that James had "an extraordinary faculty of creating vivid pictures of persons in words. He adds, quite slowly, always taking his time about getting it precisely, the right epithet, one touch after another, until the whole portrait stands out clearly." What emerges from the diary of the diplomat is a sense of James's conversational improvisation, his continually skilled exercise in finer discrimination.

III

If a new circle of friends replaced the dead—friendships formed all in the new century, among Edwardians—James still kept in touch with certain old American friends; in his later years Howells crossed the Atlantic more frequently than before; and on each occasion, in London and in Paris, James saw him and revived in their talk many memories; in private and in print, his old friend, by now the *doyen* of American critics, remained loyal to his original admiration of James. James had also kept up a strange friendship out of his old 1874–5 New York days with the Manton Marbles—a Jamesian name if there ever was one. Marble was a famous bi-metallist; he had been an editor of the *World*; and James used to disappear for week-ends at their home near Brighton. It was a little corner of America which James could visit. Edith Wharton later said that she and her friends had a theory James "luxuriated" in the Manton Marble bathroom, rumoured to be one of the best-appointed in England. Marble's interests were only peripherally literary; he and James wrote doggerel to one another, and in the large batch of letters to Marble which survives, is to be found James's recantation of his early criticism of Walt Whitman and a fine letter expressing his doubts about the Shakespeare of legend and the Shakespeare of the plays.

Lady Ottoline Morrell now became a friend and James's visits to her are recorded in her diaries. There remained his old attachment to the crippled Jonathan Sturges, who was increasingly ill. "Sturges, poor unspeakable little demon, is at present at an hotel at Eastbourne with a nurse (and more or less without a bottle!). He has charming rooms over the sea, he motors a little; and this bland summer (I went over the other day to see him, and shall renew the pilgrimage) will have done something for him." But at Christmas of 1908 James made the journey again and found Jonathan "at the best, more and more, but the ghost of his former self." It was "pure tragedy—unrelieved."

One of James's less chronicled friendships was with Antonio de Navarro and his actress wife Mary Anderson who had retired from the stage on her marriage in 1890 and lived in Broadway, which James had often visited in the past and where he still maintained his friendship with the American painter Frank B. Millet. They had friends in common, particularly Sturges. Navarro was the son of an engineer who had created a steamship line to Cuba; he often wrote candidly to James about himself and his idleness. One answer suggests the tone of this friendship and the tenderness James could bring to his relations with friends.

I am very sorry to hear of your depressions and lassitudes, I scarcely know what to say to you about them. The want of a commanding, that is of an imperative occupation is a fertile source of woe—to an *âme bien née*—and you are in some degree paying the penalty of your "material" advantages themselves, your freedom of expatriation, your fortune, your living in a terrific "modernity" of cosmopolite ease (which has the drawback of not working you actively into the scheme of things here.) My own conditions resemble yours—that is as to ease of expatriation, and putting aside fortune and other *agréments*!—but I am luckily possessed of a certain amount of corrective to our unnatural state, a certain amount of remedy, refuge, retreat, and anodyne! From the bottom of my heart I pity you for being without some practicable door for getting out of yourself. We all need one, and if I didn't have mine I shouldn't—well, I shouldn't be writing you this now. It takes at the best, I think, a great deal of courage and patience to live—but one must do everything to invent, to force open, that door of exit from mere immersion in one's own states. You are young and gallant and intelligent—so, *allons donc*, there are still horizons!

Thus the fatherly Master who signed himself "my dear Tony, your always affectionate old friend."

IV

Max Beerbohm belonged to an older generation of James worshippers. He was of the 1890's and he had caricatured James first as a bearded Victorian and later as the clean-shaven ecclesiastical-looking Edwardian. Still later he would parody his style. His parodies had in them a great affection for the Master, a love that amounted to veneration. Max was also slightly afraid of the massive overpowering personality—he having remained the eternal mischievous small boy who mocked his elders. James was very much an Elder. Max's notes as reported by Lord David Cecil suggest what he saw—"priest—fine eyes—magnificent head—strong voice." He also noted: "Henry James took a tragic view of everyone, throwing up his hands and closing his eyes to shut out the awful vision. Rocking his chair and talking with tremendous emphasis . . . His talk had great authority; there was a great deal of hesitation and gurgitation before he came out with anything: but it was all the more impressive, for the preparatory rumble."

One of Max's most charming anecdotes was how one day, after lunching with Somerset Maugham, he strolled along Piccadilly debating whether to see an art show or to go to the Savile Club to read Henry James's new story in the *English Review*—"The Velvet Glove." While engaged in this debate he met Henry James himself, who asked about the art shows and expressed regret Beerbohm was walking in the other direction. "Now if only you were coming in *this* direction, and if we two together, could visit the collection you recommend . . ." Beerbohm always wondered why he lied: "Ah, if only I could! But I have to be in Kensington at four!" and went instead to the Savile and read James's story. It was a case, he used to say, of his "preferring the Master's work to the Master."

Max always regarded himself as James's disciple and this has led to the impression that they were great friends. But perhaps the reason Max walked away from James on this day in 1909 was that he sensed a certain reserve in the Master. Henry James was of two minds about Max. He liked his praise and his wit; at the same time he experienced the element of hostility implicit in caricature and parody even when it also contains a large measure of affection. This he explained one Sunday in February of 1913 during a walk with Sydney Waterlow. He had just read Max's "The Mote in the Middle Distance." James was "delighted with Max's parody of himself, only it affected him in a curious way: whatever he wrote now, he felt that he was parodying himself. He said the book was a little masterpiece, but deplored the cruelty of some of the attacks." James went on to say there was "something unpleasant about a talent which turned altogether to exposing the weaknesses of others. It was indelicate." And, said the Master, "the older I get, the more I hate indelicacy."

During these later years his public appearances were few; he avoided them as always, in spite of the extent to which he had displayed himself during his American tour. But buried in the London newspapers is an account of a rare occasion in which Henry James presided at a French lecture, by André Beaunier. The visitor spoke on Madame Récamier, and the reporter for the London *Times* seems to have captured the tone of James's talk. "Mr James intimated the sphere in which French literature delights, but where Anglo-Saxon literature, not possessing the precious secret, falls heavily. This was the sphere of 'the complex relations between the sexes; of the subtler shades of passion; of the mysterious justice, of sensibility in regard to give and take.'" James, said the reporter, deplored the Anglo-Saxon's lack of appetite for the finer and deeper meaning of these things. "The quality of his curiosity was not rightly tempered; his intellectual feeling lacked the light pressure natural to minds which breathed an atmosphere so drenched in literature as that of France." James went on to say that Frenchmen did not confine their taste for exercises and sports to the physical world. "The position of the person called 'lady friend' in Anglo-Saxon was ambiguous—she was either in Byron's company 'the unlady' or in Carlyle's 'the lady'—she was not herself." James ended by complimenting M. Beaunier on his novel *Siméon et Picrate* "as unlike an English novel as an orchid is unlike a cabbage."

THE YOUNGER GENERATION

A FTER forty-five years of "the literary life" Henry James's
reach could now go far beyond the memory of the young.
He could evoke Thackeray out of his childhood, Dickens out of
his youth, Flaubert and the heart-warming Turgenev out of his
maturity. He remembered Tennyson and Browning, Trollope
and George Eliot. And then there was his trans-Atlantic reach as
well: he talked of Emerson and Lowell as friends and neighbours.
He was that strange "relic," unique and larger than life because he
had become legendary—an Anglo-American Victorian. Now he
was meeting the young, of the unpredictable future, the "Bloomsbury Group" in especial, before it became Bloomsbury or, in the
public mind, a "group." At one time or another his path crossed
that of every member of "Old Bloomsbury," as Leonard Woolf
would characterize the first generation of the gifted men and
women who were dedicated to the overthrow of the Master's
world—who sought the New at the very moment he cherished
the Old; and yet who looked at him with a mixture of affection
and veneration. It was strange that Lytton Strachey, in full revolt
against the Victorians, should still scan the windows of Lamb
House and there see—as large as life—Henry James, looking
into the street. The New faced the Old for one brief minute, the,
as yet, beardless Strachey and the clean-shaven Master who had
once worn a beard. Strachey wrote to his friend Virginia Stephen
that the face he saw through the glass seemed like "an admirable
tradesman trying to give his best satisfaction, infinitely solemn
and polite." Strachey wondered how such an individual, with his
large embonpoint, could be the author of *The Sacred Fount* or
those late novels to which he had thrilled as an undergraduate at
Cambridge. "Perhaps if one talked to him one would understand." The next day James walked into the Mermaid Inn, in Rye,
where Strachey was staying, to show the antique fireplace to a

Spanish painter named Gustave Bacaresas, a friend of Hendrik Andersen's who had come to Rye for the day. Strachey described James as looking "colossal;" "I long to know him," he wrote to Virginia. This was in 1907.

E. M. Forster had tea with the Master once in 1908 in Lamb House. James mistook him for G. E. Moore, the Cambridge philosopher whom he had met with that other future member of Bloomsbury, his neighbour Sydney Waterlow. Forster's diary records, "we sat in a detached room—glimpse of fine study as we passed. H.J. very kind. Laid his hand on my shoulder and said: 'Your name's Moore.'" Forster also noted, "Head rather fat, but fine, and effectively bald. Admired the Queen's letters." (A. C. Benson's edition of Queen Victoria's letters had been published in the autumn of 1907.) James remarked, "She's more of a man than I expected." When one of the guests said that the Queen "underlines her words so," James rejoined, "Well, she's an underlined man." Forster also remembered James talking of Mrs Eddy. James believed Mrs Eddy must have said to herself, "hitherto things have been done *gratis* for the poor. I will provide for the rich and charge enormously." Forster's diary note concludes, "He was very anxious one should eat and drink. First great man I've ever seen—not alarming but that isn't my road." He would always be affectionately critical of the Master.

Desmond MacCarthy would be the most admiring of the "Bloomsberries." He had been at Cambridge with Woolf, Strachey, Waterlow, and Saxon Sydney-Turner, and had met James in 1901. The Master left a profound impression on the sensitive and critical MacCarthy, himself a novelist *manqué*. MacCarthy would be one of the great conversationalists of his time: James had long been a master of that art. The younger man remembered the extraordinarily unhurried quality of James's talk and his thought; and he recalled fumbling the first time he met him for what to say. He asked James if he thought London "beautiful." The Master gave this casual question the deepest cerebration. "London? Beautiful?" Then, "No, hardly beautiful. It is too chaotic, too——" A discourse on London followed that contained a remembered remark about "craving for a whiff of London's carboniferous damp." James also said "my books make no more sound or ripple now than if I dropped them one after the other into mud." MacCarthy assured the Master that in Cambridge he had been religiously read. James was sceptical. "I doubt if he believed," said MacCarthy, "that anybody thoroughly understood what, as an artist he was after." MacCarthy recalled that women seemed to open up volubly to James "as though they were sure of his complete understanding." The Master disliked poverty and was himself a great seeker of comfort, remarking after visiting what seemed to MacCarthy a reasonably prosperous home, "Poor S., poor S.—the stamp of unmistakable poverty upon everything." It is possible, however, that James may have caught certain tell-tale signs not seen by MacCarthy, to whom James also remarked "I can stand a great deal of gold." They were at that moment in an exceptionally gilded drawing-room. In a moment of insight, MacCarthy once expressed to James a thought about his problems as a writer—he was never capable of a sustained work. Perhaps, he said, writing made him feel "absolutely alone." James's answer was, "Yes, it is solitude. If it runs after you and catches you, well and good. But for heaven's sake don't run after *it*. It is absolute solitude."

A late visit to James was recorded by MacCarthy in an unpublished letter to Virginia Woolf. James had been ill. MacCarthy was admitted to the Cheyne Walk flat into which James had recently moved by the diminutive "rock-faced" Burgess who said the Master was unwell. MacCarthy turned to leave. James summoned him. He found him sitting in an armchair with a foot rest, his eyes half-shut. He seemed to speak with difficulty, "as though whenever his lips closed, they were stuck together and the wheels of his mind turned with a ponderous smooth difficulty, as though there was not steam enough to move so large an engine." James asked MacCarthy not to smoke; he rang for tea. "If I take tea it will either kill me or do me good, what shall I do?" MacCarthy refused to take so momentous a decision. The conversation laboured.

Gradually I became aware, however, that we were making progress. We began to talk about the power to visualize memories and imaginary scenes.

He seemed to think that a novelist's power depended on it. I admitted that in his own case the dependence was masked, but in that of others was not the ocular nerve of the reader often positively starved—and with admirable results? Fielding for example—there wasn't a picture on a single page of him! Then we went through the novelists with this idea in our heads, and he read to me. All the time he was getting brisker and brisker till at last from a semi-comatose condition he began to grow positively lively—shovelling on coal and eating cold tea cake and sweet buns. I enjoyed my afternoon extremely.

II

Through Thackeray's daughter Lady Ritchie (whose sister had been the first Mrs Leslie Stephen) Henry James occasionally had news of the Stephen girls, Virginia and Vanessa—the first destined for literature as Virginia Woolf, the second for art as Vanessa Bell and both at the centre of Old Bloomsbury. He had known them as children. James had mourned the passing of their mother, the beautiful Julia Duckworth; and more recently of their father, whom he had esteemed most among the Victorians. In 1906 he was touched by still another death in that much-bereaved family, that of a brother. To Ann Ritchie he wrote: "I haven't really borne to *think* of the bereavement of those brave and handsome young Stephen things (and Thoby's unnatural destruction itself)—and have taken refuge in throwing myself hard on the comparative cheer of Vanessa's engagement—quite as if it were an escape, a happy thought, I myself had invented. So I cling to it and make grossly much of it."

He would make much more than he had anticipated; for when he met the young Clive Bell he actively disliked him. He found him crude, bohemian, earthy, wholly out of key with his image of the ethereal Vanessa and the beautiful Virginia. These opinions he confided to his old friend, the "Aunt Lucy" of his London days—Lucy Clifford. "Oh yes, I went to see Vanessa Stephen on the eve of her marriage (at the Registrar's) to the quite dreadful-looking little stoop-shouldered, long-haired, third-rate Clive Bell—described as an 'intimate' friend of poor, dear, clear, tall, shy superior Thoby—even as a little sore-eyed poodle might be an intimate friend of a big mild mastiff." He presumed Vanessa knew what she was doing. She seemed very happy and eager and "almost boisterously in love (in that house of all the Deaths, ah me!) and I took her an old silver box ('for hairpins,') and she spoke of having got a 'beautiful Florentine teaset' from you." Virginia, James reported, had "grown quite elegantly and charmingly and almost 'smartly' handsome."

He added: "I liked being with them, but it was all strange and terrible (with the hungry *futurity* of youth;) and all I could mainly see was the ghosts, even Thoby and Stella, let alone dear old Leslie and beautiful, pale, tragic Julia—on all of whom these young backs were, and quite naturally, so gaily turned. I heard afterwards that the Vanessas, so to speak—for she is the whole housefront—almost missed their marriage altogether (for the time) by scrambling into the Registrar's after their hour and just as he was about to close. What a nuptial 'solemnity!'"

The Clive Bells spent the month of September in the year of their marriage at Playden, in that part of Rye where James had lived ten years before. His further view never reconciled the Master to Bell—and as late as 1912 he told Sidney Waterlow he could not cultivate the Stephen house in Gordon Square, because of the presence of "that little image." Waterlow recorded, "Tell Virginia—tell her—how sorry I am that the inevitabilities of life should have made it seem possible even for a moment that I would allow any child of her father's to swim out of my ken." And Waterlow, noting this, observed that under "all his absurdities" he found James "impressive for his real greatness and breadth of mind, as if an oracle spoke."

Virginia Stephen, during the 1907 summer at Playden, went to tea with the Master. She described on 27 August her progress down the High Street with James. He "fixed me with his staring blank eye, it is like a child's marble," (so would she years later describe the eye of Shakespeare in *Orlando*) and she then caricatured one of James's sentences: "My dear Virginia, they tell me, they tell me, they tell me, that you—as indeed being your father's daughter, nay your grandfather's grandchild, the descendant, descendant of a century—of a century—of quill pen and ink, ink, in, pots, yes, yes, yes, they tell me ahmmm, that you, that you, that you write in short." This went on, said Virginia, while "we all waited, as farmers wait for the hen to lay an egg, do they? nervous, polite, and now on this foot now on that." The future novelist said she felt "like a condemned person." If this made her uneasy it did not prevent her from noting the way James "made phrases over the bread and butter, 'rude and rapid' as it was, and told us of the scandal of Rye, 'Mr Jones has eloped I regret to say to Tasmania leaving twelve little Jones's and a possible thirteenth to Mrs Jones, most regrettable, most unfortunate, and yet not wholly an action to which one has no private key of one's own so to speak.'"

Leonard Woolf would wryly comment on James's dislike of Clive Bell and Saxon Sydney-Turner, two who "understood and admired him" far more profoundly than Sydney Waterlow and Hugh Walpole. Yet "all that the sensitive antennae recorded was that the young man was small, silent, and grubby." There was no accounting for antipathies; and Woolf did not know how much there was of admiration for "the crushed strawberry glow of Vanessa's beauty and credibility and the promise of Virginia's printed wit." To his old friend, Sara Norton, James recorded a glimpse of these fair visitors to Rye of that year. "Leslie Stephen's children (three of them—the three surviving poor dear mild able gigantic Thoby gathered in his flower) have taken two houses near me (temporarily) and as I write the handsome (and most loveable) Vanessa Clive-Bell sits on my lawn (unheeded by me) along with her little incongruous and disconcerting but apparently very devoted newly acquired *sposo*. And Virginia, on a near hilltop, writes reviews for *The Times*—and the gentle Adrian interminably long and dumb and 'admitted to the bar' marches beside her like a giraffe beside an ostrich—save that Virginia is facially most fair."

Some sense of his lost youth, his distant days with the parents of these girls, the feeling of the "generation gap," seems to have touched him profoundly at this moment. He had written to Lucy Clifford of "the hungry futurity" of youth. Now, with a flourish of the pen, he added in this letter to Sara Norton: "And the hungry generations tread me down!"

III

The future Bloomsbury males were of the generation of the turn of the century at Cambridge. Almost a decade later a new generation at Cambridge was still reading Henry James and worshipping him quite as much. On New Year's eve in 1907 Geoffrey Keynes, then at Pembroke, Charles Sayle, under-librarian at the University Library, and Theodore Bartholomew, an assistant librarian, decided to send a card of greeting to the Master. To their surprise he replied: "I am extremely touched and very grateful and all responsively yours, Henry James." Emboldened, they invited James to visit them at Cambridge. He was then involved in his second series of theatricals. No answer survives. They tried again on the eve of 1909. This time there came an encouraging response: "Yes, I really will come this year—about the May time I promise myself." They were strangers to him, but the Master now entered fully into the fun and admiration, which he found "most sustaining."

To his American friend Gaillard Lapsley, who was a don at Trinity, James wrote: "I literally go to Cambridge to stay for forty-eight hours, at 8 Trumpington Street with my bevy of 'admirers'—Charles Sayle, Geoffrey Keynes and the elusive Bartholomew (none of whom I have ever seen.) I feel rather like an unnatural intellectual Pasha visiting his Circassian Hareem!" The minutely-planned occasion began on 12 June 1909 and James returned to London on 14 June. Again to Lapsley he reported, "My Cambridge adventure was the lively exemplification of a leap in the dark—I having absolutely no données on my hosts, or host. But they were as kind to me as possible and I *liked* it, the whole queer little commerce, and *them*, the queer little all juvenile gaping group, quite sufficiently; so that the leap landed me on my feet and no bones are broken." His hosts had arranged a strenuous programme. He was given dinner on arrival, taken to a concert—Parry, Stanford, Mendelssohn, Wagner. James did not conceal his boredom. After the concert, back in Trumpington Street, they talked until late. One subject was Walt Whitman. James maintained that it was impossible for any woman to write a good criticism of Whitman or get near his point of view. The host, Charles Sayle, made one serious mistake: like James's typists, he tried to supply a word during a long-pondered sentence. James waved it aside. Sayle continued to try. The members of the triumvirate suffered. Breakfast, the next morning, was pleasant. James was escorted to King's Chapel and the University Library. At Pembroke, Keynes gave them lunch and guests were a professor of genetics; Sydney Cockerell, the director of the Fitzwilliam Museum; and Rupert Brooke. There was no question in the minds of the participants that the future war poet "made" the occasion memorable for the Master. We know that James visited the Fitzwilliam and talked of Byron and Tolstoy to Cockerell, that he met Francis Cornford, later professor of Greek, that he lunched with two future Bloomsburians, John Maynard Keynes (Geoffrey's brother), and H. J. Norton. Desmond MacCarthy, arriving late at this luncheon, claimed to remember James sitting "with a cold poached egg in front of him bleeding to death upon a too large, too thick helping of bacon, and surrounded by a respectful circle of silent, smoking, observant undergraduates." MacCarthy later claimed, though some disputed this, that James cross-examined him about Rupert Brooke. He told the Master the youth wrote poetry which however was no good. James was quoted as replying he was relieved "for with *that* appearance if he had also talent it would be too unfair." James was said to have advised Brooke "not to be afraid of being happy." This was Lambert Strether talking to Little Bilham. Other memories are of James telling of Carlyle's manner of lecturing, discussing the Russian ballet, and describing Ann Ritchie "her style, all smiles and wavings of the pocket handkerchief." The Master dismissed J. K. Huysmans and Pierre Louÿs "with opprobrium." "Excrement," he said of Louÿs. And he called *Kipps* "the best novel of the last forty years." The best-remembered episode was James reclining in a punt on velvet cushions—the image of the Pasha had come true—"gazing up through prominent half-closed eyes at Brooke's handsome figure clad in white shirt and white flannel trousers." Cockerell recalled James later saying he had been entertained "by young men whose mother's milk was barely dry on their lips." To Sayle James wrote a formal letter of thanks. He recalled he had been made to "loll not only figuratively but literally on velvet surfaces exactly adapted to my figure." He sent thanks to all "with a definite stretch towards the Rupert—with whose name I take this liberty because I don't know whether one loves one's love with a (surname terminal) *e* or not." In Brooke James had found one friend during that week-end. One of the last sentences the Master would write, after Brooke's death in the war, was in the preface to Brooke's *Letters from America*—recalling how he "unforgettingly" met him early in June 1909. Brooke reappeared in the memory "in that splendid setting of the river . . . as to which indeed I remember vaguely wondering what it was left to such a place to do with the added, the verily wasted, grace of such a person, or how even such a person could hold his own, as who should say, at such a pitch of simple scenic perfection."

HUGH

HUGH WALPOLE occupied a place apart among the younger generation in the Master's life. Leonard Woolf had wondered what James saw in Hugh when he could have admired the intelligence and perceptions of Clive Bell or Saxon Sydney-Turner. James hardly admired Hugh as an intelligence: there was something else which drew him to this young man who descended on London in 1909 hungry for success and invited the literary establishment to love him. He was ingenuous, good-looking and a bit pathetic in his reaching-out to people. "A nice boy, full of anxiety and good feeling," A. C. Benson wrote in his diary. Hugh continued to be anxious, and nice, and to possess good feeling. He had had a fragmented childhood. Born in New Zealand, uprooted when his clerical father moved to New York to teach theology, Hugh was sent to school in England at a tender age and had experienced the cruelties which older boys are apt to visit on the younger. His schooldays were a nightmare of pain and loneliness, during years when many children are accustomed to parental love. Things were better at Cambridge; Hugh went through exultations, agonies, a religious crisis. Now he faced the world, with a forward-thrusting chin and a boundless need for love. Sir Rupert Hart-Davis, in his admirable biography of Hugh, suggests this in the epigraph from Jean Paul: *Er liebte jeden Hund, und wunschte von jeden Hund geliebt zu sein.*

Hugh was unashamedly "on the make" as he settled into his small rooms in Chelsea; he got work as a reviewer; he clipped and sent his reviews to authors he wanted to meet. His letters were candid and naïve. He nearly always succeeded. To Henry James he wrote late in 1908 invoking Benson's name. James found the young man's candour appealing. He responded with a character-istic mixture of kindness and caution. "I rejoice that you were

406

moved to write it." On the verge of accepting the invitation of the Cambridge group James added "I always find myself (when the rare and blest revelation—once in a blue moon—takes place) the happier for the thought that I enjoy the sympathy of the gallant and intelligent young." He warned Walpole on the dangers of "the deep sea of journalism" and concluded "let me believe that at some propitious [hour] I may have the pleasure of seeing you." Walpole answered promptly and James replied. A. C. Benson had written him, he said, "that I shall not make a mistake in attempting, within my compass of the safely combustible, to feed your flame." Unable to resist a touch of irony, he added that "so dancing and aspiring" a flame scarce required "more care than you yourself can give it." He encouraged the young aspirant, "write me the letters and send me Books and pay me the visits; and above all keep as tight hold as you can of the temper and the faith of your almost unbearably enviable youth. I am a hundred years old—it's my one merit—but the breath of your enviability (that name says all for it,) quickens again, after all, yours with every good wish Henry James." James had sized up his young man, for he also would write him "you bleat and jump like a white lambkin on the vast epistolary green which stretches before you co-extensive with life . . . I positively invite and applaud your gambols." Thus began the friendship of Hugh Walpole and the Master.

I

They faced each other for the first time in February 1909 when James came up to London to attend a matinée of *The High Bid*. He gave the young Hugh dinner at the Reform Club. A bout of ill-health, his new involvement with the theatre, his sense of the passing years—James would be sixty-six that April—made him particularly receptive to the ardent worship of the outgoing young man. Walpole's diary records: "Dined with Henry James alone at the Reform Club. He was perfectly wonderful. By far the greatest man I have ever met—and yet amazingly humble and affectionate—absolutely delightful. He talked about himself and his books a good deal and said some interesting things. It was a wonderful evening." Never one to be shy, young Hugh also talked a great deal about himself.

The invitation to Rye followed. "Can you come some day—some Saturday—in April? I mean after Easter. Bethink yourself." And referring to Hugh's novel *The Wooden Horse* about to be published James added: "I am tender-hearted enough to be capable of shedding tears of pity and sympathy over young Hugh on the threshold of fictive art—and with the long and awful vista of large production in a largely producing world before him. Ah, dear young Hugh, it will be very grim for you with your faithful and dismal friend Henry James."

It wouldn't be in the least grim for the success-hungry Hugh. To be sure James would always be critical where craft was concerned; but he gave Hugh a very large measure of tenderness and affection. This was what the young man wanted. And if the Master was critical, the public was less inclined to be so. Hugh was a born story-teller. His novels flowed with the same steadiness as they had flowed from his predecessor and in some ways model, Sir Walter Scott. In future years, Walpole would be two or three novels ahead of his publisher; the printers could hardly keep up with him.

The aspirant came to Rye towards the end of April 1909. "I shall be here, at your carriage door with open arms (and with my handy man for your bag.) Bring a love-scene or something, and read it to yours immensely Henry James." The love-scene Hugh brought was his own responsive affection and his bright habit of demanding total commitment from those who showed any inclination to give it. As with Hendrik Andersen, as with Jocelyn Persse, the first visit and the chance for private communion in the Rye setting, had its effect on both Master and disciple. Youth responded to affection; age and loneliness to youth. Hugh's diary offers its testimony—"a wonderful week-end with Henry James. Much more wonderful than I had expected. I am very lucky in my friends. The house and garden are exactly suited to him. He is beyond words. I cannot speak about him." If he did not speak in his diary, Hugh would later record in *Fortitude*, one of the most successful of his early novels, the lessons of the Master; still later we can find the emotion of their meeting—Hugh's unbounded admiration and worship, James's unbounded delight in Hugh's brashness—in a tale called "Mr Oddy." James would always seem odd to Hugh, who felt overpowered by him. He named his fictitious novelist, both in novel and tale, Henry Galleon; James, in his obesity, his large Johnsonian body set on his short legs, must have seemed like some great old ship—and like those ships he was also, to Hugh, a great prize or catch. In *Fortitude*, Galleon talks to the young aspirant in simplified Walpolian sentences, but we catch the reverberation of the great style; the feeling rings true. The invocation to "the sacredness of your calling," the discourse on the treacheries of the market-place. "Some will tell you that you have no style—others will tell you that you have too much. Some again will tempt you with money and money is not to be despised." There would be publicity, lecture offers, dinners

... Worst of all there will come to you terrible hours when you yourself know of a sure certainty that your work is worthless. In your middle age a great barrenness will come upon you. You have been a little teller of little tales, and on every side of you there will be others who have striven for other prizes and have won them. Sitting alone in your room with your poor strands of coloured silk that had once been intended to make so beautiful a pattern, poor boy, you will know that you have failed. That will be a very dreadful hour—the only power that can meet it is a blind and deaf courage. Courage is the only thing that we are here to show ...

and again "Fortitude is the artist's only weapon of defence ... I have hurried, I have scrambled, I have fought and cursed and striven, but as an Artist only those hours that I have spent listening, waiting, have been my real life ... You are here to listen ... There must be restraint, austerity, discipline ... the Artist's life is the harshest that God can give to man ... I am at the end of my work. I have done what I can. You are at the beginning of yours. You will do what you can. I wish you good fortune."

Such words sealed their friendship. As with the young sculptor, James would have been glad to have the young writer stay on at Lamb House indefinitely. James talked of Thackeray and Dickens, Carlyle and Stevenson. "And then all his talk about the Novel and his own things is quite amazing," the ebullient

Hugh informed his mother. "It is a wonderful thing for me and will of course alter my whole life. He is, I think, really a great man." On another occasion, Hugh's diary again offers, "Such a day! H.J. talking all the time. Described Daudet's meeting with Meredith, smashed *Mrs Tanqueray*, argued with Robbie about the drama, long walk with me during which I told him about *Fortitude* and he approved. Final summing-up of everyone to me in the small hours of the morning." Robbie was Oscar Wilde's friend, Robert Ross, and the occasion for this diary entry was a week-end spent by James and Walpole at the home of Lady Lovelace.

To Benson, James wrote that he felt for "the delightful and interesting young Hugh Walpole . . . the tenderest sympathy and an absolute affection." He said that he was inclined to be sorry for "the intensely young, the intensely confident and intensely ingenuous and generous" but this was not the case with Hugh. "I somehow don't pity *him*, for I think he has some gift to conciliate the Fates. I feel him at any rate an admirable young friend, of the openest mind and most attaching nature." This was in June 1909. A month later he told Benson, "We have become fast friends; I am infinitely touched by his sympathy and charmed by his gifts . . . I wish him no end of ardent existence—feeling as I do that he can handsomely and gallantly carry it."

II

It must be recorded that in matters of craft very few of the Master's lessons rubbed off on young Hugh. He had talent and a kind of invincibility of desire that nothing could arrest in its impulse to self-indulgence and gratification. He had need of the fortitude but not of the courage that James preached. James was talking from the high places of art and from his arduous career in which his passion had been so largely present. We can quite believe Hugh's record in his diary of James's saying, "I've had one great passion in my life—the intellectual passion. What that has been for me I cannot say. Make it your rule to encourage the impersonal interests as against the personal—but remember also that they are interdependent." Hugh tended to do the reverse. He followed the personal rather than the impersonal. His nature spilled out everywhere and he found universal goodwill. He possessed neither James's sense of craft, nor his dedication; he was always active, always spontaneous. Success came to him easily. Perhaps it was his uncomplicatedness that appealed to James. Hugh would find love—the love of men, for he feared women, though he was attractive to them—and wealth, and be knighted, and lecture in America and have an honourable career and a loyal public. Of his relation with James he would write, a dozen years after the novelist's death, "I knew him only during the last ten [it was actually the last seven] years of his life. I loved him, was frightened of him, was bored by him, was staggered by his wisdom and stupefied by his intricacies, altogether enslaved by his kindness, generosity, child-like purity of his affections, his unswerving loyalties, his sly and Puck-like sense of humour." He also said, "I was a young man in a hurry, ambitious, greedy, excitable. I was not really vain. When he told me gently that I was an idiot and that my novels were worthless, I believed that, from his point of view, it must be so, and that if the world had been peopled with Henry Jameses I should certainly never publish a line. The world was not."

The letter James wrote to Hugh after his first visit to Rye suggests a kind of pact of affection between them. To "my dear, dear, Hugh," James writes that his "confidence and trust and affection are infinitely touching and precious to me, and I all responsibly accept them and give you all my own in return. Yes, all 'responsibly,' my dear boy—large as the question of 'living up' to our splendid terms can't but appear to loom to me." James seems to be speaking of his age, as he would speak in a later letter of his yearning for Hugh "in the most motherly, not to say grandmotherly, way." But now he wrote:

Living up to them—for *me*—takes the form of wanting to be more sovereignly and sublimely—and ah so tenderly withal!—good for you and helpful to you than words can well say. This is, in vulgar phrase, a large order, but I'm not afraid of it—and in short it's inspiring to think how magnificently we shall pull together, all round and in every way. See therefore how we're at one, and believe in the comfort I take in you. It goes very deep —deep, deep, deep: so infinitely do you touch and move me, dear Hugh. So for the moment enough said—even though so much less said than felt.

Hugh had asked James how he might address him and the novelist replied that "for the present" he might call him *très cher maître* or "my very dear Master." Hugh complied. The Master on his side was less solemn. He wrote "belovedest little Hugh," "beloved boy;" on one occasion "darling darling little Hugh" which in the same letter he laughingly abbreviated to "d.d.l.h." There were moments in which his passion overwhelmed him and the letters (very early in their friendship) spoke of his loneliness and betrayed a curious dependency. "I only want to be *in* your mind, and not a whit grossly 'on' it, while you can always believe and know that you're in mine quite as entirely. I am yours, yours, yours, dearest Hugh, *yours*! H.J." From Hugh's own remarks, and a later novel he dedicated to James's memory, one gathers that the young man saw the Master as a figure of physical as well as artistic power and sensed the masculine side of James within the "grandmotherly." A strong possessiveness is to be found in these letters as well. James pictures himself on occasion as an "old ponderous Elephant" reaching out to grasp Hugh with an embracing trunk. On another occasion the Elephant "paws you oh so benevolently;" still another assures him that the Master is "a steady old beast." James could however turn the Elephant into a faithful canine. "The old grizzled and blear-eyed house-dog looks up, that is, and grunts and wags his tail at the damaged but still Delectable Prodigal Son"—this when Hugh had written James of some bout of illness. There are all kinds of hints and allusions and bursts of jocular jealousy as when James chides Hugh for a dedication. "Who the devil is the Dedication-wretch of 'Mr Perrin' who has—the brute—'more understanding and sympathy than any one you have ever met.'" James most assuredly thought himself Hugh's most "understanding" friend. The Master proceeded then to dissect the novel, *Mr Perrin and Mr Traill*, mercilessly. Hugh did not have an "operative centre" in it; Mr Traill came through as someone with no capacity for experience. As with his critiques of Howard Sturgis, James brought heavy critical artillery into play, after which there followed an expression of love. "Don't feel that your infatuated old friend discriminates only to destroy—destroy, that is, the attachment to him that it is his very fondest dream all perpetually and intensely to feel in you."

There was no compromise on craft. He might flatter, praise, smother Hugh with affection; yet he gave him no quarter as a writer. In that respect he was the law-giving Master. His love was earthly; his philosophy of craft Olympian. They had been friends but a few months when Walpole sent James his second novel *Maradick at Forty*. James's answer was to say he had "in a manner" read it. He reminded Hugh he was "the grim and battered old *critical* critic." As always he complimented the young man on his love of life. However he found the book "nearly as irreflectively juvenile as the Trojans"—an allusion to Hugh's first novel *The Wooden Horse*. Hugh had written, said James, about "the marital, sexual, bedroom relations of Maradick and his wife" but "you don't tackle and face them— you *can't*. Also the whole thing is a monument to the abuse of voluminous dialogue, the absence of a plan of composition, alternation, distribution, structure, and other phases of presentation than the dialogue—so that the *line* (the only thing *I* value in a fiction, etc.) is replaced by a vast formless featherbediness—billows in which one sinks and is lost. And yet it's so loveable—though not so *written*. It isn't written *at all*, darling Hugh." Then James was contrite. "Can you forgive all this to your fondest old reaching-out-his-arms-to-you H.J.?"

Hugh forgave James inevitably, and did not betray the hurt. This he buried very deeply, and it did not surface until long after James's death when he wrote out a primordial fantasy in which a slayer becomes the man he slays and dedicated the book to the memory of the Master. This suggests the extent to which Hugh identified with James. It suggests also the inner mechanisms by which Hugh had learned to cope with the school bullies of his childhood—by becoming the bullies.

James's letters, even the most critical, breathe a cheerful affection, that of a man who enjoys Hugh's company enormously —whenever he can have it—loves his easy enthusiasms and his prattle and wants to do everything he can for him. He sent Hugh a large desk for his seaside cottage; he inscribed books; he insisted that Hugh pocket a £5 note during the first Christmas of their acquaintance. Hugh himself told the humorous incident of James's insistently giving him his top hat at the Reform Club in which Hugh felt uncomfortable and did not wear until middle age. On one occasion at Rye, when Hugh kept asking the Master what time it was (he wanted to catch a train), James took his watch from his pocket and gave it to him. He always dined him in London. Hugh's diary tells us 6 July 1909; "Had a ripping dinner with H.J. on Friday night. That is a quite perfect affair in its way and one begins to feel that the *one* thing that one really demands of the friend is perfect comprehension." The three-score letters which testify to this relationship are among the finest James ever wrote, in their playfulness, their mixture of affection and literary doctrine, their shrewdness, their breadth of feeling. At times these feelings become intense, although there is never in this correspondence quite the same "tactile" quality, the laying on of hands, which is to be found in the letters to Hendrik Andersen. James wrote with freedom both to Hugh and Hendrik, apparently on the assumption they were destroying his letters. "Chuck this straight into the fire," writes James at one point to Hugh, mainly because the letter is full of gossip. He adds, "I count on that being, by the way, where you *always* chuck me." Hugh no more could have chucked a James letter into the fire than could Hendrik. James's letters to Jocelyn Persse offer us a distinct contrast: they are less effusive and the affection in them seems to run deeper, it does not require articulation. With James and Hugh the correspondence is of writer to writer. The verbalization of love was important to both.

III

Hendrik Andersen was twenty-seven when James met him; Jocelyn was thirty; Hugh was twenty-four. James had loved Hendrik when he himself was in his fifties. He had reached his sixties and was increasingly ill when he met Hugh. They saw very little of each other during the first year of their friendship. The Master's illness of 1910 culminated in his going to America for a year, and the friendship was not resumed until late in 1911;

by that time Hugh was in the first great whirl of success; and the best part of their friendship, and James's finest letters, belong to the short time when James was turning seventy in that season of the century soon to be betrayed by 1914. Of these three significant late friendships, only that with Jocelyn seems to have had a genuine continuity; the friendship with Hendrik was doomed to be distant and James made an image of the sculptor that did not correspond to the reality. James saw brightness where there was dullness; and intelligence where there was mediocrity. With Hugh there was intelligence and the community of literature. With Jocelyn there seems to have existed a permanent sense of comradeship and unquestioned love. Still James could write to Hugh in the autumn of their first year of "our admirable, our incomparable relation," and echo the words he had used of his relation with Jocelyn, "we are in such beautiful, such exquisite, relation."

What that relation was must remain—beyond the evidence of the letters and the testimony of Hugh's diaries—a matter for conjecture. With James there is always a touch of "too late, too late" as with Lambert Strether, in his meetings with the young man. "I think I don't regret a single 'excess' of my responsive youth," James wrote on one occasion to Hugh, "I only regret in my chilled age, certain occasions and possibilities I *didn't* embrace." According to Hugh there was one occasion which James did not embrace. In his later years Hugh told the young Stephen Spender that he had offered himself to the Master and that James had said "I can't, I can't." Somerset Maugham, as we have earlier recorded, also told this story. It is interesting however to note how often Hugh, in later times, would emphasize James's "puritanism." Thus in his most important reminiscence of James, he wrote: "He was curious about everything, he *knew* everything, but his Puritan *taste* would shiver with apprehension. There was no crudity of which he was unaware but he did not wish that crudity to be named. It must be there so that he might apprehend it, but it must not be named. I was, alas, too crude myself to present anything without naming it, and I learnt to dread that shy look of distress that would veil his eyes as he apprehended my clumsy intrepidities."

A striking incident throws doubt on this. Hugh went regularly to Edinburgh, where his father was Bishop. There he met the Catholic priest, John Gray, who had been a friend of Oscar Wilde. He also met André Raffalovich, a European-Russian, author of a book on homosexuality, who was said to have wooed John Gray away from Wilde. Raffalovich had contributed to the building of St Peter's in Father Gray's parish and maintained a ritualized cultural salon in Edinburgh. To some it seemed as if the friendship of Gray and Raffalovich had been translated into religious emotion. Not to Hugh. In his life, religion and homosexuality had been carefully separated. He disapproved of Gray and Raffalovich but instead of saying this to James, or offering any gossip, he simply wrote—rather angrily—of "immorality on stone floors." Hugh said he couldn't say more: it made him suffer so. James's rejoinder was a mixture of laughter and affection. "That's the very *most* juvenile logic possible," wrote the Master. "*There* was exactly an admirable matter for you to write me *about*—a matter as to which you are strongly and abundantly feeling; and in a relation which lives on communication as ours surely should." Thus prodded, Hugh seems to have offered a fuller account. James was still not satisfied. "I could have done even with more detail—as when you say '*Such* parties!' I want so to hear exactly what parties they are. When you refer to their 'immorality on stone floors,' and with prayerbooks in their hands, so long as the exigencies of the situation permit of the manual retention of the sacred volumes, I do so want the picture developed and the proceedings authenticated."

This was doubtless what Hugh meant when he described how "curious" James could be. In public James was shocked by crudity. James saw Raffalovich shortly after this exchange, for in a note to Hugh he writes "Raffalovich of Edinburgh ('immorality on stone floors!') comes on Tuesday." And it was Raffalovich who told of an incident reflecting what Hugh called James's "puritanism." According to Raffalovich James once called on the Beardsleys "and Aubrey's sister (a beautiful and charming girl) pointed out to him on the stairs a Japanese print which shocked him. He called it a 'disconcerting incident' and always afterwards fought shy of her, though the print on the stairs was nothing startling. I remember once teasing him with a friend to know what the Olympian young man 'in the Cage' had done wrong. He swore he did not know, he would rather not know."

IV

Henry James once said to Hugh about a friend, "I not only love him—I *love* to love him." This was the way in which he loved Hugh. Years later Hugh would write: "His tenderness of heart was unequalled in the world." This he described as "a power of generosity, of loyalty and forgetfulness of self. It had a quality of sweetness quite unmistakable." James lived, Hugh said, "deeper down than the rest of us . . . had had experiences that he could communicate to no one . . . He was also a sick man during a great part of the time that I knew him, and I was then extremely healthy and as filled with vitality as a merry-go-round at a fair. It was this vitality that attracted and bewildered him. How could I have so much eagerness, so much real curiosity about life, so much interest in so many *different* things and yet penetrate life so thinly? Why, if I wanted to know so much, didn't I see that I knew more? When I visited Lamb House I must give in every detail, the full account of every adventure. There he would sit, listening, his head on one side like a stout and very well-dressed robin. But at the end of it I had omitted, it seemed, every essential."

In the year of his seventieth birthday James wrote a letter to Hugh, filled with deep emotion. "Cultivate with me, darlingest Hugh, the natural affections, so far as you are lucky enough to have matter for them. I mean don't wait till you are eighty to do so—though indeed *I* haven't waited, but have made the most of them from far back." In another passage the letter says:

Don't say to me, by the way, apropos of jinks—the "high" kind that you speak of having so wallowed in previous to leaving town—that I ever challenge you as to *why* you wallow, or splash, or plunge, or dizzily and sublimely soar (into the jinks element) or whatever you may call it: as if I ever remarked on anything but the absolute inevitability of it for you at your age and with your natural curiosities, as it were, and passions. It's good healthy exercise, when it comes but in bouts and brief convulsions, and it's always a kind of

o

thing that it's good, and considerably final to *have* done. We must know, as much as possible, in our beautiful art, yours and mine, what we are talking about—and the only way to know is to have lived and loved and cursed and floundered and enjoyed and suffered.

He went on to say to Hugh that the advice he was giving was bad doctrine for "a young idiot or a duffer; but in place for a young friend (pressed to my heart,) with a fund of nobler passion, the preserving, the defying, the dedicating, and which always has the last word."

A PASSION ON OLYMPUS

HENRY JAMES had spoken of Mrs Wharton as being "almost too insistently Olympian." It is doubtful, however, whether he would have written "The Velvet Glove" had he known how troubled and difficult life had become on Olympus. Her high life of the intellect had been a way of escape from a frivolous and imprisoning society and from a stifling marriage with a good-natured easy-going man who had no interest in his wife's ethical, moral, and artistic passions. Teddy was handsome, a perfect gentleman of his world, a bit eccentric; he was bored by his wife's constant reference of life to the things of the mind. He was bored too by some of her artist friends. He once remarked to James, "Puss wants to come over, but I feel much too well to want to stand her crowd." James replied: "But my dear Teddy, what's the use of a 40 horsepower Pierce Arrow if you can't fly away in it from any high-browed crowd?" For years Edith had closed her eyes to his indifference; she had taken him for granted; it had been pleasant in the earlier years to have him around, and he always let her go her own way. Otherwise she would not have registered with so great a sense of shock, in 1908 — when she was forty-six — a small episode which suggests that she had had an illumination. Reading John Locke and "struck by a curious and rather amusing passage" she held it out to her husband saying "Read that!" Teddy dutifully looked at the page. He answered with characteristic candour, "Does that sort of thing really amuse you?"

This had probably happened many times before and Mrs Wharton had shrugged it off without pain. Now, however, she seems to have listened with her whole being — and received a very clear message. "I heard the key turn in the prison lock," she confided to her diary. "Oh, Gods of derision! And you've given me twenty years of it! Je n'en peux plus." A breaking-point had been reached. She was finally facing the truth of her marriage, perhaps because she had also allowed herself to face the truth of her love for Walter Van Rensselaer Berry. They had known each other for years. She had taken him as much for granted in her life as she took Teddy. She would later say "he found me when my mind and soul were hungry and thirsty, and he fed them till our last hour together." Mind and soul! They no longer seemed to suffice. Suddenly she saw that Eros too lived on Olympus. Walter Berry had been appointed a judge of the International Tribunal sitting in Egypt and was leaving to spend three years in Cairo. Mrs Wharton had invested the passion of her younger years in freeing herself from her society and in becoming an artist. Other passions now seemed to assert themselves. With Berry gone and Teddy increasingly eccentric and irresponsible, she felt that her stable world was in collapse—in the very midst of her literary and social triumphs.

How intense her love for Berry had become we may judge from certain passages of feeling recorded in her journal, to which, however, Henry James understandably did not have access. Otherwise he would have known that the proud Diana—or Astarte—was no longer on her pedestal. "I am a little humbled, a little ashamed, to find how poor a thing I am, how the personality I had moulded into such strong firm lines has crumbled to a pinch of ashes in this flame!" She had said that "There is a contact of thought, that seems so much closer than a kiss." Now she discovered that "thought may be dissolved in feeling." It was a terrible—and a joyful discovery. She told herself that she had endured her marriage "all these years, and hardly felt it, because I had created a world of my own, in which I had lived without heeding what went on outside." Henry James had spoken of this to certain of his friends and had characterized the blindness of those who have been too "facilitated." Mrs Wharton had said to herself that one hour of love "ought to irradiate a whole life." Now she exploded, *Eh bien bon, ce n'est pas assez!*

Teddy was actually more ill than Mrs Wharton knew; he would eventually have to be committed to a sanitorium. Berry would remain a valuable intellectual friend. The world wondered at Edith Wharton's admiration for this smooth, impersonal, hand-

some and handsomely turned-out chamber-of-commerce man.
Percy Lubbock would speak of Mrs Wharton's "surrender" to a
man "of a dry and narrow and supercilious temper." "Life is not
a matter of abstract principles," she had lately written in *The Fruit
of the Tree* "but a succession of pitiful compromises with fate, of
concessions to old tradition, old beliefs, old charities and frailties
. . . that was the word of the gods to the mortal who had laid a
hand on their bolts. And she had humbled herself to accept the
lesson." It was a hard lesson: and it was the central drama in the
life of this brilliant woman who had fascinated and irritated Henry
James, and who now, bit by bit, began to discover, like her
heroine, new realities within the house of mirth. Edith began to
confide in the Master only after his second visit in 1908. And she
found at this time a new friend, who was also James's, the
journalist Morton Fullerton. The sentimental *homme de cœur* was
by now more French than the French. French poetry was constantly on his lips. He had written a small book in French. He
had some of the dignity and the bearing of Walter Berry; but he
was also softer, more gentle; there was a touch of the feminine in
his make-up. James had always been fond of him; and he now
appears in company with Mrs Wharton—they turn up at Lamb
House together. James goes on excursions with them; and
Morton's name begins to figure in the Master's letters to Mrs
Wharton. It is significant that in her memoirs Morton Fullerton
is not mentioned, although he appeared so much in her daily life
during the years that Walter Berry was away. Was she consoling
herself with Fullerton? A hypothesis might be advanced, with the
recollection that James had invoked Astarte among the goddesses
in "The Velvet Glove" and that the rites of that goddess were
celebrated by men dressed as women. James would say that in her
novels "the masculine conclusion" tended "so to crown the
feminine observation." Having grown up in a houseful of males
with her father and two brothers much older than herself, she was
most at home in the company of men; her intellectual masculinity
made it possible for a man of Berry's temperament to accept her
almost as if she were a man. But Fullerton's component of
femininity may have made him in turn highly acceptable to her.

Some such chemistry of personality was at work among Edith's friendships—certainly at Qu'Acre where the rite of Astarte was performed by a circle of younger men, not least the embroidering host, Howard Sturgis.

I

When Edith Wharton began to tell her troubles to Henry James he offered her the advice he had always given his friends—that one must "live through" an experience and try not to avoid it; that in life it was better to give way to tears than to hold them back; and also that one had to continue with the everyday things of existence—in a word keep a hold on reality. He warned Mrs Wharton against acting impulsively. The letter he wrote to her has long been known. Mrs Wharton herself allowed it to be published; but she removed certain passages from it. How much she told James about Walter Berry is not clear; but she seems to have frankly confided to him her unhappiness in her marriage. "Only sit tight yourself and *go through the movements of life,*" James replied, "live it all through every inch of it . . . waitingly." She must not, he said in a passage she withheld, let herself conclude anything in a hurry. "Anything is more creditable—conceivable—than a mere inhuman *plan.*"

Edith Wharton had by no means fully confided in James; for the Master remained curious as well as concerned. "I suffer almost to anguish for the darkness in which I sit," he wrote to her in April 1909, the month in which "The Velvet Glove" was published in a magazine. "I haven't for a long time known as little of you as these weary weeks—in fact *never* known as little probably in proportion to what there is to know. You must have been living very voluminously in one way or another—and however right it may serve me not to possess the detail of that, I have to invoke a terrible patience—which precludes no gnashing of teeth."

To this Mrs Wharton seems to have responded with greater candour. For in his next letter James told her he now saw "with all affectionate participation" that her anxiety had been "extreme." He added, "Poor dear Teddy, poor dear Teddy, so little made by all the other indications as one feels, for such assaults and such

struggles! I hope with all my heart his respite will be long, however, and yours, with it, of such a nature as to ease you off." He
urged her to "live in the day—don't borrow trouble, and remember that nothing happens as we forecast it—but always with
interesting and, as it were, refreshing differences."

Edith Wharton having had her conquest of Paris, had come to
England late in 1908—to English hospitality and rounds of
country visits of the kind the Master had long ago relished. She
also came and went in Lamb House. Writing to Walter Berry in
Cairo, Henry James described how Edith had been having "after
a wild, extravagant, desperate, detached fashion, the Time of her
Life. London, and even the Suburbs have opened their arms to
her; she has seen everyone and done everything and is even now
the occasion of some grand houseparty away off in the Midlands
whence she comes back to more triumph and will, I imagine, be
kept on here, in one way or another, till the New Year or the
arrival of Teddy." James was writing in December of 1908 before
Edith had confided in him. He went on to say that with Edith's
"frame of steel it has been remarkably good for her. But what a
frame of steel and what a way of arranging one's life! I have
participated by breathless dashes and feverish fits, but then had to
rush back here to recuperate and meditate."

II

To the young Cambridge men who gathered round the Master in
Trumpington Street in June 1909 and listened to his suavities he
seemed a quiet, sedentary slightly prickly figure. It little occurred
to them that Henry James was at the centre of a series of dramas
of passion. He had come to Cambridge from having seen Morton
Fullerton off to America. The bare notations in James's date-
books tell us how much he was moving about in the Whartonian
Olympus:

4 June 1909 Dine with Morton Fullerton and E. W. Charing Cross Hotel.
5 June Saw W.M.F. off to N.Y. at Waterloo 10 a.m. Went by motor with
E.W. to Guildford and thence by beautiful circuit to Windsor and Queen's
Acre.
7 June E.W. motored me long and beautiful run (to Wallingford.)

He was at Cambridge from 12 to 14 June. On the 15th he dined with Minnie Jones, Edith's sister-in-law and on the next "Dine with Mrs Wharton at Lady St Helier's." However, Jocelyn Persse and Hugh Walpole have to be squeezed into the crowded schedule. He lunches with Hugh, dines with Mrs Wharton; goes to Queen's Acre on 26 June with Mrs Wharton and motors the next day with her to see Mrs Humphry Ward at Stocks; on 28 June he motors with her and Howard Sturgis to Hurstbourne. During the first week of July he is at the Reform Club and then retreats to Lamb House where Jocelyn Persse spends the week-end of 10 July. On the 12th Persse leaves and "E.W. and Morton Fullerton arrived to dinner and for night." (Fullerton's trip to America had been brief.) On the next day Mrs Wharton motors James to Chichester and en route they stop at Eastbourne for lunch with Jonathan Sturges. On 15 July "Motored with Edith Wharton and Morton Fullerton to Folkestone and thence Canterbury where we lunched. They return to Folkestone for France—I returning to Lamb House by train." Two days later Hugh Walpole arrives to spend the week-end.

What these bare entries do not reveal is a drama within the drama. While Edith Wharton was living-out furiously her crisis of middle age, and consoling herself with Morton Fullerton (and the company of a young Englishman, A. John Hugh-Smith, a classmate of Percy Lubbock) the Gallo-American Fullerton was working out a crisis of his own—with the intimate participation and help of Mrs Wharton and Henry James. Some of the details are to be found in a series of letters Fullerton separated from his personal papers and entrusted to his sister Mrs Gerould. Fullerton had finally broken through a long reticence and confessed to James late in 1907 that he had been having a complicated love affair in Paris. He had rarely been available to come to Lamb House when the Master had beckoned and this had been a source of chagrin to James. James told him he stirred "my tenderness even to anguish." In language of reproach and caress he told Morton to have no compunction or apology for having "so late, so late, after long years, brought yourself to speak to me of what there was always a muffled unenlightenment and ache for my affection in not knowing." He had guessed at "complications" in Morton's life, yet had been "utterly powerless to get any nearer to." He was certain he might have been able to offer some moral help "and I think of the whole long mistaken perversity of your averted *reality* so to speak, as a miserable *personal* waste, (that of something—ah, so tender!—in *me* that was only quite yearningly ready for you, and something all possible, and all deeply and admirably appealing in yourself, of which I never got the benefit." The "clearing of the air," said James, "lifts, it seems to me, such a load, removes such a falsity (of defeated relation) between us."

The plot was thicker than a mere love affair in Paris. Fullerton had been driven to speak to James, who now offered so much fatherly love, because the woman was blackmailing him. It was like some plot in a Sardou play. Morton, conscious of his position as representative of the London *Times* in Paris, was a man with a sense of his importance; he was the old-fashioned "journalist" and a "voice" of the august Thunderer, and he felt himself vulnerable. The woman apparently could be bought off. But Morton had no money. He did not appeal for financial help to James—he simply seems to have conveyed to the Master in his anguish—the sense of his dilemma.

James consoled him, suggested he was suffering from "exacerbated and hypnotized nerves," urged him to get away from his "damned circle" in Paris; in a word, as with Mrs Wharton, James urged Morton to "keep very still and very busy and very much interested in things." "Throw yourself on your work, on your genius, on your art, on your knowledge, on the Universe in fine (though letting the latter centrally represent H.J.)—throw yourself on the blest *alternative* life which embraces all these things and is what I mean by the life of art." The life of art would see Morton through everything, James said. "She has seen *me* through everything and that was a large order too." But Morton was not an artist, he was simply a journalist—even though it was flattering to be accorded equality with the Master.

Further letters elicited information that Morton was living in the same house, if not the same apartment, as the blackmailer; that

James regarded her as "a mad, vindictive, and obscure old woman" who was simply angry because Morton hadn't married her. The Master advised Morton to stop breathing "the poisoned air of her proximity." He believed that if Morton broke with the woman he would find himself "free" and he would leave her "merely beating the air with grotesque *gestes*." This apparently was more easily said than done. By early 1909 Mrs Wharton had become a party to the drama. She and James now actively intrigued to discover how they could extract the journalist from the blackmailer. In January 1909 James wrote Mrs Wharton "Glad am I that we 'care' for him, you and I, for verily I think I do as much as you, and that you do as much as I. We can help him— we even can't *not*. And it will immensely pay." Help Morton they did, by an ingenious piece of plotting. The question was how to get enough money to him to pay off the blackmailing woman and recover the incriminating papers. Apparently this was one of the subjects discussed during the June–July meetings of 1909 recorded in James's date-books. Morton suggested, or was induced to suggest, that he write a book on Paris for Macmillan. He was eminently qualified to do so. Macmillan would offer an advance. However, the advance would be made more substantial by Mrs Wharton paying to James a sum of money, which James would induce the Macmillans to include in their offer. Morton would know only that Macmillan thought highly enough of the project to be extremely generous.

In a letter to Frederick Macmillan of 26 July 1909 (shortly after he saw Edith and Morton off to France), James wrote that Fullerton "may have to write and ask you for some advance on the money he is to receive from you, for getting more clear and free for work at his book—and I should like to send you a cheque for £100, say, that he may profit to that end, *without his knowing it comes from me*." James said Fullerton would probably send the money "back to me were I to propose it to him straight." What Macmillan could not know was that Edith Wharton on her side would supply the £100 to James. It was a goodly sum at that time. In the end, Macmillan paid the advance to Morton and James gave surety for it if the book were not produced.

"I hope the sum he has to pay to the accursed woman isn't really a very considerable one," James wrote to Edith. He also said, "I will play my mechanical part in your magnificent combination with absolute piety, fidelity and punctuality." The plan worked, for on 3 August 1909 James wrote to Mrs Wharton how delighted he was to learn of "the change wrought in Morton by recent events." It brought home "with a force with which one fairly winces as for pain, the degree of the pressure of the incubus under which he had so long been living." The "normal and possible expanding and living man was lost in it, lost to himself and lost to *us*. Now that we have got him—and it's *you* absolutely who have so admirably and definitely pulled him out—we must keep him and surround him and help to make up for all the dismal waste of power—waste of it in merely struggling against his (to put it mildly) inconvenience." Fullerton apparently had recovered the papers and the whole matter disappears from the correspondence. The Eumenides had been driven off.

III

In all this there was a side-plot as well. While Edith Wharton intrigued with James, and James intrigued with Macmillan, she was urging and helping Morton Fullerton perform an act of friendship for Henry James. The New York Edition had been completed. The last volume had now been published. But it had passed almost unnoticed. Morton wrote a long and full article on the Edition and on the significance of James's career in the history of the novel. He had no difficulty placing it in the *Quarterly Review*. Mrs Wharton tried to induce *Scribner's Magazine* to publish it in America; the journal was not interested and her own editor at Scribner's told her the reception of the Edition was "disappointing." "I have had a hand—or at least a small finger—in the Article, and I think it's good . . ." Edith Wharton wrote to the magazine. "I long so to have someone speak intelligently and resolutely for James." This Morton had done. James was shown the article in manuscript. He kept it for some time; he said he was "embarrassed . . . fairly to anguish." It reads indeed as if the Master had inspired it: but he had talked often enough with

Morton and Edith for them to have imbibed a great deal of his doctrine. If certain sentences sound as if James himself wrote them, we must also remember that Fullerton had long been accused of writing his dispatches for *The Times* in a Jamesian style. The article appeared in the *Quarterly Review* in April 1910 and was reprinted in America in the *Living Age*. It points directly at James's discoveries in the handling of "the states of mind of the actors *through whom his story became a story*" and discerned his having found a solution "in the art of passing, at the inevitable moment, from the consciousness of one character to that of another." Fullerton discussed the prefaces and James's late style. He defended it as providing tone, richness, depth, and "completeness." He speaks of James's subjects and the hundreds of characters he had created in his tales—seeing him as "the historiographer of that vast epic—the modern Iliad, when its peripatetic and romantic elements do not make it more like an Odyssey—the clash between two societies, the mutual call of two sundered worlds, with not one Helen but a thousand to create complications and to fire the chivalry of two continents. As a sociological phenomenon, no 'Return of the Heracleidae' mythic or real, is comparable to the invasion of Europe by American women, backed by their indispensable heads of commissariat, the silent, clean-shaven American men. The emigration required its Homer," said Fullerton, "and Mr James was there."

With his saturation in things French, Fullerton wrote that James could be compared only with Balzac "as to methods and to aims." He echoed James's views of Tolstoy of whom he spoke as "merely a deeper and richer Maupassant." In the latter part of his essay he touched on the quality many contemporary critics would later describe in James—the unity of his imagination with the power of his intelligence. Fullerton likened the mystery of James's creativity in a long passage to the qualities of "radioactivity"—"Nature, the world, life impinge on, punctuate, his consciousness with a myriad of tiny unmeaning holes, and that consciousness has the magic capacity of transmuting these perforations, these nothings into intelligible signs . . . A consciousness so completely alive is the rarest state of human activity."

James may have felt uneasy over some of the Fullertonian journalese. However, the sentiments were genuine and its insights make of this essay an important contemporary document in discerning critically the high originality of James's work.

Thus in an ironic way Edith Wharton reversed the situation of "The Velvet Glove" and secretly repaid James with kindness. If the Master hesitated to "puff" his acolytes, the acolytes could, with energy and sincerity, laud the Master. The essay James liked best was written by Percy Lubbock. It appeared anonymously in *The Times Literary Supplement*, on 8 July 1909; James soon learned the identity of the author and wrote to Mrs Humphry Ward on 11 July 1909 that the article "does that gentle and thoroughly literary and finely critical young man great honour, I think—but it does me no less; and I somehow feel as if it drove in with an audible tap a sort of shining silver nail and marked, in a manner, a date." Unfortunately there would be few such dates. The Edition had its discriminating readers, but they belonged usually to the inner circle of the Master himself.

WOMAN-ABOUT-TOWN

FROM the passions of Olympus to the depths of blackmail—Henry James had run that gamut during 1909; and in the same year he was himself at the centre of a pathetic minor comedy, a comedy of mere mortal passion involving his old acquaintance of Winchelsea, Ford Madox Hueffer and his friend Violet Hunt. Since the days at the turn of the century when he had waylaid the Master on his daily strolls, Hueffer had had a troubled time. He had had a breakdown in 1903 and gone to Germany for a cure. James had written sympathetically to his wife. He recognized her difficulties and the "very pathetic story . . . an almost tragic one." "You had, together, the sad fortune, inevitable at certain moments of life, that things—things of hard friction—accumulated on your exposed heads and spent their fury." Germany was just the place "to muffle and pacify . . . intenser and finer vibrations. . . . Give him my friendliest remembrance . . . but don't be precipitate even about that." The letter has in it James's ironic detachment. He could perform the offices of friendship with loyalty and devotion as he did with Mrs Wharton and Fullerton. But the world seemed to find too much comfort in him and he had often to protect himself against its weeping too profusely on his shoulder. The emotional wear and tear was too great. He could cultivate when necessary "the voice of stoicism."

James had known Violet Hunt since she was a young girl. She was the daughter of Alfred Hunt, an Oxford don, who at the urging of Ruskin had become a water-colourist. James had visited his artistic-bohemian house on Campden Hill. Violet Hunt's girlhood memories were of a silken-bearded Henry James with "deep, wonderful eyes," who looked as if he might have worn earrings and been an Elizabethan sea captain. In her youth she possessed a certain pre-Raphaelite beauty; she was pursued by men and she pursued them. She wrote tales and novels, and James occasionally invited her to Lamb House and listened to her sex-charged gossip. Her diaries show that he shied away from listening to her love affairs. During 2 and 3 November 1907 she recorded her attempt to tell James how she had loved Oswald Crawfurd, whom James had known, "and poor H.J. got up from the table like a dog that has had enough of his bone and closed the discussion." She wrote "he always wants my news but never more than half of it, always getting bored or delicate." On this particular week-end we receive an image in the diary of Miss Hunt's being seductive even with the Master—she speaks of "drifting as I know how" in her "white Chinese dressing gown," into the Lamb House draw-ing-room. She had been unwell after dinner, and the Master was "all solicitude and I do believe pleasure"—but unapproachable; the best Miss Hunt could do was to have a conversation with him about Mrs. Humphry Ward's novels. James's letters to her are coy and telegraphic. He poses as a "man-about-town" who will be happy to see the "woman-about-town" when he is in London. One gets a sense of how James felt about her, for he called her his "Purple Patch."

The Purple Patch was eleven years older than Hueffer; she was almost fifty in 1909, he not yet forty. They had become lovers; and the discrepancy in their ages made Miss Hunt wish ardently for marriage. Elsie Hueffer, however, was unwilling to give Hueffer a divorce, claiming she was Catholic (actually she was Anglo-Catholic). In due course she sued for "restitution of conjugal rights." The case got into the newspapers. James happened to have invited Miss Hunt to visit him at Lamb House just before the scandal broke—"I am more and more aged and infirm and unattractive, but I make such a stand as I can . . . We can have a long jaw (with lots of arrears to make up) and, weather permitting, eke a short talk." That was on 31 October 1909. Two days later, with strange paragraphs appearing in the press, James apparently decided that it would be wise to avoid the possible publicity of offering even a week-end's hospitality to the third party in the Hueffer family feud. He may have had memories of Miss Grigsby. He wrote to Miss Hunt: "I deeply regret and deplore the lament-able position in which I gather you have placed yourself in respect to divorce proceedings about to be taken by Mrs Hueffer: it affects me as painfully unedifying, and that compels me to regard all agreeable and unembarrassed communication between us as impossible. I can neither suffer you to come down to hear me utter those homely truths, nor pretend, at such a time, of free and natural discourse of other things, on a basis of avoidance of what must now be most to the front in your own consciousness and what in a very unwelcome fashion disconcerts mine."

The letter sounds cruel, and Miss Hunt understandably resented having the door of Lamb House slammed in her face. She felt James was "disloyal" and proving himself a fair-weather friend. She argued that he was passing judgment on her private life in deploring her "lamentable position." James replied that he hadn't "for a moment tried to characterize her relationship with Hueffer." This was "none of my business at all." He had merely spoken of her "*position*, as a result of those relations." And we may judge that by this he meant essentially the fact that she had got herself into the newspapers. His old abhorrence of the publicizing of the private life seemed to be at the heart of his seeming rudeness. He did not speak of this, however, in his answer. He confined himself to insisting that hospitality for Violet Hunt would involve him with Hueffer's "and his wife's private affairs, of which I wish to hear nothing whatever." James added "you immediately illustrate this by saying 'as you know' they have been separated for years. I neither knew, nor know, anything whatever of the matter; and it was exactly because I didn't wish to, that I found conversing with you at all to be in prospect impossible."

To Hueffer, who wrote in remonstrance, James reiterated "what I wrote to her that I deplored and lamented was the situation in which . . . her general relations with you had landed or were going to land her—the situation of her being exposed to figure in public proceedings. I don't see how any old friend of hers can be indifferent to that misfortune." He denied that he had "pretended to judge, qualify or deal with any act or conduct of Violet Hunt's in the connection . . . that whole quantity being none of my business and destined to remain so."

The affair developed further complications when Hueffer went to Germany, claimed German nationality and pretended to get a divorce there. Violet promptly began to use the name of Mrs Hueffer. Elsie Hueffer sued for libel. She was the only legitimate Mrs Hueffer under English law; she had received no bill of divorcement. She won; and the effect was to involve Hueffer and his common-law wife in new scandal. James was in America much of this time and by his return the affair was ancient history. He continued to correspond with Violet Hunt; and he saw both her and Hueffer in London on at least one occasion, in April 1912, for a note in his pocket diary records: "Met Violet Hunt and F. M. Hueffer and went home with them for half an hour."

Two facts remain to be recorded in the story of Henry James's relations with Hueffer. One was that during Hueffer's editorship of the *English Review* in 1908 and 1909 he published four of James's late tales, including "The Jolly Corner" and "The Velvet Glove." The publication was arranged by James's literary agent and there was no contact to speak of between editor and author. Hueffer paid James the regular rate from £50 to £75 for each tale, according to its length; and James wrote to his agent that he was pleased with the typography and presentation of his stories. Then, in 1913, Hueffer brought out a book on James, the first "critical" study of the novelist to appear, although an earlier expository book about him by Elisabeth Luther Cary had been published in the United States. "Mr James is the greatest of living writers," Hueffer wrote in his introduction, "and in consequence, for me, the greatest of living men." The volume is as discursive as most of Hueffer's critical writing; but he showed his literary judgment by singling out the works in which James had developed his late techniques, notably *The Spoils of Poynton*, *Maisie*, and the tales published in the *English Review*. A few weeks after its appearance Archibald Marshall asked the novelist how he felt about Hueffer's book. James replied:

You commiserate me for my exposure to the public assault of F. M. Hueffer, but I assure you that though I believe this assault has been perpetrated I have not had the least difficulty in remaining wholly unconscious of it. I am vaguely aware that his book is out, but he has at least had the tact not to send it to me, and as I wouldn't touch it with a ten-foot pole nothing is simpler than for it not to exist for me.

Book Six

The Finer Grain
1910–1913

★

THE BENCH OF DESOLATION

THE first royalty statement for the New York Edition had reached Henry James in October of 1908 while the final volumes were still in preparation. These figures, James immediately wrote to his agent, knocked him "rather flat"—"a greater disappointment than I have been prepared for." After his long labour he experienced "a great, I confess, and bitter, grief." "Is there anything for me at all?" he asked. "I don't make out or understand." James had not recognized that his earnings would be reduced by heavy permissions fees due to the publishers participating in the edition—Houghton Mifflin Company, Harper and Brothers, and The Macmillan Company, who had published him before Scribner's. His agent explained this to him. But the Master had had his shock. "I have been living in a fool's paradise," he wrote. His four years of unremunerated labour, the gathering in of his work of a lifetime, on which he had counted to yield revenue for his declining years showed signs of being a complete failure. Three days later James wrote that he had recovered a bit since "the hour of the shock, but I think it would ease off my nerves not a little to see you." He felt his reaction was in part a result of his having no clue as to the possible yield. He had built up high hopes on the strength of the "treasures of ingenuity and labour I have lavished on the amelioration of every page of the thing." As yet his new fling at the theatre had brought him no great returns. "The non-response of *both* sources has left me rather high and dry."

It left him, emotionally, higher and drier than he knew. The effect, though delayed for a few months, was as if he had faced a booing audience again, and were being told that his life-work were no good, and that he was unwanted. He had written his way out of depression thirteen years before—it had been a long and difficult ordeal—but now he tumbled right back into it. He had

437

then been fifty-two; he was now approaching his sixty-sixth year. It was harder to take defeat at this advanced age. Re-reading the sales figures he discerned that his first payment on the Edition would total $211. "And I have *such* visions and arrears of inspiration." A brief note in Miss Bosanquet's diary tells us much about the Master. "Mr James depressed," she wrote. "Nearly finished *Golden Bowl* preface—bored by it—says he's 'lost his spring' for it." Some of that depression crept into a letter to Howells on the last day of 1908. "It will have landed me in Bankruptcy" he said of the Edition. "It has prevented me doing any other work." Later he would say it had been "the most expensive job of my life."

I

The shock of *Guy Domville* had brought James long ago to the verge of a nervous breakdown. He had staved it off by hard work and by discovering within himself the themes which resolved his anxieties and restored his self-confidence. This time the breakdown occurred in a very clear way and it is not difficult to recover its stages. Early in 1909, little more than three months after the news had "knocked me flat" he noted that he felt sharply unwell for the first time in six years. Miss Bosanquet's diary of 17 January says simply, "Mr James unwell (heart trouble)." At least that was what he thought he had. There were some palpitations, a little shortness of breath, but no pain to speak of. The local doctor prescribed digitalis. He found nothing ominous and urged James to take more exercise. The Master had become too fat. He wasn't walking enough. Henry James, with his empathy with his brother William, seems to have decided he was having, or about to have, a heart condition such as William had lived through, in Lamb House, almost a decade before. In writing to his brother and describing his symptoms Henry also said he was "a little solitarily worried and depressed." As in the old days he appealed to his brother's knowledge of medicine, even though William had never practised.

In due course, with increasing anxiety, Henry James wrote to Sir William Osler, who had examined William at the time of his ttack. The great doctor recommended that Henry see the renowned heart specialist of the time, Sir James Mackenzie. The novelist paid his visit 25 February 1909. We have access to this consultation since Sir James wrote it up in his book *Angina Pectoris* as Case 97, after the novelist's death. He did not name his patient; yet he gave away his identity by describing him as a novelist who had written a ghost story about mysterious occurrences to two children, one of whom "died in the arms of the narrator." The physician's notes tell us that he found the patient "stout and healthy-looking." His heart was slightly enlarged but "there is no murmur present." "The blood pressure varied curiously. He was a nervous man, and on one visit I noticed that when I first took the blood pressure it was 190 mm Hg. After a few minutes it was 170 and later 160 mm Hg." He prescribed exercise and moderate eating, and addressed himself to James's anxieties. Sir James Mackenzie used the novelist as a case history because he wished to demonstrate how (in a manner that would today be called psychotherapeutic) he reassured a patient who thought he had a heart condition. He made James explain what he had tried to do in his ghost story ("The Turn of the Screw" wasn't named) and when the Master admitted his use of ambiguity to make the reader's imagination "run riot and depict all sorts of horrors," the learned doctor tapped Henry on the chest and said: "It is the same with you, it is the mystery that is making you ill." The doctor continued,

You think you have got angina pectoris, and you are very frightened lest you should die suddenly. Now, let me explain to you the real matters. You are 66 years of age. You have got the changes in your body which are coincident with your time of life. It happens that the changes in the arteries of your heart are a little more advanced than in those of your brain, or of your legs. It simply follows that if you be more judicious in your living, and give your heart less work to do, there is no reason why you should not reach the ordinary span of human life.

The doctor reported his patient was "greatly cheered by this," and that he remained in good health. But apparently Henry did not believe all that Sir James Mackenzie told him. He continued to speak of having had a "cardiac crisis." He had apparently decided he was as ill as his brother. Still, he followed the doctor's orders and during the rest of 1909 found himself much improved. He worked, he entered into the casting of *The Outcry*, and he was preoccupied with the affairs of his Olympian friends. In October came the second annual royalty returns for the Edition. This time it yielded $596.71—hardly reassuring for his old age. He told his agent that in no year had he so "consummately managed to make so little money as this last." Notes in the back of his date-book indicate that he reported his earnings to the income tax as £1096 in 1908, £1020 in 1909, and £1309 in 1910. His income was thus adequate for the time, and especially for his bachelor needs, but offering him slim margin if his powers should fail. His property in America yielded him $3500 in 1910 and in that year he reported earnings by his pen of $2500. He makes no note of savings; there is simply a note of his having a balance of $2089 at Brown Brothers, and some £89 in his bank at Rye.

One day, shortly after this, in a fit of sadness, perhaps prompted by fantasies of death, he gathered his private papers—forty years of letters from his contemporaries, manuscripts, scenarios, old notebooks—and piled them on a rubbish fire in his garden, including a carbon copy of a recent tale "A Round of Visits" which his agent would ask of him a few days later. He was ruthless. A great Anglo-American literary archive perished on that day. His act was consistent with his belief that authors were themselves responsible for clearing the approaches to their privacy. "I kept almost all my letters for years," he wrote to his old friend Mrs Fields, on 2 January 1910, "till my receptacles would no longer hold them; then I made a gigantic bonfire and have been easier in mind since." He had done this he said in obedience to a law "as I myself grow older and think more of my latter end: the law of not leaving personal and private documents at the mercy of any accidents." He was destroying a part of his personal past. As for the past which was enshrined in the New York Edition, the public had spoken.

He had, preceding his illness, a lonely and sad Christmas at Rye. An old friend "considerably lone and lorn" passed the holiday with James, "a little lugubriously." And then he went over to

Eastbourne to see sick Jonathan Sturges "ever a stiff bit of discipline for me." He spoke of Sturges, with whom he had passed so many cheerful Christmases in the past, as "that tragic and terrible little figure," and "the ferocious nature of his deeply congenital little egoism now so exasperated by disease and suffering."

His last effort to work off his depression occurred on 4 January when in the early morning, he began to make notes in pencil, in a large scrawl, for a new fiction which the Harpers had asked him to write. It would be his last recorded invocation of the Muse:

> I must now take up projected tasks—this long time *entrevus* and brooded over—with the firmest possible hand. I needn't expatiate on this—on the sharp consciousness of this hour of the dimly-dawning New Year. I mean, I simply invoke and appeal to all the powers and forces and divinities to whom I've ever been loyal and who haven't failed me as yet—after all: never, never yet! . . . Momentary sidewinds—things of no real authority—break every now and then to put their inferior little questions to me; but I come back, I come back, as I say, I all throbbingly and yearningly and passionately, oh, *mon bon*, come back to this way that is clearly the only one in which I can do anything now . . . *Causons, causons, mon bon*—oh celestial, soothing, sanctifying process, with all the high sane forces of the sacred time, fighting through it, on my side.

It seemed to him he was emerging from his recent "bad days" and "the prospect clears and flushes, and my poor blest old Genius pats me so admirably and lovingly on the back that I turn, I screw round, and bend my lips to passionately, in my gratitude, kiss its hand."

The "sane forces of the sacred time"—that time when he could write scenarios and plan great novels—refused to stay with him. Shortly after writing this supreme appeal to his "blest Genius" he collapsed. Some vague discomfort in the stomach: inability to take food, a certain amount of nausea. It was indeed difficult to swallow the fact that his work of a lifetime had not met with a greater reception and brought him the recognition he craved and the money that would have given him a greater sense of security. After some weeks he admitted to being attacked by "the black devils of nervousness, direst damndest demons." The beast in his private jungle had jumped and this time there was no turning away.

II

Henry James's illness had been signalled also just before the new year by two bad attacks of gout, first in one foot and then the other. Then had come, early in January, his "food-loathing" and general debility; he lingered in bed mornings, dozing in a kind of withdrawal from his daily existence. Hugh Walpole asked to come to see him and he answered, scrawling his letters in pencil on his knee, that "I am not fit company for you." His state was "obscure." He was Hugh's "dilapidated friend." He would announce improvement for forty-eight hours and then relapse. The local doctor, Ernest Skinner, still found nothing seriously wrong except his loss of appetite and his general weakness. Miss Bosanquet was laid off for the time. There was no work for her. She had, however, regularly answered queries addressed to her by James's friends and in particular, at Mrs Wharton's insistence, sent bedside bulletins. After some three weeks of recurrent illness of this sort the doctor put Henry to bed, insisted on great regularity in his life, and induced him to have a nurse. "I am so glad that he has decided to submit to the Doctor's orders," Mrs Wharton wrote to Miss Bosanquet. On 25 January he penned a postcard to Mrs Wharton, "Your beautiful letter this a.m. welcomed. I am doing admirably, mending fast, though sitting up but an hour for the first time (these several days) this afternoon. Beseech you kindly send me *Tales of Men* [*and Beasts*]. I want so awfully to see how you do it. More very soon. Am forbidden 'style.' Yours H.J. P.S. All my sympathies in your immersion— which must be grand and horrible."

The Master could be brief when he had to be. "A digestive crisis making food loathsome and nutrition impossible—and sick inanition and weakness and depression," he wrote to Bailey Saunders. "I lie here verily as detached as a sick god on a damp Olympus," he wrote to Miss Robins. Dr Skinner had him fed every two hours. He was reduced to an infantile regimen. Mrs Wharton discreetly wrote and asked if he was in need of funds. He replied gratefully he was on a decent financial basis "with a margin of no mean breadth and most convenient balance at my bank and a whole year quite provided for even if I should do no work at all." She made him promise that if he should be in need he would let her know. Once he was on a regular regimen Mrs Wharton sent him great clusters of grapes. By early February the doctor, treating Henry as essentially a case of "nerves," began to take him out daily in his car as he made his calls—to provide an airing and change of scene. Henry wrote a full account of his illness to William and blamed his condition on his having for so long "Fletcherized" his food—the fad involving lengthy mastication.

Although Henry had cabled cheerfully to Irving Street, William James dispatched his eldest son, Harry, to visit the novelist. He crossed the mid-winter seas very promptly and arrived at Lamb House on 24 February. Henry was touched. By that time the novelist had begun to speak candidly of his "black depression" and his "beastly solitudinous life." He welcomed the "priceless youth" with open arms. Harry, firm, managerial, sized up the situation at once and wrote a letter to his father and mother which gives us a sharp picture of the Master's condition. Two things were required, he said: get James out of Rye to London; and have him thoroughly examined by an eminent medical authority. He turned to Sir William Osler.

Harry described his uncle as having been, on his arrival, on an "upward wave" but secretly Fletcherizing again, feeling he had "got hold of something." Then there was a new collapse. At this moment Henry talked freely and it is possible to see what his deeper anxieties were. He remembered his sister's protracted illness; he remembered William's heart attack. Harry described how he found him both depressed and excited one day. The nurse gave the Master some bromide but after supper she hurried to Harry and said his uncle wanted him. He found him in the little oak bedroom in a state of complete despair:

There was nothing for me to do but to sit by his side and hold his hand while he panted and sobbed for two hours until the Doctor arrived, and stammered in despair so eloquently and pathetically that as I write of it the tears flow down my cheeks again. He talked about Aunt Alice and his own end and I knew him to be facing not only the frustration of all his hopes and ambitions, but the vision looming close and threatening to his weary eyes, of a lingering illness such as hers. In sight of all that, he wanted to die . . . He didn't have a good night and the next day the same thing began again with a fear of being alone.

When Harry announced he was writing at once to Osler, the Master "stopped panting and trembling, and from that moment began to revive." There was a change of mood. In the evening he was vivacious and jocular. Then a further picture was painted by the nephew, who possessed a certain touch of his father's style —and some of his father's critical attitudes—towards his uncle. Harry realized the great authority and solemnity of the Johnsonian dictator that was co-existent with the death-haunted mortal lying there on his bed. With a truly Jamesian touch, Harry called his uncle "a portentous invalid."

The magnificent solemnity of process that marks as momentous even the taking of his temperature overwhelms one. This afternoon I watched him begin to stir a cup of beef tea with an expression like a judge about to announce an opinion, and a gesture by which he ladled teaspoonfuls eighteen inches into the air and poured them splashing back again. His mind running off on something else, he continued this splendidly wasteful process unconsciously until I made a movement that brought him back to earth. Nothing is too small to be given its fullest measure and emphasis. Yesterday while taking some milk he handed an open envelope to Burgess, who was to mail some letters, and told him to lick it and close it. Burgess did so, not copiously but promptly, and quite well. "Oh!" cried Uncle Henry, "Oh-oh! Burgess not that way; you must wet it *more*." "Iss-sir," said Burgess and aplied himself to the more abundant insalivation of the envelope until I was afraid its contents would be drowned. Luckily Burgess is entirely incapable of reflection when he is in Uncle Henry's presence."

Thus the nephew, who understood the immediate realities of the case, but not the intensities of the Master or the temperament of genius. He reported that he was well cared for in Lamb House and he described the staff with their "endless polishings and cleanings and arrangings at all hours of the day" and "their cheerful, self-respecting well-defined dutifulness." Harry went to London; he saw Sir William Osler and arranged to bring his uncle to the great man.

They came up to town together to Garland's Hotel in Suffolk

Street, and on 14 March Osler gave Henry James the most complete physical examination he had ever had. He found nothing seriously wrong. He thought him "splendid for his age." The novelist's eating habits had done no damage to his stomach; what was needed was reform. Heart, lungs, arteries, were fine, and he said that Henry had "the pulse of a boy." William had written to Henry that perhaps he ought to recognize that what he had was something in the nature of a "nervous breakdown." The novelist, telling William of Osler's examination, denied this. "My illness had no more to do with a 'nervous breakdown' than with Halley's comet." He insisted it was a stomach condition. William continued to call it "melancholia," and after a while Henry accepted the idea, writing to Edmund Gosse that he had had "a sort of nervous breakdown." Hugh Walpole, who came to see the novelist at Garland's hotel found him "most frightfully depressed —most melancholy conversation." But life in a hotel was no solution for the nervous Master who nevertheless managed to see Galsworthy's *Justice* in London before Harry took him back to Rye. Osler prescribed massage, and walks, and a general routine intended to make James take an interest in everyday occupations.

III

Even before Harry returned to America, satisfied with Osler's examination, William and Alice James had sailed to be with Henry. They had decided from Henry's letters that he needed family, distraction, company, and William knew how fond his brother was of Alice. He planned himself to take a further cure at Bad Nauheim, for his heart was troubling him again after several comfortable years. They arrived in April and Alice took over in Lamb House. What William would not face, and Alice did not sufficiently perceive, was that the older brother had a serious bodily illness while Henry's illness was one of the spirit. From this time on we have a guide, the daily sentence or two Mrs William James wrote in a little date-book. It is a sad little personal document—oscillating from day to day in its description of William's increasing debility and Henry's constant changes of mood, from deep depression, to partial calm, and then a relapse into depression. An entry she set down in June is eloquent: "William cannot walk and Henry cannot smile." Mrs Wharton provided a motor that spring for Henry and William and they went on long drives. In May Edward VII died; and in the period of mourning and the funeral all the London theatres were closed. This proved a death blow to Frohman's repertory and the impending production of James's play. Frohman paid James $1000 forfeit as agreed. By this time Henry was indifferent to his work in the theatre. He talked of his "nervous upsets." "But I am emerging," he wrote to his agent.

To Jocelyn, who was in Ceylon, he wrote of his "nervous condition—trepidation, agitation, general dreadfulness." Things had been "in short, dismally bad." William with his diagnostic psychiatric eye judged his brother's case "more and more plainly one of melancholia, 'simple,' in that there are no fixed or false ideas," apart from Henry's belief the cause had been diet. "He fluctuates a great deal from day to day." He had complete confidence in the local doctor. In due course, William and Alice convinced Henry that the best thing for him to do would be to return to America with them. William would go to Nauheim first. Alice would remain in Lamb House with Henry. They would then join William and travel in Switzerland. Henry and William both had memories of their youth in that country; and while such a trip might be helpful to Henry there seems to have been no realization on Alice's part that her husband was too ill to travel.

They carried out their plan. In Lamb House Alice tried to distract Henry. On one day, when he could not read, and sat in glum despair, she tried to teach the Master to knit. He was beyond occupational therapy. Yet he was able to gather his most recent tales into a volume to be called *The Finer Grain*. He led off with "The Velvet Glove" and concluded with a long tale of passivity and despair called "The Bench of Desolation." Scribner and Methuen agreed to do the book and each paid him $1000 advance. By now he was taking more food; and walking almost daily. For a fortnight in May Alice took Henry to visit Mrs Charles Hunter, the hostess of Hill Hall and patroness of the arts, in the hope that in a great establishment and with the comings and goings of guests Henry would be distracted. It was only a partial success. Sargent was there; one of his sisters, Mrs Ormond and her husband; Percy Grainger, the pianist; Viola Tree; there were assorted peers and James posed for his portrait which was painted by Mrs Swynnerton. James had "dark and difficult days" in the "vast, wondrous, sympathetic house." "I am unfit for society," he wrote to Goody Allen; however, he recognized that the visit on the whole was beneficial.

Early in June they made the trip to Bad Nauheim. William had not benefited by the cure; he was much weaker. From Nauheim the novelist wrote to Mrs Wharton that he was going to America. "I am wholly unfit to be alone—in spite of amelioration." They stayed a while in Nauheim. They went on excursions. One gets glimpses of these two tired sick brothers trying to keep up a show of activity and wearing on Mrs William's nerves. William was having the last of his "curative" baths. Again to Mrs Wharton, the Master wrote, "I eat, I walk, I *almost* sleep—and what I shall most have done, if things go on as I hope, will be to have walked myself well." "Your noble image," he told Edith, "is cherished by your affectionate H.J." To his friends the Protheros in Rye Henry James wrote, "I have really been down into hell and stayed there for months since I saw you . . . I keep hold of my blest companions, I intensely clutch them, as a scared child does his nurse and mother."

They went to Zürich; they visited scenic views and palaces, William dragging himself along. Then to Lucerne, and Geneva, scene of their youth; here the news reached them that Robertson James, the Civil War veteran, had died in America in his sleep of a heart attack. Alice told Henry and they agreed to withhold the news from William for the time being. "Dark troubled sad days," wrote Henry in his little date-book, recording an attack of gout which a Swiss doctor arrested. Early in July they reached London; Henry went to stay at the Reform Club and was visited by Jocelyn, back from his eastern trip. William and Alice stayed in a hotel. Henry began to note "William great source of anxiety." Dr Mackenzie cared for him in London. He mustered enough strength to do some London shopping with Alice. But he had several sharp attacks of chest pain and several times took to his bed.

IV

On the morning of 21 July 1910 Henry James awoke in his room at the Reform Club from a good night's sleep. He felt well again. The only clues we have to this moment of experience are in his date-book in which he scribbled "woke up in great relief." Then two months later, on 12 September he wrote "woke up with a return of the old trouble of the black times, which had dropped comparatively, yet as markedly on red-letter day July 21st with that blessed waking in my London room." We may ask ourselves what there was about that summer's awakening that made it a "red-letter day" and also "blessed." The date-books for that year guard their secret, but they contain a certain amount of mysterious ritual. It begins in October with Henry James using red and black crosses in great profusion. Thus on 24 October there are no less than fifteen red crosses instead of his usual record of engagements, and on 25 October there are twenty-seven such crosses. Various numbers are marked in the book from 26 to 30 October but on 31 October the colour changes to black: there are four black crosses on that day and from 2 to 10 November the crosses continue to be black, most often five in number. On 11 November a variation occurs: they are alternately red and black—thus on this day there are five in all and the second and fourth are red. On 12 November the system changes. He starts with red and then changes to black, the first, third and fifth crosses are in red. Throughout the remainder of November the markings are exclusively red save on 21 November when he makes four black ones. They are red again on 14 December and the system of alternation again occurs. And so on, with variations until the end of the year when the ritual is abandoned.

We have no clues to this personal code save the fact that he spoke of the red-letter day, and then of "black times." This would suggest that the red crosses marked the days on which James felt comparatively well and the black recorded his more depressed

THE CHARIOT OF FIRE
Edith Wharton and the Master in the Panhard with Edward Wharton
(on the chauffeur's right) in 1907

A TERRACE AT VALLOMBROSA 1907

The Master (cigarette in hand), Howard Sturgis and Mr and Mrs
Edward Boit

days. The variations in number may or may not have significance
or may simply record the extent of his well-being or discomfort.
One other speculation: the day of the splendid awakening in the
Reform Club may have been the morning of his dream of the
Louvre which he commemorated vividly in *A Small Boy and
Others*. Indeed his account of this dream begins "I recall to this
hour, with the last vividness, what a precious part it [the Galerie
d'Apollon in the Louvre] played for me . . . on my waking, in a
summer dawn many years later, to the fortunate, the instantaneous
recovery and capture of the most appalling yet most admirable
nightmare of my life." It can only be conjecture, but the dream
was of the sort—in its components of fear, anxiety, and frustration, and then its triumph—that might indeed have resolved his
long weeks of depression. Certainly from the time of that
awakening, recorded in so enigmatic a form, we may date his
gradual recovery from his severe illness of 1910. Since the dream
contained a vigorous moment of self-assertion and putting to
flight of a frightening other-self (or brother) it may have helped
restore to James that confidence and faith in himself which had
crumbled in his life when he received the news of the failure of the
Edition.

After this stay in London, Henry, William, and Alice went
briefly to Rye to enable William to have several days of complete
rest before sailing. Henry noted "Poor—very bad, nights and
days for William. Difficult days—dreadful gloomy gales—but I
feel my own gain in spite of everything. Heaven preserve me."
And again, "Ah these dark days of farewell to this dear little old
place—saturated now with *all* associations. William just a little
better." Mrs Wharton arrived with her motor, accompanied by
Walter Berry; they took Henry to Windsor, stopping for lunch
at Tunbridge Wells. They visited Howard Sturgis at Qu'Acre.
"The dark cloud of William's suffering state hangs over me to the
exclusion of all other consciousness—though I am struggling
back to work. The weather hot and magnificent; the house ample
and easy; the 'pathos' of the whole situation wrings my heart."
Henry wrote this on 11 August.

The Jameses sailed on 12 August on the *Empress of Britain* for

P

Quebec, Henry accompanied by Burgess. In his date-book he wrote, "extraordinarily peaceful and beautiful voyage with no flaw or cloud on it but William's aggravated weakness and suffering—to see which and not to be able to help or relieve is anguish unutterable; now more and more." The voyage lasted six days. At Quebec Harry was on hand to help his parents and uncle. They then took the day-long journey to Chocorua. William was home at last. Billy James, William's second son, would remember how he met the voyagers at North Conway in a car and drove them to Chocorua. He was appalled at his father's weakened condition. At first the philosopher still sat at table finding it easier to breathe while erect. On one occasion Henry expatiated on the dreariness of that part of Canada through which they had passed "that flat desert of fir trees broken only here and there by a bit of prehistoric swamp!" William mustered enough strength to reply "better than anything in Europe, Henry—better than anything in England." The end was not in doubt. William James was suffering too much to want to live. On 26 August his younger brother wrote to Grace Norton "my own fears are of the blackest, I confess to you and at the prospect of losing my wonderful beloved brother out of the world in which, from as far back as in dimmest childhood, I have so yearningly always counted on him, I feel nothing but the abject weakness of grief and even terror." Grief, not terror, made James reopen this letter after he sealed it to add a postscript: "I open my letter of three hours since to add that William passed unconsciously away an hour ago—without apparent pain or struggle. Think of us, dear Grace—think of us!"

NOTES OF A BROTHER

WILLIAM JAMES died on a Friday and on Monday Henry rose at four-thirty and journeyed from Chocorua with his brother's family to Cambridge where in Appleton Chapel the Harvard University service was held—or as Henry, in a less emotional moment would say, Harvard "meagre mother, did for him—the best that Harvard can." The philosopher was cremated and his ashes were placed in a grave beside his parents in the Cambridge Cemetery. "Unutterable, unforgettable hour—with those that have followed . . . all unspeakable," the son and brother wrote in his date-book when they were back in Chocorua.

In the setting of mountain and valley and lake, Henry and Alice, his niece Peggy and the nephews, spent the following days. Henry's mourning was profound. He had always loved his brother with a strong devotion and admiration in which he diminished himself in the belief in William's superiorities; he had been also the rejected one for William always held and maintained his status of elder brother—"ideal Elder Brother" as Henry now wrote in answer to the condolences that came pouring in. "I was always his absolute younger and smaller, hanging under the blest sense of his protection and authority," he told an old friend of their Newport time. Henry James had lost, within weeks, his youngest brother Robertson and his oldest, William. He was now alone, sole survivor of that branch of the James family which had given America two remarkable men, a philosopher-psychologist, and an artist. Like one of his heroes in many of his stories, Henry James now wore the mantle of Family; he was the last heir, the final voice; his would be the last word. Out of this came, indeed, during the next three years, the Master's auto-biographies, *A Small Boy and Others* and *Notes of a Son and Brother*. A third volume, *The Middle Years*, which had himself for subject, and the beginning of his career abroad, was never

451

completed, although Henry lived long enough and had the vigour to write it. He had achieved solitude in his art; but the subject of his art had always been family relations, and personal relations. In reality there was no personal autobiography that he wanted to write, once removed from the frame of Family.

I

The letters Henry James wrote during these weeks were filled with an intense grief, a powerful emotion of helplessness but also of strength. "My beloved brother's death has cut into me, deep down, even as an absolute mutilation," the Master wrote to Edith Wharton. As with his "other-self" in "The Jolly Corner," the mutilation only gave him a greater sense of power. He could "only feel stricken and old and ended," in the first moments and the American landscape seemed haunted with associations. William's "extinction changes the face of life for me," he wrote to their oldest friend, T. S. Perry. It changed his life in quite another sense from that which Henry believed. His strength was returning, even if he still had "black," depressed days. He had always found himself strong in William's absence. Now he had full familial authority; his nephews deferred to him; his brother's wife now became wife to him, ministering to his wants, caring for him as she had cared for the ailing husband and brother. Henry had ascended to what had seemed, for sixty years, an inaccessible throne.

The Master was deeply touched by the world's tributes and particularly by words written by H. G. Wells. "That all this great edifice of ripened understandings and clarities and lucidities should be swept out of the world leaves me baffled and helplessly distressed," Wells wrote and James commented to his friends "a really beautiful eloquence — and he is not often beautiful." Henry (and Burgess with him) stayed on with his brother's family and in due course moved with them back into Irving Street where life was resumed on a normal basis. Henry began to work again. He would spend the winter in America, he announced, to give support to his brother's family; and there was another purpose in his remaining, for Mrs William James had promised her husband that she would hold seances and try to communicate with his spirit. William's lifelong interest in extra-sensory and extra-human experience had prompted him to tell her that he, in turn, would seek, from the Other World, to continue research beyond the grave. What attempts were made in Irving Street are not known; although the matter was not kept secret. Somerset Maugham, who dined with Henry James and Mrs William during that winter, remembered that Henry told him he and his sister-in-law were available as "two sympathetic witnesses on the spot ready to receive" any spiritualist messages, if they should come. None came; and when Henry received a document describing a seance at which William's voice was heard, he denounced it as "the most abject and impudent, the hollowest, vulgarest, and basest rubbish . . . utterly empty and illiterate, without substance or sense, a mere babble of platitudinous phrases."

In Irving Street James converted *The Outcry* into a novel and read the last proofs of *The Finer Grain*. He walked a great deal. Maugham quoted him as saying, "I wander about those great empty streets of Boston and I never see a living creature. I could not be more alone in the Sahara." He was bored, and his letters show it. "This is a hard country to love," he wrote to Emily Sargent, the painter's sister. And to Rhoda Broughton he spoke of "the tedium of vast wastes of homesickness here." Better, he said "fifty years of fogland—where indeed I have, alas, almost *had* my fifty years."

After a number of weeks in Irving Street—in mid-October—it was a relief to hear the sound of "the silver steam-whistle of the Devastating Angel." Mrs Wharton had crossed the Atlantic to spend a fortnight in America. She was staying at the new and splendid Hotel Belmont in Times Square. Emerging from his period of retirement, the novelist took train for the city of his birth.

11

On 17 October 1910 John Quinn, a wealthy Irish-American lawyer and patron of the arts, friend of Yeats and Lady Gregory, future friend of Conrad, Joyce, Eliot, Pound, and collector of their works and manuscripts, dining at the Hotel Belmont, suddenly had one of the "moments" of his life which he recorded. An enthusiast, a lover of literary celebrity, he recognized Henry James, massive, slow-moving, awe-inspiring, at dinner with two gentlemen and a lady. He would never know that he was witness to an unusual gathering of the Angel of Devastation's acolytes. It was not so much James dining with these three, as Edith Wharton, dining with three men of great importance in *her* life. With her at the Belmont were Walter Berry, on one of his holidays from his post in Egypt and W. Morton Fullerton—and the Master, who was friend and party to those other friendships. It was almost like the story by Mrs Wharton of the much-divorced lady who is able to achieve her ambition of having to tea at one time all of her former husbands.[1] Mrs Wharton was, as it were, with two major characters—and Henry James had joined the party in quarters in the hotel "that were as those of the Gonzagas, as who should say, at Mantua." Henry was delighted that he had answered the summons of the Angel—"the being devastated," he wrote to Howard Sturgis "has done me perceptible good." Edith he said was "as sublime and as unsurpassable" as ever.

He enjoyed Manhattan, although he would tire of it and say it was "the eternal Fifth Avenue." He found "the rhythm and beat and margin were all scant and inadequate" compared with "the vast circular Babylon" of London. Still, it was infinitely more interesting than Boston "so far as either of them is interesting." New York was "a queer mixture of the awful and the amusing, the almost interesting and the utterly impossible." He had a sneaking feeling of kindness for it—for its "pride and power." As for the United States (he wrote to his walking mate, Sydney Waterlow) the country was "prodigious, interesting, appalling." To Dr J. William White he spoke of "this babyish democracy."

During this year in America, in which he avoided all publicity and refused to lecture, James kept Irving Street in Cambridge as his base and periodically came to New York, usually staying with Mrs Cadwalader Jones in familiar lower Fifth Avenue. He was

---

[1] "The Other Two" in *The Descent of Man* (1904).

given a guest membership at the Century Club and there among painters, writers, and amateurs of the arts he often lunched: he visited art galleries; he attended the business meetings of the American Academy held at the University Club and the impression was "simply sickening." Everywhere in America he deplored the lack of ritual, the absence of standards. Above all he saw great affluence, great waste, and he was disturbed by the life of the rich who seemed to have no sense of *noblesse oblige*. He was revolted by the growth of advertising and publicity; and it seemed to him that a great national selfishness existed in America from which all kindness had been banished. His nephew took him to visit the Rockefeller Institute, where he met the director Dr Simon Flexner, and certain of the research scientists. Harry was then the business manager of the Institute. Dr Peyton Rous remembered this visit. He remembered James's serious face and the "banker's eyeglasses" he wore, large lenses held together by a black horizontal bar, with a black ribbon arching from them, past a black waistcoat striped with white. His boots were "almost arrogantly British," very thick-soled. Dr Flexner introduced Dr Rous as in charge of cancer research. Henry laid a heavy hand on his shoulder and said: "How magnificent! To be young and to have divine power!" The Master paused before the mouse cages. "May I ask, has the individuality, I might say the personality of these little creatures impressed itself upon you?" Dr Rous told James that one of the female mice had breast cancer and that a strange thing had happened recently. He had given the young to a healthy mouse to be suckled; she had accepted them as if they were her own. Stimulated by curiosity, Rous had supplied a second litter. Then a third. She patiently nursed these till they were about an inch long. Then "during a single night she killed them all. It was an act of self-preservation; the urge to live had overcome maternal feeling."

Dr Rous, who many years later would win the Nobel prize for his researches, told the story in a matter-of-fact way. The Master stood deeply thoughtful. He was about to speak when Dr Flexner put his head through the door and called. Dr Rous ever after told the anecdote with a sense of frustration.

In the spring James accepted an honorary degree from Harvard
"with deference to William's memory—though he was so infinitely more to Harvard than Harvard ever was to, or for, him."
He visited his Emmet cousins in Connecticut. He revisited Newport. He was still in the hands of doctors. In Boston he consulted
Dr James Jackson Putnam, a neurologist, and seems to have had
what might be called today a number of "therapeutic sessions."
Dr Putnam was in touch with Freud and Ernest Jones and the
psychologist Morton Prince. He had known William James. In
his office in Marlborough Street the discussion seems to have been
—to judge from a letter written by the novelist—about Henry's
depression and ways of eating sensibly and walking a great deal.
The novelist had made the mistake of trying to reduce by starving
himself; in keeping up his walks on so slender a diet he had
exhausted himself. This in part seems to have contributed to his
1910 illness. "You tided me over three or four bad places during
those worst months," James wrote to Dr Putnam. In New York
he consulted the fashionable doctor, Joseph Collins, who seemed
as much interested in writing a popular series of books on "the
doctor looks at . . ." life, literature, and so on, as in medicine.
After the novelist's death, Dr Collins wrote an account of
James's calls on him. This was included in his volume *The
Doctor Looks at Biography*. "He put himself under my professional care and I saw him at close range nearly every day for
two months; and talked with him, or listened to him, on countless
subjects." Dr Collins's conclusion was that Henry James had
"an enormous amalgam of the feminine in his make-up; he displayed many of the characteristics of adult infantilism; he had a
singular capacity for detachment from reality and with it a dependence upon realities that was even pathetic. He had a dread of
ugliness in all forms . . . His amatory coefficient was comparatively low; his gonadal sweep was too narrow." Dr Collins's
therapy consisted of "baths, massage, and electrocutions." James
found Dr Putnam more helpful.

Henry spent pleasant hours with Howells; he had long talks
with his old friend Grace Norton. Somerset Maugham, during
his dinner in Irving Street, found the Master nervous and ill at

ease; and while Maugham is not always a reliable witness—for he disliked James and envied him his vogue as theorist of fiction— he told how Henry escorted him to the street-car on Massachusetts Avenue and described his obsessive concern that Maugham get safely aboard. Henry told Maugham that American street-cars were of a savagery, an inhumanity, a ruthlessness beyond conception.

Thus the winter passed. The early summer brought intense heat and Henry fled to the cooling breezes of a house at Nahant, that of an old friend, George Abbot James. Near here James, who had glimpsed Blériot in flight over the Channel, saw a Wright bi-plane and found it of "extraordinary thrilling beauty." Mrs Wharton was back at The Mount trying to decide whether to sell it or not and whether to part from Teddy. James spent a very hot week-end there, Gaillard Lapsley also being present. "You must insist on saving your life by a separate existence," he told Mrs Wharton. The heat was intense and Mrs Wharton remembered "his bodily surface, already broad, seemed to expand to meet it, and his imagination to become a part of his body, so that one dripped words of distress as the other did moisture." Electric fans, iced drinks, cold baths, didn't seem to help, but motoring did, and Mrs Wharton drove him across miles of landscape, in order to provide coolness. Mrs Wharton felt a great desire to pack James off to Europe on the next ship, he seemed so miserable. To have an idea was, for Mrs Wharton, to translate it into action. She got James a booking on a liner sailing from Boston but he had planned his sailing and wasn't going to change it with great suddenness. "Good God, what a woman—what a woman! Her imagination boggles at nothing! She does not even scruple to project me in a naked flight across the Atlantic." It was of a piece with his remark, quite in the manner of "The Velvet Glove," in a letter to Lapsley that he could not help regretting "that an *intellectuelle*—and an Angel—should require such a big pecuniary basis."

James made his farewells in Irving Street; he said good-bye to Grace Norton, now one of the very few left out of his distant past. He felt it was their last meeting. He sailed for England on 30 July

1911. He had been in his native land for almost a year. The first anniversary of William's death was approaching. Shortly before sailing he learned that the crippled Jonathan Sturges, "the little demon," companion of his earlier days at Lamb House, whom he had known so long and cared for so deeply, had died in England. John La Farge had died while he was in America.

On the *Mauretania* he saw "the great bland simple deaf street boy" Thomas A. Edison and "I have talked with him." The smooth ocean liner of the new century lifted James across the sea "as if I had been carried in a gigantic grandmother's bosom and the gentle giantess had made but one mighty stride of it from land to land."

III

Re-established in Lamb House, he recognized very quickly the realities of his situation. Rye had been splendid for him when he was working on his big novels and living himself into retreat from so many years of London. But its rural life and its loneliness had had a great part in his depression; and after a very short time he found himself slipping again into despair. His remedy was to leave at once for London, for his perch at the Reform Club. He began also to look for a flat in Bloomsbury but found nothing to suit him. "Dear old London and its ways and works, its walks and conversations, define themselves as a Prodigious Cure," he wrote. He feared the "immobilization, incarceration" of Lamb House; his early sense of being "caged" in Rye had distinctly returned. His problem was what to do with his servants, who remained in idleness—and how to arrange his work. The Reform Club allowed him to have a typist in his rooms, but not a female, and he was in touch with Miss Bosanquet. She was willing to resume on the old basis. It was she who provided a temporary solution. She had two rooms available at one end of her flat at No. 10 Lawrence Street in Chelsea. These could be furnished for the Master; one of them had a bathroom and he could use it as a dressing-room. There was a separate entrance. James was enchanted; he very quickly organized his "Chelsea cellar" as he called it—because the workroom was long, narrow, and dark.

He found that he could take a taxi in the morning at the Reform Club for a few pennies, and in ten minutes be at work. He came to call it his "little Chelsea temple, with its Egeria." Here he began dictating the memorial to his brother, his notes as son and brother. He soon found himself writing instead the story of his earliest years—the book that would precede his tribute to William, *A Small Boy and Others*. Miss Bosanquet has given us a vivid picture of this dictating. Each morning, after reading the pages he had written the day before, he would pace up and down the room "sounding out the periods in tones of free resonant assurance. At such times he was beyond reach of irrelevant sounds or sights. Hosts of cats—a tribe usually routed with shouts of execration—might wail outside the window, phalanxes of motor-cars bearing dreaded visitors might hoot at the door. He heard nothing of them. The only thing that could arrest his progress was the escape of the word he wanted to use. When that had vanished he broke off the rhythmic pacing and made his way to a chimney-piece or bookcase tall enough to support his elbows while he rested his head in his hands and audibly pursued the fugitive."

In a certain sense the recall of his childhood in that dim Chelsea room, to the accompaniment of the familiar typewriter, ministered to his further physical recovery. It held in it the same form of release from discouragement and depression he had experienced a decade earlier when he had written out of his fantasies a series of novels and tales about children. Now he could draw directly upon the experiences of the little boy who had played in the streets around lower Fifth Avenue, travelled in the river steamer to visit his grandmother in Albany and eaten peaches from remembered trees in her large yard. An old America of small brick and frame houses and muddy streets, arose out of the past; and he found himself remembering Emerson and Thackeray in Fourteenth Street and his one-legged father with his long beard and his hours at his writing desk and the name of Swedenborg constantly evoked in the James's household. There came back to him the London of Dickens and du Maurier, the Paris of the Second Empire, the hours in the National Gallery and the first visit to the

Galerie d'Apollon. He saw himself and his brother as pious little American "pilgrims" abroad, decked out in their best, discovering the paintings of Delacroix, or at home his attendance at old melo-dramas in the Bowery. The memories may have seemed like anachronisms in a new London in which he could taxi every morning from his club to his workroom, but they danced vividly before his eyes and in the resonances of his style—quite like Proust, who was making similar discoveries of the "lost time" of his childhood. One reads *A Small Boy and Others* and hears the personal voice in every line; by degrees what is built up for us in this unique autobiography is the development of an artistic sensibility and the education of an imagination, and that capacity for observing "by instinct and reflection" with irony "and yet with that fine taste for the truth of the matter which makes the genius of observation." The James family with its innumerable cousins and its blighted lives, its galaxy of eccentric uncles and aunts, came to life again. Where other writers remember by simply recounting a curriculum of their lives, James embroidered a *petit point* of memory that showed the weavings to and fro across the Atlantic of the Jameses and the way in which they became—the younger members at least—citizens of two worlds.

He wrote now in the voice of his father and his brother. When he quoted from their letters he freely revised, as if their texts needed the same retouching given his own work in the New York Edition. When his nephew protested, after *Notes of a Son and Brother* was published, at this violation of William's language, Henry explained that he was showing it a marked respect. He could hear, he said, the voice of William saying to him, "Oh, but you're not going to give me away, to hand me over, in my raggedness and my poor accidents, quite unhelped, unfriendly: you're going to do the very best for me you *can*, aren't you?" His goal was to make the documents (and his own text) "engag-ingly readable and thereby more tasted and liked." He admitted that "I did instinctively regard it at last as all my truth, to do what I would with." And while he pleaded that he retouched only form, he subtly altered content as well. Part of the family history had to be written as art: life in its raw state was inartistic. This was why James joined two trips to Europe into one, and made his father write a letter to Emerson in stronger language than was in the manuscript. The novelist's visual memory for ancient detail was extraordinary; he calls up the size, shape, and appearance of objects; he remembers the essential physiognomical characteristic of long-dead personages; he is aware of old smells and sounds and when it comes to food he has all the taste of a hungry young boy. His "dive into the past" was hardly "free" association—but it was a return to a very old reservoir of experience. And if the old man pacing the narrow room, superimposed himself on the bright-eyed small boy or the meditative youth, it was through insights into the stages of his growth, the process that had made him artist and ultimately Master. He recreated as he said "the vivid image and the very scene; the light of the only terms in which life has treated me to experience"—in a word "the fine substance of history"—personal history.

The autobiographies evolved by stages. *A Small Boy* took James to his fifteenth year, when he had had typhoid at Boulogne-sur-Mer. He then embarked on a second volume calling it at first "Early Letters of William James with Notes by Henry James." When Harry sent him from America letters of the elder Henry James, he added—as the manuscript shows—a long section on his father, and in this fashion there evolved *Notes of a Son and Brother*. To his nephew, the busy Uncle kept explaining that he worked "expensively;" he was writing much more than he would use; that ultimately the "Family" book would be carved out of this material. In reality Henry James, in accordance with the imperious impulses of his nature, was pre-empting the family scene. Ultimately Harry James himself would edit his father's letters in two volumes. But the Master's enterprise yielded two volumes of rare autobiography in a most original vein. James gave the volumes to the Macmillans—he had owed them a book ever since his promise of the never-written work on London. In America the autobiographies were published by Scribner's appearing successively in 1913 and 1914. He was paid £500 in advance by each publisher.

Late in 1911, shortly after installing himself in his workshop in Chelsea, Henry found a solution for his "lonely" servants in Rye. His favourite nephew Billy married that autumn in America Alice Runnells, daughter of an affluent railroading family. The Uncle very promptly offered them Lamb House as a honeymoon house, an idea the young couple accepted with delight. Henry could remain at the Reform Club, his house tenanted by the attractive young people, who were there to take care of him when he stayed in Rye, and even to nurse him through a brief illness. He worked happily in London; and when the honeymooners came to the city the Uncle opened up for them all the avenues of English life. Billy, with his interest in painting, was taken to museums, to studios, to inspect the royal Holbeins at Windsor. The newest Alice in the James family—now the third—enjoyed meeting James's writer friends. Henry went shopping with them for furniture for their American home—"two hours of expensive acquisition." They went to the British Museum. He took them to see Pavlova, in all the freshness of her genius, and they saw the Princess Bariatinsky in a production of *Thérèse Raquin*; one evening when the Irish players came to London they saw *The Playboy of the Western World*. Long remembered by both was a week-end at Mrs Hunter's in Hill Hall, with notables of art and music present, and George Moore at the dinner table insisting on the interest of adultery. Out of this time there remained an anecdote of the Master's going for a stroll with Moore. He was asked on his return whether he had enjoyed his walk. Henry made a long speech—he talked of the many people he had known, and the delightful women, but he had never met, he said—never in all his experience—anyone who was quite so "unimportantly dull" as George Moore.

Billy and Alice remained in Lamb House throughout that winter and Henry remained happily in London. The couple returned to America in June; and James resettled in Lamb House for the summer. Summers were never lonely in Rye; it was the winters he feared. Summers, however, brought their own moments of terror—the "eagle pounce" of the Angel of Devastation—and her motor, and his usual ambivalence; he wanted to go with her, and he had his work. During this particular summer he wanted to finish *Notes of a Son and Brother*. The result was a period of large-scale diplomacy to which James brought all the power of his pen and all the energies of his mind.

THE FIREBIRD

Henry James had been seeing the Russian ballet—and he had his name for Edith Wharton. She had been an eagle and an Angel; now she was a Firebird—with "iridescent Wings." Bird imagery combined with motor imagery—the Firebird and her Chariot of Fire. She had been in touch with the Master throughout his illness. In 1911 she had commissioned a charcoal drawing of him by John Singer Sargent. The artist was delighted to have his old friend for a sitter; but things did not go well. The painter tried once or twice; finally he created a stern, heavy-lidded, accusing-eyed Master. James felt he could not regard the portrait objectively. Mrs Wharton did not like it. Sargent first thought of destroying it. It survives however. It ended up in the Royal Collection in Windsor Castle, where neither Henry James nor Mrs Wharton ever expected it would be. It was acquired to figure with the portraits of holders of the Order of Merit, which would be bestowed on the Master in due course.

I

The Master had hardly resettled into Lamb House for the summer when he wrote a beguiling—and also a cunning—letter to Mrs Hunter, the hostess of Hill Hall. There had been some question of his visiting there with Mrs Wharton and motoring in the surrounding countryside. He suggested tactfully and firmly that Mrs Hunter should try to stay her hand a little "as regards marked emphasis or pressure" in urging Mrs Wharton to come. He would be "a little in a false position . . . if one puts out a very persuasive hand to draw her over." If she came, there would be the motor, and he was busy with his writing. "Pleading with her to come does imply such a pledge—her motoring habits and intentions being so potent and explicit." In sum: "I think that what

464

my little plea really amounts to is that you should most kindly not appear to throw *me* into the scales of persuasion."

It didn't help. Little more than a fortnight later James was wiring Mrs Hunter that the Firebird was about to sweep "and to catch me up in her irresistible talons." To Mrs William James he explained "the pressure on me is great, and I am going and probably shall enjoy it as much as I *can* enjoy it with an irritated and distressed sense of interruptions and deviation." The question of this motor episode became for him, somehow, a matter of serio-comic urgency. Dispatches were sent to Edith's friends and his own, describing the inexorable advance of the authoress on Lamb House. The first in this series is dated "Reign of Terror, *ce vingt juillet*, 1912" to Howard Sturgis. It was "a sort of signal of distress" thrown out confidentially "at the approach of the Bird o'freedom—the whirr and wind of whose great pinions is already cold on my foredoomed brow! She is close at hand, she arrives tomorrow, and the poor old Ryebird, . . . feels his barn-yard hurry and huddle, emitting desperate and incoherent sounds, while its otherwise serene air begins ominously to darken." *Bref*, said James, the Angel—"half-angel and half-bird" as Browning had prefigured her—"has a *plan* of course." They would go to Qu'Acre, then dine with Lady Ripon; the Master was dissociating himself from this in advance. He had wired the Angel in Paris to say so. "I foresee," he added, "that on Edith's arrival the battle will be engaged."

To his Rye confidante, Fanny Prothero: "I clutch at anything to hang on by—Mrs Wharton being due in her motor-car half an hour hence, straight from Paris . . . and designing, with a full intensity, to whirl me away for several days—into the land at large. Nothing could suit me less . . . Ah our complicated mo-dernity! Yes, pray for me while I am hurried to my doom."

To Goody Allen in London: "An hour ago there arrived Mrs Wharton from Paris, by motor car from Folkestone—it is now 7 p.m. and she left this a.m. and she stays till Tuesday. I shall not get off without *some* surrender; when a lady has motored straight across the channel to ask one to oblige, one must go some little part of the way to meet her—even at the cost of precious hours and blighted labours and dislocated thrift and order."

What particularly troubled James was that Miss Bosanquet had gone away for a holiday; she had provided a temporary substitute, Miss Lois Barker, who would now collect pay while her employer had to go off with Mrs Wharton. "I feel better," he told Goody Allen, "for this (intensely *private*, please,) howl already. But oh one's *opulent* friends—they cost the eyes of the head."

II

The comedy of the Firebird resolved itself into a series of compromises. Henry sent her off alone; he promised to go with her to Howard Sturgis and to spend four or five days at Hill Hall. "The horrible thing about it is that it will be most interesting and wonderful and *worth while* and yet even this won't solve effectually my inward ache." Meanwhile Miss Barker, the typist, a parson's daughter, would have "elegant leisure" and James would be doing "the charmingly right thing at the hideously wrong time."

July 27, 1912—Queen's Acre. Motored to Cliveden with Edith Wharton after lunch; had tea there and promised Mrs Waldorf [Astor] to come back on Tuesday till Thursday.

July 28—Motored with E.W. beautifully, in afternoon (lovely day) over to Newbury to see Lady St Helier but found her away and her house let. Had tea at Inn—and most wonderful and beautiful run back to Qu'acre.

July 29—Motored with E., Howard and Babe over to tea with Ranee [of Sarawak] at Ascot. Vernon Lee there, with whom I had a good deal of talk.

It was his first meeting with Vernon Lee since she had caricatured him in a novel almost twenty years earlier.

July 30-31—Afternoon run to Cliveden. Three New Yorkers (*such* New Yorkers!) staying for night with Nancy Astor. Beautiful walk on the slopes down to and by river 6-8 with E.W. Americans left—day wet.

Spencer Lyttelton arrived . . . Day better p.m. Walked with E. through grounds, over slopes and by river—into Taplow Woods. Evening Arthur Ainger, Mrs John Astor and son Vincent.

Aug. 1—Agreed to stay over today Thursday . . . Second stroll with E. but had pectoral attack after lunch—through too much hurry and tension on slopes and staircase. Quiet till dinner—but second attack on mounting room 10.30. Lord Curzon at dinner.

Edith was understandably upset by Henry's heart flurries—apparently induced by his conflict between duty and pleasure and the Firebird's importunities. They left on 2 August and went back to Howard Sturgis's where they lunched. Then Mrs Wharton sent James back to Lamb House in her car.

. . . had admirable car and dear Cook lent me by Edith for most beautiful and merciful return, by myself, across country, back to Rye, where I write this. Admirable afternoon; admirable run through so lovely interesting land from about 2 to 6.30. Gave Cook forty shillings. Went straight to bed on arriving last night.

James stayed in bed the following day, but felt he needed "movement." He renewed his long walks and experienced immediate relief. "The only proper place for me is home," James wrote to Mrs Hunter.

James's impression of Nancy Astor, the future hostess of the "Cliveden Set" and Member of Parliament were that she was "full of possibilities and fine material—though but a reclaimed barbarian, with all her bounty, spontaneity and charm, too." He thought Cliveden "a creation of such beauty and distinction that the mere exposure of one's sensibility and one's imagination to the effect and the 'message' of such a place (in itself) becomes a duty if the opportunity arises." Thus he justified to himself his absence from his work.

Mrs Wharton returned to Lamb House early in August just before taking flight for the Continent. "The firebird perches on my shoulder," James wrote to Howard Sturgis on 12 August. Edith had held James and two other visitors "spell-bound, by her admirable talk. She never was more wound up and going, or more ready, it would appear, for new worlds to conquer." The only thing was, said James, what new worlds were left for her? "She uses everything and every one either by the extremity of strain or the extremity of neglect—by having too much to do with them (when not for *them* to do), or by being able to do nothing whatever, and passes on to scenes that blanch at her approach."

To Mrs Cadwalader Jones he gave the ultimate summary of "Edith's prodigious visit." "She rode the whirlwind, she played with the storm, she laid waste whatever of the land the other raging elements had spared, she consumed in fifteen days what would have served to support an ordinary Christian Community for about ten years. Her powers of devastation are ineffable, her repudiation of repose absolutely tragic, and she was never more brilliant and able and interesting."

Lois Barker, Miss Bosanquet's substitute, remembered vividly her summer's work in Lamb House. She took lodgings in Rye and turned up at Lamb House each morning where Burgess ushered her into the Green Room, and occasionally the Garden Room. James was often late. More than once on arriving she met him in the hall dressed only in pyjamas, carrying a large bath sponge. He beamed at her in his informality with his "large blue eyes" and always reassuringly said he would be with her in a few moments. He dictated his autobiographies without notes, though occasionally he darted to a drawer to return with a letter or other document. He dictated that summer the passage in *A Small Boy* in which Thackeray admired the buttons on James's boyhood jacket; he held in his hand the daguerreotype by Brady of the small boy wearing the jacket which would later be the frontispiece to the book. Suddenly in the midst of dictating the passage he left the room and returned. He was carrying the original jacket, buttons and all — those buttons which had fascinated Thackeray more than half a century before in New York.

A BROWNING CENTENARY

THE Master had avoided public appearances during all the years of his residence in England. *Guy Domville* had been an exception and an indiscretion for which he had paid a heavy price. He had done nothing abroad comparable to his lectures on Balzac in America. Nevertheless, in the fullness of age, during that spring of 1912 in London, James faced a distinguished audience to deliver a commemorative tribute to his old friend of the London drawing-rooms, to the poet of his youth — Robert Browning. The occasion was Browning's hundredth birthday, 7 May 1912. James had long ago enshrined the double-personality of Browning in his small tale "The Private Life;" now he offered a full-length paper, and read it himself. He called it "The Novel in *The Ring and the Book*." He spoke in an upper chamber of Caxton Hall with its pictured windows recording famous events in Westminster. Edmund Gosse presided. The other speaker was Arthur Pinero, the playwright, whose subject was Browning as a dramatist. The ceremony was under the auspices of the Academic Committee of the Royal Society of Literature to which Henry James had been elected some years before. It was one of those occasions relished by men of letters, proud of their craft, with the full sense of their profession and their status. It was also an odd occasion. In celebrating the centenary of Browning the two speakers were each dealing with him through their particular art — Pinero's address, long, loud, delivered with oratorical flourish and booming voice, was designed to show that Browning had been in no way a playwright; Henry James's tribute analysed *The Ring and the Book* to show how it might have been written as a novel — a novel, to be sure, by the author of *The Golden Bowl*.

"Pinero who thunderously preceded me," said James afterwards, "spoke twice as long as I had been told he was to; and this made me *apprehensive* and hurried and flurried and worried and faint through the sense that we were all *spent* — and the hall vast."

It was too vast to carry James's voice when he let it fall, so that his talk was intermittently inaudible to some parts of the audience. And yet the audience never became restless. It sat indeed as if hypnotized. It murmured approval. As in America at the Balzac lectures there were bursts of applause; and when the Master came to a particularly fine passage describing the sense of place — Tuscany and Rome — in Shelley, Swinburne, and Browning, a great stir and a great flutter greeted his words:

Shelley, let us say in the connection, is a light, and Swinburne is a sound — Browning alone is a temperature.

This was the Master's unique way of putting things; it resembled his memorable passage in his Balzac lecture on the quality of light he found in the great novelists. He compared Browning's re-creation of history with *Romola*. Browning stirred up "a perfect cloud of gold dust" whereas George Eliot "leaves the air about us clear, about as white, and withal about as cold, as before she had benevolently entered it."

Then James began to rewrite *The Ring and the Book* into a novel; he would bring the Canon Caponsacchi on earlier, "ever so much earlier, turn him on, with a brave ingenuity, from the very first," and in the city of Rome perhaps, "place him there in the field, at once recipient and agent, vaguely conscious and with splendid brooding apprehension, awaiting the adventure of his life, awaiting his call, his real call (the others have been such vain show and hollow stopgaps), awaiting in fine, his terrible great fortune." With delicate touches James also painted the background "*my* Italy of the eve of the eighteenth century — a vast painted and gilded rococo shell roofing over a scenic, an amazingly figured and furnished earth, but shutting out almost the whole of our own dearly-bought, rudely-recovered spiritual sky."

James was clear throughout — as he expounded doctrine out of the New York Edition prefaces — that his was an act of homage to Browning. "We move with him but in images and references and vast and far correspondences; we eat but of strange compounds and drink but of rare distillations; and very soon, after a course of this, we feel ourselves . . . in the world of Expression at any cost." He compared poets and novelists by saying the reader of fiction walks with the novelist on the same side of the street, whereas the poet is always "elegantly" walking on the other side, across the way "where we greet them without danger of concussion."

James singled out one quality in especial in Browning's work —"the great constringent relation between man and woman at once at its maximum and as the relation most worth while in life for either party." This remained, said James, the thing of which "his own rich experience most convincingly spoke to him." He had figured it "as never too much either of the flesh or of the spirit for him, so long as the possibility of both of these is in each, but always and ever as the thing absolutely most worth while." Was it worth while for *them* or for the reader? "Well, let us say worth while assuredly for us, in this noble exercise of the imagination." But there wasn't a detail of the "panting" flight of Caponsacchi and Pompilia over the autumn Appenines "the long hours when they melt together only *not* to meet—that doesn't positively plead for our perfect prose transcript."

The lecture had elegance; it had authority; it spoke for a powerful directing mind. James created seemingly impossible sentences, and made them somehow meaningful to the audience. Lord Charnwood, biographer of Lincoln, said there was an "extreme point-lace kind of refinement and elaboration of phrase and thought which makes me, personally, sick when I see a page of Henry James in cold print," but listening that afternoon it was "fascinating, soothing, elevating, even in parts intelligible to me when I heard it from the living voice of a quite living man." And then Lord Charnwood was arrested by the way James left him aware in his talk of Browning, "of one thing that might really satisfy a man's desire of life, namely to love a woman." A reporter present spoke of the "visible movement of enjoyment" in the listeners "over some more than usually musical and in every way beautiful sentence." When James stopped and sat down it seemed "as if the applause would never cease."

He had richly paid his debt to the remembered Browning, who had taught him so much about "point of view" long ago; about

entering into the thoughts of characters. But now the audience of
literary England, of his peers and of his readers, paid its homage
to him. It had never had such a chance in all the years of his
English life; and it did so with a fullness of measure that perhaps
James, in his flustered state, and high nervousness, did not
appreciate—until he read the reports in the papers. One journalist
spoke of sentences so musical and "so charged with criticism and
insight that one would strive to fix it in the memory; and then,
just as one thought one had succeeded, another as significant and
as rhythmical, would sound forth, and drive the predecessor
away." James began by reading the expository part of the lecture
rapidly; then he slowed down. His tone was conversational, his
voice mellow. "All true charm is indescribable, and that of Henry
James is more indescribable than most," the reporter wrote. The
press spoke of his "magic" very much as Max Beerbohm had
described it. "I noticed," wrote Filson Young in the *Pall Mall
Gazette* "that even the most experienced reporters gave it up in
despair, laid down their pencils, and sat hypnotized. . . . One
merely listened to the voice of this charming old artist as though
in the enchantment of a dream."

I was sitting near him and could hear every word; I am afraid that at least
half of the audience could hear nothing at all; but such was the charm in the
voice, such was the magic of this dear old man's personality, and such were
the affection and regard in which he was held by his audience, that not a
sound or movement disturbed the silence of the room during the whole of
that long and infinitely complicated address.

The Master to the Firebird:

"It might indeed have diverted you to be present at our Browning commemoration—for Pinero was by far the most salient
feature of it (simple, sensuous, passionate—that is artless, audible,
incredible!) and was one of the most amusing British documents
we had had for many a day. He had quite exhausted the air by the
time I came on—and I but panted in the void. But dear Howard
and dear Percy held each a hand of me—across the width of the
room—and I struggled through."

James was pleased nevertheless, for he clipped Filson Young's
comments and sent them to Cambridge, Massachusetts.

LA FOLIE DES GRANDEURS

THE years had passed and Hendrik Andersen had produced no memorable work; he had been young and ambitious in his twenties, when James met him. Now he was forty and dull. He showed no signs of maturity. The Master had had great expectations, and from time to time in their letters of love Henry James admonished him to do the practical artistic thing. But Andersen went on multiplying, as James ruefully specified, buttocks and breasts and penises, in the massive fountains he designed, with no visible sign that America was interested in such a quantity of nudity. After their brief meeting in America, in 1905, when James and Andersen had gone to Newport together, James had written to him "it's all pretty wretched, this non-communication —for there are long and weighty things about your work, your plan, your perversity, your fountain, your building, on and on and, up and up, *in the air*, as it were, and *out of relation to possibilities and actualities*, that I wanted to say to you." He went on to urge him once again to "*make the pot boil, at any price, as the only real basis* of freedom and sanity."

What American community, James wondered, "is going to want to pay for thirty and forty stark-naked men and women, of whatever beauty and lifted into the raw light of one of their public places. Keep in relation to the *possible* possibilities, dearest boy." He returned frequently to the charge. He spoke of "your horribly expensive family of naked sons and daughters, of all sizes, and ages . . . And then I reflect that you are always (terrible fellow!) begetting new ones as fast as possible—and I do lie awake at night asking myself what will become either of them or of you." James continued to tell Andersen that he would do better to create marketable potboilers; these at least would have some relation to reality.

In 1906 Andersen sent James a photograph of a statue of two

lovers in embrace. James said the work was the finest of the long "and interminable" series. He went on to analyse the statue's qualities:

I don't think I find the *hands*, on the backs, *living* enough and participant enough in the kiss. They would be, in life, very participant—to their finger-tips, and would show it in many ways. But this you know, and the thing is very strong and (otherwise) more complete. There is more flesh and *pulp* in it, more life of *surface* and of blood-flow *under* the surface, than you have hitherto, in your powerful simplifications, gone in for. So keep at *that*—at the flesh and the devil and the rest of it make the creatures palpitate, and their flesh tingle and flush, and their internal economy proceed, and their bellies ache and their bladders fill—all in the mystery of your art.

Thus the artist who had once described a parsimonious kiss in one of his famous novels and lately revised it in the sense in which he now wrote. His words fell, however, on emptiness. Andersen neither understood, nor did he listen. In another letter of this year James is again wondering "where this colossal multiplication of divinely naked and intimately associated gentlemen and ladies, flaunting their bellies and bottoms and their other private affairs, in the face of day, is going, on any *American* possibility, to land you." He complained that Andersen's figures were too stocky, "the faces too blank and stony." Andersen's women and men were also too undifferentiated—"*the* indispensable sign apart." There was a statue of a ballerina: he had not allowed her "a quite sufficient luxury—to my taste—of hip, or to speak plainly, Bottom. She hasn't *much* more of that than her husband and I should like her to have a good deal more." He adjures him to "stop your multiplication of unsaleable nakedness for a while and hurl yourself, into the production of the interesting, the charming, the vendible, the *placeable* small thing." He urged him to get at busts, "for it is fatal for you to go on infinitely neglecting the Face never doing one, only adding Belly to Belly—however beautiful —and Bottom to Bottom, however sublime. It is only by the Face that the artist—and the sculptor—can hope *predominately* to live and steadily to live—it is so supremely and exquisitely interesting to do." Such passages usually ended with "dear, dear Hendrik, have patience with my words and judge of the affection that prompted them."

II

In a letter of 1908, after he had had his reunion in Rome with Hendrik and watched him work in his studio, Henry James returned to his usual warning. He had seen the assembled works, the great impractical fountains, the lifeless nudes, *tutti bravi signori*, brave men, and beautiful women; and he remarked ironically "we shall have to build a big bold city on purpose to take them in." He added, not realizing how thoroughly he had diagnosed Hendrik Andersen, "I daresay you would take a contract for that, too, yourself." James probably forgot that he had written this. Yet he could not have put his finger more accurately on Andersen's vaulting fantasy, a kind of megalomania of the colossal, as James would call it, that he possessed.

Early in 1912, Hendrik sent the Master plans, circulars, appeals for funds, which he was distributing throughout Europe. He wanted indeed to build a "World City," a "world centre of communication." The motto for it would be "Love—Equality—Peace." His idea was that nations separated by oceans and mountains, language and custom, politics and prejudice, religion and culture—these phrases were in the prospectus—might here "imbibe living and vibrating knowledge at a great fountain, and offer of their best." To that end Hendrik envisaged, and had elaborate architectural drawings made by forty architects, of a vast Paris-like metropolis, a long mall, resembling the Tuileries, with a Palace of Nations, like the Louvre, with an Olympic athletic area at one end and a vast Palace of the Arts at the other, with a tremendous tower—a kind of mixture of the leaning tower of Pisa and the Eiffel Tower—presiding over the whole show. It was an architect's and sculptor's dream of a kind of permanent, super-World Fair. The buildings were all of the Grand Palais style, Graeco-Roman; one has a feeling that Hendrik Andersen planned this city around the huge fountains he had been designing for years. The photographs of the fountain-figures quite fit the descriptions of them in James's letters. One might add that both men and women look like heavyweight boxers—the women formidable with only the slightest of breasts, and their limbs set and masculine, poised in their frozen ballet. The plan would later elaborate the economy of the city down to the central heating. Andersen's idea was that it could be placed anywhere, he had no particular site in mind. He finally got up a big two-volume printing of three hundred copies of his plans and sent them to the millionaires of the world. And he travelled about Europe soliciting help for his idea. The King of the Belgians received him and gave him his blessing. The statues continued to multiply in Rome. The sculptured utopia remained stillborn.

The whole scheme was too much for the Master. James's reply 14 April 1912 had a portentous beginning. "Not another day do I delay to answer (with such difficulty!) your long and interesting letter . . . Brace yourself . . . though I don't quite see why I need, having showed you in the past, so again and again, that your mania for the colossal, the swelling and the huge, the monotonously and repeatedly huge, breaks the heart of me for you." His only answer to this waste of money and time on a "ready-made City" was to "cover my head with my mantle and turn my face to the wall, and there, dearest Hendrik, just bitterly *weep* for you—just desperately and dismally and helplessly water that dim refuge with a salt flood." He warned him of "dread Delusion"—medical science had a name for it, MEGALOMANIA and Henry wrote it in capital letters adding "look it up in the Dictionary." He also gave it to him in French, *la folie des grandeurs*. The dictionary wasn't necessary, for James went on to explain it was "the infatuated, and disproportionate love and pursuit of, and attempt at, the Big, the Bigger, the Biggest, the Immensest Immensity, with all sense of proportion, application, relation, and possibility madly *submerged*." The idea of a city built *de chic* filled the Master "with mere pitying dismay, the unutterable Waste of it all makes me retire into my room and lock the door to howl! Think of me as doing so, as howling for hours on end." He would continue to howl, he said, until he heard that Hendrik had chucked the whole thing into the Tiber. Cities he explained to Andersen, were "living organisms." They grew from within, piece by piece. There could not be a "ready-made city, made-while-one-waits." He closed asking Hendrik to understand "how dismally unspeakably much these cold hard, desperate words, witholding sympathy, cost your ever-affectionate, your terribly tender old friend." The world, James explained to Andersen, was no place for castles in the air given "this terribly crowded and smothered and overbuilt ground that stretches under the feet of the for the most part raging and would-be throat-cutting and mutually dynamiting nations." He also said that "things struggle into life, even the very best of them, by slow steps and stages and rages and convulsions of experience, and utterly refuse to be taken over ready-made or *en bloc*."

When Hendrik wrote again a year later, James had to recognize that "evidently, my dear boy, I can only give you pain." He repeated he did not understand "your very terms of 'world' this and 'world' the other." He told him "you take too much for granted, and take it too sublimely so, of the poor old friend who left you such a comparatively short time since in all contentment, as he supposed, in a happy Roman studio." The Master went on to say that he would feel quite the same about such vague immensities "even if I were not old and ill and detached, and reduced to ending my life in a very restricted way." Hendrik had dragged it out of him; he had to say to him, "I simply loathe such pretentious forms of words as 'world' anything—they are to me mere monstrous sound without sense. The World is a prodigious and portentous and immeasureable affair, and I can't for a moment pretend to sit in my little corner here and 'sympathize' with proposals for dealing with it. It is so far vaster in its appalling complexity than you or me, or than anything we can pretend without the imputation of absurdity and insanity to do to it, that I content myself, and inevitably *must* (so far as I can do anything at all now), with living in the realities of things, with 'cultivating my garden,' (morally and intellectually speaking) and with referring my questions to a Conscience (my own poor little personal), less inconceivable than that of the globe." With the words of Voltaire, this curious friendship of the Master with the no longer young sculptor more or less came to an end. James referred again to "the dark danger" of megalomania, "that way, my dear boy, Madness simply lies. Reality, reality, the seeing of things as they *are*, and not in the light of the loosest simplifications—come back to *that* with me, and then, even now we can talk!" And James signed himself "your poor old weary and sorrowing and yet always so personally and faithfully tender old Henry James."

We must recognize that in the inner world of the Master some deep dream of grandeur also existed—a dream of triumph amid the art works of the great world—as in the Galerie d'Apollon of the Louvre where he could defeat and feel the exaltation of power. It may be that Hendrik Andersen, in addition to having been an image in a mirror of youth in 1899, when James was reaching the farther limit of middle age, was also James's "secret sharer" of those drives of craft and glory. But Andersen did not really possess them, save in "the Big" and in Utopian fantasies. James had been able to control and channel his drive to greatness into the realities of his time and his world. Andersen would live to old age in Rome and leave his great unsold collection of statues; some would be used in buildings projected by another individual with a *folie des grandeurs*. Andersen's art was that kind of blind cold frozen art that could adorn great Mussolini manifestations of public frenzy and national megalomania so that the irony grew larger with the passage of time. The ornaments of an intended city of peace became the ornaments of a government of war. This, however, was far beyond the lifetime of the Master.

A DETERMINED WOMAN

ONE of the consequences of the Firebird's vision of Henry James during the motor tours of 1912 was her growing belief that he needed money. He had complained to her once too often of his low royalties; his ironies about his unprincely scale of life were taken seriously. During 1912 Walter Berry sent James a beautifully fitted leather suitcase lined with morocco leather. James had written an elaborate thank-you letter telling Berry how the beautiful object made everything else in Lamb House seem poverty-stricken. The letter was a bit overdone. James found the conceit too enticing to let go without an even more than customary recourse to hyperbole. *"Très cher et très-grand ami!"* he began, and after referring to Berry's "ineffable *procédé*" he spoke throughout the letter of the suitcase as "him" and said "I can't live with him, you see, because I can't live up to him." With his customary operative irony he went on to speak of "his claims, his pretensions, his dimensions, his assumptions and consumptions, above all the manner in which he causes every surrounding object (on my poor premises or within my poor range) to tell a dingy, and deplorable tale—all this makes him the very scourge of my life, the very blot on my scutcheon . . . I simply can't afford him, and that is the sorry homely truth. He is out of the picture—out of *mine*" and so on for nearly 2000 words. Mrs Wharton saw this letter. She probably noted the phrase "I simply can't afford him." She had heard James say this often enough. James was in reality telling Berry that he didn't need so grandiose an article (certainly he planned no further travels) but Mrs Wharton must have received quite another message.

In the preceding year she had quietly organized, with the help of Edmund Gosse in England, and with that of William Dean Howells in America, a vigorous campaign to obtain the Nobel prize for Henry James. It had never been given to an American and would not be until 1930. The Swedish Academy was thoroughly documented; appropriate letters were written emphasizing the Master's supreme position in Anglo-American letters. But the northern judges of the world's literature had not read Henry James and had not read about him in the newspapers; he was an intensely private figure; moreover, they tended to be influenced by the degree to which foreign writers were popular in other countries than their own and the extent to which they were translated. James had been very little translated. He did not permit it. He considered himself—and most translators agreed—untranslatable. In a word James was not as "visible" as Kipling, who had received the prize in 1907. Even the Firebird, with her tremendous energy and enthusiasm, could not convince the Academicians that a writer who belonged so intensely to the Anglo-American world deserved the great prize. It was much easier for the Academy to award it that year to Maurice Maeterlinck.

Edith Wharton was not to be frustrated. She remembered the highly successful device by which she—and the Master himself—had provided much-needed funds to Morton Fullerton when he was being blackmailed. She accordingly entered into secret correspondence with Charles Scribner who was her publisher in America—and also Henry James's. She and Scribner agreed that $8000 could be safely diverted from her royalties to the Master's Scribner account without arousing suspicion. They could hardly falsify the earnings on the New York Edition which were by now minimal. Scribner therefore wrote a letter to James which the novelist read with a certain amount of surprise, pleasure, and a touch of suspicion. The letter was a model of discretion. Scribner expressed delight at the chance to publish the autobiographies. James's agent had, moreover, said that the Master was working on a novel of American life—an allusion to his sketching out of *The Ivory Tower* just before his 1910 illness. "As the publishers of your definitive edition we want another great novel to balance *The Golden Bowl* and round off the series of books in which you have developed the theory of composition set forth in your prefaces." Scribner felt such a book would be of great advantage

W. MORTON FULLERTON

HENRY JAMES AT SEVENTY
Portrait by John Singer Sargent

both to publisher and author; it should be written as soon as possible. It obviously would demand much time, and Scribner's had decided therefore to make an "unusual proposal." If James could begin the book soon, the publisher was prepared to pay him an advance of $8000 (£1500), perhaps half on signing the contract and half on delivery of the manuscript. The novel would form an additional volume or volumes of the New York Edition.

James had never received so handsome an offer from any publisher. It was settled that he would be given a 20 per cent royalty and Scribner would have world rights and would thus arrange publication in England. Also that James would write the novel as soon as possible after the completion of the autobiographies. James B. Pinker, the novelist's agent, was not fooled; he ultimately fathomed the intrigue, for a note in Miss Bosanquet's diary, made after James's death, tells us that Pinker "has been convinced by his recent communications with Scribner's that his guess as to Mrs Wharton having subsidized the Scribner novel contract was quite correct." The agent was discretion itself. If he was suspicious, no sign was given to James, who simply remarked he could hardly believe in the bounty of publishers, but that he should certainly accept.

Mrs Wharton was disturbed that James handed the matter over to his agent. This meant that almost $1000 of the sum—or to be exact $800—would be paid to Pinker as his fee. She did not see why Pinker should get anything; and caused Scribner to suggest to James that since the initiative had been taken by the publisher no negotiation with the agent was needed. James, however, insisted that Pinker handle the contract and receive his due. The first instalment of the advance was $3600—which James happily pocketed, still surprised, but also greatly delighted.

II

The Scribner letter could not have come at a better moment, and Mrs Wharton's initiative, while meddlesome and not required, since James's financial position, if modest, was sound, helped greatly to give James's morale a lift at a crucial moment. For in

Q

the autumn of 1912, when he seemed to have fully recovered from
his depression and illness of two years earlier, he suddenly came
down with the painful systemic virus disease known as *herpes
zoster*—in a word "shingles." The evenly spaced skin eruption,
from which the ailment takes its name, appeared across the chest
and round to his back; since it follows the line of a cutaneous
nerve, it was painful in the extreme. James had a very bad case of
it—it laid him low for the next four months and while he could
have been ambulatory, he spent much time in bed since he found
that his clothing irritated his skin. A consequence of this was that
he did not get the exercise he required, given his obesity and the
condition of his heart. His letters of this time, some scrawled in
pencil in bed, betray the intense irritation and suffering he under-
went. And yet he kept up his friendships and his interests, and
managed to do a considerable amount of reading and planning,
and even dictation, so that *A Small Boy and Others* was completed, and *Notes of a Son and Brother* got under way. In the mid-
winter, in February of 1913, the prolonged inactivity produced an
accumulation of fluid at the bottom of James's lungs. This was
not at first diagnosed, and as James's breathing became more
difficult, and his discomfort acute, alarms went out to his friends.
Mrs William James offered to come from America. Mrs Wharton
was prepared to "rush over for two or three days at once" from
Paris. She ventured to be "insistent" because in the absence of
James's family the doctor should know there was someone to
whom the "exact facts" could be reported.

James's loyal housemaid, Minnie Kidd, at this moment was
called to her aged mother who was ill and the doctor brought in
a nurse to replace her. The Master called the latter "a mild
dragon." Mrs Wharton secretly provided funds for a nurse for
Kidd's mother and restored the faithful maid to James's bedside—
this being arranged through Miss Bosanquet. James's nurse was
speedily dismissed. Once diagnosed, James's oedema was readily
treated and he rapidly recovered. "My vitality, my still sufficient
cluster of vital 'assets,'" James wrote to his nephew Harry, "to
say nothing of my *will to live and to write*, assert themselves in
spite of everything." This was true. There was little depression

in this illness. The prospect of doing a new novel for Scribner, the handsome sum advanced, the progress of the autobiographies, prevailed over the ills of the flesh. James went through the siege surrounded by friends, ministered to by his servants, and after the first eight or ten weeks was able to move about during the daytime though quite eager to tear off his clothes and get into bed as quickly as possible at the day's end. For a while in the later stages massage was prescribed but it coincided with the onset of the oedema and was not successful. There is an interesting footnote to the massage by way of a remark made by a Swedish masseur to a lady in Sweden who incorporated it in her memoirs. The Swedish authoress, Mia Leche Löfgren, recorded a conversation with a "medical gymnast" who said he had worked for Henry James and "didn't like him." Wasn't he friendly? the authoress asked, and the answer was, "Yes, he was *too* friendly."

III

In the weeks preceding his illness, Henry James had been extraordinarily active. He was delighted that his old friend Edmund Gosse had become librarian of the House of Lords and had tea with him in the lordly surroundings. At the beginning of 1912, dining at Edmund Gosse's, he met the young French writer André Gide, "an interesting Frenchman" James noted. He took him in his cab back to his hotel. It was their only meeting.

James's date-books show that during this period he met May Sinclair, attended a reception at Sir Edward Elgar's, saw again his old friend Lady Gregory, with whom he shared in common an interest in Paul Harvey, now having a distinguished career in the diplomatic service. William Lyon Phelps, the Yale *literatus*, turned up in London. James described him as "the boring and vacuous (though so well-meaning) Yale chatterbox Phelps." The Master took a lively interest in suffragette activities. He saw something of Lady Ottoline Morrell "always touching and charming; and yesterday (8 May 1912) she was very interesting; and also beautiful. But I wish she didn't run so much to the stale, but a little more to the fresh, in costume." He referred to her "window-curtaining clothes." Lady Ottoline did affect elaborate and eccentric garb; one might meet her on occasion dressed as a shepherdess.

On 26 June 1912 Oxford bestowed the honorary degree of doctor of letters on the Master and he may have remembered how years before he had given a dinner in London to celebrate bestowal of that honour on Turgenev. Attired in the academic gown he heard himself described as "fecundissimum et facundissimum scriptorem, Henricum James."

He wrote during that year a long and warm letter of praise for William Dean Howells's seventy-fifth birthday to be read at one of Colonel Harvey's great dinners in New York. It was almost as long as an essay and surveyed Howells's work with affection and friendliness out of their lifetime of friendship. He reminded Howells that Taine had once greeted him as "a precious painter and a sovereign witness," and he told him that "the critical intelligence—if any such fitful and discredited light may still be conceived as within our sphere—has not at all begun to render you its tribute." He told Howells, "It's a great thing to have used one's genius and done one's work with such quiet and robust sincerity." In the letter James recalled the encouragement Howells, during his *Atlantic* editorship, had given him long ago, the first editor to believe in and proclaim the genius of Henry James.

Reading that autumn the letters of George Meredith, just published, he was led to reflect on the way in which greatness is reduced in the posthumous world. He complained at the letters chosen by Meredith's son, their scantness and their failure to convey the charm and magic of the Meredith he had so long known. In a series of letters to Gosse, James wrote "what lacerates me perhaps most of all in the Meredith is the meanness and poorness of the editing—the absence of any attempt to project the Image (of character, temper, quantity and quality of mind, general size, and sort of personality,) that such a subject cries aloud for; to the shame of our purblind criticism. For such a Vividness to go a-begging . . . When one thinks of what Vividness would, in France, in such a case, have leaped to its feet in commemorative and critical response." On further acquaintance with the volumes he grew critical; he complained that the "aesthetic range" of the letters was meagre; Meredith had lived, James felt "even less than one had the sense of his doing, in the world of art—in that whole divine preoccupation . . . His whole case is full of anomaly . . . He was *starved*, to my vision, in many ways—and that makes him but the more nobly pathetic." It was Meredith's lack of "aesthetic curiosity" that bothered James most.

The Master's date-books do not record his encountering a young American with thick fluffy brown hair growing back from a very straight line along his forehead and a little pointed moustache and beard, and as Miss Bosanquet would note "slightly aesthetic clothes." Ezra Pound spoke with a drawl; he lowered his voice so as to become inaudible. This may have been the awe in which he stood of the Master. Pound wrote home that he and Henry James "glared at one another across the same carpet" and he remembered James's saying of America, that it was "strange how all taint of art or letters seems to shun that continent." In Pound's *Cantos* years later was recorded a memory of the Master, a glimpse at the Reform Club:

> And the great domed head, *con gli occhi*
> *onesti e tardi*
> Moves before me, phantom with weighted motion,
> *Grave incessu*, drinking the tone of things
> And the old voice lifts itself
>   weaving an endless sentence.

This was indeed Henry James; and on 15 April 1913 he would be seventy.

IV

Shortly before the onset of his attack of the shingles, Henry James had found a flat in London, in Cheyne Walk, in Chelsea. His room at the Reform Club had served him for more than ten years; now, with his intermittent illnesses, and his need to have Miss Bosanquet available, and above all remembering how his "hibernation" at Rye bred loneliness and depression, he had decided to return to the metropolis. He would use Lamb House only in the summers. No. 21 Carlyle Mansions suited him in every way. It was an L-shaped apartment, with two large rooms hanging over the Thames; these could serve as study and dining-room. Off the long corridor there was a series of smaller rooms, a master bedroom for himself and further down rooms for his cook, a maid, and the indispensable Burgess. There were five bedrooms in all. It would cost him only £60 a year more than his pied-à-terre at the Reform. He was a little touchy about the fact that the landlord hadn't heard of Henry James and asked for references; but Edmund Gosse, with his address at the House of Lords, provided the kind of *cachet* that seemed to be needed. He would have as a neighbour his old friend, Emily Sargent, sister of the painter. The rooms over the river gave him a southern view: they had a great deal of sun. The scene had been painted many times by Whistler, whose studio had been in nearby Tite Street where Sargent now lived. James had fond memories of the area; in 1869, during his first adult trip abroad, he had been taken here to visit Dante Gabriel Rossetti by Charles Eliot Norton. He liked the pompously-embanked river which offered him a walk all the way to Westminster; and the neighbourhood was associated with Carlyle, Turner, Leigh Hunt, George Eliot.

Since he was still ill in January 1913, when he took possession of the apartment, the move was made by his servants, who brought various pieces of furniture from Lamb House, and settled everything for the Master. He arrived to a tolerably organized establishment, whose occupation Fanny Prothero had supervised with great efficiency.

And so Henry James formerly of 34 De Vere Gardens, Kensington, who had forsaken London in the late 1890's, now returned to the metropolis. He was again near his clubs and a host of friends—a whole new generation of friends. He could watch the boats on the river; and feel himself again in harmony with the great rumbling city. He now had a telephone; the days of "calling" and leaving cards were being supplanted by that device. Taxicabs were handy. He was ready to settle down to work again. But he knew—he felt—that this was his last harbour; and the voyage was nearly over.

THE MASTER AT SEVENTY

LATE in 1912 or early in 1913 Edith Wharton caused to be circulated a form letter among figures of society and finance in the United States proposing that a substantial sum be raised in honour of Henry James's seventieth birthday. She regarded the secretly diverted royalty as a stop-gap: she wanted the Master to receive a large purse. If the Swedish Academy would not give him the Nobel prize his own countrymen should do something quite as handsome. The circular letter suggested that a series of large contributions would be welcomed and named a bank into which the sums should be paid. It was a characteristic example of the generous—and thoughtless—impulses of the Firebird; she had acted quickly and imperiously, but without sufficient attention to Henry James's feelings. One of her thoughts seems to have been that James might purchase a car from the proceeds of this subscription.

While the appeal was made with discretion, was private and wholly unpublicized, word of it reached Henry James's nephew Harry, at the Rockefeller Institute in New York, and Billy, who had settled in Boston after his honeymoon in England. Billy cabled his uncle at once. The reply could not have been more prompt. "Immense thanks for warning taking instant prohibitive action. Please express to individuals approached my horror money absolutely returned. Uncle." This was followed by a letter to Billy saying he wanted the appeal for funds "stamped out by any violent means (not, of course, of the newspaper)." With Harry acting in New York, and Billy in Boston, he was certain they would easily "break the back of the thing." He added: "A more reckless and indiscreet undertaking, with no ghost of a preliminary leave asked, no hint of a sounding taken, I cannot possibly conceive—and am still rubbing my eyes for incredulity." He wanted it given out, privately and socially, "to all it may concern, this my all but indignant, and my wholly prohibitive protest." The money was returned. Among the papers of Mrs Wharton there is no letter from Henry James on the subject, and the chances are he said not a word to her. Their friendship continued unchanged; however misguided the attempt, her motive had been generous. She had been guilty of a failure in empathy—and in strategy.

I

Henry James's friends in England, practised in the arts of homage, had quite another scheme. Percy Lubbock, Hugh Walpole, Edmund Gosse, Lucy Clifford, and others, a small informal committee, issued an appeal to the Master's friends and admirers. His seventy years of art and distinction should be honoured, and in a fitting public fashion. James got wind of this initiative from loyal Goody Allen and asked very promptly they put a stop to it. He explained to Miss Bosanquet he didn't want it bruited abroad "that I'm a fabulous age when I'm trying to put forth some further exhibition of my powers." Lucy Clifford flatly told him he was "cold, callous, and ungracious." He capitulated. No one was allowed to contribute more than £5. Nearly three hundred persons subscribed, and with this sum a silver-gilt Charles II porringer and dish was purchased for £50 to be presented to the author of *The Golden Bowl*. The balance was offered to John Singer Sargent to paint a portrait of the Master. Sargent, as a friend of many years, refused to take any honorarium; and the sum was used to commission a bust of Henry James by a young sculptor suggested by Sargent, Derwent Wood. In this way, and with all the niceties observed, the Master awoke on 15 April to discover himself, at least for the day, a great public figure.

The bell at No. 21 began to ring early; by forenoon the apartment was filled with flowers; cables and telegrams arrived from everywhere. On behalf of friends and admirers the Golden Bowl was presented and accepted by James with his customary elegance. Inscribed on the bowl were the simple words "To Henry James from some of his friends." He announced he would sit for the portrait (and later consented to sit for the bust) but that he would not accept the painting as belonging to himself; it belonged to his admirers. He agreed to be its custodian and publicly willed it to the National Portrait Gallery; if it should be judged unacceptable by that institution, he suggested it be offered to the Metropolitan Museum in New York. He thus gave the country of his adoption "first refusal," but he did not forget the city of his birth. The portrait hangs today—one of Sargent's masterpieces—in the National Portrait Gallery in London.

He had felt so many times in his life that the world did not want his art and did not recognize his genius. But on this day he was given a full measure of the world's affection. Lucy Clifford, one of James's most cherished friends, wrote to Scribner's, her publisher in America, "we have just had a high jubilation over Henry James's birthday, given him an address, a really beautiful golden bowl. I went to see him on the great morning and found him bewildered—his staircase a sort of highway for messengers and telegraph boys carrying messages, wonderful flowers arriving, the telephone bell going like mad; his faithful servants standing on their heads, and a general effect of joy, congratulations, and delightful lunacy. I happen to adore him very much, so after an hour of it, I carried him off to lunch peacefully at my club and then returned him to the rejoicings at his flat."

Opening the *Pall Mall Gazette* on that day the Master found in it an editorial entitled "Henry James." The newspaper spoke of the "spontaneous impulse" of James's innumerable friends in England and on the Continent but "thousands of others who will only hear of it today, will be with the participants in their hearts." The editorial referred to James's "immense achievement" and the appearance at this moment of *A Small Boy and Others*. It expressed the wish that "this keen observer, very great artist, and brilliant and generous critic of men and manners, may, in the best of health and the fulness of power, enjoy many more birthdays; and that that great delight, 'a new book by Henry James,' may be often in store for the public in the future." In an age of "much hurry, superficiality, and meanness," said the editorial, it had been shown that "a great and deliberate artist and a generous spirit can still win its proud and affectionate recognition."

The name of Edith Wharton was not in the list of subscribers because the committee had known of her separate initiative and had not approached her; but James added her name afterwards and that of Walter Berry, and he quietly added the names of a few others who had been informed too late or who were not known to the committee when the appeal went out. He did this because he had decided to print and send to the donors a formal letter of thanks, and inserted all their names at the bottom of the letter. Later he arranged for all of them to receive a photograph of the Sargent portrait signed on the left by Sargent and on the right by himself. Sargent's name has all but faded from such of these as survive; but James's name, with its customary largeness and boldness, remains visible.

All of James's epistolary art is in the letter of thanks. "Dear Friends All," he began, "let me acknowledge with boundless pleasure, the singularly generous and beautiful letter, signed by your great and dazzling array and reinforced by a correspondingly bright material gage, which reached me on my recent birthday, April 15th." It had moved him "as brave gifts and benedictions can only do when they come as signal surprises. I seem to wake up to an air of breathing good-will the full sweetness of which I had never yet tasted." He had been drawn to London, he wrote, long years before, by the sense "of all the interest and association I should find here, and now I see how my faith was to sink deeper foundations that I could presume ever to measure." It was wonderful to count over "your dear and distinguished friendly names, taking in all they recall and represent, that I permit myself to feel at once highly successful and extremely proud." His friends and admirers "making one rich tone of your many voices," told him "the whole story of my social experience . . . there is scarce one of your ranged company but makes good some happy train and flushes with some individual colour." He accepted the "admirable, the inestimable bowl;" he engaged to sit for Sargent, "but with this one condition that you yourselves, in your strength and goodness, remain guardians of the result of his labour." Then in a postscript he wrote "and let me say over your names."

The list is a roll call of splendour in the annals of the arts, politics, and the social life of the time. The nobility of England and the Rye neighbours; James's physicians; the personalities of the stage, a great many novelists; one notes the absence of Conrad and Hardy, who may have been overlooked when the appeal went out. His French friends, however, were not forgotten.

II

James posed that spring for Sargent in his studio, about a dozen times. Sargent painted him in a characteristic pose, his left thumb catching his striped and elegant waistcoat. He is wearing a bow tie and starched collar, and the watch chain dangles across the ample embonpoint at the lower end of the picture. On the strong hand holding the waistcoat may be seen the topaz ring James had worn for many years, an American ring, probably a family heirloom. For the rest, the picture fades into chiaroscuro, since Sargent painted always from dark to light; the full highlight accentuates the great forehead, as Pound describes it in the Cantos, the eyes half closed as if in the middle of thought, but with all their visual acuteness, which so many of his contemporaries had described; and the lips are formed as if the Master were about to speak. In every way it was a portrait of power and mastery so that some disliked it, feeling that it looked more like a painting of a corporation president or a titan of finance. A careful study of the picture shows that beyond the portliness Sargent has caught the sensitivity of the Master; if he had had difficulty with the charcoal sketch earlier, it now constituted an exercise for this performance. There is a great feeling of life in it. The Master is caught in one of the moments of his greatness—that is a moment of "authority." James felt this as he saw himself take form on the canvas. He was a patient sitter but Sargent had him invite friends to talk to him and distract him while he was being painted "to break the spell of a settled gloom in my countenance," said James. Jocelyn Persse was summoned and came; and also the young Ruth Draper, freshly descended on London from America to do her inimitable monologues at that time in some of the great houses of England; later and for many years she would perform publicly in the theatre. James was fascinated by her from the first. "Little

Ruth is a dear of dears," he wrote, "and her talent has really an extraordinary charm." Inspired by her work he would write a monologue for her which, however, she never performed, for she always created her own. James greatly enjoyed his sittings in Sargent's high cool studio which opened on a balcony and a green Chelsea garden. He found himself saying that he looked more and more like Sir Joshua's Dr Johnson, and others who saw the picture had the same impression—certainly it was true of the massiveness of the figure if not of the features—James's having a delicacy not visible in the coarser face of the eighteenth-century's literary dictator. To Rhoda Broughton, James wrote that the picture was "Sargent at his very best and poor old H.J. not at his worst; in short a living breathing likeness and a masterpiece of painting. I am really quite ashamed to admire it so much and so loudly it's so much as if I were calling attention to my own fine points. I don't, alas, exhibit a 'point' in it, but am all large and luscious rotundity—by which you may see how true a thing it is." He would have liked to go on sitting; it made the mornings of the early summer by the Thames so pleasant, even if it took him from his work.

James had always been fond of Sargent from the first days when he had met him in Paris almost three decades before and urged him to settle in London. He liked his geniality and good nature, and was struck again as he sat for him by "the large ease and modesty of his intercourse, his liberal hospitable way altogether." It was the sort of thing (he told his niece Peggy who came to England that summer) that "one always finds, I think, in the truly great—when they are great enough." As for the portrait itself, he told Peggy that Sargent had scarce ever done anything of a "higher class." The face "has such extraordinary life, such inward being, behind it," and he repeated he was ashamed of his admiration for the picture since he was admiring himself.

Since the picture had been commissioned, in effect, by some three hundred persons, Sargent held a special showing of it in his studio in December 1913 during three consecutive days. This provided the novelist with an opportunity to thank the donors personally. They flocked to see portrait and subject in great numbers and "I really put myself on exhibition beside it," James wrote to Gosse, "each of the days, morning and afternoon, and the translation (a perfect Omar Khayyam, *quoi*!) visibly left the original nowhere." It had been an "exquisite incident . . . most beautiful and flawless." The work was acclaimed "with an unanimity of admiration, and literally, of *intelligence*, that I can testify to."

THE INFINITE OF LIFE

THE following spring—early in May 1914—an elderly white-haired woman, placid-looking and wearing a loose purple overcloak, entered the rooms of the Royal Academy in London. It was the opening day of the spring show. She walked from room to room until she came to Room III. Here, under glass, she found the portrait by John Singer Sargent of Henry James. It was attracting attention in the press. Suddenly those in the room heard the sound of shattering glass. The peaceable-looking lady was wielding with vigour a meat-cleaver she had concealed beneath the purple cloak. Several women pounced on her—but already Sargent's masterpiece had in it three ugly gashes. She had cut through the left side of the head, the right side of the mouth and below the right shoulder. A man who attempted to defend the violent lady from the irate women had his glasses broken. The police arrived promptly.

At the station the woman gave her name as Mrs Mary Wood. She had never heard of Henry James. Her assault on the picture was for reasons that had nothing to do with the novelist or with Sargent. She explained it, in the most explicit manner, in the police court that day. "I did it as a protest," she said. A militant suffragette, she said that she had read that the picture was valued at £700. A woman painter, she said, would not have received anywhere near such a sum. "I have tried to destroy a valuable picture," said Mrs Wood, "because I wish to show the public that they have no security for their property, nor for their art treasures, until women are given their political freedom."

"Academy Outrage," the newspaper headlines screamed that day. An urgent meeting of the Council of the Academy was called with Sargent present; the experts believed the picture could be repaired and restored. The weekly meeting of the Women's Social and Political Union voted Mrs Woods "a brave woman."

In jail Mrs Woods went on a hunger-and-thirst strike and after a few days was released. Edmund Gosse wrote a letter to *The Times* saying it had been a "horrible" outrage since the picture had been "the emblem of private affection and regard" for a great artist—a great man "who has nothing to do with politics." James's old novel about feminism, *The Bostonians*, which might have provided still another motive, went unmentioned.

"Most gentle friend," Henry James wrote to Goody Allen after the onslaught, "I naturally feel very scalped and disfigured, but you will be glad to know that I seem to be pronounced curable ... The damage, in other words, isn't past praying for, or rather past mending, given the magic of the modern mender's art." His table was strewn, he said, with three hundred and ninety kind notes of condolence. The suffragette had only caused him to receive, less than a year after his seventieth birthday, still another ovation. To William Roughead, the Edinburgh Jurist, with whom James had been having a lively correspondence about old Scottish murder trials, the Master wrote that it was a sad fact that all that could be done after such violent events was "to lock the stable door after the horse is stolen." The "smash of an object really precious to the general mind" should be acclaimed only "for the light and wisdom and reason that they shall bring to our councils."

To Howells James was less urbane. "Those ladies really outrage humanity, and the public patience has to me a very imbecile side." Another portrait had been hacked with a chopper on the day he was writing—such events being contagious—"and the work goes bravely on." The Sargent portrait was restored before the end of the month and exhibited again under watchful guard.

I

Henry James remained in London until late in the spring of 1913 after his birthday celebrations and the painting of the portrait, in order to pose for his bust. A few days before his scheduled departure for Rye, he felt ill, went to bed and lost consciousness. He had never had a fainting spell and it frightened him. "I was *consciously* sure I was dying," he said. His doctor brought in a nurse; within twenty-four hours the Master—after a "wretched time"—was able to have lunch at home with his nephew Harry; Peggy and Fanny Prothero came at once to give him support. His specialist, Dr Des Voeux, was "very reassuring and interesting" James noted in his date-book. He said the novelist had "*very* great powers of recuperation." Thus heartened James left as he had planned for Lamb House accompanied by his niece. He had begun to restrict his activities even before this brief illness. He had once described the predicament of a novelist who feels the world shrinking around him: in his tale of "The Middle Years" he had made the novelist muse that "he was better of course, but better, after all than what? He should never again, as at one or two great moments of the past, be better than himself. The infinite of life was gone, and what remained of the dose was a small glass scored like a thermometer by the apothecary . . . It was the abyss of human illusion that was the real, the tideless deep."

What was real now for James was that "the evening of life is difficult." So he wrote to his old friend Helena De Kay Gilder. "One always supposed it would be—and now one knows. One *has* to take it, however, which is rather grim so I try to see it, or feel it, rather as much as I can by exemptions and simplifications." He tried to cultivate "a grand serenity." His friends saw this serenity during 1913–14, when he constantly apologized for not dining out, but occasionally on good days lunched in town when he was not working, and took tea after his long walks—for he kept up his walking. To Hugh Walpole he wrote with a certain anguish of "increasing limitations of ease and dilapidations of state." "We communicate across the gulf of Time, awful Time, while I grow relentlessly older and you shamelessly younger, but let us none the less do it as we can and under whatever disadvantage—let us keep the possibility just enough *ahead* of the difficulty."

He was able during the summer at Lamb House in 1913 to put last touches to *Notes of a Son and Brother*. He had many good days and a feeling of the old time. His nephew Harry came for almost a fortnight; Peggy was with him much of the time, and he invited Logan Pearsall Smith down for a long week-end. They had never known each other well. Logan would greatly exaggerate their friendship and like Hueffer tell many spurious anecdotes—but they had lately exchanged letters and the future author of *Trivia*, descended from Philadelphia Quakers, seems to have been quite in character during his stay. "Logan Pearsall Smith was just with me for 36 hours—and the tide of gossip between us rose high, he being a great master of that effect." Logan Pearsall Smith was especially lurid about elderly stout Constance Fletcher, James's old friend, and he would have an elaborate anecdote about her much later—about her adventures in a bathtub in Lamb House from which, because of her obesity, she could not extricate herself. On another occasion, in the last year of James's life, Pearsall Smith arranged for the Master to lunch with Santayana in St Leonard's Terrace and quoted him as saying he would walk barefoot through the snow to meet the philosopher. Actually what James had written to Gaillard Lapsley was "I envy you the intercourse of Santayana, whom I don't know and have never seen, but whose admirable mind and style I so prize that I wish greatly he sometimes came to London." In his memoirs Santayana speaks of the meeting. "In that one interview," he wrote, the Master "made me feel more at home and better understood than his brother William ever had done in the long years of our acquaintance. Henry was calm, he liked to see things as they are, and be free afterwards to imagine how they might have been." Other visitors that summer were Joseph Conrad "poor queer man," who came to Lamb House for lunch. Wells's new novel *The Passionate Friends* arrived and James read it, and his letter of criticism was quite as sharp as always. He had for a long time been giving Wells private full-dress reviews of each book. James always began with praise; then with the statement that it was his habit to rewrite people's novels "rehandling the subject according to my own lights and overscoring the author's form and pressure with my own vision." Almost as if he were addressing young Hugh and not the experienced Wells, James went on to say he found him "perverse" and "on a whole side, unconscious, as I can only call it, but my point is that *with* this heart-breaking leak even sometimes so nearly playing the devil with the boat your talent remains so savoury and what you do substantial. I adore a rounded objectivity." James explained that he objected to Wells's use of the autobiographical form. He had said this many times before—the use of the first person led to too much fluidity, brought in too many extraneous elements. He then dissected the novel but ended as always with sincere admiration—"your temper and your hand form one of the choicest treasures of the time; my effusive remarks are but the sign of my helpless subjection and impotent envy." Wells, whether in irony or truth, replied that his book was "gawky," it had been thrust into the world too soon; he abjectly added "my art is abortion—on the shelves of my study stand a little vain-gloriously thirty-odd premature births . . . But it is when you write to me out of your secure and masterly *finish*, out of your golden globe of leisurely (yet not slow) and infinitely *easy* accomplishment that the sense of my unworthiness and rawness is most vivid. Then indeed I want to embrace your feet and bedew your knees with tears—of quite unfruitful penitence." To Walpole James said that this reply showed Wells "profusely extravagantly apologetic and profoundly indifferent." He added that artistically Wells had "gone to the dogs"; his work, however, still expressed his temperament and "that self remains to me demonic—for life and force, cheek and impudence and a wondrous kind of vividness *quand même*. He inveterately goes to pieces about the middle—in this last thing the first half promised and then the collapse was gross. And he will never do anything else, and will never dream of so much as wanting to. They all seem to me money-grabbers pure and simple, naked and unashamed; and Arnold Bennett now with an indecency, verily, an obscenity of nudity!"

How demonic Wells could be James would find out. And as for the rest, there was still a great power of assertion in the Master and he was about to have his say in an article that would reverberate through the British literary establishment.

II

That autumn in London he received from André Raffalovich a volume of Aubrey Beardsley's last letters, edited by Father John

Gray. "I knew him a little, and he was himself to my vision touching, and extremely individual; but I hated his productions and thought them extraordinarily base—and couldn't find (perhaps didn't try enough to find!) the formula that reconciled this baseness, aesthetically, with his being so perfect a case of the artistic spirit." The letters had disclosed this personal spirit to James. "The amenity, the intelligence, the patience and grace and play of mind and of temper—how charming and individual an exhibition!" He said that "the poor boy remains quite one of the few distinguished images on the roll of young English genius brutally clipped, a victim of victims, given the vivacity of his endowment. I am glad I have three or four very definite—though one of them rather disconcerting—recollections of him."

James had a fairly decent winter of 1913–14. Van Wyck Brooks, then in London, remembered his glimpse of the novelist at a lecture given by Georg Brandes over which Edmund Gosse presided. He had heard James lecture at Harvard; and now he saw him rise at the end of the evening and climb to the platform to salute Brandes. The young continued to come to James; and he took great pleasure in the arrival of Compton Mackenzie on the literary scene with *Sinister Street*. He remembered young "Monty" Compton (Compton Mackenzie was his writing name) as a boy—the son of Edward Compton the actor who had produced *The American* and his wife Virginia Bateman who had played Madame de Cintré. He had toured with their company as long ago as 1890 enraptured by the production of his first play. There was perhaps this partiality of memory which led James to praise extravagantly *Sinister Street*. He quite made Hugh Walpole jealous. Then the second volume came out and James had to climb down. He was frankly disappointed. But he continued to write affectionate letters to Mackenzie, who in his late years, like Pearsall Smith, like Hueffer, like so many others, had his hoard of cherished and embellished anecdotes, and helped build the "legend" of the Master.

In the spring of 1914 James showed an active interest in the plight of Robert Ross, Oscar Wilde's friend and executor. Ross had, in the years since Wilde's death, slowly rebuilt the reputation of his friend, and brought the estate from bankruptcy to stability. He was avowedly homosexual, but enjoyed the friendship of the literary world, not least of Gosse and it was with the latter that James gossiped about Ross as he had about Symonds long ago. Ross was now suing Lord Alfred Douglas for libel, a repetition as it were of the Wilde case itself, but in a new and less exercised age. Behind the trial there were old animosities and old jealousies. It was, said James, an "infamous history" but he felt haunted by Robbie Ross's "demoralized state." The thing was, he wrote to Hugh, "to try to help him to keep his head and stiffen his heart."

Early in 1914 James went to lunch with A. B. Walkley, the drama critic of *The Times*, whose work he admired. Walkley wanted him to meet Henry Bernstein, the French dramatist. Bernstein talked to James of a new writer across the channel named Marcel Proust and of his novel *Du Côté de Chez Swann*. He promised to send the book, just published. When he didn't, James accepted a copy from Edith Wharton; he received it, acknowledged its arrival, said he could not at the moment read it. The remark is tantalizing for we do not know whether he did. There is no evidence save Mrs Wharton's remark that "his letter to me shows how deeply it impressed him." Beyond the letter saying he would read *Swann*, no other letter mentioning Proust has survived.

III

James had dispatched the manuscript of *Notes of a Son and Brother* before leaving Rye late in the fall of 1913. This left him free for other work. He had promised Bruce Richmond, the editor of *The Times Literary Supplement* an article on "the new novel" and this he now wrote. It was so long that it appeared in two instalments —entitled "The Younger Generation." It dealt with the generation younger than James, but certainly not the youngest save for Hugh Walpole, Compton Mackenzie and Gilbert Canaan. It revealed the old and vigorous James, but it might be said that for the first and only time in his long critical career he had not read all the novels carefully nor surveyed the entire horizon. His most remembered lapse was his speaking of D. H. Lawrence's *Sons and*

Lovers as a novel that might be mentioned "should we wish to be *very* friendly to Mr Lawrence." In reality the entire article seems to have been a mixture of things; a failure in discernment if not in power. He began by wanting to say publicly why he disliked Wells and Bennett whose money-opportunism he had deplored—that is their willingness to compromise art; then he found himself wanting to say something approvingly about Conrad's *Chance*, and he had at last an opportunity to praise Mrs Wharton for he had liked *Ethan Frome*, and commended *The Reef*—writing her a letter comparing it to Racine—and had been delighted by the satire of *The Custom of the Country*. Then he wanted to be nice to Hugh, in his old way, and to pat young Monty Mackenzie on the back. The mixed motives of the article made it a grab-bag of comment; the old mastery is still there, the old lessons of the master are repeated, but the attack is principally on the *saturated* novel, of which Tolstoy was the supreme example, and Wells and Bennett lesser English counterparts. His image for them was that of the squeezing of the sponge dry (sometimes he changed the sponge to orange), an image to which he often returned. Thus James brought his criticism of Wells into the open; this may have been in part due to the fact that Wells, two years earlier, in a lecture on "The Scope of the Novel" had denied that the novel could be an aesthetic and artistic end in itself; in effect offering another version of Shaw's criticism of James in the theatre. Shortly after, James had insisted at the Royal Society of Literature that Wells be elected, saying that it was difficult to vote for other candidates so long as his particular talent was not represented. Wells, to James's surprise, declined election: he wasn't going to allow himself to be voted into the Establishment. After a private talk with Wells, James wrote to Gosse that Wells "has cut himself loose from literature clearly—practically altogether."

In his article James described Wells and Bennett as squeezing "to the utmost the plump and more or less juicy orange of a particularly acquainted state." They "let this affirmation of energy, however directed or undirected, constitute for them the 'treatment' of the theme." Tolstoy, James argued, was "the great illustrative master-hand on all this ground of disconnection of method from matter." He repeated what he had said both publicly and privately, that the Russian master stood as "a caution" and only "execrably, pestilentially, as a model." Just as there was no "centre of interest" or sense of the whole in *War and Peace* so there was none in *The Old Wives' Tale* or *The Passionate Friends*. The reader was left with the simple amusement of watching the orange being squeezed.

We have already seen how deeply Conrad was disturbed by the passages devoted to him. Hugh, whose youth rather than his work was praised, felt that he had got off lightly; the other young men were pleased to have some notice, and Mrs Wharton could not but derive satisfaction at having finally had public notice from the man she so intensely admired—even more as man than as artist. All the English novelists of the time read the article and many felt themselves ignored; the title "younger" generation exempted Hardy, but then James had dealt with Conrad, who was certainly no longer young, and whose reputation dated from the 1890's. The Master, undisturbed, had had his say. He revised the article and gathered it in with the series of brilliant and definitive essays he had written on Balzac, Flaubert, Zola, and George Sand earlier in the century. The book was his last critical collection and he called it *Notes on Novelists*.

THE IVORY TOWER

PUBLICATION of *Notes of a Son and Brother* on 7 March 1914 was the occasion for many new tributes to the Master and he received as well letters from many of his old friends. All were moved by the pages he consecrated in the book to the memory of Minny Temple, his long-dead cousin. Memories of her had been incorporated in Isabel Archer. She had become Milly Theale. She had been from the beginning to the end of James's life "the heroine of the scene." He had lately re-read his own letters to his mother on the death of Milly; he wrote out of refreshed memory; and he used the letters she had written to John Gray, the lawyer, who had ended his career as head of the Harvard Law School. These were sent to him by Gray's widow. Harry James had a theory that James revised these letters; and he also believed that the novelist then destroyed them. They are not extant. A note Harry made in his own copy of the book, however, casts a particular light on these pages. "Everything said about [Minny] by H.J. seems to me to be as appropriate as possible to W.J. allowing for differences of sex. They were clearly chips of the same block. It is as if time and distance had enabled H.J. to see in her and to describe traits conspicuous to me in W.J. which he doesn't refer to in his allusions to his brother." We might speculate that the love that Henry had for William—but could not offer or express because William so stubbornly would not accept it—found its expression in the book of memory: there was also in Minny something boyish, vigorous, passionate. She had been for Henry long ago cousin, brother, sister, sweetheart, all in one. She had burned herself out in the flames of her own passion. Whatever the truths of this long-ago relation, it is clear that Minny Temple remained, as James predicted in his twenty-ninth year, a living figure within "the crystal walls of the past." Now he had placed her at the very centre of his and his brother's

early lives. It was true, he had said then, that he did not love her.
He *adored* her—he worshipped her. She had been a Diana in the
temple of his life; and he had offered his genius to her memory—
and in doing so offered it also to his brother.

Such were the psychological complexities and ambiguities of
Henry James. Henry Adams, reading the book, which James sent
him promptly, had other feelings. His memory went back to the
old years; his wife, Clover Hooper, had belonged to that period
—and he looked across the gulf of time with the dry pessimism
of his old age. "I've read Henry James's last bundle of memories
which have reduced me to a pulp," Adams wrote to Mrs Cameron.
"Why did we live? Was that all? . . . Poor Henry James thinks
it all real, I believe, and actually still lives in that dreamy, stuffy
Newport and Cambridge, with papa James and Charles Norton."
Henry Adams embodied these feelings in a letter to the novelist
which does not seem to have survived. James's reply, however,
was an elegant and highly documentary expression of the new-
found emotional energies of his old age. In spite of illness and
reduced activity and much suffering, all vestiges of his old depression seem to have left him. He wanted to live; and he was
determined to take from life all that it would offer him.

He had received, he said, Adams's "melancholy outpouring."
The only way to acknowledge it was to recognize "its unmitigated
blackness."

Of course we are lone survivors, of course the past that was our lives is at the
bottom of an abyss—if the abyss *has* any bottom; of course, too, there's no
use talking unless one particularly *wants* to. But the purpose, almost, of my
printed divagations was to show you that one *can*, strange to say, still want
to—or at least can behave as if one did.

He went on to say that he found his consciousness still interesting
"under *cultivation* of the interest." Why it yielded the interest, he
did not know. He wasn't challenging it or quarrelling with it—
he was encouraging it "with a ghastly grin."

You see I still, in presence of life (or of what you deny to be such), have
reactions—as many as possible—and the book I sent you is proof of them.
It's, I suppose, because I am that queer monster, the artist, an obstinate
finality, an inexhaustible sensibility. Hence the reactions—appearance,

memories, many things, go on playing upon it with consequence that I note and "enjoy" (grim word!) noting. It all takes doing—and I *do*. I believe I shall do yet again—it is still an act of life.

I

Old, tired, Henry James continued to perform the acts of life and nothing testifies to this more than his last writings. *The Finer Grain*, his volume of tales of 1910, assembled just before his brother's death, and the novel he was trying to write, subsidized by Edith Wharton's wealth, which he called *The Ivory Tower*, show that James had found new themes and grandiose subjects during his two visits to America. The stories, nearly all set in New York, and the fragment of the novel—for he never finished it—set in Newport and Manhattan have within them recurrent themes. In effect James was saying that certain members of the American wealthy had too much wealth; that this wealth was corrupting—and corruption; and that he had been robbed of his national birthright. The theme of his tale of "A Round of Visits" and of *The Ivory Tower* is of Americans who inherit great wealth only to have it stolen by other Americans. The American world was a great predatory competitive world; and James, had he had the strength would have completed—as some critics have held— one of his finest novels. The title of *The Finer Grain*, as he explained in a memorandum he wrote for his English publisher, was supposed to suggest "the finer grain of accessibility to suspense or curiosity, to mystification or attraction—in other words, to moving experience." His heroes are sentient, perceptive, reflective, and engaged in "the personal adventure." But what the sentience reflected was an anger more fully expressed than in earlier works. A single paragraph in the story "Crapy Cornelia" contains James's vision of the future in America:

This was clearly going to be the music of the future—that if people were but rich enough and furnished enough and fed enough, exercised and sanitated and manicured and generally advised and advertised and made "knowing" enough, *avertis* enough, as the term appeared to be nowadays in Paris, all they had to do for civility was to take the amused ironic view of those who might be less initiated. In *his* time, when he was young or even when he was only but a little less middle-aged, the best manners had been the best kindness, and the best kindness had mostly been some art of not insisting on one's luxurious differences, of concealing rather, for common humanity, if not for common decency, a part at least of the intensity or the ferocity with which one might be "in the know."

The women particularly in these tales are devoid of all sympathy; fat and fatuous, ugly, rich, cruel, they seem to have lost the meaning of kindness. Civilization, as he had shown in his three great novels, had many masks and it was by its masks that it could survive. Behind them lay the terror in the heart of man.

II

The Ivory Tower was to have been written in ten books and in the manner of *The Awkward Age*—that is each section was to have been devoted to a different character, and the whole designed to illuminate the central situation. That situation seemed as fantasy to be a continuation of "The Jolly Corner," the question of what America did to individuals and what one "escaped" by being in Europe. If *The Golden Bowl* had resolved certain old difficulties, and enabled Henry James to return and claim his American heritage, *The Ivory Tower* questioned the worth of the heritage— implied that someone had absconded with its riches. The novel has in it no sign of James's old age save that the images are overweighted and the prose is heavy and "difficult," shot through with the symbolic imagery he had been cultivating ever since *The Wings of the Dove*. *The Ivory Tower* combines the themes of his last three novels—the American innocent, called here Graham Fielder, who, however, returns to America rather than Paris; the couple in love, Horton ("Haughty") Vint and Cissy Foy, like Kate Croy and Merton Densher, who cannot marry and plot to obtain the millions Fielder inherits from his uncle. In the opening scenes we have the old rivalries of James's works re-expressed in two former business partners who are both dying—of their millions—full of guilt and unforgiveness. One partner bears the Biblical name of the archetypal rival—Abel; and as in *Roderick Hudson* the Cain figure seems to be regarded as the better of the two; James gives him, indeed, the name of Betterman. Possessed of the riches of their lives, they seem adumbrations of William and Henry James at the end of time, with their intellectual and artistic capital. They are even rivals in the process of dying; Abel Gaw wants to outlive Betterman but dies of a stroke when he learns that his former friend has improved—a symbolic rehearsal of the Cain and Abel story. The great scene that survives is the interview between Betterman and Fielder in the second part of the novel, in which Fielder is judged sufficiently innocent and worthy to inherit the huge fortune which he is not sure he wants. The stage for this interview is set by Gaw's daughter Rosanna, the Jamesian heiress of the ages now revived as an obese good-natured woman who has loved Fielder from the days of her young years in Europe. She now plays "angel" to him as Ralph Touchett did to Isabel in *The Portrait of a Lady*.

All the Jamesian ingredients were present as James planned this novel, reworking an old theme found among his papers and called "The K.B. Case"—an allusion to Mrs Bronson of Venice and C.F.—probably the other Venetian of his later years, Constance Fletcher, who had some of Rosanna's rotundity. If the ingredients are familiar the background is new. The novel would have been the story of a year, like Henry's own year in America in 1904–5. From Newport it would move to New York and later to the world of Edith Wharton at Lenox. What James intended to bring into this novel was American wealth, the "money-passion," the spirit of "ferocious acquisition." The question was whether a life built on such gains was any life at all. Christopher Newman had been proud of his "pile," but he had talked of thousands. James's rich now talk of millions. The central symbol of the novel is the ivory tower, an *objet d'art* in which Fielder chooses to place an unread document left him by Gaw, the better-man's rival. He had been offered a cigar case but rejected it as wrong—doubtless too symbolic of the wealth about which he has such misgivings. The ivory tower is represented as "the most distinguished retreat"—from commerce, from sex, from all the turbulence and passion of this world. In his own way, Fielder is suggesting that the American values—the accumulation of money—are not his values; the ivory tower, or escape into Europe, was perhaps the only way to escape the curse and guilt of wealth. In a sense therefore *The Ivory Tower* is not the pagoda of *The Golden Bowl*. The pagoda was a symbol of innocence and escape from reality; the ivory tower was a symbol of conscious withdrawal from reality looked in the face. And in *The Ivory Tower* James had projected also his chorus-like Assinghams of the *Bowl*; here they would have been the Bradhams.

James's last novel was emerging as an apologia for his own life; it would have denounced with all the delicacy and subtlety of his style, the world of the American rich which he had seen, at Biltmore, at Lenox, in Washington in the great houses of New York and in the new palaces at Newport: a richness so gross and devoid of the humane that he had fled back to England never to return. He had reclaimed his American heritage, but he seems to have felt it wasn't worth reclaiming. The absconders could have it. "You seem all here so hideously rich," says his hero.

III

James wrote Howells who urged him to return in May of 1914 for still another visit to the United States, "I don't like to frequent the U.S. . . . weigh *prosperity* against posterity . . . That autumn, winter and spring (1910–11) which I spent in Cambridge and New York—well, I shall go down to my grave without having breathed to another ear what I went through with then." And to Alice James his sister-in-law he had written a year earlier: "Dearest Alice, I could come back to America (could be carried back on a stretcher) to *die*—but never, never to live . . . but when I think of how little Boston and Cambridge were of old ever *my* affair, or anything but an accident, for me, of the parental life there, to which I occasionally and painfully and losingly sacrificed, I have a superstitious terror of seeing them at the end of time again stretch out strange individual tentacles to draw me back and destroy me ... You see my capital—yielding all my income, intellectual, social, associational, on the old investment of so many years—my capital is *here*, and to let it all slide would be simply to become bankrupt."

The Ivory Tower re-created the old myths of Henry James's life in what would have been a dense and powerfully conceived work.

Even in the fragment—like some fragment of partially chiselled marble in Florence—we can discern the shapes of strong highly individualized characters, the American versions of Cain and Abel, of Jacob and Esau, of rapacity and violence and greed. James was drawing upon the oldest material he possessed—his early tales of "Guest's Confession" and "A Light Man" had foreshadowed such themes—tales of treachery and fraternal humiliation. And the crowning irony was that as he worked innocently on this book, he could not know that it had been subsidized by the very kind of wealth he condemned. *The Ivory Tower* remains a remarkable fragment, for the Master was old and ill; he no longer could work regularly, as of old. He had begun at last to falter.

Book Seven

Within the Rim

1914–1916

★

A WRECK OF BELIEF

THE year 1914 began for Henry James with the extraction of most of his teeth, "the wounds, the inconvenience, the humiliations," not to speak of the effects of the anaesthetic. He relied heavily now on nitroglycerin tablets for his heart discomfort; he spoke frequently of his "desiccated antiquity." In the midst of the dentistry, however, he had told Henry Adams to cultivate an interest in life; and he was vigorous enough that spring to welcome and entertain his niece and his youngest nephew, Peggy and Alex, and be highly critical of their American companions. Peggy had with her in Europe this time a young lady he believed to have had the kind of background about which he had written so often in his fiction. She was like Daisy Miller, a product of the permissive vacuity of a childhood without direction. James had pity, he said, "for a poor young creature whose elders and home-circle have handed her over, uncivilized, untutored, unadvised, and unenlightened to such a fool's paradise of ignorance and fatuity." He was no less concerned about the boon companion of his nephew, who was silent and unsociable, with no grace of communication and no subject but athletics—and he discoursed at great length about the cultural environment William James had created for his young and the environment from which these other young Americans had come. They had affluence, a large measure of it, but no enlightenment.

He had seen Edith Wharton in recent weeks; the previous autumn he had found she had lost her "harassed look;" a few weeks later he saw her as "a figure of entire unmitigated *agitation*." It was this way with Edith, there were often ups and downs. Still, she was "so clever, powerful, and stimulating that I think one forgives her very much." For the rest, he kept up his social life and Peggy noted the general level of his strength was better than the previous year. His date-book of the spring of 1914 shows him as active and as observant as of old. Thus on 25 March he goes to the London Zoo, with Mrs Sutro, conveyed there in her motor "we walked about a long time to my benefit; then to tea at Mrs S's." On 28 March he joins Lucy Clifford and Ethel Dilke in a box at the Vaudeville Theatre for "deplorably platitudinous performance—dramatization of Arnold Bennett; drove her home and then came by apartment and had tea (5.30) with Emily Sargent. Dined with Lady Lovelace 8.15." The next day he lunches with Owen Lankester in Upper Wimpole Street, goes to an art exhibition and pays a call on Lady Courteney. He still had his London life.

A note of 3 April in his appointment book records however, "Bad days: climax of the long effect of privation of exercise— more intense demonstration of imperative need of sacrificing *everything* to this boon . . . Long resolute walk from Piccadilly Circus down to Westminster and thence all along the Embankment to the corner of Chelsea Barracks and Hospital Road. I was more than three hours—nearer four—on foot—the length of the effort was the effective benefit—and this benefit was signal. I broke the hideous spell of settled *sickness*, which had become too cruel for words—and if I haven't now learned the lesson ——! I worked in consequence well again yesterday (Friday) forenoon; but renewed my locomotion in due measure again in the afternoon. That is I called on Rhoda Broughton but walked both there and back—with better and better effect."

His niece provided him with company for his walks. They went to the cinema; to the Royal Academy: to the British Museum. He dined at the Philip Morrells', Prime Minister Asquith being present. He took Peggy and her companion to the House of Commons for the third reading of the Home Rule Bill, the government obtaining a majority. He took Lady Ottoline, Morrell's wife, home. "Rather historic occasion," he noted. A note of 9 June records he had tea at the Athenaeum where he talked with a man who "did me good by telling me of a friend of his, of 78, who had lived with bad *angina pectoris* for 25 years and is now much better than formerly, having swallowed enough 'dynamite' to blow up St Paul's."

The Master stayed in London into July and on the 14th he went to Lamb House. A long entry in his appointment book of 30 July begins with his trying to remember the date on which he sent Ellen Terry his one-act play of 1895; he then recalls his stay in Torquay, when he got the idea of *The Ambassadors* from Jonathan Sturges. "Oh the full De Vere Gardens days of those years!" he writes and recalls how he began dictating to the type-writer in 1897. He then notes, with some minuteness, all his comings and goings of that summer but breaks off in the middle. There is no further entry until 4 August. On that day he scrawled: "Everything blackened over for the time blighted by the hideous Public situation. This is (Monday) the August Bank Holiday but with horrible suspense and the worst possibilities in the air. Peggy and Aleck came down on Saturday to stay."

I

The coming of the war was, for Henry James, "a nightmare from which there is no waking save by sleep." Later he would say that it "almost killed me. I loathed so having lived on and on into anything so hideous and horrible." The letters which he wrote during the early days of August—days of blandness and blueness at Rye—are among the most eloquent of his life. He pictured himself dipping his nose into the inkpot "but it's as if there were no ink there and I take it out smelling gunpowder, smelling blood, as hard as it did before." He believed civilization had collapsed totally into barbarism and that this had turned his life into a gross lie. "I write you under the black cloud of portentous events on this side of the world, horrible, unspeakable, iniquitous things—I mean horrors of war criminally, infamously precipitated." Thus to his old Newport friend Margaret La Farge. "These are monstrous miseries for *us*, of our generation and age, to live into; but we wouldn't not have lived—and yet this is what we get by it. I try to think it will be *interesting*—but have only got so far as to feel it sickening." To Edith Wharton in Paris he wrote in some anxiety, for he had had no news of her. She had been on the verge of a motor tour in Spain, with Walter Berry—"even like another George Sand and another Chopin." Now he wrote her (on 6 August) of "this crash of our civilization. The only gleam in the blackness, to me, is the action and the absolute unanimity of this country."

However, it was to the old irascible and undividedly British Rhoda Broughton, whom he had known for so many years, that he poured out his anguish two days later. "Black and hideous to me is the tragedy that gathers and I'm sick beyond cure to have lived on to see it. You and I, the ornaments of our generation should have been spared this wreck of our belief that through the long years we had seen civilization grow and the worst become impossible. The tide that bore us along was then all the while moving to *this* as its grand Niagara—yet what a blessing we didn't know it. It seems to me to *undo* everything, everything that was ours, in the most horrible retroactive way—but I avert my face from the monstrous scene."

He could not avert his face. He had always lived too close to the realities behind human illusion. He was nervous and tense. He felt that the exquisite summer mocked him. The "shining indifference" of nature chilled his heart. "Never were desperate doings so blandly lighted up." He had been betrayed. All that he had done, the little private adventures that he had chronicled were suddenly "so utterly blighted by the public." His mind went back to the other war, the Civil War, and Mr Lincoln's call to arms. He remembered the hushed crowds, the solemnity; for a while everyone seemed to walk on tip-toe. Now everything moved with extraordinary speed. James awoke each day to find the same light, the same air, the same sea and the sky, "the most beautiful English summer conceivable." This was "the sole, the exquisite England, whose weight now hangs in the balance." He had remained an American all his years. Now he began to speak of "we" and "us." He walked to the Ypres tower, relic of the Napoleonic day, and looked out from the heights of Rye in the direction of France. His imagination could not encompass the horrors. "I go to sleep, as if I were dog-tired with action," he wrote to Mrs Wharton, "yet feel like the chilled *vieillards* in the old epics, infirm and helpless at home with the women, while the plains are ringing with battle."

Mrs Wharton was in Paris when Belgium was invaded; she came over to England and visited James briefly at Rye. Peggy found "a cleverness and insight and economy of words about her that is masterly." She liked in particular the fact that Mrs Wharton was "tactful and non-fatiguing" for her uncle. James felt unwell; he had a spell of illness in late August. He ate little; his nerves remained on edge. But he summoned all his strength and in September began to speak of returning to London. He couldn't work. He found it difficult to read. He wanted to mitigate "the huge tension and oppression" he felt in the Sussex solitude. He described himself as living under "the funeral spell of our murdered civilization." He wanted to be nearer to some source of information and contact. His old need for action was strong; his sense of drive and power remained in spite of his infirmities. In the days before his departure, his restlessness was increased by the war activities in Rye; the local enlistments, the drilling of recruits, the continual marching of men. Then Burgess announced he was joining up. He was sturdy and athletic, a bantam-weight fit for military service. His master gave him his blessing. "It's like losing an arm or a leg," James wrote to Mrs Wharton. She promptly sent one of her menservants, Frederick, to help James for the time being. James wrote to Burgess, "I see you are going to make a first-rate soldier and nothing could give me greater pleasure." His job would be kept for him; James hoped he would visit him during his leaves. "If it's *socks* you will throughout most want, I will keep you supplied," James wrote in his most maternal vein; he also kept Burgess supplied with goodies and pocket change.

Two or three nights before James's departure from Rye the first Belgian refugees arrived, assigned to the small Catholic congregation of the town. James had offered his Watchbell Street studio as a gathering place. They were awaited all day, from train to train. In the evening a sound of voices made the Master go to his door at the top of the winding street. Over the grass-grown cobbles came a procession of the homeless. "It was swift and eager, in the autumn darkness," the Master would write, "and under the flare of a single lamp—with no vociferation and, but

for a woman's, scarce a sound save the shuffle of mounting feet
and the thick-drawn breath of emotion." James saw a young
mother carrying her child. He heard "the resonance through our
immemorial old street of her sobbing." History had reached his
doorstep.

SOLDIERS

EVEN before he left Rye, James heard from Hugh. It was a brief letter and it told him that he was leaving for Russia. Hugh had been turned down by the Army; he was helpless without his glasses. But the thought of inaction was as painful to him as to the Master. "Think of me as I cross the North Sea," Hugh wrote, "I shall think of you continually." James replied he was "deeply moved," and said that Hugh—who was to be war correspondent on the eastern front for the *Daily Mail*—was showing "the last magnificence of pluck, the finest strain of resolution." James added, "I bless and cheer and honour it for all I am worth." From Jocelyn Persse came word almost at the same time. He had joined the Royal Fusiliers and was in a camp in Essex. The strenuous life, the English damp and cold, soon caught up with Jocelyn and he came down with pneumonia and was sent on a sick leave. Desmond MacCarthy was among the early callers at Carlyle Mansions once the Master was reinstalled. He "looked remarkably well and solid in his khaki." He had joined the Red Cross and was leaving for France. This would give him much experience, said James, and "can only contribute hereafter to his powers of conversation."

"We must for dear life make our own counter-realities," James wrote to Lucy Clifford. Having all his life declined to serve on committees, he immediately threw himself into Belgian relief in Chelsea; and when it was suggested that he visit Belgian wounded in St Bartholomew's Hospital because he could speak French to them, he went eagerly. Presently he was moving from bedside to bedside talking to the English wounded as well. "I am so utterly and passionately enlisted," he wrote to his nephew, "up to my eyes and over my aged head in the greatness of our cause, that it fairly sickens me not to find every imagination not rise to it." His date-book provides a record of constant visits and of aid to in-

dividual soldiers. "Took three maimed and half-blind con-
valescent soldiers from St Bart's to tea 24 Bedford Square and
delivered them home again." The Protheros lived at No. 24. The
next day he "telephoned Dr Field inquiring about his attending
to Private Percy Stone who has practically lost an eye." He sends
chocolates to St Bartholomew's. He visits St George's. He notes
"the deaf soldier in Harley Ward—John Willey. The others in
the same ward with wounded arm." He sends a pocket comb to
one soldier, cigarettes to others. One soldier, a sapper of the
Royal Engineers, found in James a loyal friend. On leaving the
hospital he was invited to the Master's flat for meals; presently
James arranged for him to have his teeth taken care of "at very
reduced military rates." Sapper Williams had been a great runner;
James liked his vitality. Friends of the Master wondered how the
soldiers reacted to his subtle leisurely talk—but he seemed quite
capable of entertaining and comforting them. He likened himself
to Walt Whitman during the Civil War. It made him feel less
"finished and useless and doddering when I go on certain days
and try to pull the conversational cart uphill for them."

He had long ago written about the British soldier. Ever since
his visit to a Civil War camp, where he had gone to see his
younger brothers, he had had an image of men committed to
heroism and to death. He was appalled by war as he had shown in
his tale of "Owen Wingrave," but thrilled to human endurance
and strength. The sense of power and glory in James made him
an admirer always of the soldier—"such children of history"—
and he said "there is nothing, ever, that one wouldn't do for
them." He stopped soldiers on the street and astonished them by
emptying his pockets of small change for them. He couldn't keep
away from the windows of his flat if he heard the sound of a bugle,
or a band, or the skirl of the bagpipe. Saturated reader of
Napoleonic memoirs, admirer of the kind of action he himself had
never had, he interrupts a letter to his nephew "to watch from my
windows a great swinging body of the London Scottish, as one
supposes, marching past at the briskest possible step with its long
line of freshly enlisted men behind it. These are now in London,
of course, impressions of every hour, or of every moment; but

there is always a particular big thrill in the collective passage of the stridingly and just a bit flappingly kilted and bonneted when it isn't a question of mere parade or exercise, we have been used to seeing, but a suggestion, everything in the air so aiding, of a real piece of action, a charge of an irresistible press forward, on the field itself."

Of his visits to the hospitals he left a record in an essay written for a book edited by Edith Wharton to raise funds for refugees. It is called *The Book of the Homeless* and James's essay is entitled "The Long Wards." In it one can discern the quick human sympathies James brought to the bedside. Certain observers might wonder what this super-subtle civilized man could offer the "Tommies;" the essay shows the precise nature of the relations he established. James came to the soldiers not as a great writer or an admirable intellect of the age; the men probably didn't know who he was. What came through to them was his kindness, his warmth. He told himself that to sit and help them complain against fate was useless. "The inmates of the long wards have no use for any imputed or derivative sentiments or reasons." He did ask himself how these quiet, patient, enduring men, who seemed so amiable and now so helpless could have welcomed "even for five minutes the stress of carnage?" And how could "the murderous impulse at the highest pitch, have left so little distortion of the moral nature?" To ask himself these questions was to dismiss them. It was clear to him that the soldiers wanted a complete rest "from the facing of generalizations." Out of this, and in his characteristic way, James seems to have found the right human note "of one's poor bedside practice." The master of wit and irony simply fell back on the solace of small talk; and apparently with great success. His portly presence, quiet, authoritative, composed, conveyed almost in silence admiration without condescension, trust without question, an air of acceptance. All his life he had preached the thesis of "living through" and of "infinite doing." Now he practised it in full measure. It gave him new reason for existence; and through the rest of 1914 and well into 1915, until recurrent illness slowed him up, he surrendered himself to the British soldier. His essay contains much reflection on the peace-time soldier, the figure he had found absent from the American cities during his recent visits to his homeland. Such soldiers were familiar to him from all the years of his European residence. The professional soldier was "rooted in the European basis." But even such reflections, he recognized, belonged "to the abyss of our past delusion." Now there was only one thing— human suffering. He did what he could.

He enlisted himself in the same way in the service of the particular American activity that arose in England during the early days of the war before America's entry which he would not live to see. He accepted the chairmanship of the American Volunteer Motor-Ambulance Corps in France. Richard Norton, the son of his old friend Charles Eliot Norton, a friend of Mrs Wharton, had thrown himself into this work, and James and Mrs Wharton were committed to help. James wrote a long letter to the American press on the nature of this endeavour. It was designed to be informative as an appeal for funds. The Corps was one of the pioneer enterprises in the new age of the motor; it helped change the care of the wounded; it made possible rapid transportation to hospitals and care centres. At first tentative and experimental, it grew rapidly in importance; and in Russia, Hugh Walpole, tired of inaction in Moscow, enlisted in the first hospital units on that front and saw action in this way—even while certain ladies in London gossiped fiercely about his absence from England and imputed to him an attempt to dodge military duty— a matter which led James to outbursts of anger.

James's work among the Belgian refugees in Chelsea was recorded in an essay which also solicited contributions. It was first published in *The Times Literary Supplement*. His essay was a report—"the statement of a neighbour and an observer deeply affected by the most tragic exhibition of national and civil prosperity and felicity suddenly subjected to bewildering outrage that it would have been possible to conceive." The headquarters in Chelsea were in Crosby Hall, in the ancient suburban site of the garden of Sir Thomas More. Here was Chelsea's hospitality "to the exiled, the broken, and the bewildered." James joined their hours of relaxation which had the nature of a "huge, comprehensive tea-party." The Belgians seemed to James persons who had "given up everything but patience." They lived now from hour to hour. He brought to them the same qualities he took into hospitals. Early in June 1915 he noted "I give tea to Belgians at Crosby Hall." It seemed to him a great and painful irony that these people, with their local, "patriarchal beatitude" so rooted in their "teeming territory" should have been among the first up-rooted—"the Belgian ideal of the constituted life, dismembered, disembowelled, and shattered." To those who had been injured and wounded James gave his greatest attention. And again, what emerges from James's observations is his careful diagnosis of what had to be done. These were people who illustrated "the seated and saturated practice" of "close and comfortable household life." One had to recognize "the infamy of the outrage" suffered, and minister to the shock.

II

With the pain—and resolution—of helping the wounded and the victims, James experienced the anguish of the wives and the widows. He scanned casualty lists, and had constant news of the decimation of youth. Clare Sheridan, daughter of Moreton Frewen, his neighbour at Brede and a cousin of Winston Churchill's, wrote to James of her loneliness when her husband went off to the front. James gave her his usual prescription, in a letter that spoke for his own pain as well as hers. "I am incapable of telling you not to repine and rebel, because I have so, to my cost, the imagination of all things, and because I am incapable of telling you not to feel. Feel, *feel*, I say—feel for all you're worth, and even if it half kills you, for that is the only way to live, especially to live at *this* terrible pressure, and the only way to honour and celebrate these admirable beings who are our pride and our inspiration." There came moments, however, when the feeling got too intense for the Master. At the end of August 1915 he went to lunch with Wilfred Sheridan going "back to front after a week's leave; he splendid and beautiful and occasion somehow such a pang—all unspeakable: 8 or 10 persons: sat between Mrs Frewen and Lady Poltimore. Afterwards at tea at Lady C's—very interesting (splendid) young *manchot* [armless] officer, Sutton." To which he adds the words: "They kill me!"

He died a thousand deaths with the deaths of these handsome uniformed men who dined in London one week and were dead the next. Wilfred Sheridan was killed at the front three weeks after this entry, and James could only resume, in the vein in which he had written to Sheridan's wife earlier. He wouldn't pretend to offer consolation—"who can give you anything that approaches your incomparable sense that he was yours, and you his, to the last possessed and possessing radiance of him?" He had "sight and some sound of him during an hour of that last leave just before he went off again; and what he made me then feel, and what his face seemed to say amid that cluster of relatives in which I was the sole outsider (of which too I was extraordinarily proud), is beyond all expression. . . . I live with you in thought every step of the long way."

The first elation and tension of the war, with the seizing at any and every rumour, the quiet passing on of "inside" information gleaned out of thin air, gave way in James to an overwhelming sense of the loss of youth—"the destruction, on such a scale, of priceless young life, more and more reiterated, poisons and blackens one's whole view of things, and makes one ask what the end, *anywhere*, will be." Thus to his niece in America. He was writing two months after the death of Rupert Brooke—the shining youth of his 1909 visit to Cambridge. Rupert remained in his mind, a bright vision of another time—another century, so it seemed. He had died of blood poisoning on a French hospital ship after serving with the Royal Naval Division. "He isn't tragic now—he has only stopped," James wrote to Edward Marsh, Brooke's closest friend. Of his poems he had written "Splendid Rupert—to be the soldier that could beget them on the Muse! and lucky Muse, not less, who could have an affair with a soldier and yet feel herself not guilty of the least deviation." He foresaw "a wondrous romantic, heroic legend will form." He had known Rupert enough "exceedingly to prize him . . . He was an interesting young poet—he has left things, and they'll be gilded. But he was also such a beautiful young being. *Youth*, however, was his sense, his scope, his limit—and we shall think of him as of the family of Keats and Shelley." James agreed to write a preface to Rupert's posthumous book, *Letters from America*.

Closest of all perhaps, because it touched him intimately, was the army experience of his man Burgess, to whom James wrote as a father to a son, letters of the greatest simplicity and concreteness, in declarative sentences as simple as his characteristic sentences were complex. "What things you are seeing, and perhaps will still more see, and what tremendous matters you will have to tell us! . . . I think it wonderful for you to be able in the midst of such things to write to us at all, and we are very grateful, but want you not to worry when you can't, to leave it alone always till you can, and to believe that we always understand your difficulties, just as much as we rejoice in your news." James added, "my life manages in spite of the horrible sad difference the War brings with it to be so quiet and regular that I want very little waiting upon beyond what Minnie is able very devotedly and easily to do. She and Joan bear up admirably, though they miss you very much and often tell me so." (Joan had succeeded Mrs Paddington as cook; the latter had retired prior to the move to Cheyne Walk.)

Burgess was wounded early in his service. In mid-1915 he was back in England in a Leicester hospital with thirty shrapnel wounds, none of them serious. What was serious was that the exploding shell had deafened him, as it turned out, for life, although there was some improvement in later years, thanks to a hearing aid. "You have clearly been very bravely through very stiff things, but have paid much less for it than you might," James wrote him. "I hope your hospital is a good and kind one and that they take the best care of you, but am very sorry you couldn't have been sent to London or to somewhere nearer to us here, and where we could have got to see you . . . Keep up your heart—there are many so much worse," the Master wrote. Burgess was ultimately invalided home. Later by special dispensation he was allowed to remain with Henry James.

STATESMEN

HENRY JAMES had a last meeting with Henry Adams his friend of so many years in the opening weeks of the war. Adams had crossed from Paris, and remained in England until he could sail to America. Aileen Tone, his secretary-companion, a woman of distinction and beauty, remembered to the last the encounter of the two Henrys; how they threw their arms around each other, as if bridging a great chasm. James's report to Mrs Wharton was that "Henry, alas, struck me as more changed and gone than he had been reported, though still with certain flickers and *gestes* of participation, and a surviving capacity to be very well taken care of: but his way of life, in such a condition, I mean his world wandering, is all incomprehensible to me—it is so quite other than any I should select in his state."

The historian and amateur of the arts had had a stroke a few years earlier. He would return to Washington and there outlive Henry James. The novelist saw other Americans in London; for he fell into the habit of periodically calling on Ambassador Walter Hines Page, and discussing with emotion America's failure to come to the aid of the Allies. He resented the continuing amenities between Berlin and Washington. And he waited eagerly for news, when Walter Berry went to Berlin on a mission. Berry was not reassuring. German morale was too high. The Fatherland was confident, arrogant. James's nephew Harry also came abroad on a Belgian relief mission and went to the Continent. He brought back to his uncle some weeks later eye-witness experiences which the latter seized upon eagerly. Finally he had continuing news from Mrs Wharton herself, her accounts of her visit to Verdun, and other visits in fighting France. He wrote to her with passion and fervour—and great admiration. "I am too aged and too battered to do almost anything but feel."

We get a glimpse of this in the diary of John Bailey, an English critic. "Old Henry James asked me to come," wrote Bailey, in his diary in October of 1914. He went on to say that James received him, "kissing me on both cheeks when I arrived and thanking me enormously for coming. He is passionately English and says it is almost good that we were so little prepared, as it makes our moral position so splendid. He almost wept as he spoke."

It was of such utterances that Percy Lubbock—who knew best the James of this time—wrote, when he came to edit the Master's letters. "To all who listened to him in those days, it must have seemed that he gave us what we lacked—a voice; there was a trumpet note in it that was heard nowhere else and that alone rose to the height of the truth."

II

Walmer Castle, in Kent, near Deal and not far from Dover, a thick-walled machicolated old fortress with embrasures twenty feet deep, was used late in 1914 and early 1915 as a half-way point to the front by the Prime Minister, Herbert H. Asquith. Pitt had lived here; Wellington had died here. The wartime leaders would congregate, with members of the Army and Navy, for conferences; at Walmer too, on week-ends, Margot Asquith, the former Margot Tennant, wife of the Prime Minister, gathered notables with the art of an old and practised imperious hostess. To Walmer Castle Henry James came on 16 January 1915. He was an old friend of Margot's; he had known Asquith in the 1890's before high office had come to him. He remembered the high-flying Margot from her hunting and riding days, as one of a group of daughters of a Scottish border landlord, a Liberal baronet. He had seen her when he was a frequent visitor at the Henry Whites of the American Embassy. Margot had heard the "trumpet note" of James, and had lost no time in having him to lunch in recent weeks at No. 10 Downing Street. Her luncheons were famous—a gathering, very casual, of prominent figures in the London world—the world of war and the arts, of men and women whose vitality and leadership counted for so much in the national morale. The Prime Minister, coming in from his morning's conferences never knew whom he would find at table. He found again, after many years, Henry James.

In December 1914, at one such luncheon, the Master had chatted with General Sir Ian Hamilton; and it had led to his dining with Haldane, the Lord Chancellor, in the company of Ambassador Page and Winston Churchill, First Lord of the Admiralty, and his wife Clementine. There is no record of that first encounter between the forty-year-old Winston, not then the bulky bulldog of his old age, and Henry James, almost seventy-two, who bulked much larger. Churchill was straight, athletic; and as always articulate and incisive; he was at the top of his younger form when James met him: he breathed war and action; he had wit and eloquence. James's comment after this occasion was simply that he found in the war leadership "no illusions, no ignorances, no superficialities"—and "deep confidence." He seems to have been remembering some of Churchill's talk in an interview he gave a few weeks later to the New York *Times* on behalf of the American Volunteer Motor-Ambulance Corps. "A distinguished English naval expert happened to say to me that the comparative non-production of airships in this country indicated a possible limitation of the British genius in that direction." Then on James's asking this distinguished person why airships shouldn't be within the compass of the greatest makers of sea-ships the person had replied, "Because the airship is essentially a bad ship, and we English can't make a bad ship well enough."

It is possible that Churchill read this interview. For in it there was a sentence of Henry James's that seems to have lodged in his memory. "English life," said Henry James, "wound up to the heroic pitch, is at present most immediately before me, and I can scarcely tell you what a privilege I feel it to share the inspiration and see further revealed the character of this decent and dauntless people." James's rhetoric of the First World War thus seems to have made its contribution to one of the most characteristic Churchillian utterances of the Second World War.

III

"Mr James being away weekending with Mr Asquith and his daughter Elizabeth, who is decidedly cultivating him, I had a free morning," Miss Bosanquet recorded in her diary. Both Violet

Asquith, later Lady Bonham-Carter and Elizabeth, then a precocious seventeen, but already a lively companion of her father
on the political scene, liked James; and he was charmed by them.
Violet was the child of Asquith's first marriage, Elizabeth was
Margot's daughter. James brought with him Frederick, Mrs
Wharton's man, who was still serving him. The Master was eager
and curious. "I don't do things easily nowadays," Henry James
wrote to his nephew on the day that he made the trip to Walmer
Castle. "But I thought this, in all the present conditions, almost
a matter of duty, really not to be shirked." More than "duty" it
was an occasion to assuage curiosity about the conduct of the war,
the personalities involved, the social fabric in which England's
leaders moved in a time of high stress. James added that "one
'hears' and 'learns' on such occasions much less than one might
fancy—officialdom never turns its official side outward: only,
mostly, some *other* pleasant comparatively not at all thrilling
side." Still "the great Winston" was expected and other important guests.

The day was bright and cold. Walmer Castle was picturesque
—a great terrace over the Channel—and James was thrilled to
see the ships of England "going about their business in extraordinary numbers." On arrival he had tea with Violet Asquith.
Before dinner, writing to Edith Wharton to tell her that without
the aid of Frederick he would not have been able to accept this
invitation, James said that "the sentiment the place makes one
entertain in every way for old England is of the most acutely
sympathetic, and the good kind friendly easy Asquith, with the
curtain of public affairs let thickly down behind him and the foot-
lights entirely turned off in front, doesn't do anything to make it
less worth having." James had had a bitter cold motor run
around the Isle of Thanet with the Prime Minister and the actress
Viola Tree. "The car was practically open, but the friendly sight
of all the swarming khaki on the roads made up for that."

Of that week-end we know very little. There seems, however,
to have been a collision between the First Lord of the Admiralty
and the Master—the two most articulate men present on the
occasion. Churchill, jaunty, full of his characteristic note of pride,

confidence, assurance, faith, and swagger, accustomed to having
the centre of the scene found Henry James at that centre.
"Winston," said one who was present, "was at his very worst."
He had never read Henry James; he was impatient at the respect
and deference shown this old man who was so slow-spoken, even
though his rhetoric was so remarkable—when he finally got it
out. Everyone listened to Henry James in awe. Winston was
impatient, irritable; he could not wait for the end of such long and
intricate sentences. He disregarded the Master; or he interrupted
him. He showed him "no conversational consideration." He
used a great deal of slang. Some of it James must have liked, for
he himself appreciated the colloquial, decorously placed between
quotation marks, in his novels. Some of it, however, apparently
grated on him. Churchill had piqued his curiosity; but this re-
encounter of two men of personality possessed of a great sense of
their dignity and power was not a happy one for the Asquiths,
who were very fond of Henry James.

When James was about to leave, at the end of the week-end, he
said to Violet that it had been a very interesting "very encouraging
experience to meet that young man. It had brought home to me
very forcibly—very vividly—the *limitations* by which men of
genius obtain their ascendancy over mankind. It," said the
Master, fumbling apparently for a bit of *argot* in the Churchill
manner, "bucks one up."

IV

He lunched again with the Prime Minister late in March of 1915—
"on the chance of catching some gleam between the chinks—
which was idiotic of me, because it's mostly in those circles that
the chinks are well puttied over." James had to content himself
with the same rumours as everyone. To Mrs Henry White he
wrote of the Asquiths, saying that Margot, in the setting "appears
a fairly weird fruit of time." She was, he said "a voluble restless
ghost." She had acquired remarkable Asquith sons, but she
looked "as if she had lost her luggage, that of the past we originally knew her in, at a bustling railway station." The indefatigable
Margot had sent James her diaries and he read all the old gossip

with great relish. He was probably being ironic, however, when he wrote her that she was "the Balzac of diarists." He said "St Simon is in forty volumes—why should Margot be put in one?" Margot herself acknowledged some years later that her diaries seemed an assemblage of trivialities and gossip. James observed the amenities by telling her her diaries had created "an admirable portrait of a lady, with no end of finish and style . . . if I don't stop now, I shall be calling it a regular masterpiece." He stopped.

He worked hard at this moment on the interview he had agreed to give to the New York *Times*. Or, as Miss Bosanquet put it in her diary, "his consent was given on condition that he might see the Copy produced. H.J. finding that it wouldn't do at all from his point of view, has spent the last four days redictating the interview to the young man who is, fortunately, a good typist. I think the idea of H.J. interviewing himself for four whole days is quite delightful!"

The result, published in the *Times* of 21 March 1915 belongs in the Jamesian canon. It is doubtful whether the reporter was allowed to write a single sentence of his own. James artfully introduced sections on style, achievement, revisions in the New York Edition; but he focused mainly on the courage of England at war and the appeal for funds on behalf of the Ambulance Corps which was the main reason for the interview. Again and again the great rhetoric of valour, the cadences foreshadowing the future Churchill are striking:

"It is not for the wounded to oblige us by making us showy, but for us to let them count on our open arms and open lap as troubled children count on those of their mother."

"We welcome any lapse of logic that may connect inward vagueness with outward zeal!"

"The horrors, the miseries, the monstrosities they are in presence of are so great, surely, as not to leave much of any other attitude over when intelligent sympathy has done its best."

"The war has used up words; they have weakened, they have deteriorated like motor car tires; they have like millions of other things, been more overstrained and knocked about and voided of the happy semblance during the last six months than in all the long ages before, and we are now confronted with a depreciation of all our terms, or, otherwise speaking, with a loss of expression through increase of limpness, that may well make us wonder what ghosts will be left to walk."

There is one passage which may have been the work of the reporter, although even here one senses Jamesian revision. This was his description of the Master:

"Mr James has a mobile mouth, straight nose, a forehead which has thrust back the hair from the top of his commanding head, although it is thick at the sides over the ears, and repeats in its soft gray the colour of his kindly eyes. Before taking in these physical facts, one receives the impression of benignity and amenity not often conveyed, even by the most distinguished. And, taking advantage of this amiability, I asked if certain words just used should be followed by a dash and even boldly added: 'Are you not famous, Mr James, for the use of dashes?' 'Dash my fame!' he impatiently replied. 'And remember, please, that dogmatizing about punctuation is exactly as foolish as dogmatizing about any other form of communication with the reader.'"

LOYALTIES

EARLY that summer Henry James, friend of the Prime Minister, great figure in England's literary establishment, incessant worker among the wounded and the refugees, discovered to his deep chagrin that he was considered still—officially—an alien. It was a rude shock. He had lived in England for forty years. Yet when the time came to plan a summer at Rye, he learned that he would have to report to the police. Rye was a forbidden zone. Aliens—however friendly—had to have permission to go there. This gave James some troubled hours. With his inveterate logic, he felt that the situation should be rectified. The upshot of this was his writing a carefully worded letter to his nephew Harry, telling him he had decided to become a British subject. He had felt he should do this ever since the war began, but his feeling had become "acute with the information that I can only go down to Lamb House now on the footing of an Alien under Police supervision." It labelled him a "technical outsider to the whole situation here, in which my affections and my loyalty are so intensely engaged." He wanted to take the only logical step that would "rectify a position that has become inconveniently and uncomfortably false." He would make his civil status agree with his moral and his material status. "Hadn't it been for the War, I should certainly have gone on as I was, taking it as the simplest and easiest and even friendliest thing; but the circumstances are utterly altered now."

"I have spent here all the best years of my life—they practically have *been* my life: about a twelvemonth hence I shall have been domiciled uninterruptedly in England for forty years, and there is not the least possibility, at my age, and in my state of health, of my ever returning to the U.S. or taking up any relation with it as a country." He was telling Harry this simply to let him know; his mind was made up and he hoped his nephew would understand why he had taken such an important decision. In fact, if his nephew had any reserves, Henry "should then still ask you not to launch them at me unless they should seem to you so important as to balance against my own argument, and frankly speaking, my own absolute need and passion here; which the whole experience of the past year has made quite unspeakably final."

He did not wait for Harry's answer. He found out readily enough from his solicitor that all he needed was to apply for British citizenship, surrender his American passport, and have four persons testify—it amused him greatly—to his literacy as well as his good character. He turned to Gosse, in his exalted position as librarian of the House of Lords. And then it occurred to him that he could call in another excellent witness. Why not the Prime Minister himself? There went forth on 28 June a letter from Henry James to Herbert H. Asquith at No. 10 Downing Street:

> I am venturing to trouble you with the mention of a fact of my personal situation, but I shall do so as briefly and considerately as possible. I desire to offer myself for naturalization in this country, that is, to change my status from that of American citizen to that of British subject.

He wished "to testify at this crisis to the force of my attachment and devotion to England and to the cause for which she is fighting." He had made up his mind. It was beyond all doubt, and brooked "no inward denial."

> I can only testify by laying at her feet my explicit, my material and spiritual allegiance, and throwing into the scale of her fortune my all but imponderable moral weight—"a poor thing but mine own." Hence this respectful appeal.

Would the Prime Minister join with Edmund Gosse, in offering his testimony and bear witness to Henry James's "apparent respectability, and to my speaking and writing English with an approach to propriety?" The Master's solicitor would wait on the Prime Minister with a paper requiring simply his signature "the affair of a single moment."

Prime Minister Asquith was delighted. He went beyond the act of bearing witness to asking the Home Secretary Sir John Simon to facilitate the Master's desire to become a subject of the

King. Asquith, Gosse, George Prothero, editor of the *Quarterly Review*, and James's agent J. B. Pinker were the four witnesses. The application went through in record time. Henry imaged himself in his letters to his friends as offering, like Martin Luther, his testament, "Here I stand, I can no other." On 29 June he surrendered his passport. His application for citizenship contained the following formal statement:

Because of his having lived and worked in England for the best part of forty years, because of his attachment to the Country and his sympathy with it and its people, because of the long friendships and associations and interests he has formed there these last including the acquisition of some property: all of which things have brought to a head his desire to throw his moral weight and personal allegiance, for whatever they may be worth, into the scale of the contending nation's present and future fortune.

At 4.30 p.m. on 28 July, accompanied by his solicitor, Henry James took the oath of allegiance to King George V. "*Civis Britannicus Sum*" he proudly announced. He added: "I don't feel a bit different."

II

The news was formally proclaimed by *The Times*: "Mr Henry James. Adoption of British Nationality." "We are able to announce," said the newspaper, "that Mr Henry James was granted papers of naturalization on Monday and took the oath of allegiance as a British subject. All lovers of literature in this country will welcome the decision of this writer of genius, whose works are an abiding possession of all English-speaking peoples, and they will welcome it all the more on account of the reasons which Mr James gives in his petition for naturalization."

The Master had expected the avalanche of mail that descended upon him from all parts of England—from all those friends who two years before had honoured him, and from many strangers. What he had not expected was the sharpness of the reaction in America. Perhaps it was the sensitivity of some Americans before the spectacle of the European horror; the ambiguity of feeling among those who wanted to help England and France while at the same time being eager to keep the country out of the war. Certainly the gesture made by James was distorted in the United States out of all proportion. He had after all kept his American citizenship for four decades. Yet to many Americans his swearing allegiance to the English King seemed an act of disloyalty; a confirmation of the long-nurtured legend that James was "anti-American." Long after his death, the issue would be kept alive. James in the end simply shrugged his shoulders. It seemed to him highly irrational of a country which measured aliens by the speed with which they became naturalized Americans, to judge him so severely because he had performed the same kind of act in the country of *his* residence.

He could go and come now freely. But his life had become constricted. The "wear and tear of discrimination," as he put it, was now beyond his endurance. He was eloquent on this subject in a letter to Edith Wharton:

> I myself have no adventure of any sort equal to just hearing from you of yours—apart I mean from the unspeakable adventure of being alive in these days, which is about as much as I can undertake at any moment to be sure of. That seems to go on from day to day, though starting fresh with *aube* and getting under way in fact always then with such difficulties, such backings and tanglings and impossible adjustments . . . I stagger out of my dusk to follow the path of the hours, and I *have* followed them I suppose, when I flop back to my intersolar swoon again—though with nothing whatever to show for them but that sad capacity to flop . . .

He was learning to take for granted, he said, "that I shall probably on the whole *not* die of simple sick horror—than which nothing seems to me at the same time more amazing. One aches to anguish and rages to suffocation, and one is still there to do it again, and the occasion still there to see that one does." He lived now in a world of death. Everyone is killed, he remarked, who belongs to anyone, and one was getting the habit of looking "straight and dry-eyed, hard and arid, at those to whom they belonged." There was a final question in the letter about Fullerton. What had become of him? He had seemed to be, even before the war, without ambition, without focus, without anything but a kind of mild continuity. "The non-eventuation of him!" He signed the letter to Edith "*Je vous embrasse, je vous vénère.*"

TREACHERIES

ON 5 July 1915, during the period when James was awaiting British citizenship, he stopped one day at the Reform Club and was handed a book parcel which had lain there some time unforwarded. The book was by H. G. Wells, who for years had sent the Master everything he published. It had an elaborate title-page *Boon, The Mind of the Race, The Wild Asses of the Devil,* and *The Last Trump,* and purported to be "a first selection from the literary remains of George Boon." It was edited by one Reginald Bliss who was mentioned as the author of *The Cousins of Charlotte Brontë, A Child's History of the Crystal Palace,* a book on *Whales in Captivity,* and there was "An Ambiguous Introduction by H. G. Wells." Clearly some kind of literary spoof was intended. Wells said he had not read the book through "though I have a kind of first-hand knowledge of its contents" and he added "it seems to me an indiscreet, ill-advised book." The preface ended with the statement that "Bliss was Bliss and Wells is Wells. And Bliss can write all sorts of things that Wells could not do."

The design of this became clear to James. It was a long and witty joke, and it poked fun at many things and named many writers by their name, not least Henry James who was indeed the very centre of the joke. In a word, Wells himself could not sign such a book; its authorship could be imputed to the demonic *gaminesque* side of him, the little boy with the pea-shooter who behind the prophet, seer, scientist–journalist–historian, was treating himself to a lark. James turned to "Chapter the Fourth" which was entitled "Of Art, of Literature, of Mr Henry James." In this chapter, with more impishness than was apparent to outsiders, Wells constructed a dialogue on the novel between George Moore and Henry James: he knew James's opinion of Moore; and Hueffer was brought into the picture as well. With considerable wit, and a great deal of animus, Wells let loose all his bottled up irritation against James's essay on "The Younger Generation" and the endless unsolicited reviews of his novels the Master had sent Wells in their private correspondence. He laughed at the entire concept of fiction as a "craft." In reality he echoed his lecture on the novel in which he had argued for the loose "usable" novel as against the *organic* creation the Master had always espoused. James had called Wells "cheeky" once too often, and Wells now proved his cheekiness. "Your cheek is positively the very sign and stamp of your genius," Henry James had once said to Wells and in half a hundred letters he had spoken of "your sublime and heroic cheek," and exploded into "cheeky, cheeky, cheeky" when he praised three of Wells's utopias.

This is what James read in *Boon*:

In practice James's selection becomes just omission and nothing more. He omits everything that demands digressive treatment or collateral statement. For example, he omits opinions. In all of his novels you will find no people with defined political opinions, no people with religious opinions, none with clear partisanships or with lusts or whims, none definitely up to any specific impersonal thing. There are no poor people dominated by the imperatives of Saturday night and Monday morning, no dreaming types—and don't we all more or less live dreaming? And none are ever decently forgetful. All that much of humanity he clears out before he begins his story.

In this vein, the character Boon starts to write a novel in the James manner. What ensued was an elaborate parody of *The Spoils of Poynton* interlarded with echoes from "The Turn of the Screw." The crucial passage, which would be quoted across the years, read as follows:

The thing his novel is *about* is always there . . . It is like a church lit but without a congregation to distract you, with every light and line focused on the high altar. And on the altar, very reverently placed, intensely there, is a dead kitten, an egg-shell, a bit of string . . . Like his "Altar of the Dead," with nothing to the dead at all . . . For if there was they couldn't all be candles and the effect would vanish . . . He splits his infinitives and fills them up with adverbial stuffing. He presses the passing colloquialism into his service. His vast paragraphs sweat and struggle; they could not sweat and elbow and struggle more if God himself was the processional meaning to which they sought to come. And all for tales of nothingness . . . It is leviathan retrieving pebbles. It is a magnificent but painful hippopotamus resolved at any cost, even at the cost of its dignity, upon picking up a pea which has got into a corner of its den. Most things, it insists, are beyond it, but it can, at any rate, modestly, and with an artistic singleness of mind, pick up that pea.

II

James read these passages with bewilderment. He had always considered himself Wells's friend and their discussions of art to have been on the level of "profession" without any thought of any kind of *ad hominem* penetration. He wrote to Wells promptly and with great simplicity, but also in pain. "I have more or less mastered your appreciation of H.J., which I have found very curious and interesting, after a fashion—though it has naturally not filled me with a fond elation. It is difficult of course for a writer to put himself *fully* in the place of another writer who finds him extraordinarily futile and void, and who is moved to publish that to the world—and I think the case isn't easier when he happens to have enjoyed the other writer enormously, from far back; because there has then grown up the habit of taking some common meeting-ground between them for granted, and the falling away of this is like the collapse of a bridge which made communication possible."

He said that "the fact that a mind as brilliant as yours *can* resolve me into such an unmitigated mistake . . . makes me greatly want to fix myself, for as long as my nerves will stand it, with such a pair of eyes . . . I try for possible light to enter into the feelings of a critic for whom the deficiencies preponderate." He couldn't keep it up, it was too difficult; he had to fall back on his sense of his "good parts." And the Master concluded by saying that "my poetic and my appeal to experience" rested upon "*my* measure of fulness—of fulness of life and of the projection of it, which seems to you such an emptiness of both." The fine thing about the fictional form was that it opened "such widely different windows of attention."

Wells replied by being contrite. James had written "so kind and frank a letter after my offences that I find it an immense embarrassment to reply to you." He confessed to having set before himself a *gaminesque* ideal—he had a natural horror "of dignity, finish, and perfection." There was "a real and very fundamental difference in our innate and developed attitudes towards life and literature. To you literature like painting is an end, to me literature like architecture is a means, it has a use. Your view was, I felt, too dominant in the world of criticism and I assailed it in tones of harsh antagonism." He confessed *Boon* was "just waste-paper basket." He had written it to escape from the war. Wells ended, "I had rather be called a journalist than an artist, that is the essence of it, and there was no other antagonist possible than yourself." He had regretted a hundred times that he had not expressed "our profound and incurable difference and contrast with a better grace." He signed himself James's "warm if rebellious and resentful admirer, and for countless causes yours most gratefully and affectionately."

James's answer to Wells was his last letter to that writer. It is dated 10 July 1915. He began by saying that he didn't think Wells had made out any sort of case for his bad manners. One simply didn't publish the contents of waste-baskets. He wasn't aware that his view of life and literature had as much of a following as Wells imputed to it. He believed literature lived on the individual practitioner. That was why he had always admired Wells. "I live, live intensely and am fed by life, and my value, whatever it be, is in my own kind of expression of that. Art *makes* life, makes interest, makes importance," James told Wells, adding he knew of no substitute whatever for "the force and beauty of its process." He rejected the idea that literature was like architecture. Both were art. He rejected the "utility" idea of the arts.

Years later Wells in his autobiography, apparently still feeling some twinges of guilt over his behaviour, sought to justify his attack on James. In reality his reminiscences, often quoted, were a renewed attack, and revealed that the differences between the two ran deeper than doctrine. Wells had never got over his below-stairs origins; he resented James's easy acceptance of his place in the world and his aristocratic view of man-made hierarchies. Wells was in open revolt against these hierarchies. James had come to represent for Wells the sovereignty and established power of the aristocracy and no matter how genial and accepting the American was, Wells faced him with an under-edge of hostility. The American wielded his pen as if it were a sceptre; Wells's pen was a dagger, a sabre, a gun.

The autobiography tells us much about how Wells saw James. Where other writers are described—the brilliant fire in Conrad's eyes, the deportment of Shaw, the aspect of Crane—we see James only in externals. With all his comings and goings at Lamb House, Wells could paint only the formal side of the novelist, his habits and rituals, the special hats he wore for different occasions, the matching sticks, the regularity with which he dictated in his "charming room in his beautifully walled garden"—dictated "with a slow but not unhappy circumspection." The picture seems drawn in malice; it is in reality a below-stairs view of a settled aristocrat—for when did aristocrats possess a single hat or a single stick? As Wells had over-dressed himself for the first night of *Guy Domville* compared with Shaw, so he singled out as formality those very objects which made James in reality look informal. Snapshots of the novelist in his peaked cap or his knickerbockers, his colourful waistcoats and his varied walking sticks convey the opposite of what Wells suggested. Wells was intent, however, on showing that James "never scuffled with Fact." This was true to the extent that James did not need to "scuffle" as Wells did. James could re-imagine Fact, could remake the world in his mind and his sentience, Wells could remake it only by writing utopias.

"He saw us all as Masters or would-be Masters, little Masters and great Masters, and he was plainly sorry that *Cher Maître* was not an English expression," Wells remembered. "One could not be in a room with him for ten minutes without realizing the importance he attached to the dignity of this art of his. I was by nature and education unsympathetic with this mental disposition. But I was disposed to regard a novel as about as much an art form as a market-place or a boulevard. It had not even been necessarily to get anywhere. You went by it on your various occasions."

Thus the fundamental dynamics of this friendship always remained the same. James had an easy acceptance of himself and the world; Wells worked hard to make the world accept him. In the end Wells would try to excuse himself by calling James "a little treacherous to me in a natural sort of way." Certainly there had been no treachery in James's attempt to have him elected to the Royal Society of Literature: it was Wells who had refused. But the Master had criticized his work with too much candour. The victory long after was James's. Wells's social novels have been judged at this distance obsolescent. James's novels, those which left out fact but dealt truthfully with human dilemmas, have more vogue today than they ever did.

The literary quarrel was fast forgotten by James in the announcement of his newly-acquired citizenship. The Prime Minister entertained him at dinner on the day of his nationalization. It was one of the last dinners James attended in London.

THE MULBERRY TREE

IN January of 1915 Henry James received word that the large mulberry tree in the very centre of his garden at Lamb House had been toppled by a violent storm. To Mrs Dacre Vincent, a Rye friend who sent him these tidings, he answered, "He might have gone on for some time, I think, in the absence of an *inordinate* gale—but once the fury of the tempest really descended he was bound to give way, because his poor old heart was dead, his immense old trunk was hollow. He had no power to resist left when the southeaster caught him by his vast *crinière* and simply twisted his head round and round. It's very sad for he was the making of the garden—he was *it* in person."

I

James had hoped to go to Rye shortly after his naturalization in the mid-summer of 1915. But he was ill throughout August and finished with effort his preface to Rupert Brooke's *Letters from America*. The prose of that essay shows, however, little strain; it is a beautiful eulogy and was his last piece of writing. Long before, he had stopped his work on *The Ivory Tower*. That novel was too actual; the war seemed to make it obsolete. Instead he turned to the unfinished *Sense of the Past*, which he had set aside in 1900. The story of an American walking into a remote time seemed more possible to James in the midst of headlines and casualty lists. He worked intermittently on this, but in reality half-heartedly. Its subject had always been difficult.

He did not get to Rye until 14 October, going down with Burgess, recently returned to him, his cook Joan Anderson, and his maid, Minnie Kidd. He had loaned Lamb House during the year he had been away to various persons who needed temporary housing, and he was turning it over to still another tenant. Apparently his trip was mainly to take care of certain of his papers, for Mrs William James later said "he burned up quantities of papers and photographs—cleared his drawers in short." In the midst of this he developed acute symptoms and sat up for three nights breathing with difficulty. With his addiction to self-diagnosis, he treated himself for a gastric upset. But on calling in the local doctor, Ernest Skinner, he was told that there was a change in his heart rhythm—he seems to have had intermittent tachycardia or auricular fibrillation. Skinner gave him digitalis, and he was able to return to London, where Sir James Mackenzie confirmed the doctor's diagnosis and the medication.

In November James wrote to Rhoda Broughton "I have really been miserably ill these three months, but only during the latter half of them have I emerged into a true intelligence of the source of my woe—which has been a bad heart crisis . . . Bustling is at an end for me for ever now—though indeed, after all, I have had very little hand in it for many a day." Hugh returned from Russia at this time and talked to the Master over the phone from Cornwall. "I hear that people have been seeing you so that I hope that means that you are better," he wrote him. James replied tenderly: "The past year has made me feel twenty years older, and, frankly, as if my knell had rung. Still, I cultivate, I at least attempt, a brazen front. Do intensely believe that I respond clutchingly to your every grasp of me, every touch, and would so gratefully be a reconnecting link with you here." Hugh wrote in his diary, "delightful letter from H.J.—one of the most truly affectionate I've ever had from him."

II

A few weeks earlier Mrs Wharton had arrived in London for a brief visit. She telephoned James one morning wanting to drive him to Qu'Acre to see Howard Sturgis. He told her he was too ill. She then asked him whether he could lend Miss Bosanquet to her for the day. "I suppose," Miss Bosanquet noted, "he could hardly say he was well enough to work if he was not well enough to go to Windsor." Excited at the prospect of getting to know Mrs Wharton better, Miss Bosanquet hastily tidied herself up and then "made a rather flurried way" to Brook Street, to Buckland's

Hotel. She found the lady novelist in a very elegant pink négligée, wearing a cap of *écru* lace trimmed with fur. "Her arms," Miss Bosanquet wrote in her diary, "were very much displayed, coming from very beautiful frills of sleeve, and they were good arms, not either scraggy or too fleshy, but just the right plumpness and ending up in hands most beautifully manicured." Her only complaint was that Mrs Wharton used too intense a perfume. The central heating was turned up too high for Miss Bosanquet's comfort. Mrs Wharton's face was "squareish" and finely wrinkled; her complexion was "browny-yellow." She had "good eyes and a strong mouth."

"Of course, Miss Bosanquet," said the Firebird, "I didn't really want you to come here to write letters for me, but just so that we might have a quiet talk." Miss Bosanquet, knowing the closeness of Mrs Wharton's relation to James, spoke candidly of his ever-increasing illnesses. Mrs William James and Peggy had wanted to come over during the previous summer but James had not wanted them to risk a voyage amid prowling enemy submarines and they had gone to California instead. The doctors now considered that James had a real, not a simulated, heart condition.

Miss Bosanquet confided to her diary: "I was rather unhappily conscious all the time we were talking that I wasn't as much charmed as I ought to be. I could *see* the charm and I couldn't feel it—and that was so disappointing." She decided that Mrs Wharton "so evidently depends on fascinating people all about her, her sole effect makes one continually conscious of that." Mrs Wharton did turn to literature once or twice, but Miss Bosanquet didn't feel like pursuing the subject.

The importance of this meeting was that Mrs Wharton established a bond of friendship with Miss Bosanquet, and a link within the Master's household. It ministered to her need for omniscience and power. And it would enable her to act, if some emergency occurred.

A TERROR OF CONSCIOUSNESS

EARLY in the morning of Thursday, 2 December 1915, Henry James's maid, Minnie Kidd, came to Miss Bosanquet's flat in nearby Lawrence Street and told her that Mr James seemed to have had "a sort of stroke." The maid had been in the dining-room at eight-thirty and heard the Master calling. She entered his bedroom. He was lying on the floor; his left leg had given way under him. She called Burgess. Between them they got Henry James into bed; it wasn't easy—the Master was heavy. Miss Bosanquet came at once to Carlyle Mansions. James was lying in bed. He was open-eyed and calm. He had had, he told her, a stroke "in the most approved fashion." The most distressing thing, he said, was that in wanting to ring for his servants he had found himself fumbling with the electrical wiring of the bed-lamp. He had then called for help. Mrs Wharton years later said that Howard Sturgis was told by James that his first thought as he fell was "so it has come at last—the Distinguished Thing." Minnie Kidd reported she heard James say, "It's the beast in the jungle, and it's sprung."

Dr Des Voeux arrived promptly and confirmed that it was a stroke, a slight one. The Master then dictated a cable to his nephew: "Had slight stroke this morning. No serious symptoms. Perfect care. No suffering. Wrote Peggy yesterday." James had written a long letter to his niece the previous day. He had re-counted his recent illnesses; described life in London; complained of his sleepless nights. Peggy had told him of Frank Duveneck's being "lionized" in Cincinnatti. He wondered why Lizzie Boott's husband should be lionized at this time when his work belonged "to such an antediluvian past. His only good work was done in his very few first years, nearly fifty years of these ago." However, he had heard Duveneck was a fine art teacher; perhaps that was the reason for his acclaim. He told Peggy of Burgess being back. He was on an extended leave from service. Then he felt tired and ended his letter with the words "the pen drops from my hand!"

It had indeed dropped, and for all time. Mrs William James cabled she was sailing at once; she had long ago promised her husband she would "see Henry through when he comes to the end." Miss Bosanquet meanwhile took charge. Having no specific instructions, she answered queries, sent daily bulletins to Mrs Wharton, and instructed the servants. She took control of James's friends who flocked to see him, flocked in such numbers that the doctor had to restrict visiting drastically.

On the second day, Dr Des Voeux announced that James had had a second stroke. The paralysis of his left side was more complete. He called in Sir James Mackenzie. They pronounced the novelist to be in grave condition, and that night Emily Sargent and her sister Mrs Ormond stayed up in the flat in case they should be wanted. Miss Bosanquet had in the meantime obtained the services of a male nurse; he proved inefficient and the doctor brought in two regular nurses. Miss Bosanquet sent a second cable to Harry James and also telegraphed Mrs Wharton. The Firebird would have come directly, but she was at Hyères. Within twenty-four hours, the patient had rallied and was calling for a thesaurus to discover the exact descriptive word for his condition. He didn't think "paralytic" was right. He told Miss Bosanquet to write to Mrs Wharton and to Hugh Walpole. Mrs Wharton wired "can come if advisable" but with Mrs James en route and the novelist improving, Miss Bosanquet suggested there was no need of her for the present. A week after the first stroke Miss Bosanquet noted that the Master was "more himself." In the interval proofs of the Rupert Brooke preface arrived and she read them.

I

Two diaries were kept during Henry James's last illness. Miss Bosanquet's records with some minuteness the comings and goings, the daily reports of the doctors, and such talk of the Master's as she heard. Mrs William James began a diary shortly after her arrival. She principally wrote down certain remarks made by James. These show a distinct pattern of confusion; they reveal that he was from the first confused about his "sense of place," and then, as he struggled to orient himself in the scale of his mental wanderings he experienced a mounting and strange terror. He began to think he was mad—and that his visitors would notice he was mad.

This condition went at first unnoticed; he seemed simply to be rambling. On 10 December Miss Bosanquet noted "mind clouded this morning and he has lost his own unmistakeable identity—is just a simple sick man." He was running a temperature; the doctors found he had "embolic pneumonia" due to a clot in his lung. In this condition, James spoke to Miss Bosanquet very strongly and clearly about wanting to take Burgess to Lady Hyde's with him. He would then send Burgess back. "Where am I?" he asked. "What is this address?" When Miss Bosanquet told him it was 21 Carlyle Mansions, he answered "How very curious, that's Lady Hyde's address too." On the next day he spoke of himself as being in a strange hotel far away from London and when Mrs Charles Hunter came to see him he couldn't account for her presence in this hotel. He was delirious at moments. On 13 December he wanted to know where certain manuscripts were, he thought they had gone to Ireland. In the latter part of the day he spoke of himself as being in Cork. In the evening he asked whether the "plumbers had carried out the alterations in the bathroom," a corollary to his having dictated to Miss Bosanquet certain paragraphs about alterations in the Tuileries. Then he spoke of "the curious annexation of Chelsea to Cork." He told Miss Bosanquet, she recorded, he felt "the mantle of her protection was flung over him to a far greater extent than he was at all conscious of."

Mrs William James arrived on the evening of 13 December after a stormy crossing. James seemed glad to see her. He patted her hand and said, "I don't dare to think of what you have come through to get here." Then he began to speak of being in California, probably because Mrs James had been there with Peggy during the preceding summer. Mrs William said to him, "You remember Mr Bruce Porter in San Francisco. He and Peggy have made fast friends on the basis of their love of you." The Master rejoined "they have a pretty feeble basis." He complained that he was constantly surrounded by women. "The absence of the male element in my entourage is what perplexes me." On 22 December he told one of his visitors "this is a desperately long tunnel I see." He held his thumb and forefinger up to form a circle, then added there was "a gleam of blue" at the tunnel's end. On another day Mrs James brushed his hair and he said "that ardent brushing does not mitigate my troubles."

II

The confusion returned on 16 December when the barber came to shave the Master. Later James summoned Miss Bosanquet. He told her it was "most painful and distressing" to be spoken of as if he were in London. He found it "equally painful" that when he asked for an account of the country and the people round no one seemed able to give an intelligible answer. "Even the barber who came to shave me this morning is in on the conspiracy. I had last seen him in London and when I asked him this morning if he'd been in London recently he actually said he was here now."

After tea on this day he returned to the subject. He wanted to know whether someone could help clear up his mystification. "Someone whom I could ask if this extraordinary state of utter dependence upon the good offices of these quite well-meaning nurses doesn't strike them as uncanny in the same way in which it strikes me." Miss Bosanquet told him he had been ill. The mystery would resolve itself when he was stronger, and "I tried to impress on him the idea that eating would help to make him stronger."

"I have a curious sense," Henry James said, "that I'm not the bewildering puzzle to all of you that you are to me." He returned to the absence of males in his entourage with the "negligible exception of Burgess and the doctor."

The next day James again said he was in Cork. His return, again and again to Cork, may have been a memory of the death of his mother. He had been in that city only once—on his journey back to England after Mary James had died. He had found Cork full of soldiers, and had not lingered.

On 21 December Miss Bosanquet came into the bedroom. Minnie Kidd was by his bed. He opened his eyes, looked towards his amanuensis, and Kidd said: "You know who that is, don't you, sir?" He replied, "Oh, Miss Bosanquet." She went beside the bed and took James's hand. He said:

"Miss Bosanquet, there were two or three things I wanted to say to you. We had some talk, you remember, two or three days ago." Miss Bosanquet said everything was perfectly clear. He said: "This place in which I find myself is the strangest mixture of Edinburgh and Dublin and New York and some other place that I don't know."

Miss Bosanquet mentioned Mrs Wharton, and James asked: "Does she seem at all aware of my state?" Miss Bosanquet said she seemed aware. James may have been talking of his mental state; Miss Bosanquet believed he was referring to the state of his illness. His message was "tell Mrs Wharton that I thank her very kindly for her inquiries and that at present I'm entrusting the answers to you, but that I hope very soon to get into closer relation with her."

There seems to have been considerable strain between Mrs James and the nurses: she constantly interfered. On 22 December Miss Bosanquet noted that "he looked desperately ill—his face all drawn and wasted and unshaved, head falling right over to the paralysed side, and his body barely covered by a brownish Jaeger blanket—his feet sticking out beyond it at the bottom. He was uncomfortably propped on a variety of pillows and many-coloured cushions and each arm rested on a pillow too. If ever a man looked dying, he did."

During Christmas James suddenly became restless with what Miss Bosanquet called "a passion for motion." He was moved into the drawing-room and then from one chair to another. "He was furiously angry with everyone who tried to reason with him." In the afternoon the whole household was prostrate, "Kidd and Burgess flat in the kitchen, the nurse hysterical in the passage and Mrs James more miserable than she has ever been before, which is saying a very great deal."

The next day some movement seemed to have returned to

James's arm and leg. Dr Des Voeux had a wheel-couch brought in and James was easily moved into the drawing-room. He asked for Miss Bosanquet. She found him looking "a complete wreck of his former self now, and his eyes have a strained, wandering expression—they don't look intelligently at one a bit." She gave him messages from Miss Allen and Lucy Clifford. She mentioned Mrs Clifford was reading proofs of an article and noted that his face clouded when she mentioned proof—evidently the idea of proof-reading gave him a momentary pang. On the next day he was profoundly depressed. He kept saying good-bye to each member of his household.

During the early days of January there seemed to be some improvement and on 12 January the Master asked if he mightn't go to Rye. Then he seems to have made the journey in his mind for he spoke to Burgess of how nice it was to be back in Lamb House. There was an increasing concern about the effect he was having on other people. He asked Burgess whether his muddled condition of mind didn't make people laugh. Mrs James intervened defensively, "Never, Henry, no one wants to smile." The Master fixed her with his right eye—the left eyelid was drooping because of the stroke—"What is this voice from Boston, Massachusetts breaking in with irrelevant remarks in my conversation with Burgess?"

On another occasion he seems to have been imagining one of his plays was being produced. He asked Mrs James, "What effect will my madness have on the house?" He also wanted to know about "Fanny." When he was asked if he meant Fanny Prothero he said no. Apparently he was thinking of Fanny Kemble. Then he waved to Mrs James "not to speak before them" meaning the nurses. He indicated he wished to conceal his "madness" from them.

III

Read in their fragmented form, these partial records of Henry James's mental confusion suggest a kind of heroic struggle to retain his grasp on reality in the midst of his death-in-life. Taken together they suggest that in some mysterious way the Master may have been living out that "terror of consciousness" with which he had sought to endow his hero in *The Sense of the Past*, the unfinished novel he had been trying to complete. He had actually turned over some of its pages on the evening before his stroke. In his notes for this novel James had spoken of his hero, walking into the year 1820, with his knowledge of the future, as being "in danger of passing for a madman." He feels "cut off . . . and lost." We are indeed in the presence of the uncanny when we think of James's sense of being cut off from those around him, in the grim comedy of confusing London and Cork. He was apparently living out a part of his fiction. Perhaps some of his remarks related to the continuation of his creative work on this novel; and then, in his confused memory, shuttling between the cities of his pilgrimages—the Ireland of his father and grandfather, the London, Rome, Edinburgh, of his own experience, he had to cope with the disoriented sense of being in two places at once. Memory became actual; the actual of the sickroom intruded on memory. This, in another form, was a part of the fantastic idea for *The Sense of the Past*—it had been designed as a novel dealing with "the conscious and understood fusion" taking place between the hero and his ancestral self; it was as if the Jamesian character in "The Jolly Corner" and his *alter ego* were no longer distinct from one another. His original fantasy of 1900, seemed to come true now within his dispossessed imagination. He had written of "scared and slightly modern American figures" moving against the background of three or four European environments. "I seem to see them *going*—hurried by their fate—from one of these places to the other, in search of, in flight from, something or other." And the danger of his being thought mad was a terror imposed on the terror of death. During his last hours he would speak of nights "of horror and terror." His imagination, cut loose perhaps by the stroke from temporal moorings, floated through such moments of nightmare all the more ghastly for the disconnection.

FINAL AND FADING WORDS

A STRANGE thing had occurred during the first period of his confusion, before the arrival of Mrs William James. In his delirium, when his fever was high, Henry James had wanted to write. He kept asking for paper and pencil. When he got it, his hand would make the movements of writing. Then he wanted to dictate. The typewriter was brought into the sickroom. The familiar sound pacified him. Miss Bosanquet took his dictation. "I find the business of coming round about as important and glorious as any circumstances I have had occasion to record, by which I mean that I find them as damnable and as boring," he dictated. He said it was "not much better to discover within one's carcass new resources for application than to discover the absence of them; their being new doesn't somehow add to their interest but makes them stale and flat, as if one had long ago exhausted them." Miss Bosanquet said these sentences were spoken slowly and with many pauses, as if he were making a great effort to mobilize his thoughts. "Such is my sketchy state of mind, but I feel sure I shall discover plenty of fresh worlds to conquer" and he added "even if I am to be cheated of the amusement of them."

The Master's mind was disintegrating; but it still had its force and its logic. On the afternoon of Saturday, 11 December, he called once more for the typewriter and dictated words about touching "the large old phrase into the right amplitude . . . we simply shift the sweet nursling of genius from one maternal breast to the other and the trick is played, the false note averted." Then he exclaimed: "Astounding little stepchild of God's astounding young stepmother!" There followed a passage that seemed to contain a recall of the war, and to become confused with his reading of Napoleonic memoirs. He was back in the Paris of the Second Empire which he had known in his boyhood: back in the Louvre. This was his dictation; sometimes Miss Bosanquet missed a word; sometimes there was discontinuity of thought:

. . . on this occasion moreover that, having been difficult to keep step . . . we hear of the march of history, what is remaining to that essence of tragedy, the limp? . . .

. . . mere patchwork transcription becomes of itself the high brave art. We . . . five miles off at the renewed affronts that we see coming for the great, and that we know they will accept. The fault is that they had found themselves too easily great, and the effect of that, definitely, had been, within them, the want of long provision for it. It wasn't why they [were] to have been so thrust into the limelight and the uproar, but why they [were] to have known as by inspiration the trade most smothered in experience. They go about shivering in the absence of the holy protocol—they dodder sketchily about as in the betrayal of the lack of early advantages; and it is upon *that* they seem most to depend to give them distinction—it is upon that, and upon the *crânerie* and the *rouerie* that they seem most to depend for the grand air of gallantry. They pluck in their terror handfuls of plumes from the imperial eagle, and with no greater credit in consequence than that they face, keeping their equipoise, the awful bloody beak that vindictive intention, during these days of cold grey Switzerland weather on the huddled and hustled after campaigns of the first omens of defeat. Everyone looks haggard and our only wonder is that they still succeed in "looking" at all. It renews for us the assurance of the part played by that element in the famous assurance [divinity] that doth hedge a king.

During recent months James had met various Bonaparte descendants: he had seen his old Roman friend Count Primoli and Princess Victor Napoleon of Belgium. Perhaps some recollection of this caused him to dictate on the next day—12 December—the sentence "the Bonapartes have a kind of bronze distinction that extends to their fingertips and is a great source of charm in the women." He went on to say "therefore they don't have to swagger after the fact; fortune has placed them too high and anything less would be trivial. You can believe anything of the Queen of Naples or of the Princess Caroline Murat." He rang in a change: "There have been great families of tricksters and conjurors; so why not this one, and so pleasant withal?" Whether he was moving in consciousness from the Napoleonic family to the James family is not clear; this is suggested, however, by the sentence immediately following, as if he were dictating a passage in *Notes of a Son and Brother*: "Our admirable father keeps up the pitch. He is the dearest of men." Then he went back to the Napoleonic legend:

I should have liked above all things seeing our sister pulling her head through the crown; one has that confident . . . and I should have had it most on the day when most would have been asked. But we jog on very well. Up to the point of the staircase where the officers do stand it couldn't be better, though I wonder at the *souffle* which so often enables me to pass.

We are back from . . . but we breathe at least together and I am devotedly yours . . .

The sudden transition, as if he were ending a letter, suggests that in his mental confusion Henry James was busy writing recent and old books, and also thinking of himself as dictating letters. At one moment there is a recollection of Mrs Wharton, "We squeeze together into some motor-car or other and we so talk and talk and what comes of it?" Then another fragmentary thought, "Yes, that is the turn of public affairs. Next statement is for all the world as if we had brought it on and had given our push and our touch to great events."

"After luncheon," Miss Bosanquet noted at the time (this was on 12 December) "he wanted me again and dictated, perfectly clearly and coherently two letters from Napoleon Bonaparte to one of his married sisters—I suspect they weren't original compositions, but subconscious memory—one letter about the decoration of the Louvre and the Tuileries and the other about some great opportunity being offered them which they mustn't fall below the level of. After he had finished the second letter he seemed quite satisfied not to do any more and fell into a peaceful sleep."

Actually the first letter was the Bonaparte letter, and he signed it with Napoleon's original Corsican form "Napoleone," apparently having dictated the exact spelling he wanted. The second letter, no less Napoleonic in its sharpness of tone and military eloquence, was signed with his own name. Again his memory was mingling Napoleonic family affairs and James family affairs. It sounded as if he had gone out into the world and had conquered, and was allowing William and Alice to share in the spoils. William had been dead now almost six years; and Henry in alluding to him during his delirium spoke always of his being in some other room. Following are the letters, with Miss Bosanquet's notes of the time:

Dictation resumed at 2.10 p.m. on the same day.

The letter following originally began "Dear and highly considered Brother and Sister" but after its conclusion, H.J. reconsidered the opening words and changed them.

Dear and most esteemed Brother and Sister,

I call your attention to the precious enclosed transcripts of plans and designs for the decoration of certain apartments of the palaces here, the Louvre and the Tuileries, which you will find addressed in detail to artists and workmen who are to take them in hand. I commit them to your earnest care till the questions relating to this important work are fully settled. When that is the case I shall require of you further zeal and further taste. For the present the course is definitely marked out and I beg you to let me know from stage to stage definitely how the scheme promises and what results it may be held to inspire. It is, you will see, of a great scope, a majesty unsurpassed by any work of the kind yet undertaken in France. Please understand I regard these plans as fully developed and as having had my last consideration and look forward to no patchings nor perversions, and with no question of modifications either economic or aesthetic. This will be the case with all further projects of your affectionate

Napoleone.

My dear Brother and Sister,

I offer you great opportunities, in exchange for the exercise of great zeal. Your position as residents in our young but so highly considered Republic at one of the most interesting minor capitals is a piece of luck which may be turned to account in the measure of your acuteness and your experience. A brilliant fortune may come to crown it and your personal merit will not diminish that harmony. But you must rise to each occasion—the one I now offer you is of no common cast, and please remember that any failure to push your advantage to the utmost will be severely judged. I have displayed you as persons of great taste and judgment. Don't leave me a sorry figure in consequence but present me rather as your fond but not infatuated relation, able and ready to back you up, your faithful Brother and Brother-in-law,

Henry James.

The remaining passages of James's dictation were taken down at various times, some in longhand by James's niece. This part comes closest to the modern "stream of consciousness," for there is fragmentation and discontinuity:

across the border
all the pieces
Individual souls, great of . . . on which
great perfections are If one does . . . in the fulfilment with the neat and pure
and perfect—to the success or as he or she moves through life, following
admiration unfailing . . . in the highway—Problems are very sordid.

He wandered off to allude to Robert Louis Stevenson in a less
fragmentary way and perhaps to Henry Adams who had visited
at Vailima.

One of the earliest of the consumers of the great globe in the interest of the
attraction exercised by the great R.L.S. of those days, comes in, afterwards.
a visitor at Vailima and . . . there and pious antiquities to his domestic annals.

At the end, on a day of sore throat and much malaise, he dictated
a cogent passage which seemed to show an awareness that he no
longer could command his old coherence. "These final and faded
remarks," he dictated, "have some interest and some character—
but this should be extracted by a highly competent person only—
some such whom I don't presume to name, will furnish such last
offices." Implicit in this was still the lingering of an old curiosity,
his sense that all of life, even the act of dying, had interest in it, to
be discerned and recorded. The rest of the passage, however, has
in it a note of despair and then of resignation:

invoke more than one kind presence, several could help, and many would—
but it all better too much left than too much done. I never dreamed of such
duties as laid upon me. This sore throaty condition is the last I ever invoked
for the purpose.

There would be another Napoleonic stance, some time later. In
talk with Mrs William James one day he asked if his nephew Billy
had friends and said he wished one of the boys had connections in
England. The conversation could have occurred in a tale by
Henry James:

"You are their connection with England and Europe," Mrs William James
said.
"Yes, I know, and I should say, without being fatuous, with the future."
"With the future always. They will try to follow you."
"Tell them *to follow, to be faithful, to take me seriously.*"

OVER THE ABYSS

LORD MORLEY, later Viscount Morley of Blackburn, statesman and man of letters, had always regarded Henry James as a superficial and trivial person. To be sure, James had written one of the most successful volumes in the "English Men of Letters Series" which Morley edited for the Macmillans—his study of Hawthorne—but he had also written on French writers and on France and Lord Morley considered his aesthetic view and concern with French novelists simply "honest scribble-work." Morley's subjects were grandiose—Voltaire, Rousseau, Diderot, and then he had done a large life of Gladstone. Thus it was that when Prime Minister Asquith told Morley that he was thinking of recommending James for the Order of Merit, the greatest distinction conferred by the Crown on civilians, and that James as a British subject was now eligible for this honour, held by Thomas Hardy and George Meredith, Morley opposed him. What had James done but write of the idle rich as compared with Hardy's personages? In the face of Morley's vigorous opposition, Asquith wavered. He was fond of Henry James. He knew that he was gravely ill. And the New Year's honours list was almost ready.

Edward Marsh, who had served as Winston Churchill's secretary, was now attached to the Prime Minister's office. He had known James for some years. When he read James's preface to the Ruper Brooke volume he was profoundly moved. On 18 December he wrote a long and remarkable memorandum to the Prime Minister. "May I write a few words in the hope that the question of the Order of Merit for Henry James has not been irrevocably set aside?"

There was, he argued, little doubt of James's right to stand beside Meredith and Hardy, the only novelists admitted thus far to the Order. If they had qualities not in James, it was equally true James had qualities which they did not possess.

It has been said that the great French novelists are conscious artists, the English inspired amateurs. Henry James is the exception. No writer of his time gives the same impression of knowledge and mastery in the architectural structure of his works, and in the gradual building up of atmosphere, character, and situation.

Marsh reminded Asquith that James's three hundred friends and admirers had said in presenting him with the portrait and a Golden Bowl, "You are the writer, the master of rare and beautiful art, in whose work creation and criticism meet as they have never met before in our language." Marsh continued:

> He is sometimes blamed for dealing only with characters drawn from the hothouse life of the leisured classes, hypertrophied in intellect and emotion; but an artist should be judged not by his choice of material but by his treatment. It would be equally fair to rule out Thomas Hardy for his complete failure to represent any educated person. Henry James's shorter stories are certainly not inferior to those of any English writer. His style may be criticized as mannered, and sometimes obscure; on the other hand it is one of the most individual that has ever been evolved; it is infinitely expressive, except when it defeats itself by trying to express too much; and it rises at times to the height of beauty.

In his thorough way Marsh proceeded to describe James's qualifications as a critic. He mentioned the prefaces to the New York Edition, "a uniquely illuminating account of an artist's creative processes." He then pointed to James's influence on other writers —listing Bennett, Wells, Mrs Wharton, Anne Douglas Sedgwick. He invoked Stevenson's regard for James; he mentioned Edmund Gosse. He said he was certain "the profession of letters as a whole would warmly welcome this appointment." There were two extraneous considerations. One was James's generous and impressive gesture of adherence to England's cause. And the other was that the United States would appreciate the compliment to an American-born writer such as James. "I understand Lord Morley is against the proposal; but with the greatest respect for him I could wish that some opinion might be taken which would be representative of a later epoch in taste."

The effect of this vigorous memorandum was immediate. Asquith needed just such arguments to stiffen the case for James against Morley. Two days after Marsh submitted the memorandum, a message came from Buckingham Palace, signed by the King's secretary. "The King, acting upon your recommendation of the case, will be prepared to confer the Order of Merit upon Henry James."

I

It was announced on New Year's day. A great pile of telegrams and letters descended on Carlyle Mansions. One was a note from George Alexander, who said that he was proud to have produced *Guy Domville* even though it had not been a success. How much of this mail Henry James saw we do not know. Lord Bryce brought the insignia of the rare order to James's bedside. The distinguished invalid seemed pleased. Minnie Kidd reported that he said to her "turn off the light so as to spare my blushes." Mrs James read him some of the telegrams and he said "what curious manifestations such occasions call forth!" The occasion was muted; the novelist did not need excitement. Miss Bosanquet was a little disturbed at Mrs William James's nonchalance when word arrived from Buckingham Palace that Sir Harry Legge wanted to know when he could see Mr James to deliver a message from the King.

Things had become a little easier during the first days of the new year. Peggy after a rough wintry voyage reached his bedside. James's mind seemed clearer; he signed a power of attorney for Mrs William James to allow her to take care of all the servants and the bills. But at this time Miss Bosanquet received a jolt. She found a note written by Peggy criticizing her for having taken too much upon herself and that she had seemed to be getting pleasure "managing things in a heartless sort of way while the faithful servants have slaved to the breaking-point." The real meaning of this was something quite different. Mrs William did not like Miss Bosanquet's writing about Henry James's condition to Mrs Wharton—she so intensely disliked Mrs Wharton, partly from her puritanical revulsion at the adultery in *The Reef*. From this time on James's amanuensis found herself more and more excluded from 21 Carlyle Mansions. Miss Bosanquet was deeply hurt. She noted "it was none of my wish to be alone with the household."

She had done what she felt was her duty. She was, however, summoned when James wanted her. Otherwise there was little for her to do except occasional typing jobs. On the day in which her diary records the criticism of her work, she sets down also the message dictated by James for Edmund Gosse—"tell Gosse that my powers of recuperation are very great and that I'm making progress toward recovery without withdrawal."

II

There were moments when James seemed to be entirely in the past. He spoke for example of having tea at Carlyle's house with his father. There were further incidents between Miss Bosanquet and Mrs William. Miss Bosanquet asked whether she was to write to Mr Pinker about a contract and was told "I'll see Mr Pinker myself if necessary."

Peggy and Mrs James were distinctly hostile—"the presumptuous secretary being put in her place and slinking out of the presence of righteousness" Theodora wrote in her diary. From then on she came daily to inquire about her employer but stayed only if asked to do a specific bit of work. Occasionally the New Englanders were more friendly. One morning Peggy said her uncle was remembering things more clearly as for instance the English clothes she was wearing. He had helped her buy them a year before. Apparently Edith Wharton sensed that all was not well, for she wrote to Miss Bosanquet asking her whether she would like to be her secretary. "I don't think I shall," Miss Bosanquet noted, "it's too alarming a prospect." She declined the offer on the ground she did not know French well enough. Actually she was proficient in the language.

In January, James's nephew, Harry, arrived "nearly white-haired, but still black-moustached. He has a tremendous chin—the most obstinate-looking jaw," Miss Bosanquet noted. He asked her to go through the unfinished typescripts and make lists. He went to Rye and had inventories made of the furniture and the books. Mrs James gave Miss Bosanquet her cheque for her month's salary. Miss Bosanquet returned it. Mrs James, contrite, insisted that she keep it.

T

Intrigue surrounded the Master to the end. His sick-life was now reduced to a routine. Harry prepared himself, to be James's executor. Mrs William wondered which furniture to take back to America from Lamb House. But what is most interesting, in reading her letters to her children, and her diary, is the dawning on her that Henry James was a great and important figure; that the English stood in awe of him. She had for so long accepted the idea that he was simply William's artistic brother, a kind, amiable, gentle, idiosyncratic man. In her letters this light grows and grows. Some of her letters to her sons in America are touching in their picture of the Master finally at bay:

He seems like a tired child but tranquil, comfortable, enjoying his food and the sitting on a big lounge in the window whence he can look out at the river, with the ever-creeping barges and the low-lying clouds. He thinks he is voyaging and visiting foreign cities, and sometimes he asks for his glasses and paper and imagines that he writes. And sometimes his hand moves over the counterpane as if writing. He is never impatient, or contrary or troubled about anything. He still recognizes us and likes to have us sit awhile beside him. He very especially likes Burgess—"Burgess James" he called him yesterday. It is a touching sight to see little Burgess holding his hand and half kneeling in the chair beside him, his face very near to Henry, trying to understand the confused words Henry murmurs to him.

James thought as he watched the passing boats on the Thames that he was on a ship. When he asked for Burgess on one occasion, Mrs James said he was out doing errands. "How extraordinary that Burgess should be leaving the ship to do errands!" he exclaimed. To Peggy he turned one day and asked "I hope your father will be in soon—he is the one person in all Rome I want to see." And again "I should so like to have William with me."

The Master continued on this plateau until the last week of February. On the 23rd when Mrs William came into the sick-room he said to her "Beloved Alice" and then told her to tell William he was leaving in two days. And then to Alice he said "helpful creature to William and to me." He may have been having a premonition of death. Two days later he was seriously ill. On the 24th he spoke of "a night of horror and terror." On the next day "stay with me, Alice, stay with me." He lapsed into unconsciousness on that day. On 27 February the nurse summoned Mrs William. The novelist was breathing hard and trembling. She sat beside him till the symptoms passed and he slept. His pulse and temperature were normal. He tried to speak during the day but his words were unintelligible. On 28 February he could take no nourishment. At four that afternoon the doctor said "this is the end." James was breathing in short gasps. He had oedema. At six he sighed—three sighing breaths, at long intervals, the last one, Mrs William James noted, "very faint." She wrote, "He was gone. Not a shadow on his face, nor the contraction of a muscle."

III

Miss Bosanquet, arriving at Carlyle Mansions that evening, met Emily Sargent in the hall and learned the news. She left a note for Mrs James and then wired Edith Wharton who wrote her a day or so later that James had been "one of the wisest and noblest men that ever lived. We who knew him well know how great he would have been if he had never written a line."

The long cruel dying was at an end. Howard Sturgis called it that. James's will to live had been strong and he had died with the same tenacity as he had lived. On the 29th Miss Bosanquet asked if she could be of help; she was assured that "everything had been provided for." There was talk of a service in Westminster Abbey; it was however not feasible and Mrs William decided in favour of a funeral in Chelsea Old Church. The body remained in Carlyle Mansions. Burgess gave his master his last shave. The coffin was brought and James was placed in it. Miss Bosanquet returned on 1 March and was taken into the drawing-room by Minnie Kidd. Henry James O.M. lay in his coffin. It was covered with a black pall and there was a white square over his face which Minnie Kidd the maid folded back. The face was bandaged to keep the jaw from falling. "It looked very fine," Miss Bosanquet wrote, "a great work of art in ivory wax. Perfectly peaceful, but entirely dissociated from everything that was his personality. I quite understand what Mrs James meant by speaking about the great feeling of tenderness one has for the dead body that is left behind.

One feels that the spirit that inhabited it isn't there to care for it any longer."

She went back and viewed the body on the next day. The Master looked more like his living self because this time there was no bandage around his face. "Several people who have seen the dead face are struck with the likeness to Napoleon which is certainly great."

And so the funeral of the Master was held, in the little old Chelsea church which had seen much literary history. There came to it, in the midst of war, those who had known Henry James and cherished him — Sargent and his sister, Kipling, Gosse, swollen-eyed Goody Allen, Lucy Clifford, representatives of the Prime Minister and the war group James had met. Dickens's daughter, Mrs Perugini was there, and Howard Sturgis, the Colvins, the Pollocks, and many others including Ellen Terry. The coffin was carried in and placed in the chancel. Mrs James, Peggy, Sargent and his sister sat in the front pew; the servants sat on the opposite side. Fanny Prothero wandered in looking lost, and found herself a seat far back. Whether Persse was there, we do not know. Hugh was back in Russia; he did not get the news until some days later. The service was conventional — the lesson from I Corinthians and two hymns "For all the Saints" and "O God, our help in ages past." But it wasn't the beautiful singing or the service so much as the emotion of the mourners, a kind of universal love that held them together for this strange lonely man from America who had lived so much and so intensely in their midst and was now gone.

Henry James had inscribed *Notes on Novelists* at the outbreak of the war to Edmund Gosse with the words "Over the Abyss." Gosse conveyed the emotion of the mourners who overflowed Chelsea Old Church in a letter to *The Times* on the day after the funeral. "As we stood round the shell of that incomparable brain of that noble and tender heart, it flashed across me that to generations yet unawakened to a knowledge of his value the Old Chelsea Church must for ever be the Altar of the Dead . . . He was a supreme artist; but what we must remember and repeat is that he was a hero . . . an English hero of whom England shall be proud." A plaque honouring James and speaking of "amenities of brave decisions" hangs on the wall of the church.

The body was cremated at Golders Green. Mrs James later took the ashes back to America. She smuggled them in; it was wartime and she took no chances. The urn was buried beside the graves of Henry's mother and sister. He had stood there in 1904 and looked at the Medusa Face of life and cried *Basta! Basta!*

The will was simple. James left all his property to Mrs William James and after her to her children. Harry received Lamb House and its contents. Peggy got his insurance. The Sargent Portrait was left as promised to the National Portrait Gallery. James bestowed gifts of £100 on Jocelyn Persse, Hugh Walpole, and Lucy Clifford. All the servants were provided for. James left gifts to various nephews and nieces, children of his younger brother, but a codicil withdrew the gift from his nephew Edward Holton James, Robertson's son, because the anti-royalist pamphlet he had written a few years before had embarrassed his uncle.

The obituaries—in newspapers filled with the war—were of great length. The homage was profound. One newspaper inquiring into the status of James's works found that very few of the Master's novels were in print, and the late ones were expensively available in the New York Edition. James would indeed sink from sight; swallowed up by the war, his would be among the forgotten reputations of the 1920's, although an occasional subject of controversy, mainly about his expatriation. It would take time for the world to rediscover him. When the Second World War came he was, however, remembered and read, and his centenary awoke new interest in a new generation. The author of *The Portrait of a Lady* and *The Wings of the Dove*, of *The Ambassadors* and *The Golden Bowl* had sensed in his own life that somehow he would be, as he had spoken of Pater, a Figure. Unlike Pater's, his work itself gained an audience, slowly at first, until in the mid-twentieth century his books were in print in great numbers, as many as five editions in paperback of *The Ambassadors* alone. His letters were saved in quantities that would have astonished him and became expensive autographs. He became a word, an image, a symbol long after his death. He was constantly quoted—certain of his phrases reverberating beyond the grave into modernity. The secret of his enduring fame was a simple one: he had dealt exclusively with the myth of civilization; he had written about men and women in their struggle to control their emotions and passions within the forms and manners of society. He understood human motive and behaviour and was the first of the modern psychological novelists. He had carried his art into a high complexity and he had endured because he had fashioned a style. Long ago he had said that a style is a writer's passport to posterity. He had issued such a passport to himself. He had had great ambitions; he had sought power in craft and had found it; he had fashioned a trans-Atlantic myth; he had learned that artists take the chaos of life and shape it into forms that endure. "The older civilisation gave him the wonderful things he wanted: but the wonder was his own," said G. K. Chesterton in one of the most discerning and eloquent of the tributes. "His whole world is made out of sympathy; out of a whole network of sympathy." To his nephews and nieces his message had been that they be kind, and *kind*, and *kind*! Younger men would find him a sign-post, a guide, a vast encompassing intelligence. Ezra Pound would speak of him as a Baedeker to a Continent. Unlike Browning, his disciples formed no "James Societies." They simply read him and wrote about him. His centenary in 1943 found him claimed by the two great literatures of the English-speaking peoples. His influence was pervasive—the entire "modern movement" drew upon his explorations of subjective worlds, from Joyce to Virginia Woolf. He had given his message, "tell them to follow, to be faithful, to take me seriously." He would be taken seriously. But the memory of his wit also re-mained, and of his courage. He had indeed planned a career and carried it out as a general plans his campaigns and wins his vic-tories. His elegy of Jeffrey Aspern might have been written of himself

... at a period when our native land was nude and crude and provincial, when the famous "atmosphere" it is supposed to lack was not even missed, when literature was lonely there and art and form almost impossible, he had found means to live and write like one of the first; to be free and general and not at all afraid; to feel, understand and express everything.

Long before he had urged young novelists to "be generous and delicate and pursue the prize." He had been generous; he had been delicate; and the prize for him had been always the treasure of his craft. He felt powerful because he knew that his imagination could transfigure life; and he said that the greatest freedom of man was his "independence of thought," which enabled the artist to enjoy "the aggression of infinite modes of being."

He had written some years before his death an essay, "Is There a Life after Death?" If one meant physical life, he believed there was none. Death was absolute. What lived beyond life was what the creative consciousness had found and made: and only if enshrined in enduring form. Like Proust he saw that art alone retains and holds the life—the consciousness—of man long after the finders and the makers are gone. The true immortality was the immortal picture or statue, the immortal phrase whether of music or of words. This was his deepest faith. He sought beauty instead of ugliness, kindness instead of cruelty, peace instead of violence; he preferred the poetry of prose, the magic of style, the things shaped within the past given sacredness by their survival. In one of the last sentences of his essay on life after death he wrote: "I reach beyond the laboratory brain."

This was his final word to the new age.

New York 1950
Honolulu 1971

NOTES AND ACKNOWLEDGMENTS

I WISH to express my thanks to Alexander R. James, grandson of William mes, for generously maintaining my priorities in certain materials essential to the writing of the present volume. I am indebted to the late John James, who before his untimely death in 1969 maintained an interest in this work shown by his father William and his uncle Henry, sons of William James who originally held the rights in the James papers. I also had materials in this volume from the late Frederika James, widow of Alex James; and from Catherine P. Short, daughter of Peggy James who provided me with documents relating not only to her mother but also to her father the late Bruce Porter of San Francisco.

As before, I am indebted to the President and Fellows of Harvard College for continued access to the James papers; to Dr William H. Bond, director of the Houghton Library, who, with his predecessor, William A. Jackson, always showed my work the greatest consideration; and once again I thank Carolyn Jakeman, librarian of the Houghton Library, for unfailing kindness and interest.

Outside the James family, my greatest debt is to C. Waller Barrett, whose major collection of manuscripts and books contains, in particular, the letters of Henry James to Hendrik Andersen. Mr Barrett allowed me access to much of this material long before his gift of it to the Alderman Library of the University of Virginia. I am indebted to the Collections of the Humanities Research Center, The University of Texas at Austin for reserving for my use the important collection of James letters to Sir Hugh Walpole which I had seen when they were in the hands of Sir Rupert Hart-Davis, Walpole's executor. In a similar way I am indebted to the late Dr John D. Gordan of the New York Public Library, curator of the Berg collection, and his successor, Mrs Lola Sladitz, for assistance in the use of invaluable materials ranging from Lady Gregory's papers to those of Sir Edward Marsh, and certain Bloomsbury documents as well as the important diary of Sir Sydney Waterlow. When I quote from these I do so with permission of the Henry W. and Albert A. Berg Collection of the New York Public Library, Astor, Lenox, and Tilden Foundation. At Yale University, Dr Herman W. Liebert, librarian of the Bienecke Library, and Donald Gallup, curator of the American Collection, gave me access in 1969 to the Edith Wharton materials which had been locked away by her orders until the end of 1968. I also appreciated the courtesy of R. W. B. Lewis, Mrs Wharton's biographer, in allowing me access to these letters. I was fortunate in having the help and advice of

Frederica Rhinelander Landon and Frederick Rhinelander King, cousins of Mrs. Wharton and of Louis Auchincloss, whose writings and collection of Edith Wharton materials — and whose intimate knowledge of her world — have put Wharton scholars profoundly in his debt. I wish to thank him for the admirable portrait of Mrs Wharton.

I want in particular to thank again Mr George Stevens of J. B. Lippincott Company in America and Sir Rupert Hart-Davis in England for their recognition, from the beginning, of the nature and scope of this work. I have drawn on my own memories of talks long ago with Mrs Wharton, W. Morton Fullerton, Bernard Shaw, Harley Granville Barker, the Forbes-Robertsons, and others, and on correspondence with Jocelyn Persse and Hugh Walpole. Dr John Waterlow and Professor Charlotte Waterlow allowed me the use of their father's diary; Rev. H. P. Kingdon and Miss C. F. Kingdon, showed me Miss Weld's diary; and Miss Bosanquet's executor, Professor Teresa J. Dillon, the diaries of Miss Bosanquet. My friendship with Theodora Bosanquet was of long standing. I discussed James and the Qu'Acre circle with Percy Lubbock shortly before his death, and I am grateful to John Ormond of the National Portrait Gallery for materials relating to his grand-uncle John Singer Sargent. Others who communicated letters or helped in various ways are Dr Nathan G. Hale Jr, Heywood Hill, James F. Beard, Lady Mander, Richard L. Purdy, James Osborn, Anna Lee Mitchell, Michael Millgate, Stanley Weintraub, David Robertson, John S. Van E. Kohn, Michael Papantonio, Raleigh Parkin, Sybille Pantazzi, Rosamond Gilder, Wallace Fair, Dr Gregg M. Sinclair, and Marjorie Sinclair. As with earlier volumes, Simon Nowell-Smith in England generously followed clues for me when I could not cross the Atlantic myself. He originally made the letters of James to H. G. Wells available to Dr Gordon N. Ray and myself for our editing. The Wells letters are now in the Bodleian Library.

I continue to be in debt to my old friend Donald Brien, to Mrs John Hall Wheelock, and to Dr Roberta R. Edel. And I wish to recall again the names of three admirable Jamesians whose help in this volume extended beyond their death—Edna Kenton, Allan Wade, and LeRoy Phillips. I had the active help of Alvin Langdon Coburn in reconstructing his photographic adventures on behalf of the New York Edition. Howard C. Rice Jr, curator of manuscripts, aided my research at Princeton where the Scribner archive now reposes. I was helped by Leonard Woolf and Douglas Goldring; F. B. Adams and Herbert Cahoon of the Morgan Library; Professor James Thorpe of the Henry E. Huntington Library; Alan S. Bell of the National Library of Scotland; Mrs J. Pingree, archivist of Imperial College, London; R. A. Storey of the United Kingdom National Register of Archives; Charles W. Mann of the Pattee Library, Pennsylvania State College. My debt to others are recorded in the notes.

I have used as before abbreviations in these notes for the James family (AHJ for Mrs William James) and to avoid confusion refer to HJ's nephews as Harry and Billy. Since my material is largely unpublished I can only source it in a general way, but I make known where it is to be found.

BOOK ONE: *Notes on Novelists*

Vie de Province: Memoir writers have left many pictures of Henry James in Rye. The account here given is drawn from the reminiscences of James's relatives; from Gosse, Ford Madox Ford, A. C. Benson, A. C. Bradley; the diaries of James's typists and of Sir Sydney Waterlow; also Edith Wharton; Percy Lubbock; David Garnett; Gaillard Lapsley; Virginia Woolf, and others. Reubell, 11 Oct. 1900, 22 Dec. 1903; Gosse, 22 Sept., 18 Nov. 1900; Miss Mackenzie, 15 June, 17 Oct. 1901, 9 Mar. 1902; W. M. Fullerton, 27 Jan., 21, 26 Sept. 1900, 12 Mar. 1901; Hay, 3 April 1900; Godkin, 1 April 1900; Wells, 20 Jan. 1902; Sturges, 10 July 1900; AHJ, 31 Jan. 1899; Mrs Clifford, 24 Jan., 25 May 1900; C. E. Norton, 24 Nov. 1899; Lady Wolseley, 10 June 1900.

A Letter to Rhoda: Letters to Rhoda Broughton are in the Public Records Office in Chester, England. I wish to thank Mrs Tamie Cole for her help. Michael Sadleir on Miss Broughton, *Things Past* (1944). Francis Boott, 10 Feb. 1897; Norton, 26 Dec. 1898; Sturgis, 1 April 1915. Percy Lubbock, *Mary Cholmondeley: A Sketch from Memory* (1928).

An Innocent Abroad: WDH, 19 Aug. 1879; WJ, 22 May 1900; Mark Twain to WDH, 21 July 1885, 23 Oct. 1898, 31 Jan., 22 May 1900, 19 April 1904. *Mark Twain–Howells Letters:* The Correspondence of Samuel L. Clemens and William Dean Howells, 1872–1910 (eds Smith and Gibson 1960); Justin Kaplan, *Mr Clemens and Mark Twain* (1966); Van Wyck Brooks, *The Ordeal of Mark Twain* (1920).

A Natural Peculiarity: I listened to Ford Madox Hueffer's reminiscences of Henry James at his flat in Paris in 1930. See his *Henry James:* A Critical Study (1913); *Return to Yesterday* (1932); *It Was the Nightingale* (1934); and *Portraits from Life* (1938) published in England as *Mightier Than the Sword*. HJ's fourteen letters to Hueffer (Ford) and to his wife are in the Houghton Library. Arthur Mizener kindly shared these with me while working on his life of Ford. HJ's story "The Liar" first appeared in the *Century* May–June 1888 and was reprinted in *A London Life* (1889); Hueffer, 23 May 1900. Archibald Marshall, *Out and About* (1934). I corresponded with Douglas Goldring about Hueffer and Violet Hunt. Richard Garnett arranged for my use of the Olive Garnett diaries.

A Master Mariner: I am grateful to Frederick R. Karl of City University of New York, editor of the Conrad letters, for help with this chapter. Gosse, 20 June 1902; Hueffer, 8 Jan. 1904; Mrs Hueffer, 12 Oct. 1909; Mrs Wharton, 27 Feb. 1914. The inscribed copy of *The Nigger of the Narcissus* is in Houghton; the inscribed *Spoils of Poynton* is in Berg. William (Billy) James described to me Conrad's and Hueffer's visits to Lamb House; Bernard Meyer, *Joseph Conrad, A Psychoanalytic Biography* (1967); Jocelyn Baines,

Joseph Conrad (1960); G. Jean-Aubry, Joseph Conrad, *Life and Letters* (1927); Edward Garnett (ed.), *Letters from Joseph Conrad* 1895–1924 (1928); Joseph Conrad, *Lettres françaises* (1929).

A Ghostly Rental: HJ's letters to Cora Crane are in the Columbia University Library. I have found no extant HJ letters to Crane. See also the biographies of Crane by Thomas Beer (1923), John Berryman (1951) and R. W. Stallman (1968), and Lilian Gilkes, *Cora Crane* (1960). Cmdr Melvin E. Schoberlin supplied some of the data. The account of the Christmas play is based on John Gordan's "The Ghost at Brede Place," Bulletin of the New York Public Library (Dec. 1952). C. Lewis Hind, *Authors and I* (1921); H. G. Wells, *Experiment in Autobiography* (1934); Wells, "Stephen Crane from an English Standpoint," *North American Review* (Aug. 1900); Anita Leslie, *Mr Frewen of England* (1966). Stephen Crane: *Letters*, ed. Stallman and Gilkes (1960). HJ letters to Pinker are in Beinecke Library, Yale.

The Ambassadors: The origin of this novel is described in *The Treacherous Years* in the chapter "The Figure in the Carpet." The Emmet portrait: Sturges, 10 July 1900; Bay Emmet, 20 Oct. 1901, 11 Oct. 1903; Pinker, 19 April, 9 May, 30 June, 10 July, 13 Sept. 1901; Duchess of Sutherland, 23 Dec. 1903; Sturgis, 16 Dec. 1903; Mrs Green, 10 Jan. 1904. The history of the misplaced chapter is described in Edel and Laurence *Bibliography of Henry James* and in Edel "The Text of *The Ambassadors*" Harvard Library Bulletin XIV:3 453–460 (Autumn 1960).

BOOK TWO: *The Beast in the Jungle*

A Poor Ancient Lady: HJ letters to Peggy, are in Houghton. WJ, 26 April 1900, 24 Jan. 1901; Mrs Benedict, 24 Dec. 1900; Jessie Allen, 25 Dec. 1900; Gosse, 22 Jan. 1901; AHJ, 30 Jan. 1901; Bourget, 30 March 1901; Miss Robins, 9 Feb. 1901; Fullerton, 12 Mar. 1901; Contessa Rucellai, 15 Feb., 27 Feb. 1901; Sutherland, 11 June 1901; Peggy James, 14 Aug. 1902; Bay Emmet, 11 Oct. 1903; Mrs Curtis, 3 Feb. 1901.

Miss Weld: This chapter is based on the Weld diaries and related papers kindly furnished by Miss Weld's son Rev. H. P. Kingdon and her daughter Miss C. F. Kingdon. WJ, 17 Nov., 9 Dec. 1900; AHJ, 27 May 1901; Duchess of Sutherland, 11 June 1901; Peggy James, 17 Aug. 1902; Bay Emmet, 11 Oct. 1903; Benedicts, 22 Jan. 1901; Holmes, 20 Feb. 1901.

A Family Summer: Rostand was completed 26 Aug. 1901; Flaubert, 17 Nov. 1901; Maurice Maeterlinck described his meetings with HJ to me some years before his death. Fullerton, 9 Aug. 1901; Curtis, 7, 13 Sept. 1901; E. L. Childe, 25 Sept. 1901; Gosse, 10 Oct. 1901; Mrs Clifford, 13 July 1901. HJ's memories of Gissing are in Waterlow; Robins, 22 April. 1901; Allen, 26 Sept. 1901.

A Domestic Upheaval: WJ, 19, 25 Sept. 1901; Peggy James, 20 Oct. 1901. Ford Madox Ford's account of Smith is in *Return to Yesterday* (1932).

Aunt Lucy: I have never seen the originals of James's letters to Mrs W. K.

Clifford, but copies of more than fifty were made for Percy Lubbock and these are in Houghton. Mrs Clifford, 24 Jan., 25 May 1900, 6 Oct. 1901. She is described in Marie Belloc Lowndes, *The Merry Wives of Westminster* (1946); Mackenzie, 17 Oct. 1901.

The Wings of the Dove: Godkin letters (Harvard) and Pinker letters (Yale); HJ's illness in letters to WJ and AHJ; Graham Balfour letters in National Library of Scotland; HJ's visits to Palazzo Barbaro are recounted in *The Middle Years.* See also Preface to New York Edition XX. The correspondence with Dr Baldwin is in the Morgan Library; WDH, 25 Jan. 1902; Hueffer, 9 Sept. 1902; Clifford, 27 Aug. 1902; Mrs Jones, 23 Oct. 1902.

Billy: Much of the material in this chapter was derived from talks with William James, second son of the philosopher, and his wife Alice Runnells. Most of HJ's letters to them were shown to me in transcript and I later saw the originals. I lived for one summer in their house in Cambridge and was able to consult many volumes from HJ's library which Billy brought over from Lamb House after his uncle's death; also various manuscripts, papers, and photographs which they had accumulated. Harry James, 13 Oct. 1902; Billy, 2, 11 Nov. 1902, 10 April, 1 Sept. 1903; Bay Emmet, 11 Oct. 1903.

In the Workshop: This chapter is composed from various allusions to his work made by James to assorted correspondents. The number of desks in Lamb House is mentioned to W. E. Norris. James's daily routine and life "below stairs" in Lamb House was minutely described to me by Burgess Noakes, James's valet. HJ discussed problems of dictation with Miss Bosanquet, Mrs Cadwalader Jones, and Morton Fullerton. Theodora Bosanquet, *Henry James at Work* (1924).

The Impenetrable Sphinx: "The Beast in the Jungle" was published for the first time in *The Better Sort* (1903). See my chapter on Miss Woolson in *The Middle Years* (1962). The quotations in that chapter from this tale were from the first edition; quotations used here are from the revised edition.

The Real Right Thing: HJ, 2 Jan. 1910, to Mrs Fields (Huntingdon) contains the account of the burning of the papers. HJ to Graham Balfour, National Library of Scotland. George Sand essays are in *Notes on Novelists* (1914). Manton Marble letters, Houghton; Manton Marble papers, Library of Congress. Preface to *The Tempest*, Vol. 16 of "The Renaissance Edition" of Shakespeare Sir Sydney Lee (ed) 1907.

BOOK THREE: *The Better Sort*

Goody Two Shoes: Miss Allen, 6, 25 Dec. 1900, 12, 14, 15 Dec. 1902, 20 June, 25 Aug., 23 Nov. 1903, 1 July 1904. More than two hundred HJ letters to Miss Allen are in Houghton. Lady Meyrick, Miss B. M. Allen, and David McKibbin of the Boston Athenaeum kindly gave me details about her life. Mr McKibbin also supplied many details concerning the Palazzo Barbaro gathered in his lifelong study of John Singer Sargent and the history of those who sat for him.

A Queer Job: HJ's letters to Waldo and Maud Story, University of Texas library; WDH, 25 Jan. 1902; Mrs Wister, 21 Dec. 1902; Henry Adams to HJ, 18 Nov. 1903; HJ to Adams, 19 Nov. 1903. Houghton Mifflin Co., 29 Dec. 1902, 25 Jan. 1903. I wish in particular to thank the late H. M. Landon and Frederica R. Landon for making available to me material relating to James, Browning, and the Storys. *Story and his Friends*, Blackwood, Edinburgh, two volumes, and Houghton Mifflin Co., Boston, October 1903. HJ to Blackwood in National Library of Scotland.

The Master at Sixty: Many anecdotes and descriptions of HJ may be found in Simon Nowell-Smith, *The Legend of the Master* (1947). Grace Norton, 18, 20 Dec. 1902; Holmes, 10 Dec. 1902, 12 Aug. 1903. James's opinions of Gosse are in his correspondence with W. E. Norris in the Beinecke Library, Yale.

The Reverberator: I first had the Grigsby story from Logan Pearsall Smith in 1930. She is mentioned only twice in HJ's letters, to Jessie Allen, 5 May 1903, and WJ, 6 May 1904. The article from the New York *Evening Journal*, 4 Jan. 1906, was kindly given me by Edna Kenton. The late Lloyd Morris told me he dined once at the home of Miss Grigsby in New York and was shown some HJ letters but was not allowed to read them. Herbert Mitgang of the New York *Times* kindly facilitated my examination of the newspaper's file on Miss Grigsby.

An Exquisite Relation: Although I corresponded briefly with Jocelyn Persse in the 1930's, and he sent me at that time his letters from HJ dealwith their theatregoing, I could find out very little about him. Sir Shane Leslie published his reminiscences of Persse in *Horizon* "A Note on Henry James" VII:42 (June 1943) but did not identify him; however, he furnished me with some details and generously copied out the James letters for me in England. Later I saw the originals in their dilapidated condition at Harvard. Hugh Walpole speaks of him briefly in "Henry James: A Reminiscence" *Horizon* I:2 (Feb. 1940) and occasionally in his diaries. The details of the Colvin–Sitwell wedding are in E. V. Lucas, *The Colvins and Their Friends* (1928). Most of the Colvin letters are in the Beinecke library at Yale. Mrs Colvin, 14 July 1903; Persse, 16, 21 July, 15 Sept. 26, 27 Oct. 1903, 3, 21 March, 4 July, 16 Aug., 6 Sept. 1904, 24 Aug., 11 Sept. 1905, 22 Jan., 9 Dec. 1907. "This exquisite relation," 22 Oct. 1908.

Lessons of the Master: For a detailed account of the writing of *Belchamber*, see Elmer Borklund, "Howard Sturgis, Henry James and *Belchamber*," *Modern Philology* LVIII:4 255–69 (May 1961). Sturgis, 19 May 1899, 2, 25 Feb. 1900, 30 Sept., 8, 18, 23 Nov., 2, 7, Dec. 1903. Sturgis is described in Lubbock, *Mary Cholmondeley* (1928), and George Santayana, *The Middle Span* (1945).

An Agreeable Woman: The chapters on Edith Wharton in this book are based in great part on one hundred and seventy-seven letters from HJ in the Beinecke Library where Edith Wharton's papers were locked away until 1968. I have also drawn on my talks with Mrs Wharton in 1931 and 1936; on HJ's letters to Mrs Wharton's friends; on the Edith Wharton letters in the Louis Auchincloss collection. Frederick R. King showed me Mrs Wharton's letters to Minnie Jones, now at Yale. HJ's letters to Minnie Jones are in Houghton. I long ago had access to a portion of HJ's letters to Mrs Wharton in the Lubbock typescripts at Houghton; this batch was selected by Mrs Wharton herself and constituted less than a third of the correspondence. The HJ and Edith Wharton letters to Scribner are now in the Princeton University Library; I saw them in the offices of the firm thanks to the late Charles Scribner Jr. Bourget, 23 Nov. 1899; Minnie Jones, 26 Oct. 1900, 31 Dec. 1903; WDH, 25 Jan. 1902, 28 May 1904; Reubell, 22 Dec. 1903; Margaret La Farge, 9 Jan., 10 June 1904; Persse, Mar. 1904; Walter Berry, 13 Nov., 20 Nov. 1904. HJ's letters to the La Farges are in the New York Historical Association.

The Golden Bowl: Mrs Bellingham, 31 Dec. 1902. Notebooks, 22 May 1892. Miss Weld's diaries. *The Golden Bowl* was begun with the tentative title "Charlotte." HJ began to write it 25 May 1903 and by September had written two-thirds of it. By 25 Oct. 1903 he estimated he had written 110,000 words. He began extensive revision and rewriting in November. On 8 Jan. 1904 he wrote WDH he was finishing the novel but actually did not complete it until May 1904. The last parts were sent to Pinker, 20 May, 21 July 1904.

A Passion of Nostalgia: Grace Norton, 22 Jan. 1902, 27 July 1903; WJ and AHJ, 21 Dec. 1902, 10 April, 24 May, 6 July 1903, 19 Jan., 5 July 1904; Louisa Loring, 22 Sept. 1903; Gaillard Lapsley, 15 Sept. 1902; Benedicts, 21 Nov. 1903, 3 Feb. 1904; H. G. Wells, 27 Nov. 1903; WDH, 8 Jan., 5 Aug. 1904; WDH to Elizabeth Jordan, 1 Jan. 1904; Pennell, 23 June 1904; Jessie Allen, 29 June, 1 July 1904; Peggy James, 21 July 1904. Letters to Elizabeth Jordan are in the manuscript division, New York Public Library.

BOOK FOUR: *The American Scene*

The Jersey Shore: This and the ensuing chapters are drawn from HJ's letters to his friends abroad, press reports of the time and published writings, notably *The American Scene*. For details of HJ's itinerary see my edition of this book (1968) Arrival: N.Y. *Sun*, 31 Aug. 1904. Letters to Col. Harvey, Library of Congress. Willis F. Johnson, *George Harvey* (1929); Eugene Exman, *The House of Harper* (1967).

A New England Autumn: I visited the summer house of William James at Chocorua a number of times as guest of the Billy Jameses. Letters to Horace Fletcher are in Houghton. New York *Herald* 2 Oct. 1904. Letters to Katherine Wormeley, Yale. Letters to Bay Emmet, Houghton. Visits to Jackson N.H., Concord and Salem, *The American Scene*.

The Lady of Lenox: Jessie Allen, 22 Oct. 1904. Wharton, *A Backward Glance* (1934) contains substantial passages of recollection of HJ; while Mrs Wharton is not mentioned by name, at least one of the American motoring episodes is in *The American Scene.* HJ *Letters to Walter Berry*, the Black Sun Press, Paris (Harry and Caresse Crosby) 1928. Minnie Bourget to EW, 5 Nov. 1904 (Yale).

The Medusa Face: The American Scene, Chap. 7; *Notebooks* (1937) 29 Mar. 1905, 317–24.

City of Conversation: The American Scene, Chaps. 9, 11; Margaret Chanler, *Autumn in the Valley* (1936); Raleigh Parkin of Montreal, made available the relevant letters concerning his father's visit to Philadelphia now in the Public Archives of Canada at Ottawa.

Castle of Enchantment: Letters to Gosse, Mrs Wister, the William Jameses and Mrs Wharton, 3–5 February 1905. *The American Scene*, 396.

The Blighted Invalid: The American Scene, Chaps. 12–14.

A Western Journey: Howells and James: A Double Billing, ed. Edel and Powers, New York Public Library (1958) contains HJ's letters to Elizabeth Jordan; also E. Jordan, *Three Rousing Cheers* (1938); Marie P. Harris, "Henry James, Lecturer," *American Literature*, XXIII No. 3 (Nov. 1951); Charles E. Burgess, "Henry James's 'Big' Impression," Missouri Historical Society, Bulletin 17 Oct. 1970, documents the session at the University Club; Robert Herrick, "A Visit to Henry James," *Yale Review*, July 1923, 724–41; Hamlin Garland's diaries and notes are in the Henry E. Huntington Library, San Marino, California; "The Lesson of Balzac," *Atlantic Monthly*, August 1905; a fuller text is in *The Question of Our Speech*, *The Lesson of Balzac*, two lectures (1905). I had from Edna Kenton and Van Wyck Brooks their memories of HJ as lecturer. Edward Holton James's account of his uncle's visit to Seattle is in a privately printed pamphlet written for his children.

The Terrible Town: The American Scene, Chaps. 2–5; Witter Bynner, "A Word or Two With Henry James," The *Critic*, XLVI, Feb. 1905.

The Brothers: I am indebted to the National Institute of Arts and Letters, and in especial, Miss Felicia Geffen, assistant secretary-treasurer of the American Academy of Arts and Letters, for access to the WJ letter to the Academy; Robert Underwood Johnson, *Remembered Yesterdays* (1923). WJ's letters on HJ's style, in *Letters of WJ* (1920); WJ to AHJ, 31 March 1905. The inscribed *American Scene* is in the Barrett Collection. Robert Cortes Holliday, *Walking Stick Papers* (1918). Elizabeth Robins described the adjective-hunt game to me.

BOOK FIVE: *An Elaborate Edifice*

The Supreme Relation: The Garland visit occurred 21–22 June 1906. Pinker, 4 Aug. 1906; Lady Ottoline Morrell, *Diaries* (ed. Gathorne Hardy) (1963); Harper's *Bazar*, "The Speech of American Women," Nov. 1906 to

Feb. 1907; "The Manners of American Women" April–July 1907. Mrs Wharton, 4 Dec. 1912; Wells to HJ, 20 Mar. 1907.

The Better Chance: The primary material for this chapter is drawn from the Scribner archive. HJ's memorandum, 30 July 1905; to Scribner, 8 March, 9 May, 17 Aug. 1906, 26 Feb., 10 Mar., 14 Dec. 1908; Bourget, 22 Nov. 1899; Brander Matthews, 16 Nov. 1903; WDH, 1 Nov. 1906, 2 Aug., 17 Aug. 1908; Mrs Wharton, 7 Mar. 1908, 20 Dec. 1911; Grace Norton, 5 Mar. 1907; Robert Herrick, 7 Aug. 1905; Harry James, 1 April 1908; Pinker, 11 May, 6 June, 29 Sept. 1905, 8 Jan., 8 March, 9 May, 8, 10 June 1906, 31 Dec. 1907, 20, 23 Oct. 1908, 19 April, 19 May 1909; Bosanquet, 21 Feb., 28 Oct. 1908; Coburn, 2, 6 Oct., 7, 9 Dec. 1906. See also Leon Edel, "The Architecture of the New York Edition," *New England Quarterly*, XXIV (June 1951), 169–78.

I am indebted to the late Alvin Langdon Coburn for many details of his quest for the New York Edition frontispieces and for access to his papers. These and his negatives are now in the George Eastman House in Rochester, N.Y. For the collation of different editions of *The Portrait of a Lady* I am indebted to the unpublished dissertation of Anthony J. Mazzella (Columbia 1970). See also Simon Nowell-Smith, "Texts of *The Portrait of a Lady* 1881–1882: The Bibliographical Evidence," P.B.S.A., 63 (1969), 304–10.

Mr Francis J. B. Watson, director of the Wallace Collection, showed me the furniture James had photographed for *The Spoils of Poynton.*

The House of Mirth: E. L. Childe, 19 Feb. 1907 (courtesy, Countess de Sartiges); Sturgis, 20 Mar., 13 April, 14 May 1907, 27 April 1908; WJ, 30 April, 11 Aug. 1907; Jessie Allen, 28 Mar. 1907; Protheros, 13 April 1907; T. S. Perry, 17 April 1907; Persse, 4 May 1907; Margaret Chanler, *Autumn in the Valley* (1936); Edith Wharton, *A Motor Flight Through France* (1908); HJ's letters to the Benedicts are in the appendix of Jörg Hasler, *Switzerland in the Life and Work of Henry James* (1966); excerpts from this correspondence appeared earlier in the privately printed *The Benedicts Abroad.* Jacques Émile Blanche, *Mes Modèles* (1929); Bay Emmet, 26 Nov. 1908.

The Velvet Glove: I talked with Mrs Wharton in 1931 about this story. She told me substantially what she later wrote in *A Backward Glance,* and made the remark that she would never have asked James for a preface. I am indebted to Edna Kenton's notes for collation of the quotations from *The Fruit of the Tree.* As I was completing this book I received from Adeline Tintner, long a student of James's relation to the plastic arts, a fascinating essay in which she had deduced the connection by a study of the story's pastoral imagery and the correspondence in Millicent Bell, *Edith Wharton and Henry James* (1965). "The International Press Service" of New York headed by a man named Markeley asked Pinker for the article on Mrs Wharton. Wharton, 4 Oct., 24 Nov. 1907; Grace Norton, 5 Mar. 1907.

Miss Bosanquet: I knew Miss Bosanquet for thirty years and talked with her many times about her role in the last years of HJ's life. Professor

Teresa J. Dillon generously made Miss Bosanquet's diaries available to me. The diaries are now in Houghton.

Theatricals: Second Series: Sources for this chapter can be found in *The Complete Plays of Henry James* (1949). Mrs Clifford, 20 Oct. 1907, 21 Mar. 1908; Miss Broughton, 8 Nov. 1907; Waterlow, 8 Jan. 1908; Persse, 22 Feb., 6 Mar. 1908; Mrs Wharton, 23 Mar. 1908; Jessie Allen, 12 Aug. 1908. The HJ–Bernard Shaw letters are in *Complete Plays*. Granville-Barker, 10 Jan., 22 Jan., 7 Feb. 1908. I have never seen the originals of HJ's letters to Granville-Barker but used typed copies furnished me by Allan Wade. I discussed *The High Bid* with Sir Johnston Forbes-Robertson and Gertrude Elliott in London in 1937. Elizabeth Robins provided the original version of this play, now at the University of Texas. Granville-Barker, in Paris in 1931, told me of casting *The Outcry* and provided a memorandum on his work with James. Bernard Shaw and Allan Wade gave me details of the Frohman repertory.

The Tone of Time: Norris, 23 Dec. 1907; Mrs Clifford, 7 April 1908; HJ's tribute to Harland, *Fortnightly Review*, April 1898; Broughton, 21 Dec. 1906; Margaret Brooke, Ranee of Sarawak, 27 Dec. 1906; Curtis, 3 Jan. 1908; WJ, 2 Nov. 1908. Leonard Woolf and David Garnett gave me their reminiscences of Waterlow; Dr John Waterlow and Professor Charlotte Waterlow allowed me to use their father's diary on which I based my article in *The Times Literary Supplement* "Henry James and Sir Sydney Waterlow," 8 Aug. 1968. The diary is in the Henry W. and Albert A. Berg Collection of the New York Public Library, Astor, Lenox, and Tilden Foundation. I corresponded with Mary Anderson; her son J. M. de Navarro and his wife Elizabeth Hoare gave me access to this correspondence. Navarro, 1 Nov. 1905. Beaunier, *The Times*, 11 Mar. 1909. Lord David Cecil gave me access to his James material relating to Beerbohm.

The Younger Generation: Leonard Woolf furnished Bloomsbury and Jamesian details and the Desmond McCarthy letter to Virginia Woolf. See also Leonard Woolf, *Sowing* (1960) and *Beginning Again* (1964). I had also information from David and Angelica Garnett. In 1961 Clive Bell talked to me about HJ's strange antipathy. Quentin Bell, biographer of Virginia Woolf, made available certain relevant material. See *Letters of Virginia Woolf and Lytton Strachey* (1956). E. M. Forster copied for me the passage from his diary describing tea at Lamb House; Michael Holroyd, *Lytton Strachey* (1967); Lucy Clifford, 6 Nov. 1907, 3 Dec. 1908; Lady Ritchie, 21 Dec. 1906; Virginia Stephen's tea with HJ, 27 Aug. 1907; Sara Norton, 11 Sept. 1907. For the Cambridge week-end, see Geoffrey Keynes, *Henry James in Cambridge* (1967). Lapsley, 17 June 1909.

Hugh: Sir Rupert Hart-Davis, Hugh Walpole's biographer and executor, allowed me to read Walpole's diaries and the HJ letters. I also saw the manuscript of *The Killer and the Slain* in his possession. Walpole, 13, 19 Dec. 1908, 8 Jan., 28 Mar., 20, 27 April, 24 July 23, 26 Oct., 10, 21 Nov. 1909,

12 April, 13 May 1910, 15 April, 13 Oct. 1911, 18 April, 27 Sept. 1912, 5 Mar., 21 Aug., 10 Nov. 1913. Stephen Spender gave me recollections of his talk with Hugh Walpole. Allusions to Gray and Raffalovitch, 2, 6, 29 Jan. 1914; Raffalovitch, 5 Feb. 1914. Hugh Walpole, *The Apple Trees* (1932).

A Passion on Olympus: Mrs Wharton's diary, Wayne Andrews (ed), *The Best Short Stories of Edith Wharton*, 1958. The late Martha Hyde, Caresse Crosby, and Edith Wharton described Walter Berry to me. See also Percy Lubbock, *Portrait of Edith Wharton* (1947), and Olivia Coolidge, *Edith Wharton* (1964). Louis Galantière shared with me his memories of a visit to Marcel Proust in the company of Walter Berry. I met W. Morton Fullerton in 1930, corresponded with him and saw him again in his old age, after the liberation of Paris in 1944. Certain of HJ's letters to him are in Houghton; others are in the Princeton University Library; still others in the Barrett Collection. Fullerton, 17 Dec. 1905, 4 Jan. 1906, 11 Sept., 14, 19, 26 Nov. 1907, 11, 31 Jan., 14, 19 April, 9, 16 May, 28 July, 3, 15, 20, 23 Aug., 8, 29 Oct., 24 Nov., 13, 24, 26, 30 Dec. 1909; Edith Wharton, 7, 11 Mar., 13 Oct. 1908, 14, 24 April, 10 May, 26 July, 9, 19, 21, Nov., 16, 17 Dec. 1909. Fullerton figures in the following HJ letters to Mrs Wharton: 30 Aug., 11 Sept., 14, 19 Nov. 1907, 7, 11 Mar., 16 April 1908, 11, 31 Jan., 19 April, 9 May, 3, 15, 20, 23 Aug., 8, 29 Oct. 1909, 25 April, 10 June, 19 Nov. 1910, 13 Mar. 1912, 10, 16, Sept. 1913, 23 Mar., 13 Aug. 1915; HJ's letter to Macmillan, 26 July 1909. HJ's date-books from 1908 to 1915 are in Houghton, and contain innumerable diary notes not used by Matthiessen and Murdock in the *Notebooks*.

Woman-About-Town: HJ to Violet Hunt in Barrett. Violet Hunt, *The Flurried Years* (1926). HJ's letters to Mrs Hueffer, Houghton. David Garnett, *The Golden Echo* (1954). Charles W. Mann, curator of the rare book room in the Pattee Library at Pennsylvania State College gave me access to some of Miss Hunt's diaries. Archibald Marshall, *Out and About* (1933). See also Arthur Mizener, *The Saddest Story:* A Biography of *Ford Madox Ford* (1971).

BOOK SIX: *The Finer Grain*

The Bench of Desolation: Pinker, 20, 23 Oct. 1908, 4 Oct. 1909; WDH, 31 Dec. 1908; Wharton, 2 Feb. 1910, 20 Dec. 1911; WJ, 3, 26 Feb. 1909. Sir James Mackenzie's book *Angina Pectoris* (1923) contains a full account of HJ's visit to him without naming the novelist. Walpole, 10 Jan. 1910; Pinker, 16 Jan. 1910; Bosanquet to Harry James, 23 Jan. 1910; Harry to WJ, 9 Mar. 1910; Wharton, 25 Jan., 2 Feb., 10, 21 June 1910; WJ, 15 Mar., 4 April 1910; Benson, 9 May 1910; AHJ's diary, 8 May, 9, 29 June 1910; Gosse, 10 Sept. 1910; Persse, 28 April 1910; WJ to Osler, 3 May 1910.

Notes of a Brother: Somerset Maugham's preface to *Great Short Stories* (1943) contains his recollections of the Jameses. B. L. Reid, *The Man from New York* (1968), the Quinn dinner, 17 Oct. 1910. I had the anecdote of

HJ's visit to the Rockefeller Institute from Dr Peyton Rous. Letter to Dr Putnam, courtesy Dr Nathan G. Hale Jr; Joseph Collins M.D., *The Doctor Looks at Biography* (1925); Waterlow, 19 Jan. 1911; Lapsley, 1 Jan. 1910; Walpole, 27 Oct. 1910, 15 April 1911; Persse, 27 Oct. 1910; J. William White, 12 May 1911; Protheros, 6 May, 5 Sept. 1911; Broughton, 25 Feb. 1911; Wharton, 19 July, 19 Sept. 1911; G. A. James, 12 Aug. 1911; Emily Sargent, 1 Oct. 1910. Dr Gordon N. Ray allowed me to examine the manuscript of *Notes of a Son and Brother* in his possession; Billy and Alice James, 9 Sept. 1911; Sir Harold Nicolson told me the anecdote about George Moore. Minnie Jones, 30 Sept., 17 Oct. 1911.

The Firebird: Lapsley, 12 Jan., 13 Feb. 1912; Sturgis, 20, 22 Feb., 1, 20 July, 9 Aug., 11 Sept., 10 Dec. 1912; Wharton, 5, 24 Feb., 29 Mar., 12 May, 3, 6 Aug., 18 Nov. 1912; AHJ, 23, 31 July, 1912; Berry, 28 Oct. 1912. Simon Nowell-Smith supplied notes of Lois Barker's recollections.

A Browning Centenary: HJ's lecture on Browning, *Transactions of the Royal Society of Literature*, Second Series XXXI, Part IV, 1912. Reprinted revised in *Notes on Novelists* (1914). My quotations are from the original lecture. I am indebted to Dr Gordon N. Ray for the letter from Lord Charnwood to Stuart Sherman.

La Folie des Grandeurs: Anderson, 11 May, 6 Aug., 5 Nov. 1905, 31 Jan., 31 May, 20 July, 25 Nov. 1906, 18 July 1907, 24 Jan., 22 Sept. 1908, 14 April, 10, 12 Nov. 1912, 4 Sept. 1913.

A Determined Woman: Nobel prize efforts: Wharton to WDH, 18 Feb. 1911; WDH to Wharton, 3 Mar. 1911; Gosse to Wharton, 14 Feb. 1911; Minnie Jones to WDH, 28 Feb. 1911. Mrs Wharton's letters to Gosse are in the Brotherton Library at Leeds. The Scribner offer: 22 Sept., 10 Oct. 1912; Pinker to Scribner, 15 Nov. 1912; Wharton, 15 Mar. 1913. HJ on Meredith, letters in Barrett. Ezra Pound details, Miss Bosanquet's diary; the quotation is from Canto VII:24. Cheyne Walk: AHJ, 17 Jan. 1913; Grace Norton, 6 Feb. 1913. Miss Bosanquet arranged for my inspection of the flat in Carlyle Mansions. See also letters to the Protheros (Harvard).

The Master at Seventy: HJ's cable, 28 Mar. 1913. Scribner archives: Broughton 20, 28 June 1913; Peggy, 19 June 1913; letter of acknowledgment, 15 April 1913.

The Infinite of Life: Wells, 21, 22 Sept., 14 Oct. 1913. See Edel and Ray (eds), *Henry James and H. G. Wells* (1958). Van Wyck Brooks described the Brandes lecture to me. Sir Compton Mackenzie gave me access to the letters of HJ to himself and parents. Henry Bernstein told me in 1943 of meeting HJ. Sir Bruce Richmond told me of HJ's writing of the *TLS* articles. H. Adams, 21 Mar. 1914; Mrs Gilder, 23 June 1913; Hugh Walpole, 3 Nov. 1913, 29 Jan. 1914; AHJ, 11 Oct. 1913; L. P. Smith, 25 Dec. 1913.

The Ivory Tower: The notes and MS versions of *The Ivory Tower* are in Houghton. Adams, 21 Mar. 1914; AHJ, 11 Oct. 1913; WDH, 13 May 1914.

BOOK SEVEN: *Within the Rim*

A Wreck of Belief: Broughton, 1 Oct. 1914; Peggy James, 2 Dec. 1914; Scribner, 12 Dec. 1914; Reubell, 10 Dec. 1914; Mrs Balestier, 27 Dec. 1914. HJ's letters to Burgess Noakes are in Houghton. See "Refugees in Chelsea," first published as "Refugees in England," in the N.Y. *Times* and Boston *Sunday Herald*, 17 Oct. 1915, in *Within the Rim* (1919).

Soldiers: Harry James, 30 Oct. 1914; *The Book of the Homeless* (ed. Wharton) (1916); "The Long Wards" was reprinted *Within the Rim* (1919); HJ's letter in behalf of the American Volunteer Motor-Ambulance Brigade first appeared as a pamphlet 1914 and was reprinted in the American press. HJ to Clare Sheridan, 26 June, 4 Oct. 1915; Mrs Clifford, 26 Aug. 1914; Peggy, 18 June 1915. Edward Marsh, 24 April 1915; Marsh papers, Berg Collection, N.Y. Public Library; Lubbock, 25 April 1915; Burgess Noakes, 22 Mar., 25 May 1915.

Statesmen: Last meeting with Adams, Wharton, 20 Oct. 1914; the late Aileen Tone described the occasion to me. Margot Asquith, 9 April 1915; Mrs Henry White, 11 April 1915; "Henry James's First Interview" by Preston Lockwood, New York *Times Magazine*, 21 Mar. 1915. Lady Bonham Carter (Violet Asquith) recalled the week-end at Walmer Castle in correspondence with Billy James; Mrs Wharton, 16 Jan. 1915; Harry James, 16 Jan. 1915.

Loyalties: Harry James, 24 June, 20, 28 July 1915; Gosse, 25 June 1915; Asquith, 28 June 1915; Statement to *The Times*, 14 July 1915; AHJ, 2 Jan. 1915; Mrs Wharton, 23 May 1914.

Treacheries: Wells, 5, 10 July 1915; Wells to HJ, 8 July 1915. *Boon* (1915); *Henry James and H. G. Wells*, Edel and Ray (eds) (1958).

The Mulberry Tree: Mrs Dacre Vincent, 6 Jan. 1915. Miss Bosanquet's visit to Mrs Wharton is in the Bosanquet diaries.

A Terror of Consciousness: Miss Bosanquet's diaries contain a detailed account of HJ's last days. The late John James made available Mrs William James's diary.

Final and Fading Words: The text of HJ's final dictation was originally published by me in the *Atlantic Monthly*, "The Deathbed Notes of Henry James," CCXXI (June 1968) 103–5, and in *The Times Literary Supplement*, "Henry James's Last Dictation," 2 May 1968. Portions of the last dictation were taken down by Miss Bosanquet and are in her diaries; certain sentences were dictated to Peggy James and were in her handwriting. To the best of my knowledge the original document was destroyed by order of Henry James's executor without his knowing that I had already taken a copy of it.

Over the Abyss: A draft of Edward Marsh's memorandum is among his papers in the Berg Collection. The funeral: Bosanquet's diaries; contemporary press reports. HJ's essay on *Is There a Life After Death?*, Harper's *Bazar*, Jan.–Feb. 1910, reprinted in *In After Days* (1910).

INDEX